Introduction to
Educational Research

TEXTBOOKS IN EDUCATION
William H. Burton, *Consulting Editor*

An Approach to Guidance, by Edna Dorothy Baxter.

Growth and Development of the Preadolescent, by Arthur Witt Blair and William H. Burton.

The Diagnosis and Treatment of Learning Difficulties, by Leo J. Brueckner and Guy L. Bond.

Student Teaching in the Elementary School, 2nd ed., by James R. Burr, Lowry W. Harding, and Leland B. Jacobs.

Guidebook for Elementary Student Teachers, by Isabel Miller, George E. Dickson, and Loren R. Tomlinson.

Supervision, 3rd ed., by William H. Burton and Leo J. Brueckner.

Education and Morals, by John L. Childs.

Public Education in America, by George R. Cressman and Harold W. Benda.

Supervision as Co-operative Action, by Muriel Crosby.

The Third Curriculum, by Robert W. Frederick.

Educational Psychology, by Karl C. Garrison and J. Stanley Gray. Also accompanying *Workbook,* by Karl C. Garrison, Ira E. Aaron, and Joseph C. Bledsoe.

Introduction to Educational Research, by Carter V. Good.

Methods of Research, by Carter V. Good and Douglas E. Scates.

Human Relations in School Administration, by Daniel E. Griffiths.

Guidance in Democratic Living, by Arthur Hollingshead.

The Guidance Function in Education, by Percival W. Hutson.

Early Elementary Education, by Myrtle M. Imhoff.

The Child and His Curriculum, 2nd ed., by J. Murray Lee and Dorris May Lee

The Child and His Development, by J. Murray Lee and Dorris May Lee.

The Preadolescent, by Mary Jane Loomis.

Changing the Curriculum, by Alice Miel.

Teaching Adolescents in Secondary Schools, by Harry N. Rivlin.

Education and the Democratic Faith, by Ephraim Vern Sayers and Ward Madden.

Statistical Methods in Educational and Psychological Research, by James E. Wert, Charles O. Neidt, and J. Stanley Ahmann.

Introduction to
EDUCATIONAL RESEARCH

By

CARTER V. GOOD, Ph.D.

Director of Graduate Studies and Dean
Teachers College, University of Cincinnati

New  York

APPLETON-CENTURY-CROFTS, Inc.

Preface

This is an introductory book on research methods for field workers, graduate students in the early stages of their work, and seniors in the undergraduate college. It is intended to serve the purposes of both producers and consumers of research, with research presented as a method of problem-solving or of finding answers to significant hypotheses or questions.

The series of chapters follows the sequence or steps of reflective thinking or problem-solving, although it is recognized that there is frequently a shuttle-like movement from hypothesis to data to tentative conclusions and often back to formulation and testing of a new hypothesis until the correct answer or interpretation is found. These steps in research and in development of a graduate thesis or project include formulation of the problem, together with a survey of the pertinent literature; selection and use of an appropriate data-gathering procedure, including analysis and interpretation of the evidence; and preparation of the research or technical report. In this book analysis and interpretation of data are presented in the functional setting of the chapters on research methods rather than as separate discussions.

By delimitation of scope, this text has left to the many specialized graduate courses and books the quantitative details of testing and statistics (except as mentioned briefly from time to time for illustrative purposes): intelligence tests and measures of general mental ability, measurement and prediction of special abilities or aptitudes, personality and character tests, measures of attitudes and interests, projective methods and other devices for the study of personality, psychometric and sociometric techniques with emphasis on standardized testing and statistics, and educational or accomplishment tests in schools and elsewhere.

This is not a "rule book" of research methods, but is a discussion of concepts, principles, and procedures. Under each chapter on a particular research method the plan of presentation is to identify areas appropriate for investigation, to characterize the research procedure or data-gathering technique, and to summarize illustrative studies. Many details must remain for treatment in the voluminous literature, as listed in the chapter bibliographies and in footnotes, since it is common for a book of several hundred pages to be devoted to a single data-gathering technique or procedure.

The author has not strained at creating artificial dichotomies in research approaches: the scientific versus the philosophical, the quantitative versus the qualitative, the mathematical versus the descriptive, or the statistical versus the clinical. These are complementary procedures in problem-solving, probably different aspects of the purposes of inquiry or research.

Since an interdisciplinary view of research now recognizes the increasing interdependence of problems and procedures in education, psychology, sociology, and certain other social areas, a number of illustrative studies and techniques have been drawn from these fields. In a sense, a common pattern of research methodology has been presented for the educational, psychological, sociological, and related social fields, with primary emphasis on education.

The footnotes and bibliographies indicate the indebtedness of the author to hundreds of research workers and writers on investigational procedures.

C.V.G.

Contents

Contents

Introduction to
Educational Research

1

The Hallmarks of Scientific Method

This chapter deals with science and research in relation to scientific method in the educational, psychological, and social areas, interdisciplinary co-operation, role of values, hallmarks of the scientist, freedom and responsibility, participation of the teacher, graduate education, and responsibility to society.

CHARACTERISTICS OF SCIENCE AND RESEARCH

Varying Frames of Reference

The characteristics of science have been analyzed in terms of varying frames of reference. One description of science, both as substantive theory and as methodology, uses such phrasing as empirical, propositional, logical, operational, public (subject to communication to other scientists), problem-solving, abstract, tending toward a system, and on-going.[1] Other current interpretations of the term *science*, or notions about the scientist and his work, are in relation to subject-matter fields, complicated gadgets, universal laws, systematic procedures, technical methodology, and pseudo-scientific schemes (for example, astrology, phrenology, physiognomy, palmistry, and graphology).[2]

An older description of science and research was in terms of mathematical precision and accuracy, objectivity, verifiability, impartiality, and expertness, with the first letters of these five characterizations spelling out

[1] John T. Doby, Editor, *An Introduction to Social Research*. Harrisburg, Penn.: The Stackpole Co., 1954. p. 6–10.
[2] Clarence W. Brown and Edwin E. Ghiselli, *Scientific Method in Psychology*. New York: McGraw-Hill Book Co., 1955. p. 3–4.

the word *movie*. We now recognize, however, that many historical, descriptive-survey, and case-clinical studies cannot be phrased or reported in mathematical terms, and that precision may be in either mathematical or verbal terms. In many instances the criteria of objectivity and verifiability can be only partially satisfied in the educational, psychological, and social areas.

It may be that the following bit of verse will not take us too far afield. Moving up the page, the letters in italics spell out the word *movie*.[3]

    M–O–V–I–E
    Deep, how deep
    The wisdom of Old China!
    Unfathomable,
    Illuminating;
    Wisdom gained by reflection,
    Introspection,
    Conversation with sages
    Long lost in sleep;
    *E*xpertly data all arrived at,
    Ergos cunningly connived at,
    Fallacies fully contrived at,
    *I*mpartial in their scope
    And comprehension;
    *V*erifiable in their minutest dimension
    By laws of calculation
    And mensuration;
    *O*bjectively observed
    By millions contemplative;
    *M*athematically demonstrable
    Before and after Euclid
    That VIRTUE consists simply
    In being
    TU-YUNG-TU.

        By Ira L. Harrison, Leitchfield, Ky.

Nature of Modern Research

Over the course of time man has used other than scientific methods or sources for arriving at answers to his questions or problems, including mythology and personification, supernatural explanation, personal experience, custom and tradition, the voice of authority, and syllogistic reasoning. While man has ordinarily found his answers to perplexing or inter-

[3] It was written by a graduate student with tongue in cheek.

esting questions through other than research methods, he is engaged in research if he follows a procedure substantially as follows:[4]

If he questions his explanations, the stage is set for research. If he goes further and challenges the methods by which he arrived at his conclusion; if he critically and systematically repeats his observations; if he devises special tools for taking, recording, and analyzing his observations; if he tests the reliability and the validity of these tools and evaluates his data in other ways; if he scrutinizes the thought processes by which he passes from one step of his logic to another; if he gradually refines his concept of what it is he is trying to explain and considers anew the necessary and sufficient conditions for proof; if at every step he proceeds with the utmost caution, realizing that his purpose is not to arrive at an answer which is personally pleasing, but rather one which will stand up under the critical attacks of those who doubt his answer—if he can meet these criteria and steadfastly hold to his purpose, then he is doing research.

The characteristics of research have been identified concretely in an analysis (of two studies) made to determine whether research was represented rather than a more casual or routine piece of work.[5] The major characteristics of research, as identified, were: inclusion in the report of a description of methodology and sources, original observations, careful planning step by step in gathering and evaluating data, systematic organization and summarization of data, and a background of general competence on the part of the investigator.

Steps or Sequence in Research

It should not be assumed that any given list (series) of steps in scientific or reflective thinking (research or investigation) follows some invariable sequence. In actuality, the steps in research or problem-solving may move backward and forward in a "shuttle-like" fashion. The investigator may go from the hypothesis to the data and, if the hypothesis proves invalid, he will return to formulation of a new hypothesis. With the possibility of this shuttle-like movement always present in research, it is helpful to identify the more important steps in problem-solving. Although the temporal order is substantially as enumerated below, we should recognize that these steps in scientific investigation represent a somewhat idealized account of how the scientist actually does his work.[6]

   1. Selection of problem area

   2. Acquaintance with current theory and knowledge in the area

---

[4] Quoted from Carter V. Good and Douglas E. Scates, *Methods of Research*: Educational, Psychological, Sociological. New York: Appleton-Century-Crofts, 1954. p. 11.

[5] *Ibid.*, p. 269–71.

[6] John T. Doby, Editor, *op. cit.*, p. 12–15.

3. Definition of the problem

4. Development of hypothesis

5. Development of the formal argument

6. Delineation of the source of data

7. Creation of the instrument

8. Writing a "dummy argument"

9. Pretest of the instrument, and possible revision

10. Formal acquisition of data

11. Analysis of the data

12. Formal write-up of conclusions reached.

A briefer, consolidated list of steps in research, similar to the sequence of chapters in this book, is as follows:

1. Definition and development of the problem, including the survey of the related literature and formulation of the working hypothesis

2. Selection or creation of appropriate data-gathering techniques and actual collection of data

3. Classification and analysis of data

4. Conclusions, generalizations, and applications (with due attention to reporting).

Fallacy of Dogmatic Finality

In discussing the importance of open-mindedness on the part of the scientist and scholar, Whitehead has expressed himself forcefully on what he terms "the fallacy of dogmatic finality":[7]

The Universe is vast. Nothing is more curious than the self-satisfied dogmatism with which mankind at each period of its history cherishes the delusion of the finality of its existing modes of knowledge. Sceptics and believers are all alike. At this moment scientists and sceptics are the leading dogmatists. Advance in detail is admitted; fundamental novelty is barred. This dogmatic common sense is the death of philosophic adventure. The Universe is vast.

I was in Cambridge in the 1880's, first as an undergraduate, later as one of the staff. It was from two hundred to two hundred and fifty years since mathematics had had its fresh impetus from men like Descartes and Sir Isaac Newton; there were certain borderlands where affairs in that science were considered indefinable, but in the main, mathematical physics looked sound and solid. . . . By the turn of the century, nothing, absolutely nothing was left that had not been challenged, if not shaken; not a single major concept. This I consider to have been one of the supreme facts of my experience.

[7] Quoted from *Dialogues of Alfred North Whitehead*. As Recorded by Lucien Price. New York: New American Library of World Literature, 1954. p. 12, 175.

Misconceptions Concerning Social Science

Among the wrong attitudes and misconceptions concerning social science, as held by many college freshmen (and others), are six common fallacies.

1. Science is techniques and gadgetry. The average student judges the merits of a particular scientific endeavor by certain superficial "techniques" which are easily grasped. He sees the scientist as a man in a white coat, working alone in a laboratory full of test tubes, gurgling retorts, and flashing electronic signals. This concept would rule out most physical scientists, more biological scientists, and all social scientists.

2. In some cases he has the stereotyped idea that a scientific law must be an algebraic equation. This would rule out many biological and social generalizations. For example, the principle of blood constancy (homeostasis) can be stated clearly in words. It applies to all human beings and has many useful applications in "life and death" problems.

3. Then there is the misconception that "it must be infallible or it isn't science." We have found that the student rejects the I.Q. test as a social invention because it has certain flaws. But he does not reject the products of the physical sciences on the same grounds. Yet anyone who has a TV set knows that it distorts reality and breaks down on occasion.

4. The social scientist is perceived as "studying people" as unique personalities and "the basic units of society"; therefore, to predict anything which will happen in society, we must know all of the unique characteristics of each individual. But to expect any social scientist to know what Mary Jones will be doing on her twenty-first birthday is as hopeless as asking the physical scientist when a cork thrown in the Mississippi River will arrive in New Orleans. Pure scientific investigation is more likely to focus on such basic variables as conformity, rumor, decision-making, role conflict, attitude, etc.

5. Another interesting belief is that, in the physical sciences, the basic theoretical concepts are more "real" and tangible than in the social sciences. For example, the majority of the freshmen classify the atom as something that has been proven beyond a shadow of a doubt, but the "subconscious mind" as having never been proven to exist—"It's just a theory." Yet, it is simpler to demonstrate the existence of the subconscious mind than the concept of the atom.

6. A large proportion of the freshmen share the misconception that "science is successful insofar as it contributes to the manufacturing of more gadgets."[8]

Scientific Method and Educational Research

A definition of research which ends with an analysis of the characteristics of scientific method emphasizes that:[9]

[8] Quoted from Raymond L. Gorden, *Antioch Notes* 33: 1–8; May 1956.
[9] Quoted from Francis G. Cornell, "Research and Science in Education," *Report of the First International Conference on Educational Research.* Educational Studies and Documents, No. 20. Paris: UNESCO, 1956. p. 26–30.

1. Research is a form of human behavior or activity.

2. Many educational investigations are applied research, made for the purpose of solving an immediate concrete problem, sometimes utilizing the tools and techniques of other disciplines.

3. Scientific method involves purpose, theory, and verification of hypothesis or theory by observation and/or experiment.

At least one general definition of research would be that which refers to the *activity* of collecting information (or observing reality) in an orderly and systematic fashion. The quality of such activity presumably varies with the dependability of the information collected, whether that be a count of the number of test items passed on a test administered to *n* groups of pupils or the descriptions of class and grade organization in *k* different schools. But there is no need here to dwell at length upon what is good and what is poor research. To be sure, the best research is that which is reliable, verifiable and exhaustive, so that it provides information in which we have confidence. The main point here is that research is, literally speaking, a kind of human behaviour, an *activity* in which people engage. By this definition all intelligent human behaviour involves some research. . . .

In education, teachers, administrators, scholars, or others engage in *educational* research when they systematically [and purposefully] assemble information about schools, school children, the social matrix in which a school or school system is determined, the characteristic of the learner or the interaction between the school and the pupil. . . .

Hence, by literal definition, the collection of data [according to a purpose and plan] concerning a vast array of subjects about education may be considered educational research. Educational research is an *applied* research and may be undertaken for the purpose of solving an immediate concrete problem or satisfying an action taken, or of converting people to a point of view. It may also be undertaken simply for the purpose of the doing of it. On the other hand, if it possesses characteristics of the methods of *science*, it may be as basic and fundamental as the subject matter of educational research can be basic—unless, of course, we stray entirely from the educational arena and become purely psychological, sociological, historical, economic, anthropological, political, or some other form of researchists. The educational arena is certainly interdisciplinary. An educational problem can require the characteristics of several disciplines. . . .

There have been many learned analyses defining and describing the methods of science. The layman is largely unaware of science as a way of human behaviour. To him science is a storehouse of knowledge, a *product* of the processes or methods of science. I shall limit my discussion only to the methods, since it seems evident that the characteristics of research, scientific or otherwise, are best determined by the processes of arriving at the end product and not the product itself.

As has been suggested, the activities which we call educational research may be guided by many purposes besides the purposes of science. There is a level of *activity* classified as educational research but which might also be eliminated from our definition because of the absence of purpose. It is easy for the purposes of the testing of pupils, or the collection of statistics about school populations, school attendance, or school finances and the like, to become lost when the operation becomes repetitive over a period of time and practical needs for such information change. Programmes of intelligence and achievement testing were adopted by many school systems in America two decades or so ago simply because it was recognized in the most respected professional circles of the day that that was the proper thing to do. The tools of research, the means of achieving some end, appeared before the acceptance of ideas more important in their actual use—the concepts and perspectives of learning and of teaching, of child study and of guidance, which are now more commonly understood by American teachers and administrators. Many of the statistical manoeuvres of the educational technician adopted during this period became standard operations for the "treatment of data"—but not always methods of achieving an end other than the end of processing the data. . . .

Scientific method possesses these features:

1. *Purpose*—Scientific method deals with problems to be solved. It is therefore highly purposive since there are specific goals that guide the activities of persons who engage in it.

2. *Theory*—There is usually a step which involves a "theory," or as sometimes might be said, an hypothesis or hypotheses concerning the explanation of a phenomenon or a solution of a problem.

3. *Verification*—The establishing of an hypothesis or of a theory is followed by observation and/or experiment. Scientific method is distinct from speculation by this step consisting of tests in reality.

The more that educational research possesses characteristics such as the above, the more it contributes to one category of research which some people have called "basic research." However, since education deals to a very great extent with day-to-day matters and real phenomena, it is expected to bear on the solution of practical problems. Therefore, all educational research need not be "basic" nor of a type which is directed toward the solution of generalizable theory. Much of what is considered educational research would be classified as "development," "demonstration," or "operations research." Since education is certainly an applied field this must be an important area. This is research of a type which works day in and day out to help the teacher, or the principal or agencies in authority over school systems. Then whether our orientation is science or practice, desiring as researchers to be orderly and systematic we justifiably examine the paraphernalia with which we work. As long as such examination of our techniques, our instruments of measurement, our devices of analysis, or other activities of research is guided by their usefulness in the solution of problems, we are certainly justified in this process. We could easily unbalance our view of the scope of educational research by limiting our discussion to techniques and methods.

Pure Research and Practical Research

Reference has been made in the preceding section to the "pure" and to the applied aspects of research in education. In pure research the investigator may attack any problem anywhere that appeals to his fancy. After he has selected his problem he need only apply scholarly methods to its solution and publish the results, with no concern about any practical social use of his findings. In practical research the problem is localized within practice, and the results are to be applied to the improvement of practice.

Both pure and practical research should be encouraged and supported. While pure research, at the time the particular investigation was made, may have been evaluated chiefly in terms of the satisfaction afforded the research worker, at a later date the same pure research may have practical and social value. The work of Benjamin Franklin, as he played with his kite and key in studying electricity, probably would be regarded as pure research that did not take on practical and social values until Thomas A. Edison much later worked out his numerous inventions utilizing electricity. In attempting to classify pure research and practical research, we do not have a dichotomy but a continuum. The efforts of the extreme purist and of the extreme technologist are complementary, contributing to a range of research and a diversity of attitude beneficial to society.[10] (During recent years the term *action research* has become widely accepted, as discussed in the chapter on descriptive-survey studies.)

INTERDISCIPLINARY AND BEHAVIORAL SCIENCE

Reference has been made earlier in this chapter to the interdisciplinary aspects of research, with special application to education as a field of instruction and investigation. A scientist, Bush, comments on the general desirability of professional collaboration, with particular emphasis on medicine.[11]

There are other ways, worth-while no doubt, in which the professions may be brought to a better understanding of one another. It is not necessary that they be brought to a full understanding of one another's subject matter; that would be impossible. For, if they grasp one another's mores and traditions, methods of thought, deep convictions, and motivations, there will be no further need to stimulate collaboration of the highest sort. It will occur automatically. And from it will result a surge forward on that complex task of understanding life, where the skill of all professional groups will be strained to the utmost, a new accomplishment which will place a firmer foundation under the keystone of that honorable profession to which medical men belong, ministry to the

[10] Benton J. Underwood, *Psychological Research*. New York: Appleton-Century-Crofts, 1957. p. 8–13.
[11] Quoted from Vannevar Bush, "Professional Collaboration." *Science* 125: 49–54; January 11, 1957.

people. May that ministry always be conducted with pride and dignity. And may the gratitude of humble men always remain the primary compensation and reward.

Hallenbeck designates five types of specialties (disciplines) or specialists appropriate as resources or teams for interdisciplinary research.[12]

Interdisciplinary research is a team job in which specialists in different areas, using different approaches to their study, work together on a problem requiring research in order to analyze various aspects of the problem in their relationships. This raises two important questions: first, what are the disciplines from which specialists might be selected for such research; and second, what are the principles of selection and operation?

Looking only at the practical problem of resources for the team of specialists which interdisciplinary research requires, it is possible to designate five different types of specialties or specialists—some would say disciplines.

1. There are the traditional disciplines of the social sciences, long recognized and established—history, economics, anthropology, psychology, sociology, and perhaps a few others. Usually the major line of study will fall into one of these more general areas. Perhaps all of the team could be made up of what would now be called generalists in these fields. This would depend upon the focus of the study, the relationship of breadth to depth in what was planned. The particular fields to be represented would be dictated by the requirements of the particular research.

2. A great number of specialties come within each of these general areas. These are perhaps most likely to be needed when the research is directed toward a clearly defined problem. Such specialists as demographers, labor economists, criminologists, child psychologists, specialists in government or in family life, and dozens of others are of great use in building teams.

3. Cross-disciplines have come into prominence recently. In the social sciences, social psychology and social anthropology are best known, but there are other combinations only one side of which is social science, such as psychiatry or home economics.

4. There are specialists in each of the general disciplines who are concerned with technical processes. These fields have in some cases been followed with such intensive study that the techniques have lost contact with the purposes for which they were developed, but they can be exceedingly useful when teamed up with other specialties. There are many of these—a few of which are sociometry, polling, propaganda analysis, psychological measurement, group dynamics, statistics.

5. Finally, there are what are sometimes called the applied disciplines. These are the operational areas within which, through experience and experiment, conceptual frameworks, organizations, and techniques for carrying on the social services have developed. There are more of them than would at first be thought and they cover a wide range. Public administration, city planning, community organization, public relations, social case work, group development,

[12] Quoted from Wilbur C. Hallenbeck, "Interdisciplinary Research in the Social Sciences." *Teachers College Record* 58: 129–36; December 1956.

guidance, personnel administration, psychological counseling, and education in its many phases and divisions are particularly important.

It should prove especially profitable to bridge some of the remaining gaps between sociology and psychology.[13] Although differences in the historical roots of psychology and sociology in the realms of assumption, theory, and method have often prevented effective communication and collaboration between these two disciplines, relations are now so mature that it is profitable to make explicit some of the remaining gaps between sociology and psychology. From the beginning, sociology has considered as its central problem the question of how individuals learn to act together and to adjust to one another, while the basic question posed by psychologists about social factors is what effect they have on individual behavior. Typically the psychologist has adopted the experimental method as his basic research approach, and the sociologist has emphasized observation, frequently in the form of diaries and other personal documents, questionnaire responses, scales, and similar procedures, as basic techniques of gathering evidence. Psychologists and sociologists need to give further study to differences in their approaches to problems in such areas as heredity and environment, intelligence, learning, and personality.

As the result of co-operative work on certain common problems, however, a number of theoretical concepts and propositions are now more or less the shared property of psychology, sociology, anthropology, and education, or, at least, such concepts are reasonably meaningful in theoretical discussions of an interdisciplinary nature that cross departmental boundaries. Certain interdisciplinary agreements in these fields may be found with respect to the human organism, human behavior, interaction, grouping, culture, social structure, personality, and symbolization and communication.

Thus we must admit that there are difficulties, technical and of a psycho-socio-cultural nature, along the way toward the achievement of general theory and wider collaboration among specialists in the study of social man. But we do not regard such difficulties as insuperable. Already we have a vast amount of data and understanding concerning mankind. On the basis of the science we already have we know that time after time men have reached their goals in the face of what seemed to be insurmountable obstacles. It would be ironic indeed if we as scientific students of man should in our own case remain paralyzed in the face of difficulties that are actually rather trivial and that we should thereby be blocked from our goal—which after all, is nothing more and nothing less

[13] Arnold M. Rose, "The Hiatus Between Sociology and Psychology," *Theory and Method in the Social Sciences*. Minneapolis: University of Minnesota Press, 1954. p. 220–27.

than a reliable understanding of social man, an understanding constantly increasing in breadth, in truth, and in clarity.[14]

The present national and international scene makes imperative an evaluation of the role and potential contribution of behavioral science, which is characterized as follows by a special committee:[15]

This is the combined endeavor of many fields investigating all aspects of behavior, leading to understanding of human beings as individuals and in social relations. Behavioral science therefore includes many studies in the fields of anthropology, biochemistry, ecology, economics, genetics, geography, history, linguistics, mathematical statistics, neurology, pharmacology, physiology, political science, psychiatry, psychology, sociology, and zoology. Applications ramify into advertising, business administration, education, government, human engineering, labor relations, law, medicine, military science, operations research, personnel selection, public relations, and many other aspects of human endeavor. Some of these sciences are still in early stages of development, but American research in them at the moment has a clear lead over Russian, which is constricted by Communist dogma.

Behavioral science has demonstrated its usefulness to human welfare and national security. Its further development could increase its contribution in areas of international relations, military defense, and national vigor.

According to the same committee in this field, applications of basic research in behavioral science have led to significant advances that already have had an impact on society. This progress includes:

Intelligence and aptitude testing; techniques to speed learning and increase the effectiveness of education; use of drugs in alleviating or curing certain mental illnesses; sample survey methods using mathematical statistics for measuring and predicting social trends; development of increasingly reliable economic indicators fundamental to planning in government and industry; use of group dynamics to improve the efficiency of face-to-face working groups; and many others. Such achievements make for widespread general acceptance—sometimes too enthusiastic and uncritical—of behavorial science.

Throughout the ages when man has gained more knowledge he has gained more freedom. His understanding of physical laws increasingly has enabled him to control the natural environment, protect himself from heat and

[14] Quoted from John Gillin, Editor, *For a Science of Social Man*: Convergences in Anthropology, Psychology, and Sociology. New York: The Macmillan Co., 1954. p. 263–76.

Also see Margaret B. Luszki, *Interdisciplinary Team Research:* Methods and Problems. No. 3 of the Research Training Series. New York: New York University Press (for the National Training Laboratories), 1958. 382 p.

[15] Quoted from James G. Miller and Others, *National Support for Behavioral Science*, February 1958. 24 p. At time of publication, obtainable from James G. Miller, 1025 Connecticut Avenue, N.W., Washington 6, D.C.

Also see Karl W. Deutsch, "The Place of Behavioral Sciences in Graduate Training in International Relations." *Behavioral Science* 3: 278–84; July 1958.

cold, and travel speedily and comfortably. Expanding biological science has freed him from pestilences, most of the terrors of childbirth, the feebleness of malnutrition, many forms of pain and physical misery. His life span has been prolonged and made more healthy.

Similarly behavioral science, directly probing man's central nature, gives promise of increasing his degrees of freedom and expanding his effectiveness and creativity. He can be released from the constriction of life by neurosis and feeblemindedness and the tragedy of psychosis; the limitation of opportunity from inadequate education, associated prejudice and bias; the diminishing of contentment and effectiveness from marital strife, industrial unrest, crime and delinquency; and perhaps most of all, the fear of international conflict which constrains the free expression of the world's peoples. To these central problems of human existence the sciences of man ultimately address themselves.

We are coming to accept as likely in the future a sort of physical existence which would have been unimaginable a few years ago. But the potential benefits which can flow from basic study of our behavior are not so clearly seen.

ROLE OF VALUES IN RESEARCH AND EDUCATION

Educational research and social investigation in general, including the behavioral sciences, owe a prominent place to certain concepts that are common in our culture: purpose, motive, teleology, values, feelings, and emotions. These values are basic to human living, a view that has received greatly increased support since the 1930's. At that time, there was an over-emphasis in many graduate departments of education and psychology on statistical and measurement techniques, to the partial exclusion of certain other problem-solving procedures. There were even some graduate bulletins where the term *philosophy* was not permitted to appear in a course title or description. That this view has changed materially can be amply documented in the literature of education, psychology, and sociology.[16]

The "pure" scientist traditionally prided himself on his concern for fact and his indifference to value, an attitude that influenced Titchener, who imitated the classical physicist in his zeal to make psychology scientific and excluded value, along with meaning and utility, from the new science of psychology. It is true that some schools of psychology have centered their problems around purpose, personality, adjustment, or *Gestalten*, rather than around sensation, with at least some place for value

[16] Carter V. Good, "The Role of Values in Educational and Social Research." *Peabody Journal of Education* 33: 259-71; March 1956.
Carter V. Good and Douglas E. Scates, *op. cit.*, p. vii.

in their world of facts, and yet other psychologists have reserved for values a central place in their system. From this varied background psychology in the 1930's developed applications of the scientific method in attacking various aspects of the problem of values. A comprehensive review of psychological studies of values, based on a bibliography of 211 items, covers the following problems:[17]

1. Measuring the values of groups of individuals and relating the results to other data concerning the groups (individual differences)

2. The origin and development of values within the individual

3. The influence of an individual's values on his cognitive life.

By way of definition and delimitation, Dukes concludes from his review that such terms as attitude, interest, motive, need, sentiment, or valence are often used interchangeably with value, or at least refer to some aspect of value, and that investigations of level of aspiration, character, or the superego almost necessarily involve evaluations.

As pointed out in the preceding section of this chapter, dealing with the interdisciplinary aspects of research, scientists and scholars are coming to recognize that there is really no essential conflict between the problem-solving procedures of science, philosophy, logic, history, statistics, and case-clinical study, whether our concern is with values or some other major question. Therefore, in offering graduate instruction, particularly in research courses, and in our discussions of research, we should make only moderate use of the term *scientific*. The methods of science (and technology) and of philosophy (and logic) are complementary techniques, perhaps different aspects of the general purpose of a single discipline of inquiry, in the development of problem or concept and in the gathering of evidence with which to test or modify the concept. It is held that science without philosophy is blind, while philosophy without science is empty.

This point of view is in keeping with evidence of an interdisciplinary approach and of close co-operation between the different areas of behavioral and human and social science, as found in the literature and in certain graduate programs and research centers that utilize the combined resources of psychology, sociology, anthropology, education, and a number of other social fields. This larger movement toward co-operation in all the human sciences makes it possible to develop a common pattern of research methodology (and to some extent theory, as well as background for study

[17] William F. Dukes, "Psychological Studies of Values." *Psychological Bulletin* 52: 24–50; January 1955.

of values), with appropriate applications to each special field of investigation.

By way of an illustration of research in the realm of values, as summarized by a reviewer, Morris studied the preferences of college students in several countries with respect to "ways to live."

The larger conceptions of the good life—the "schemata of value" as Gordon Allport has called them—have seemed either so complex and shifting, or so vaguely transcendental as to resist empirical study. Their analysis and dynamics traditionally have been left to the humanist, the professional philosopher, or the theologian. In the main the social scientist has avoided them. The psychologist, it is true, has achieved a certain methodological rigor and elegance in the study of such molecular phenomena as motives, attitudes, beliefs, goals, ethical judgments, and the like, all of which are, however, peripheral to the larger problem.

There have been some notable attempts to study values in the global sense. Witness the widely contrasting value patterns identified in various cultures by Ruth Benedict and Margaret Mead, and the democratic and anti-democratic polarities isolated by Adorno, Else Frenkel-Brunswik et al. in the study of authoritarian personality. The clinical psychologist has become increasingly aware that, as a matter of therapeutic strategy, implicitly or explicitly he must commit himself to some broad conception of the good life, and such a shrewd observer as Erich Fromm raises the disturbing question of the universality of the value norms by which mental health and ill health are to be judged.

A study of values which is intended to make an empirical contribution to a science of man must take into account the nature and extent of cultural influences. Although anthropologists are not in complete agreement as to its interpretation, there is an impressive amount of evidence indicating that all experience, including values, is partially or wholly culturally determined. The basic requirement of Professor Morris' research is a measuring instrument capable of use across cultural boundaries.

In the present study the basic instrument consisted of thirteen summaries of "ways to live," and the respondents rated their preferences of each Way on a sevenfold scale. The Ways were given no formal labels, but they embody the conceptions of the good life as expressed in various religious and ethical systems. The respondents were approximately 6,000 college students in the United States, Canada, China, India, Japan, and Norway.[18]

To cite another example of problems of values, Lasswell suggests four types of contributions needed in the field of political science.[19]

[18] Quoted from review by Franklin Fearing, *Contemporary Psychology* 2: 157–59; June 1957, of Charles Morris, *Varieties of Human Value*. Chicago: The University of Chicago Press, 1956. xv+209 p.

[19] Quoted from Harold D. Lasswell, "Political Science of Science." *Scientific Monthly* 84: 34–44; January 1957.

One professional contribution, it appears, is to project a comprehensive image of the future for the purpose of indicating how our overriding goal values are likely to be affected (if current policies continue).

A closely related contribution consists in clarifying the fundamental goal values of the body politic. We are accustomed to confront political ideologies with new factual contingencies and to suggest appropriate specific interpretations. We also confront political doctrines with rival doctrines and with comprehensive theological and metaphysical systems. I have called attention to the point that the basic value systems of European civilization, in particular, are likely to be exposed to sweeping challenge as biology and engineering narrow the obvious differences between man and neighboring species and between man and centrally operating machines. The crisis will be peculiarly sharp if we create or discover forms of life superior to man in intellect or instinctual predispositions. Our traditions have not been life-centered, but man-centered. We possess various paranoidlike traditions of being "chosen." Clearly a difficult task of modifying these egocentric perspectives lies ahead.

The third task is historical and scientific. It is historical in the sense that by mobilizing knowledge about the past we are enabled to recognize the appearance of new patterns and the diffusion or restriction of the old. It is scientific in the sense that we summarize the past in order to confirm (or disconfirm) propositions about the interplay of predisposition and environment. If we are to serve the aims of historic recognition and of scientific analysis, one of our professional responsibilities is to expedite the development of more perfect institutions specialized to continual self-observation on a global scale. Self-observation requires guidance by a system of theoretical models of the political process in which a continuing gradation is maintained between the most inclusive model and submodels adjusted to more limited contexts in time and space. Continual self-observation renders it necessary at each step through time to reevaluate the appropriateness of the operational indices for the variables and concepts employed at the most recent step. In this way, all the concepts that figure in systematic, descriptive political science can be kept chronically pertinent to the ordering of political events as the future unfolds.

The fourth task is inventive and evaluative. It consists in originating policy alternatives by means of which goal values can be maximized. In estimating the likely occurrence of an event (or event category), it is essential to take into account the historical trends and the scientifically ascertained predispositions in the world arena or any pertinent part thereof.

Many of our values are the result of tradition, experience, and environment, rather than education. Some of our highest values are emotionally, rather than intellectually, transmitted. Education as to values is considered the very essence of living.

How-one-feels is possible of education, and needs education as surely as what-one-thinks.

Education as to values should decrease indifference, the trivial, the medi-ocre, the accidental, the incongruous. It should increase sensitiveness to what clarifies and enlarges life and gives it greater promise and more direction, to what enlarges aspiration and intelligent purpose. It should aim at a sense of significance for our lives and for life in general. It is chiefly people who care and who feel that the effort is worth while who change the world for the better.

How will such education take place? We are educated in values by think-ing, by doing, and by feeling. Intellectual understanding grows by thinking; education in the functioning of body and mind comes largely by doing, by development of muscle and nerve in strength, staying power, and skill, as with the pianist, the tennis player, the housekeeper, the craftsman. Education of the emotions—that is, of values—comes first by contagion from the example of others, and then from experience, teaching, the cultivating of inner desire, and above all by living the best we know.

In a college the fire of purpose and aspiration is caught mainly from the faculty, but also from fellow students. If one already has the flame, he can increase it from great books, which, like fuel, feed the flame once it has been lighted. Intellectual study is greatly important to clarify, discipline, and inform purpose and aspiration; but unless the spark is there, intellectual education alone will not supply it. Some of the least desirable of men have been intelligent and educated.

Our values increase and are educated by persistent daily practice. Every day on a college campus, as elsewhere, there are occasions for exercise of courage, integrity, responsibility, friendship. The actual direction of life is largely determined by the qualities men and women develop in daily living. It is principally in that way that the values develop out of which history is made.

There is such a thing as authority concerning values. The intelligent, experienced physician is a better authority on health and disease than the banker or farmer. So, as to values in general: exceptional intelligence, ex-perience, and insight have produced patterns of value that, though not in-fallible, have degrees of authority.[20]

[20] Quoted from Arthur E. Morgan, "The Value of Values." *Antioch Notes* 34: 3–5; March 1957.

Also see H. J. Muller, "Human Values in Relation to Evolution." *Science* 127: 625–29; March 21, 1958. "We may place in the foremost positions among psy-chological needs, and we may accord the highest value to, for one thing, the grati-fication of curiosity—that is, the pursuit of truth for its own sake, by methods of the most effective kind (the kind used by science)—and, for another thing that is no less important, the fulfillment of love in its varied aspects. Among other values, the cultivation of which is also highly important, we may mention here as a few examples, largely overlapping with one another and with the two already given, the zest for making one's own decisions (that is, for the exercise of freedom), for achievement, creativity, variety, and adventure, and the appreciation of nature, art, and artifice. All of these overlapping values can be harmonized with one another, and the seeking of them will play major functional roles in our objective as well as subjective progression."

HALLMARKS OF THE SCIENTIST

What are the major characteristics or hallmarks of the scientist and scholar?[21] Although at times some investigators may fail to recognize urgent problems pressing for attention, or may lack essential training for undertaking a particular study, or may hesitate to pay the full price for an unusually time-consuming or complex investigation, most scientists and research workers possess in some form or measure the characteristics described below. Many additional illustrations of these traits of the scientist or scholar may be found in the chapter on the formulation and development of the problem.

Problem Awareness

The alert scholar or scientist has a sensitivity to problems or a problem awareness, although at times even able scientists and inventors overlook problems and solutions close at hand. All too frequently the beginner in research suffers from the handicap of "problem blindness." In investigating his problem, the scientist may see fit to duplicate an experiment, may extend his study in time or scope, or may follow an "offshoot" of an investigation in progress that "buds out."

Appropriate Specialization

In modern times sound scholarship requires considerable specialization, although a caution against overspecialization is in order. It was much easier in Helmholtz's day, however, for him to consider all experimental physical science as his field and to attribute much of his success to this breadth of interest and talent: "Possessing some geometrical capacity, and equipped with a knowledge of physics, I had, by good fortune, been thrown among medical men, where I found in physiology a virgin soil of great fertility; while, on the other hand, I was led by the considerations of the vital processes to questions and points of view which are usually foreign to pure mathematicians and physicists."[22]

[21] Carter V. Good, "The Hallmarks of Scholarship and Research," *The Good Education of Youth*. Forty-fourth Annual Schoolmen's Week Proceedings. Edited by Frederick C. Gruber. Philadelphia: University of Pennsylvania Press, 1957. p. 101–110.

Also see Harold K. Schilling, "A Human Enterprise." *Science* 127: 1324–27; June 6, 1958. Science as lived by its practitioners, especially in its human and social aspects, bears but little resemblance to the stereotypes of science as described in print.

[22] Howard Gruber and Valmai Gruber, "Hermann von Helmholtz: Nineteenth-Century Polymorph." *Scientific Monthly* 83: 92–99; August 1956.

Acquaintance with Related Research

In all scientific endeavor, research workers have recognized their interdependence in the identification and solution of problems. In spite of difficulties in securing the works of other scholars, even such early investigators as Roger Bacon and Leonardo da Vinci reveal an extensive knowledge of the writings of other scholars in their special fields of interest. On the other hand, it must be admitted that certain able scientists and scholars have considered it undesirable or even unwise to study closely the related literature dealing with the particular problem under study, fearing that these earlier studies would condition the investigator's mind to see the problem in the same way and thus overlook a new or more promising approach. It would seem essential and reasonable to read critically in the related literature as a stimulus to thinking.

Intellectual Curiosity and Drive

The pages of the history of science and scholarship are filled with the names of workers led or driven to their discoveries by consuming intellectual curiosity or by some compelling drive. Historians especially have been prodigious workers with remarkable powers of concentration. Pavlov's parting advice to young investigators was to become familiar with the groundwork of the science, to become accustomed to simple scientific tools, to penetrate beneath the surface of things, to remain modest, and to develop a compelling intellectual curiosity: "And lastly, science must be your passion. Remember that science claims a man's whole life. Had he two lives they would not suffice. Science demands an undivided allegiance from its followers. In your work and in your research there must always be passion."[23]

Willingness to Pay the Price

Research workers frequently encounter certain costs and hazards (financial, physical, or otherwise). Wallin[24] tells of the early difficulties of clinical psychologists in securing recognition and prestige, as compared with the M.D. In one of his early clinical positions he did all the indi-

---

[23] Ivan Pavlov, *Scientific Monthly* 81: 129; September 1955.
Also see Clarence Leuba, "A New Look at Curiosity and Creativity." *Journal of Higher Education* 29: 132–40; March 1958.
[24] J. E. Wallace Wallin, *The Odyssey of a Psychologist*: Pioneering Experiences in Special Education, Clinical Psychology, and Mental Hygiene with a Comprehensive Bibliography of the Author's Publications. Wilmington, Del.: The Author, 1955. p. 43–51.

vidual and group testing, scored the papers, made the records, compiled the results, did the transcribing (as much as could be done), and the clerical work (filing, indexing, typing case reports, letters, write-ups of results, articles, and answering phone calls). He did not even have the use of a typewriter but had to purchase his own machine, on which he did all of the official typing. He paid for his own stationery and stamps. Wallin encountered serious obstacles in the early days of his clinical work, an experience that he shared with many other psychologists, in securing recognition as a professional staff member, in studying psychological phenomena of certain patients, in freedom of movement on the grounds of the institution, in association with medical members of the staff, and in freedom of publication and attendance at professional meetings.

Creativity and Ingenuity

As to technique and equipment, the most important instrument or element in research is the mind of man. Although adequate methods, techniques, equipment, and working conditions are important in many types of research, ornate laboratory equipment and complex measuring and recording instruments will not of themselves guarantee soundness of thinking or valid evidence. Great discoveries have been made in unexpected places and in improvised laboratories.

A Negative Image of the Scientist

An executive in industry has commented on the negative image of the scientist among high-school pupils, as reported by Margaret Mead and Rhoda Metraux. He goes on to refute this false impression by data from approximately half the 2,400 technically trained specialists engaged in research for the du Pont Company. These scientists received their education in 258 colleges and universities in the United States and 34 foreign institutions, 68 per cent with doctoral degrees, with specialization chiefly in chemistry and to a lesser extent in chemical engineering, other types of engineering, physics, bacteriology, and biochemistry. The data from these specialists refute the negative image of the scientist as follows:[25]

1. "A scientist should not marry. No one wants to be such a scientist or to marry him." For the sample, 88 per cent of the scientists are married, with an average of two children per family.

2. "His work may be dangerous. Chemicals may explode. He may be hurt

[25] Samuel Lenher, *The Scientist as a Person.* Tenth Annual Management Conference, Graduate School of Business and Public Administration, Cornell University, Ithaca, N.Y., April 18. 1958. E. I. du Pont de Nemours and Co., 1958. 15 p.

by radiation, or may die." The injury frequency rate for the scientists was lower than the over-all company rate during the same period.

3. "He may not believe in God, or may lose his religion." Seventy-five per cent of the research workers mentioned church in listing their activities.

4. "He is a brain; he is so involved in his work that he doesn't know what is going on in the world. He has no other interests and neglects his body for his mind. . . . He has no social life, no other intellectual interests, no hobbies or relaxations." Among 37 per cent of the scientists there was a range of 64 different civic activities.

5. "His work is uninteresting, dull, monotonous, tedious, time-consuming, and, though he works for years, he may see no results or may fail, and he is likely to receive neither adequate recompense nor recognition. He may live in a cold-water flat; his laboratory may be dingy." Only a few scientists found research dull. One out of four of these scientists decided upon his career before reaching the age of fifteen, and most of these specialists had a strong personal interest in the field of research represented.

6. "If he works by himself, he is alone and has heavy expenses. If he works for a big company, he has to do as he is told, and his discoveries must be turned over to the company and may not be used; he is just a cog in a machine." It is common for the scientist to share through a bonus system in the rewards resulting from his discoveries. Although scientists are different from ordinary people, in terms of creativity, it is this difference that contributes to the understanding of our world.

Attitudes in Educational Research

The practical approach, informal language (probably unacceptable to many scientists), and human (even sentimental) qualities represented in a description of the research worker's attitudes toward attacking curriculum problems may prove appealing to many beginning graduate students and field workers of limited experience. The concrete suggestions, as abbreviated and summarized below, will help answer two major questions: "What sorts of attitudes do I want to guide me as I do research?" and "What sorts of problems do I want to work on?"[26] The list is presented with full recognition of the possibility that arch critics of education may object to both the language and the sentiment.

1. In doing research, I do not have to act like somebody who isn't "me"; I can do research so that what I do is more and more clearly mine.

2. Research is an operation by which I am trying to become a better

[26] Quoted from Ross L. Mooney, "The Researcher Himself," *Research for Curriculum Improvement.* 1957 Yearbook. Washington: Association for Supervision and Curriculum Development, a Department of the National Education Association, 1957. p. 179–81.

Also see Abraham Shumsky, "Teachers Explore Their Attitudes toward Research." *Educational Research Bulletin* 37: 31–38, 56; February 12, 1958.

self-teacher so that my experience can say more things to me, give me more to think about and feel.

3. I can do research just for myself if I want to. However, I can have more fun, if, on some things at least, I can share my experiences with others.

4. A man doesn't have to publish to do research; he can communicate the shape of his experience in a lot of ways, and often the best way is right on the job with those with whom he associates daily.

5. There is very little to differentiate a good teacher from a researcher since both are avid inquirers.

6. It is no disgrace not to know a particular skill; I need not apologize for that. What would embarrass me in my own eyes would be to forget that my authority has to come from my own handling of myself.

7. A good place to think about doing research is in the middle of some activity where I am trying to do something that is important to me. My research is then my attempt to improve my actions in getting the values I want out of my experience.

8. My research will require a clarification of what I want just as much as it will require a clarification of how to get what I want in the most effective ways.

9. Teaching is at the very heart of life's most cogent situations. Human behavior is then as complex as it ever gets. Research depends on a willingness to accept the complexity and work within it.

10. The curriculum can be thought of in a number of different ways.

11. Proof is not a sledge hammer which can drive things into other people's heads. Proof is an "illustration," a "suggestion," an "offering"—not a bludgeon.

12. When I hit the "intangibles," as I most certainly will, I will consider them as useful constructions of mine which I can make more useful by (*a*) specifying what is meant in concrete situations and (*b*) showing how the constructions fit into a larger system of constructions. To run from engagement with the intangibles is to run from the problem of organizing one's experience.

13. In curriculum building, I cannot stop with a naming of "activities" I feel are valuable for children to do; I have to know what the children are actually experiencing while they are acting.

14. The critical unit is the experience of an experiencer. This means I am not down to basic data until I know what's going on in an individual child's experiencing.

15. Studying behavior is not the same as studying experience. I can watch a child's behavior without relating the action I see to what I think the child is experiencing.

16. To be sensitive to the experiencing of a child, I have to be able to posit myself as if I were in the center of experiencing of the child.

17. I can never be the child, of course, nor can I ever know what the

full inclusion of his experience may be, but there is no escape for me—my primary data are my "as if" projections.

18. These projections are, of course, within my experience. I do not get outside my experience. Projections are a function of myself.

19. The more "as if" selves I can differentiate in myself, the richer my humanity and the greater the resources for projecting reliable data in the next "as if" case.

20. What is important in "objectifying" is the capacity to hold a form in the center of attention while differentiating it from as many other forms as possible. This makes a form stand out for easy and reliable grasping.

21. Objectivity can be fostered by the way I give my attention to the field in which the form is taken to appear, i.e., by looking at the whole with the intention of seeing the whole while, at the same time, noting as many differentiations as possible within the whole. When this happens, I have a maximum of relations by which to structure forms in the field. My judgments are then more reliable.

22. Scientists who deal with inanimate material use the same basic methods I do; it is only that they can check their "as if" position in their on-going experience with greater ease than I. My compensation is that I am already nearer what I value in life at the point where I get my data. The physical scientist has a long way to go to make wisdom out of his knowledge.

23. I will know I'm off the track if, at any time, my getting of data seems to require that I treat others in ways I would not treat myself.

24. I will not be a failure in research as long as I'm learning better how to make good use of me. I am my own final judge in this matter.

25. When I seek criticism of what I'm doing in research, I'm asking my critics to tell me how they organize their experience in situations similar to those I present. This is a good sharp way of challenging a sharing right at the point where communication can be most poignant.

FREEDOM AND RESPONSIBILITY FOR RESEARCH

External Inhibiting Factors

Certain conditions external to the investigator himself may inhibit freedom for research:[27]

1. Tradition in the school or community may prove a powerful retarding influence.

2. Lack of time, energy, and resources has been a block for most teachers and administrators.

[27] Ronald C. Doll, "Freedom for Research," *Research for Curriculum Improvement*. 1957 Yearbook. Washington: Association for Supervision and Curriculum Development, a Department of the National Education Association, 1957. p. 249–68.

Also see William H. Blanchard, "Intellectual Inhibition and the Search for Scientific Truth." *Journal of Social Psychology* 47: 55–70; February 1958.

3. A climate of co-operative group work is lacking in many schools.

4. Research activity has failed significantly in one or more instances, and it has been deemed unworthy of further expenditure of time and money.

5. A particular research project is believed to have endangered the educational welfare of children.

6. Research looks so much like John Dewey's "experimentalism" that it is out of step with the prevailing educational philosophy.

7. Research procedures have been found difficult—even incomprehensible.

8. Research is considered to be the business of a few administrators.

9. Research has threatened the strongly held but vaguely supported opinions of certain supersensitive and influential teachers and administrators.

Internal Inhibiting Factors

Internal factors, such as feelings of fear, threat, and uncertainty, may inhibit freedom for research on the part of school people and others:

1. They are afraid to experiment with public money and with other people's children.

2. They fear starting research activity in the wrong situation or in the wrong way.

3. They feel threatened when they are urged to do research concerning matters about which they are already insecure.

4. They believe they lack the necessary understanding and skill to make the end result satisfactory in their own and other people's eyes.

5. They are wanting in the adventuresome spirit that would impel them to take calculated risks in solving their problems.

Obstacles to Research in Social Science

Similar inhibiting conditions restrict research in the various social fields. Chapin points out that application of social-science knowledge to the solution of problems of human relations is hampered by existing habits of thought and action, with at least eight social obstacles to the acceptance of current knowledge or evidence in the social-science field:[28]

1. The subject matter of social science is emotion-arousing.

2. The normative set and value-judgment approach tend to attach "praise" and "blame" to natural situations in human relationships.

3. The scientific social observer is himself a part of the social process he tries to observe.

4. The confidential and privileged character of much sociological in-

[28] Francis S. Chapin, *Experimental Designs in Sociological Research*. Revised Edition. New York: Harper & Brothers, 1955. p. 250–66.

formation makes scientific or objective formulation of knowledge a difficult process.

5. "Conspiracies of silence" involve conventions that often block social research or implementation of evidence.

6. There may be unpleasant consequences to minority groups when social-science knowledge is applied.

7. Much of the subject matter of social science consists of verbal behavior, which frequently is intangible and trite.

8. Concentrated and continuous mental effort is required to know that such concepts as intangibility, relativity, and probability are basic to social understanding.

Ways to Promote Freedom in Research

Specific ways in which school personnel can overcome obstacles to freedom in research, especially in the curriculum field, have been simply phrased, in terms of the language, principles, and procedures of action research:[29]

1. Building a feeling among potential researchers that it is all right to have problems.

2. Design researches that will satisfy the needs people feel.

3. Start gently, perhaps on a modified-voluntary basis.

4. Talk often about the importance of getting evidence.

5. Help people find security in groups, and help them work together successfully as group members.

6. Provide safety valves through which to "blow off steam" when things do not go well.

7. Allow for the lone researcher as well as for the researcher who wishes to work with only one or two other persons.

8. Use every legitimate means to build understanding of the research process.

9. Involve in research activities those teachers, parents, and other persons who are high in the power structure of school and community.

10. Provide all the time, resources, and help you can.

11. Attend to the climate of the school as a whole, as a valuable stimulus to research.

12. Be realistic about the limits, internal and external.

13. Resolve to press against the limits that actually exist.

14. Capitalize on growing expertness by urging its use in additional research.

[29] Ronald C. Doll, *op. cit.*

Responsibility and Opportunity of the Teacher for Research

The university staff member is generally expected to engage in research and to communicate the results to others.

For years it has commonly been accepted that research and the communication of its results to the world is a basic duty of the university to society. Indeed, the scholar's intellectual drive to inquire has been regarded almost as powerful as the physical urge to eat and sleep. The nature of this research has often been discussed. . . .

But here we are more concerned with the results of research—the transmission of its fruits to others. Quite properly this may be regarded as the return to society of society's investment in the university and in the scholar. The researcher who does not report the results of his inquiry has failed to live up to one of his basic obligations. He has kept information to himself which belongs to all. Thus the first objective of the writing up of research is the preparation of information for the use of others. A second purpose lies in making available such research for scrutiny and objective judgment by others in the same field. This invites the judgment of peers—the soundest and most searching of all criticism. Viewed in this light, research may be said to be incomplete until it has been prepared for the examination of other inquirers in the same subject-matter area. It is at this point that the quality of research is tested. Although not always promptly expressed, penetrating judgment is made; the fourflusher, the incompetent, and above all, the dabbler are discovered. Third, the formal presentation of the results of investigation compels the scholar to summarize his work and come to logical conclusions based on assembled evidence. All too often, half-completed or poorly organized investigation leads to fallacious or illogical impressions which color the thinking of the scholar, may warp his whole outlook, and mislead others.

Certainly, the faculty adviser who aspires to direct graduate degree candidates or to examine them should be currently alive to the problems of research. Far too many advisers appear content to rest on the laurels of their own dissertations, a doubtful resting place in many cases. How often we hear the phrase on the lips of one many years out of graduate school, "Now in my dissertation, I. . . ." It is the research beyond the dissertation which is the most significant and which qualifies a teacher to direct the studies of younger people. Is it too much to expect that every graduate faculty member should progress beyond his first dissertation stage in the great intellectual adventure of scholarship? Essentially, graduate education involves investigation; individual faculty members as well as the entire graduate school must demonstrate the spirit of inquiry. We would do well to recall the words of President William Rainey Harper of the University of Chicago, who asserted fifty years ago that "it is only the man who has made investigation who may teach others to investigate. Without this spirit in the instructor, and without his example, students will never be led to undertake the work."

A person who professes to follow an intellectual career should thrill to active research which includes the transmission of results to others. Not only does it make for an intellectually alert person but it makes for a better teacher. The teacher who carries on an active research program has at his command a sense of awareness and of deep understanding which others who plow conscientiously but dully through lectures of many years standing cannot possibly possess. He has at his fingertips illuminating examples and searching questions which can give his lectures or discussions that vibrancy and sparkle which make for real teaching.[30]

After traveling in the United States, Canada, England, Scotland, and France, inquiring into the organization and structure of educational research (especially in the United States), an Australian investigator has reported favorably, even highly optimistically, on the possibilities for research by workers in elementary and secondary schools.[31]

Can schools as we know them undertake research? This reduces to the questions whether the staff has the ability, the time, the interest, and the power to undertake it. As far as ability is concerned, on every staff there must be some with the power to formulate questions about their activities, to analyse these, to clarify the assumptions behind practices, to consider how to evaluate the result of their activities, to question the effectiveness of the relationship of school to community, of teacher to pupil, of learning experiences to reality. Something must depend on the size of the school; it is too idealistic to expect every staff to be concerned with all problems, but every staff is concerned with some. I have no doubts about the ability of a big segment of the teaching strength of my own country to make lucid analyses of the problems facing them in educating children.

Have they the ability to devise techniques, or to use those already devised? There are many simple tools available to teachers for many enquiries and others that they can fashion for themselves with a little expert assistance. I believe we must expect teachers to know how to collect data about a problem, how to measure results, and where to get assistance. This means devoting some time to training; if research is accepted as an important attitude, or even a useful technique, there is no real problem here.

Can they interpret data and apply conclusions? They are doing it every day. We have no right to assume they cannot and should not do it; rather I think it an obligation to assume that they can, and to try to develop their ability in this way.

Have teachers the time for research? If it is regarded by them as important, they have, and will always have, the time. If we believe that progress comes only from ceaseless questioning of customs and practice, we should be encouraging teachers never to cease from such questioning, putting on them

---

[30] Quoted from Everett Walters, "On the Results of Research." *Graduate School Record* 8: 1, 3; March 1955.

[31] Quoted from W. C. Radford, "The Function of the School, Department of Education, University, National Centre and Independent Body in Educational Research," *Report of the First International Conference on Educational Research.* Educational Studies and Documents, No. 20. Paris: UNESCO, 1956. p. 36–40.

the onus of much enquiry taking it for granted that they have enough interest in their job to pursue it in their own time if necessary. But there is much research in classroom practices that does not need additional time or additional preparation—only the interest to undertake it.

Have teachers the interest in research?—Interest, that is, to initiate it and undertake it? The realistic view in most countries is, I fear, that not many teachers have. But this is probably more a matter of approach and training than of natural disinterest. My own view is that we cannot expect *all* teachers to have an interest in it, but a substantial proportion—enough to ensure that in any staffed school about two or three teachers in every five should be doing something in the way of research into their own school problems. Administrative authorities, and teacher training institutions, have an obligation here which, with a few outstanding exceptions, I do not think they have accepted.

Have they the power to undertake it? I have yet to hear of any school, or teacher, forbidden to experiment in some way. Every society has its limits, and I would not question these here; but within these limits we should as educators be urging those to whom the schools belong, or those who administer them, to encourage teachers to enquire, to research their opinions, assumptions, techniques, and results.

In sum, I believe the teachers in every country have the opportunity and the capacity to undertake some research. Such research, carried out in the day-to-day work of the school, should be concerned directly with the problems of that school. It can properly concern itself with such matters as child development, class organization, teacher-pupil relationships, interaction with the community, curriculum matters, teaching techniques, and many others.

A more critical survey concludes that many useful activities conducted under the name of educational research are incorrectly labeled research in the accepted meaning of the term, particularly in the research offices of large city school systems, state departments of education, and state education associations. It has been suggested that progress may be made toward meeting the need for basic research, if persons trained and experienced in research, such as the members of the American Educational Research Association, will increase their efforts to help teachers and administrators in the public schools realize the essential nature of research and its contribution to school practice and to education in general.[32]

RESEARCH AND GRADUATE EDUCATION

Research and its encouragement constitute a natural domain and an inevitable commitment for every great graduate school. And in this area there are some current popular fallacies that we need to join in refuting. We

[32] David G. Ryans, "Are Educational Research Offices Conducting Research?" *Journal of Educational Research* 51: 173–83; November 1957.

need to make plain what research is—hard and sustained work by competent and highly trained people in fields of their choice. It is not some species of magic. There are no incantations or tricks, and nobody waves a wand.

Research invites many and various figures of speech. People say it is the lifeblood of the professions, the key to our future, battle and conquest (though often they forget that it can be frustration and failure), a race, the exploration of frontiers, the study of submerged icebergs, a Sherlockian unraveling of clues. Such figures may have value for their insights, but our best approach is to point to a few common research elements, recognizing differences in techniques and objectives. We need to stress intelligence, integrity, training, imagination, and work. And we need to give a large role to investigation, experiment, hard thinking, freedom, time, self-criticism. There is also the little matter of patience. We should never judge the quality of scholars by measuring their lists of publications with administrative rulers. A medical colleague of mine worked for twenty years on a research, the first ten without coming to any turning point, and then ten more. At the end he had discovered cortisone and, with a fellow researcher, he became a Nobel Prize winner.

Research looks for principles. Research works out from principles. In the past we have understandably depended much, as indeed we still do, on the richness of European basic research. Research should, and in the long run does, jump provincial and national boundaries. But I think we of the American university world will have to depend much more upon ourselves in the future, and the graduate schools are logical centers for our fundamental research—the kind that Mr. Conant describes as prospecting for oil in unexplored country as contrasted with applied research, which is also highly important, but which Mr. Conant says is drilling for oil where you know you are likely to strike it. From ideas and principles born of imaginative basic research, applications flow out in an almost endless stream, as is illustrated by modern medicine with its myriad uses of the germ theory, nutrition, hormones, genetics, and cells.[33]

In analyzing the satisfactions in graduate education, a graduate dean identifies six possible and desirable accomplishments.[34]

The years in the graduate school constitute the educational period when self-responsibility asserts itself, the processes of inquiry and research in particular are learned, a subject-matter area is staked out and explored, ability to express thoughts and to write creatively is acquired, an intellectual career is anticipated, and professional responsibilities and behavior are understood.

Usually the modern graduate school serves two major purposes or provides two types of opportunity for the student: to extend his range of knowledge and understanding in a field of special interest, and to engage in creative research.

[33] Quoted from Theodore C. Blegen, "Graduate Education and Research: Problems and Prospects." *Graduate School Record* 11: 3–7; December 1957.

[34] Quoted from N. P. Hudson, "On Satisfactions in Graduate Education." *Graduate School Record* 9: 1, 3; December 1955.

By creative research is meant the active utilization of the techniques of research by the student to discover for himself basic insights into certain areas of knowledge. Therefore, creative research cannot be a means of piling up fact upon fact but rather it must yield knowledge of the elemental. . . .

Research serves to reveal the inner workings of the simple elements which heretofore have been taken for granted. If research becomes an end in itself it falls into disrepute, but if it provides the necessary building blocks for the establishment of theory and ideas where such theory and ideas are needed, or if it helps revitalize theory by calling into question dogmatic proposition, then theory becomes an ennobling venture which finds in the graduate school a haven which permits it to flourish. . . .

Graduate education ought eventually to take the student back to the simple; that is, graduate education, whatever else it accomplishes, should lead to knowledge of the fundamental processes and concepts which give root to a discipline or a profession. And since root concepts and processes adhering to a discipline or a profession must be subjected to modification and at times revision, the graduate school needs to keep open the avenue of basic research. Stagnant theory leads not to knowledge but to dogma. Research is perhaps the only assurance we have that a discipline or a profession will not decay into meaningless scraps of dogmatic utterances.[35]

SCIENTIFIC PROGRESS AND SOCIAL RESPONSIBILITY

Research in the physical sciences developed much earlier than in the social fields because of certain favorable factors and conditions: greater freedom of inquiry, seemingly more urgent problems, financial support, objectivity of problem and procedure, invention of instruments for recording and measuring, standardization of terminology, collection of specimens such as in museums, emphasis on scientific training, and publication of scientific materials.

A number of factors have favored educational research in the United States: a democratic philosophy, decentralized schools, financial support, research departments and bureaus, teacher training and graduate work, and publication facilities.

In general, the accomplishments of science in our time are almost miraculous, with the rate of progress still accelerating. Research can continue to expand as long as society is friendly toward this form of progress. There is evidence of stress and strain, however, between the great accomplishments of the physical sciences and the much slower development of the social sciences (which provide the controls for human behavior). At times an impossible course of action has been suggested, to the effect that physical research should take a holiday until social science catches up, since certain discoveries (as in the domain of

[35] Quoted from Bernard Mehl, "Graduate Education and the Teaching Profession." *Graduate School Record* 9: 3–4; July 1956.

atomic energy) involve the potential for great harm to, or even destruction of, society when wrongly applied. Scholars and scientists have a grave social obligation to see that scientific and technological (and social) discoveries are used for the benefit of society and that appropriate controls of human behavior are developed, with the aid of knowledge in social science, psychology, education, and religion.

Specific examples of advances in science that also generate new hazards of unprecedented magnitude include certain dangers to life from widely disseminated radiation, the burden of man-made chemicals, fumes, and smogs of unknown biological effect which we now absorb, large-scale deterioration of our natural resources, and the potential of totally destructive war.

The determination that scientific knowledge is to be used for human good or for purposes of destruction is in the control of social agencies. For such decisions, these agencies and ultimately the people themselves must be aware of the facts and the probable consequences of action. Here scientists can play a decisive role: they can bring the facts and their estimates of the results of proposed actions before the people.[36]

Many of our modern scholars and scientists recognize that we cannot and must not impose upon the social scientists alone the burden of solving our social, economic, and political problems.

Public issues, and especially those of world-wide portent, are the concern of all of us, and scientists of every kind (as well as nonscientists) must learn to think constructively about them, to speak out, and to make their voices heard. For this, we need to find efficient organizational patterns through which scientists may effectively express their views on vital issues. The annals, brief though they are, of such an organization as the Federation of American Scientists demonstrate, I think, that vigilant action groups of this type are indispensable in our society.

But we must not forget that the American Association for the Advancement of Science itself is constitutionally committed "to improve the effectiveness of science in the promotion of human welfare" as well as "to increase public understanding of the importance and promise of the methods of science in human progress." It is my firm hope that the Association will quickly find ways for an increasingly effective implementation of these mandates.

It has recently been said that the record of the past decade amply justifies the statement that the scientific community has a social conscience as well as a newly heightened social role. I am certain that the social consciences of the

---

[36] Quoted from Ward Pigman and Others, "Association Affairs: Preliminary Report of AAAS Interim Committee on the Social Aspects of Science." *Scientific Monthly* 84: 146–51; March 1957.

scientists will insure that they will find the way to fulfill the solemn obligations of that role.[37]

Lasswell emphasizes that the impact of science and technology does not occur in a social vacuum but in a context of human identifications, demands, and expectations. He proposes that it is appropriate for political scientists, in company with other scientists and scholars dealing with human affairs, to improve our procedures of continuous deliberation on the potential impacts of science and technology upon human affairs.

No doubt the American Political Science Association and other professional societies constitute an appropriate network for the purpose. We can sustain continuing conferences devoted to the examination of emerging developments. As fellow professionals, we have special responsibility for giving thought to the aggregate effects of any specific innovation.[38]

The Parliament of Science, sponsored by the American Association for the Advancement of Science, illustrates a way whereby scientists may appropriately consider the social consequence of their findings or explore the problems of science and public policy. The general principles (which underlie a larger number of specific conclusions) are as follows:[39]

1. Scientific endeavor is one phase of human intellectual effort; the degree to which it flourishes depends largely upon the extent to which intellectual effort generally is supported and encouraged.

2. Optimal progress in science requires increased support for basic research.

3. As funds for the support of science increase, it becomes increasingly necessary to formulate appropriate plans and procedures for the administration and correlation of the total scientific effort and to give closer scrutiny to national scientific policy.

4. In order that science may progress most effectively, and in order that science may be wisely used for the improvement of human welfare, scientists must have the maximum possible freedom to communicate with each other, both in person and by publication, and to communicate with the public.

5. Scientists are dedicated to the finding of new knowledge. As citizens, they have the responsibility to concern themselves with the social consequences of their scientific findings and to inform the public of the consequences they foresee.

6. The primary goal of education is the intellectual development of the individual. The primary need of education is to employ quality and to raise standards—of teachers, of curricula, and of what is expected of students.

[37] Quoted from Laurence H. Snyder, "What We Most Need to Know." *Scientific Monthly* 84: 17–23; January 1957.
[38] Quoted from Harold D. Lasswell, *op. cit.*
[39] Quoted from American Association for the Advancement of Science, "1958 Parliament of Science." *Science* 127: 852–58; April 18, 1958.

7. In the assignment of funds to the improvement of education, first priority should go to improvements in curricula, teaching, and the status and salaries of teachers.

Sears maintains that, among the practical problems of humanity today, our relation to the immediate space in which we live is of greater critical importance than man's dramatic invasion of outer space. Our concern with the technological applications of mathematics, physics, and chemistry may have beclouded the fact that we need biology in general and ecology in particular to illuminate man's relation to his environment. It is not enough that the biological sciences are supported primarily in the fields of medicine and agriculture, and that social sciences are used for dealing with the immediate ills of society; we need general encouragement and utilization of all science to guide the cultural and physical aspects of future evolution. We need more and better science teaching, not merely to produce scientists, but also to develop scientific literacy among our citizens in general, in order that society may support a science whose results are applied for the welfare of mankind. From this point of view, "our future security may depend less upon priority in exploring outer space than upon our wisdom in managing the space in which we live."[40]

The preceding paragraphs of this section indicate that much has been said about the social responsibility of the scientist, frequently meaning the physical scientist. The rapid increase of knowledge about the control of the physical world, as illustrated in the preceding paragraphs, has posed the question of whether society will be able to direct this knowledge, applying it for the benefit of mankind rather than for the destruction of man and his civilization. The social responsibility of the social scientist is equally great in the sense of discovering enough knowledge about society so that society can, if it wishes to employ this information, control the use of physical knowledge. The next question logically follows: Once the social scientists gain the social knowledge that is needed to control physical knowledge and society, how will this social evidence be controlled and what is to prevent a social scientist from taking advantage of such social knowledge to expedite the enslavement or the destruction of society? What is there to prevent one group in society from exploiting this social knowledge for the purpose of controlling another group? Examples of this problem may be found in the fields of market research, public opinion, industrial relations, and

[40] Paul B. Sears, "The Inexorable Problem of Space." *Science* 127: 9–16; January 3, 1958.

economic control (as in price and monetary controls). The social scientist's activities should be an asset to democratic society.[41]

The view just expressed implies that the social scientist must be continually conscious of his obligation as a member of society.

He may not, any more than anyone else, violate the law or general moral understandings. It is no defense to say that he has techniques that enable him to do so—so does the gangster. Nor may the social scientist feel any special pride in the fact that the indirect nature of his techniques makes detection unlikely. He cannot conceive of himself as an observer only, as one who stands off and surveys the world as a kind of curious drama. If it is a drama, then he is on-stage himself. The social scientist tries to keep values out of his research; they are felt to interfere with objectivity. A favorite way of putting the matter is this: "We all have many roles. I have a role as a citizen and with it go certain faiths and beliefs. But when I enter my laboratory, I am a scientist, and I leave my values at the door, along with my galoshes." This sort of schizophrenia may be possible for the physicist, but it is not for the social scientist. For it is as a social scientist that he is a citizen. This is his position in society, just as others are blacksmiths, physicians, or newsdealers, and society pays him for it because he makes a contribution it values. But society will not long pay a man who violates its laws, its mores, or its tacit understandings. And if the man claims that his work demands it, society is likely to put an end to his work. Nor is the social scientist abroad immune from the controls of our society. He is still a member of our society, nay more, a representative of our society, and he has the same obligations that we enjoin on any visitor to a foreign land.

The question remains of how these controls are to be enforced. I doubt that legal protections alone would be sufficient. Even in the case where a subject's legal rights may have been violated, he may not, in practice, be able to protect himself. He may not have the money to fight a difficult case through court, and even if he has, a court case is likely to force him to reveal, for all the world to hear, the very secret things he did not want even the social scientist to know. He may prefer to salvage some solace from the fact that few people read professional social science journals.

In order to have controls that work, they must come from within the profession itself, just as the strongest controls on any professional come from his own colleagues. Now I am well aware of the fact that many, perhaps most, social scientists feel no need for controls. In practice, although they might do so, they do not lie to their subjects or ever violate a confidence. They are extremely careful of a subject's personal or private life and accord him complete respect for any rights that he claims. But they do so not because they have been formally trained to do so as researchers, but because of their own upbringing as individuals. From this point of view, the social scientist learned more at his mother's breast than he did at his professor's feet. It is no contradiction to point out that in research courses the student is told that

[41] Arnold M. Rose, "The Social Responsibility of the Social Scientist," *Theory and Method in the Social Sciences, op. cit.*, p. 179–92.

he should not violate confidences and should respect a subject's rights. These suggestions are justified, not in moral terms, not in terms of the understandings that a member of our society should respect, but as being, simply, good for research. It seems to me that the responsibility of graduate schools of social research extends further than this, for the university, the social scientist it produces, and the subjects he studies are united as members of the same moral community.[42]

CONCLUDING STATEMENT

It is both logical and functional to discuss research in terms of the characteristics and sequence of scientific method. Interdisciplinary research and professional collaboration have led to the development of certain theoretical concepts and propositions that are regarded as the common property of education, psychology, sociology, and anthropology. Values are inescapably present in research, in the form of such factors as purpose, motive, aspiration, interest, need, attitude, feeling, emotion, and sentiment. The hallmarks of the scientist are typically problem awareness, appropriate specialization, intellectual curiosity and drive, willingness to encounter hazards in research, and creativity and ingenuity. Although certain external and internal factors may inhibit freedom for research, there are definite ways in which the investigator, including school personnel, may overcome obstacles to freedom in research. Graduate education may well serve the two purposes of broadening and deepening the student's knowledge in a particular field, and of creative investigation. It is not enough to emphasize the social responsibility of the physical scientist. The social scientist has an equally great obligation, that of using his knowledge so as to be an asset to democratic society.

SELECTED REFERENCES

American Association for the Advancement of Science. "1958 Parliament of Science." *Science* 127: 852-58; April 18, 1958.

ANDREWS, F. Emerson. *Philanthropic Foundations*. New York: Russell Sage Foundation, 1956. 459 p.

BAITSELL, George A., Editor. *Science in Progress*. Series 9. New Haven: Yale University Press, 1955. 343 p.

BARBER, Bernard. *Science and the Social Order*. Glencoe, Ill.: Free Press, 1952. xxiii+288 p.

BATES, Ralph S. *Scientific Societies in the United States*. Second Edition. New York: Technology Press and Columbia University Press, 1958. 308 p.

---

[42] Quoted from Edward Gross, "Social Science Techniques: A Problem of Power and Responsibility." *Scientific Monthly* 83: 242–47; November 1956.

BECK, William S. *Modern Science and the Nature of Life*. New York: Harcourt, Brace and Co., 1957. 319 p.

BECKER, Howard, and Others. *For a Science of Social Man*. New York: The Macmillan Co., 1954. 289 p.

BERGMANN, Gustav. *Philosophy of Science*. Madison: University of Wisconsin Press, 1957. xiii+181 p.

BLANK, David M., and STIGLER, George J. *The Demand and Supply of Scientific Personnel*. New York: National Bureau of Economic Research, 1957. xiv+200 p.

BOGARDUS, Emory S. *The Development of Social Thought*. Third Edition. New York: Longmans, Green and Co., 1955. x+660 p.

BORING, E. G. *A History of Experimental Psychology*. Second Edition. New York: Appleton-Century-Crofts, 1950. xxi+777 p.

BRAITHWAITE, Richard B. *Scientific Explanation*. Cambridge, England: Cambridge University Press, 1953. 376 p.

BRODBECK, May. "The Philosophy of Science and Educational Research," in "Methodology of Educational Research." *Review of Educational Research* 27: 427-40; December 1957.

BRODIE, Bernard. "Scientific Progress and Political Science." *Scientific Monthly* 85: 315-19; December 1957.

BRONOWSKI, Jacob. *The Common Sense of Science*. Cambridge: Harvard University Press, 1953. 154 p.

BROWN, Clarence W., and GHISELLI, Edwin E. *Scientific Method in Psychology*. New York: McGraw-Hill Book Co., 1955. xii+368 p.

BROWN, Harcourt, Editor. *Science and the Creative Spirit*: Essays on Humanistic Aspects of Science. Toronto: University of Toronto Press, 1958. xxvii + 165 p.

BROWN, Harrison, BONNER, James, and WEIR, John. *The Next Hundred Years*: Man's Natural and Technological Resources. New York: Viking Press, 1957. xi + 193 p.

BURCHARD, John E., Editor. *Mid-Century*: The Social Implications of Scientific Progress. Cambridge: Massachusetts Institute of Technology Press, 1950. xx + 549 p.

BUSH, George P., and HATTERY, Lowell H., Editors. *Teamwork in Research*. Washington: American University Press, 1953. xii + 191 p.

A Century of Progress in the Natural Sciences, 1853–1953. Published in celebration of the centennial of the California Academy of Sciences. San Francisco: California Academy of Sciences, 1955. 807 p.

CHAMBLISS, Rollin. *Social Thought*: From Hammurabi to Comte. New York: Dryden Press, 1954. ix + 469 p.

CLARK, Kenneth E. *America's Psychologists*: A Survey of a Growing Profession. Washington: American Psychological Association, 1957. ix + 247 p.

Committee on Institutional Research Policy. *Sponsored Research Policy of Colleges and Universities*. Washington: American Council on Education, 1955. vii + 93 p.

CONANT, James B. *Science and Common Sense*. New Haven: Yale University Press, 1951. xii+371 p.

COOLEY, William W. "Attributes of Potential Scientists." *Harvard Educational Review* 28:1-18; Winter 1958.

COREY, Stephen M. *Action Research to Improve School Practices*. New York: Bureau of Publications, Teachers College, Columbia University, 1953. xii+161 p.

COREY, Stephen M. "The Support of Research in Education." *Teachers College Record* 59:129-36; December 1957.

COUNTS, George S. "Education and the Technological Revolution." *Teachers College Record* 59: 309-18; March 1958.

CURTI, Merle, Editor. *American Scholarship in the Twentieth Century*. Library of Congress Series in American Civilization. Cambridge: Harvard University Press, 1953. vii+252 p.

DENNIS, Wayne, and Others. *Current Trends in Psychological Theory*. Pittsburgh: University of Pittsburgh Press, 1951. 213 p.

DINGLE, Herbert, Editor. *A Century of Science*: 1851-1951. New York: Roy Publishing Co., 1951. ix+338 p.

DOBY, John T., Editor. *An Introduction to Social Research*. Harrisburg: The Stackpole Co., 1954. x+275 p.

DUNSHEATH, Percy, Editor. *A Century of Technology*: 1851-1951. New York: Roy Publishing Co., 1951. ix+346 p.

EHLERS, Henry, Editor. *Crucial Issues in Education*. New York: Henry Holt and Co., 1955. 277 p.

ELMER, M. C. *Contemporary Social Thought*: Contributors and Trends. Pittsburgh: University of Pittsburgh Press, 1956. viii+256 p.

FEIGL, Herbert, and BRODBECK, May, Editors. *Readings in the Philosophy of Science*. New York: Appleton-Century-Crofts, 1953. ix+811 p.

FESTINGER, Leon, and KATZ, Daniel, Editors. *Research Methods in the Behavioral Sciences*. New York: Dryden Press, 1953. xi+660 p.

FLUGEL, J. C. *A Hundred Years of Psychology*. Revised Edition. New York: The Macmillan Co., 1951. 424 p.

FOSHAY, Arthur W., and Others. *Research for Curriculum Improvement*. 1957 Yearbook. Washington: Association for Supervision and Curriculum Development, National Education Association, 1957. x+348 p.

FRANK, P. *Philosophy of Science*. Englewood Cliffs, N. J.: Prentice-Hall, 1957. xxii+394 p.

FULLER, B. A. G. *A History of Philosophy*. Third Edition. Revised by Sterling M. McMurrin. New York: Henry Holt and Co., 1955. 618 p.

FULTON, James S. *Science and Man's Hope*. New York: Bookman Associates, 1955. 179 p.

GLASS, Bentley. "The Scientist in Contemporary Fiction." *Scientific Monthly* 85: 288-93; December 1957.

GOOD, Carter V., and SCATES, Douglas E. *Methods of Research*: Educational, Psychological, Sociological. New York: Appleton-Century-Crofts, 1954. xx+920 p.

HALL, Everett W. *Modern Science and Human Values*: A Study in the History of Ideas. Princeton: D. Van Nostrand Co., 1956. 483 p.

HILLWAY, Tyrus. *Introduction to Research*. Boston: Houghton Mifflin Co., 1956. p. 3-53.

HUTCHINGS, Edward, Jr., Editor. *Frontiers in Science*: A Survey. New York: Basic Books, 1958. 362 p.

IRVING, John A. *Science and Values*: Exploration in Philosophy and the Social Sciences. Toronto: Ryerson Press, 1952. xi+148 p.

JACOB, Philip E. *Changing Values in College*: An Exploratory Study of the Impact of College Teaching. New York: Harper & Brothers, 1957. x+178 p.

JEFFREYS, H. *Scientific Inference*. Second Edition. Cambridge, England: Cambridge University Press, 1957. 236 p.

KANTOR, J. R. *The Logic of Modern Science*. Bloomington, Ind.: Principia Press, 1953. xvi+359 p.

KOMAROVSKY, Mirra, Editor. *Common Frontiers of the Social Sciences*. Glencoe, Ill.: Free Press, 1957. viii+439 p.

LANGFELD, Herbert S., and Others, Editors. *A History of Psychology in Autobiography*. Vol. 4. Worcester, Mass.: Clark University Press, 1952. xii+356 p.

LAZARSFELD, Paul F., and ROSENBERG, Morris, Editors. *The Language of Social Research*: A Reader in the Methodology of Social Research. Glencoe, Ill.: Free Press, 1955. xiii+590 p.

LIKERT, Rensis, and HAYES, Samuel P., Jr., Editors. *Some Applications of Behavioural Research*. New York: Columbia University Press, 1957. UNESCO Publication. 333 p.

MACE, C. A., and VERNON, P. E., Editors. *Current Trends in British Psychology*. London: Methuen, 1953. viii+262 p.

MARCUSE, F. L., Editor. *Areas of Psychology*. New York: Harper & Brothers, 1954. viii+532 p.

MASON, S. F. *Main Currents of Scientific Thought*: A History of the Sciences. New York: Abelard-Schuman, 1954. viii+520 p.

McCORMICK, Thomas C., and FRANCIS, Roy G. *Methods of Research in the Behavioral Sciences*. New York: Harper & Brothers, 1958. Chapter 1.

MURDOCK, George P. "Anthropology as a Comparative Science." *Behavioral Science* 2: 249-54; October 1957.

NESS, Frederic W., Editor. *A Guide to Graduate Study*. Washington: American Council on Education, 1958. xi+335 p.

New Frontiers of Knowledge: A Symposium. Washington: Public Affairs Press, 1957. 125 p.

ODUM, H. W. *American Sociology*: The Story of Sociology in the United States through 1950. New York: Longmans, Green and Co., 1951. vi+501 p.

Office of Scientific Personnel, National Academy of Sciences-National Research Council. "Production of U. S. Scientists: Trends in the Number of Doctorates Granted in the Major Fields of Science and in the Humanities." *Science* 127: 682-86; March 28, 1958.

PERRY, Ralph B. *Realms of Value*: A Critique of Human Civilization. Cambridge: Harvard University Press, 1954. xii+497 p.

POOLE, Lynn. *Frontiers of Science*. New York: McGraw-Hill Book Co., 1958. 173 p.

ROBACK, A. A. *History of American Psychology*. New York: Library Publishers, 1952. xiv+426 p.

ROBACK, A. A., Editor. *Present-Day Psychology*: An Original Survey of Departments, Branches, Methods, and Phases, including Clinical and Dynamic Psychology. New York: Philosophical Library, 1955. 993 p.

ROE, Anne. *The Making of a Scientist*. New York: Dodd, Mead and Co., 1953. ix+244 p.

ROSE, Arnold M. *Theory and Method in the Social Sciences*. Minneapolis: University of Minnesota Press, 1954. xii+351 p.

RUMMEL, J. Francis. *An Introduction to Research Procedures in Education*. New York: Harper & Brothers, 1958. p. 1-19.

RUSSELL, Bertrand. *The Impact of Science on Society*. New York: Simon and Schuster, 1953. 114 p.

SARTON, George. *A Guide to the History of Science*. Waltham, Mass.: Chronica Botanica Co., 1952. xvii+316 p.

Scientific and Technical Societies of the United States and Canada. Sixth Edition. Washington: National Academy of Sciences-National Research Council, 1955. 441 p.

SEARLES, Herbert L. *Logic and Scientific Methods*: An Introductory Course. Second Edition. New York: Ronald Press, 1956. 378 p.

SEARS, Paul B. "The Inexorable Problem of Space." *Science* 127: 9-16; January 3, 1958.

STARK, Werner. *The Sociology of Knowledge*: An Essay in Aid of a Deeper Understanding of the History of Ideas. London: Routledge and Kegan Paul, 1958. xi+356 p.

STEVENS, S. S. "Measurement and Man." *Science* 127: 383-89; February 21, 1958.

STORR, Richard J. *The Beginnings of Graduate Education in America*. Chicago: The University of Chicago Press, 1953. x+196 p.

TATON, R. *Reason and Chance in Scientific Discovery*. New York: Philosophical Library, 1957. 171 p.

TOULMIN, Stephen. *The Philosophy of Science*: An Introduction. New York: Longmans, Green and Co., 1953. xiii+176 p.

TRAVERS, R. M. W. *An Introduction to Educational Research*. New York: The Macmillan Co., 1958. Chapters 1-3.

TYLER, R. W., and Others. *Graduate Study in Education*. Fiftieth Yearbook, National Society for the Study of Education. Chicago: The University of Chicago Press, 1951. xix+369 p.

UNDERWOOD, Benton J. *Psychological Research*. New York: Appleton-Century-Crofts, 1957. ix+298 p.

WATSON, Robert I. *Psychology as a Profession*. Garden City, N. Y.: Doubleday & Co., 1954. x+65 p.

WEAVER, Warren. "Science and the Citizen." *Science* 126: 1225-29; December 13, 1957.

WHITE, Lynn, Jr., Editor. *Frontiers of Knowledge in the Study of Man.* New York: Harper & Brothers, 1956. xii+330 p.

WIENER, Philip P., and NOLAND, Aaron, Editors. *Roots of Scientific Thought*: A Cultural Perspective. New York: Basic Books, 1957. x+677 p.

WILSON, J. T., and Others. *Current Trends in Psychology and the Behavioral Sciences.* Pittsburgh: University of Pittsburgh Press, 1954. xvi+142 p.

WOLFLE, Dael. *America's Resources of Specialized Talent.* The Report of the Commission on Human Resources and Advanced Training. New York: Harper & Brothers, 1954. xviii+332 p.

YOUNG, Pauline V. *Scientific Social Surveys and Research.* Third Edition. Englewood Cliffs, N. J.: Prentice-Hall, 1956. xx+540 p.

2

Problem and Hypothesis

This chapter discusses problem awareness, sources for identification of problems, factors in selection of the problem, initial statement and fuller definition of the problem, and formulation and testing of hypotheses.

AWARENESS OR IDENTIFICATION OF PROBLEMS

Many beginners in research and graduate students are prone to conclude that most of our educational problems have been solved. They may be overawed by the large number of research studies in print (considerably more than 100,000) and the more than 1,400 doctoral dissertations and studies per year in education. To these figures should be added a considerable number of master's theses and projects, although many master's degrees are awarded without a thesis requirement.

The difficulty for many beginners in research lies in an insensitivity to problems or "problem blindness." Later chapters of this book will present many examples of studies essential to future progress in education. Historical sources accumulate with each passing event, making necessary the extension of earlier historical narratives and sometimes a reinterpretation of older accounts. Descriptive-survey studies are soon out of date and must be repeated, as in the annual school census for a local system. Controlled experiments are repeated to test the validity of earlier investigations.

It may seem surprising that, early in the development of public schools in the United States, some educators mistakenly concluded that most of our educational problems had been solved, as expressed by the writer of more than a century ago in the *Ohio Journal of Education* (1856).

The popular interest, which has, of late years, attached to everything connected with Education, has prompted inquiry into all the departments of the subject; and to such a degree has the general surface of the subject been examined and expounded, that it is difficult to find a point of space unoccupied, or at least unnoticed. We have abounded in lectures, on all the theories, and all the arts of teaching; we have had volumes of codes for the government of schools.

At times, able scientists and scholars have overlooked problems and answers nearby. Moses G. Farmer said that the discovery of a telephone had flaunted itself before him a dozen times within ten years before release of the first description of Bell's telephone.

The poet at times has recognized the human tendency to overlook problems close at hand or even in one's "backyard." Lowell, in his "The Vision of Sir Launfal," tells of the young knight who scornfully tossed the leper a piece of gold as he left the castle gate to seek the Holy Grail. Later the knight, returning old and broken after a fruitless search, found in this same beggar and in the wooden bowl the object of his quest:

> In many climes, without avail,
> Thou hast spent thy life for the Holy Grail;
> Behold, it is here,—this cup which thou
> Didst fill at the streamlet for me but now.

The insight essential to recognition of research problems differs from the background necessary for sensing and doing practical or routine tasks in the school. Frequently the answers to these practical questions are provided in terms of judgment or experience, without resort to an investigational approach. The beginner in research may have to reorient his thinking to achieve the research perspective or may even find it necessary to undertake a more difficult task, an intellectual reorganization so as to interpret his educational world in the form of problems to be solved. The graduate student or field worker may make his choice with respect to investigating problems close at hand or more distant in time or space.

SOURCES FOR IDENTIFICATION OF PROBLEMS

Advanced Study and Critical Reading

The background of scholarship resulting from thorough training in a particular field of specialization and research should identify both the available evidence and the unsolved problems. Helpful related activities may include instruction, administration, reading, writing, and investigation. It has been typical for the graduate student to select a thesis problem in his major field of concentration and quite common for the more mature research worker to follow up the area of interest represented in his doctoral dissertation. As a caution against too narrow specialization, however, we are reminded of the current interest in interdisciplinary training and research, as described in Chapter 1.

Stimulating contacts between professor and student inside and outside the classroom or seminar, or between the senior scholar and younger worker, frequently have been profitable in selection and development of problems for investigation. Well-known examples are the influence of William James on Dewey, Thorndike, and Woodworth; Wundt on Cattell, Stanley Hall, Judd, and Titchener; and Dewey, Thorndike, and Judd on many educational and psychological investigators active in the mid-twentieth century.

In his autobiography Wallin cites a number of examples of the influence of able psychologists on their students. He characterizes J. Mark Baldwin of Princeton as debonair, companionable, popular, fluent, brilliant, resourceful, and creative, with great charm as a classroom lecturer, in spite of a slight lisp or speech mannerism. Wallin speaks of Henry H. Goddard as personable, kindly, a good social mixer, a productive worker with a flair for popular presentations of scientific data, and as a practical worker who was the trail blazer for the Binet-Simon scale in the United States.

Wallin describes Stanley Hall as a genial, stimulating, and helpful teacher, but one who knew how to "put the heat" on graduate fellows if they appeared to be loafing on the job or if they failed to produce research results.[1] This may explain in part why the Clark fellows majoring under Hall were so productive, although an important cause was also the fact that Hall was an inspiring teacher and writer with a brilliant, retentive, and encyclopedic mind. Wallin speaks of Hall as having enormous breadth of erudition, fertile imagination, catholicity of view, effective presentation, untiring industry, and prodigious productivity.

The following is a rather dramatic example of instruction. When Lester F. Ward began a summer class in 1909 at the University of Wisconsin, he reached into his pocket and pulled out two peach stones. He threw one of them out of the window and said: "That peach stone may fall upon responsive soil and may grow into a peach tree.

---

[1] J. E. Wallace Wallin, *The Odyssey of a Psychologist*: Pioneering Experiences in Special Education, Clinical Psychology, and Mental Hygiene with a Comprehensive Bibliography of the Author's Publications. Wilmington, Del.: The Author, 1955. p. 19, 24, 39.

This other peach stone will be planted in soil which has been discovered to be suitable for peach trees. The young seedling will be grafted upon a sturdy root stock. It will be protected from disease, San Jose scale, and insect pests. As all the established knowledge of peach culture will be applied to aid the growth and protection of this tree, we are more certain of having a satisfactory peach tree." Ward concluded his remarks with the assertion that those students who understood what he had said already knew everything that would be presented to the class group, and persons who wished further discussion of this problem might find some profit in remaining in the class.[2]

On the other hand, great men have sometimes been dull in their class-lecture presentation. Albion W. Small's lectures were occasionally very monotonous. At times his graduate students developed a plan to break the monotony of these lectures. A student was assigned each day to ask questions for the purpose of interrupting the lecture. The questions would stimulate Small to lay down his sheaf of papers, step forward, and launch into an interesting discussion of the point concerning which he had written rather ponderous notes in preparation for the lecture. In general, Small was an able teacher and author, with a dynamic personality.

Franklin H. Giddings of Columbia University (1855-1931) found time to encourage younger workers in sociology. When a young teacher in a small western community reported a local study in the village newspaper, with some wider publicity, he received a long-hand letter from Giddings, suggesting continuation of the study, some advice about publication, and ideas for future investigations. For several years, whenever this young teacher published anything, Giddings wrote to him, giving advice and suggestions.[3] A long list of Ph. D. candidates completed their work under Giddings' guidance, and scattered throughout the United States and to foreign lands.

During his senior year at Indiana University, 1890-91, Ellwood P. Cubberley had an unusual opportunity to become well acquainted with David Starr Jordan, the president of Indiana University. Jordan had gained wide recognition as a speaker and was accustomed to traveling and speaking on a variety of subjects, illustrating his lectures at times with slides projected by a stereopticon lantern. Cubberley accompanied Jordan on these tours and operated the lantern. The long hours together on slow

[2] M. C. Elmer, *Contemporary Social Thought*: Contributors and Trends. Pittsburgh: University of Pittsburgh Press, 1956. p. 12, 25.

[3] *Ibid.*, p. 16–17.

Emory S. Bogardus, *The Development of Social Thought*. New York: Longmans, Green and Co., 1955. p. 436–61.

trains, the prolonged stay at stations between trains, and occupancy of the same hotel room provided opportunities for conversation and exchange of ideas that influenced the younger man throughout his long career in education.[4]

In all scientific endeavor the interdependence of research workers is recognized in the identification and solution of problems. In spite of difficulties in securing the works of other scholars, even such early investigators as Roger Bacon and Leonardo da Vinci relied on extensive knowledge of the writings of others in their special fields of interest. The inspiration for many of Bacon's experiments may be found in the work of other scholars. The 5,000 manuscript pages of Leonardo's notebooks disclose his indebtedness to other workers and his wide reading (he quotes from 72 medieval and classical authors).

Charles H. Judd had exceptional opportunities for extensive reading in his undergraduate training in the United States and in his graduate work in Germany; his advice to beginning students is that they select teachers with broad interests and read widely. Although Edward L. Thorndike considered himself an investigator or experimenter rather than a scholar, in the sense of devoting his time to books and the literature, he estimated in 1936 that he had spent well over 20,000 hours reading and studying scientific books and journals. The extensive reading, erudition, and range of information of William James may well explain his success in bringing together the work of the Scottish, English, French, and German schools of psychology.

Cubberley's meticulous habits of work and extensive reading are illustrated by the manner in which he prepared for the teaching of a new course.[5] He began immediately to develop syllabus outlines with references for reading. For his history of education course, the syllabus developed in the direction of a history of culture. For his first course in school administration he drew upon collections of documents. A typical scene was that of Cubberley leaving his office after class in the evening with an armful of school laws and reports. Next morning he would lug them back to their shelves in the library. Night after night he read, made notes, and kept his syllabus growing. Sometimes when he had left the campus for lectures at institutes, his notes were not far ahead of the class. Even after retirement in 1933, Cubberley did a great deal of reading on a wide variety of subjects. After each title he placed a

---

[4] Jesse B. Sears and Adin D. Henderson, *Cubberley of Stanford: And His Contribution to American Education.* Stanford, Calif.: Stanford University Press, 1957. p. 15–16.

[5] *Ibid.*, p. 69, 83.

rating such as he was accustomed to do in his entries of stocks or bonds—double "A" if excellent, etc. He left notes on 25 books read in 1934 and 46 in 1935.

As background for his major contributions to philosophy, Whitehead had the benefit of extensive reading in the classics (Latin and Greek), mathematics, science, theology over a period of some eight years, and philosophy. His varied experience and teaching at Cambridge University, London University, and Harvard University profoundly affected the development of his philosophy.

In view of the size of Whitehead's library, his remark to a friend about not having read a great quantity of books should be taken relatively.

"I read very slowly," said Whitehead. "Sometimes I see myself referred to as 'a well-read man.' As a matter of fact, I have not read a great quantity of books; but I think about what I read, and it sticks."

"Speed is not for me. On the other hand, some of my reading is 'skippy.' Last night, for example, I was rereading that book in your lap on the Jesuits, but finding, at the beginnings of successive chapters that he was still on the same aspect of a subject whose point I had already grasped, I did not hesitate to skip."[6]

The youthful reading of Thomas Huxley, the scientist, foreshadowed his later interests:

He consumed popular novels, histories of Europe, works on science, philosophy, and religion, idling away the hours thumbing through a large, illustrated Bible that delighted him. Although he had no formal schooling for 10 years, like Herbert Spencer and others of the self-educated greater Victorians, he occupied himself advantageously in his spare time, speculating on the causes of sunset colors and inventing what he fondly thought was a perpetual-motion machine. After explaining the latter to Michael Faraday, who received him kindly but the machine rather unfavorably, the young boy vowed that some day he would have something of more import to show Faraday.[7]

It should be pointed out, however, that some scholars and scientists have not been interested in making a study of the earlier writings or related literature in their fields of specialization and research. Agassiz found the study of things themselves more attractive than what was printed in books about the particular subject; he usually was satisfied with paging through the volumes of natural history, so that he might later identify the objects he examined in nature. Comte, in the latter part of his life, practiced what he called "cerebral hygiene," i.e., he refrained

[6] Quoted from *Dialogues of Alfred North Whitehead*. As Recorded by Lucien Price. New York: New American Library of World Literature, 1954. p. 140, 320.
[7] Quoted from Charles S. Blinderman, "Thomas Henry Huxley." *Scientific Monthly* 84: 171–82; April 1957.

from reading the books of other social thinkers, which meant that he was not always abreast of the times, although in his synthetic thinking and encyclopedic work Comte borrowed ideas from many predecessors. W. G. Sumner, the sociologist, paid little attention to the work of other writers in his field, not even mentioning in bibliography or index the names of Comte, Ward, and Giddings, although he did draw upon the ideas of other scholars.

Some of these scientists and scholars have considered it undesirable or even unwise to study closely the related literature, fearing that the research worker's mind might be conditioned to see the problem in the same way or in a traditional manner and thus overlook a new or more fruitful approach. Charles Kettering, a research specialist in industry, believes that, as a result of studying conventional textbooks, we fall into a rut, escape from which may take as much effort as the solution of the specific problem. He has chided men of science who "create obstacles to their progress by referring to theories which say certain matters cannot be accomplished." Kettering's unorthodox advice to specialists is "to throw away the books and work toward the objective," based on his opinion that "the smaller the library the less chance to find excuses that it can't be done."

The poet, Byron, has aptly expressed the dilemma of creative workers: "To be perfectly original one should think much and read little, and this is impossible, for one must have read before one has learnt to think." It would seem that for most graduate students and research workers the solution of this dilemma does depend on critical reading as a stimulus to thinking.

Analysis of Evidence, Practices, Trends, or Needs in a Particular Area

When a field of knowledge is being analyzed to identify problems for study, the particular research area should be sufficiently limited to serve effectively as sources of specific problems for investigation; for example, physical growth, mental development, or reading readiness rather than child psychology or abnormal psychology. On the other hand, the research area under analysis should be large enough to permit development of meaningful, integrating concepts of interpretation; for example, language development rather than the phonetic range of the one-year-old. Much of the background for separating a subject into its constituent parts and for identifying the research problems in each subarea is derived from the programs of reading and instruction described in the preceding section of this chapter.

Beginners in research frequently are not sensitive to problems, practices, trends, and needs close at hand, as illustrated earlier in this chapter. To cite another example, even as early as 1915, when a young sociologist went to teach at the University of Kansas, Frank W. Blackmar asked, "Young man, what do you know about the people of Kansas?" When the new staff member admitted his ignorance, Blackmar said, "You can't teach young people without knowing something about their background." He handed the new teacher a copy of the *Kansas City Star*, with the question, "Do you see anything about Kansas that interests you?" When the young man replied that he saw the name of a city, Beloit, Kansas, Blackmar answered: "All right, I have arranged for a fund of $900. You will teach five hours a week this semester. Next week, you go to Beloit, spend a couple of days there, talk with anyone and everyone until you have an idea of what people around Beloit do and think."[8]

An analysis of the field of sociology identifies seven significant changes or trends:[9]

1. A science of society based on empirical research

2. Division of sociology into subject-matter areas

3. Specialization of personnel

4. Application of sociology in applied fields

5. Creation of research methods and techniques

6. Interdisciplinary collaboration

7. Integration of theory and research.

An illustration in the field of education identifies fifteen trends and areas of needed curriculum research:[10]

1. We have developed more effective research techniques for studying social and economic trends than we have research techniques for the derivation and validation of values.

2. We have clearer analyses of the social and economic trends in our society than we have of our value systems.

3. We have more analyses of aspects of our society from specific disciplines than we have interdisciplinary studies exploring the implications of such findings for human living.

[8] M. C. Elmer, *op. cit.,* p. 48.
[9] Ernest W. Burgess, "Seven Significant Changes in Sociology." *Sociology and Social Research* 40: 385–86; July-August 1956.
[10] Quoted from Margaret G. McKim, "Curriculum Research in Historical Perspective," *Research for Curriculum Improvement.* 1957 Yearbook. Washington: Association for Supervision and Curriculum Development, a Department of the National Education Association, 1957. p. 34-35.

4. We know more about trends in our society than we do about the implications of these trends in terms of children and youth growing up in that society.

5. We know more about norms for separate aspects of development than we do about the interrelationships among these aspects of development in the growing organism.

6. We have more techniques for studying the learner in the light of norms and averages than we have techniques for studying him in the light of his goals and his concept of himself.

7. We know more about learners as individuals than we do about the interrelationships among learners in groups.

8. We know more about learners' interests than we do about day-by-day problems of living they are trying to handle.

9. We know more about general processes of maturation than we do about the developmental tasks which each new stage of maturity brings.

10. We know more about how to organize a classroom or school for effective learning than we do about how to decide what should be taught.

11. We know more about how to develop skills such as reading and handwriting, and about how to teach facts, than we do about how to develop concepts or attitudes.

12. We know more about how to study the outcomes of a child's work than we do about how to study the processes by which he works—the steps he takes in solving an arithmetic problem, the way he reasons in drawing conclusions.

13. We have more techniques for evaluating growth in skills and knowledge than we have techniques for evaluating growth in such areas as attitudes and feelings.

14. We know more about planning for the effective learning of children and youth than we do about planning for the effective learning of those who are to teach them.

15. We know more about achieving effective interpersonal relations in the classroom than we do about achieving effective interpersonal relations in the faculty of a whole school system.

As another example in education, nine types of problems for research in the classroom setting indicate urgent needs that have developed over a half century:[11]

1. We accept the general assumption that the role of the school is to prepare the learner for effective living in our society, but we have little evidence regarding the type of curriculum design most likely to achieve this goal.

2. We are in substantial agreement that it is important to develop ability

[11] Quoted from *ibid.*, p. 35–36.

to think creatively, to be self-directing, to work cooperatively, but we are just beginning to learn what classroom practices will best achieve these goals.

3. We assume that the most effective motivation is intrinsic, but we have much to learn about the respective roles of teacher and pupils in the determination of goals; about the respective roles of pupil interest, need and purpose in the establishment of goals; and about the most effective functioning of pupil-teacher planning. We have much to learn, also, about how to study the learner in order correctly to identify his goals.

4. We accept the concept of maturation, but we have much to learn regarding the degree to which physiological growth patterns actually affect learning.

5. We accept the concept of readiness, but we have meager evidence regarding the role of classroom experiences in developing readiness, and much to discover regarding the appropriateness of various methods for pupils of different maturity levels.

6. We accept the concept of individual differences, but we do not yet have the evidence we need to plan the most effective program for gifted children; we do not yet have much research as a guide to the developmental tasks faced by slow learners; neither have we tested thoroughly in practice the range of possibilities for the effective grouping of learners.

7. We operate on the general assumption that learning comes through experience, but we need more evidence regarding the types of experiences most effective for different maturity levels, backgrounds and levels of intellectual ability. We also need more help in determining how the goals, needs and background of the particular learner influence the structure of an experience for him.

8. We accept the concept that we are teaching the "whole" child, but we have much to discover regarding the influences upon learning of the affective tone of the classroom, of the child's feeling of security and of his personality patterns.

9. We are in substantial agreement that evaluation should be a continuous process, but we do not yet possess the techniques we need to measure progress toward all our goals, nor do we know much about the effect of various methods of evaluation upon the learning process.

By way of a quite detailed illustration of needed research, a committee of psychologists has located and formulated the troublesome, unanswered questions about gifted children. Each of the following questions probably would encompass a family or cluster of research studies.[12]

1. Educational administrative procedures.
   A. What are the relative merits (emotional, social, and intellectual effects) of various administrative plans for the gifted such as the following?

[12] Quoted from Harriet E. O'Shea and Others, "Needed Research on Gifted Children." *American Psychologist* 9: 77–78; February 1954.

a. Keeping the child with his chronological age group and "enriching the curriculum."

b. Locating the individual close to his mental age level in school class with chronologically older children.

c. Retaining the child in his chronological age group for some subjects and advancing him in others.

d. Establishing special classes for children who have high rates of mental growth.

e. Utilizing no special administrative plan for the gifted.

B. What preceding or concomitant conditions can be recognized that are correlated with varying results from a given administrative plan such as any of the foregoing or any combination of such plans?

C. Which of these administrative procedures (or others not listed or any combination of procedures) has the best over-all results for the gifted child?

2. What is the effect (emotional, social, and intellectual) upon the gifted child of organizing his school work:

A. In terms of greater quantity of work of the same level of difficulty as that which he has been doing?

B. In terms of introducing additional new subject matter (both in classroom and extramural)?

C. In terms of advancing to higher levels of organization and abstraction in whatever experience is provided for him?

3. Relationship between ability and performance.

A. To what extent is there "concealed failure" among gifted children; that is, are they operating below their appropriate achievement level although not failing by the school's standards?

B. What personality correlates are there to such "concealed failure"?

C. What factors have contributed to such "concealed failure"?

D. What are the over-all effects of various procedures intended to raise the gifted child's performance to its optimum level?

4. What is the teacher's distinctive role in training the gifted?

A. What effects upon a gifted child result from various characteristics of his teacher?

B. Are special qualifications necessary in the teacher of the gifted and if so, what are they?

5. Life work.

A. Is it desirable or undesirable to explore vocational interests and aptitudes earlier in the life of the gifted child than in the life of other children?

B. What are the effects of beginning vocational planning and vocational preparation at various times in the life of the gifted child?

6. Personal relationships.

A. Do close personal relationships become established between children of widely different mental age?

B. Does the gifted child have to have companions at or close to his mental age in order to experience close personal relationships?

7. Special frustrations.

A. Are there special frustrations that impinge upon the gifted child that less often affect other children:
   a. in his family,
   b. in his neighborhood,
   c. in the classroom,
   d. in extracurricular activities,
   e. in job placement?

8. Special satisfactions.

A. Does the gifted child experience special satisfactions?

B. If so, what are they and what are their effects upon the gifted child?

9. What factors account for any undesirable personality traits that may be found among the gifted?

10. Status as a group.

A. Do the gifted in effect constitute a minority group receiving some of the typical hostilities directed toward such a group?

B. What are the effects upon the gifted of such treatment when it does occur?

C. Are there recognizable elements in a community that attack gifted children?

D. What are the effects of various procedures instituted to make favorable changes in attitudes toward gifted children?

11. Does the gifted child have special needs with respect to his ultimately developing desirable citizenship traits, needs either in terms of the subject matter or in terms of the age at which subject matter (classroom and extramural) is introduced?

Repetition, Extension, or "Budding Out" of Problems

In this chapter we have already indicated that history is never complete, that descriptive-survey studies are accurate only for the time and sample represented, and that many experiments should be repeated under the same or different conditions for purposes of verification. The scientist favors duplication of experiments under various conditions, lest some uncontrolled factor be present in the original experiment. At times, however, even the experienced investigator has failed to follow up a discovery in the direction of even more important conclusions or applications. Fleming described crude preparations of penicillin in 1929, but he left this work after a time, without developing a therapeutic agent, and it remained for Florey to complete the task of developing penicillin as a therapeutic agent. In 1912, nearly a decade before the discovery of insulin by Banting and Best, one of Anton J. Carlson's graduate students isolated a crude extract of insulin which mitigated the effect of diabetes in dogs. Carlson freely admitted to what he called his "stupidity" in not following up this promising line of investigation.

In many instances an "offshoot" of a problem under study or of a technique in use leads to more fruitful results than the original problem or approach; for example, the idea of the delayed-reaction experiment, as a method of studying animal mentality, came to Edward L. Thorndike after two years of work with animals. Willis R. Whitney's apt statement concerning the "budding out" of problems is:[13] "We found nature easy to follow and difficult to drive. We usually wanted what she gave for our seeking, but we could seldom get exactly what we thought we wanted at the time. We wanted light. She gave us rectifiers."

Sometimes the "bypath" in an investigation proves to be a blind alley, but careful reporting of this fact may prevent other research workers from wasting time on the same project. By way of illustration, when an enthusiastic but immature student proposed a research project dealing with attempts to standardize an aspect of social research, he first sought assistance from two other professors in sociology, without success. As a last resort, the graduate student went to Albion W. Small and received the following reaction:[14]

> Young man, I believe you are on the wrong track. I believe that you will find your search for research methods leading you into a blind alley. That, however, is perfectly satisfactory. Do your job so well that no one need ever waste any time on that project again. I spent three years of hard work on a study of the Cameralists. I think it was largely futile. But I covered the ground completely enough that no one needs to go over it again. Therefore, I consider it three years well spent.

FACTORS IN SELECTION OF THE PROBLEM

The investigator usually considers a number of external factors in choosing a problem for study: novelty, significance, sources, technique, equipment, working conditions, sponsorship, and co-operative relationships. He also evaluates such internal or personal factors as interest, motivation, intellectual curiosity, background of scholarship and training, temperament and personal characteristics, costs, risks, and timing.

[13] T. A. Boyd, *Research*. New York: D. Appleton-Century Co., 1935. p. 270.
[14] Quoted from M. C. Elmer, *op. cit.*, p. 24.

Novelty and Significance

The next chapter describes the library guides or keys for determining the research completed in a particular sphere of investigation. As pointed out earlier in the present chapter, when it seems desirable to repeat or extend earlier experiments or investigations, what is implied is deliberate and systematic planning rather than accidental or random duplication of earlier studies through ignorance of the research literature. We have already noted that even able scientists and scholars sometimes have been negligent or indifferent to the literature in their particular fields of specialization.

The question of overlapping of dissertation problems sometimes arises when two or more graduate students engage in a co-operative program of research, which is a type of investigation that has come into increasing use on the part of commissions, survey teams, and research agencies (often with the assistance of graduate students). Many teams of scholars or inventors have found it profitable to work co-operatively in seeking answers to their problems.

To cite a specific example of co-operation in the graduate field at the University of Texas, team studies have been undertaken, in order that broader research problems may be studied than is usually possible when the responsibility is carried by one person. Four doctoral candidates have co-operated in attacking the problem of class size, two such candidates have worked together to discover what happens to children whose parents insist that they enter the first grade below the age of six, and four students have been investigating methods of reporting to parents at the elementary-school level.

Two graduate students at the University of Cincinnati worked together on a two-part master's study, "Simplified Versions of the *Constitution* and the *Declaration of Independence* for Use in the Junior High School, Parts I and II."

It should be recognized that some contributions to the literature are valuable for purposes other than novelty or creativity; for example, Charles A. Ellwood (1873-1946) did not produce particularly new ideas in especially brilliant style, but he wrote in such a clear, logical manner that his work was readily understood and easily translated. Ellwood's discussion of methods in sociology vigorously criticized the tendency to overemphasize objective and statistical methods, and did much to revive interest in nonstatistical procedures.[15]

[15] *Ibid.*, p. 35.
Emory S. Bogardus, *op. cit.*, p. 590–604.

The criterion of significance or importance for the field represented and for the individual involves the realm of values. The discussions of the role of values in research and of the social responsibility of the scientist in Chapter 1, as well as certain topics of the present chapter, deal with values that frequently play a prominent part in the selection of problems for study. The literature includes a large number of analyses of problems for research, frequently with an indication of the importance or significance for the field represented (as listed in the chapter bibliography).

Curiosity and Drive

Many scientists and scholars have been urged forward by an insatiable curiosity, driving interest, or other powerful motivation, sometimes to extremes in concentration, withdrawal from social contacts, or neglect of health. Historians frequently have been prodigious workers with remarkable powers of concentration. Ranke continued incessantly busy at work until the age of ninety-one, driving his assistants to the point of exhaustion. He lived a long life, during which he produced some 50 volumes of history. Lord Acton tells of his last meeting with Ranke, who at that time, in 1876, was past eighty. Acton says of him: "He was feeble, sunken, and almost blind, scarcely able to read or write. He uttered his farewell with a kindly emotion, and I feared that the next I should hear of him would be the news of his death."[16] However, Ranke produced another group of volumes before his death in 1886, including a *World History*, which was broken off somewhere in the late Middle Ages.

It is not strange that strong motivation should play a prominent role in the life and work of psychologists. Edwin G. Boring attributes his achievements in research and writing to certain irresistible compulsions, to a capacity for hard work, and to a persistent sense of insecurity during the earlier decades of his life. Edward C. Tolman speaks of his compelling drive as an attempt to be creative; this motivation took the form of a compulsive academic ambition or drive, a self-ideal of becoming truly successful in the academic world.

When Lewis M. Terman died, near the end of his 80th year, he was working on the manuscript of volume 5 of *Genetic Studies of Genius* and was simultaneously planning the next 3 years' research on his group of 1500 "gifted children." No other facts could mark the man so well. From 1903,

---

[16] Pieter Geyl, *From Ranke to Toynbee*: Five Lectures on Historians and Historiographical Problems. Northampton, Mass.: Smith College Studies in History, 1952. p. 3.

when he arrived at Clark University to begin graduate work, until his death, his career was a continuous sequence of research and writing, broken now and then by illness and accident but never interrupted in its main course.[17]

Illustrations of the driving force of intellectual curiosity and of related types of motivation are available in the field of sociology.[18] The sociologist, Lester F. Ward (1841-1913), was the youngest of ten children, whose mechanic father had a tendency to drift from place to place in his work. When Ward was sixteen his father died, and the boy went to Pennsylvania to live with a brother, where he worked on a farm and in a sawmill for his board and room. In his spare time he made wagon hubs, which were traded for books, articles of clothing, and other things that he needed. Ward picked up a scattered education, largely undirected, although he attained some proficiency in French, German, Greek, and Latin. Later in Washington, while an employee of the government, he was able to earn the A.B., LL.B., M.A., and LL.D. degrees. When Ward left government service in 1906 and went to teach sociology at Brown University at the age of sixty-five, he had achieved a full lifetime of outstanding work in botany, geology, and paleontology, and was regarded as the leading sociologist in America. Ward was characterized by an impressive command of his subject and by a "terrific mental drive."

A rugged physique and dogged determination helped George Lundberg accomplish tasks that others thought very difficult. One night in Wisconsin, when driving with another professor, the car stopped because of carburetor trouble. Lundberg walked eight miles to the next town, found a place to buy repair parts, then walked back to the car and put it in running order. His philosophy of work was: "When anything needs to be done—do it." Lundberg considered large-scale studies and quantitative methods important, but said, "I sometimes wonder whether the most important research done in the world is not what people steal time from the regular employment to do, rather than what they are paid and honored for doing."

Strong motivation impelled Ellwood P. Cubberley to draw up careful plans for retirement, with his projects scheduled by years and the achievements checked against the calendar. He expected his program of writing to continue after retirement, including the editing of his series

---

[17] Quoted from Robert R. Sears, "L. M. Terman, Pioneer in Mental Measurement." *Science* 125: 978-79; May 17, 1957.

[18] Emory S. Bogardus, *op. cit.*, p. 305-23.
M. C. Elmer, *op. cit.*, p. 11, 127-28.

of professional textbooks in education. As early as 1913, Cubberley estimated what his income would be that year, at the age of forty-five, again for 1915, and at five-year intervals to the age of seventy-five.[19]

A psychologist-psychiatrist said of the drive behind W. K. Kellogg:[20]

Dominated as he was by an older brother for many years, Will Kellogg developed what is known today as an inferiority complex. In overcompensating for this complex, Mr. Kellogg went to limitless bounds and it is likely this was the greatest driving force behind the success. He was going to show his brother, himself, and the world that he, too, had superior qualities and that only an unfortunate set of circumstances had prevented him from being as eminent as the Doctor. Those circumstances he eliminated.

Alexandre Dumas wrote day and night, working with and without collaborators. On one occasion, when he returned to Paris by night train after a long absence, his son was waiting to take him home. However, the father demanded to be taken at once to the home of a friend, where they gossiped until four o'clock, finally reaching home at six. The elder Dumas immediately demanded a lamp. "A lamp? But why?" asked his son. "To see by, of course. I am going to get to work." Forthwith the elder Dumas began work on another novel.

Seeking to explain these extraordinary manifestations of concentration and intensity in the form of powerful driving impulses or compulsions, we enter the realm of depth psychology.

What is the significance of this extraordinary concentration and intensity? What powerful impulses are driving their way at such moments? For there is every reason to suppose that men of genius are characterized by possessing exceptionally strong emotions and usually a correspondingly strong capacity for containing them. The tension induced by the preceding efforts to find a solution gradually mounts until it reaches a climax. The great mathematician of genius, Henri Poincaré, in describing how he made his own discoveries, said: "One is struck by these appearances of sudden illumination, obvious indications of a long course of previous unconscious work. . . . These sudden inspirations are never produced except after some days of voluntary efforts which appeared absolutely fruitless." Einstein has given a very similar description, and in the Fliess correspondence there are numerous allusions to the exhausting stress and strain Freud experienced in the continuously hard work of attaining his various pieces of insight. Kretschmer speaks of the great scientists' "passionate emotions developing which drive their thought constantly in the same direction, producing the utmost tension until

[19] Jesse B. Sears and Adin D. Henderson, *op. cit.*, p. 229–30.
[20] Quoted from Horace B. Powell, *The Original Has This Signature—W. K. Kellogg*. Englewood Cliffs, N. J.: Prentice-Hall, 1956. p. 182.

at last a short-circuit occurs: somewhere a spark leaps to a new spot where up till then no human thought had ever passed."[21]

Background of Scholarship and Personal Characteristics

The analysis of the hallmarks of the scientist and scholar in Chapter 1, and the earlier section of the present chapter dealing with advanced study and reading, are pertinent to a discussion of criteria for selection of the problem for investigation. Illustrations of the part played by training and certain personal or temperamental characteristics in choice and development of research problems will be drawn from such fields as psychology, sociology, history, education, and other areas of scholarship and research. Frequently, training or scholarship in other fields (for example, physics, mathematics, physiology, biology, medicine, philosophy) has provided important background for the early development of psychology and psychologists, and later through psychology for the field of education.

An example of productive activity is found in the life and work of Ellwood P. Cubberley, who made early contributions to educational history, administration and school surveys, and textbook editing. Early in his career Cubberley learned certain elementary but useful concepts of research,[22] at a time during the first decade of the twentieth century when the field of education was just beginning to develop. Cubberley had studied some phases of the method of historical research while preparing his syllabus in the history of education. During his graduate work at Columbia University he secured what was then an acceptable introduction to statistical method, a new field being developed by Edward L. Thorndike. In the course of his doctor's dissertation he learned useful procedures of a descriptive-survey type, as he found his way factually into the then unexplored field of school administration.

Cubberley's long and busy life was spent in building a small department of education into a school of wide reputation, developing his own field of work, carrying a full-time schedule of teaching, writing and editing books, and serving as consultant and adviser. Of the 106 books in the professional series that Cubberley edited, he wrote ten, fifteen others bore the names of his colleagues, and a number of others were prepared by his former students. Cubberley's ten books in this series sold to the number of 341,000 copies, and the figures for the entire series of 106 books amounted to "approximately 3,070,000 copies."

[21] Quoted from Ernest Jones, "Nature of Genius." *Scientific Monthly* 84: 75–83; February 1957.

[22] Jesse B. Sears and Adin D. Henderson, *op. cit.*, p. 87–88, 97–98.

In summary, Cubberley contributed to five areas of activity: as teacher, educational historian, writer in school administration, investigator and consultant, and editor and author of textbooks. His insight in developing and editing the series of professional textbooks in education is significant, especially as viewed against the background of the undeveloped status of education when plans were first made for the series in 1911:

> School administration was scarcely recognized as a field of study. The curriculum, as a field, had hardly been thought of. The psychology was at most only partly applicable and parts of it were being questioned as to their validity. The literature on methods and management and on supervision was little more than armchair opinion. Educational theory was vague and general at best. There were books promoting special systems of arithmetic or of reading but the systems had been conjured from successful experience, not from careful observation and experiment.[23]

Terman's long lifetime of research and writing followed up the pioneer area of his doctoral dissertation:

> The half-century since Terman finished his doctoral training is almost coincident with the history of mental testing. So is Lewis Terman. From the first, there was something provocative and exciting to him in the very idea of measuring complex psychological qualities. His doctoral dissertation was a comparison of seven bright and seven dull schoolboys. He gave each child a battery of more than 40 hours of individual tests, probably the most overwhelming test-assault inflicted on any child up to that time. Nothing much came of the study, but it did give Terman a chance to try his hand at making up tests. He loved it, and he went right on loving it to the end of his life. He built test after test for 40 years, all of them good (technically) and nearly all of them useful.[24]

To cite specific instances of the contributions of other fields of scholarship to the background of psychologists, Wundt, physician and physiologist, accepted a chair of philosophy at Leipzig in 1875, although his place is that of a founder in the history of psychology. Stanley Hall came into psychology with a diversified background of theological preparation, European study, college teaching, and physiology. The broad training and experience of Edward B. Titchener covered music, collection of coins, classical languages, half a dozen modern languages, linguistics and philology, biology, physiology, and anthropology.

Although many of the founders of modern psychology came from philosophy or other disciplines, it is also true that a number of modern

---

[23] Quoted from *ibid.*, p. 191–94.
[24] Quoted from Robert R. Sears, *op. cit.*

psychologists have entered the field as graduates of other areas of specialization: Edwin G. Boring, L. L. Thurstone, and Edward C. Tolman from engineering, Godfrey Thomson from physics, Jean Paget from natural science. Tolman speaks of a number of sources that influenced his psychological points of view: the Gestalt psychologists, a year's stay in Vienna (involving both the academic and psychoanalytical traditions of European psychology), war experiences that developed points of view relating to personality psychology, and contacts with a group of workers interested in sociology, anthropology, personality, and social psychology. Walter Bingham's interest in music as a hobby led to a topic for his doctoral dissertation dealing with the nature of melody.

Many historians have drawn on an exceptional background of training and scholarship. Barthold Niebuhr at the age of eighteen knew 18 European languages, as well as Hebrew, Persian, and Arabic. His phenomenal memory was an enormous asset as he went on to master philosophy, mathematics, physics, chemistry, natural history, history, Roman law, and practical politics and administration. The great German scholar, Theodore Mommsen, published 1,513 different titles, and was a scholar in at least six fields of knowledge: epigraphy, numismatics, history, law, archaeology, and early Italian philology. Adolf von Harnack published at least 1,800 titles of books and articles, a record that invites comparison with Mommsen.

Examples from sociology indicate the varied training, broad scholarship, and wide reading of the pioneers in this field. Lester F. Ward studied and read philosophy, medicine, law, botany, geology, and anthropology. William G. Sumner had at his command a dozen languages in studying cultural-anthropological problems, and did extensive reading in history, theology, metaphysics, and general literature. Franklin H. Giddings read extensively in European philosophy and sociology, and had six years of experience in journalism and six years of teaching in experimental school situations.

The earlier discussions of advanced study, critical reading, and creative scholarship, as well as the illustrations just presented, remind us that classroom instruction and the library are only part of the background for the accomplishments of scientists and scholars. Able scientists sometimes have not appeared to good advantage in meeting formal examination requirements. The examiners recognized the special talents of Paul Ehrlich, and somewhat reluctantly passed him on his final medical examinations. History records that Einstein failed at the entrance examinations to the Polytechnic School. It is possible that the inventive scientist or creative scholar may even be at a disadvantage in accumulating the factual information frequently tested on formal examinations, in contrast to the bright student with a good memory who accepts uncritically what he is told or what he reads.

For some scientists and scholars certain traits of personality or temperament have helped at times; others have been hindered in their work and influence on advanced students. From a long life of direct contacts with psychologists, Wallin sketches many interesting pictures of personalities. For example, Wallin[25] speaks of Howard C. Warren of Princeton as lacking the glamour or capacity for social contacts of J. Mark Baldwin, and as reserved and somewhat inhibited (possibly because of a physical blemish). Warren was a rather uninspiring classroom lecturer, unable to arouse much enthusiasm among his undergraduates; yet he possessed a keenly critical and orderly mind and business acumen, with far more ability than appeared on the surface. He slavishly followed his lecture notes, with few interest-provoking asides.

Wallin characterizes W. B. Pillsbury as somewhat reticent and uncommunicative, rather fidgety, nervous, and apparently inhibited. Pillsbury's lectures were well organized and effectively documented, but with the presentation somewhat marred by a rather halting and jerky manner of speaking. Nevertheless, Pillsbury made substantial contributions to the literature of experimental and theoretical psychology, and was a solid scientist. Edward W. Scripture was said to be somewhat nervously unstable but very approachable, helpful, and sympathetic, with energetic, inventive, and imaginative traits, as well as great capacity for original research in psychology and something of a popularizer in his writings.

Ladd is characterized by Wallin as a scholar of profound erudition, an indefatigable worker, and an amazingly productive author. Wallin draws a picture of Ladd as a somewhat aloof person, with a coldly analytical mind, endowed with the rare power of systematically pursuing a sustained line of thought in his class lectures without recourse to, or with very little dependence on, notes, and with the same inexorable logic, precision of verbal expression, and freedom from rambling that characterized his textbooks. Ladd's sentence structure was so exact that it gave the impression that he was reading chapters verbatim from one of his books. He was the author of some 33 books, including revisions but exclusive of articles, at least 28 of which were in the fields of psychology, philosophy, ethics, religion, and education. Unfortunately, his style of writing was ponderous and involved, which robbed him of the recog-

[25] J. E. Wallace Wallin, *op. cit.*, p. 12–24.

nition from his colleagues he so richly deserved, and he was not accorded the acclaim by psychologists at large that was his just due by virtue of outstanding ability and accomplishments. One of Ladd's anecdotes was to the effect that one day on the campus a former student accosted him and said about one of Ladd's most recent books: "Professor, that was a corking book you issued recently, but it is way above my head." Ladd's quick retort was: "The book may be above your head, but God understands it, and so does Ladd, and possibly President Hadley [of Yale] also."

Newton had a markedly irritable and suspicious temperament, and much of the controversy that disfigured his life arose from his credulous belief in the statements of overcandid friends. In later life these qualities deteriorated for a while into paranoic delusions of persecution; perhaps in this connection it is not irrelevant to remark that Newton never fell in love and never married.

Faraday, the supreme physicist of the 19th century, had also his vein of credulousness. He said: "In early life I was a very imaginative lively person who could believe in the *Arabian Nights* as easily as in the *Encyclopaedia*, but facts were important to me and saved me." Throughout his life he was an adherent of the obscure sect of Sandemanians, followers of the religious prophet Robert Sandeman, and for 3 years regularly preached sermons before them. One must place this in contrast with Faraday's exceptional intelligence in other spheres, since it would be commonplace otherwise.

Darwin was a man of far more placid temperament, and it is probable that any turmoil of emotions found their expression in the psychosomatic afflictions to which he was a martyr. But his skepticism was tempered by a credulous attitude toward other authorities. Even after his great discovery of the operation of evolution through natural selection he still believed in Lamarck's doctrine of evolution through the inheritance of acquired characters, a doctrine his own work had rendered superfluous and indeed erroneous.

His friend and contemporary Huxley offers a very interesting contrast to the genius Darwin. Although possessing a wider knowledge than Darwin, and gifted with more originality and a greater intellectual daring, Huxley's actual achievements are of a different order. On first reading Darwin's theory he exclaimed: "How extremely stupid of me not to have thought of that." Now, Huxley was endowed with any amount of skepticism, of indeed a rather pugnacious brand. It has been said of him: "He allowed himself no prejudice, no sentimentalities, no illusions." But there is no record in his life of any evidence of credulousness to match it and, according to my view, to enable him to make really great discoveries.[26]

At times, traits of personality or temperament (or a feeling of self-sufficiency) have influenced able scholars to disregard the work of their fellows or to disagree sharply among themselves. Lester F. Ward had a feeling of self-sufficiency and finality about his own views and statements, and was outspoken in his rejection of other points of views. An-

[26] Quoted from Ernest Jones, *op. cit.*

other sociologist once commented on certain of Ward's conclusions as follows:[27] "It appears to me that Ward's conclusions are not correct. However, I may not be a competent critic since Ward has stated that, because of my different point of view, I am not a sociologist."

William G. Sumner (1840-1910) was one of the first teachers of sociology in the United States. He was never quite accepted by Small, Ward, or Giddings as a sociologist, but neither did Sumner accept them. Small expressed surprise when Sumner was elected president of the American Sociological Society: "It came to me consequently as a surprise and a shock that he was thought of as second president of the American Sociological Society. At that time (1907) he was not within my field of vision as even nominally a sociologist."

On the other hand, many scientists have been extremely modest people. Stating that the number of men widely recognized as possessing the attributes of genius is very small (Newton, Darwin, and Einstein), Jones speaks of Freud's disclaimer:[28]

"The genius of Freud" is a phrase that has been used so widely that I think we must subscribe to a truth contained in it. Characteristically enough, Freud himself vehemently dissented from its being applied to him. Even as far back as 1886, when he was 29, he wrote to his betrothed: "There was a time when I grieved that Nature had not, in one of her gracious moods, impressed on me that stamp of genius as she sometimes does. Since then I have long known that I am no genius, and I no longer understand how I could have wished to be one. I am not even very talented; my whole capacity for work probably lies in my character attributes." On one occasion in later life when it was applied to him he burst out with the protest: "Geniuses are unbearable people. You have only to ask my family to know how easy a person I am to live with. So I cannot be a genius." This disclaimer, however, was based on a very partial definition of genius, so we need not take it too seriously.

Pavlov has provided an inspiring statement that seems an apt partial summary of the requirements for sound scholarship: sound basic training, thorough acquaintance with the factual evidence, and devotion to the scientific approach.

What shall I wish for the young students of my country? First of all, sequence, consequence and again consequence. In gaining knowledge you must accustom yourself to the strictest sequence. You must be familiar with the very groundwork of science before you try to climb the heights. Never start on the "next" before you have mastered the "previous." Do not try to conceal the shortcomings of your knowledge by guesses and hypotheses.

[27] M. C. Elmer, *op. cit.*, p. 16, 21–22.
Emory S. Bogardus, *op. cit.*, p. 305–51.
[28] Quoted from Ernest Jones, *op. cit.*

Accustom yourself to the roughest and simplest scientific tools. Perfect as the wing of a bird may be, it will never enable the bird to fly if unsupported by the air. Facts are the air of science. Without them the man of science can never rise. Without them your theories are vain surmises. But while you are studying, observing, experimenting, do not remain content with the surface of things. Do not become a mere recorder of facts, but try to penetrate the mystery of their origin. Seek obstinately for the laws that govern them. And then—modesty. Never think you know it all. Though others may flatter you, retain the courage to say, "I am ignorant." Never be proud. And lastly, science must be your passion.[29]

Sources, Technique, Equipment, and Working Conditions

The problems in selection of sources and method are closely related to the scholar's background of training and personal characteristics. The several methodological chapters of this book provide appropriate orientation for selection of a suitable technique for the problem at hand, although we should remember that investigators vary in their degree of devotion to highly formalized methods. When a group of young sociologists, overimpressed by the rigors of formalized approaches in gathering data, quizzed Edward A. Ross about his methods of research, he smiled and replied:[30]

I am not a research man, I just write what I think best explains a process or a situation. For example, a number of years ago I decided to spend some time in China. I told everybody I was going to China and asked if they knew anybody there. By the time I left for China I had three thousand names and addresses of people: Chinese officials, Chinese scholars, coolie brothers of laundry men, beach combers, missionaries, teachers, relatives. I made up a list of five things I would like to know about changes taking place in China. I contacted, wherever possible, the names I had and countless others. When I talked with them at first our general conversation might lead to the person expressing himself on one or more of these five questions. If the answer did not come up naturally, I asked him questions. After the interview I would sit down on the side of the road on a stone or back in my room and write up, as nearly as possible, an exact account of what had been said to me. I returned to Wisconsin with many boxes full of notes and with the aid of some intelligent assistants classified these notes and put them in the form of a little book, *The Changing Chinese*. Nothing scientific about it, it was just what I had gathered from hundreds of sources.

Ross traveled widely in the United States and abroad; he was a keen observer and recorder of social life.

As illustrated in the later chapters on research methods, special

---

[29] Quoted from Ivan Pavlov, *Scientific Monthly* 81: 129; September 1955.
[30] Quoted from M. C. Elmer, *op. cit.*, p. 33-34.
Emory S. Bogardus, *op. cit.*, p. 523-39.

equipment or tools must be devised or adapted for certain types of investigation. Favorable working conditions are usually helpful, but not an absolute prerequisite to successful research or productive scholarship. The quality of scientific work depends much less on the complexity of the equipment or instruments than on the soundness of the thinking and the validity of the evidence, since the most important instrument or element in research is the mind of man. Work in improvised laboratories sometimes has produced remarkable results. There are many examples of great discoveries outside the laboratory or study.

With John MacGillivray, son of the famous ornithologist, Huxley improvised dredging nets, often finding his specimens kicked off the deck by sailors; nevertheless, the lack of scientific instruments, the necessity of lashing his microscope to the mast, the paucity of scientific literature, and the presence of unsympathetic mates merely threw him upon his own resources.[31]

Appropriate illustrations may be drawn from the field of psychology. William James contended that he began instruction in experimental psychology at Harvard either in 1874-75 or 1876 with equipment described by Stanley Hall as a "tiny room under the stairway of Agassiz Museum . . . with a metronome, a device for whirling a frog, a horopter chart, and one or two bits of apparatus." However, as early as 1879 Stanley Hall exposed the fallacy of theatrical methods and "brass-instrument" psychology, insisting that curves, instruments, and flashing charts of themselves would not insure the accuracy of a doubtful generalization, and objecting to the fad of reducing everything to mechanics and motion (a movement that was spreading even in the 1870's).

Edward L. Thorndike modestly underrates his background in mentioning an extreme ineptitude and distaste on his part for using machinery and physical instruments. He regrets the absence in his training of a systematic course in the use of standard physiological and psychological apparatus for exposing, timing, and registering, and of extended preparation in mathematics. On the other hand, the work of many psychologists has benefited from their considerable ingenuity in devising equipment or apparatus. Clark L. Hull conceived the idea of building a machine that would do nearly all of his correlation work automatically. Although Hull could not make mechanical drawings and his assistant could not read such drawings, they achieved their purpose by making marks free-hand on bits of paper at the mechanic's work bench; both had an idea of how the wheels should go around to do certain things.

Varied conditions of work and environment have contributed to the

[31] Quoted from Charles S. Blinderman, *op. cit.*

solution of important problems, depending in part on the temperament of the scientist or scholar. Helmholtz has said that, after working on a problem for some time, happy ideas for a solution frequently came to him at some place other than his working table. Some scientists have claimed that an unexpected insight or intuition, at times in sleep, produces the answer to a problem, although these solutions probably do not take place spontaneously; rather, such "insights" come from a mind with a rich background of knowledge. Scientists and scholars have reported certain conditions or environmental settings as favorable to the emergence of solutions to problems: freedom from competing problems or worries, periods of relaxation or sleep, and recovery from fatigue. In so far as Helmholtz offers an explanatory theory, it is based on fatigue and recovery from fatigue. In 1896, at a dinner in honor of his seventieth birthday, Helmholtz spoke of his methods of work on original problems as follows:[32]

> I must say that those fields of work have become ever more agreeable to me in which one need not depend on lucky accidents and "happy thoughts." But as I have found myself pretty often in the uncomfortable position of [waiting for thoughts my story is useful to others]; . . . they never came to a fatigued brain and never at the writing desk. It was always necessary, first of all, that I should have turned my problem over on all sides to such an extent that I had all its angles and complexities "in my head" and could run through them freely without writing. To bring the matter to that point is usually impossible without long preliminary labor. Then, after the fatigue resulting from this labor had passed away, there must come an hour of complete physical freshness and quiet well-being, before the good ideas arrived. Often they were there in the morning when I awoke, just according to Goethe's oft-cited verses, and as Gauss also once noted. But they liked specially to make their appearance while I was taking an easy walk over wooded hills in sunny weather. The smallest amount of alcohol seemed to frighten them away.

A characterization or analysis of the nature of genius takes cognizance of examples of intuition or spontaneity in problem-solving, but recognizes that this feature is not always present in research and scholarly activity.

This seems to accord with the frequency with which geniuses often receive their inspiration in a sudden flash that startles the recipient himself. It is a feature that has always been recognized. Both Plato and Aristotle commented on it, and they associated it with the divine source of the inspiration. The description of Apollo in the third book of *Hyperion* seemed to Keats to have come by chance or magic—to be, as it were, something given to him. He said

[32] Quoted from Robert S. Woodworth and Harold Schlosberg, *Experimental Psychology*. Revised Edition. New York: Henry Holt and Co., 1954. p. 838.

also that he had often not been aware of the beauty of some thought or expression until after he had composed and written it down. It had then struck him with astonishment and seemed rather the production of another person than his own. Alfred Russell Wallace wrote: "Finally both Darwin and myself, at the critical period, had our attention directed to the system of *positive checks* as expounded by Malthus in his *Principles of Population.* The effect was analogous to that of friction upon the specially prepared match, producing that flash of insight which led us immediately to the simple but universal law of the 'survival of the fittest.'" This is, however, a feature by no means always present. The flash of insight which Wallace described did presumably happen to him, but Darwin himself seems to have reflected on the suggestion more calmly. No one can have accepted revelation more tardily and gradually, even cautiously and very timidly, than Darwin, whose dawning vision came only as the result of many years of hard work.[33]

Sponsorship and Co-operation

In selection of a thesis or research adviser, it is essential to reflect carefully on the availability and personality characteristics of the particular professor or staff member under consideration; among the important factors are leave of absence, a heavy teaching schedule, a large number of advisees, concentration on writing or research, numerous speaking engagements, ill health, or temperamental difficulties. For certain types of studies sponsorship, co-operation, or special permission from responsible school officers may be necessary; for example, to administer tests to pupils, to interview employees, to distribute questionnaires, to observe pupils and teachers at work, to evaluate buildings or equipment, to try out innovations in curriculum or method, or to make case studies of pupils.

The present chapter and other sections of this book identify directly or indirectly many instances of helpful co-operation between professor and student. It is only honest to say that graduate students and others sometimes have suffered from lack of intelligent advising, appropriate sponsorship, or administrative co-operation. To cite an example, Wallin believes that the dissension caused by the ouster of certain psychologists from Yale University in the first decade of this century proved especially disastrous for Yale psychology graduates over a number of years, with respect to securing major positions in philosophy or psychology. He speaks of the young Yale graduates in psychology of those early days as a "lost generation," in terms of finding or being recommended for attractive positions in psychology.[34]

[33] Quoted from Ernest Jones, *op. cit.*
[34] J. E. Wallace Wallin, *op. cit.*, p. 12, 15–16.

Scripture's sudden severance from Yale University made it impossible for him to do the editorial work on Wallin's thesis, which had been accepted for publication in the Studies from the Yale Psychological Laboratory (Scripture was the editor). Wallin himself had to do all the editorial work at a time when he had no experience in scientific publication. The one suggestion Scripture had made was that the copy for publication should be boiled down about 50 per cent, not by eliminations but by condensing the sentences and by packing them brim full of content. (Scripture said that he scarcely recognized his own thesis when Wundt, the great German psychologist and founder of the world's first psychological laboratory in 1879, got through with it.)

Risks and Costs

In the selection and development of certain types of problems there are sometimes special risks, penalties, handicaps, or costs of a physical, financial, personal, social, or professional character. Fortunately the costs of graduate study and research have been considerably eased during recent years through a variety of financial resources.

The risks in educational research, where human relationships usually are involved, may include problems of professional ethics.

To what extent is the investigator free to tamper with complex organisms and their relationships to one another?

To what extent is he free to set up conditions which are strictly his—conditions with which the subjects of research may not even be familiar and which are not of their making?

Are the proposed risks in research legitimate? For example, to what extent does one have the right to use an untried method of instruction? On the other hand, to what extent is one obligated to try out new methods of instruction in order that progress might be made?

Do the child and his parents have the right to expect that the school will make use in its instructional program of those methods and procedures which have been found somewhat productive, or is the child's school experience to be a testing ground for untried, albeit promising hypotheses?

What is the effect on the learner whose opportunity to learn has been impeded by the research process (the process to produce the information that the procedure in question was not efficacious)? Would the deprived learner have legitimate grounds for complaint, and would his parents?

To what extent does the learner bear a part of the burden of extending knowledge as to how learning takes place?

To what extent is the research worker free to disregard the expectations of the learner in a given situation?

If a deficiency discovered in a survey has been corrected, should the results of the survey be published?

Should we be as assiduous in trying to find external factors which might cause substantially better performance than was anticipated, as we are in seeking such explanations for performances which are not up to our expectations?

If the unfortunate personal traits of a staff member in a school system have created a barrier to research, to what extent should he be informed of the effects of his own personal idiosyncrasies?

To what extent are we justified in using students and faculty members as unwitting guinea pigs? Can we excuse this type of procedure on the grounds that their awareness of the nature of the research would invalidate the findings and make these less generally applicable? Or can we justify giving full information with the general conclusion that people will do better and behave more intelligently if they know what they are doing and why they are doing it?[35]

Occasionally a professional risk or hazard is involved in a disagreement between graduate student and professor. Hugo Münsterberg disagreed with Wundt in setting up a dissertation problem in the Leipzig laboratory and was shifted to another (less important) problem which was accepted. Although Münsterberg later adapted the rejected dissertation for another purpose, he lost the favor of Wundt and as a result was handicapped in securing a position.

The hazards of research in the field of medicine and health are well known to the doctors, scientists, interns, medical students, research workers, patients, and others who test new treatments for disease, new drugs, or new scientific equipment. Selected research volunteers for service in this field have formed the Walter Reed Society, named after Major Walter Reed of Spanish-American War fame, who dramatized the use of human volunteers in medical experience and helped to solve the riddle of yellow fever.

Men of high achievement have often accomplished their work in spite of physical or health handicaps. Sir Walter Scott was lame as a result of a childhood attack of polio and was ill for much of his life. At times he dictated while racked by pain from gallstone and stomach cramps.

Samuel Johnson achieved greatness in spite of lifelong suffering from a compulsive neurosis, the distorting convulsions of his severe tic, and his attacks of depression. It has been suggested that, had Johnson lived at a later date, science would have been able at least to name his oddities, if

[35] Quoted from James A. Hall, "Some Ethical Problems," *Research for Curriculum Improvement.* 1957 Yearbook. Washington: Association for Supervision and Curriculum Development, a Department of the National Education Association, 1957. p. 269–77.

not to cure them. His habits with respect to eating, drinking, and personal cleanliness should be viewed in the perspective of the eighteenth century rather than in terms of standards or customs two hundred years later.[36]

A number of psychologists have been confronted with physical and health problems. A nervous disorder William James had during his twenties may have contributed indirectly to his intellectual development, since it gave him psychological insight into abnormal conditions and took him abroad in search of a cure, with profitable visits to the intellectual and artistic centers of Europe. The tic (blinking) of Edward B. Titchener may have struck the young student as a strange flaw in a famous psychologist, but Titchener's personality was so natural and spontaneous that in the course of the seminar or lecture the tic was disregarded and forgotten. Clark L. Hull was handicapped by a severe attack of typhoid fever that left him with a generalized bad memory for names; an attack of polio left one leg badly paralyzed and crippled; and his earlier years of psychological study were made much more difficult because of his weak eyes. James R. Angell, near the end of his college course, considered medicine as a career, but weak eyes caused him to believe that he could not do the exacting microscopic work required as part of the medical program.

For sixteen years at Cambridge University, Whitehead had a constant struggle with insomnia, and each September, after a summer's vacation in the country or by the sea, he would wonder whether he could endure another year of teaching.[37] However, the insomnia never seemed to affect his work, and when he moved to London University it diminished and finally ceased.

The sociologist, Charles H. Cooley (1864-1929), spent seven years as an undergraduate student at the University of Michigan because of ill health. We do not know how much effect his ill health, and the influence of his able jurist father, may have had on his quiet, effective thinking and writing. Most of his work assumed the form of digesting and interpreting the writings of others, and in applying the conclusions to life around him.[38]

Ellwood P. Cubberley produced a large volume of published material and edited works, in spite of colds, stomach ulcers, and sinus disturbances

---

[36] Edward Hitschmann, *Great Men*: Psychoanalytic Studies. New York: International Universities Press, 1956. p. 176.

[37] *Dialogues of Alfred North Whitehead*. As Recorded by Lucien Price. New York: New American Library of World Literature, 1954. 320 p.

[38] M. C. Elmer, *op. cit.,* p. 36.

Emory S. Bogardus, *op. cit.,* p. 492–504.

that caused him frequent discomfort for many years. His notebooks record the symptoms and the treatment, often including a record of temperature and blood pressure together with the physician's diagnosis. Later he was hospitalized a number of times, and underwent several serious operations, the details of which he set down in his notebooks.[39] His major illnesses included surgery for an ulcer in 1918, removal of his appendix in 1934 and of a kidney in 1935, and the handicap of a serious heart ailment.

Scientists and scholars frequently have encountered financial difficulties or have sacrificed their personal resources. Sir Walter Scott's badly managed ventures in printing and publishing failed, with debts of 130,000 pounds charged against him. Refusing bankruptcy, during the last six years of his life Scott produced a nine-volume life of Napoleon and in two years turned over 40,000 pounds to his creditors. He continued writing best sellers until his frail health cracked, and he died at the age of sixty-one. Later, the sale of Scott's works settled the last of the debts that helped kill him.

Herbert Spencer was an invalid most of his life, with an uncertain income. He invested more in his early books than he received from them, since he usually employed an amanuensis. In the early days of the *American Journal of Psychology*, Stanley Hall had to spend $8,000 of his own money on the publication, in order to keep it going.

In many instances scientists have disregarded monetary costs and returns, particularly when their work was supported by educational institutions and agencies. Pasteur declared, "I could never work for money, but I would always work for science," and Agassiz said, "I have no time to make money."

Some scientists have had the benefit of large personal resources for conducting their research. Roger Bacon was a member of a wealthy family and probably earned substantial fees for lecturing. He spent 10,000 pounds, in modern money, on the purchase of books, experiments and instruments, journeys to meet scholars, and secretaries. Charles Darwin was an English gentleman of wealth and leisure, with favorable conditions for making his scientific studies.

Occasionally a specialist in psychology or education has made himself financially independent. Edward L. Thorndike made it a rule early in his career to spend so little and earn so much that he would be free from financial worry, and in so doing became a person of considerable means. Ellwood P. Cubberley was able to accumulate a fortune, derived chiefly from royalties on books and fees for editorial services, with

[39] Jesse B. Sears and Adin D. Henderson, *op. cit.*, p. 82–83, 233, 247–48.

smaller sums from services as consultant, investigator, and lecturer. These sums were increased greatly through investments that proved sound. The gifts by Cubberley and his wife to Stanford University totaled more than three quarters of a million dollars, including more than a half million dollars for a new School of Education building.[40]

Timing

The variables of worker, problem, technique, adviser, sponsorship, and working conditions are such that it is extremely hazardous to predict the length of time required to complete a specific investigation. Beyond a certain point additional money, equipment, and personnel resources will not shorten the period of development and maturation essential for successful research. Charles F. Kettering once estimated that a certain project would require a year for completion. When urged to double his force and reduce the time to six months, his reply was, "Do you think that by putting two hens on the nest a setting of eggs could be hatched out in less time than three weeks?"

The need for relatively long periods of sustained effort in research is aptly expressed by Cannon:[41]

An investigator may be given a palace to live in, a perfect laboratory to work in, he may be surrounded by all the conveniences money can provide; but if his time is taken from him he will remain sterile. On the other hand, as the history of science abundantly shows, an investigator may be poverty-stricken, he may be ill-clothed, he may live in a garret and have only meager appliances for his use; but given time he can be productive.

It is unusual to have as exact (and surprisingly short) a time schedule for completion of a dissertation as that left on record by Ellwood P. Cubberley, who made a study of state school laws on finance under the title, "School Funds and Their Apportionment." This dissertation was the beginning of many years of study by Cubberley of the financing of public-education administration. He began the research for his dissertation on January 24, 1905; Mrs. Cubberley began the typing on March 17, and Cubberley presented the dissertation to his adviser on April 14. In his diary he entered the comment: "Handed it to Dr. Perry, returned borrowed sections of Teachers College Library, and breathed a sigh of relief—Done!" He took his oral examination on May 19 and received the Ph.D. degree on June 14, 1905, at Columbia University.[42]

[40] *Ibid.,* p. 267, 280.
[41] Quoted from Walter B. Cannon, *The Way of an Investigator.* New York: W. W. Norton and Co., 1945. p. 87.
[42] Jesse B. Sears and Adin D. Henderson, *op. cit.,* p. 81.

William James was relatively slow in his development and program of writing; he required considerable persuasion to complete a textbook in psychology, his famous *Principles of Psychology* (1890), after twelve years of hard work. On the other hand, John Dewey was only 26 years of age when he produced his *Psychology*, which means that he was engaged in writing this book at the age of 24 or 25 (an unusual accomplishment for so young a man).

One aspect of timing involves historical or research perspective—the ability to evaluate one's work or the efforts of others in the contemporary setting and also in relation to changed conditions or new evidence after a period of time. For example, Edward A. Ross (1866-1952) was outspoken in criticism, even of his own works, when conditions changed or new evidence appeared: [43]

> In the thirty-five years since the book left my anvil, I have scrutinized society in many countries and a society which "controls" does not look so global to me now as it did to me in 1900. . . . I doubt if "lessons from history" will have much to do with shaping humanity's future. Basic conditions are changing so rapidly that most of the old techniques of control are junk. . . . Science and invention—together with applied psychology open vistas into a wondrous new age with its own problems of control, in which control devices will be employed that the past never heard of.

Ross, speaking of his 1920 book on *Principles of Sociology*, stated that when published he thought it sound, but "even then sensed that certain parts were labored and foggy." He said that almost every month fresh shortcomings had appeared and that, if by 1960 it should prove forty to fifty parts sound, he would be content.

INITIAL STATEMENT OF THE PROBLEM

Focusing Topics for Research

After the title of a thesis or investigation has been phrased within one or two lines, the next step is to provide an adequate statement of the problem in one or more paragraphs in the introductory chapter. Certain errors in the phrasing of thesis or research topics should be avoided:

1. Naming a broad field or area of study instead of a specific problem for investigation; for example, "the effect of various factors on learning," which might be delimited as "the effect of three thirty-minute periods of practice

---

[43] Quoted from M. C. Elmer, *op. cit.*, p. 29–30.
Emory S. Bogardus, *op. cit.*, p. 523–39.

versus five eighteen-minute periods on learning silent reading in the fifth grade"; or the history of music the world over for all time, which was delimited by one student to present a history of a particular conservatory of music.

2. Narrowing or localizing a topic to such an extent that it may prove a "pinpoint" problem; for example, a proposed history of a one-room school might be broadened to deal with the history of the school district or even the history of the county school system in which the one-room school is located.

3. Wording of a hortatory or biased character, or citing undigested data without identifying a problem; for example, "an argument for free textbooks in the public schools" might better be phrased as "the practices of public schools in a particular area in providing free textbooks." "Fifty tape recordings of home room programs" might become "an analysis of the content of home room programs, based on tape recordings."

The problem may be stated in the form of a question (or series of questions) or as a declarative statement (or series of statements). The question form may have an advantage in sharpening or focusing the issue, but the declarative statement probably is more common. The following example[44] combines the two ways (question and declarative statement) of phrasing the problem:

The purpose of this study, broadly stated, was to investigate the effectiveness of a method of teaching arithmetic in which children's immature procedures in dealing with number are accepted as normal and valuable steps toward their achievement of competent, mature behavior with reference to number. More narrowly, the objective of the investigation was to determine the effect upon the arithmetical development of children of their temporary use of certain immature procedures, when careful guidance is given by teachers. These procedures are designated as "intermediate," since they occur between the initial awareness of number and the achievement of mature modes of dealing with number relationships. The study was limited to the development of understanding in the four fundamental processes, on the part of the second-grade children.

Preliminary problems.—Two preliminary problems which were basic to the major purpose of the study may be stated as follows:

1. The discovery of the intermediate procedures that were being used by children at the beginning of the study.

2. The selection of those intermediate procedures which showed promise as aids to more mature understanding of number ideas by pupils.

Sub-problems.—In the evaluation of a teaching technique in which the immature or intermediate procedures of children are regarded as of central

[44] Quoted from Edwina Deans, "The Effect of Certain Immature Procedures on the Learning of Arithmetical Processes by Second-Grade Children," *Abstracts of Graduate Theses in Education*, 1944-54, Vol. 5. Cincinnati: Teachers College, University of Cincinnati, 1955. p. 129–47.

importance, a number of pertinent questions arise. Such questions, which may be regarded as sub-problems, include the following:

1. In what ways can experience be provided for all children on the selected intermediate procedures?

2. Is it possible for some children to bypass some intermediate procedures without jeopardizing understanding?

3. Do some children tend to move to more advanced procedures before understanding is present?

4. How can readiness for a more advanced intermediate procedure be determined?

5. Do children willingly discontinue the use of immature procedures?

6. Under what circumstances are less mature methods dropped and replaced by more mature methods?

7. What steps can be taken by the teacher to encourage children to discontinue the use of immature methods?

8. As children are taught intermediate procedures, to what extent is their later thinking characterized by increasingly higher levels of maturity in dealing with number situations?

9. What problems do teachers encounter as they attempt to guide children through succeeding maturity levels in dealing with number situations?

FULLER DEFINITION OF THE PROBLEM

The brief introductory statement of the problem usually is followed by a fuller definition and development of background concerning sub-problems, scope, related literature, sources of data, method, significance, terminology, assumptions, and hypotheses. Of course it may not be appropriate for a particular study to include all of these items of background as part of the fuller development of the problem.

Constituent Elements and Scope

The preceding illustrative study of arithmetical processes by Deans also shows how the major problem is divided into subproblems, constituent elements, or questions to answer. A statement of the limits or scope of the investigation well may provide information concerning "who, what, when, where, and how many."

Thoughtful analysis of problems for action research involves answers to such questions as the following:[45]

1. What conditions need to prevail both to allow and to invite teachers to state problems of importance to them?

[45] Hilda Taba, "Problem Identification," *Research for Curriculum Improvement.* 1957 Yearbook. Washington: Association for Supervision and Curriculum Development, a Department of the National Education Association, 1957. p. 42–71.

2. In what context do problem identification and analysis produce the maximum of identification, allow for varied levels of involvement depending on the capacity and the insight of individuals, and permit significant problems to emerge?

3. What is the sequence in opening up a problem for research with teachers?

4. What is the timing factor? How is one to gauge how fast or how slowly to proceed, at which point to introduce which considerations?

5. What is a team pattern in guiding action research which yields the greatest possible combined competence? What is the role of the research consultants? of the supervisor? of teachers?

The analysis of action-research problems should proceed in an atmosphere that provides for at least three conditions:[46]

1. It is necessary to provide a climate which facilitates an analysis of the factors which those who propose a "problem" may not be quite ready to see.

2. It is necessary to proceed so as to maintain an optimum identification with the problem. It is easy to "detach" a teacher from his concern by suggesting a greater complexity or a greater change in approach than the teacher can take for the time being. This means that the levels of analysis or of investigation need to be gauged to each individual's ability and insight, so as to maintain his self-respect, while challenging some assumptions and cherished concepts.

3. This in turn means that the steps in the analysis need to be broken down to provide an "easy road in." One needs to gauge the speed with which to proceed with each individual.

Related Literature and Terminology

We have already noted the importance of the literature in the selection of problems for investigation. The next chapter presents the keys to the related literature, from which may come explanatory hypotheses, techniques for gathering evidence, and comparative data for purposes of interpretation. The orientation provided by a survey of the related research is helpful in making a straightforward statement of the need for the investigation, avoiding the two extremes of an apologetic attitude and exaggerated claims or boastfulness. Chapters of the *Encyclopedia of Educational Research, Review of Educational Research,* and the *Annual Review of Psychology* may serve as useful examples of summaries of the research literature on specific topics.

Certain specialized terms in the technical report or in the related

[46] *Ibid.*, p. 53–54.

studies may require definition. Comprehensive dictionaries[47] are available for the fields of education, psychology, and sociology.

Sources of Data and Method

An introductory section of the technical report should include appropriate information concerning sources of evidence and techniques of data-gathering, including a frank admission of any weaknesses or short-comings. Detailed discussions of sources and methods are found later in this book in the several chapters on research methodology. The fol-lowing illustrative statement of sources and method involves a case-study procedure.[48]

The fifty-five subjects represented consecutive cases seen in the psycho-logical clinic of the Juvenile Court of Hamilton County, Ohio, from Novem-ber 1, 1947, to May 1, 1948, who had attended public schools for one month or more of this period. Every subject was given Form L of the Stanford Binet Intelligence Test, Form D of the Stanford Achievement Tests, and a structured interview. Probation officers checked questionnaires which provided pertinent social history material about each child. All thirty-two schools attended by subjects were visited and the principals or assistant principals, counselors, homeroom teachers, and classroom teachers of each child were interviewed by a structured procedure. Cumulative and other available records in the schools and the work of the court and clinic were used as research data.

Basic Assumptions

In social investigations and in school and community life, certain premises or assumptions are generally accepted, frequently without identification in the technical or research reports; for example, in a democracy we assume that co-operation rather than strife and respect for the individual rather than rigid regimentation are desirable. We accept the premise that schools and education are necessary, and that transporta-tion of pupils in rural areas is desirable.

[47] Carter V. Good, Editor, *Dictionary of Education.* Second Edition. New York: McGraw-Hill Book Co., 1959. xxx+676 p.

Philip L. Harriman, *New Dictionary of Psychology.* New York: Philosophical Library, 1947. 364 p.

H. C. Warren, Editor, *A Dictionary of Psychology.* Boston: Houghton Mifflin Co., 1934. x+372 p.

Horace B. English and Ava C. English, *Comprehensive Dictionary of Psycho-logical and Psychoanalytical Terms.* New York: Longmans, Green and Co., 1958. xiv+594 p.

H. P. Fairchild, Editor, *Dictionary of Sociology.* New York: Philosophical Library, 1944. viii+342 p.

[48] Quoted from Vera C. Edwards, "A Study of the School Adjustment of Fifty-Five Delinquent Children," *Abstracts of Graduate Theses in Education,* 1944-54, Vol. 5. Cincinnati: Teachers College, University of Cincinnati, 1955. p. 266-76.

The scientist typically accepts two basic assumptions:[49]

1. That there is lawfulness in the events of nature as opposed to capricious, chaotic, or spontaneous occurrences (in other words, determinism).

2. That every natural event or phenomenon has a discoverable and limited number of conditions or factors which are responsible for it (an assumption of finite causation).

To the extent that basic assumptions are open to question, the results of the particular investigation are subject to challenge. Many assumptions or premises in the social areas involve the realm of values and are not subject at present to validation through any known scientific procedure. Underlying assumptions should be stated as part of the definition and development of the problem, and also in connection with the conclusions of the investigation.

DEVELOPMENT AND TESTING OF HYPOTHESES

A hypothesis is an informed or shrewd guess or inference, with a reasonable chance of being right, formulated and tentatively adopted to explain observed facts or conditions and to guide in further investigation, in other words, to serve as the investigator's "eyes" in seeking answers to questions. The scientist's hypothesis parallels the common man's personal opinion or hunch.

Hypotheses may serve the following functions:[50] They may contribute as explanations, stimuli to research, sources of methodology, criteria for evaluating experimental and other techniques, and as organizing principles. In thus limiting the area of investigation, sensitizing the worker to pertinent data and relationships, and providing a unifying concept, the single hypothesis should not blind the research worker's observation of all pertinent data, even though some facts may not contribute to validation of the chosen hypothesis. As emphasized later, it is common for a particular study to involve formulation and testing of more than one hypothesis.

Factors that contribute to the emergence of hypotheses[51] include generalizing beyond the results of previous investigations, analyzing factual conditions requiring explanation, intellectual equipment and resources of the scientist, and inspiration. Expressed otherwise, hypotheses

[49] Benton J. Underwood, *Psychological Research*. New York: Appleton-Century-Crofts, 1957. p. 3–6.

[50] Clarence W. Brown and Edwin E. Ghiselli, *Scientific Method in Psychology*. New York: McGraw-Hill Book Co., 1955. p. 157–59.

[51] *Ibid.*, p. 162–63.

originate from substantially the same background as that which serves to identify problems: the insight and imagination that should result from a sound instructional program, extensive and critical reading, knowledge of existing practices and needs, and meaningful contact with pertinent data.

There is no sharp line of demarcation between hypothesis and theory, since the basic difference is one of complexity and the extent of testing against the evidence. In its early stages of testing a theory usually has been called a hypothesis but, as the hypothesis is checked against the data and their logical implications toward a successful conclusion, it may become known as a theory. A law represents an order or relation of phenomena that is invariable under the given conditions and permits of no exception in its operation.

The working hypothesis, when checked against the data, may emerge as a central explanatory theme for purposes of interpretation; for example, the formulation and development of three hypotheses which became central themes in a history of music education in the city school system of Cincinnati:[52]

1. Music in the schools has been an important factor in the cultural life of the city.

2. The background of the people who came to live in the city has exerted a strong influence on the development of public-school music in the city.

3. One of the educational results of the interaction of these two groups was a systematic method of instruction in music.

A parallel history of music instruction in the parochial schools of the Archdiocese of Cincinnati identifies three hypotheses which became unifying themes of interpretation:[53]

1. Little success was met in the efforts to develop an organized system of music education in the parochial schools as long as there was no centralized control.

2. Training in music found a natural place in the Catholic schools from the beginning.

3. An interplay of influence between the Church and the school was evident in the development of the instructional program in music.

[52] Charles L. Gary, "A History of Music Education in the Cincinnati Public Schools," *Abstracts of Graduate Theses in Education*, 1944-54, Vol. 5. Cincinnati: Teachers College, University of Cincinnati, 1955. p. 158–68.
[53] Sister Mary Joeline Ebertz, "A History of the Development of Music Education in the Archdiocese of Cincinnati." Unpublished Doctor's dissertation. Cincinnati: University of Cincinnati, 1955. vii+259 p.

The hypothesis may be evaluated in terms of agreement with and explanation of the evidence, absence of conflict with satisfactorily proved generalizations, success for purposes of prediction, simplicity and clarity of statement, and logical consistency.[54] Although a specific investigation usually involves the development and testing of more than one hypothesis, many scientists and scholars have been reluctant to describe their rejected hypotheses or failures. This means that it is frequently impossible to learn about the blind alleys traveled by earlier investigators. Since the technical report is usually prepared at the conclusion of the study, the author commonly tells a simple story of "smooth sailing." If research workers are overly cautious about making and reporting mistakes, they are not likely to make either errors or discoveries. As Whitehead says, "Panic of error is the death of progress." According to Humphrey Davy, "The most important of my discoveries have been suggested to me by my failures." It may be surprising that so able a scientist as Charles Darwin could not recall a single first-formed hypothesis, with the exception of the Coral Reefs, which had not after a time been given up or greatly modified.[55]

This reluctance to describe the scientist's mistakes to the reader is aptly described by Helmholtz, in commenting on his work during 1891, including the solution of certain problems in mathematics and physics over which great mathematicians had puzzled in vain:[56]

But any pride I might have felt in my conclusions was perceptibly lessened by the fact that I knew that the solution of these problems had almost always come to me as the gradual generalization of favourable examples, by a series of fortunate conjectures, after many errors. I am fain to compare myself with a wanderer on the mountains, who, not knowing the path, climbs slowly and painfully upwards, and often has to retrace his steps because he can go no farther—then, whether by taking thought or from luck, discovers a new track that leads him on a little, till at length when he reaches the summit he finds to his shame that there is a royal road, by which he might have ascended, had he only had the wits to find the right approach to it. In my works I naturally said nothing about my mistakes to the reader, but only described the made track by which he may now reach the same heights without difficulty.

A similar view concerning the development and testing of hypotheses has been expressed by Cannon, a research worker in medicine and physiology:[57]

[54] Morris R. Cohen and Ernest Nagel, *An Introduction to Logic and Scientific Method*. New York: Harcourt, Brace and Co., 1934. p. 207–15.
[55] Allen Johnson, *The Historian and Historical Evidence*. New York: Charles Scribner's Sons, 1926. p. 166–67.
[56] Quoted in William H. George, *The Scientist in Action*: A Scientific Study of His Methods. London: Williams and Norgate, 1936. p. 229–30.
[57] Quoted from Walter B. Cannon, *op. cit.*, p. 22.

Investigators do not march straight to their goal with ease and directness. In their imagination they see a possible fact and they set forth to learn whether their foresight can be realized. Or they come upon something which is puzzling and challenging and which they wish to explain; then they try in various ways to relate it to other phenomena that would solve the riddle. Obstacles and difficulties are sure to be encountered. The search for understanding is an adventure or, more commonly, a series of adventures. If an attempt in one direction fails, the failure is not discouraging to an eager explorer. There are other possible approaches to the end in view and relentlessly, one after another, these are tried.

CONCLUDING STATEMENT

The investigator is aided in identifying significant problems through advanced study and critical reading, analysis of practices and needs, and repetition or extension of earlier studies. (The chapter bibliography includes references dealing with surveys of progress and critiques of research, trends, prophecies, and needed research.) Important factors in selection of the problem include: novelty and significance, intellectual curiosity and drive, scholarship and personal characteristics, sources and technique, sponsorship and co-operation, risks and costs, and timing. The initial statement and fuller definition of the problem involve appropriate focusing of the topic, constituent elements and scope, related literature and terminology, sources of evidence and methodology, and basic assumptions. The hypothesis may serve the purposes of explanations, stimuli to research, sources of methodology, criteria for evaluating research techniques, and organizing principles.

SELECTED REFERENCES

ABEL, Theodore, BOCK, Kenneth E., and REED, Stephen W. "The Present Status of Social Theory." *American Sociological Review* 17: 156-67; April 1952.

ACKERMAN, Nathan W. "Mental Hygiene and Social Work, Today and Tomorrow." *Social Casework* 36: 63-70; February 1955.

ANDERSON, G. Lester. "Unsolved Problems in Teacher Education." *Third Yearbook*, American Association of Colleges for Teacher Education. Oneonta, N.Y.: The Association, 1950. p. 22-33.

ARENSBERG, Conrad M., and Others. *Research in Industrial Human Relations: A Critical Appraisal.* New York: Harper & Brothers, 1957. x+213 p.

AUSUBEL, David P. "Relationships between Psychology and Psychiatry: The Hidden Issues." *American Psychologist* 11: 99-105; February 1956.

BAIL, Milo. "Six Decades of Progress." *North Central Association Quarterly* 30: 193-207; October 1955.

BAITSELL, George A., Editor. *Science in Progress.* Ninth Series. New Haven: Yale University Press, 1956. 482 p.

BARR, Arvil S., DAVIS, Robert A., and JOHNSON, Palmer O. *Educational Research and Appraisal.* Philadelphia: J. B. Lippincott Co., 1953. p. 5-13, 308-13, 335-39.

BARZUN, Jacques, and GRAFF, Henry F. *The Modern Researcher.* New York: Harcourt, Brace and Co., 1957. p. 18-27.

BELSON, William A. "New Developments in Audience Research Methods." *American Journal of Sociology* 64: 174-79; September 1958.

BERDIE, Ralph F. "A Program of Counseling Interview Research." *Educational and Psychological Measurement* 18: 255-74; Summer 1958.

BIGELOW, Karl W. "New Directions in Teacher Education Appraised." *Teachers College Record* 59: 350-56; March 1958.

BOGARDUS, Emory S. *The Development of Social Thought.* Third Edition. New York: Longmans, Green and Co., 1955. x+660 p.

BOGARDUS, Emory S. "Forty Years of 'Sociology and Social Research.'" *Sociology and Social Research* 40: 426-32; July-August 1956.

BORDIN, Edward S., and Others. "Anticipations of Developments During the Next Decade Which Will Influence Psychology." *American Psychologist* 11: 686-88; December 1956.

BORGATTA, Edgar F., and COTTRELL, Leonard S., Jr. "Directions for Research in Group Behavior." *American Journal of Sociology* 63: 42-48; July 1957.

BORGATTA, Edgar F., and PHILIP, Hugh. "The Definition of Some Problem Areas for Research: A Theoretical Formulation of Some Problems of Relevance to Diagnostics." *Group Psychotherapy* 6: 90-101; 1953.

BORING, E. G. *A History of Experimental Psychology.* Second Edition. New York: Appleton-Century-Crofts, 1950. xxi+777 p.

BORROWMAN, Merle L. "Teacher Education in the Past Decade: A Review." *Teachers College Record* 58: 446-57; May 1957.

BOWEN, Howard R. *The Business Enterprise as a Subject for Research.* Social Science Research Council Pamphlet 11. New York: The Council, 1955. viii+103 p.

BOWMAN, Claude C. "Research in Family Dynamics: A Criticism and a Proposal." *Social Forces* 34: 201-7; March 1956.

BREEN, Leonard Z. "Some Problems of Research in the Field of Aging." *Sociology and Social Research* 41: 412-16; July-August 1957.

BRIGGS, Thomas H. "The Secondary School Curriculum: Yesterday, Today, and Tomorrow." *Teachers College Record* 52: 399-448; April 1951.

BRODERICK, Catherine M. "Research in the Use and Purposes of Instructional Materials." *Educational Leadership* 13: 425-29; April 1956.

BROOKOVER, Wilbur B. "Research on Teacher and Administrator Roles." *Journal of Educational Sociology* 29: 2-13; September 1955.

BROWN, Clarence W., and GHISELLI, Edwin E. *Scientific Method in Psychology.* New York: McGraw-Hill Book Co., 1955. p. 133-76.

BROWN, Harrison, BONNER, James, and WEIR, John. *The Next Hundred Years:*

Man's Natural and Technological Resources. New York: Viking Press, 1957. xi+193 p.

BROWNELL, Samuel M. "Unsolved Problems in American Education." *School Review* 62: 519-26; December 1954.

BRUNO, Frank J. *Trends in Social Work, 1874–1956*. New York: Columbia University Press, 1957. xv+462 p.

BUCK, Roy C. "School District Reorganization: Some Considerations for Sociological Research." *Journal of Educational Sociology* 28: 25-29; September 1954.

BURGESS, Ernest W. "Seven Significant Changes in Sociology." *Sociology and Social Research* 40: 385-86; July-August 1956.

BURGESS, Ernest W., and Others. "Symposium: Important Changes in Sociology During the Past Forty Years." *Sociology and Social Research* 40: 383-432; July-August 1956.

BUROS, Oscar K., Editor. *The Fourth Mental Measurements Yearbook*. Highland Park, N.J.: Gryphon Press, 1953. 1,189 p.

BURROWS, Raymond. "Present-Day Trends in Music Education." *Teachers College Record* 52: 213-25; January 1951.

BURTON, William H., and Others. "Needed Research on Textbooks." *Phi Delta Kappan* 33: 297-300; January 1952.

BUSWELL, G. T. "Needed Research on Arithmetic," *The Teaching of Arithmetic*. Fiftieth Yearbook of the National Society for the Study of Education, Part 2. Chicago: The University of Chicago Press, 1951. p. 282-97.

CARPENTER, Finley. "Wanted: More Descriptive Research in Education." *Educational Research Bulletin* 33: 149-54, 167-68; September 15, 1954.

CARTER, G. S. *A Hundred Years of Evolution*. New York: The Macmillan Co., 1957. x+206 p.

CASSEL, Russell N. "Delineating the Areas of Educational and Clinical Psychology." *Journal of Educational Psychology* 45: 292-99; May 1954.

CASWELL, Hollis L. "Great Challenges for Education." *Teachers College Record* 59: 69-75; November 1957.

"Centenary of Psychology: 1856–1956; Celebration at Washington University, St. Louis." *American Psychologist* 11: 558-62; October 1956.

A Century of Progress in the Natural Sciences, 1853–1953. Published in celebration of the centennial of the California Academy of Sciences. San Francisco: California Academy of Sciences, 1955. 807 p.

CHAMBERLAIN, N. W., and Others. *A Decade of Industrial Relations Research, 1946–1956*. New York: Harper & Brothers, 1958. 212 p.

CHAMPLIN, Nathaniel L. "Some Neglected Philosophic Problems of Education." *Educational Theory* 7: 122-27; April 1957.

CHARTERS, W. W., Jr. "Research on School Board Personnel: Critique and Prospectus." *Journal of Educational Research* 47: 321-35; January 1954.

CHASE, Francis S. "The Status of Research in Education." *School Review* 62: 457-64; November 1954.

CLARK, John R. "Issues in Teaching Arithmetic." *Teachers College Record* 52: 205-12; January 1951.

CLIFT, Virgil A. "Needed Changes in Higher Education for the Decades Ahead." *Journal of Negro Education* 23: 428-35; Fall 1954.

COHEN, Morris R., and NAGEL, Ernest. *An Introduction to Logic and Scientific Method.* New York: Harcourt, Brace and Co., 1934. p. 207-15.

COHEN, Wilbur J. "Current and Future Trends in Public Welfare." *Social Service Review* 29: 247-59; September 1955.

COMBS, Arthur W., FISK, Robert S., and Others. "Problems and Research Needs in Administration." *Journal of Social Issues* 10: No. 2; 49-66; 1954.

COOPER, Shirley, and Others. "A Symposium on Needed Research in District Reorganization." *Phi Delta Kappan* 32: 356-59; April 1951.

COTTRELL, Leonard S., Jr. "New Directions for Research on the American Family." *Social Casework* 34: 54-60; February 1953.

COTTRELL, W. Fred. "Research to Establish the Conditions for Peace." *Journal of Social Issues* 11: No. 1; 13-20; 1955.

CRANDALL, Vaughn J. "Some Problems of Personality Development Research." *Child Development* 27: 197-203; June 1956.

CRISWELL, Joan H. "Sociometric Measurement: Some Practical Advantages and New Developments." *Sociometry* 18: 383-91; December 1955.

CRONBACH, Lee J., Editor. *Text Materials in Modern Education:* A Comprehensive Theory and Platform for Research. Urbana: University of Illinois Press, 1955. 216 p.

CRUMMEL, Robert A. "The Development of Higher Education in the United States, 1900–1955." *Educational Record* 38: 320-28; October 1957.

CUMMINGS, H. H., and Others. *Looking Ahead in Secondary Education.* Report of the Second Commission on Life Adjustment Education for Youth. Office of Education Bulletin No. 4, 1954. Washington: Government Printing Office, 1954. iv+105 p.

DANE, Chase. "The Need for a Research Program in Library Problems." *College and Research Libraries* 16: 20-23; January 1955.

DANIEL, Glyn E. *A Hundred Years of Archaeology.* New York: The Macmillan Co., 1950. 343 p.

DARLEY, John G. "Psychology and the Office of Naval Research: A Decade of Development." *American Psychologist* 12: 305-23; June 1957.

DAVIES, Daniel R. "Educational Administration at Mid-Century." *Teachers College Record* 54: 125-30; December 1952.

DENNIS, Wayne, and Others. *Current Trends in Psychological Theory.* Pittsburgh: University of Pittsburgh Press, 1951. 213 p.

DINGLE, Herbert, Editor. *A Century of Science: 1851–1951.* New York: Roy Publishing Co., 1951. ix+338 p.

DUNSHEATH, Percy, Editor. *A Century of Technology: 1851–1951.* New York: Roy Publishing Co., 1951. ix+346 p.

DUSHKIND, Donald S. "Special Problems in Sociological Research." *Sociology and Social Research* 41: 42-45; September-October 1956.

DYER, Henry S. "The Need for Do-It-Yourself Prediction Research in High School Guidance." *Personnel and Guidance Journal* 36: 162-67; November 1957.

EDGERTON, Harold A. "Some Needs in Training Research." *Personnel Psychology* 8: 19-25; Spring 1955.

EELLS, Walter C. "Journals Publishing Articles on College Teachers and College Teaching." *American Association of University Professors Bulletin* 43: 458-60; September 1957.

EHLERS, Henry, Editor. *Crucial Issues in Education.* New York: Henry Holt and Co., 1955. 277 p.

ELLIS, Albert. "Critique of Systematic Theoretical Foundations in Clinical Psychology." *Journal of Clinical Psychology* 8: 11-15; January 1952.

ELMER, M. C. *Contemporary Social Thought:* Contributors and Trends. Pittsburgh: University of Pittsburgh Press, 1956. viii+256 p.

ENTERLINE, Herman G. "Summary of Needed Research in Business Education Administration and Supervision." *National Business Education Quarterly* 20: 43-52; May 1952.

EURICH, Alvin C. "Mid-point: The Vision of the Future." *North Central Association Quarterly* 25: 168-73; October 1950.

EVANS, Francis C., and Others. "Symposium on Viewpoints, Problems, and Methods of Research in Urban Areas." *Scientific Monthly* 73: 37-50; July 1951.

FARBER, Maurice L. "New Directions in the Study of National Character." *Journal of Social Issues* 11: 3-56; 1955.

FARBER, Maurice L. "Psychoanalytic Hypotheses in the Study of War." *Journal of Social Issues* 11: No. 1; 29-35; 1955.

FAUNCE, William A., and FULTON, Robert L. "The Sociology of Death: A Neglected Area of Research." *Social Forces* 36: 205-9; March 1958.

FAURI, Fedele F., and COHEN, Wilbur J. "Twenty Years of Progress in Social Security." *Public Welfare* 13: 143-51; October 1955.

FELIX, R. H. "New Scientific Developments in the Mental Health Field." *Social Service Review* 31: 123-34; June 1957.

FIELD, G. Lowell. "Hypotheses for a Theory of Political Power." *American Political Science Review* 45: 716-23; September 1951.

FINCH, James K. "A Century of Engineering Progress: 1852-1952." *Scientific Monthly* 75: 99-108; August 1952.

FITZPATRICK, E. A. "Need for Catholic Studies in the History of Education." *Catholic School Journal* 51: 148-49; April 1951.

FLANAGAN, John C., and Others. *Planning for Progress.* Proceedings of an A.I.R. Planning Conference on What Advances in Psychological Knowledge Could Make the Greatest Practical Contribution to the Welfare of the Nation in the Next Ten Years, March 22, 1956. Pittsburgh: American Institute for Research, 1956. 44 p.

FLUGEL, J. C. *A Hundred Years of Psychology.* Revised Edition. New York: The Macmillan Co., 1951. 424 p.

FOOTE, Nelson N., and COTTRELL, Leonard S., Jr. *Identity and Interpersonal Competence:* A New Direction in Family Research. Chicago: The University of Chicago Press, 1955. ix+305 p.

FOSHAY, Arthur W., and Others. *Research for Curriculum Improvement.* 1957 Yearbook. Washington: Association for Supervision and Curriculum Development, National Education Association, 1957. p. 42-71.

FREEMAN, Howard E., and KASSEBAUM, Gene G. "The Illiterate in American Society: Some General Hypotheses." *Social Forces* 34: 371-75; May 1956.

FREUDENTHAL, Kurt. "Need for Research in the Area of Treatment Relationships." *Social Casework* 36: 369-71; October 1955.

FURFEY, Paul H. "The Humanitarian Philosophy and the Acceptance of Sociological Generalizations." *American Catholic Sociological Review* 16: 117-22; June 1955.

GAGNE, Robert M. "Training Devices and Simulators: Some Research Issues." *American Psychologist* 9: 95-107; March 1954.

GANS, Herbert J. "The Sociology of New Towns: Opportunities for Research." *Sociology and Social Research* 40: 231-39; March-April 1956.

GARRETT, Henry E. *Great Experiments in Psychology*. Third Edition. New York: Appleton-Century-Crofts, 1951. 400 p.

GASKILL, Evelyn R., and MUDD, Emily H. "A Decade of Group Counseling." *Social Casework* 31: 194-201; May 1950.

GEMMELL, James, and Others, Editors. "Needed Research in Economic Education," *Economics in General Education*. Proceedings of the Riverdale Conference, Sponsored by the Joint Council on Economic Education, 1954. New York: The Council, 1954. p. 141-47.

GERARD, R. W. "Problems in the Institutionalization of Higher Education; An Analysis Based on Historical Materials." *Behavioral Science* 2: 134-46; April 1957.

GEWIRTZ, Jacob L. "A Program of Research on the Dimensions and Antecedents of Emotional Dependence." *Child Development* 27: 205-21; June 1956.

GIBSON, A. J. "Trends in Secondary Schools." *North Central Association Quarterly* 31: 209-18; October 1956.

GOETHALS, George W. "A Framework for Educational Research." *Harvard Educational Review* 28: 29-43; Winter 1958.

GOLDSCHMIDT, Richard. "Fifty Years of Zoology." *Scientific Monthly* 71: 359-69; December 1950.

GOLDSMITH, Maurice. "One Hundred Years of British Science." *Scientific Monthly* 74: 170-79; March 1952.

GOLLIN, Eugene S. "Some Research Problems for Developmental Psychology." *Child Development* 27: 223-35; June 1956.

GOOD, Carter V. "Educational Research After Fifty Years." *Phi Delta Kappan* 37: 145-52; January 1956.

GOOD, Carter V., and SCATES, Douglas E. *Methods of Research*: Educational, Psychological, Sociological. New York: Appleton-Century-Crofts, 1954. p. 33-132.

GOODE, William J., and HATT, Paul K. *Methods in Social Research*. New York: McGraw-Hill Book Co., 1952. Chapters 6, 7.

GRAY, A. L. "Needed Research in the School-Plant Field." *Review of Educational Research* 21: 63-68; February 1951.

GRAY, W. S. "Needed Research in Reading." *Elementary English* 29:100-8; February 1952.

GREENWOOD, Ernest. "Recent Trends in Social Work Research." *Sociology and Social Research* 35: 250-59; March-April 1951.

GREENWOOD, Ernest. "Social Work Research: A Decade of Reappraisal." *Social Service Review* 31: 311-20; September 1957.

GREENWOOD, Ernest. "Social Work Research: The Role of the Schools." *Social Service Review* 32: 152-66; June 1958.

GUILFORD, J. P., Editor. *Fields of Psychology*. Second Edition. New York: D. Van Nostrand Co., 1950. 779 p.

HALL, Oswald. "Sociological Research in the Field of Medicine: Progress and Prospects." *American Sociological Review* 16: 639-44; October 1951.

HALPERN, Ben. "History, Sociology, and Contemporary Area Studies." *American Journal of Sociology* 63: 1-10; July 1957.

HAMILTON, C. Horace. "Some Current Problems in the Development of Rural Sociology." *Rural Sociology* 15: 315-21; December 1950.

HANSON, Robert C. "Evidence and Procedure Characteristics of 'Reliable' Propositions in Social Science." *American Journal of Sociology* 63: 357-70; January 1958.

HARLOW, Harry F. "Current and Future Advances in Physiological and Comparative Psychology." *American Psychologist* 11: 273-77; June 1956.

HARMS, Ernest. "Child Guidance Yesterday, Today, and Tomorrow." *School and Society* 72: 129-32; August 26, 1950.

HARRIS, Chester W., Editor. *Encyclopedia of Educational Research*. Third Edition. New York: The Macmillan Co. Scheduled for 1960.

HASKEW, L. D. "Teacher Education in the Years Ahead." *Educational Research Bulletin* 36: 189-98; September 11, 1957.

HAYES, Samuel P., Jr. "Some Psychological Problems of Economics." *Psychological Bulletin* 47: 289-330; July 1950.

HENDRICKSON, Gordon. "Some Needed Research in Elementary Education." *Elementary School Journal* 51: 127-35; November 1950.

HERRICK, Virgil E. "Our Future in Teacher Education." *Teachers College Record* 57: 323-32; February 1956.

HILL, Reuben. "A Critique of Contemporary Marriage and Family Research." *Social Forces* 33: 268-77; March 1955.

HILLWAY, Tyrus. *Introduction to Research*. Boston: Houghton Mifflin Co., 1956. p. 95-119.

HODNETT, Edward. *The Art of Problem Solving*: How to Improve Your Methods. New York: Harper & Brothers, 1955. ix+202 p.

HORN, Francis H. "Problems Facing Higher Education." *Teachers College Record* 57: 360-70; March 1956.

HOSELITZ, Bert F. "The Social Sciences in the Last Two Hundred Years." *Journal of General Education* 4: 85-103; January 1950.

HUNT, Herold C. "Midpoint: A Challenge to Education." *North Central Association Quarterly* 25: 163-67; October 1950.

JACOBSON, P. B. "Research Shows Twelve Changes in Fifty Years of Secondary Education." *Nation's Schools* 49: 38-41; January 1952.

JAHODA, Marie, DEUTSCH, Morton, and COOK, Stuart W. *Research Methods in Social Relations*. Part 1, Basic Processes. New York: Dryden Press, 1951. Chapter 2.

JAMES, C. Evan. "Trends in Child Development Research." *Childhood Education* 29: 73-76; October 1952.

JOHNS, R. L., and MORPHET, E. L., Editors. *Problems and Issues in Public School Finance*: An Analysis and Summary of Significant Research and Experience. New York: Bureau of Publications, Teachers College, Columbia University, 1952. xiv+492 p.

JOHNSON, B. Lamar. "Opportunity Ahead in Higher Education." *School and Society* 84: 115-18; October 13, 1956.

JOHNSON, Leighton H. "Education Needs Historical Studies." *Phi Delta Kappan* 36: 157-59; January 1955.

JONES, Archie N., and EVANS, G. K. "Areas of Needed Research in Music Education." *Education* 72: 23-27; September 1951.

JONES, G. P., and POOL, A. G. *A Hundred Years of Economic Development*. New York: The Macmillan Co., 1950. 420 p.

JUDD, C. H., and Others. *A Century of Social Thought*. Durham, N.C.: Duke University Press, 1939. vii+172 p.

KANDEL, I. L. "Problems of Comparative Education." *International Review of Education* 2: 1-15; 1956.

KANDEL, I. L. "Some Unsolved Issues in American Education." *Educational Forum* 20: 269-78; March 1956.

KAVRUCK, Samuel. "Thirty-Three Years of Test Research: A Short History of Test Development in the U. S. Civil Service Commission." *American Psychologist* 11: 329-33; July 1956.

KINNEY, Lucien B. "New Horizons in Research." *Journal of Teacher Education* 5: 292-97; December 1954.

KIRK, Samuel A. "Needed Projects and Research in Special Education," *The Education of Exceptional Children*. Forty-ninth Yearbook, National Society for the Study of Education, Part 2. Edited by Nelson B. Henry. Chicago: The University of Chicago Press, 1950. Chapter 17, p. 320-34.

KNOWLES, Asa S. "Emerging Features of Tomorrow's Higher Education." *Educational Record* 38: 329-39; October 1957.

KOCH, Sigmund. "The Current Status of Motivational Psychology." *Psychological Review* 58: 147-54; May 1951.

KOMAROVSKY, Mirra, Editor. *Common Frontiers of the Social Sciences*. Glencoe, Ill.: Free Press, 1957. viii+439 p.

KONOPKA, Gisela, and VINTER, Robert D. "Group Work with Children and Youth: Unanswered Questions and Research Problems and Possibilities." *Social Service Review* 30: 300-21; September 1956.

LA BRANT, Lou. "Needed Research in Language Expression." *Elementary English* 29: 35-38; January 1952.

LANGFELD, Herbert S., Editor. *A History of Psychology in Autobiography*. Vol. 4. Worcester, Mass.: Clark University Press, 1952. xii+356 p.

LARSON, Olaf F., and HAY, Donald G. "Hypotheses for Sociological Research in the Field of Rural Health." *Rural Sociology* 16: 225-37; September 1951.

LEE, Harold N. "Theoretic Knowledge and Hypothesis." *Psychological Review* 57: 31-37; January 1950.

LIONBERGER, Herbert F. "The Diffusion of Farm and Home Information as an Area of Sociological Research." *Rural Sociology* 17: 132-43; June 1952.

LIVELY, Charles E., and GREGORY, Cecil L. "The Rural Sociocultural Area as a Field for Research." *Rural Sociology* 19: 21-31; March 1954.

Lomax, Paul S. "Needed Research in Basic Business Education in the Secondary Schools." *United Business Education Association Forum* 5: 11-13; March 1951.

Lorge, Irving D. "Research Needs." *Adult Education* 1: 73-79; December 1950.

Luck, J. Murray. "Man against His Environment: The Next Hundred Years." *Science* 126: 903-8; November 1, 1957.

Luszki, Margaret B. "Some Social Problems of Social Research." *American Sociological Review* 22: 333-35; June 1957.

Maas, Henry S., and Gould, Raymond F. "Psychiatric Clinic Services for Children: Unanswered Questions and Research Strategy and Possibilities." *Social Service Review* 30: 276-99; September 1956.

Maas, Henry S., and Others. "Proceedings of the Conference on Research in the Children's Field." *Social Service Review* 30: 237-357; September 1956. (Research problems and techniques in the areas of foster-care and adoption, residential treatment, psychiatric clinic services, and group work.)

Maaske, Roben J., and Others. *Needed Research in Teacher Education.* Oneonta, N.Y.: American Association of Colleges for Teacher Education, 1954. 62 p.

Mace, C. A., and Vernon, P. E., Editors. *Current Trends in British Psychology.* London: Methuen, 1953. viii+262 p.

Marcuse, F. L., Editor. *Areas of Psychology.* New York: Harper & Brothers, 1954. viii+532 p.

McCarthy, Dorothea. "Trends in the Psychological Appraisal of Children." *Child Development* 26: 213-22; September 1955.

McCollum, E. V. "Fifty Years of Progress in Nutritional Research." *Scientific Monthly* 71: 376-79; December 1950.

McConnell, T. R. "The Diversification of American Higher Education: A Research Program." *Educational Record* 38: 300-15; October 1957.

McConnell, T. R. "Some Unresolved Problems of Secondary Education." *North Central Association Quarterly* 27: 258-66; January 1953.

McCormick, Thomas C., and Francis, Roy G. *Methods of Research in the Behavioral Sciences.* New York: Harper & Brothers, 1958. Chapters 2, 3.

McGrath, Earl J. "Need for Experimentation and Research," *General Education in Transition.* Edited by H. T. Morse. Minneapolis: University of Minnesota Press, 1951. p. 16-28.

McGuigan, F. J. "A Crash Research Program for Peace." *American Psychologist* 13: 224-28; May 1958.

McLean, Dorothy. "Child Development: A Generation of Research." *Child Development* 25: 3-8; March 1954.

Meisels, Joseph F., Loeb, Martin B., and Brieland, Donald. "Foster-Care and Adoption: Unanswered Questions About Foster-Care and Current Research on Adoption." *Social Service Review* 30: 239-59; September 1956.

Melton, Arthur W. "Present Accomplishment and Future Trends in Problem-Solving and Learning Theory." *American Psychologist* 11: 278-81; June 1956.

Merton, Robert K. "The Role-Set: Problems in Sociological Theory." *British Journal of Sociology* 8: 106-20; June 1957.

MILLS, Theodore M. "Some Hypotheses on Small Groups from Simmel." *American Journal of Sociology* 63: 642-50; May 1958.

MOEHLMAN, Arthur H. "Fifty Years of Educational Thought." *Phi Delta Kappan* 37: 131-40; January 1956.

MORRISON, J. Cayce, and Others. "Twenty-five Years of Educational Research." *Review of Educational Research* 26: 199-344; June 1956.

MOWRER, O. Hobart. "Learning Theory: Historical Review and Reinterpretation." *Harvard Educational Review* 24: 37-58; Winter 1954.

MOWRER, O. Hobart. "Some Philosophical Problems in Psychological Counseling." *Journal of Counseling Psychology* 4: 103-11; Summer 1957.

MURPHY, Gardner. *An Historical Introduction to Modern Psychology*. Revised Edition. New York: Harcourt, Brace and Co., 1949. xiv+466 p.

NAHM, Helen. "Trends in Nursing Education as Seen from a National Organization Point of View." *Teachers College Record* 55: 438-45; May 1954.

"Needed Research in Teacher Education." *Phi Delta Kappan* 32: 144-46; December 1950.

NEHNEVAJSA, Jiri. "Sociometry: Decades of Growth." *Sociometry* 18: 48-95; December 1955.

NEUMEYER, Martin H. "International Trends in Juvenile Delinquency." *Sociology and Social Research* 41: 93-99; November-December 1956.

NEWBURY, Edward. "Philosophic Assumptions in Operational Psychology." *Journal of Psychology* 35: 371-78; April 1953.

ODUM, Howard W. *American Sociology*: The Story of Sociology in the United States through 1950. New York: Longmans, Green and Co., 1951. vi+501 p.

ODUM, Howard W. "Folk Sociology as a Subject Field for the Historical Study of Total Human Society and the Empirical Study of Group Behavior." *Social Forces* 31: 193-223; March 1953.

OGBURN, William F. "Social Trends." *Sociology and Social Research* 42: 3-9; September-October 1957.

O'SHEA, Harriet E., and Others. "Needed Research on Gifted Children." *American Psychologist* 9: 77-78; February 1954.

PAULSEN, F. Robert. "Basic Assumptions of Educational Administration." *Peabody Journal of Education* 34: 270-82; March 1957.

PEIK, W. E. "Looking Ahead in American Teacher Education." *Third Yearbook*, American Association of Colleges for Teacher Education. Oneonta, N.Y.: The Association, 1950. p. 9-21.

PENNIMAN, T. K. *A Hundred Years of Anthropology*. Revised Edition. London: Duckworth and Co., 1952. 512 p.

PIERCE, Truman M., and WILSON, Craig. "Research in County Educational Administration." *School Executive* 72: 96-106; March 1953.

POLLAK, Otto, and ORMSBY, Ralph. "Design of a Model of Healthy Family Relationships as a Basis for Evaluative Research." *Social Service Review* 31: 369-76; December 1957.

POWELL, F. De Sales. "Recent Trends in Industrial Sociology." *American Catholic Sociological Review* 18: 194-204; October 1957.

REED, Glenn A. "Fifty Years of Conflict in the Graduate School." *Educational Record* 33: 5-23; January 1952.

REINER, William B. "Needed Research in Evaluation in Science Teaching." *High Points* 34: 13-19; November 1952.

REISS, Albert J., Jr. "Research Problems in Metropolitan Population Redistribution." *American Sociological Review* 21: 571-77; October 1956.

"Report of California Planning Conference on Leadership in Secondary Education: Secondary Education During the Next Half Century." *California Journal of Secondary Education* 27: 330-64; October 1952.

Research Methods Applied to Health, Physical Education, and Recreation. Revised Edition. Washington: American Association for Health, Physical Education, and Recreation, N.E.A., 1952. p. 42-83.

Research Needs in Traffic Safety Education: A Questionnaire Survey Prepared by the N.E.A. Research Division for the National Commission on Safety Education, N.E.A. Washington: National Education Association, 1956. 20 p.

RICE, Arthur H. "For Teacher Organizations—A Century of Progress." *Nation's Schools* 49: 102-6; June 1952.

RIEMER, Svend. "Prehypothetical Studies in Sociology." *Sociology and Social Research* 42: 37-43; September-October 1957.

ROBACK, A. *A History of American Psychology.* New York: Library Publishers, 1952. xiv+426 p.

ROGERS, Carl R., and SKINNER, B. F. "Some Issues Concerning the Control of Human Behavior." *Science* 124: 1057-66; November 30, 1956.

ROSE, Arnold M. "Generalizations in the Social Sciences." *American Journal of Sociology* 59: 49-58; July 1953.

RUMMEL, J. Francis. *An Introduction to Research Procedures in Education.* New York: Harper & Brothers, 1958. p. 20-56.

RUSSELL, Roger W. "Contemporary Issues of Concern to Psychologists." *American Psychologist* 13: 199-216; May 1958.

SANFORD, Fillmore H. "Psychology and the Mental Health Movement." *American Psychologist* 13: 80-85; February 1958.

SARASON, Seymour B. "The Psychologist's Behavior as an Area of Research." *Journal of Consulting Psychology* 15: 278-80; August 1951.

SHANE, Harold G. "Recent Developments in Elementary School Evaluation." *Journal of Educational Research* 44: 491-506; March 1951.

SHEPS, Cecil G., and TAYLOR, Eugene E. *Needed Research in Health and Medical Care*: A Biosocial Approach. Chapel Hill: University of North Carolina Press, 1954. ix+216 p.

SHERER, Lorraine M. "Some Implications from Research in Arithmetic." *Childhood Education* 29: 320-24; March 1953.

SIEGEL, Bernard J. "High Anxiety Levels and Cultural Integration: Notes on a Psycho-Cultural Hypothesis." *Social Forces* 34: 42-48; October 1955.

SILBERMAN, Leo. "Problems of Evaluation Research." *Rural Sociology* 20: 229-41; September-December 1955.

SIMEY, T. S. "Social Investigation: Past Achievements and Present Difficulties." *British Journal of Sociology* 8: 121-29; June 1957.

SIMMONS, Ozzie G., and DAVIS, James A. "Interdisciplinary Collaboration in Mental Illness Research." *American Journal of Sociology* 63: 297-303; November 1957.

SIMON, Abraham J., and GERSHENSON, Charles P. "Residential Treatment of Children: Unanswered Questions and Research Problems and Possibilities." *Social Service Review* 30: 260-75; September 1956.

SINGLETON, W. Ralph. "Some High Lights of the First Half Century of Genetics." *Scientific Monthly* 71: 401-7; December 1950.

SJOBERG, Gideon. "Urban Community Theory and Research: A Partial Evaluation." *American Journal of Economics and Sociology* 14: 199-206; January 1955.

SMIGEL, Erwin O. "Trends in Occupational Sociology in the United States: A Survey of Postwar Research." *American Sociological Review* 19: 398-404; August 1954.

SMITH, M. Brewster. "Cross-Cultural Education as a Research Area." *Journal of Social Issues* 12: 3-8; 1956.

SMITH, M. Brewster. "A Perspective for Further Research on Cross-Cultural Education." *Journal of Social Issues* 12: 56-58; 1956.

SMITH, Nila B. "Areas of Research Interest in the Language Arts." *Elementary English* 29: 31-34; January 1952.

SNYDER, Laurence H. "What We Most Need to Know." *Scientific Monthly* 84: 17-23; January 1957.

SOUTHWORTH, W. H. "Research Needs in School Health." *American Journal of Public Health* 42: 133-38; May 1952.

SPALDING, Eugenia K. "Current Problems of Nurse Educators." *Teachers College Record* 57: 38-46; October 1955.

SPENCE, Ralph B. "Role of Research in Adult Education." *Adult Education* 3: 76-79; February 1953.

STANDLEE, Lloyd, and MECH, Edmund. "A Brief Note on Trends in School Learning Research." *Journal of Educational Research* 48: 355-67; January 1955.

STEPHENS, J. M. *Educational Psychology:* The Study of Educational Growth. New York: Henry Holt and Co., 1951. Chapter 4.

STEWART, Lawrence H. "Some Needed Research on Problems of Retirement." *Educational Administration and Supervision* 42: 68-71; February 1956.

STONE, L. Joseph. "A Critique of Studies of Infant Isolation." *Child Development* 25: 9-20; March 1954.

STORY, M. L. "Fifty Years of Secondary Education: A Midcentury Appraisal." *School Review* 59: 153-56; March 1951.

STROUP, Herbert. "Some Unexplored Problem Areas in Student Activities." *Teacher College Record* 57: 469-74; April 1956.

SUPER, Donald E., and Others. *Vocational Development:* A Framework for Research. New York: Bureau of Publications, Teachers College, Columbia University, 1957. xiv+142 p.

TAYLOR, Griffith, Editor. *Geography in the Twentieth Century:* A Study of Growth, Fields, Techniques, Aims, and Trends. New York: Philosophical Library, 1951. x+630 p.

THOMAS, John L. "Theory and Research in Family Sociology." *American Catholic Sociological Review* 16: 104-16; June 1955.

THOMAS, Lawrence G., and Others. "Prospects of Scientific Research into Values." *Educational Theory* 6: 193-214; October 1956.

TRAVERS, R. M. W. *An Introduction to Educational Research.* New York: The Macmillan Co., 1958. Chapter 4.

TRAXLER, Arthur E. "Emerging Trends in Guidance." *School Review* 58: 14-23; January 1950.

TRAXLER, Arthur E. "Some Comments on Educational Research at Mid-century." *Journal of Educational Research* 47: 359-66; January 1954.

TRAXLER, Arthur E., and Others. "Symposium: Future Progress in Educational and Psychological Measurement." *Educational and Psychological Measurement* 14: 245-82; Summer 1954.

TYLER, Ralph W. "Next Steps in Improving Secondary Education." *School Review* 60: 523-31; December 1952.

TYLER, Ralph W. "Trends in Teaching—How Research Is Affecting Our Understanding of the Learning Process." *School Review* 59: 263-72; May 1951.

VINACKE, W. Edgar. *The Psychology of Thinking.* New York: McGraw-Hill Book Co., 1952. 369 p.

VINCENT, Clark E. "Trends in Infant Care Ideas." *Child Development* 22: 199-209; September 1951. (Based chiefly on periodical literature.)

WALLACE, Anthony F. C. *Human Behavior in Extreme Situations:* A Survey of the Literature and Suggestions for Further Research. Disaster Study No. 1; Publication No. 390. Washington: Committee on Disaster Studies, National Academy of Sciences-National Research Council, 1956. v+35 p.

WALLACE, Earle S. "Trends in Junior Colleges During the Past Decade." *Junior College Journal* 26: 273-80; January 1956.

WATSON, R. I. "Measuring the Effectiveness of Psychotherapy: Problems for Investigation." *Journal of Clinical Psychology* 8: 60-64; January 1952.

WEATHERFORD, Allen E. "Major Research Problems in Recreation." *Journal of the American Association for Health, Physical Education, and Recreation* 23: 19-20; December 1952.

WEAVER, Warren. "Fundamental Questions in Science." *Scientific American* 189: 47-51; September 1953.

WEBSTER, Harold. "Dynamic Hypotheses in Psychology." *Psychological Review* 59: 168-71; March 1952.

WELLEMEYER, J. F., Jr. "Survey of United States Historians, 1952, and a Forecast." *American Historical Review* 61: 339-52; January 1956.

WEST, S. S. "The Hypothesis of Slow Cyclical Variation of Creativity." *American Journal of Sociology* 63: 143-51; September 1957.

WEY, Herbert. "The South Calls for Research." *Phi Delta Kappan* 38: 19-24; October 1956.

WHITE, Lynn, Jr., Editor. *Frontiers of Knowledge in the Study of Man.* New York: Harper & Brothers, 1956. xii+330 p.

WHITNEY, F. L. *The Elements of Research.* Third Edition. New York: Prentice-Hall, 1950. p. 68-96, 446-59.

WILLIAMS, C. B., and STEVENSON, A. H. *A Research Manual*. Revised Edition. New York: Harper & Brothers, 1951. p. 62-75.

WILLIAMS, Robin M., Jr., FISHER, Burton R., and JANIS, Irving L. "Educational Desegregation as a Context for Basic Social Science Research." *American Sociological Review* 21: 577-83; October 1956.

WILLIS, Ivan L. "Education at the Mid-Century: An Appraisal of Its Present Status." *North Central Association Quarterly* 25: 195-202; October 1950.

WILSON, J. T., and Others. *Current Trends in Psychology and the Behavioral Sciences*. Pittsburgh: University of Pittsburgh Press, 1954. xvi+142 p.

WRIGHT, Quincy. "The Peaceful Adjustment of International Relations: Problems and Research Approaches." *Journal of Social Issues* 11: No. 1; 3-12; 1955.

YOUNG, Pauline V. *Scientific Social Surveys and Research*. Third Edition. Englewood Cliffs, N.J.: Prentice-Hall, 1956. p. 115-27.

ZIRBES, Laura. "Needed Research in Education." *Educational Leadership* 10: 129-31; November 1952.

ZNANIECKI, Florian. "Basic Problems of Contemporary Sociology." *American Sociological Review* 19: 219-24; October 1954.

3

Keys to the Literature

The importance of the related literature as background for problem-solving has already been emphasized in Chapter 2. The present chapter describes the guides or keys to the vast storehouse of research (books, periodicals, and theses) now available in education, psychology, sociology, and cognate social fields. This chapter also presents certain problems closely related to library technique, such as note-taking, although the topic of documentation and bibliographical form is reserved for the last chapter, dealing with the technical report. The present chapter can do no more than mention briefly a few of the most generally used library tools (including extensive bibliographies, exhaustive summaries of research, and biographical, institutional, and statistical directories or handbooks), leaving for the guides to reference works the detailed information concerning several hundred helpful titles of reference books.[1] In the description later in this chapter of the guides to the literature, it will be helpful to identify major subdivisions or the larger subheadings in education, psychology, and sociology, under which the related studies usually are classified or indexed.

[1] Carter Alexander and Arvid J. Burke, *How to Locate Educational Information and Data.* Third Edition. New York: Bureau of Publications, Teachers College, Columbia University, 1950. xix+441 p.
  I. G. Mudge, *Guide to Reference Books.* Sixth Edition. Chicago: American Library Association, 1936. xii+504 p. Also see earlier editions and the informal supplements.
  Constance M. Winchell, *Guide to Reference Books.* Seventh Edition. Chicago: American Library Association, 1951. xvii+645 p.
  Constance M. Winchell and O. A. Johnson, *Guide to Reference Books.* Seventh Edition Supplement, 1950-52. Second Supplement, 1953-55. Chicago: American Library Association, 1954, 1956. 140 p., 134 p.
  Louis Shores, *Basic Reference Sources.* Chicago: American Library Association, 1954. ix+378 p.

INTEGRATION OF PUBLISHED FINDINGS[2]

It is generally recognized that a field of knowledge makes progress as a scientific discipline through the activities of the worker who is engaged in conducting and interpreting research. There is another function, however, that involves important activities of integration and assimilation of the bodies of data and published findings in the many sub-areas of such fields as education and psychology. Unless the research findings from many thousands of individual studies are incorporated within appropriate theories, it is virtually impossible for graduate students and others to assimilate the knowledge in a particular field of specialization. It is possible that data and published studies are accumulating more rapidly than they can be integrated or summarized effectively, as witnessed by recent difficulties in securing qualified persons to prepare summarizing articles for the *Review of Educational Research, Encyclopedia of Educational Research,* and *Psychological Bulletin.* Therefore, it seems appropriate to give due recognition to the scholar who does his work in the library, sorting research findings according to an integrating scheme, summarizing sound empirical findings, noting contradictory findings, identifying needed research, and noting the status of explanatory efforts. This type of assimilating or integrating work may prove more valuable as a summary of several hundred research reports than for a scholar to spend the same amount of time in collecting original data.

The survey of the related literature may provide guiding hypotheses, suggestive methods of investigation, and comparative data for interpretative purposes. Sometimes textbooks and subjective critiques of a problem area provide important insights and hypotheses that may well have a place in the summary of the related literature. The summarizer of research always has before him the problem of striking a balance between tedious detail and superficial sketchiness. One technique is to group similar studies, with a representative investigation analyzed in some detail. The weaknesses of unsound studies and the merits of outstanding investigations should be indicated in a constructive manner, but without the ordinary adjectives of denunciation or praise as such.

Careful handling of references is imperative in relation to effective summarizing. In the matter of bibliographical work, even as experienced

[2] Benton J. Underwood, *Psychological Research.* New York: Appleton-Century-Crofts, 1957. p. 290–91.
Carter V. Good and Douglas E. Scates, *Methods of Research*: Educational, Psychological, Sociological. New York: Appleton-Century-Crofts, 1954. p. 84–86.

and prolific an author as Ellwood P. Cubberley encountered criticisms that seemed merited. A reviewer of Cubberley's *Syllabus of Lectures on the History of Education* thought the bibliographies were useful but complained of the defective or incomplete references, having found 39 on a single page. The number of such faulty references throughout the book caused the reviewer to wonder whether much of the bibliographical work had not been done by students. For the careless reference work, Cubberley could have no excuse, except that he had only a master's degree at that time, with no record of bibliographical training. His later reference work evidenced improvement.[3]

LANGUAGE SKILLS

Although the traditional acceptance of the basic position of foreign languages in the qualifications for the doctoral degree has been considerably modified since the 1930's, especially for professional degrees, a reading knowledge of one or more modern foreign languages should prove helpful in canvassing the related literature on a problem for investigation. It has been typical to stress the "tool" aspect of the foreign language, supporting the view that a doctoral candidate should be able to read German or French, so that he can translate the most recent technical articles relating to his special field or problem. This use of a foreign language is similar to the study of statistics in psychology, education, sociology, or economics, as a necessary or practical tool or technique. On the other hand, many graduate students and some professors maintain that all the important literature has been translated into English or is being translated, so that there is no longer a need for the foreign-language requirement in the doctoral program. One answer to this view is that it smacks of provincialism, and that something usually is lost in translation. Many scientists and scholars still take pride in the ability to translate for themselves, supporting the adage, "Never read a book about a book, read the book."

Another important advantage of foreign-language facility as a tool is its practical employment by the scholar or scientist who travels abroad. With an increasing number of overseas fellowships and scholarships available, and more American specialists in demand as technical advisers to foreign governments and American overseas financial enterprises, more academic people now are enabled to travel abroad. When such persons

[3] Jesse B. Sears and Adin D. Henderson, *Cubberley of Stanford: And His Contribution to American Education.* Stanford, Calif.: Stanford University Press, 1957. p. 119–20.

have been able to converse directly with men in their own fields, the value of a foreign language has been demonstrated, not only on the practical grounds of communication, but also as a means of better understanding of another nationality, with some lessening of the narrow provincialism of which our nation and our higher institutions have sometimes been guilty.[4]

NOTE-TAKING

It is essential, especially in summarizing the literature and in historical studies, to collect the material systematically, with a well-arranged plan of note-taking.[5] A note system should be flexible, to permit addition of new material, without disarranging the older notes, and with the possibility of rearranging the notes as desired. To make this possible, it is necessary that the notes be taken on separate sheets of paper, slips, or cards.

Three kinds of notes are regularly made by historical workers and are also appropriate, with some adaptations, for summarizing studies. The bibliographical note includes the standard data, author, title, pages, place and date of publication, and other formal facts about the document or study. The subject note contains one item of information about a specific topic, with the source indicated; most notes collected by the summarizer or historian usually are of this type. The "method" notes include suggestions or ideas useful in interpreting the facts.

Some preliminary reading and note-taking probably have taken place before the major topics of the outline begin to stand out in relief, and in turn the tentative outline and its headings serve as a guide for further reading, study, and note-taking. Expansion of the bibliography, analysis of content, and gathering of notes probably continue until the actual writing of the report begins and even later.

Although able historians like George Bancroft, J. B. McMaster, James

[4] Everett Walters, "Foreign Languages: Benefit or Barrier?" *Graduate School Record* 9: 1, 3; January 1956.

[5] Carter Alexander and Arvid J. Burke, *op. cit.*, p. 52–57, 179–93.

Jacques Barzun and Henry F. Graff, *The Modern Researcher*. New York: Harcourt, Brace and Co., 1957. p. 18–39.

William W. Brickman, *Guide to Research in Educational History*. New York: New York University Bookstore, 1949. p. 191–200.

E. W. Dow, *Principles of a Note-System for Historical Studies*. New York: Century Co., 1924. vi+124 p. plus numerous illustrations.

Homer C. Hockett, *The Critical Method in Historical Research and Writing*. New York: The Macmillan Co., 1955. p. 89–142.

Robert E. Tuttle and C. A. Brown, *Writing Useful Reports*: Principles and Applications. New York: Appleton-Century-Crofts, 1956. p. 263–76.

Ford Rhodes, and Edward Gibbon have used bound notebooks instead of a flexible system, it can only be said that they succeeded in spite of it. During the 1840's Bancroft had a number of quarto-size blank books, in which one or more pages were allocated to the successive days of the years, and the data were entered on the page corresponding to the day and year when the event occurred. Even as late as the 1890's, Rhodes used blank books for his notes, since the card system at that time was something of a novelty.

William G. Sumner, the sociologist, had no financial assistance for research and little help, yet his files of notes compared favorably with many later research workers supported by relatively large financial grants. Sumner filled 52 drawers and boxes of notes, averaging 3,000 sheets each.

Soon after Clark Hull, the psychologist, began graduate study, he initiated a permanent notebook system of the original ideas on psychological subjects that came to him on reading a new book, agreements or disagreements with the author, and views on subjects discussed in class or seminar. Near the end of his career, this series of notebooks totaled 27 volumes. To his surprise Hull discovered that the notes were valuable not so much as aids to memory, but as stimuli to systematic thinking. Hull confesses that he had little success in persuading promising graduate students in his seminars to keep similar notebooks, even when he presented notebooks to the students.[6]

Throughout his life Ellwood P. Cubberley kept notes on a wide variety of subjects which interested him, particularly matters revealing significant trends (by studying data in series). Cubberley left an unusual record for his biographer: a long series of pocket calendar notebooks which he kept with regularity through the years from 1905 to 1940. These booklets were filled with facts about home, work, travel, accounts, attendance at operas and concerts and dinner meetings, illnesses, books he was working on as author or editor, trips for business or pleasure, expenses for clothes, lecture dates and topics, life-insurance policies with dates when premiums were due, library interests, his college program of study and reading, notes on the weather, and other memoranda of items he liked or wanted to remember or think about. Although Cubberley said that he did not want to be run by a card catalogue and seemed to dislike the thought of a system of formal records, in his notebooks there is

[6] Herbert S. Langfeld, Editor, *A History of Psychology in Autobiography.* Vol. 4. Worcester, Mass.: Clark University Press, 1952. xii+356 p.

evidence of care and considerable labor in recording a mass of detail, but detail dictated by his own personal interests and tastes rather than by any scheme of logic or plan of systematic accounting.[7]

CLASSIFICATION SYSTEMS

The reader who uses such documentary materials as books is indebted to the workers who have given their attention to classification for the purpose of affording order and system, without which library work would be virtually impossible. The two principal systems of library classification in the United States are that worked out by Melvil Dewey and published in 1876, commonly referred to as the "Dewey decimal" system, and the Library of Congress system (devised because developments in certain fields seriously crowded the older Dewey scheme). In addition to the basic systems, many special rules are necessary to cover detailed questions that arise, and some libraries have issued their own rule publications.

These classification schemes or systems are supplemented from time to time by efforts toward classification in special fields, as in education,[8] psychology, and sociology. The first extensive list of subject headings in education was prepared by Voegelein, *List of Educational Subject Headings*, 1928, which influenced the *Education Index*, first published in 1929. A later list by Pettus, *Subject Headings in Education*, 1938, was arranged in classified rather than dictionary (alphabetical) form, and included definitions of various heads and subheads. Other sources that indicate the scope of a particular field or discipline are the *Review of Educational Research*, *Encyclopedia of Educational Research*, *Dictionary of Education*, *Psychological Abstracts*, *Annual Review of Psychology*, and *Sociological Abstracts*, as illustrated by the lists of subtopics later in this chapter. If librarians, professors, and graduate students will learn to think outside the limitations of the Dewey decimal system and the Library of Congress system, there is opportunity for a much closer relationship between bibliographical organization in the social fields and its physical implementation in libraries, thus furthering an interdisciplinary approach to problems in the behavioral and human sciences.

[7] Jesse B. Sears and Adin D. Henderson, *op. cit.*, p. 82.
[8] L. Belle Voegelein, *List of Educational Subject Headings*. Columbus: Ohio State University Press, 1928. xiv+338 p.
　　Clyde Pettus, *Subject Headings in Education*: A Systematic List for Use in a Dictionary Catalogue. New York: H. W. Wilson Co., 1938. 188 p.

EDUCATIONAL AND GENERAL GUIDES

Before beginning a systematic examination of the titles in the library guides, it may prove desirable to secure certain background concerning the problem by reading the kind of overview treatment commonly found in textbooks and general reference works. From this more general reading should come at least an initial list of subtopics for use in examining the library guides.

The beginner in research or graduate student probably will start with the *Education Index*, which lists virtually all the educational materials in published form in the United States, except elementary and high-school textbooks. For research materials the summaries in the *Encyclopedia of Educational Research* (published in 1941, and revised in the 1950 and 1960 editions) are useful. For current research studies and to supplement the *Encyclopedia of Educational Research*, the *Review of Educational Research* is the chief summarizing guide (beginning in January, 1931). The *Review* originally planned to cover fifteen major subdivisions of education within a three-year cycle, but as the years passed the number of topics increased and the appearance of a particular topic once in three years was not always possible or desirable. It will be of interest to examine the following list of topics covered in the *Review*, noting the subjects that have been treated rather regularly at three-year intervals; for example, curriculum, guidance and counseling, mental and physical development, and teacher personnel.

REVIEW OF EDUCATIONAL RESEARCH

ADMINISTRATION: I:3 (June 1931); II:2 (April 1932); II:5 (December 1932); III:5 (December 1933); IV:4 (October 1934); V:2 (April 1935) V:4 (October 1935); VII:4 (October 1937); VIII:2 (April 1938); VIII:4 (October 1938); X:4 (October 1940); XI:2 (April 1941); XII:2 (April 1942); XIII:4 (October 1943); XIV:2 (April 1944); XV:1 (February 1945); XVI:4 (October 1946); XVII:2 (April 1947); XVIII:1 (February 1948); XIX:4 (October 1949); XX:2 (April 1950); XXI:1 (February 1951); XXII:4 (October 1952); XXV:4 (October 1955); XXVIII:4 (October 1958).

CURRICULUM: I:1 (January 1931); IV:2 (April 1934); VII:2 (April 1937); XII:3 (June 1942); XV:3 (June 1945); XVIII:3 (June 1948); XXI:3 (June 1951); XXIV:3 (June 1954); XXVI:2 (April 1956); XXVII:3 (June 1957).

EDUCATIONAL MEASUREMENT: II:3 (June 1932); II:4 (October 1932); III:1 (February 1933); V:3 (June 1935); V:5 (December 1935); VIII:3 (June

1938); VIII:5 (December 1938); XI:1 (February 1941); XIV:1 (February 1944); XVII:1 (February 1947); XX:1 (February 1950); XXIII:1 (February 1953); XXVI:1 (February 1956); XXIX:1 (February 1959).

EDUCATIONAL PSYCHOLOGY: I:4 (October 1931); I:5 (December 1931); II:1 (February 1932); III:4 (October 1933); IV:5 (December 1934); V:1 (February 1935); VI:3 (June 1936); VII:5 (December 1937); VIII:1 (February 1938); IX:3 (June 1939); XVIII:6 (December 1948).

EDUCATIONAL SOCIOLOGY: VI:4 (October 1936); VII:1 (February 1937); IX:4 (October 1939); X:1 (February 1940); XIII:1 (February 1943); XVI:1 (February 1946); XIX:1 (February 1949); XXII:1 (February 1952); XXIII:4 (October 1953); XXV:1 (February 1955); XXVIII:1 (February 1958).

GUIDANCE AND COUNSELING: III:3 (June 1933); VI:2 (April 1936); IX:2 (April 1939); XII:1 (February 1942); XV:2 (April 1945); XVIII:2 (April 1948); XXI:2 (April 1951); XXIV:2 (April 1954); XXVII:2 (April 1957).

MENTAL AND PHYSICAL DEVELOPMENT: III:2 (April 1933); VI:1 (February 1936); IX:1 (February 1939); XI:5 (December 1941); XIV:5 (December 1944); XVII:5 (December 1947); XX:5 (December 1950); XXII:5 (December 1952); XXV:5 (December 1955); XXVIII:5 (December 1958).

LANGUAGE ARTS, FINE ARTS, NATURAL SCIENCES, AND MATHEMATICS: X:2 (April 1940); XI:4, Part 1 (October 1941); XII:4 (October 1942); XIII:2 (April 1943); XV:4 (October 1945); XVI:2 (April 1946); XVIII:4 (October 1948); XIX:2 (April 1949); XXI:4 (October 1951); XXII:2 (April 1952); XXV:2 (April 1955); XXVII:4 (October 1957); XXVIII:2 (April 1958).

RESEARCH METHODS: IV:1 (February 1934); IX:5 (December 1939); XII:5 (December 1952); XV:5 (December 1945); XVIII:5 (December 1948); XXI:5 (December 1951); XXIV:5 (December 1954); XXVI:3 (June 1956); XXVII:5 (December 1957).

SPECIAL PROGRAMS: VI:5 (December 1936); X:5 (December 1940); XI:3 (June 1941); XI:4, Part 2 (October 1941); XIII:5 (December 1943); XIV:3 (June 1944); XIV:4 (October 1944); XVI:5 (December 1946); XVII:3 (June 1947); XVII:4 (October 1947); XIX:5 (December 1949); XX:3 (June 1950); XX:4 (October 1950); XXIII:2 (April 1953); XXIII:3 (June 1953); XXIII:5 (December 1953); XXIV:1 (February 1954); XXIV:4 (October 1954); XXVI:4 (October 1956); XXVI:5 (December 1956); XXVII:1 (February 1957).

TEACHER PERSONNEL: I:2 (April 1931); IV:3 (June 1934); VII:3 (June 1937); X:3 (June 1940); XIII:3 (June 1943); XVI:3 (June 1946); XIX:3 (June 1949); XXII:3 (June 1952); XXV:3 (June 1955); XXVIII:3 (June 1958).

The *Bibliographic Index* is really a cumulative bibliography of bibliographies dealing with a wide range of subjects. The first number, published in 1938, includes 4,400 references.

The monthly *Book Review Digest* takes the form of a specialized periodical index, in the sense that it provides excerpts from the reviews that appear in some eighty book-review periodicals. In the course of a year it lists approximately 4,000 books, and cumulates at intervals.

The inclusive term *serials* has been defined as any publication issued serially or in successive parts more or less regularly. The Ayer list[9] is a bibliography of newspapers and periodicals, but it includes much additional information. The Gregory union list[10] of serials indicates the extent to which more than 75,000 different serials are found in the more important libraries in the United States and Canada. Ulrich's directory of periodicals[11] lists the titles published in the United States and in foreign countries that have proved most useful in American collections.

The *United States Catalogue* lists virtually all books in print in this country on a specific subject. It is kept up to date by the monthly *Cumulative Book Index*, which cumulates at irregular intervals during the year, annually into a supplement, and after several years into a large supplement. The *Publishers' Weekly* is regarded as a supplement to the *Cumulative Book Index*, in the sense that it describes and indexes new books in a convenient reference and buying list.

Guides are available for current graduate theses[12] and dissertations in education, although a research master's study is no longer generally required for the awarding of the first graduate degree. Since many graduate institutions publish abstract volumes or lists of their graduate theses, it is fortunate that we have available a basic guide[13] to such summaries.

Starting with 1952, Phi Delta Kappa has sponsored an annual list of doctoral dissertations completed in education and a list of doctoral dissertations under way in education, classified under the following headings:[14]

[9] *Directory of Newspapers and Periodicals.* Philadelphia: N. W. Ayer and Sons, 1880—.

[10] Winifred Gregory, Editor, *Union List of Serials in Libraries of the United States and Canada.* Second Edition. New York: H. W. Wilson Co., 1943. 3,065 p. Also see supplements.

[11] Eileen C. Graves, Editor, *Ulrich's Periodicals Directory:* A Classified Guide to a Selected List of Current Periodicals, Foreign and Domestic. Eighth Edition. New York: R. R. Bowker Co., 1956. x+730 p.

[12] T. A. Lamke and H. M. Silvey, Editors, *Master's Theses in Education, 1956-57.* No. 6. Cedar Falls, Ia.: Research Publications, 1957. Also see later numbers.

[13] Thomas R. Palfrey and Henry E. Coleman, *Guide to Bibliographies of Theses—United States and Canada.* Second Edition. Chicago: American Library Association, 1940. 54 p.

[14] Stanley B. Brown, Mary Louise Lyda, and Carter V. Good, *Research Studies in Education, 1956:* A Subject-Author Index and Research Methods Bibliography. Bloomington, Ind.: Phi Delta Kappa, 1957. viii+114 p. *Research Studies in Education, 1957,* published in 1958. vi+110 p. Also see later numbers.

AREAS OF EDUCATION

Philosophy; Principles and Trends; School and Community
Foreign or International Education; United Nations
Religion in the Schools; Religious Education; Character Education
Administration: General Areas
Administration: Special Areas
Administration: School Boards; Reorganization
Supervision
Public Relations
Recruitment
Finance
School Plant; Transportation
Legislation
Educational History; Biography
Psychology of Childhood and Youth
Educational Psychology; Psychology
Studies of Childhood and Youth
Measurement and Evaluation
Teacher Training; In-Service Training
Audio-Visual Education
Curriculum; Extracurricular Activities
Teaching Methods; Teaching Aids and Materials; School Libraries
Intercultural Education
Preschool; Kindergarten; Elementary Education
Secondary Education—Senior High Schools
Secondary Education—Junior High Schools
Language Arts; Speech, Writing; Communications
Reading; Literature
Foreign Language
Aviation and Science
Arithmetic and Mathematics
Social Studies
Art; Music
Vocational and Industrial Education
Business Education
Agricultural Education
Guidance and Counseling
General Personnel Problems
Personnel Problems; Public Schools
Personnel Problems; Higher Education
Health
Physical Education
Safety Education
Recreation
Combined Physical Education, Recreation, Health, Safety, and Sports
Special Education; Exceptional Children

Education for Family Life; Consumer Education; Home Economics and
    Homemaking
Rural Education; Conservation
Teachers' Problems; Personnel and Personal Problems
Teachers' Problems; Professional Problems
Higher Education
Professional Education; Certification; Accreditation; Nursing Education
Junior College and Community College
Extension Services of Colleges and Universities
Adult Education; Continuation Education
Veterans Education
Educational Research; Biographies; Directories.

It usually is possible to borrow typewritten graduate theses or
dissertations by interlibrary loan, although occasionally it is difficult or
even impossible to secure one of the older studies. John Dewey's doctoral
dissertation (1884) at The Johns Hopkins University, dealing with the
psychology of Kant, was never published and no copy is available, since
the Johns Hopkins Library apparently did not preserve the manuscript.[15]

The *List of American Doctoral Dissertations* (covering 1912 through
1938, Library of Congress) and *Doctoral Dissertations Accepted by
American Universities* (1933-34 through 1954-55, sponsored by the Association of Research Libraries) overlapped some 5½ years. The successor
to these two series of dissertation lists appears under the title *Index
to American Doctoral Dissertations*, published by University Microfilms,
beginning in 1957. The same publisher also issues *Dissertation Abstracts*
and for each abstract makes available a microfilm of the entire manuscript.[16]

EDUCATIONAL LITERATURE IN RELATION TO
NATIONAL AND INTERNATIONAL AGENCIES

It is informative to note the major contributions to the literature
made by selected organizations or agencies in education.

[15] A. A. Roback, *History of American Psychology*. New York: Library Publishers, 1952. p. 98.

[16] Douglas E. Scates, "Changing Sources of Information about Thesis Research." *Journal of Teacher Education* 8: 210–13; June 1957.

Also see Bert Kaplan, "Dissemination of Primary Research Data in Psychology."
American Psychologist 13: 53–55; February 1958. With the development of microcopy
as a medium of scholarly publication, the financial barriers to publication are partly
eliminated, although the cost of a good microcard reader still presents a problem.
On a 3×5-inch microcard, up to 60 pages of material can be reproduced.

U. S. Office of Education

In performing its three major functions, the United States Office of Education[17] has an extensive program of publication in the fields of educational research, educational services, and administration of grants. The Office carries on its work through publishing its research studies and survey reports, participating in conferences, speaking and writing, consultation and field work, contracting with higher institutions and state departments of education to conduct research, and administering grant funds as stipulated by the Congress. Through its publications and otherwise, the Office interprets the educational needs of the nation and promotes a general understanding of educational objectives, collects and disseminates information on education in the states and territories to make possible intelligent comparison and wise decisions on programs and operations, presents proposals for improving practices and the adoption of educational standards (arrived at by co-operative planning and research), and with the aid of authentic information seeks to stimulate improvement in educational leadership. The five divisions of the Office of Education are: School Assistance in Federally Affected Areas, Higher Education, International Education, State and Local School Systems, and Vocational Education.

Through its research and statistical services, the Office of Education:

Collects, verifies, analyzes, and publishes educational statistics of wide interest and national significance.

Provides technical statistical services to the divisions of the Office, including consultation and advice on research methods, as well as operational assistance in data collection, tabulation, calculation, and analysis.

Responds to requests for information in the field of educational statistics.

Maintains liaison with other departments or agencies, especially the Office of Statistical Standards of the Bureau of the Budget.

Through its publications services, the Office of Education:

Plans and directs its over-all program of publications and information.

Maintains liaison with educational and information groups and individuals outside the Office.

Assists authors in planning individual publications, and edits, designs, and handles the technical production and distribution of all the professional publications issued by the Office.

Plans, edits, and distributes the *Education Fact Sheet* and the monthly magazine *School Life*, and produces and distributes an annual report and other reports.

[17] *Handbook, Office of Education.* Washington: Government Printing Office, 1957. 28 p. Also see later numbers.

Prepares official statements, messages, articles, scripts, speeches, and news releases, and acts as a clearing house for information requested by the Congress, the White House, other government agencies, communications media, the educational profession, and the public.

N. E. A.

Since 1922 the Research Division[18] of the National Education Association has performed the two functions of providing information required currently, and of undertaking long-time investigations in anticipation of future needs. The two major areas of operation have been the technical professional areas of instruction and administration, and the professional welfare problems of salaries, tenure, and retirement. Since 1922 the Division has answered more than 200,000 letters of inquiry, issued 155 numbers of the *Research Bulletin* (more than 3,186,000 copies printed and distributed), and prepared 71 yearbooks for the departments of classroom teachers, elementary-school principals, school administrators, and other groups (with more than 700,000 copies distributed). Other surveys and studies have dealt with tenure conditions and laws, academic freedom, teaching procedures, economic status of teachers, teacher retirement, and other special problems.

American Council on Education

The American Council on Education has served as a clearing house for the exchange of information and opinion, has conducted numerous inquiries into specific educational problems, and has secured the cooperation of appropriate agencies (especially higher institutions) for the solution of such problems.

The Educational Record, the quarterly journal of the American Council on Education, has been issued regularly since 1920. It is a general educational periodical of considerable circulation, and numbers among its contributors many well-known college administrators, teachers, public officials, and writers. . . .

A second periodical, widely distributed, is the occasional bulletin, *Higher Education and National Affairs*, which aims to report and interpret significant federal developments and other activities of concern to educational institutions and organizations.

As the end result of its research, special studies, conferences, and surveys, the Council publishes from 15 to 20 books a year. About 200 titles are currently in print and on sale, not counting cumulative record folders, filmstrips, and filmslides.

[18] *N.E.A. Handbook*. Washington: National Education Association, 1957. p. 91-92. Also see later numbers.

Two standard directories inaugurated by the Council are the only directories composed exclusively of *accredited* institutions of higher education. They are: *American Universities and Colleges,* first issued in 1928, and the companion volume *American Junior Colleges,* first issued in 1940. These volumes are issued every four years. A third and similar, but even more complicated, project inaugurated by the Council is *Universities of the World Outside U.S.A.,* published in 1950.[19]

UNESCO

In collaboration with the Education Press of America, UNESCO[20] has produced the *International List of Educational Periodicals* as an accurate and up-to-date list representing all systems of education. The volume is divided into two parts totaling more than 3,400 periodicals from 79 countries and territories, in three languages (English, French, and Spanish).

UNESCO publishes an extensive list of periodicals and monographs in the educational and social areas. *Fundamental and Adult Education* is a quarterly technical journal, mainly for specialists. *Education Abstracts,* published 10 times a year, includes bibliographical details relating to documents, publications, and textbooks on education, with each issue devoted to a single subject. Another serial, usually with 10 numbers each year, is *Educational Studies and Documents.* A valuable recent number in this series described education clearing houses and documentation centers. Major studies have appeared as volumes of three important series. *Studies in Compulsory Education* have been made for a number of countries; these constitute major sources of information on such topics as attendance and legal provisions for education. The *Monographs on Fundamental Education* deal with such problems as literacy, the use of vernacular languages in education, and the program of fundamental education. *Problems in Education* is a series of volumes devoted to issues of international interest, such as teacher preparation and mental hygiene in the schools. UNESCO also publishes the *World Survey of Education,* a handbook of educational organization and statistics.

[19] Quoted from *A Brief Statement of the History and Activities of the American Council on Education, 1918-1957.* Washington: The Council, 1957. 48 p. Also see later numbers.
[20] *An International List of Educational Periodicals.* Educational Studies and Documents, No. 23. New York: UNESCO Publications Center, 1957. 212 p.
Colin D. Ewers, "The Education Clearing House of UNESCO." *School and Society* 82: 114-18; October 15, 1955.
Carter V. Good, "Bibliographic Sources," *Encyclopedia of Educational Research.* Third Edition. New York: The Macmillan Co. Scheduled for 1960.

PSYCHOLOGICAL GUIDES

For the field of psychology, the major guides to the literature are *Psychological Abstracts,* founded in 1927, and the *Annual Review of Psychology,* initiated in 1950, with the references classified under the following headings:

PSYCHOLOGICAL ABSTRACTS

General
    Theory and Systems, Methods and Apparatus, New Tests, Statistics, Reference Works, Organizations, History and Biography, Professional Problems of Psychology, Films

Physiological Psychology
    Nervous System

Receptive and Perceptual Processes
    Vision, Audition

Response Processes

Complex Processes and Organizations
    Learning and Memory, Thinking and Imagination, Intelligence, Personality, Aesthetics

Developmental Psychology
    Childhood and Adolescence, Maturity and Old Age

Social Psychology
    Methods and Measurements, Cultures and Cultural Relations, Social Institutions, Language and Communication

Clinical Psychology, Guidance, Counseling
    Methodology, Techniques, Diagnosis and Evaluation, Treatment Methods, Child Guidance, Vocational Guidance

Behavior Deviations
    Mental Deficiency, Behavior Problems, Speech Disorders, Crime and Delinquency, Psychoses, Psychoneuroses, Psychosomatics, Clinical Neurology, Physically Handicapped

Educational Psychology
    School Learning, Interests, Attitudes and Habits, Special Education, Educational Guidance, Educational Measurement, Education Staff Personnel

Personnel Psychology
    Selection and Placement, Labor-Management Relations

Industrial and Other Applications
    Industry, Business and Commerce, Professions.

ANNUAL REVIEW OF PSYCHOLOGY

Perception
Vision
Hearing
Physiological Psychology
Comparative Psychology
Developmental Psychology
Learning
Educational Psychology
Statistical Methods
Industrial Psychology
Engineering Psychology
Personality
Theory and Technique of Assessment
Psychotherapy
Counseling
Abnormalities of Behavior
Social Psychology and Group Processes
Recent Developments in Psychology (in Selected Countries).

SOCIAL SCIENCE GUIDES

For the social fields we have the fifteen-volume *Encyclopedia of the Social Sciences*,[21] covering the fields of anthropology, economics, education, history, law, philosophy, political science, psychology, social work, sociology, and statistics; the *Dictionary of American Biography*,[22] *Dictionary of American History*,[23] and the periodicals *Biography Index* and *Sociological Abstracts*, with the following headings:

SOCIOLOGICAL ABSTRACTS

General
Theory
Methodology-Statistics
Social Structure (Organization)
Personality
Interaction within Groups
Interaction between Groups

[21] Edwin R. A. Seligman and Alvin Johnson, Editors, *Encyclopedia of the Social Sciences*. New York: The Macmillan Co., 1930-34. 15 vols.

[22] Allen Johnson and Dumas Malone, Editors, *Dictionary of American Biography*. New York: Charles Scribner's Sons, 1928-37. 20 vols. and index, plus supplements.
  Also see *Biography Index*: A Cumulative Index to Biographical Material in Books and Magazines. New York: H. W. Wilson Co., 1946—.

[23] James T. Adams and R. V. Coleman, Editors, *Dictionary of American History*. New York: Charles Scribner's Sons, 1940. 5 vols. and index.

Rural and Urban Sociology
Sociology of Occupations and Professions
Social Stratification
Political Sociology
Communication and Public Opinion
Sociology of Knowledge, Education, Literature, Religion, Art, and Science
Demography and Ecology
Social Change and Control
Marriage and Family
Social Disorganization (Criminology)
Social Anthropology
Industrial Sociology '
Social Biology
Applied Sociology
Bureaucratic Structure.

Historical Abstracts summarizes articles on political, diplomatic, economic, social, cultural, and intellectual history relating to the period 1775-1945, published in the periodical literature (some 800 journals) the world over. The publication also includes general articles on historiography, bibliography, and research methods.

CONCLUDING STATEMENT

The keys to the vast storehouse of published literature may open doors to sources of significant problems and explanatory hypotheses, and provide helpful orientation for definition of the problem, background for selection of procedure, and comparative data for interpretation of results. In order to be truly creative and original, one must read extensively and critically as a stimulus to thinking. The major reference works and guides since the late 1920's have greatly simplified the canvass of related literature and have appeared just in time to help the graduate student and investigator explore the greatly increased volume of research published during this period. The numerous bibliographic and documentary guides and sources suggest that there has been a trend toward such aids as an ally of the scientific and experimental movement.

SELECTED REFERENCES

ALEXANDER, Carter, and BURKE, Arvid J. *How to Locate Educational Information and Data.* Third Edition. New York: Bureau of Publications, Teachers College, Columbia University, 1950. xix+441 p.
BARTON, Mary N., Compiler. *Reference Books:* A Brief Guide for Students and Other Users of the Library. Third Edition. Baltimore: Enoch Pratt Library, 1954. 100 p.

BARZUN, Jacques, and GRAFF, Henry F. *The Modern Researcher*. New York: Harcourt, Brace and Co., 1957. p. 61-87.

BATES, Ralph S. *Scientific Societies in the United States*. Second Edition. New York: Technology Press and Columbia University Press, 1958. 308 p.

BRICKMAN, William W. "Educational Reference Works." *School and Society* 79: 166-72; May 29, 1954.

BROWN, Stanley B., LYDA, Mary L., and GOOD, Carter V. *Research Studies in Education, 1956:* A Subject-Author Index and Research Methods Bibliography. Bloomington, Ind.: Phi Delta Kappa, 1957. viii+114 p. *Research Studies in Education, 1957*, published in 1958. vi+110 p. Also see earlier and later numbers.

BRYAN, Roy C. *Keys to Professional Information for Teachers*. Kalamazoo: Western Michigan University, 1957. 28 p.

BUROS, Oscar K., Editor. *The Fourth Mental Measurements Yearbook*. Highland Park, N. J.: Gryphon Press, 1953. 1,189 p.

BUROS, Oscar K., Editor. *Statistical Methodology Reviews, 1941–1950*. New York: John Wiley & Sons, 1951. 458 p.

DANIEL, Robert S., and LOUTTIT, C. M. *Professional Problems in Psychology*. New York: Prentice-Hall, 1953. xv+416 p. (Embodies a revised and enlarged edition of Louttit's *Handbook of Psychological Literature*.)

"Doctoral Dissertations in Progress, 1957." *American Journal of Sociology* 64: 74-84; July 1958. Also see earlier and later numbers.

DOWNS, Robert B. *American Library Resources*: A Bibliographical Guide. Chicago: American Library Association, 1951. 428 p.

DREVER, James. *A Dictionary of Psychology*. Baltimore: Penguin Books, 1952. 315 p.

ENGLISH, Horace B., and ENGLISH, Ava C. *Comprehensive Dictionary of Psychological and Psychoanalytical Terms*. New York: Longmans, Green and Co., 1958. xiv+594 p.

FAIRCHILD, H. P., Editor. *Dictionary of Sociology*. New York: Philosophical Library, 1944. viii+342 p.

FARNSWORTH, P. R., and McNEMAR, Quinn, Editors. *Annual Review of Psychology*. Vol. 9. Stanford, Calif.: Annual Reviews, 1958. 543 p. Also see earlier and later numbers.

FERM, Vergilius. *A Dictionary of Pastoral Psychology*. New York: Philosophical Library, 1955. xi+336 p.

GITTLER, Joseph B., Editor. *Review of Sociology*: Analysis of a Decade. New York: John Wiley & Sons, 1957. 588 p.

GOOD, Carter V. "Bibliographic Sources," *Encyclopedia of Educational Research*. Third Edition. New York: The Macmillan Co. Scheduled for 1960.

GOOD, Carter V. "Library Resources and Documentary Research." *Review of Educational Research* 21: 329-36; December 1951.

GOOD, Carter V., Editor. *Dictionary of Education*. Second Edition. New York: McGraw-Hill Book Co., 1959. xxx+676 p.

GOOD, Carter V., and SCATES, Douglas E. *Methods of Research*: Educational, Psychological, Sociological. New York: Appleton-Century-Crofts, 1954. p. 133-69.

GRAY, William S. "Summary of Reading Investigations July 1, 1956 to June 30, 1957." *Journal of Educational Research* 51: 401-35; February 1958. Also see earlier and later numbers.

HARRIMAN, Philip L. *New Dictionary of Psychology.* New York: Philosophical Library, 1947. 364 p.

HARRIS, Chester W., Editor. *Encyclopedia of Educational Research.* Third Edition. New York: The Macmillan Co. Scheduled for 1960.

"Higher Degrees in Sociology, 1957." *American Journal of Sociology* 64: 62-73; July 1958. Also see earlier and later numbers.

HILLWAY, Tyrus. *Introduction to Research.* Boston: Houghton Mifflin Co., 1956. p. 72-86.

JOHNSON, H. Webster, and McFARLAND, Stuart W. *How to Use a Business Library with Sources of Business Information.* Cincinnati: South-Western Publishing Co., 1951. vi+122 p.

KOCH, Sigmund, Editor. *Psychology:* A Study of Science. New York: McGraw-Hill Book Co. The first part (on conceptual and systematic psychology) of seven volumes is scheduled for publication late in 1958.

LAMKE, T. A., and SILVEY, H. M., Editors. *Master's Theses in Education,* 1956-57. No. 6. Cedar Falls, Ia.: Research Publications, 1957. Also see earlier and later numbers.

LATHAM, Albert J. "Guides to Psychological Literature." *American Psychologist* 9: 21-28; January 1954.

LOUTTIT, C. M. "Publication Trends in Psychology: 1894-1954." *American Psychologist* 12: 14-21; January 1957.

LYDA, Mary L., and BROWN, Stanley B. *Research Studies in Education:* A Subject Index of Doctoral Dissertations, Reports, and Field Studies, 1941-1951. Boulder, Col.: The Authors, 1953.

MARTIN, Michael, and GELBER, Leonard. *The New Dictionary of American History.* New York: Philosophical Library, 1952. vi+695 p.

McCORMICK, Thomas C., and FRANCIS, Roy G. *Methods of Research in the Behavioral Sciences.* New York: Harper & Brothers, 1958. Chapter 4.

MONROE, Walter S., Editor. *Encyclopedia of Educational Research.* Second Edition. New York: The Macmillan Co., 1950. xxvi+1520 p. Third Edition scheduled for 1960.

MORRIS, R. B., Editor. *Encyclopedia of American History.* New York: Harper & Brothers, 1953. xv+776 p.

MORRISON, J. Cayce, and Others. "Twenty-five Years of Educational Research." *Review of Educational Research* 26: 199-344; June 1956.

"Outstanding Educational Books of 1957." *NEA Journal* 47: 345, 347-48; May 1958. Also see earlier and later numbers.

PIERSTORFF, Lola R. "Research Tools: Library Resources," in "Methodology of Educational Research." *Review of Educational Research* 27: 471-75; December 1957.

Research Methods Applied to Health, Physical Education, and Recreation. Revised Edition. Washington: American Association for Health, Physical Education, and Recreation, N.E.A., 1952. p. 84-124.

RUSSELL, Harold G., SHOVE, Raymond H., and MOEN, Blanche E. *The Use of Books and Libraries.* Seventh Edition. Minneapolis: University of Minnesota Press, 1951. v+91 p.

SCATES, Douglas E. "Changing Sources of Information about Thesis Research." *Journal of Teacher Education* 8: 210-13; June 1957.

SEEGER, Ruth E. *Library Resources in Educational Research.* Columbus: Bureau of Educational Research, Ohio State University, 1957. v+26 p.

SHERA, J. H., KENT, Allen, and PERRY, James W., Editors. *Information Systems in Documentation.* Vol. 2. New York: Interscience Publishers, 1957. 639 p.

SHORES, Louis. *Basic Reference Sources.* Chicago: American Library Association, 1954. ix+378 p.

STAVELEY, Ronald. *Notes on Modern Bibliography.* London: Library Association, 1954. viii+111 p.

TAUBER, Maurice F., and Others. *Technical Services in Libraries.* New York: Columbia University Press, 1954. 487 p.

TROTIER, Arnold H., and HARMAN, Marian, Editors. *Doctoral Dissertations Accepted by American Universities 1954-1955.* No. 22. Compiled for the Association of Research Libraries. New York: H. W. Wilson Co., 1955. 298 p. Also see earlier numbers.

TRYTTEN, M. H., and HARMON, L. R. *Doctorate Production in United States Universities 1936-1956:* With Baccalaureate Origins of Doctorates in the Sciences, Arts, and Humanities. Publication 582. Washington: National Academy of Sciences-National Research Council, 1958. vii+155 p.

UNESCO, *Current Sociology.* Vol. V, No. 2, 1956. Sociology of Science. (A trend report and bibliography.) Prepared for the International Sociological Association with the support of the International Committee for Social Sciences Documentation. Paris: UNESCO, 1956. p. 89-153.

UNESCO, *International Bibliography of Sociology.* Vol. V: Works Published in 1955. Prepared by the International Committee for Social Sciences Documentation in co-operation with the International Sociological Association. Paris: UNESCO, 1957. 293 p.

VESEY, Margaret A., and ANDERSON, Earl W. "Investigations of Teacher Supply and Demand Reported in 1956." *Educational Research Bulletin* 36: 144-55; April 10, 1957. Also see earlier and later numbers.

WARREN, H. C. *A Dictionary of Psychology.* Boston: Houghton Mifflin Co., 1934. x+372 p.

WENDT, Paul R. *Audio-Visual Instruction.* What Research Says to the Teacher, No. 14. Washington: National Education Association, 1957. 32 p.

"What Research Says about Teaching and Learning." *Phi Delta Kappan* 39: 241-304; March 1958.

WILKINS, W. D., and GROSS, Lucy. "Usefulness of Educational Periodicals for Research." *School and Society* 79: 9-11; January 9, 1954.

WILLIAMS, C. B., and STEVENSON, A. H. *A Research Manual for College Studies and Papers.* Revised Edition. New York: Harper & Brothers, 1951. p. 16-61.

WINCHELL, Constance M. *Guide to Reference Books.* Seventh Edition. Chicago: American Library Association, 1951. xvii+645 p.

WINCHELL, Constance M., and JOHNSON, O. A. *Guide to Reference Books.* Seventh Edition Supplement, 1950-52. Second Supplement, 1953-55. Chicago: American Library Association, 1954, 140 p.; 1956, 134 p.

WINICK, Charles. *Dictionary of Anthropology.* New York: Philosophical Library, 1956. vii+579 p.

YOUNG, Pauline V. *Scientific Social Surveys and Research.* Third Edition. Englewood Cliffs, N. J.: Prentice-Hall, 1956. p. 127-36.

YOUNG, Raymond J., Compiler. *A Directory of Educational Research Agencies and Studies.* Bloomington, Ind.: Phi Delta Kappa, 1957. 80 p.

4

History and Historiography

This chapter presents the major steps, processes, or aspects of historical research and historiography: collection of data, with consideration of sources as documents and remains, and as primary and secondary; evaluation of data, including external and internal criticism; and presentation of the facts in readable narrative form, including problems of organization, composition, and interpretation.

HISTORY AS A FIELD OF KNOWLEDGE AND RESEARCH

Definition and Scope of History[1]

Viewed as research, history may be defined as an integrated narrative or description of past events or facts, written in the spirit of critical inquiry, to find the whole truth and report it.[2] A newspaper or journalistic report of some current event, or a debate in Congress or a state legislature, is not history, because it is not typically an inquiry into the *whole* truth. The campaign book of a political party summarizing the events and activities of the party for the four years preceding the election is not history, since it was not written as a *critical* inquiry into the truth.

[1] Herman Ausubel, *Historians and Their Craft*: A Study of the Presidential Addresses of the American Historical Association, 1884-1945. New York: Columbia University Press, 1950. p. 300-358.

Jacques Barzun and Henry F. Graff, *The Modern Researcher*. New York: Harcourt, Brace and Co., 1957. p. 3-17, 43-56.

Gilbert J. Garraghan, *A Guide to Historical Method*. Edited by Jean Delanglez. New York: Fordham University Press, 1946. p. 1-32.

Louis R. Gottschalk, *Understanding History*: A Primer of Historical Method. New York: Alfred A. Knopf, 1950. p. 26-37.

Homer C. Hockett, *The Critical Method in Historical Research and Writing*. New York: The Macmillan Co., 1955. p. 237-54.

[2] Allan Nevins, *The Gateway to History*. Boston: D. C. Heath and Co., 1938. p. 22-23.

The historical novel is not history, even though incorporating certain events and threads of historical truth, but rather it seeks to entertain the reader. Biography or autobiography becomes history when adequate historical perspective enables the author to see the individual in relation to the society and events of his time, but is not history when the account is limited to a single life in isolation. Antiquarian research or writing does not become history merely through the process of preserving material or records in almanac or museum-like fashion.

As to scope, history embraces the entire field of the human past and is as broad as life itself. Our human past includes many areas of social experience and activities that frequently have proved more significant than political history or military campaigns; for example, culture, ideals, institutions, law, religion, literature, art, travel, engineering, industry, technology, medicine, science, philosophy, economics, education, psychology, anthropology, and sociology. There is general agreement among modern historians concerning the richness of the content of history, including social, cultural, economic, and intellectual developments, and on a broad view of past events, extending far beyond the study of politics, diplomatics, constitutions, and "drum and trumpet" war materials.

Interrelationships of History and Science

It is without profit to argue the question of whether history is science or art. History qualifies as science in the sense that its methods of inquiry are critical and objective, and that the results are accepted as organized knowledge by a consensus of trained investigators. The research aspects of history in dealing with sources are scientific in approach, while narration and historiography commonly involve the art of expression and philosophy of the author.

Until recent years the natural sciences and the cultural sciences were generally regarded as far apart, yet these two fields of research are parts of a meaningful whole when we think of scientific knowledge not merely as a finished product but as a historical development, with a dimension of historic depth. On the other hand, the unique or disparate events of human history may fit into a unified, integrated pattern or process, if we view the gradual advance of man's knowledge as a central theme of historical development. These interrelationships of history and science make it important that the modern historian be well grounded in the natural sciences.

A glance at the present era suffices to convince us that science makes history, that the growth of our knowledge is a compelling force in historical events—and here I am far from thinking of atom bombs alone, for the past teaches the same lesson. The historic changes in the life of man are an expression and consequence of intellectual development; a new manner of thinking, a new way of seeing the world, inevitably brings about changes in man's activity, even in his everyday life. True, it seems to many of us today that our century is dominated, to a terrifying degree, by ruthless brute force; that an unrestrained lust for pleasure or profit or power has triumphed over all spiritual forces. But even these manifestations are conditioned by the spiritual and intellectual state of our world: our own day-to-day life is shaped by what the philosophers and scientists of the last two centuries have thought and expounded.

Thus it is to be expected that the ideas which are taking form today, the knowledge which is being acquired in our time, will be the crucial factors in tomorrow's decisions. And an awareness of the headlong intellectual transformations taking place today will give us an idea of the momentous changes that the future has in store for us.[3]

History differs in method[4] from the natural sciences, since it is not a discipline of direct observation or experimentation, but utilizes reports of observations that cannot be repeated; the historian cannot recall the actors of the past to reproduce the famous scenes of history on the stage of today. Instead of the direct observations used in science, the historian usually must depend on the observations of others (often untrained observers). Therefore, the historical method involves a procedure supplementary to observation, a process by which the historian seeks to test the truthfulness of the reports of observations made by others. Both historian and scientist examine data, formulate hypotheses, and test the hypotheses against the evidence until acceptable conclusions are reached. A number of historians, in emphasizing the interpretation and meaning of facts, have sought to identify tendencies, themes, patterns, and laws of history, while some of these investigators have dealt with such philosophical or theoretical problems in history as discovery of laws, unity and continuity, possibility or impossibility of prediction, and oversimplification growing out of the search for clues or keys.

History in Relation to Other Social Fields

History has close interrelationships with other social fields. The economists have introduced a quantitative emphasis into modern history; for example, citing numerical data such as the United States census for a given year, or basing certain computations upon such data, in calculating

[3] Quoted from Pascual Jordan, *Science and the Course of History*. Translated by Ralph Manheim. New Haven: Yale University Press, 1955. p. vii–viii, 3–4.

[4] Homer C. Hockett, *op. cit.*, p. 7-8.

by decades the rate of increase of the population of the United States. Handling of quantitative material is important in economic history, in sound social history (with its dependence on knowledge of population movement, inheritance, and social mobility), and sometimes in military history.

As another example of close interrelationships between the social fields, history and sociology are complementary, in the sense that both areas seek to explain the past, although the sociologist is interested primarily in generalized descriptions and in types of societal evolution, without the historian's concern with time-and-place relationships and unique events. It is true that American sociologists by choice ignore the bulk of historical findings by restricting themselves to a single culture and to the short time span they consider relevant to contemporary conditions. Even within the present, the interests of sociologists are normally narrower than those of historians, who deal with the contemporary national scene in relation to foreign, political, legal, and economic issues, as well as the rise and decline of communities, corporations, families, ideologies, and the fortunes of ethnic groups. When it serves its purpose, to clarify an argument or exposition, the historian does introduce new elements of explicit theory (economic, social, political, or legal). Specific ways in which history and sociology can learn from each other involve questions of the observation, selection, and organization of factual evidence or data:

> Does firsthand observation, the overwhelming detail of the living scene, give an unqualified advantage, or are there compensating advantages in the severity of the criticism that the historian has to apply to his more limited sources? To him, every personal record is a psychological document, the shades of validity in its testimony to be checked by other kinds of evidence. Should the interview report, said now to be the key tool in the sociologist's kit, be similarly handled? Can the historian's techniques of criticism help the sociologist to counteract the bias of his interview work, which excludes those important classes of people who resent the interviewer's intrusion? In return, can the sociologist help the historian counteract the bias of his written sources, which too often reveal the lowest classes only in their economic relations or in their tangles with the law? How far is the sociologist's fuller observation of short-run change colored by his own effect upon the situation? Is any community quite the same after an interpersonal rating survey?[5]

Values of History

Historians of the twentieth century have commonly emphasized the immediate usefulness of history in dealing with contemporary problems. They have stressed the importance of a social consciousness for the histo-

---

[5] Quoted from Sylvia L. Thrupp, "What History and Sociology Can Learn from Each Other." *Sociology and Social Research* 41: 434-38; July-August 1957.

rian, use of history to throw light on the present, inquiry into the past for solutions to contemporary problems, and avoidance of the charge of antiquarianism. Modern historians, like economists, political scientists, sociologists, and psychologists, have maintained that they too have answers to contemporary social problems. History may enable communities to grasp their relationship with the past and to plan more intelligently for the future; it may give to people a sense of continuity and a consciousness of unity in their efforts and achievements. "Seated at the roaring loom of time, for six thousand years man has woven a seamless garment. But that garment is invisible and intangible save where the dyes of written history fall upon it, and forever preserve it as a possession of generations to come."[6]

The wide-ranging mind of Charles A. Beard grasped the significance of Lord Acton's precept: "Study problems, not periods." In Collingwood's language, "Scissors-and-paste historians study periods; they collect all the extant testimony about a certain limited group of events, and hope in vain that something will come of it. Scientific historians study problems; they ask questions, and if they are good historians they ask questions which they see their way to answering." Beard was forever asking questions, and, following in the train of European scholars (notably Croce) who were more than a generation in advance of Americans in this matter, he and Carl Becker asked fellow historians to consider the meaning of their research and their writing. Beard reminded them that in every era contestants had used the writing of history to capture the human mind. Catholics and Protestants had done so, and Voltaire had made history "a dynamic force for the French Revolution." At a later time, "under the guise of romanticism, history had served the reaction." Every history, it was maintained, was "a selection of facts made by some person or persons and is ordered or organized under the influence of some scheme of reference, interest or emphases—avowed or unavowed—in the thought of the author or the authors." As Collingwood expressed it, "history is nothing but the re-enactment of past thought in the historian's mind." Modern historians, said Beard, "working in the scientific spirit, seeking emancipation from the tyranny of old assumptions" should legitimately use their discipline to illuminate "all divisions of contemporary thought and all formulations of public policy." Historical writing, he believed, was to be an instrument for the advancement of social reform.

More than anyone else, Beard stimulated scholars to recognize frankly the functional nature of historical knowledge and to make them aware of what they were doing. "Just what intellectual operations does the historian perform in studying and writing history?" he asked. "For what reason . . . are particular aspects of history chosen for emphasis and other aspects excluded?"[7]

[6] Allan Nevins, *op. cit.*, p. 3, 5.
[7] Quoted from Michael Kraus, *The Writing of American History*. Norman: University of Oklahoma Press, 1953. p. 372-73.

To comment further on the concept of a historical period, it is inherently fluid and slippery.

One of the more common and successful ways for a young historian to make a reputation is to juggle this essential symbol. He may create a new period, or demonstrate that an old one has no validity. The "Renaissance" happened much earlier than is usually thought, these promising scholars will write; or they may undertake to prove that there "really" was no "Renaissance" at all. What a historian does when he consciously concerns himself with periods is to look for the existence or absence of certain common characteristics that reappear a certain number of times. What these are and how often they must reappear in order to justify the use of the symbol are matters to be determined by the writer's expert opinion. To conclude because it is opinion that the concept of a historical age has no validity, or to say that one opinion of this kind is as good as another, is a common error. It is not so common but even more of an error to conclude that something exists in nature that divides the past up into sections like those of a bamboo pole.[8]

To cite another example, in order to understand education as a social process with a long history, and to evaluate school theories and plans, we need to know the historical evidence or approach in the form of origins that have influenced the present state of education and of the schools, serial or temporal data for identification of significant causal factors, and the insights of educational thinkers in appraising panaceas, half-truths, and fads or frills. Specific competencies[9] to be developed through instruction in the history of education have been listed as follows:

1. Understanding the dynamics of educational change
2. Increased understanding of the relationship between education and the culture in which it operates
3. Increased understanding of contemporary educational problems
4. Understanding the functions and limitations of historical evidence in analyzing educational problems
5. Development of elementary ability in locating, analyzing, and appraising historical evidence
6. Development of a sense of the dignity and responsibility of the teaching profession.

Specific applications of the historical approach extend beyond the general field of educational history to comparative education; to legal

[8] Quoted from H. Stuart Hughes, Editor, *Teachers of History*: Essays in Honor of Laurence Bradford Packard. Ithaca, N. Y.: Cornell University Press for Amherst College, 1954. p. 314-17.
[9] Committee on Historical Foundations of the National Society of College Teachers of Education, R. Freeman Butts, Chairman, *The Role of the History of Education in the Professional Preparation of Teachers*. Ann Arbor, Mich.: The Society, 1957. p. 19-29, 65-66, 84-98, 123-29.

research in education, with the statutory law and the case or common law as the sources; to thorough bibliographical and summarizing studies, as illustrated by the *Encyclopedia of Educational Research* and *Review of Educational Research;* to psychology, as illustrated by biographical and autobiographical narratives, general histories of psychology, and the *Annual Review of Psychology;* and to the biographical, case-history, and life-history materials and other historical approaches of sociology and certain related social disciplines.

Especially during the second quarter of the present century and later, historical studies have made important contributions to psychology, as illustrated in a five-fold classification:[10]

1. Topical surveys, dealing with specific psychological concepts, such as Greek theories of cognition

2. Surveys of periods, and expositions of the views of particular men or groups, such as the history of Greek psychology

3. Source books, sometimes making available important materials in foreign languages

4. Biography, providing accounts of the lives of men who have made significant contributions to psychology

5. General histories of psychology, some devoted to the late modern period, and others purporting to cover the entire scope of psychological history.

In the field of psychology many genetic, biographical, autobiographical, case, and clinical studies are essentially historical in approach. One of the areas for further development in psychology is the training of specialists to do research and to give instruction in the history of psychology.

Problem and Process

The selection and development of the problem for study, and the chief library guides, have been discussed in earlier chapters. As in other fields, the beginner in historical research frequently chooses too broad a topic. As examples of delimitation of an overly large topic, a history of political parties in the United States became a treatment of a presidential campaign in one state, and a study of Negro land-grant colleges in the United States became the story of a particular land-grant college. Less frequently the historical problem is broadened as the study pro-

---

[10] Knight Dunlap, "The Historical Method in Psychology." *Journal of General Psychology* 24: 49-62; January 1941.

Also see A. A. Roback, Editor, *Present-Day Psychology.* New York: Philosophical Library, 1955. xiv+995 p. Chapter 20 lists and reviews contemporary histories of psychology.

gresses, as when the history of a small church-related college became a history of the program of higher education supported by the specific church denomination. In the background program of reading for development of the problem, the investigator may proceed from the best general treatises to specialized volumes and printed collections of sources, then to calendars of documents, expert bibliographies, and reviews in historical and other appropriate journals. Specialized and detailed advice for selection and development of the historical problem[11] is available.

Historical research and historiography involve three major steps, processes, or aspects:

Collection of data, with consideration of sources as documents and remains or relics, and as primary and secondary

Criticism of the data, including the process of external criticism (questions of authorship, time, place, genuineness, and actual language or text of the original document) and the process of internal criticism (questions of accuracy and value of the statements made)

Presentation of the facts in readable narrative form, including problems of organization, composition, exposition, and interpretation.

HISTORICAL SOURCES

A classification of sources[12] appropriate for history, as well as other social fields, is as follows:

1. Physical remains: historic sites, roads, aqueducts, pyramids, fortifications, buildings ruined or whole, furniture, human remains, clothing, food, utensils, pottery, implements, weapons, machinery, industrial processes, and fine arts and museum pieces of many kinds

[11] Carter Alexander and Arvid J. Burke, *How to Locate Educational Information and Data.* Third Edition. New York: Bureau of Publications, Teachers College, Columbia University, 1950. p. 320-25.
Jacques Barzun and Henry F. Graff, *op. cit.,* p. 18-27.
William W. Brickman, *Guide to Research in Educational History.* New York: New York University Bookstore, 1949. p. 1-8.
Louis R. Gottschalk, *op. cit.,* p. 62-70, 174-78.
Homer C. Hockett, *op. cit.,* p. 86-89, 184-86.
[12] Jacques Barzun and Henry F. Graff, *op. cit.,* p. 4-15.
Gilbert J. Garraghan, *op. cit.,* p. 103-23.
Louis R. Gottschalk, *op. cit.,* p. 41-61, 70-73, 86-117, 179-80.
Allan Nevins, *op. cit.,* Chapters 3, 4.
Thomas Woody, "Of History and Its Method." *Journal of Experimental Education* 15: 175-201; March 1947.
Pauline V. Young, *Scientific Social Surveys and Research.* Third Edition. Englewood Cliffs, N. J.: Prentice-Hall, 1956. p. 127-33.
Also see Walter C. Langsam, "Truth in History." *Bulletin of the Historical and Philosophical Society of Ohio* 16: 95–103; April 1958. "Today, practically speaking, we have five groups of sources for our contemporary history: the accounts of par-

2. Orally transmitted material (sometimes in writing), such as folklore, legends, ballads, tales, anecdotes, sagas, traditions, customs, manners, burials, ceremonials, social institutions, and language

3. More elementary and durable kinds of representative or artistic materials, not written in the ordinary sense, such as inscriptions baked upon clay, chiselled stones, monuments, stamped coins, woven tapestries, vases, scenic or portrait sculptures, historical paintings, and portraits

4. Hand-written materials (sometimes in print), including papyri, bricks bearing cuneiform writing, vellum or parchment manuscripts, and such more recent documents as chronicles, annals, biographies, memoirs, diaries, and genealogies

5. Printed books, papers, and literature

6. Motion-picture film, microfilm, and recordings, including radio and television

7. Personal observation (by the writer or by people whom he interviews).

Documents and Remains

The preceding classification of sources suggests that the earlier simple categories have become more complex and probably will continue to expand in the future. In illustrating the varied sources in educational history, it is reasonably satisfactory to use two broad divisions: documents and remains or relics. Documents are reports of events, consisting of impressions made on some human brain by past events and consciously or deliberately recorded for the purpose of transmitting information. The observer's or eye-witness's impression of the event is illustrated by such documents as the opinion of a judge, minutes prepared by the secretary of a board of education, a superintendent's annual report, the director's report of a school survey, a college catalogue prepared by a dean, or a course of study transmitted to the superintendent by the chairman of the particular curriculum committee. Relics are physical objects (sometimes written materials of historical value) produced without the conscious intention of imparting connected information. Through documentary sources one sees not the event of the past, but what the eye-witness thought the act was. In remains or relics one sees the actual objects as handed down from the past. Sometimes man more nearly reveals

---

ticipants, the reports of observers, the publications of government agencies, the researches of scholars, and the writings of popularizers. Each of these groups possesses certain advantages for collecting and presenting materials—and certain disadvantages. And the task of the intelligent reader and citizen is to take from each contributing source what is, or what within a framework of historical background appears to be, nearest the truth. Only thus can one create a synthesis that is based on a relatively high degree of probability."

the truth unconsciously through these physical objects or remains than through the documents that he deliberately records. For example, a schoolmaster may write in his annual report or diary (documentary source) of the humane and kindly methods of discipline employed, whereas the remains in the form of his devices for physical punishment (bundle of switches, iron-bound ruler, and whipping post) may reveal the truth and the inaccuracy of the documentary source.

A useful list of sources[13] in educational history is especially appropriate for modern materials in the form of documents or remains:

Documents

1. Legislative acts such as constitutions, laws, charters

2. Court decisions

3. Executive and other official records
   a. Proceedings of administrative officers and bodies
       (1) Minutes of boards of education
       (2) Reports and orders of principals, superintendents, presidents
       (3) Reports of committees, including recommendations for executive action
       (4) Systems of student records and salary lists
   b. Proceedings of deliberative bodies, such as the National Education Association and the North Central Association
   c. Reports of commissions; for example, the Educational Policies Commission
   d. Reports of school surveys and of official observers; for example, the report of Victor Cousin
   e. Courses of study
   f. Catalogues, prospectuses, advertisements

4. Newspapers and periodicals
   a. Articles
   b. News notices
   c. Advertisements

5. Personal materials
   a. Autobiographies, memoirs, reminiscences, and biographies
   b. Annals and histories written by actors in the events narrated
   c. Letters
   d. Legal instruments executed by individuals in a personal capacity, contracts, wills, and deeds
   e. Legal instruments conferring powers upon individuals; for example, certificates
   f. Lecture notes

6. Literary materials, as the novels of Charles Dickens or Edward Eggleston. (All literature has a potential use in the history of edu-

[13] H. G. Good, "Historical Research in Education." *Educational Research Bulletin* 9: 7-18, 39-47, 74-78; January 8, January 22, and February 5, 1930.

cation. A great amount of such material is found in the publications of the Early English Text Society and similar bodies.)

Remains

1. School buildings and their furnishings
2. Photographs of buildings or furnishings, or of children, teachers, and parents engaged in educational activities
3. Forms of diplomas, attendance, and certificates; and record blanks
4. Various physical devices of the school for teaching, punishment, exercise, or health
5. Textbooks, manuscript exercise-books made by pupils, and pupils' maps and drawings (for example, the collection of more than eight thousand old textbooks in the library of the University of Pittsburgh)
6. Under certain conditions all kinds of written materials, if the problem is to observe what people unconsciously reveal about themselves rather than to determine what they consciously or deliberately say about themselves.

The two preceding classifications of historical sources suggest that many types of materials have not been fully utilized, especially remains or relics. In the writing of history, physical remains usually have been considered more valuable for social and economic history than for political history, and more useful for descriptive than analytical phases of history. Some remains or relics are called "memorials," with the characteristics of both remains and documents. A gravestone including only a name is a relic, but with the addition of dates of birth and death, and possibly other information, it becomes a "memorial." The cornerstone or dedication plaque of a school building, including identifying dates, architect, or school board, has the characteristics of both remains and documents. The significance of educational remains has not been fully recognized, and space for housing bulky collections of remains has not been so commonly provided as for documents.

The same source at different times may be classified as either a document or a remain, when used for different purposes; for example, when letters written by George Washington and others (before Noah Webster's efforts toward standardization of spelling) are studied to determine variations in spelling, rather than the messages deliberately recorded in the letters, these sources would serve the purposes of remains and would be so classified. If the historian searches the same letters to identify attitudes toward public education, his interest is in the recorded messages, which means that the source serves the purposes of a document and is so classified. A printed diploma or report card in blank is a remain, but when the name of a pupil and his attainments are entered in the proper blanks, the source presents a message and becomes a document. School textbooks are remains, since they do not deliberately or consciously record information concerning school practice or teaching procedure, although they do throw considerable light on such problems for a particular period of time. As a rule, the author's preface in a textbook comments on certain curricular, teaching, or learning problems and as such is a documentary source. The school textbook in some instances illustrates the relative values of documents and remains in the search for truth; in the preface the author may deliberately or consciously lay claim to modern curriculum materials and methods, but the discussion and exercises in the body of the textbook, serving as a silent witness, may testify that the materials and methods are obsolete.

Primary and Secondary Sources

An earlier section of this chapter has characterized sources as documents and as remains or relics. Another possible classification of sources[14] is as primary or secondary, and even tertiary or a greater number of times removed from the eye witness or direct observer of the event. Primary sources are the original documents or remains, the first witnesses to the event, with only the mind of the observer or eye witness coming between the original event and the user of the source. The preceding lists of documents and remains provide numerous examples of primary sources. The secretary's minutes of a school-board meeting are primary, but the newspaper editor's comment on the meeting of the board, even though based on the minutes of the meeting, is secondary, since both the secretary and the editor have come between the event and the person who reads the newspaper comment. If the editor is present in person at the meeting of the school board, then his comments are primary.

The primary sources for writing the history of equipment in the science laboratories of secondary schools would include the equipment itself as preserved in storerooms or museums, pictures of apparatus, state or local manuals specifying laboratory equipment, written records by science teachers describing their laboratory apparatus or procedures, order blanks for requisitioning science materials, and the oral testimony of pupils and teachers who worked in the science laboratories of the

[14] Jacques Barzun and Henry F. Graff, *op. cit.*, Chapters 1, 3-5.
William W. Brickman, *op. cit.*, p. 91-116.
H. G. Good, *op. cit.*, p. 43-47, 74-76.

past. Secondary sources for the same topic would include such materials as portions of histories of education, special bibliographies, and parts of books on the teaching of science, which usually are several times removed from the original event or have several minds between the laboratory equipment described and the user of the source.

The official registration cards for students in a school are a primary source for analyzing age, sex, and geographical distribution, but a newspaper report based on this analysis is a secondary source.

The nature of the problem and its purpose sometimes determine whether a particular source is primary or secondary. For most purposes, textbooks in the history of education are secondary sources, with most chapters and sections of the book many times removed from the original event; the author actually witnessed only a few of the events during the modern period in writing a history of education in the United States. If the problem and purpose of the historical study should change to the organization of materials, philosophy of interpretation, and style of writing employed by certain authors, then their books become primary sources; the author's book is as close as one can come to his philosophy of interpretation and style of writing. In the initial stage of a particular problem, a secondary source (such as a history of education) may prove more helpful and even more accurate than a primary source, if the educational historian has been successful in evaluating primary sources, interpreting meaning, and writing the narrative. As a first step in writing a history of reading instruction in the elementary school for a stipulated period of time, it probably is desirable to begin with such secondary sources as historical chapters in books on the teaching of reading.

The vitality of history is enhanced not only through reading the original sources but also through visitation of place of origin of events. Aristotle says that a Libyan, when asked to name the best manure, replied: "The land-owner's footprints." When asked about the best feed to fatten a horse, a Persian answered: "His master's eye." If Livy had paid more attention to factors of geography and topography, and had he visited Lake Trasimenus, only some thirty miles from his birthplace, he would have written differently about that famous battlefield.[15]

An interesting example of modern literary scholarship and extensive travel in the recovery of a large quantity of manuscripts involves the papers of James Boswell, the biographer of Samuel Johnson. Through painstaking efforts an American professor became acquainted with Boswell's descendants and located the Boswell manuscripts in Ireland, after

[15] Thomas Woody, *op. cit.*, p. 175-201.

which the papers were purchased and brought to the United States.

Without papers and documents from the past, the historian of science would be helpless. Unfortunately, these valuable source materials are being destroyed at a startling rate in present-day America. Children today do not carry on a long family tradition, and heirlooms and papers kept for decades are being disposed of summarily.

Professor W——, for example, was a key figure in American science at the turn of the century. He carried out impressive research at one of our leading universities, founded an important journal, and organized one of our great research laboratories. His ideas were provocative and influential, and his pupils rose to eminent positions in the world of science. Yet today there exist no primary source materials relating to his work. His correspondence, notebooks, photograph albums, and manuscripts have disappeared.

What is needed to correct the situation is a Commission to Preserve the Private Papers of American Scientists. Whether the commission is set up as a private or government agency, its members would represent such institutions as the National Academy of Sciences, the Library of Congress, and the National Archives and such organizations as the Society of American Archivists and the History of Science Society. The commission would have a twofold task. It would be a central agency carrying on a systematic and comprehensive search for source materials for the history of science, and, in this regard, it ought to be empowered to establish a national history of science archives in Washington.

It is doubtful whether any single collection, however grand, can do the job on the comprehensive scale required. As its second, and more important task, the commission should take action to stimulate and coordinate the archival work of the present scientific institutions and organizations. It is not enough that we have the papers of an Einstein. We need material concerning the *hundreds* of top-notch men doing important creative work in theoretical science and in the applied fields—medicine, engineering, industry, and so on. And we cannot predict which of these men will be of greatest interest to the future. Each scientific and educational institution—be it a university, museum, library, or research laboratory—has a part to play in finding and storing papers of potential historical value. And every scientific organization should have collections of relevant data at the national, regional, and local levels.

The heroic age of American science began shortly after the Civil War and reached its climax just after World War II. These years, during which we won a position of world leadership, will be of unique interest to future historians of science. Already we have let much of this rich heritage slip through our fingers. A strong and active commission of the kind proposed can still repair some of the damage. But time is running out.[16]

The answer which Le Play sought was suggested to him by the experience he gained in extensive travels. Le Play began these excursions in the summer of 1829, before his accident, as part of the fieldwork required of

[16] Quoted from Gerald J. Gruman, "Preserving the Stuff of History." *Science* 127: 1471; June 27, 1958.

students in the Ecole des mines, and he resumed them as soon as his health permitted. In the course of some twenty years, he thus visited, at various times, Spain and Italy, England, Scotland, Ireland, the Low Countries and Germany, Scandinavia, Russia, the Balkans, and Asia Minor. Some of these journeys he undertook on his own initiative, giving over his summers to them, while others were occasioned by invitations to study or advise upon mining and metallurgical technics. His sojourn in Russia, for instance, was at the request of Prince Anatole Demidov, who asked him to survey the mining operations on the estates of the Demidov family in the Donetz basin. In all, Le Play traveled some two hundred thousand miles, much of this distance on foot.

Although Le Play made his trips mainly to inspect mines and forges, he became a serious observer of social conditions in the lands he visited. Wherever he went, he made it his practice to inquire as to which family in each locality, whether rich or poor, was widely regarded as an example of well-being and virtue, and he attempted a systematic study of such families.[17]

Both historians and sociologists are agreed on the importance of such nonofficial documents as personal letters, autobiographies, diaries, life histories, and similar records. Especially of late, a keen public interest in such historical sources has developed, as witnessed by accounts in popular magazines of collections relating to Lincoln, the Lewis and Clark explorations, Boswell, and works of art.

Collections of private letters have certain limitations when published by the writer himself or by a literary executor, since damaging passages or even entire letters may be omitted; an editor without personal relations with the author of the letters is much more likely to present an unbiased treatment. Diaries and autobiographies edited and published by the author are subject to the same limitations mentioned for letters. It is only natural that many self-centered persons who write letters, diaries, and autobiographies will describe themselves and their motives, and edit their collections, as they wish to appear to the public rather than as they actually are. An exception to this characterization is Samuel Pepys, who presumably wrote with candor and honesty in his diary, since he probably did not expect anyone to decode his special system of shorthand. Although James Boswell was almost ideally qualified to write the *Life of Johnson*, in view of his close relationships with his subject, Boswell omitted interesting details in following what he considered the dictates of good taste in biography.

Essentially similar views are expressed in the discussion between Whitehead, his wife, and Lucien Price.[18]

---

[17] Quoted from H. Stuart Hughes, *op. cit.*, p. 63-65.
[18] Quoted from *Dialogues of Alfred North Whitehead*. As Recorded by Lucien Price. New York: New American Library of World Literature, 1954. p. 43.

"I think you get a truer picture of a period from intimate letters written spontaneously and without a thought of publication than you do from its fiction and often better than from its historians."

"And women write better than men in that vein," said his wife.

"Certainly better than authors writing letters to each other with an eye to future publications," he agreed.

"Edmund Gosse used to complain that while the letters Robert Louis Stevenson wrote him were works of art and literature they didn't tell him what he wanted to know about his friend—which touched off Carolyn Wells to write that ballade with the refrain, 'They must look well in print!' "

EXTERNAL CRITICISM: AUTHENTICITY

The historian is obligated to determine the authenticity and meaning of sources. Many writers on the historical method and on historiography have labeled these processes of criticism and evaluation as external criticism and internal criticism, while other historiographers have avoided the formality or logic of such a classification of the aspects of criticism. For present purposes it seems helpful to employ the terms *external* and *internal criticism.*

External criticism[19] deals with the genuineness of the document, whether it is what it seems to be and reads true to the original. It is concerned with form and appearance of the document rather than meaning of the contents, although external criticism at times may employ internal evidence from the document through a study of its contents, in an attempt to establish questions of authorship. Problems of external criticism, in testing the genuineness of a document or remain, involve questions about the characteristics of the author and his qualifications as a reporter; factors or conditions that may have influenced the production of the document, such as time, place, purpose, and circumstances of composition; and the extent to which the document and its parts read true to the original.

The work of external criticism has been greatly facilitated through the development of a number of auxiliary sciences, and of printing and photography, especially in dealing with older sources. A partial list of the important auxiliary aids or fields includes: anthropology, archaeology,

[19] William W. Brickman, *op. cit.,* p. 116-60.
Gilbert J. Garraghan, *op. cit.,* p. 168-231.
H. G. Good, *op. cit.,* p. 17-18.
Louis R. Gottschalk, *op. cit.,* p. 118-38.
Homer C. Hockett, *op. cit.,* p. 13-82.
Allan Nevins, *op. cit.,* Chapters 5, 6.
Chauncey Sanders, *An Introduction to Research in English Literary History.* New York: The Macmillan Co., 1952. p. 95-124, 142-206.

astronomy, cartography, chemistry, chronology, diplomatics, economics, education, epigraphy, exact sciences, genealogy, geography, geology, heraldry, historical method and philosophies, languages, law, literature, military affairs, natural history, numismatics, paleontology, paleography, philately, philology, philosophy, politics, prehistory, and psychology. Before the invention of printing, when manuscripts were copied by hand, there were frequently inadvertent errors in the form of unintentional omissions or insertions, and sometimes deliberate changes in the text. During recent years microphotography has made it possible to reproduce and transmit entire books, bulky records, newspapers, and other manuscripts for projection in some distant library or research center, thus obviating the type of error that arises in copying.

It is true that students in education and other social fields do not often encounter problems of actual genuineness in dealing with modern documents, especially printed sources. There is little temptation to forge a modern arithmetic textbook, a course of study, or school-board minutes. Even though there may not be any great incentive to perpetrate frauds or forgeries in the modern literature of the social fields, there is still the question of authorship (external criticism) in determining the extent to which a city superintendent has written his annual report rather than his assistant superintendents and supervisors, and the part played by a university president in preparing his annual report as compared with contributions by the deans of his several component colleges.

Typical motives for deception[20] in the preparation of older documents were: use of a well-known name to increase the sales or prestige of a manuscript, enhancement of the reputation of prominent persons through employment of "ghost" writers, and use of pseudonyms to stimulate the curiosity of the public. Types of invention or forgery that have appeared in the past include: witty sayings of famous persons, invented speeches placed in the mouths of famous personages by the older historians, insertion of applause in the written record of legislative speeches never delivered, genealogies and family trees, interpolations or insertions for deceptive purposes by copyists or others, and business documents, works of art, and antiques.

Merton presents a sociological interpretation of the frequently puz-

[20] Gilbert J. Garraghan, *op. cit.*, p. 81-99.

H. G. Good, *op. cit.*, p. 13-14.

Robert K. Merton, "Priorities in Scientific Discovery: A Chapter in the Sociology of Science." *American Sociological Review* 22: 635-59; December 1957.

Chauncey Sanders, *op. cit.*, p. 408-11.

Thomas Woody, *op. cit.*, p. 175-201.

zling aspects of conflicts over priority or originality in scientific discovery. His interpretation is that, like other social institutions, science has its characteristic values, norms, and organization, including emphasis on the value of originality. As emphasis upon originality and its recognition is stepped up, the greater becomes the involvement of the scientist in the successful outcome of inquiry and his emotional vulnerability to failure. This cultural and social background can lead scientists to develop an extreme concern for recognition, which is in turn the validation by peers of their work, and can lead to reprehensible conduct on the part of individual scientists. The history of science reports many instances of deviant behavior in the form of contentiousness, self-assertive claims, secretiveness lest one be forestalled, reporting only the data that support a hypothesis, false charges of plagiarism, even the occasional theft of ideas and, in rare cases, the fabrication of data. This misbehavior is in response to a discrepancy between the great emphasis in the culture of science upon original discovery and the actual difficulty many scientists experience in making an original discovery, with the result that, in a situation of stress and strain, various forms of questionable adaptive behavior are adopted.

Frauds and Forgeries

Interesting examples[21] of hoaxes, frauds, and forgeries from a number of fields may be cited to illustrate the range and complexity of problems of genuineness in external criticism. For example, a painting is brought to the United States labeled as a self-portrait done by a great Dutch artist. The authenticity of the painting is challenged by the artist's nephew, and a battle develops between art experts in the United States, in Europe, and in the U. S. Treasury Department. The customs officers are interested because original works of art are duty-free, whereas copies and reproductions are not. One group of experts on art, handwriting, pigment, and language decides that the picture is genuine, so it is admitted to this country duty-free, but another group of specialists is unwilling to accept the painting as an original work by the Dutch artist.

Forgery was practiced even thousands of years ago. The Egyptian pharaohs often claimed for themselves the deeds of their ancestors by

---

[21] Jacques Barzun and Henry F. Graff, *op. cit.*, p. 88-114.
William W. Brickman, *op. cit.*, p. 156-57.
Gilbert J. Garraghan, *op. cit.*, p. 184-85.
Tyrus Hillway, *Introduction to Research*. Boston: Houghton Mifflin Co., 1956. p. 138.
Homer C. Hockett, *op. cit.*, p. 26-28.
Allan Nevins, *op. cit.*, p. 124-25, 131-37.
James W. Thompson and Bernard J. Holm, *A History of Historical Writing*. Vol. 1, New York: The Macmillan Co., 1942. p. 6.

erasing the name of the hero on the wall and by chiseling in their own names. Sometimes the pharaohs reproduced on another slab or monument the record of the hero's achievements, with their own names inserted to receive credit.

Ultraviolet rays and fluorescence photography have been developed as new methods of examining documents, especially in detecting alterations and erasures. Through such techniques it has been discovered that numerous changes were made in the personal journals of Nathaniel Hawthorne by Mrs. Hawthorne after her husband's death. By reading even heavily blacked out portions of Hawthorne's journals, the scholar has found him a man of real vigor and some bluntness of expression, although Hawthorne's widow had toned down his writing to sound more genteel or inoffensive.

It is difficult to believe that a standard encyclopedia of American biography included at least 47 sketches of the lives of men who never existed. The author (paid according to amount of space) sought to increase his remuneration by creating characters out of his imagination, including a scientist who supposedly won fame by combating the Asiatic cholera in South America, in 1783, 52 years before the disease first appeared there.

In a letter under an 1834 date, attributed to Lincoln, is an expression "that North East quarter of Section 40" of which Lincoln as an experienced surveyor could hardly have been guilty, since he knew quite well that a Congressional township was made up of 36 sections. The same letter included the geographical term *Kansas;* the territory of Kansas was not organized and open for settlement until 1854, and the term probably was not in use as early as 1834. The fact that the handwriting bore no resemblance to Lincoln's authenticated style helped establish the letters as forgeries. One of the spurious letters attributed to Ann Rutledge mentions a Spencerian copybook not in use until 1848; Ann died in 1835.

A striking example of a hoax or fraud is *The Diary of James Gallatin, Secretary to Albert Gallatin, A Great Peacemaker, 1813-1827,* edited by Count Gallatin and published in London and New York late in 1914.

In the preface, Count Gallatin explained that thirty-nine years before, in 1875, his grandfather had handed him "a large sealed packet, telling me it contained his Diary . . . also many important documents. I was not in any case to publish any part of it until 1900. . . . It lay unopened and nearly forgotten until last year. On reading it, I found it of the deepest interest. This decided me (after weeding out large portions and suppressing anything that might offend) to offer it to the public."[22]

[22] Quoted from Raymond Walters, Jr., "The James Gallatin Diary: A Fraud?" *American Historical Review* 62: 878-85; July 1957.

The authenticity of the *Diary* has been questioned for the following reasons:

1. Critics observed that the text of the *Diary* is not "pure" and contains a number of "aberrations."

2. Among the entries in the *Diary* are many expressions that seem to throw doubt on its authenticity as a whole, including expressions that were not in use at the time the *Diary* was supposed to have been written.

3. Many of the persons described in the *Diary* as having been at a particular place on a given date are known, on the basis of standard sources, to have been elsewhere at the time.

4. Members of the family and others were unable to find any trace of the original manuscript of the *Diary* or of anyone who had ever seen it.

5. The *Diary* does not check with other sources; for example, it includes many obvious inaccuracies about the French political and social scene.

6. Neither the literary style of the *Diary* nor the personality it displays of its supposed author jibes with the style or personality of James Gallatin exhibited elsewhere.

7. It is unlikely that the *Diary* was written earlier than 1879, at least three years after James Gallatin died, because much of the material is obviously drawn from two works published in that year by Henry Adams, dealing with the life and writings of Albert Gallatin. Of the twenty-nine letters and documents reproduced in the *Diary*, all but three appeared in one or both of Adams' works. Numerous entries in the *Diary* simply paraphrase passages found in Adams.

8. There are many discrepancies in matters of dates and events. The author of the hoax or fraud probably is the "Count Gallatin" who is listed as the editor of the *Diary* and signed its Preface. This man is James Francis Gallatin, grandson of the ostensible keeper of the *Diary*. This grandson was born in New York City in 1853, and had sufficient motivation and background for perpetrating the hoax.

An instance of forgery in the 1930's came to light when two young English book dealers were exposed as having printed certain rare and expensive books by well-known British authors, books presumed to have been published in limited or small editions about the middle of the nineteenth century. The temptation for a clever printer to issue these forged editions was the high price of the original editions in the rare-book market.

Piltdown Man, the so-called "Eoanthropus dawsoni," was generally (although not universally) accepted for approximately 40 years as an important fossil link in the chain of human evolution. His exposure as a fraud—as a synthetic monster compounded of the brain-case of a relatively recent, modern type of man and the doctored lower jaw of a recent anthropoid ape—rocked paleontological and anthropological circles in 1953.

The story of the hoax, as now revealed, is presented in detail by J. S. Weiner, the Oxford anthropologist who first suspected that the Sussex "fossil" was a concatenated chimera, and at whose insistence the anatomical and chemical investigations were undertaken which proved beyond doubt that the "earliest Englishman" was a diabolically clever forgery. The discovery of the skull, the ensuing scientific controversies, the problems that acceptance of the skull as an actual fossil entailed, and the events leading to the exposure of its true nature, are set forth by Weiner in an absorbing manner. No detective story or fiction could be more engrossing or more challenging. The personalities involved receive considerable attention.[23]

Inventions and Distortions[24]

Thucydides, the Greek historian, created elaborate speeches or orations for his leading characters, intended not merely for rhetorical effect but also to set forth the politics and diplomacy of his philosophy of history. The Roman dictator, Sulla, after his retirement from public life wrote a fabulous autobiography, pointing to a series of miraculous occurrences coincident with his public work, for the purpose of showing that the hand of the Goddess Tyche was visible throughout his activities. In marked contrast, Caesar's Commentaries present at least an external illusion of impartiality and self-restraint, although we should remember that Caesar wrote primarily to justify himself before the Roman people. When Alexander the Great was listening to an account of how he slew his opponent's elephant with a single blow of his spear, the young conqueror's sense of historical accuracy could not condone such exaggerated hero worship, and he snatched the book and threw it into the water with the comment that the author of such untruth also should be ducked.

In the writing of Thucydides, rhetorical speeches had served a genuinely dramatic purpose, but many of his successors made these inventions occasions for dramatic flourishes and illustrations of their command of style.

In most humanist historical writing of the fifteenth century the device of imaginary direct discourse was used not only to conform to rhetorical rules but also to construct idealized portraits. In this way individual historical

[23] Quoted from review by William L. Straus, Jr., *Scientific Monthly* 83: 209-10; October 1956, of J. S. Weiner, *The Piltdown Forgery*. New York: Oxford University Press, 1955. xii+214 p.

[24] Gilbert J. Garraghan, *op. cit.*, p. 228, 265.
Michael Kraus, *op. cit.*, p. 14-18, 39, 51, 80, 305.
Allan Nevins, *op. cit.*, p. 134, 139-40, 162-63.
J. T. Shotwell, *The History of History*. Vol. 1. New York: Columbia University Press, 1939. p. 210, 184-86.

characters came to exemplify abstract virtues and vices and thus serve as material for moral instruction. A great gulf separated the purpose of this use of direct discourse from that of a realist like Guicciardini, who in his masterpiece which covered the years of Erasmus' mature life used the same rhetorical device to underline the ironic difference between what men said and what they did. Erasmus' position in the *De copia* is that of traditional humanism.[25]

Parson Weems' rhetorical *Life of George Washington* includes many inventions in the form of dialogues, speeches, and anecdotes. The pioneer historian, Jared Sparks, edited the everyday language of George Washington and corrected his spelling, in order to picture Washington as a character of almost superhuman traits. Sparks has been accused of omitting materials that did not support his purpose of exalting some individual, and even of manufacturing a source or narrative as needed.

Belated appearance of a tradition, especially after the death of the person involved, may give rise to doubt. Captain John Smith's second version of his adventures in Virginia describes dramatically how Pocahontas saved his life, whereas she was barely mentioned in the first version. The story of Ann Rutledge and Abraham Lincoln is thought to be mainly legendary, since no mention of the episode appeared until 31 years after her death.

Authorship and Borrowing

Problems of external criticism are much less those of forgery or invention than of authorship, time, dependence of documents upon each other, and borrowing.[26] It has already been pointed out in this chapter that annual reports of university presidents and school superintendents pose a problem of determining authorship in relation to the contribution of their assistants. A difference in style or language in the several parts of such an annual report is not so important as whether the president's or superintendent's ideas are accurately presented in the phrasing of a dean or assistant superintendent. Washington's "Farewell Address" raises the question of what contribution Madison and Hamilton made to it. A similar question of authorship is present in identifying the numbers of *The Federalist* written by Madison, Hamilton, and Jay. Prominent persons in governmental positions and in other walks of public life

---

[25] Quoted from H. Stuart Hughes, *op. cit.*, p. 14-15.
[26] H. G. Good, *op. cit.*, p. 16.
Homer C. Hockett, *op. cit.*, p. 23-24.
Michael Kraus, *op. cit.*, p. 4, 13, 93-99, 105-14, 123-27, 140-47, 164, 316.
Allan Nevins, *op. cit.*, p. 153-56.
Thomas Woody, *op. cit.*, p. 175-201.

frequently have employed "ghost" writers. It is believed that Bancroft, the historian, wrote the message that Andrew Johnson sent to Congress in December 1865, although the discovery was not made until some forty years later.

Borrowing has been common, especially during earlier periods when authors copied freely from a variety of sources without acknowledgment of the borrowing. For more than a century John Marshall's *Life of George Washington*, published in 1804, was considered a great original work and a classic in its defense of federalism. The work has now been pronounced a mosaic of borrowings, carelessly pieced together, with unacknowledged instances of copying found on 268 of the 488 pages in one volume.

INTERNAL CRITICISM: CREDIBILITY

Internal criticism[27] deals with the meaning and trustworthiness of statements remaining within the document after any spurious or interpolated matter has been removed from the text, in other words, it weighs the testimony of the document in relation to the truth. These questions of accuracy and value of the statements made (credibility) normally come in sequence after questions of authorship, genuineness, time, place, and actual language or text of the original document have been answered through the processes of external criticism. The shift of emphasis in internal criticism is from the document as such to statements within the document. Many authentic or genuine documents (so determined by external criticism) may not be completely accurate or truthful, and require the processes of internal criticism in the form of textual criticism, as well as investigation of such factors as the competence, good faith, position, and bias of the author of the document.

There is no sharp dividing line between the external and internal phases of historical criticism, and the two processes may progress simultaneously, with a considerable amount of overlapping. Internal criticism may use external evidence concerning authorship, or time and place of writing, in determining the truthfulness and accuracy of the statements made in the document. The terms *external* and *internal* refer to the

[27] William W. Brickman, *op. cit.*, p. 161-79.
Gilbert J. Garraghan, *op. cit.*, p. 232-317.
H. G. Good, *op. cit.*, p. 39-47, 74-76.
Homer C. Hockett, *op. cit.*, p. 41-82.
Louis R. Gottschalk, *op. cit.*, p. 139-71.
Allan Nevins, *op. cit.*, Chapter 7.
Chauncey Sanders, *op. cit.*, p. 207-52.

purpose of the criticism and not to a specific method of dealing with sources, or whether one looks within or without the document for evidence to accomplish the particular purpose.

Before proceeding with specific illustrations, it is helpful to summarize basic principles[28] of internal criticism:

1. Do not read into earlier documents the conceptions of later times.

2. Do not judge an author ignorant of certain events, necessarily, because he fails to mention them (the argument *ex silentio*), or that they did not occur, for the same reason.

3. Underestimating a source is no less an error than overestimating it in the same degree, and there is no more virtue in placing an event too late than in dating it too early by the same number of years or centuries.

4. A single true source may establish the existence of an idea, but other direct, competent, independent witnesses are required to prove the reality of events or objective facts.

5. Identical errors prove the dependence of sources on each other, or a common source.

6. If witnesses contradict each other on a certain point, one or the other may be true, but both may be in error.

7. Direct, competent, independent witnesses who report the same central fact and also many peripheral matters in a casual way may be accepted for the points of their agreement.

8. Official testimony, oral or written, must be compared with unofficial testimony whenever possible, for neither one nor the other is alone sufficient.

9. A document may provide competent and dependable evidence on certain points, yet carry no weight in respect to others it mentions.

Literal Meaning and Real Meaning

Internal criticism is concerned with questions of the real meaning as distinguished from the literal meaning, the competence of the observer for careful and accurate reporting, and the good faith of the observer in making statements without bias or prejudice. The virtues[29] of the historian include accuracy, love of order, logic, honesty, self-awareness, and imagination.

The attempt to discover the literal meaning and the real meaning of the document is a positive aspect of internal criticism. While the literal meaning and the real meaning are usually the same in modern documents, except for rhetorical figures of speech and ambiguities in political speeches and platforms, many of the older sources present a

[28] Thomas Woody, *op. cit.*, p. 175-201.
[29] Jacques Barzun and Henry F. Graff, *op. cit.*, p. 56-60.

difficult task of determining the real meaning, because of unfamiliar or obsolete terms and reference to strange institutions or customs. The language of Cotton Mather must be interpreted, to understand what he is saying about certain events in the lives of the colonists that might seem trivial to the outside world: "If a war between us and a handful of Indians do appear no more than a Batrachomyomachie [battle of frogs and mice] to the world abroad, yet unto us at home it hath been considerable enough to make a history." Even in modern history we find rhetorical figures and literary artifices such as allegory, symbolism, irony, satire, jests, hoaxes, allusions, implications, metaphors, and hyperboles. George Bancroft's high-flown rhetoric needs tempering in determining an appropriate shade of meaning: "History has ever celebrated the heroes who have won laurels in scenes of carnage. Has it no place for the founders of states; the wise legislators, who struck the rock in the wilderness, so that the waters of liberty gushed forth in copious and perennial fountains?"[30]

There is an ever-present inclination of the uneducated to transform an allegorical allusion into a literal reality, to bring a metaphor clumsily and inappropriately to earth. Once a history student, presented with the statement that Napoleon "cut" the Austrian lines of communication in the Italian campaign of 1796, pictured the operation in its most literal sense. There had to be something physical if one was to cut as with a pair of shears. Hence he imagined railway, telephone, and telegraph lines—snip, snip, snip. When, pushed to further investigation, he discovered that humanity was blessed with none of these conveniences at the time, his picture disintegrated, leaving only a blank canvas and the conviction, which still prevailed, that something had been cut. And it is likely that he was unusual only in making further investigation. Most students never come to a position where they can hear with comfort an argument to show that there was no "Renaissance," or that the "fall" of Rome was not noticeable at the time.[31]

Competence and Accuracy of the Observer

To question either the competence and accuracy or the truthfulness and honesty of the observer is a negative aspect of internal criticism, in that every possible reason for disbelieving is sought and every statement is questioned as long as any reasonable doubt remains. An observer's competence is evaluated in relation to his status as a trained eye witness, presence of emotional stress or pressure that might affect observation, extent to which the position for observing was favorable, and extent to which memory was used after a lapse of time.

[30] Michael Kraus, *op. cit.*, p. 14, 115-27.
[31] Quoted from H. Stuart Hughes, *op. cit.*, p. 312.

Even the secretary of a professional organization is not always an accurate observer and reporter. A history[32] of the American Psychological Association indicates that the minutes of a recording secretary cannot always be trusted as evidence of what actually happened at a particular meeting. The published facts of the founding of the A.P.A. indicate that seven psychologists (Hall, Fullerton, James, Jastrow, Ladd, Cattell, and Baldwin) met at Clark University on July 8, 1892, to discuss the advisability and possibility of forming an association of psychologists. At the time the history was prepared Cattell and Jastrow were still living, but when asked to recall any important events concerning this founding meeting both replied that they had been unable to attend the meeting of July 8, 1892. It is true that sometimes a secretary lists in full the committee members in reporting the minutes, not noting absences, especially if the absent members have made recommendations by mail in advance of the meeting.

As an example of the problem of accuracy in determining a date of birth, when institutions were celebrating in 1944 the one hundredth anniversary of the birth of G. Stanley Hall, it was found that different sources gave three birth dates for him. A biography of Hall, written by a man who had worked closely with him, included the date of February 1, 1846. Another investigator found that the vital records of Ashfield, Massachusetts, Hall's apparent birthplace, did not contain the name of G. Stanley Hall, that Hall himself did not refer to his birth date in a biographical article, that different editions of *Who's Who in America* mention different dates, and that Hall's monument in Ashfield carried the inscription, "Born, February 1, 1844," which was accepted by the second investigator. A third author communicated with all the institutions with which Hall had been affiliated, with Hall's son, and with the General Land Office, and concluded that the most probable month and day of Hall's birth appeared to be February 1, although he was not certain about the year. Despite certain evidence favoring 1844, this third investigator (a scholar and research specialist in educational history) concluded that Hall was evidently confused about his own birth date and that no final answer can be reached until some indisputably authentic record of his birth date is discovered.[33]

---

[32] Samuel W. Fernberger, "The American Psychological Association, 1892-1942." *Psychological Review* 50: 33-60; January 1943.
    Wayne Dennis and Edwin G. Boring, "The Founding of the APA." *American Psychologist* 7: 95-97; March 1952.
[33] William W. Brickman, *op. cit.*, p. 121-22.

Another illustration of internal criticism relates to determining the first American work in the field of education.

Many writings on American educational history refer to Samuel R. Hall's *Lectures on School-Keeping* (1829) as the first American work in the field of education. Knight and Monroe, for example, make this statement in their respective textbooks. J. P. Gordy describes Hall's volume as "the first book on the subject ever written in this country" (*Rise and Growth of the Normal-School Idea in the United States*, p. 12). In their foreword to their Hall's *Lectures on School-Keeping*, Arthur D. Wright and George E. Gardiner refer to it as the "first book on education published in the United States in the English Language." This leaves out of account Christopher Dock's *Schulord-nung* (1770), and Joseph Neef's *Sketch of a Plan and Method of Education* (1808) and *Method of Instructing Children* (1813), all three published in Philadelphia. Of course, the claim may be made that Dock's book was written in German and that Dock and Neef were born abroad. In that event, the statement should read, "the first book on education written by an American."[34]

When Ellwood P. Cubberley, in 1898, started to teach at Stanford University, he had never studied the history of education, as such, although his undergraduate specialization in science may have thrown some light upon the history of science. If Cubberley had had the benefit of graduate work in history, he would have read and heard much about scientific procedure, historical method, analysis of documents for evidence, and in some universities might have heard criticism of the older concepts of history, including hints concerning a new outlook. Highly desirable as this preparation for his new position might have been, Cubberley had to face the task with the equipment he had, and he developed his course in the history of education as time, energy, and insight made possible.[35]

Critics of Cubberley's publications in the history of education have questioned the quality of his books as historical works. The criticisms have been concerned with the method of writing history, erroneous views of history, wrong interpretations, easy generalizations, and errors in fact. Certain of these defects may have been due to Cubberley's rapid methods of work. When reading history or studying documents, he quickly perceived a major trend, and became less concerned with minor considerations, at times appearing too quick in drawing conclusions. Although Cubberley never overcame completely his lack of technical

[34] Quoted from *ibid.*, p. 129.
[35] Jesse B. Sears and Adin D. Henderson, *Cubberley of Stanford: And His Contribution to American Education*. Stanford, Calif.: Stanford University Press, 1957. p. 104-5.

training in historical method and based much of his writing upon secondary sources, he had extensive acquaintance with a wide range of original papers, records, and documents. His contribution to the history of education has been evaluated by an enthusiastic colleague as follows:[36]

To have begun with no technical preparation and to have written so much and to so many different purposes; to have written in terms of an essentially new idea of the task in hand; to have chosen as the aims of his major works two ultimate values that could scarcely fail to glorify as well as increase the efficiency of teaching; to have organized so massive an amount of fact in a clear and simple manner; to have depicted education as going hand in hand with politics, religion, industry, recreation, and family life—all building themselves separately and yet together and moving forward in terms of their great common values of freedom and democracy; all this is an achievement of high order. In contrast to this the shortcomings of his writings seem small and one cannot be surprised that his work was well received and that it was and is widely influential.

To cite other examples of the methods of different observers, Major William Jackson was the official secretary of the Federal Convention of 1787, but his minutes were little more than brief, disorderly notes. James Madison was an unofficial reporter, but he was an intelligent and careful eye witness. The conditions were therefore almost ideal for observation, note-taking, and transcription of his complete notes, with the result that posterity has depended on Madison's reporting of the Convention. Francis Parkman, in writing the narrative of the Anglo-French conflict for control of North America, during his vacations went on long walks through the woods to trace the battle lines and took trips to the West to gather information concerning the Indians. Because of the fallibility of memory, an entry in a careful diary or similar source by a reputable person probably is more accurate than recollection. John Quincy Adams in 1844 based on his notable diary the assertion that Andrew Jackson, a quarter of a century earlier, had approved relinquishment of the claim of the United States to Texas, whereas Jackson's denial was based only on memory.

Bias and Prejudice

A competent observer may know the truth, but for reasons of bias or prejudice may report the evidence only in part or in distorted form. The tests of truthfulness and honesty include evaluation of the observer's characteristics and statements in relation to personal or vested interest, race, nation, party, region, sect, social level, economic group, profession,

[36] Quoted from *ibid.*, p. 123-26.

conventional formulas rather than true sentiments, vanity or boasting, attempt to please some individual or group, exaggerations, and embellishments.

An example[37] of bias may be found in the writing of an author opposed to current tendencies in American higher education, especially at the graduate level. Flexner criticized the theses and dissertations accepted at certain institutions, confining himself to mention of the titles, without attempting to analyze the content of a sampling of such graduate studies. Flexner made certain comparisons with the dissertations completed in Germany, and apparently was still under the impression that German universities are superior institutions where trivial subjects are never accepted as doctoral dissertations and where these graduate investigations are models of scientific writing. Available evidence has indicated that many German dissertations reveal immature thinking, a superficial grasp of the problem, amateurish methods of research, and other inadequacies. Flexner's approach discloses his bias in favor of German higher education and his lack of impartiality in analyzing American higher education.

As an example of the influence of family loyalty, readers of the *Education* will recall that Henry Adams' treatment of his distinguished ancestors is both favorable and respectful.

To be sure the ironic questions are present in these earlier chapters of the *Education* but the edges are blunted by his willingness to admit the greatness of his grandfather—overpowering as it was to a mere boy. To Adams, the family heritage was symbolized in the "law of Resistance; of Truth, of Duty, and of Freedom" and, if these represented an eighteenth-century system of order no longer applicable to the nineteenth and twentieth centuries, they had made for a distinguished family tradition of political responsibility. Evidence for this respect and regard for his family can be abundantly confirmed in the letters of Henry Adams. Family loyalty, whether Adams was willing to admit it or not, was a personal solution that he always clung to in the face of his "problem" of finding direction through space, of running order through chaos.

But family tradition was more than a mere legend for Adams; it was an intellectual experience as well. From his boyhood, he had lived under the spell of his grandfather's and great-grandfather's writings. As a boy, he had helped his father with the proofs of an edition of the work of John Adams. By constant use of the magnificent Adams family library he became familiar with the papers of John Quincy Adams. At one time, when trying to find some occupation for himself after graduation from Harvard, he toyed with the idea of editing the works of J. Q. Adams, but he abandoned the project

[37] William W. Brickman, *op. cit.*, p. 177-78.
Abraham Flexner, *Universities:* American, English, German. New York: Oxford University Press, 1930. ix+381 p.

because he thought "it is not in me to do them justice"—a judgment which betrays respect and reverence as well as his own insecurity and indecision at the time. Nevertheless, it is important to remember that Henry Adams' first significant publication in the field of American history, *Documents Relating to New England Federalism, 1800-1815,* was prepared in order to defend the reputation of his grandfather and to provide documentary evidence for the high motives of John Quincy Adams in his desertion of the Federalist party in 1807. The publication of the *Documents* in 1877 began the painstaking spadework of investigation that was to result in the publication of the nine-volume *History* more than a decade later.[38]

A number of specific historical works may be cited as illustrations of the effect of bias, even in the writing and interpretation of able historians:

Livy, in his patriotic ardor, does less than justice to the enemies of Rome. Matthew Paris, a leading medieval chronicler, is influenced by anti-papal prejudice. Macaulay is notoriously unfair to the anti-Whigs. From his ultra-democratic viewpoint, Grote could see no good in the Greek "tyrants." A recent reissue of his *History of Greece,* admittedly a work of value, omits the chapter on the "Tyrants" as a distortion of the facts. Froude's *History of England* is saturated with anti-Catholic feeling. Gardiner's *History of the Commonwealth* has not escaped the imputation of bias in favor of the Cromwellians. Bancroft's exaggerated nationalism often results in one-sided presentation of the facts. Parkman's stirring narratives of the French-English conflict in North America are out of focus as a result of his preoccupation with Anglo-Saxon "superiority." Mommsen's *History of Rome* has its patent prejudices, in regard to Cicero. Motley's *Rise of the Dutch Republic* is unfair to the Spanish actors in the drama. Rhodes' *History of the United States* betrays animus against certain political figures, against Douglas, for instance, while the accuracy of the picture he draws of slavery has been called into question. Osgood's *American Colonies* has been charged with prejudice against the Quakers. Von Holst, in his *Constitutional and Political History of the United States,* is against the South.[39]

Other illustrations of bias or prejudice in historical writing may be summarized briefly. Thomas Carlyle was essentially a moralist, who sometimes was tempted to suppress evidence in favor of artistic effect. Francis Bacon altered both literary and documentary sources, in keeping with his purpose, although his intentions were not deliberately to deceive but to clarify and interpret by including his own opinions. The bias of Thomas Macaulay assumed the form of a great pride in England and a theme of English superiority that appealed to national patriotism. Cotton Mather's superstition is revealed when he says, "Molestations from evil spirits have so abounded in this country, that I question

[38] Quoted from H. Stuart Hughes, *op. cit.,* p. 124-25.
[39] Quoted from Gilbert J. Garraghan, *op. cit.,* p. 50.

whether any one town has been free from sad examples of them."[40]
Brave man though he was, John Smith's vanity and boastfulness led him to
write glowing accounts of his own achievements, picturing himself
always a match for the Indians, except where great odds overcame him.
Parson Weems glorified the name of George Washington by assigning
to a great but quite human character the traits of almost superhuman
nobility. The bias or prejudice of John Quincy Adams, in accusing
Thomas Jefferson of loose morals, of being a free thinker (irreligious
and probably atheistic), of displaying selfishness in trying to gratify
ambition, of duplicity, of treachery to superiors and friends, and of
deliberate falsehood, was occasioned by Adams' faulty memory at the
age of sixty-three, by political differences, and by his New England
attitude toward cards, horse racing, and mere amusement. George Bancroft's bias was in the form of an exaggerated patriotism; he characterized the American Revolution as a crusade of virtuous and disinterested
patriots on behalf of the liberties of civilization, and described the Constitution as the product of a group of unique mental giants, never before
equaled and not to be matched in the future.

Even the great German historian, Leopold von Ranke, was pre-
judiced in his enthusiasm for Luther, the Hohenzollerns, and Prussia,
although he is customarily considered the founder of the objective
school. Ranke said in his first book, when he was not yet thirty years
of age, that he did not presume, as did most historians, to sit in judgment
on the past, and only wished to show "what had really happened."
Although Ranke is representative of the period that instituted the modern
study of history, and sought to be critical, colorless, and new, we do
meet the mind of Ranke, or his mind is revealed, in his works. Ranke
was not successful in achieving his goal—that of repressing the poet, the
patriot, the religious or political partisan—of sustaining no cause, of
banishing himself from his books, and of writing nothing that would
gratify his own feelings or disclose his private convictions. Among
other things, there was the effect of the mystical religious faith that he
drew from his Lutheran family tradition; he experienced not merely
an aesthetic enjoyment of the ever-varying scene, but a view of God's
government as well.[41]

Macaulay's style and method of conducting an argument were those
of the orator who enjoys the clash and thrust of debate. Sometimes in

[40] Michael Kraus, *op. cit.,* p. 35.
[41] Pieter Geyl, *From Ranke to Toynbee:* Five Lectures on Historians and Historiographical Problems. Northampton, Mass.: Smith College Studies in History,
1952. p. 3-10.

the heat of debate, while remaining master of his argumentative powers, Macaulay was inclined to be swept along by antagonism and to lose respect for the personality of his opponent. At times certain characteristics of his mind or temperament seemed to be projected into his style in the form of straight, unhesitating phrasing, of surprising effect, and of sharp, dramatic contrasts. Macaulay "viewed with the eye of the zealot for public virtues and for progress and for the cause of liberty"; he could approve and admire, as well as detest and denounce, but seemed incapable of establishing "disinterested" contact with a human being in historic or even literary personages.[42]

HISTORICAL WRITING: COMPOSITION

The writing of history or historical composition is the work of synthesis that follows the evaluation and criticism of sources, including the mechanical problem of documentation, the logical problem of relative importance and arrangement of topics, and the theoretical or philosophical problem of interpretation. Since documentation is discussed in another chapter of this book, such details need not be repeated here.

Although general principles of organization and presentation of materials in the technical report have been outlined in another chapter, it is appropriate at this time to make specific applications to historiography.[43] Older types of historical writing and history textbooks usually followed a chronological arrangement of materials in the form of an almanac or calendar of dates, facts, events, and names, with the chapters covering a relatively short time span, sometimes marked off by a period of several years or even a few months. A common arrangement was to mark off the chapters in terms of presidential administrations.

A topical or thematic grouping of historical materials has been recommended as a functional organization to meet the criticism that older histories of education and courses in this field were a mass of comparatively unrelated facts, with little consideration of the pertinent social forces and of the activities and problems of schools and professional workers. Good history of education observes the conditions of good storytelling, shows purpose and meaning, and provides background for better

[42] *Ibid.*, p. 28-30.
[43] Herman Ausubel, *op. cit.*, p. 148-88.
Jacques Barzun and Henry F. Graff, *op. cit.*, p. 115-354.
William W. Brickman, *op. cit.*, p. 161-90, 201-15.
Homer C. Hockett, *op. cit.*, p. 143-80, 189-254.
Gilbert J. Garraghan, *op. cit.*, p. 321-49, 381-95.
Allan Nevins, *op. cit.*, p. 355.

understanding of current educational problems. A history of education that adopts a functional basis of organization, in the form of major problems or areas of contemporary education, includes such chapters as: the aim, method, and curriculum of education; elementary, secondary, and higher education; and the political, psychological, and philosophical bases of education.[44] Many historians of today regard overemphasis on facts as a major obstacle to good history and are convinced that facts must be selected for the sake of clarity and conciseness, with the needs of the present serving as an important criterion in the selection or omission of facts. Macaulay regarded facts in isolation as the dross of history.

Philosophies and Schools of Interpretation

History is rewritten whenever discovery of new sources and helpful reinterpretation of old data make it possible to correct the errors and inadequacies of existing history. In applying new social theory or evidence, it is essential to give appropriate emphasis to all causal factors or forces in a synthetic or eclectic treatment of data, rather than to follow narrowly a single school of interpretation that might exclude some part of the evidence. As an example of historical reinterpretation, during the latter part of the past century social and economic conditions began to receive the attention of historians, as compared with earlier preoccupation with political and military affairs. Illustrative general theories or philosophies[45] of historical interpretation may be summarized briefly. These philosophies of history are broader in scope than the specific schools of interpretation, do not lend themselves readily to pragmatic tests of their workability, and have not often touched the larger or more comprehensive works in history.

1. The Greek and Roman historians viewed Fate as controlling human destiny.

2. The Christian philosophy of history was based on the dominant ideas of divine concern for mankind and of changes in history as slowly tending toward the progress and universality of the true religion.

3. According to Voltaire's rationalistic theory, the events of history were attributable not to design but to chance or fortuity.

4. Hegel's docrine was that every epoch in history was inspired and dominated by some specific idea.

[44] John S. Brubacher, *A History of the Problems of Education.* New York: McGraw-Hill Book Co., 1947. 688 p.

[45] Allan Nevins, *op. cit.,* p. 240-50.

Harry E. Barnes, *A History of Historical Writing.* Norman: University of Oklahoma Press, 1937. p. 42-43, 147-206, 330-35.

5. The Darwinian theory of evolution, as applied to history, means that in social institutions, as well as in the animal kingdom, the rule of the survival of the fittest applies and that acquired characteristics of society are passed on to succeeding generations.

6. The Marxian philosophy applied to history is that the mode of production in economic life primarily determines the general character of the social, political, and cultural processes of life, which shift as the economic foundation changes.

7. Since the World War of 1914-18 a rhythm-philosophy explains history as a series of pulsations, the swing and counter-swing of the pendulum, a series of cycles of summer-fall-winter-spring seasons, with the present period representing a very bleak season.

Both the reader and the writer of history are interested more in the special interpretations or schools of history,[46] as listed below, than in the broad philosophies of history. The more limited scope of a specific interpretation of historical evidence permits a pragmatic test of the explanatory concept, whereas it requires many centuries to test such a broad theory as the cycle or evolutionary philosophy of history. It should be recognized that the specific schools of interpretation are not mutually exclusive, but serve supplementary purposes, and that many of our best historical works are eclectic or synthetic in interpretation rather than directly related to any special interpretation or school of thought.

1. The personal, biographical, or "great-man" theory is the best known and has been emphasized most by the conventional historians. It holds that the great personalities of history are the main causative factors in historical development, and that history is collective biography.

2. The spiritual or idealistic interpretation of history is found in the discovery of spiritual forces co-operating with geographic and economic factors to produce truly personal conditions, and in human activities finding expression in social relations for the more complete subjection of physical nature to human welfare.

3. The scientific and technological theory views human progress as directly correlated with the advances in natural science and technology, emphasizing that the prevailing state of scientific knowledge and its technical interpretation will determine the existing modes of economic life and activities.

4. The economic school of historical interpretation contends that the prevailing type of economic institutions and processes in society will, in a large measure, determine the nature of the resulting social institutions and culture.

5. The geographical theory holds that the actions of man cannot be fully understood or adequately described when divorced from their physical setting.

[46] Harry E. Barnes, *op. cit.*, p. 357-60.
Allan Nevins, *op. cit.*, p. 265-71.

6. Sociological interpretation of history draws from sociology (the science of the life and activities of men in groups) a knowledge of both the causes and the results of group life as the basis for a generalized view of the social process and of social causation.

7. The relatively recent synthetic, eclectic, pluralistic, or "collective psychological" theory is considered the most inclusive and most important type of historical interpretation, holding that no single category of causes is sufficient to explain all phases and periods of historical development, and that only the collective psychology of any period is strong enough to dominate the attendant historical development. Therefore, the new history is necessarily eclectic in approach and interpretation in contrast to the older, conventional history which overstresses political causation or holds that historical development is entirely arbitrary.

To cite examples[47] of how certain schools of history interpret historical development, Charles A. Beard rewrote, in terms of economic forces, the history of American colonization, American expansion, the Revolutionary and Civil Wars, and party conflicts, although later he recognized the effects of the heritage, politics, culture, economics, and international filiations of any civilization as interrelated factors in historical causation and interpretation. Ellsworth Huntington developed a geographical theory, stressing the stimulating effect of certain climates, together with rich natural resources and other factors, to explain the rise of great civilizations in such favored countries as the western part of Europe, the British Isles, and eastern North America. If an eclectic or synthetic point of view prevails in historical interpretation, the historian should be familiar with the literature and concepts in many fields of knowledge.

Agatha Christie, in one of her books, *The Moving Finger*, introduces a girl fresh from school and lets her run on about what she thinks of it. "Such a lot of things seem to me such rot. History for instance. Why, it's quite different out of different books!" To which the sensible elderly confidant replies: "That is its real interest."

Let me remind you of this before everything else. History is infinite. It is unfixable. We are trying all the time to reduce past reality to terms of certainty, but all that we can do is to render our own impression of it. No book can reproduce more than a part of that reality, even within the confines of its particular subject; and each book contains something else, which gets

[47] Herman Ausubel, *op. cit.*, 373 p.
Herman Ausubel, J. Bartlet Brebner, and Erling M. Hunt, Editors, *Some Modern Historians of Britain:* Essays in Honor of R. L. Schuyler. New York: Dryden Press, 1952. 385 p.
Louis R. Gottschalk, *op. cit.*, p. 193-250.
Michael Kraus, *op. cit.*, p. 38-376.
Allan Nevins, *op. cit.*, Chapters 1, 2, 9.

mixed up with historical truth in an almost untraceable manner, which does not necessarily turn it into falsehood, but which nevertheless transforms it into something different from the simple truth—I mean the opinion, or the sentiment, or the philosophy of life, of the narrator; or in other words, the personality of the historian.[48]

Hypothesis, Theme, Causation, Perspective[49]

Since an earlier chapter has dealt with the formulation and testing of hypotheses, only a few examples from history will be given at this time. Channing formulated and tested several hypotheses in seeking to determine why the Confederacy collapsed in April, 1865, with unexpected speed and completeness. He asked whether the breakdown was the result of military defeat, dearth of military supplies, starving conditions of the soldiers and people, or disintegration of southern morale and the despair of the people. Channing accepted the last hypothesis, although it is not satisfactory, since it does not tell us why morale collapsed. Multiple causation probably is the correct explanation, and Channing's interpretation would have been stronger and sounder had he assigned to each causal factor its proportionate weight. Carlyle's theory or hypothesis of historical interpretation was that great men are the major causal factors in important events, but he overlooked the effect of challenging times or crises in producing the powerful leader or hero. The hypotheses explaining the fall of the Roman Empire range from that of Gibbon on the refusal of the Roman soldiers to wear armour, to moral corruption, overtaxation, overpopulation, disintegration of the Roman army through staffing with barbarian officers, soil exhaustion, and "climatic pulsations."

Once the hypothesis has been tested satisfactorily against the evidence, it may become a central thesis, unifying theme, or principle of interpretation. Such a central theme may prove helpful in gathering evidence and in interpretation, although we must be on guard against forcing the data into some particular frame of reference. Frederick J. Turner's thesis concerning the effect of the frontier upon American life and character has influenced historical interpretation, as well as literary, social, and political thought, although needed correctives later were applied to his explanatory thesis. Charles A. Beard advanced a thesis of economic determinism, showing in his interpretation of the United States Constitution a direct relationship between the holders of the

[48] Quoted from Pieter Geyl, *op. cit.*, p. 3.
[49] Gilbert J. Garraghan, *op. cit.*, p. 350-67.
Louis R. Gottschalk, *op. cit.*, p. 209-50.
Allan Nevins, *op. cit.*, p. 214-36, 271-75, 352-53.

government debt and a strong central government that would pay it off, although later he recognized the influence of other causal factors.

Toynbee cites the history of the settlement of the North American continent to support his central thesis, namely, that it is difficulties or obstacles which lead to the flowering out of a civilization. He has labeled this notion by the striking phrase, Challenge and Response.

Challenge and Response is indeed the central theme of Toynbee's philosophy of history. To him the interest of the study of humanity lies in the indomitable quality of the spirit of man. The significance, the motive forces, the causation—to him it must all be spiritual. The lot of man is cast in a material world, but Toynbee sees his relations with the material as a struggle. Man's *significant* relations at least—his emergence into civilization, his adventures and his triumphs as a civilized being, everything that distinguishes him from the animals and from the barbarians and makes him the protagonist of what we call History—all this can never be *deduced from* the material world; it can be related to the material world only in terms of opposition, and of victory.

A striking idea! And often an illuminating one. But the point that I want to make is that Toynbee has driven it to extremes, and that the system with which he has tried to bolster it up obscures the process of history as much as the idea can occasionally illumine it.[50]

To comment further on the historical conception of a trend or central theme, it is regarded by historians as one of the most characteristic and basic of all the concepts of history.

The discernment of temporal patterns of change is what the historian regards as his main business. He observes and describes unique events, and at the same time he endeavors to establish their relation to one another. If we took from him such ideas as growth and decay, change and persistence, increase and decrease, rise and fall, he would be left with little to say.

There is no question but that the concept of a trend is highly abstract. One must conceptualize concrete actuality in order to perceive a trend. It is not the kind of thing that can be kicked or pointed at. When one speaks of a trend in temperature, there is nothing one can hold in one's hand and examine. Instead one must first create some measuring device, then read it at particular moments in time, and finally make a comparison of a number of readings over a given period of time. In the field of physics the meaning of a trend can be defined only in terms of some such set of operations.

In history, however, the operations are often forgotten, and trends seem to take on a separate existence of their own above and beyond the particular events which go to make them up. Thus, students in history courses are encouraged to recognize trends. They are sometimes told that factual materials are relatively unimportant; instead of memorizing these, they are instructed to concentrate on the larger currents in human affairs and tendencies of

[50] Quoted from Pieter Geyl, *op. cit.*, p. 68-69.

society. Trends are spoken of as "inevitable" and "irresistible." They sweep individuals along willy-nilly, and determine the course of their lives. Personalities like Napoleon's or Hitler's are said to be shaped by the trends of the age. Ultimately one approaches the conclusion (acceptable to Plato, but absurd to modern science) that the abstract determines the concrete, that the Form or the Idea is the only reality.

Few historians consciously subscribe to this conclusion. If you do not accept it (if, that is, you have some doubt that a trend belongs to a higher order of existence, a kind of supernature with an independent being of its own), then the meaning of a trend is to be determined by what a historian does. And he may do one of two things. Either he performs the sorts of operations that a physicist does in dealing with temperature trends, or he is making a literary, metaphorical, comparison.[51]

The earlier historians frequently associated trivial causes or supernatural explanations with major events and important social changes. It was said that the cackling of geese and the bite of an asp enabled Rome to develop unhindered her great power and influence. The older historians believed that the cause of the Trojan War was a quarrel over a beautiful woman, Helen of Troy. It has been said that, after the Norsemen had settled somewhere near the New England coast in 1003-4, the bellowing of a bull frightened the natives, causing them to give battle. The Norsemen returned to their own country, and therefore the bellowing of a Norse bull delayed the settlement of America for 500 years.

A more recent example of "trivial causation" is interesting, with no attempt made to establish its validity.

Trivial circumstances sometimes change the fate of nations, and so it would seem they do of cities also. North Bend might have become the great commercial metropolis of the Miami country, instead of Cincinnati, but for an affair of the heart, if we may credit the tradition preserved by Judge Burnet in his *Notes on the North-western Territory*. Ensign Francis Luce had been detailed, with a small force, for the protection of the North Bend settlement, and to locate a suitable site for a block-house. While the ensign was keenly but very leisurely on the lookout for a proper location, he made a discovery far more interesting to him—a beautiful black-eyed lady, the wife of one of the settlers. Luce became infatuated with her charms, and her husband, seeing the danger to which he was exposed if he remained where he was, resolved at once to remove to Cincinnati.

The gallant ensign was equal to the unexpected emergency, for he now began to discover what he had not discovered before, that North Bend was not, after all, so desirable a locality for the contemplated block-house as Cincinnati, and forthwith apprised Judge Symmes' of these views, who strenuously opposed the movement. But the judge's arguments were not so effective as the sparkling eyes of the fair dulcinea then at Cincinnati. And so

[51] Quoted from H. Stuart Hughes, *op. cit.*, p. 314-17.

Luce and his military force were transplanted in double-quick time to Cincinnati; and where the troops were the settlers congregated for their protection and safety. And so, the Queen City of the West followed the fortunes of this unnamed forest queen, who so completely beguiled the impressible ensign.

In this case there was no ten years' war, as in the case of the beautiful Spartan dame, which ended in the destruction of Troy; but, by Luce's infatuation and removal, North Bend was as much fated as though the combined Indians of the North-west had blotted it out of existence. Soon after this portentous removal, Luce, on May 1, 1790, resigned from the army—whether on account of his fair charmer, history fails to tell us. This romantic story has been doubted by some, but Judge Burnet was an early settler of Cincinnati, and had good opportunities to get at the facts; and when I met the judge, fully forty years ago, he seemed not the man likely to indulge in romancing. That Gen. Harmar, in forwarding Luce's resignation to the War Office, seemed particularly anxious that it should be accepted, would seem to imply that, for this intrigue, or some other cause, the general was desirous of ridding the service of him.[52]

On the other hand, it is argued by some scholars that important, crucial events in history are often determined by chance, by unpredictable events that may seem trivial in themselves.

To those who are interested in the psychology of the history of science, culture, and thought, Handlin's *Chance or Destiny* provides the occasion to reread the similar discussion in Tolstoy's *War and Peace* (1869), for the two discussions, if you take the trouble to read them both on the same afternoon, are surprisingly alike. It is true that Tolstoy makes more of the inscrutable forces of History that enslave uncomprehending kings and that promote the trivial royal intentions into the service of History's indiscernible designs, but Handlin too recognizes the existence of great trends like industrialization and democratization, trends that advance themselves—perhaps by some kind of positive feedback—and are insusceptible to influence by the individual person.

The main undertaking of Handlin's book is to show that important crucial events in history are often determined by chance, by unpredictable events that are apt to seem trivial in themselves. Cornwallis surrendered because his attempt to withdraw his army from Yorktown was ruined by a sudden storm that wrecked many of his boats and left his army divided across the York River. But for the storm, would the U. S. A. now be a Dominion? Handlin does not say that, yet the course of American history in 1781 would have been greatly changed but for the storm. The Revolution could have failed. Not all revolutions succeed. . . .

Lieutenant Commander Schweiger, commanding the German submarine U-20, was returning to his home port on May 7, 1915, discouraged at his lack of successes, when he saw through his periscope a large vessel in British waters which the Germans had proscribed. He let go a torpedo, and, as the

[52] Samuel S. Forman, *Narrative of a Journey Down the Ohio and Mississippi in 1789-90*. Cincinnati: Robert Clarke and Co., 1888. p. 32-33.

vessel went down stern-first, he could just make out the name on the bow: *Lusitania.* And so—is or isn't *so* the right word here?—the United States came into that war.

The United States Navy thought Pearl Harbor impregnable. They were prepared for attack anywhere else in the Pacific. And the Japanese, following out Admiral Tojo's perilous plan on December 7, 1941, were anything but confident. Their slim chance succeeded and the United States then was in another war. What if the majority opinion about Pearl Harbor's being impregnable, an opinion widely held in Japan too, had been right? . . .

You can find chance operating in scientific discovery and in the happy insight that leads to an important discovery, and one argument for basic research is founded on the unpredictability of the useful applications of fundamental laws; nevertheless, given motivation, there is a rational orderedness to scientific discovery that introduces into the historical process a predictability that is hindered or sped up by chance events but is not ordinarily completely stalled. This is why we speak of the Zeitgeist when we seek a concept to explain synchronous independent identical discoveries, inventions, and insights. History lords it over the scientist because history—Tolstoy's History, Handlin's Destiny—is the culture, the total accumulation of fact and value available to the individual scholar. By them is he influenced without his knowing how or how much. Because of them his contribution becomes a "next step," and often it is in spite of them that the "next step" is the unpredictable one of creative originality. So is originality necessarily chance? It can be. Remember Fermat's theorem that no one else ever proved, the theorem with the lost proof? But what about an originality's happening twice in the same year? What about Alfred Russell Wallace's and Charles Darwin's formulating the theory of natural selection independently by 1858? Adams' and Leverrier's independent discoveries of the planet Neptune in 1845? Gray's and Bell's invention of the telephone in 1876? . . .

It is a good thing to have the case for the operation of chance in history, for unpredictability, made so clearly and irrefutably. The notion of a Zeitgeist as imperative Destiny ought to be scotched. Progress is what happens, usually what has happened, as Handlin says; its direction is never certain or clear until it has entered the past. But after—with Handlin's help—you have got rid of superstitions about the inevitability of history and have fully accepted the fact that unpredictable chance may in important ways intervene in the causal nexus, there still remain the various problems as to how the total mass of available fact and value, too complex ever to be specified, influences and determines human conduct and thought, discovery and originality, governed, it seems at times, by some positive feedback that makes their course appear purposive because it is consistent and not wholly unpredictable.[53]

Sound historical perspective in using evidence and in interpretation enables us to evaluate events and personages, distant in time or space, in

[53] Quoted from review by E. G. Boring, *Contemporary Psychology* 2: 234-35; September 1957, of Oscar Handlin, *Chance or Destiny:* Turning Points in American History. Boston: Little, Brown & Co., 1955. 220 p.

terms of the contemporaneous standards and conditions then prevailing rather than in comparison with our present-day time and culture. The cruelties of the Inquisition, for example, when compared with the practices of the Middle Ages, are believed milder than the provisions of the contemporaneous civil law, although such excesses seem inhuman in the perspective of twentieth century standards. Accurate evaluation and interpretation of the personal hygiene of a people, community, or individual of a century ago must be done in relation to the general absence of central plumbing and heating at that time. Children in the elementary school gradually gain space and time perspective through early experience with home geography and with relatively recent historical materials of the home community.

Whitehead has commented on the importance of historical perspective in understanding the contributions of philosophers:[54]

The few first-rate philosophic minds need to be understood in relation to the times in which they lived and thought, and this is precisely what is not done. A philosopher of imposing stature doesn't think in a vacuum. Even his most abstract ideas are, to some extent, conditioned by what is or is not known in the time when he lives. What are the social habits around him, what are the emotional responses, what do people consider important, what are the leading ideas in religion and statesmanship?

Whitehead has been critical of historians who lack historical perspective:[55]

The more history I read, the less I think of historians. Most of them strike me as men who presume to write authoritatively about events which they are not qualified to understand. Or else they accept the official documents of an epoch at their full value, omitting to reflect that its real significance lay in the emotional atmosphere which activated its people and the general ideas under whose sway they lived. I make two exceptions: Gibbon is one and the other is Thucydides. Gibbon had had some practical experience of managing men in that regiment of his, the Hampshire Volunteers; he had had experience in politics; he had known an interesting set of literary men in London; and then just at the right moment, he emigrated to Geneva where he came into contact with the point of view of traveled and cultivated people on the Continent. These, with his other qualifications, gave him an equipment for the writing of history which is unique among modern historians. As for the ancient one, Thucydides was a general who had been a part of the life and times which he depicts.

[54] Quoted from *Dialogues of Alfred North Whitehead*, *op. cit.*, p. 186.
[55] Quoted from *ibid.*, p. 225.

Mastery of Materials, Synthesis, Style

Although the writing of the technical report is treated at some length in another chapter, certain principles[56] of presentation and literary or style aspects of historical writing may be summarized briefly at this time. Effective historical writing shows evidence of scholarship and mastery of materials. Thackeray said of Macaulay that he read twenty books to write a sentence and traveled a hundred miles to produce a line of description. Mastery of sources is always a challenge and frequently has been a burden to able historians. Livy worked with such large masses of data that he was sometimes overwhelmed and not able to synthesize or organize his materials effectively, with consequent contradictions and chronological errors. Leopold von Ranke had great respect for facts and accuracy, and found genuine history more attractive and interesting than romantic fiction, which explains in part the drive that kept him actively at work until the age of ninety-one. Failure to digest and master materials may be due to a false vanity that seeks to impress by including discarded materials and long quotations, a timidity that causes the inclusion of unnecessary data as a protection against possible attack, and lack of literary judgment, which causes some authors to believe that a patchwork of quotations and crude summaries is satisfactory history in contrast to an integrated narrative of events. With the materials carefully digested and classified in a good note system, the working outline emerges as a guide to a chronological or topical arrangement of evidence, or possibly a combination of the two.

Good history applies the principle of progression or moves forward with the story, frequently presenting an explanatory thesis or principle of synthesis as a theory of causation, as discussed earlier in this chapter. The major elements in historical writing should stand out in bold relief, as do the main parts in other technical reports. This means that some data usually must be discarded to attain condensation and to prevent minor details from obscuring the major elements of the narrative. William Douglass, a physician, in his closing chapter on the history of Virginia included a discussion of smallpox; in writing up other colonies also, he sometimes digressed to discuss problems of medicine. In the writing and

---

[56] Gilbert J. Garraghan, *op. cit.*, p. 396-407.
Michael Kraus, *op. cit.*, p. 147-49.
Allan Nevins, *op. cit.*, Chapter 13.
Chauncey Sanders, *op. cit.*, p. 125-41.
James W. Thompson and Bernard J. Holm, *op. cit.*, Vol. 1, p. 53, 76-77, 83, 120, 539-40, 613, 615, 623; Vol. 2, p. 71, 170, 253, 299, 306-7, 492-93, 633.

editing of biography it is a major problem to deal judiciously with sensational stories about the private life of the subject. Many of these stories are not true, and others are not major elements in the historical narrative; for example, the quite human foibles of George Washington should not be permitted to obscure his greatness of character.

There is every reason for history to possess literary excellence and effective style,[57] although the historian will not fill in missing details through exercise of his imagination, merely for the sake of completeness and a connected story. Good history can be written simply and clearly, without emotional dramatization or exaggerated rhetoric. Modern historians interested in the practical uses of history have emphasized the desirability of effective literary style as a means of commanding the attention of the layman and general reader. In spite of limitations in the work of the earlier historians, many could express their thoughts with simplicity and power, as quoted below:

Thucydides: "The whole earth is the sepulchre of famous men."

Byron's description of Livy's writing: "Livy's pictured page."

Tacitus: "No hatred is so bitter as that of near relations." "The more corrupt the state, the more numerous the laws."

Augustus: "I found Rome of clay; I leave it to you of marble."

Bancroft, in speaking of the failure of Raleigh to plant a colony: "If America had no English town, it soon had English graves."

On the other hand, Bancroft's rhetoric is extreme in describing the effect of the battles of Lexington and Concord: "With one impulse, the colonies sprung to arms; with one spirit, they pledged themselves to each other 'to be ready for the extreme event.' With one heart, the continent cried: 'Liberty or Death.' "

Hildreth did not often indulge himself in the flowery style in which he described Hamilton, Washington, and Jay: "We have a trio not to be matched, in fact, not to be approached in our history, if indeed, in any other. Of earth-born Titans, as terrible as great, now angels, and now toads

[57] Herman Ausubel, *op. cit.*, p. 120-47.
Jacques Barzun and Henry F. Graff, *op. cit.*, p. 229-354.
Louis R. Gottschalk, *op. cit.*, p. 13-19, 181-90.
Homer C. Hockett, *op. cit.*, p. 164-73.
W. T. Hutchinson and Others, *Marcus W. Jernegan Essays in American Historiography*. Chicago: The University of Chicago Press, 1937. p. 21, 35-36, 342, 352-54, 393-94.
Michael Kraus, *op. cit.*, p. 118.
James W. Thompson and Bernard J. Holm, *op. cit.*, Vol. 1, p. 25-26, 32-33, 70-71, 76-77, 86-88, 118; Vol. 2, p. 220-22.

and serpents, there are everywhere enough. Of the serene and benign sons of the celestial gods, how few at any time have walked the earth!"

CONCLUDING STATEMENT

Viewed as research, history is an integrated narrative of past events, written in the spirit of critical inquiry. History differs in method from the natural sciences, since it is not a discipline of direct observation or experimentation, but uses reports of observation that cannot be repeated. The earlier simple categories of sources (including documents and remains or relics) have become more complex and probably will continue to expand in the future. The historian determines the authenticity and meaning of sources through the processes of external and internal criticism. Historical composition or synthesis includes the mechanical problem of documentation, the logical problem of relative importance and arrangement of topics, and the theoretical or philosophical problem of interpretation. Especially during the second quarter of the twentieth century and later, historical studies have made important contributions to education, psychology, and the related social disciplines.

SELECTED REFERENCES

ADAMS, James T., and COLEMAN, R. V., Editors. *Dictionary of American History*. New York: Charles Scribner's Sons, 1940. 5 vols. and index.

AUSUBEL, Herman. *Historians and Their Craft:* A Study of the Presidential Addresses of the American Historical Association, 1884-1945. New York: Columbia University Press, 1950. 373 p.

AUSUBEL, Herman, BREBNER, J. Bartlet, and HUNT, Erling M., Editors. *Some Modern Historians of Britain:* Essays in Honor of R. L. Schuyler. New York: Dryden Press, 1952. 385 p.

BARNES, Harry E. *Historical Sociology:* Its Origins and Development. New York: Philosophical Library, 1948. x+186 p.

BARNES, Harry E. *A History of Historical Writing*. Norman: University of Oklahoma Press, 1937. xiii+434 p.

BARNES, Harry E. *An Introduction to the History of Sociology*. Chicago: The University of Chicago Press, 1948. xvi+960 p.

BARNES, Harry E., and BECKER, Howard. *Social Thought from Lore to Science*. Vols. I and II. Revised Edition. Washington: Harren Press, 1952. 790+cx p.; viii+1178+cxxxv p.

BARRACLOUGH, Geoffrey. *History in a Changing World*. Norman: University of Oklahoma Press, 1956. viii+246 p.

BELLOT, H. Hale. *American History and American Historians*. Norman: University of Oklahoma Press, 1952. x+336 p.

BENSON, Lee. "Research Problems in American Political Historiography," in *Common Frontiers of the Social Sciences*. Edited by Mirra Komarovsky. Glencoe, Ill.: Free Press, 1957. p. 113-83.

BLOCH, M. L. B. *Historian's Craft*. New York: Alfred A. Knopf, 1953. 197 p.

BOCK, Kenneth E. *The Acceptance of Histories:* Toward a Perspective for Social Science. Berkeley: University of California Press, 1956. 132 p.

BOGARDUS, Emory S. *The Development of Social Thought*. Third Edition. New York: Longmans, Green and Co., 1955. x+660 p.

BORING, E. G. *A History of Experimental Psychology*. Second Edition. New York: Appleton-Century-Crofts, 1950. xxi+777 p.

BRADFORD, S. C. *Documentation*. Washington: Public Affairs Press, 1948. 146 p.

BRAIDWOOD, Robert J. "Near Eastern Prehistory." *Science* 127: 1419-30; June 20, 1958. (The swing from food-collecting cultures to village-farming communities is still imperfectly understood.)

BRICKMAN, William W. *Guide to Research in Educational History*. New York: New York University Bookstore, 1949. ix+220 p.

BROWN, Truesdell S. "Herodotus and His Profession." *American Historical Review* 59: 829-43; July 1954.

BRUBACHER, John S. *A History of the Problems of Education*. New York: McGraw-Hill Book Co., 1947. 688 p.

BUTTERFIELD, Herbert. *Man on His Past:* The Study of the History of Historical Scholarship. New York: Cambridge University Press, 1955. xvii+238 p.

CHALLENER, Richard D., and LEE, Maurice, Jr. "History and the Social Sciences: The Problem of Communications." *American Historical Review* 61: 331-38; January 1956.

COHEN, Robert S. "Alternative Interpretations of the History of Science." *Scientific Monthly* 80: 111-16; February 1955.

CURTI, Merle. "Intellectuals and Other People." *American Historical Review* 60: 259-82; January 1955.

CURTI, Merle, Editor. *American Scholarship in the Twentieth Century*. Library of Congress Series in American Civilization. Cambridge: Harvard University Press, 1953. vii+252 p.

CURTI, Merle, Editor. *Theory and Practice in Historical Study:* A Report of the Committee on Historiography. Social Science Research Council Bulletin No. 54. New York: The Council, 1946. xi+177 p.

DAWSON, Christopher. *The Dynamics of World History*. Edited by John J. Mulloy. New York: Sheed and Ward, 1956. xiv+489 p.

DENNIS, Wayne, Editor. *Readings in the History of Psychology*. New York: Appleton-Century-Crofts, 1948. 598 p.

DESTLER, Chester M. "Some Observations on Contemporary Historical Theory." *American Historical Review* 55: 503-29; April 1950.

DOW, E. W. *Principles of a Note-System for Historical Studies*. New York: Century Co., 1924. vi+124 p.

DUNLAP, Knight. "The Historical Method in Psychology." *Journal of General Psychology* 24: 49-62; January 1941.

DUTCHER, G. M., ALLISON, W. H., FAY, S. B., SHEARER, A. H., and SHIPMAN, H.

R., Editors. *A Guide to Historical Literature.* New York: The Macmillan Co., 1931. xxx+1222 p. Reprinted 1949; new edition scheduled.

EDWARDS, Newton. *The Courts and the Public Schools.* Revised Edition. Chicago: The University of Chicago Press, 1955. 622 p.

FESTINGER, Leon, and KATZ, Daniel, Editors. *Research Methods in the Behavioral Sciences.* New York: Dryden Press, 1953. p. 300-326.

FLUGEL, J. C. *A Hundred Years of Psychology.* Second Edition. London: Gerald Duckworth and Co., 1951. 424 p.

FULLER, B. A. G. *A History of Philosophy.* Third Edition. Revised by Sterling M. McMurrin. New York: Henry Holt and Co., 1955. 618 p.

GARBER, Lee O. *The Yearbook of School Law 1957.* Danville, Ill.: The Interstate, 1957. 160 p.

GARRAGHAN, Gilbert J. *A Guide to Historical Method.* Edited by Jean Delanglez. New York: Fordham University Press, 1946. xv+482+30 p.

GARRATY, John A. *The Nature of Biography.* New York: Alfred A. Knopf, 1957. xi+289+xii p.

GEE, Wilson P. *Social Science Research Methods.* New York: Appleton-Century-Crofts, 1950. p. 280-99.

GEYL, Pieter. *Debates with Historians.* The Hague: Martinus Nijhoff, 1955. vii+241 p.

GEYL, Pieter. *From Ranke to Toynbee:* Five Lectures on Historians and Historiographical Problems. Northampton, Mass.: Smith College Studies in History, 1952. 80 p.

GEYL, Pieter. *Use and Abuse of History.* New Haven: Yale University Press, 1955. vi+97 p.

GOOD, Carter V. "Bibliographic Sources and Techniques," *Encyclopedia of Educational Research.* Third Edition. New York: The Macmillan Co. Scheduled for 1960.

GOOD, Carter V. "Library Resources and Documentary Research," in "Methods of Research and Appraisal in Education." *Review of Educational Research* 18: 373-81; December 1948; 21: 329-36; December 1951.

GOTTSCHALK, Louis R. "A Professor of History in a Quandary." *American Historical Review* 59: 273-86; January 1954.

GOTTSCHALK, Louis R. *Understanding History:* A Primer of Historical Method. New York: Alfred A. Knopf, 1950. 290 p.

GOTTSCHALK, Louis R., KLUCKHOHN, Clyde, and ANGELL, Robert. *The Use of Personal Documents in History, Anthropology, and Sociology.* Social Science Research Council Bulletin No. 53. New York: The Council, 1945. xiv+243 p.

HALPERN, Ben. "History, Sociology, and Contemporary Area Studies." *American Journal of Sociology* 63: 1-10; July 1957.

HANDLIN, Oscar, Compiler. *Harvard Guide to American History.* Cambridge: Harvard University Press, 1954. xxiv+689 p.

HARRIS, Chester W., Editor. *Encyclopedia of Educational Research.* Third Edition. New York: The Macmillan Co. Scheduled for 1960.

HARTE, Thomas J. "The Use of Parish Records in Social Research." *American Catholic Sociological Review* 19: 113-23; June 1958.

HILLWAY, Tyrus. *Introduction to Research.* Boston: Houghton Mifflin Co., 1956. p. 129-52.

HITSCHMANN, Edward. *Great Men:* Psychoanalytic Studies. New York: International Universities Press, 1956. xiii+278 p.

HOCKETT, Homer C. *The Critical Method in Historical Research and Writing.* New York: The Macmillan Co., 1955. 368 p.

HUGHES, H. Stuart, Editor. *Teachers of History:* Essays in Honor of Laurence Bradford Packard. Ithaca, N. Y.: Cornell University Press for Amherst College, 1954. vi+372 p.

HUTCHINSON, W. T., and Others. *Marcus W. Jernegan Essays in American Historiography.* Chicago: The University of Chicago Press, 1937. x+417 p.

IHDE, Aaron J. "Are There Rules for Writing History of Chemistry?" *Scientific Monthly* 81: 183-86; October 1955.

International Bibliography of Historical Sciences, 1926—. New York: H. W. Wilson Co., 1930—. Published annually.

JASPERS, Karl. *Origin and Goal of History.* London: Routledge and Kegan Paul, 1953. 294 p.

JOHNSON, Allen, and MALONE, Dumas, Editors. *Dictionary of American Biography.* New York: Charles Scribner's Sons, 1928-37. 20 vols. and index, plus supplements. Also see *Biography Index:* A Cumulative Index to Biographical Material in Books and Magazines. New York: H. W. Wilson Co., 1946—.

JORDAN, Pascual. *Science and the Course of History.* Translated by Ralph Manheim. New Haven: Yale University Press, 1955. x+139 p.

KOHN, Hans. "A Historian's Creed for Our Time." *American Association of University Professors Bulletin* 39: 608-15; Winter 1953-54.

KRAUS, Michael. *The Writing of American History.* Norman: University of Oklahoma Press, 1953. 387 p.

KRIEGER, Leonard. "The Horizons of History." *American Historical Review* 63: 62-74; October 1957.

LANGFELD, Herbert S., and Others, Editors. *A History of Psychology in Autobiography.* Vol. 4. Worcester, Mass.: Clark University Press, 1952. xii+356 p.

LANGSAM, Walter C. "Truth in History." *Bulletin of the Historical and Philosophical Society of Ohio* 16: 95-103; April 1958.

LAZARSFELD, Paul F., STRAYER, Joseph R., and DAVID, Henry. "History and Public Opinion Research: A Debate," in *Common Frontiers of the Social Sciences.* Edited by Mirra Komarovsky. Glencoe, Ill.: Free Press, 1957. p. 242-78.

LEE, Dwight E., and BECK, Robert N. "The Meaning of 'Historicism.'" *American Historical Review* 59: 568-77; April 1954.

LONDON, Ivan D., and POLTORATZKY, Nikolai P. "The Problem of Contemporary Analysis in History and Psychology." *Behavioral Science* 3: 269-77; July 1958.

LOWITH, Karl. *Meaning in History:* The Theological Implications of the Philosophy of History. Chicago: The University of Chicago Press, 1949. ix+257 p.

MADGE, John. *The Tools of Social Science*. New York: Longmans, Green and Co., 1953. p. 80-116.

MALIN, James C. *On the Nature of History*. Ann Arbor, Mich.: Edwards Brothers, 1954. vii+290 p.

MASON, S. F. *Main Currents of Scientific Thought:* A History of the Sciences. New York: Abelard-Schuman, 1954. viii+520 p.

MERTON, Robert K. "Priorities in Scientific Discovery: A Chapter in the Sociology of Science." *American Sociological Review* 22: 635-59; December 1957.

MILLER, Lebern N. "Using Law Case Materials to Teach Ethical Behavior." *Journal of Educational Research* 51: 39-42; September 1957.

MONROE, Walter S., Editor. *Encyclopedia of Educational Research*. Second Edition. New York: The Macmillan Co., 1950. xxvi+1520 p. Third Edition scheduled for 1960.

MONTAGU, M. F. Ashley, Editor. *Toynbee and History:* Critical Essays and Reviews. Boston: Porter Sargent, Extending Horizons Books, 1956. xvi +385 p.

MORISON, Samuel E. "Faith of a Historian." *American Historical Review* 56: 261-75; January 1951.

MORRISON, J. Cayce, and Others. "Twenty-five Years of Educational Research." *Review of Educational Research* 26: 199-344; June 1956.

MULTHAUF, Robert P. "European Science Museums." *Science* 128: 512-19; September 5, 1958. (Problems of displaying famous apparatus.)

MURPHY, Gardner. *An Historical Introduction to Modern Psychology*. Revised Edition. New York: Harcourt, Brace and Co., 1949. xiv+466 p.

NAGEL, Ernest. "Some Issues in the Logic of Historical Aanalysis." *Scientific Monthly* 74: 162-69; March 1952.

National Education Association, Research Division. "The Codification of School Laws." *Research Bulletin* 32: 1-47; February 1954.

NEVINS, Allan. *The Gateway to History*. Boston: D. C. Heath and Co., 1938. vii+412 p.

NICHOLS, R. F. "Postwar Reorientation of Historical Thinking." *American Historical Review* 54: 78-89; October 1948.

ODUM, H. W. *American Sociology:* The Story of Sociology in the United States through 1950. New York: Longmans, Green and Co., 1951. vi+501 p.

ODUM, H. W. "Folk Sociology as a Subject Field for the Historical Study of Total Human Society and the Empirical Study of Group Behavior." *Social Forces* 31: 193-223; March 1953.

PERDEW, Philip W. "Criteria of Research in Educational History." *Journal of Educational Research* 44:217-23; November 1950.

RATNER, Sidney. "Facts and Values in History." *Teachers College Record* 56: 429-34; May 1955.

READ, Conyers. "The Social Responsibilities of the Historian." *American Historical Review* 55: 275-85; January 1950.

REMMLEIN, Madaline K. *The Law of Local Public School Administration*. New York: McGraw-Hill Book Co., 1953. xi+271 p.

REMMLEIN, Madaline K. *School Law.* New York: McGraw-Hill Book Co., 1950. xxi+376 p.

REMMLEIN, Madaline K. "Tools and Procedures in School Law Research." *Growing Points in Educational Research.* Washington: American Educational Research Association, 1949. p. 166-75.

RICHEY, Herman G., and Others. "The Philosophical and Social Framework of Education." *Review of Educational Research* 28: 1-76; February 1958. (Urges preparation of scholarly biographies of important educational figures, and historical studies of the development of higher education and of public education in cities.)

ROBACK, A. A. *History of American Psychology.* New York: Library Publishers, 1952. xiv+426 p.

ROSE, Edward, and FELTON, William. "Experimental Histories of Culture." *American Sociological Review* 20: 383-92; August 1955.

SANDERS, Chauncey. *An Introduction to Research in English Literary History.* New York: The Macmillan Co., 1952. vi+423 p.

SARTON, George. *A Guide to the History of Science.* Waltham, Mass.: Chronica Botanica Co., 1952. xvii+316 p.

SCHEVILL, Ferdinand. *Six Historians.* Chicago: The University of Chicago Press, 1956. xv+200 p.

SCHWEINITZ, Karl De. "Social Values and Social Action—The Intellectual Base as Illustrated in the Study of History." *Social Service Review* 30: 119-31; June 1956.

SEARS, Jesse B., and HENDERSON, Adin D. *Cubberley of Stanford:* And His Contribution to American Education. Stanford, Calif.: Stanford University Press, 1957. xii+301 p.

SELIGMAN, Edwin R. A., and JOHNSON, Alvin, Editors. *Encyclopedia of the Social Sciences.* New York: The Macmillan Co., 1930-34. 15 vols.

SHANNON, David A. "Facts, Dates, and History." *Teachers College Record* 54: 159-64; December 1952.

SHANNON, David A. "The Study of History and the Critical Mind." *Teachers College Record* 56: 74-83; November 1954.

SHERA, J. H. *Historians, Books and Libraries.* Cleveland: Western Reserve University Press, 1953. 126 p.

SHINN, R. L. *Christianity and the Problem of History.* New York: Charles Scribner's Sons, 1953. 302 p.

SHOTWELL, J. T. *The History of History.* Vol. 1. New York: Columbia University Press, 1939. xiv+407 p.

The Social Sciences in Historical Study: A Report of the Committee on Historiography. Bulletin 64. New York: Social Science Research Council, 1954. x+181 p.

SPIELMAN, William C. *Introduction to Sources of American History.* New York: Exposition Press, 1951. 175 p.

STRAUS, William L. "The Great Piltdown Hoax." *Science* 119: 265-69; February 26, 1954.

STRAYER, Joseph R., Editor. *The Interpretation of History.* Princeton: Princeton University Press, 1943. vi+186 p.

SWABEY, Marie Collins. *The Judgment of History*. New York: Philosophical Library, 1954. x+257 p.

THOMPSON, James W., and HOLM, Bernard J. *A History of Historical Writing*. New York: The Macmillan Co., 1942. xvi+676, x+674 p. 2 vols.

THORNDIKE, Lynn. "Whatever Was, Was Right." *American Historical Review* 61: 265-83; January 1956.

THRUPP, Sylvia L. "History and Sociology: New Opportunities for Co-operation." *American Journal of Sociology* 63: 11-16; July 1957.

THRUPP, Sylvia L. "What History and Sociology Can Learn from Each Other." *Sociology and Social Research* 41: 434-38; July-August 1957.

TOYNBEE, Arnold J. *A Study of History*. London: Oxford University Press, 1934-39. Abridgement by D. C. Somervell, 1947. 6 vols.

WALLIN, J. E. Wallace. *The Odyssey of a Psychologist:* Pioneering Experiences in Special Education, Clinical Psychology, and Mental Hygiene with a Comprehensive Bibliography of the Author's Publications. Wilmington, Del.: The Author, 1955. xvii+243 p.

WALTERS, Raymond, Jr. "The James Gallatin Diary: A Fraud?" *American Historical Review* 62: 878-85; July 1957.

WATSON, Robert I. "A Brief History of Clinical Psychology." *Psychological Bulletin* 50: 321-46; September 1953.

WIENER, J. S. *The Piltdown Forgery*. New York: Oxford University Press, 1955. 214 p.

WILLIAMS, William A. "A Note on Charles Austin Beard's Search for a General Theory of Causation." *American Historical Review* 62: 59-80; October 1956.

WOODY, Thomas. "Of History and Its Method." *Journal of Experimental Education* 15: 175-201; March 1947.

YOUNG, Pauline V. *Scientific Social Surveys and Research*. Third Edition. Englewood Cliffs, N.J.: Prentice-Hall, 1956. p. 139-53.

5

Descriptive-Survey Studies

This chapter presents a variety of descriptive-survey studies and tech-niques:[1] investigations emphasizing general description, analysis, or classification; social, community, and school surveys; questionnaire inquiries; interview studies; observational investigations; small-group study or group-behavior analysis; critical-incident technique; action or co-operative research; content analysis of documentary materials; and such survey-appraisal procedures as rating scales, score cards, check lists, and index numbers. By delimitation of scope and purpose this book leaves to the numerous specialized volumes the various types of mental measure-ments and tests of achievement, intelligence, aptitude, and personality, with full recognition that many of these instruments serve data-gathering purposes in descriptive-survey investigations and in experimental, case-clinical, and developmental studies. Under each section the plan of presentation is to identify areas appropriate for descriptive-survey investigation, to characterize the research procedure or data-gathering technique, and to summarize illustrative studies. Many details must re-main for treatment in the voluminous survey literature, where it is common for a book of several hundred pages to be devoted to a single data-gathering technique or procedure. In general the processes of enumeration, measurement, and evaluation are left for the textbooks on quantitative methods that deal with statistical methods, measurement, and appraisal.

Although the theory and practice of sample surveys developed in other fields, education has come to make extensive use of this research approach. The large foundation grants of recent years usually require

---

[1] Carter V. Good and Douglas E. Scates, *Methods of Research:* Educational, Psychological, Sociological. New York: Appleton-Century-Crofts, 1954. p. 255-688.

status studies to determine the present position of education in our culture and thus provide a basis for comparison and future evaluation. The major impetus for status studies, utilizing the techniques of sample surveys, has been the need for vital statistics that can be used for social research and determination of public policy; for example, the evaluation of Salk polio vaccine, the Kinsey reports, and the election straw polls. Status studies may be artificially classified into two divisions according to goals.[2]

One type is represented by the operations of the United States Government agencies in conducting status studies on many national social and economic characteristics for the purpose of collecting and publishing vital statistics, with the results made available to government, industry, labor, and educational groups as aids in policy-making. Other specific examples of application of sample-survey techniques to status studies in education include the work of the United States Bureau of the Census, school enrollment, employment of students, summary of government finances, and school districts in the United States, all representing the collection of vital statistics rather than single studies motivated by specific educational problems.

The evaluation trials of the Salk vaccine constitute a specific goal before experimentation and technically should be classified as controlled experimentation, with difficult and technical problems of sampling. Other examples of sample surveys to explore specific educational issues include a survey of college freshmen and sophomores to assess their perceptions of the instructor, the influence of sociocultural characteristics on educational opportunities in public-school instrumental music for eighth-graders, achievement of objectives of elementary-school science by fifth-grade teachers, impact of social stratification on occupational expectations of twelfth-grade boys, attitudes of public-school teachers in a large city toward school and living conditions, and the effect of exposure to mass media of communication on readiness for desegregation among white males eighteen years of age and older.

CHARACTERISTICS OF DESCRIPTIVE-SURVEY STUDIES

Terminology

The literature and terminology of descriptive-survey investigations include such expressions as descriptive, survey, normative, status, and

---

[2] Rosedith Sitgreaves and Herbert Solomon, "Research Methods: Status Studies and Sample Surveys," in "Methodology of Educational Research." *Review of Educational Research* 27: 460-70; December 1957.

trend. Descriptive studies may include present facts or current conditions concerning the nature of a group of persons, a number of objects, or a class of events, and may involve the procedures of induction, analysis, classification, enumeration, or measurement. The terms *survey* and *status* suggest the gathering of evidence relating to current conditions. The expression "normative" sometimes is applied to descriptive investigations, because the purpose is to determine the normal or typical condition or practice, as in comparing local test results with a city, state, or national norm (central tendency). In certain other disciplines, such as ethics, philosophy, and religion, norm has another meaning (an ideal or desirable goal). For some studies "normative-survey" is an appropriate label, as illustrated by many investigations involving standardized tests. The expression "comparative method" is too limited for our purposes, since comparison is a part of description, in interpreting survey data as well as evidence gathered by other research techniques. For present purposes the more inclusive term *descriptive-survey studies* seems appropriate.

Purposes and Uses

The purposes of descriptive-survey investigations may be:

1. To secure evidence concerning the existing situation or current condition
2. To identify standards or norms with which to compare present conditions, in order to plan the next step
3. To determine how to take the next step (having determined where we are and where we wish to go).

To cite an example, the more analytical school surveys of recent years tell us not only where we are in a particular school system, but also recommend next steps by way of progress and suggest the methods of reaching the goal of an improved instructional program. This view is one answer to critics of the descriptive-survey method who sometimes say that it is not a forward-looking approach to the solution of educational problems. Certainly adequate survey data in the hands of an investigator of insight can be used for forward-looking purposes.

Another criticism of the descriptive-survey method has been that it is superficial and not worthy of recognition as a research approach to important problems. It should be pointed out that descriptive studies provide essential knowledge about the nature of objects, events, and persons. Descriptive-survey specialists have devised many tools and techniques for gathering evidence, including standard tests and norms, score cards and rating scales, inventories and schedules, and public-opinion polls.

Contributions to Other Types of Research

Descriptive-survey studies have been helpful in contributing to other types of investigation. Survey investigations of present conditions are concerned essentially with history in the making. When survey studies are repeated annually or at other intervals, such cross-section pictures of conditions at different time periods provide the data for historical studies; for example, the annual school census and the United States census make possible historical studies of school enrollment and of the growth of population in the United States. The annual reports of the school superintendent and of the university president furnish material for writing the history of the school system and higher institution.

As in many historical studies, there are occasions in descriptive-survey investigations when it is necessary to rely on verbal data or verbal statements of fact. An example of use of nonquantitative data would be a study of comparative education, involving the educational conditions and practices in another country. A survey of compulsory education in the forty-eight states would require verbal or nonquantitative data concerning the administrative machinery for enforcing the laws, the varying provisions under the state laws, and the different social and educational philosophies underlying the state legislation for compulsory education.

For some types of descriptive-survey studies data are available in the files of state departments of education, regional accrediting organizations, and national professional associations, gathered through annual reports and in other ways. If the investigator has recourse to such sources of data, it is important for his questions and the major divisions of his inquiry to correspond with the report blanks that provide the data for state departments of education, regional groups, and national organizations. Use of documentary sources for historical purposes has been discussed in an earlier chapter. Many of the library guides to the published sources are listed in the chapters on library technique and on the historical method. The basic principles of historical criticism apply in dealing with documents for descriptive-survey purposes.[3]

Genetic or growth studies secure measurements of the individual or group at different stages of development and thus may be considered a series of cross sections of growth or a sequence of survey studies separated

---

[3] Carter V. Good and Douglas E. Scates, *op. cit.*, p. 583-96.

by time intervals. It is true that genetic or developmental studies usually follow an individual or a group in terms of one or only a few aspects of growth, whereas descriptive-survey investigations usually cover a larger number of traits or characteristics of the group.

In group experimentation, the testing usually done at the beginning to determine current status or to provide the evidence for equating groups, as well as the end testing, may be regarded as forms of survey-testing or measurement, but so used as to serve as an important part of the total experimental procedure.

Analysis and Classification

Many descriptive investigations are highly analytical in character and sometimes have been characterized as "analytical studies,"[4] although analysis as a process is present in all types of research. The varieties of analysis in descriptive-survey studies may be illustrated by the buildings of a city school system. The investigator may be interested in a general aspect of the school buildings such as architectural style or in the component parts of the building (classrooms, laboratories, libraries, cafeterias, and other parts of the building). For purposes of an analytical study the interest may be in matters of form, pattern, or organization; for example, the grouping of the classrooms in relation to fire escapes, cafeteria, or library, or even the seating arrangement of the pupils in particular classrooms. Another type of analytical study in the descriptive-survey area concerns itself with the dynamics of the school, as illustrated by pupil-teacher relationships or teacher-principal relationships.

Classification,[5] the recognition of similarities and differences among experiences, is a basic process in all research, including descriptive-survey studies. Grouping or the forming of categories is conducive to economy of thought. Examples of major classification plans or schemes are the Dewey decimal and Library of Congress systems for cataloguing books, the taxonomy or classification system for animals and plants in the biological sciences, and the periodic table of elements in chemistry and physics.

The primary uses of classification are as follows:

1. To provide codified data, as in dividing the data of the United States census or school census according to sex, age, place of residence, nationality, and the like

2. To form useful classes according to kind, as in classifying and reporting

---

[4] *Ibid.*, p. 277-492.
[5] *Ibid.*, p. 493-547.

frequencies for the reasons high-school pupils give for leaving school before graduation

3. To afford logical order and system, as in cataloguing books in the library according to a system

4. To develop the meaning of class concepts, as in examining court decisions to determine the meaning of the category "discretionary powers of school boards"

5. To create cases through delimitation, as in studying parent-child relationships by taking different cultures (probably in different parts of the world) as representing varying categories of parental behavior

6. To standardize observations that describe, as in studying the behavior of mothers during their visits to pediatricians working in clinics

7. To select and categorize scale indicators, as in determining that the manner of a particular pediatrician is positive and reassuring (rather than negative, disturbing, and offensive) by counting the number of instances of detailed behavior classified under these different categories.

Criteria for Survey Research

This introductory discussion has not attempted to answer specifically whether the descriptive-survey method is a superior or an inferior approach to problem-solving. The important consideration is whether a particular technique provides answers to significant questions, which means that the descriptive-survey method is best for certain purposes. Many of the illustrative survey studies in this chapter evidence ingenuity in planning, skill in devising techniques, and insight in interpretation of data, thus providing answers to important questions, as well as helpful illustrations of technique and high standards for research. The challenge is to produce survey studies of high quality, in keeping with the criteria[6] listed below:

1. The research report usually has a distinctive form, with definite attention given to describing the methodology, the sources, the population, the trait being studied, and other appropriate methodological or technical details.

2. Presumably original observations are taken.

3. Each step in the work proceeds with meticulous care and with due consideration for the large plan and purpose of the work. The data are verified and evaluated.

4. The data are resolved, or organized into certain more general terms, and are sometimes related to a single, over-all thesis. Certainly the data will be summarized in some form or other, as systematic as possible. What is done with the data is a definite part of the contribution of the study.

[6] Quoted from *ibid.*, p. 271.

5. The background, sensitivity, and general competence of the investigator, as well as the spirit with which he works, are vital elements. As to whether a study must have more or less than the qualities in this list, probably no definite rule can be stated. These qualities vary in degree; various types of research have their own criteria. One should aim, in doing his own research, not at the minimum requirements of research, but at a fairly full-bodied attack.

Limitations of Survey Studies[7]

Although the survey method is an important tool or instrument which has developed greatly during recent years and is valuable for many purposes, it has certain limitations which restrict its use in gathering information on such a field as consumer behavior and its underlying causes:

1. Information that is not known to the respondents cannot be obtained in surveys; for example, annual increases in the value of life insurance reserves (on policies owned by individual families) and amounts of depreciation on houses or automobiles owned would be needed for the sake of an exact determination of amounts saved by individual families. As a general rule, such information is not available to individual policy holders or owners of homes and automobiles.

2. Information that is not salient to the respondents cannot be obtained in a reliable way; for example, most people have not given much thought to the amount of money spent on food or clothing, or on most individual food and clothing items, over a year. Therefore, annual surveys are not reliable or suitable for determining such amounts of expenditures.

3. A request for information that is considered secret should be avoided, as should questioning that appears to check upon the honesty of the respondent. The success of the interview will be endangered, if questions are asked about income from gambling, or about currency hidden in mattresses or locked in safety deposit boxes, or about tax returns already filed.

4. Information about activities shared by a very small proportion of the population cannot be obtained in a reliable way in cross-section surveys; for example, it has been found that over a period of years less than 3 per cent of the population purchased publicly traded common stock, while about 75 per cent of all families paid life-insurance premiums.

5. Data that can be obtained only with very great sampling error do not constitute proper topics of sample surveys; for example, it is impossible to determine through sample surveys what the highest income in a given year was. It is a matter of mere chance whether a small-sample survey finds one, two, several, or no families with an annual income of more than $100,000.

6. Information obtained from a single survey is less reliable than trend data derived from two or more consecutive surveys made by the same methods.

[7] Lawrence R. Klein, Editor, *Contributions of Survey Methods to Economics.* New York: Columbia University Press, 1954. p. 60-64.

7. Surveys cannot be aimed at obtaining exact quantitative forecasts of things to come; for example, plans to purchase houses or automobiles during the next twelve months.

In survey studies there is real need for co-operation; for some twenty years public-opinion agencies have developed rather reliable techniques for describing the attitudes of people concerning public affairs. Historians should welcome this method of obtaining information, which heretofore was available only indirectly, if at all, but in reality there has been little collaboration between historians and "pollsters." The difficulty or problem appears to be one of significance, in that the pollsters ask questions for the newspaper headlines rather than to gather data of lasting or permanent significance. The result is that the historian in the main disregards public-opinion surveys, and the pollsters work without the broader view of the historian that would lead to more meaningful studies. This separateness of the two fields of research suggests that the historian and the pollster should co-operate to their mutual benefit and to aid the future historian in interpreting our times.[8]

THE SOCIAL SURVEY[9]

In presenting the types and data-gathering techniques of descriptive-survey studies, we could begin with the larger and more complex investigations (such as the social, community, and school surveys) or with the simpler types of studies. We have chosen to present first the more complex types of surveys, which usually employ a variety of research pro-

[8] Paul F. Lazarsfeld, Joseph R. Strayer, and Henry David, "History and Public Opinion Research: A Debate," in *Common Frontiers of the Social Sciences*. Edited by Mirra Komarovsky. Glencoe, Ill.: Free Press, 1957. p. 242-78.

[9] Mark Abrams, *Social Surveys and Social Action*. London: William Heinemann, 1951. 153 p.

Leon Festinger and Daniel Katz, Editors, *Research Methods in the Behavioral Sciences*. New York: Dryden Press, 1953. p. 15-97.

Wilson Gee, *Social Science Research Methods*. New York: Appleton-Century-Crofts, 1950. p. 300-329.

Tyrus Hillway, *Introduction to Research*. Boston: Houghton Mifflin Co., 1956. p. 175-87.

Marie Jahoda and Others, *Research Methods in Social Relations:* With Especial Reference to Prejudice. Part One: Basic Processes. New York: Dryden Press, 1951. p. 47-58.

D. Caradog Jones, *Social Surveys*. London: Hutchinson's University Library, 1949. 232 p.

George Katona, "The Function of Survey Research in Economics," in *Common Frontiers of the Social Sciences*. Edited by Mirra Komarovsky. Glencoe, Ill.: Free Press, 1957. p. 358-75.

John Madge, *The Tools of Social Science*. New York: Longmans, Green and Co., 1953. 332 p.

cedures and instruments (such as questionnaires, interviews, observation, and other techniques).

The social survey is usually a co-operative study of a current social problem, situation, or population within definite geographical limits, ordinarily with some concern for a constructive program of social reform and amelioration.

European Backgrounds

The background of the social-survey movement is found in the European studies of more than a century ago. Frederic Le Play, a French social reformer and economist, used social-survey methods in his monographs on family standards of living, and at the same time combined effectively case-study and statistical procedures.

It was the Revolution of 1848, once more plunging the capital into a bloodbath, that determined Le Play at last to publish the conclusions of his thought as to the true path of peaceable social reform. This initial work took the shape of a folio volume, entitled *Les Ouvriers Européens* and published at the expense of the government in 1855, comprising an introductory essay and detailed case studies of thirty-six families which Le Play had observed in the course of his travels. In the introduction, he set forth the outline of his thought. In brief, he argued that the ultimate unit in the consideration of social problems was not the individual, but the family, and that the key to human happiness was not the freedom of the individual to seek his own pleasure, but the well-being of the family, which alone could afford the individual a complete and secure happiness. The proper method of social reform, he further held, was not a speculative discussion of one or another series of principles dealing with the state and the citizen, but rather the scientific observation of particular families. Accordingly, he specified the procedure for the compilation of case studies, or family monographs, involving an examination of the background of the family, its sources of income, the conditions of its work, its habitation and diet, recreation, and moral and religious convictions and practices. As a means of rendering the observation more precise and objective, he urged a careful inventory of all its capital, including household furnishings and wardrobe, and a budget of its annual expenditures.[10]

The English statistician and reformer, Charles Booth, was interested primarily in the conditions of poverty in the East Side of London. He

---

C. A. Moser, *Survey Methods in Social Investigation.* New York: The Macmillan Co., 1958. Chapters 1-4.

Mildred Parten, *Surveys, Polls, and Samples: Practical Procedures.* New York: Harper & Brothers, 1950. p. 1-23.

Rosedith Sitgreaves and Herbert Solomon, *op. cit.*

Pauline V. Young, *Scientific Social Surveys and Research.* Third Edition. Englewood Cliffs, N. J.: Prentice-Hall, 1956. p. 3-81.

[10] Quoted from H. Stuart Hughes, Editor, *Teachers of History:* Essays in Honor of Laurence Bradford Packard. Ithaca, N. Y.: Cornell University Press, 1954. p. 63-65.

began his seventeen-volume investigation[11] in 1886, in an attempt to help social reformers find remedies for the existing evils. Among the factors affecting life and labor in London, Booth investigated income, hours and conditions of work, housing, standards of living, number of children, size of household in relation to size and type of dwelling, type and frequency of sickness, leisure activities, and club and union membership.

A later survey of London life and labor, published in 9 volumes,[12] 1930-35, was made to discover changes in the socioeconomic life of a new generation of London workers, for comparison with Booth's earlier survey. The second survey describes the habits of laboring people after the advent of the automobile, telephone, wireless, and cinema, which had greatly changed the life and work of the people of London.

Trends in the United States

A social survey[13] in the United States was begun in 1909 by Paul Kellogg and a group of social economists and professional social workers to study the forces that affected the lives of steel workers in Pittsburgh, to discover the underlying factors in the city's growth as they affected the wage earners, to secure an inventory of an urban industrial community, and to determine how far human or social engineering had kept pace with mechanical developments in a steel district. Completion of publication of the Pittsburgh survey in 1914 stimulated many American communities to make social surveys of their own complex and changing problems. The growth of the social-survey movement was so great that by 1928 a published bibliography[14] included a total of 2,775 titles or projects.

During the 1940's and later, relatively few social surveys were undertaken by individual investigators. The increasing interest of social agencies and of the federal and state governments in social problems in local communities is evidenced by the large masses of census data and other government reports on a variety of problems, such as social security, economic conditions, employment and unemployment, wages, income, health, housing, child-welfare services, and crime and delinquency. The complexity of the social survey and the variety of research methods are

[11] Charles Booth, *Life and Labour of the People in London.* London: Macmillan and Co., 1892-1903. 17 vols.

[12] Hubert L. Smith, *The New Survey of London Life and Labour.* London: King and Son, 1930-35. 9 vols.

[13] Paul U. Kellogg, Editor, *The Pittsburgh Survey.* New York: Russell Sage Foundation, 1909-14. 6 vols.

[14] Allen Eaton and Shelby M. Harrison, *A Bibliography of Social Surveys.* New York: Russell Sage Foundation, 1930. xlviii+487 p.

illustrated by a social study of Pittsburgh,[15] which included statistical analyses; ecological studies of Pittsburgh and its satellite districts as "natural" areas; case study of agencies, families, and districts as units; group and personal interviews; and schedules and questionnaires.

THE COMMUNITY SURVEY[16]

Social surveys and community studies are similar in many respects, with no sharp dividing line. The community survey, like many school surveys, is made to provide data for planning future developments, such as an adequate system of sewage disposal or new buildings for the school system, although the recommendations of the community study frequently are broader and more general than those found in the school survey.

Characteristics and Scope

In the literature of social research the term *community* sometimes refers to small and stable communities such as a peasant village, to a large and complex urban area such as a ghetto community, to large cities and

[15] Philip Klein and Others, *A Social Study of Pittsburgh:* Community Problems and Social Services of Allegheny County. New York: Columbia University Press, 1938.

[16] Conrad M. Arensberg, "The Community-Study Method." *American Journal of Sociology* 60: 109-24; September 1954.

Ralph L. Beals, "The Village in an Industrial World." *Scientific Monthly* 77: 65-75; August 1953.

Leon Festinger and Daniel Katz, *op. cit.*, p. 15-97.

Bess Goodykoontz, "Selected Studies Relating to Community Schools," *The Community School.* Edited by Nelson B. Henry. Fifty-second Yearbook of the National Society for the Study of Education, Part 2. Chicago: The University of Chicago Press, 1953. p. 64-82.

Wilbur C. Hallenbeck, *American Urban Communities.* New York: Harper & Brothers, 1951. 617 p.

Otto G. Hoiberg, *Exploring the Small Community.* Lincoln: University of Nebraska Press, 1955. xii+199 p.

Marie Jahoda and Others, *op. cit.*, p. 611-41.

George C. Kyte, "Survey and Analysis of Community Conditions," *The Principal at Work.* Revised Edition. Boston: Ginn and Co., 1952. p. 37-58.

Stuart A. Queen and David B. Carpenter, *The American City.* New York: McGraw-Hill Book Co., 1953. 383 p.

Robert Redfield, *The Little Community:* Viewpoints for the Study of a Human Whole. Chicago: The University of Chicago Press, 1955. 182 p.

Irwin T. Sanders, *Making Good Communities Better:* A Handbook for Civic-minded Men and Women. Lexington: University of Kentucky Press, 1950. 174 p.

H. Clay Tate, *Building a Better Home Town:* A Program of Community Self-Analysis and Self-Help. New York: Harper & Brothers, 1954. xvi+236 p.

William A. Van Til and Others, "Research on Human Relations and Programs of Action." *Review of Educational Research* 23: 285-385; October 1953. Chapters 3, 5, 8 deal with community surveys and programs of action.

Arthur J. Vidich and Joseph Bensman, *Small Town in Mass Society:* Class, Power,

small towns or villages, or to a small, temporary unit such as a trailer camp. The local community or "natural area" is characterized by sociologists as having a territorial area, common interests, common patterns of social and economic relations, a common bond of solidarity from the conditions of its abode, a constellation of social institutions, and some degree of group control.

A survey of community life in urban and rural natural areas usually deals with the historical setting, social influence of physical configuration, social isolation, social contacts, economic centers, demographic characteristics, and population mobility, with an interest in the problems of social disorganization, poverty and dependency, unemployment, child labor, health, and crime and delinquency, as well as the local government and the various social institutions and organizations (economic and industrial, labor, health, religious, social welfare, delinquency control, police and criminal, educational, and recreational).[17]

The numerous studies of community schools, chiefly descriptive in character, are not as broad in scope as community surveys, but do provide answers for a number of significant questions: How can schools learn the community's needs and resources so as to serve it effectively? How have schools and communities worked together to improve the school program and the community? In what ways are community-school programs effective?[18]

Techniques and Examples

Many examples of community surveys may be found in the chapter bibliography, in the illustrations of case studies of communities in a later chapter on case and clinical techniques, and in succeeding paragraphs. It is pertinent at this time to characterize certain manuals or guides for

---

and Religion in a Rural Community. Princeton: Princeton University Press, 1958. xvi+329 p.

Roland L. Warren, *Studying Your Community*. New York: Russell Sage Foundation, 1955. xii+385 p.

S. R. Wayland and Others, *Aids to Community Analysis for the School Administrator*. New York: Teachers College, Columbia University, 1956. 51 p.

Stephen B. Withey, "Survey-Research Methods for the Study of Communities and Community Problems," in "Research on Human Relations and Programs of Action." *Review of Educational Research* 23: 329–36; October 1953.

Coleman Woodbury, Editor, *The Future of Cities and Urban Redevelopment*. Chicago: The University of Chicago Press, 1953. xix+764 p.

Coleman Woodbury, Editor, *Urban Redevelopment*: Problems and Practices. Chicago: The University of Chicago Press, 1953. xvi+525 p.

Pauline V. Young, *op. cit.*, p. 470–506.

[17] Pauline V. Young, *op. cit.*, p. 470–506.

[18] Bess Goodykoontz, *op. cit.*, p. 64–82.

studying the community and to summarize illustrative community surveys drawn chiefly from the disciplines of sociology and anthropology.

Fifteen chapters of *Studying Your Community* are devoted to specific phases of community living, such as housing, education, recreation, religious activities, social insurance and public assistance, aids to family living and child welfare, health, and intergroup relations, with each chapter serving as a guide to a study or survey of that particular aspect and including provocative questions for the survey group to ask itself in order to define and sharpen the focus of the inquiry.

These fifteen chapters are supplemented by five additional ones which deal with the larger, basic issues of survey-making, and with the "how" of community studies. This portion of the book contains some valuable pointers on such questions as the choice of the geographic area to be studied, the use of census data and other reference materials, hints about interviewers and the interviewing process, the use of the survey committee or sponsoring group, designing and compiling questionnaires and schedules, and many others. This section of the book also contains some useful observations on the general background and setting of the modern community, its economic life, its governmental structure, its social and class organizations, its primary and other interrelationships, and its readiness and ability to change.[19]

In another manual or guide, Redfield views the "little community" as an ecological system, social structure, typical biography, kind of person, outlook on life, history, community within communities, combination of opposites, and a whole and its parts, with these themes constituting ways to study the small community, or methods designed to view the object of study as a whole. Redfield illustrates the various approaches with concrete cases drawn from anthropological science, including British and American works, as well as his own adventures in Mexico, in order to understand the premises on which a scientific description of a human whole (in this case the little community) can be adequately based.[20]

EXAMPLE: GREENBELT CO-OPERATIVE COMMUNITY[21]

The author lived in Greenbelt, served on several committees, and became its mayor. His book is dedicated, "To all who confidently struggle toward a more perfect democracy." He describes in detail, as an understanding insider,

[19] Quoted from review by C. William Chilman, *Social Service Review* 29: 432–33; December 1955, of Roland L. Warren, *op. cit.*

[20] Robert Redfield, *op. cit.* Reviewed by Paul Nyberg, *Harvard Educational Review* 25: 196–98; Summer 1955.

[21] Quoted from review by Emory S. Bogardus, *Sociology and Social Research* 41:70; September-October 1956, of George A. Warner, *Greenbelt—The Cooperative Community*: An Experience in Democratic Living. New York: Exposition Press, 1956. 232 p.

the founding of this democratically functioning community. He describes its problems carefully and answers its unsympathetic critics. He traces its growth from its beginnings in 1935-37 as a community for government employees in need of housing to its achievement of an independent community functioning under the auspices of the Greenbelt Veteran Housing Corporation on December 30, 1952. On that date its former tenants (of the government) became homeowners and crossed "the threshold to a new and challenging future of complete self-reliance," a thriving community of 3,000 individuals.

This community was founded to a large extent on the Rochdale Principles of cooperation. It established its businesses on the basis of cooperative principles, "which make capitalists of all their members" and which lead to "the exact antithesis of state socialism." These cooperatives have achieved a remarkable success. The *Cooperator*, the city's newspaper, has made an unusual record. Only the health association has not succeeded, for reasons which are explained. The author thinks that the voluntary health-group plan will come into its own some day when the "people get fed up with our present antiquated method of dispensing medical care," and will see its superiority over federalized or state medicine. He believes that the achievements in cooperative living in Greenbelt are remarkable in view of the strong individualistic backgrounds of its members. Mr. Warner has rendered an important service to all who believe in what independent people working together can accomplish.

EXAMPLE: A FRONTIER COMMUNITY[22]

The book is a well-written story of contemporary ex-Texan and ex-Oklahoman pioneers seeking independence as family farmers. Rural sociologists and community planners will find in it a well-documented case history of what can happen without good planning. The villagers are "atomistic," a polite term for their lack of a strong sense of identification with the community or anyone in it except their own immediate families. Symbolic of the communal self-centeredness is the partially completed gymnasium of ten thousand disintegrating adobe bricks. A Homesteader who desires to leave the community often "up and sells out to a big rancher," with little feeling of loyalty to his fellow townsmen who might be willing to pay the same price. The idea of cooperative ownership of heavy machinery is rejected, although it would be advantageous economically. As former tenants and sharecroppers, being one's own boss is more important than monetary advantages.

People continue to express an optimistic belief in the future, despite increasing evidence that the climate promises only three good farming years in each decade. Rugged individualism motivated them to become pioneers, but it is a shaky basis for attempting to conquer the semi-desert in the face of inadequate rainfall, a marginal climate, and low prices for agricultural products. Their efforts, begun in the 1930's, to build a prosperous "pinto bean capital of the world" seem doomed to failure. Fortunately for them, their strong beliefs in

---

[22] Quoted from review by Joseph W. Eaton, *American Journal of Sociology* 62: 240–41; September 1956, of Evon Z. Vogt, *Modern Homesteaders*: The Life of a Twentieth Century Frontier Community. Cambridge: Belknap Press of Harvard University Press, 1955. xi+232 p.

rugged individualism, mastery over and exploitation of natural environment, and an optimistic faith in future progress help them to ignore possible failure. They stick tenaciously to their marginal Homestead, even if their children do not: only five out of fifty high-school graduates have remained in the village.

Example: A City Suburb[23]

Crestwood Heights is a detailed report of social life in an "upper-middle class" suburb (population circa 17,000) of a city (population circa 676,000 in 1951) "somewhere in central Canada." The study was one outcome of a national mental health project put forward by the Canadian National Committee for Mental Hygiene. It is strictly a case study; it does not relate itself to any specific theoretical framework.

The story of how Crestwood Heights was "chosen," as well as the way many other aspects of the study were decided upon, indicates that the procedure in general was astonishingly flexible. The approach is basically clinical rather than purely scientific in the general use of the latter term. Samples were apparently selected by a rather nebulous technique involving interaction between the researchers and members of the community rather than by a well-defined plan. Reporters were expected to indicate their biases and those of their respondents; it was felt that consensus and generalizations could be reached through a sort of canceling-out of bias. It is a study of the social life of an inadequately defined upper-middle class subcultural social constituency, inadequately defined at least for purposes of replication. The book abounds with general statements, which leads this reader to wish that more of the findings had been stated quantitatively rather than as generalities.

Example: An English Village[24]

Students of rural sociology seeking comparative reference materials from communities around the world will welcome this addition to the growing literature on rural life and culture. The subject of study is a small rural parish (Gosforth) in a remote section of Northwestern England. The first record of Gosforth dates back to prehistoric times and fairly complete records for the last few centuries enable the author to give a historical perspective so frequently lacking in similar studies.

Williams collected his data and information over a three year period, 1950-53. Although his methodology is not described in detail, one learns from reading the volume that field research in the nature of extensive personal interviews was supplemented by much participant observation. In addition, there is evidence of meticulous and exhaustive use of secondary source materials. The style of reporting leans towards the narrative, and this makes for easy and

[23] Quoted from review by Thomas E. Lasswell, *Sociology and Social Research* 41: 68–69; September-October 1956, of John R. Seeley, R. Alexander Sim, and Elizabeth W. Loosley, *Crestwood Heights*: A Study of the Culture of Suburban Life. New York: Basic Books, 1956. xv+505 p.

[24] Quoted from review by Alvin L. Bertrand, *American Sociological Review* 21: 646–47; October 1956, of W. M. Williams, *The Sociology of an English Village*: Gosforth. Glencoe, Ill.: Free Press, 1956. x+246 p.

interesting reading, which will appeal to the lay person as well as to the professional. The many direct quotations from natives give a decided flavor as well as an authenticity to the report.

Williams does not state specific objectives or hypotheses in connection with his study, nor does he attempt an orientation to a theoretical frame of reference. These omissions may be questioned by some professionals. He does, however, make considerable sociological interpretation of the phenomena observed. In addition a new technique for the study of social class is introduced which seems to have merit in places where the Warner techniques are not suitable. This technique makes use of indirect questions with a later analysis of statements containing a class evaluation and is worthy of further study.

Just about every aspect of life in Gosforth parish is covered in the ten detailed chapters of the book. Individual chapters are devoted to the economy, the family, some aspects of the life cycle, kinship, the social classes, formal and informal associations, neighbors, community, Gosforth and the outside world, and religion.

In studying this volume, American sociologists will find themselves making frequent comparisons with rural communities in this country. It is significant that more difference is noted in the customs relative to agriculture and religion than in anything else, although every aspect of life has comparatively unique features. The Gosforth folk, no doubt because of their isolation, are generally more conservative and traditional than rural folk in this country and exhibit more *Gemeinschaft* characteristics. Likeness to American rural communities is noted in the trend toward urbanization associated with increasing mechanization and accompanied by a decrease in population and an increasing number of special interest organizations. All in all, this volume represents one of the best community studies to date.

EXAMPLE: A BRITISH COMMUNITY[25]

Geddes' study analyzes the sustained unity of an isolated region's environment, work, and people and the manner in which small communities, in spite of poverty, once realized their vision of fellowship in labor, leisure, and spiritual life. The avowed goal of the study is service through social planning to a farming, handicraft, and fishing community threatened with disorganization precipitated by the growth of an industrial society, by invasions of religious and secular authorities, the mobility and migrations of two world wars, and international economic and political conflicts.

EXAMPLE: AN AFRICAN COMMUNITY[26]

Chapters on "The People," "Houses, Families, and Households," and "Marriage, Family Life, and Children" are placed in their proper context when

[25] Quoted from review by Donald C. Marsh, *American Journal of Sociology* 61: 652; May 1956, of Arthur Geddes, *The Isle of Lewis and Harris*: A Study in British Community. Edinburgh: Edinburgh University Press, 1955. xvi+340 p.

[26] Quoted from review by Rose Hum Lee, *American Journal of Sociology* 62: 526-27; March 1957, of Wilbur C. Hallenbeck, Editor, *The Baumanville Community*: A Study of the Family Life of Urban Africans. Durban: Institute for Social Research, University of Natal, 1955. 217 p.

occupation, education, religious and magical beliefs, leisure time, and individual and family adjustment to urban living are considered. There is a description of the historical background and administrative policies of the location, and the monograph concludes with the study of the residents' attitudes toward other racial groups and the means whereby community solidarity is attained. The appropriate chapters were written co-operatively by a sociologist, a psychologist, and a social anthropologist.

EXAMPLE: VILLAGE LIFE IN OKINAWA[27]

The opening chapter on geography and cultural history provides an excellent orientation, not to Okinawa alone, but to the Ryukyu Archipelago. Climate, soils, topography, vegetation, and human occupation are woven into a comprehensive over-all picture. The historical paragraphs lean on the able but relatively inaccessible work of George H. Kerr.

After surveying various villages, he finally concentrated on Hanashiro, an agricultural hamlet in S. E. Okinawa; on Minatogawa, a nondescript fishing and quarrying village near Hanashiro; and on Matsuda, a scattered farming and silvicultural village in N. E. Okinawa. Matsuda felt the effects of the war less directly than did the southern villages. Dr. Glacken recognizes that no Okinawan village is narrowly "typical." He allows his readers to see for themselves the kinds of local differences and general resemblances. He provides population data—sadly missing in many ethnological monographs. There are clear and often brilliant chapters on the dwelling house; on commerce and traditional finance; the family system; inheritance, tenure and use of land; agriculture; fishing and quarrying; silviculture; family and community; religion; environmental and social change. All are derived skillfully from a wealth of meticulous and intimate first-hand observation, and enriched by wide-ranging acquaintance with soils, flora, historical circumstance, and long-range human modification of geographic features.

THE SCHOOL SURVEY[28]

Historical Background

As indicated earlier in this chapter, the social surveys of the early years of the present century studied such problems as municipal organization, housing, recreation, and sometimes education. Therefore, it is a natural sequence that the beginning of the school-survey movement dates back to approximately 1910. Before that date, investigations of school

---

[27] Quoted from review by Douglas G. Haring, *American Sociological Review* 21:404–5; June 1956, of Clarence J. Glacken, *The Great Loochoo*: A Study of Okinawan Village Life. Berkeley: University of California Press, 1955. xvi+324 p.
[28] A. S. Barr, Robert A. Davis, and Palmer O. Johnson, *Educational Research and Appraisal.* Philadelphia: J. B. Lippincott Co., 1953. p. 124–57.
W. W. Charters, Jr., "Beyond the Survey in School Board Research." *Educational Administration and Supervision* 41: 449–52; December 1955.
Harold H. Church and Others, *The Local School Facilities Survey.* Bulletin

systems had been made either by the school officers as part of their regular duties or by persons interested in some particular educational problem rather than in a comprehensive survey of the school system.

During the period from 1910 to 1915 there was a tendency in school systems to invite visiting experts for a relatively short period of time, sometimes a few weeks, to make recommendations concerning such problems as buildings, teachers, curriculum, organization, educational standards and achievement, financial management, and community attitude toward the schools. The early surveys included Boise, Idaho; Montclair and East Orange, New Jersey; Baltimore; New York City; and Cleveland.

Among others, Ellwood P. Cubberley was ready to play a part as investigator and consultant in the early days of the school-survey movement by reason of his school program and interests, professional experience, and methods of work:

> Thus it happened that Cubberley grew to maturity and entered university work at a time when the scientific movement was taking hold of the country, but when such study of education was very new; when the country was greatly enthusiastic about its public schools, but also when it was beginning to find fault with them; when scientific studies were beginning to cast doubts upon the foundation of the traditional programs, but when tradition was still firmly in control; when the nature of our way of life was changing rapidly and bringing to light educational needs hitherto not recognized by the school, but when few men were scholastically equipped to enter upon a scientific study of education.[29]

of the School of Education, Indiana University, Vol. 29, Nos. 1 and 2. Bloomington: Division of Research and Field Services, Indiana University, 1953. vii+96 p.

Walter D. Cocking, "The School Survey and Its Social Implications." *Educational Research Bulletin* 30: 169–78, 196; October 9, 1951.

Carter V. Good and Douglas E. Scates, *op. cit.*, p. 567–76.

Calvin Grieder, "School Surveys." *Review of Educational Research* 19: 322–33; October 1949.

Research Methods Applied to Health, Physical Education, and Recreation. Revised Edition. Washington: American Association for Health, Physical Education, and Recreation, N.E.A., 1952. p. 315–28.

Virgil Rogers and Others, *Gary, Indiana:* A Study of Some Aspects and Outcomes of a General School Survey. Washington: National Commission for the Defense of Democracy Through Education, N.E.A., June 1957. 40 p.

Jesse B. Sears, "School Surveys," *Encyclopedia of Educational Research.* Revised Edition. Edited by Walter S. Monroe. New York: The Macmillan Co., 1950. p. 1126–33.

George D. Strayer, Jr., *Planning for School Surveys.* Bulletin of the School of Education, Indiana University, Vol. 24, No. 2. Bloomington: Division of Research and Field Services, Indiana University, 1948. 36 p.

A Survey of Surveys. Nashville, Tenn.: Division of Surveys and Field Services, George Peabody College for Teachers, 1952. 56 p.

[29] Quoted from Jesse B. Sears and Adin D. Henderson, *Cubberley of Stanford: And His Contribution to American Education.* Stanford, Calif.: Stanford University Press, 1957. p. 166.

After 1915 there was a trend toward more specialized surveys of limited aspects or problems of education, since the large number of recommendations in comprehensive surveys sometimes had proved confusing to the school staff and to the public. It was also thought desirable to add to the administrative staff of the local school system one or more specialists trained in methods of research, measurement, and survey techniques, who could assume leadership in conducting school-survey studies, rather than to depend entirely on the leadership of visiting experts. Frequently local staff members and consulting experts co-operated in conducting school surveys. As the movement spread widely through the local and state school systems, staff members of university departments of education were not able to meet the requests for leadership in surveys, with the result that a considerable part of this leadership was carried by the United States Office of Education, the educational division of the Russell Sage Foundation, and certain bureaus of municipal and governmental research. During the second quarter of the present century and later, the research and survey divisions of certain state universities, Teachers College of Columbia University, and George Peabody College for Teachers have made a large number of school surveys.

Types and Scope of School Surveys

In terms of purpose, modern school surveys may be divided into three types.[30] The comprehensive survey usually covers the following aspects of the school system:

1. Aims, outcomes, pupil achievement, curriculum, method, and instructional aids
2. Administrative problems and procedures of the schools
3. Financial policies and procedures
4. Operation and maintenance of the physical plant
5. Pupil transportation
6. Staff and personnel
7. School plant and related factors.

The educational survey deals with the instructional program and the related policies and procedures that affect the educational program. The building survey has been the most common type during recent years, because of the pressure of the greatly increased pupil population. The educational and building surveys together constitute a comprehensive survey.

[30] Harold H. Church and Others, *op. cit.*

For illustrative purposes, the steps and procedures of the plant survey may be summarized briefly. The school-building survey usually includes the community and the setting of the schools, an estimate of future school enrollment, school-plant planning, the pupil-transportation system, and the available financial resources to provide the school buildings. The co-operative building survey by members of the local staff and by a team of visiting specialists combines the advantages of the "expert" survey and self-survey, in that it costs less than the survey conducted entirely by experts, safeguards the objectivity of survey procedures and conclusions, and through co-operation between the local staff and visiting experts furthers acceptance and implementation of the survey recommendations.

The visiting survey specialist has an important role in developing procedures for setting up and conducting the survey, interpreting the findings, formulating recommendations, stimulating the local staff in answering important questions, and co-operating with the local administrator in his role of leadership.

There are some disadvantages when a single survey seeks to accomplish two separate purposes, such as administrative planning for a building program and evaluation of the efficiency of the educational program and personnel. Evaluation of the educational program and personnel (and working *with* persons for their own improvement) may prove incompatible with the purposes of a survey concerned with administrative planning.

It is possible to classify surveys in several ways (other than by plant, program, and comprehensive):

1. The major aspect of the school system: school plant, educational program, comprehensive

2. Geographical area: local, state, regional, national

3. Level of instruction: elementary, secondary, higher

4. Type of preparation: junior college, teacher education, engineering, medicine, law, social work

5. Purpose or problem: to follow up youth out of school, to describe the membership of a professional organization, to describe the characteristics of a group of institutions, to poll the opinion of a group of parents, to identify trends, to engage in survey testing

6. Data-gathering technique or procedure: questionnaire, interview, observation, group-behavior analysis, content analysis, survey-appraisal. (In the interest of emphasizing research methodology, this is the classification scheme adopted for succeeding sections of the present chapter.)

Procedures and Results of Surveys

The following summary[31] of the procedures and practical results of survey studies is drawn from an evaluation of the school surveys sponsored by George Peabody College for Teachers and from many surveys made by other agencies. A primary purpose of the evaluation of the Peabody school surveys was to study the activities in the local school system following a survey, by way of implementing the recommendations, with the evaluative data based on interviews, conferences, and documentary sources.

1. The formal request for a local survey usually came from the board of education, upon the recommendation of the superintendent, although frequently the initiative came from such groups as a citizens' committee, an education association, or a chamber of commerce. (School surveys have been sponsored by the United States Office of Education, regional accrediting associations, national professional organizations, state legislatures, state departments of education, and private philanthropic foundations.)

2. As a general rule the Division of Surveys and Field Services had complete charge of plans and procedures for making the investigation.

3. Comprehensive reports and illustrated digests were prepared by the survey staff and printed, with oral reports always made to the boards of education or survey commissions and to other interested groups invited to attend the meetings.

4. As a rule the survey reports were enthusiastically received by the public and by the press, with community groups and citizens' committees actively supporting the recommendations.

5. The superintendent of schools, more than any other individual or group, was responsible for implementing the survey recommendations, with new superintendents particularly appreciative of the guidance of the report in winning public support for school policies.

6. Members of state survey commissions played an important part in formulating survey recommendations, and assumed the responsibility for drafting bills embodying the recommendations for presentation to the legislature. It proved difficult to implement changes that depended on action by the legislative bodies of the city, county, or state, and especially when constitutional changes were necessary. Political strategy in bringing about legislative action on survey recommendations varied, with the unity of the forces supporting public education an important factor in success.

7. When survey proposals involved as a major consideration the consolidation of schools, there was always opposition in the small communities, which sometimes led to compromise or even failure in implementing the survey recommendations.

[31] *A Survey of Surveys, op. cit.*

8. Almost one-half of the survey recommendations were adopted. More immediate results were brought about in city schools than in county or state systems. Differences in favor of the city over the county systems were especially significant in the areas of administration, business management, and physical plant. (In many of our school systems the survey has been the initial stage of an educational advance, through challenging the attention of the school people and the public, even though immediate results have not always followed survey investigations.)

9. The superintendents of county and city school systems reacted favorably to recommendations for reorganization of their administrative and supervisory staffs, not only adding new members but also organizing them into a few clearly defined divisions or departments under the leadership of assistant superintendents.

10. Improvement of instruction followed slowly after a survey, although the majority of the school systems reported the adoption of many significant recommendations. (The direction of survey recommendations has been toward a positive emphasis, by way of search for and encouragement of desirable educational practices, rather than a negative emphasis in the form of a search for malpractices.)

11. The quick adoption of survey recommendations for schoolhousing reflected the critical shortage of buildings following the war years; bond issues for new school buildings were generally approved in the counties and cities.

12. Recommendations for the improvement of pupil transportation were readily adopted, with state and county systems carrying out most of the concrete proposals for a complete system of school-bus operation.

13. Proposed programs for financing the schools were frequently delayed by a variety of restrictions, although state systems made some progress in financing public education.

14. Gains in revenue receipts were only moderate in county systems, whereas the compactness and well-developed channels of communication in city schools secured relatively prompt action in increasing school funds. Recommendations concerning the business affairs of the schools were well received in both cities and counties.

15. The administrative officers in four school systems thought that the survey staff should have continuing follow-up contacts by way of consultative services in the system investigated, and suggested that survey specialists should spend more time in the classroom, as background for more accurate evaluation of the quality of teaching. Many school systems now maintain a continuing survey or study, sometimes known as an evaluation or an inventory, with a co-operative planning survey at intervals of approximately ten years, and financial and personnel provisions between surveys for securing the assistance of special consultants. (The stages of implementation of survey recommendations involve the processes of group interaction or group dynamics. Certain related techniques of group-behavior analysis and action research are summarized in other sections of this chapter.)

16. It is now recognized that many of the recommendations of school surveys are subjective (according to one specialist, 80 per cent subjective).[32] To the extent that direct observation, score cards, check lists, and rating scales are used in school surveys, there is a considerable element of subjectivity or personal reaction on the part of the investigator. Survey conclusions depend largely on committee deliberations or interpretations, with the recommendations based largely on the opinion of committee members, or the impact of opinion on facts. To cite an example, a state school survey may recommend an expanded plan of state aid for local school districts, which is a committee recommendation rather than a factual statement, although coming from or based on facts. The recommendation involves subjectivity in the frame of reference or philosophy of the survey committee: agreement on the general goal of a good school system, acceptance of the social philosophy that a good school system is desired for all, and agreement that a particular plan of equalization of support is best for the state and the local school districts.

Safeguards for School Surveys

An excellent statement of safeguards for school surveys is based on an evaluation of the Gary, Indiana, survey and its outcomes, by the National Commission for the Defense of Democracy through Education of the National Education Association.[33] After pointing out that the survey has been one of the most valuable procedures for the improvement of American school systems, the Commission emphasizes that the ultimate success of a survey depends on the interest, co-operation, good will, and confidence of the staff of the school system under study, and on the dignity and sincerity with which the survey is conducted and reported.

In considering service as a consultant on a survey, educators should give careful attention to the following safeguards:

1. If the survey agency is a profit-making group, there should be definite assurance that financial considerations will not influence the nature of the recommendations.

2. The survey agency should approach the survey in a wholly objective fashion, without predetermined findings.

3. There should be a clear understanding of the significance of the use of the names of the educators in connection with any report resulting from the survey.

[32] Dan H. Cooper, "Contributions of School Surveys to Educational Administration," *Educational Administration*: A Survey of Progress, Problems, and Needs, p. 46–59. Edited by William C. Reavis. Proceedings of the Fifteenth Annual Conference for Administrative Officers of Public and Private Schools, 1946. Vol. 9. Chicago: The University of Chicago Press, 1946. 216 p.
[33] Virgil Rogers and Others, *op. cit.*

4. The survey should emphasize constructive recommendations likely to result in improvement.

5. Consultants should be insistent that surveys shall not be staffed by people who are not familiar with the field and particularly by people who have disrespect for the areas to be studied and for the standards of the education profession.

6. There should be at least one meeting of all consultants and survey staff prior to the beginning of the survey, with adequate time devoted to a discussion of the procedures and objectives of the survey.

7. When the survey is undertaken, there should be agreement that the report represents the composite judgment of the consultants.

8. Each consultant should be assured by the survey agency that he may spend as much time as he believes necessary and desirable, in order to be sure that any findings for which he is specifically responsible may be based on adequate observation and inspection.

9. The consultant should receive and accept full authority and assume full responsibility for the preparation of the final reports, based on careful checking of factual data and inclusion in the report of adequate material to support specific findings.

10. The consultant should not permit in the report use of obnoxious and contemptuous phraseology that would tend to bring the report under suspicion as being emotional and slanted, rather than an objective and fair appraisal.

11. Following the field study, all professional consultants should meet with other survey personnel before the final report is released, in order to discuss findings and recommendations and to decide upon final approval of the complete report.

Safeguards for the school system to be surveyed are as follows:

1. Before selecting an agency to conduct the survey, the board of education and administrative staff should make a careful study of the experience and philosophy of the agencies with respect to public education.

2. An agreement should be prepared that will indicate in detail the scope of the survey, including the areas with which the recommendations will be concerned.

3. All discussion between the board of education and the survey agency should be reported in detail in official minutes of the board.

4. The number of individuals to be employed as survey staff members and consultants should be clearly noted.

5. There should be a clear commitment that, in seeking information and in studying the school system, initial approaches should be made to persons in charge of areas under study, with free access to anyone who may have information concerning agreed-on phases of the study.

6. No factual data should be presented in the report unless they have been checked for accuracy with the person in the school system responsible for such data.

7. When the report is released, it should go simultaneously to all directly concerned (preferably, prior to its public release).

8. A plan should be developed for careful study and implementation of the survey report.

To the extent that safeguards for the survey process are observed or neglected, an agency may be considered as contributing to or as destroying the values of surveys in general:

1. The agreement for conducting a survey should be openly arrived at and should be a matter of public, written record.

2. Competent and experienced educators in the areas under study should be included as members of the survey team.

3. Careful consideration should be given to involving local teachers, administrators, and other citizens of the community in the survey process.

4. The study should be unhurried, with adequate time for securing all pertinent information, including time for conferences with those most affected by the survey.

5. Careful attention should be given to viewing the system under study in the light of local historical perspective, as well as local sociological, political, and economic factors.

6. All data serving as a basis for the survey reports should be checked, not only against available figures, but also with those individuals in the school system who are in the best position to evaluate them and to indicate whether they are complete and accurate.

7. The survey staff should exercise great care to avoid any prejudging of the situation, and individuals on the survey staff who indicate such prejudgment should not be retained.

8. The wording of the report should be dignified, without being abstruse, obscure, or uninteresting, and flippant wording should be avoided.

9. The recommendations should be constructive and clear, rather than fault-finding.

10. There should be no recommendations or implications for the dismissal of personnel in the school system.

11. No survey agency that does not have reasonable respect for the process or for the agency to be studied should be included as a potential surveyor.

12. The members of the survey team, whether staff or consultants, should treat the persons under study in at least as reasonable a manner as the investigators themselves would expect to be treated.

13. Careful consideration should be given to other surveys conducted in the same school system.

14. As a general policy, the survey report should go to the individuals most affected at the same time as it is released to the board of education and to the press.

15. A part of the agreement with the employing agency should be the production of a sufficient number of copies of at least a brief form of the report, so that it may be widely distributed to the school staff and to the community.

16. The survey agency should be constantly aware that, in the conduct of the survey and in the preparation of the report, its responsibilities and influences go far beyond the boundaries of the community in which the study occurs, often setting a precedent in procedures and in outcomes.

17. Individuals participating in the preparation of the survey report should not be named generally in the report unless they are prepared to endorse it in all its aspects.

18. A proposed program for helping the board of education, school staff, and citizens of the community to study the report and implement the recommendations might well be part of the survey report, with the services of the consultants available for a period of time following the survey, and in effect constituting a continuing self-survey by the schools and the community.

THE QUESTIONNAIRE[34]

Characteristics and Uses

By the turn of the past century many psychologists were convinced that experimental and laboratory methods did not answer many of the

[34] John T. Doby, Editor, *An Introduction to Social Research*. Harrisburg, Penn.: The Stackpole Co., 1954. p. 207–19.

Sol L. Garfield, *Introductory Clinical Psychology*. New York: The Macmillan Co., 1957. p. 115–30.

Carter V. Good and Douglas E. Scates, *op. cit.*, p. 604–34.

William J. Goode and Paul K. Hatt, *Methods in Social Research*. New York: McGraw-Hill Book Co., 1952. p. 132–83.

Marie Jahoda and Others, *op. cit.*, p. 151–208, 423–62.

Robert L. Kahn and Charles F. Cannell, *The Dynamics of Interviewing*: Theory, Technique, and Cases. New York: John Wiley & Sons, 1957. p. 106–65.

C. A. Moser, *op. cit.*, Chapters 10, 12, 14.

Mildred Parten, *op. cit.*, p. 157–218, 383–484.

Stanley L. Payne, *The Art of Asking Questions*. Princeton: Princeton University Press, 1951. xiv+249 p.

J. Francis Rummel, *An Introduction to Research Procedures in Education*. New York: Harper & Brothers, 1958. p. 87–110, 361–403.

Douglas E. Scates and Alice V. Yeomans, *Developing a Depth Essay Questionnaire to Assess the Market for Further Education Among Employed Scientists and Engineers*. Washington: American Council on Education, 1950. 128 p.

Douglas E. Scates and Alice V. Yeomans, *Developing an Objective Item Questionnaire to Assess the Market for Further Education Among Employed Adults*. Washington: American Council on Education, 1950. 48 p.

Edward A. Suchman, Bernard S. Phillips, and Gordon F. Streib, "An Analysis of the Validity of Health Questionnaires." *Social Forces* 36: 223–32; March 1958.

Herbert A. Toops, "Questionnaires," *Encyclopedia of Educational Research*. Revised Edition. New York: The Macmillan Co., 1950. p. 948–51.

Pauline V. Young, *op. cit.*, p. 176–204.

questions about childhood and youth. G. Stanley Hall and his students especially promoted wide use of the questionnaire, which more recently has appeared in the form of the history blank, clinical syllabus, and personality inventory or questionnaire. The terms *questionnaire* and *schedule* may be considered equivalent for present purposes, although sometimes a technical distinction is made. The questionnaire is generally regarded as a form distributed through the mail or filled out by the respondent under the supervision of the investigator or interviewer, whereas the schedule is a form filled out by the investigator or completed in his presence.

Many beginners in research turn almost automatically to the questionnaire as a device for securing answers to problems, even before the problem and technique are fully formulated, rather than to evaluate the merits of the various data-gathering methods in relation to the particular problem. A carefully devised questionnaire technique is not a simple, quick method of investigation, but requires time, patience, ingenuity, and skill. Many of these abilities and skills are important in interview studies, and in certain other descriptive-survey techniques. Therefore, cross references are appropriate in the interest of economy of space, especially between the questionnaire and interview sections of this chapter.

As to uses and applications, the questionnaire extends the investigator's powers and techniques of observation by reminding the respondent of each item, helping insure response to the same item from all respondents, and tending to standardize and objectify the observations of different enumerators (by singling out particular aspects of the situation and by specifying the units and terminology for describing the observations). While many questionnaires seek factual information, others are concerned with opinions, attitudes, and interests. National, state, and local organizations frequently have been interested in questionnaire surveys of the status of the school personnel and current practices in school systems, including school finance. In frequency of use, the questionnaire may be outranked by the survey test; if all the practical questionnaire and testing studies are included, the two techniques probably involve more than one-half the total studies in education.

To cite a specific example,[35] the personality questionnaire or inventory attempts to measure a variety of personality attributes: rather broad categories such as emotional adjustment, social adjustment, neurotic tendency; more specific personality traits, such as introversion, extroversion, self-sufficiency, and ascendancy or dominance; and in terms of

[35] Sol. L. Garfield, *op. cit.*, p. 115–27.

specific theoretical conceptions of personality or different psychiatric categories. The personality questionnaire or inventory usually includes a specific number of questions or test items (approximately 100–500 in number) to be answered by the subject by checking one of three possible responses—"yes," "no," and a third category designated either as a question mark or as "cannot say." Among the better known examples are the Bernreuter Personality Inventory and the Minnesota Multiphasic Personality Inventory (MMPI).

Appropriateness as an Instrument

Beginners in research and many others frequently overlook the co-operative nature of the questionnaire and lack perspective concerning what may reasonably be asked of busy respondents. The questionnaire study should be important not only to the investigator and to the particular field of knowledge, but also to the respondent, whose psychology of motivation involves his attention, sympathy, interest, co-operation, and honesty in answering questions.[36] Better motivation for respondents is likely to prevail if they can see the investigator's side of the problem and procedure, and can see the end-results in the form of a concise summary of the study and possibly in the implementation of the findings.

One of the first questions the investigator should ask concerning the questionnaire is whether it is as appropriate as some other data-gathering instrument, or whether the answers may even be available in documentary sources or in the literature. Would the questionnaire be as effective as the interview in investigating the job opportunities available in the printing and tailoring trades of a large city for members of certain racial and minority groups, in studying the policy of city newspapers with respect to publication of school news, in canvassing the leisure-time activities of adolescent boys in an underprivileged area of a large city, and in asking highly personal questions such as those covered in the Kinsey reports? A sociologist's comment on a student's questionnaire is not intended to be sharp, but to emphasize the desirability and necessity of considering the appropriateness of the questionnaire in relation to other available means of gathering evidence.

First of all, you are asking in the questionnaire certain questions you could easily answer for yourself by consulting *Who's Who in America* or the university catalogues.

[36] Douglas E. Scates and Alice Yeomans Scates, "Developing a Depth Questionnaire to Explore Motivation and Likelihood of Action." *Educational and Psychological Measurement* 12: 620–31; Winter 1952.

More serious is the objection which I have to the rest of your questions; you are asking me for my opinions on very complex questions, and you formulate your questions in a way that indicates you expect a dogmatic answer. To do real justice to these questions, which concern the objectives and methods of . . . sociology, I would have to write you an essay, or several papers. It is hard to imagine that you really expect me to do this for you; if you do not, then why ask me these questions? Furthermore, it so happens that I have expressed my ideas on these matters in several publications; I admit that my opinions are in some cases not stated explicitly but by implication. Now there is an old and well established way of getting information about other scholars' opinions and theories; that is, by reading and by critical interpretation. There is no substitute for this. My advice to you is to forget about the questionnaire and to study the literature.[37]

Does the recipient of the questionnaire have the information requested, and is he free and willing to respond? Would a state survey of local administrative positions early in April find that the respondents know where they will be the following September and are willing to declare their positions vacant so early in the spring? Would a local school survey of the attitudes of parents toward curriculum and method find these citizens informed about the school program and willing to comment freely when their children are still attending school? A form of questionnaire without the signature of the respondent may encourage frank and truthful answers.

One questionnaire sought answers to the following impossible questions:

1. Consider the books, monographs, or pamphlets published between 1925 and 1949 inclusive, and list the three which you consider the most outstanding and important contributions to educational psychology. (A similar request was made for psychology as a whole.)

2. Consider the articles (theoretical, reports of research, etc.) published between 1925 and 1949 inclusive, and list the three which you consider the most outstanding and important contributions to educational psychology. (A similar request was made for psychology as a whole.)

Stages and Administrative Aspects

A check list of certain requirements, stages, and administrative aspects of questionnaire surveys is especially appropriate for large-scale studies, and also is useful in planning smaller questionnaire studies:[38]

[37] Quoted from Rudolf Heberle, "On the Use of Questionnaires in Research: Open Letter to a Graduate Student." *American Sociological Review* 16: 549; August 1951.
[38] *Standards for Statistical Surveys.* Exhibit A, Circular No. A-46. Washington: Executive Office of the President, Bureau of the Budget, March 28, 1952. 10 p.

1. Purpose of the survey
2. Relation to other surveys or programs
3. Development of the survey plan
   a. Respondents
   b. Extent of coverage
   c. Frequency and timing
   d. Method of collection
   e. Consideration of nonsampling errors
   f. Standard definitions and classifications
   g. Processing and interpretation of the data
   h. Allowance for pretests and follow-ups
   i. Comparison with data from other sources
   j. Proposed calendar
   k. Cost estimates
4. Questionnaire and accompanying instructions
5. Pretests
6. Follow-ups
7. Development of the sampling plan for partial coverage surveys
8. Supervision of field enumeration
9. Manuals and other instructions for the conduct of the survey
10. Progress and cost reporting
11. Preparation and publication of the final report.

The graduate student also must consider certain administrative aspects in choosing his problem and procedure, including sponsorship, cost, space, time requirements, clerical aid, and tabulating or calculating machine work.

Sampling and Survey Design

Sampling is a technical and statistical problem of importance in most questionnaire investigations and in many other descriptive-survey studies. The literature on application of sampling theory to practical survey problems has appeared primarily since 1940, with leadership provided in the areas of opinion-polling, market research, and census operations. Although the methodology of statistics lies outside the scope of this book, it seems appropriate to summarize the characteristics of probability samples and the limitations of "unplanned," "nonprobability," or "judgment" samples, and to refer to the literature of sample surveys in education (60 recent titles).[39]

[39] Francis G. Cornell, "Sample Surveys in Education," in "Statistical Methodology in Educational Research." *Review of Educational Research* 24: 359–74; December 1954.

Probability samples have these characteristics:

1. Each individual (or primary unit) in the sample has some known probability of entering the sample.

2. The process of sampling is automatic in one or more steps of the selection of elements or units in the sample.

3. Weights appropriate to the probabilities in (1) are used in the analysis of the sample.

The limitations of unplanned, nonprobability, or judgment sampling are represented in the following items:

1. The sample of convenience (e.g., the superintendent's office is housed in the high school; the high-school teachers being convenient, he asks some of them their opinions on a matter)

2. The canvass of experts (e.g., a questionnaire to several "informed" persons for judgment on teacher shortage or school construction needs in the United States)

3. The sample based on an obsolete list or *frame* which does not adequately cover the population (e.g., using a city directory or telephone book as a basis for sampling the adult population of a community)

4. The sample with a high proportion of nonresponse (e.g., the common questionnaire study in education)

5. The pinpoint or representative-area sample (e.g., purposive selection of typical individuals, or a typical school, typical classroom, or typical community)

6. The *quota* sample, by which there is some system of selection of primary sampling units (such as communities), and assigning interviewers *quotas* for subsampling (e.g., an interviewer is asked to select for interview 10 females who are high-school graduates between the ages of 18 and 25 living in the northeast section of a city).

To cite specific examples of design, Hyman bases much of his discussion of survey design and analysis on seven published surveys, dealing with: industrial absenteeism, public opinion and the atom bomb, American opinion on commercial radio, prejudice and personality, American sexual behavior, class consciousness, and war-bond redemption. These inquiries include certain common features, particularly with respect to the consequences of size of inquiry, organizational form, sponsorship and subsidization, and controversial subject matter. Some of these surveys present a sheer description of some phenomenon and are known as descriptive surveys, whereas other inquiries seek an explanation and are known as explanatory surveys.

Although reasonable attention has been given to problems of sampling design and theory in survey research, there has been considerable neglect of certain prior questions of the location within which the phenomenon ought to be studied, including temporal location, location in some human population, relevant units, and differentiation of the description.

Certain factors affect the quality of research findings or may lead to error in surveys:[40]

1. Variability in response
2. Differences between different kinds and degrees of canvass
   a. Mail, telephone, telegraph, direct interview
   b. Intensive vs. extensive interviews
   c. Long vs. short schedules
   d. Check block plan vs. response
   e. Correspondence panel and key reporters
3. Bias and variation arising from the interviewer
4. Bias of the auspices
5. Imperfections in the design of the questionnaire and tabulation plans
   a. Lack of clarity in definitions; ambiguity; varying meanings of same word to different groups of people; eliciting an answer liable to misinterpretation
   b. Omitting questions that would be illuminating to the interpretation of other questions
   c. Emotionally toned words; leading questions; limiting response to a pattern
   d. Failing to perceive what tabulations would be most significant
   e. Encouraging nonresponse through formidable appearance
6. Changes that take place in the universe before tabulations are available
7. Bias arising from nonresponse (including omissions)
8. Bias arising from late reports
9. Bias arising from an unrepresentative selection of data for the survey, or of the period covered
10. Bias arising from an unrepresentative selection of respondents
11. Sampling errors and biases
12. Processing errors (coding, editing, calculating, tabulating, tallying, posting, and consolidating)
13. Errors in interpretation
    a. Bias arising from bad curve fitting; wrong weighting; incorrect adjusting

[40] W. E. Deming, "On Errors in Surveys." *American Sociological Review* 9: 359–69; August 1944.

Herbert H. Hyman, *Survey Design and Analysis.* Glencoe, Ill.: Free Press, 1955. p. 143–45.

    b. Misunderstanding the questionnaire; failure to take account of the respondents' difficulties (often through inadequate presentation of data); misunderstanding the method of collection and the nature of the data

    c. Personal bias in interpretation.

Some estimation of residual errors that remain despite all pretesting may be secured through two general classes of methods available for treating this problem, namely, methods involving internal and external checks. The internal check is predicated on the logic that the meaning and quality of a given reply can be inferred from its relation to some other datum or reply. The most direct internal check involves the use of questions that require the respondent to elaborate an initial reply. Through another method, dependent variables may be arrayed for given factual categories.

The most obvious external check is the comparison of the datum under study with findings on the same or related problems collected by other agencies or individuals, on equivalent samples of the same population. Among the types of external checks in a German bombing survey were: interviewer ratings, criterion data from official records, use of other samples as informants, split-ballot procedures, comparison with earlier survey data, and "captured-mail" check.[41]

Questionnaire Construction

In questionnaire construction important decisions relate to motivation of the respondent, significance of questions, simplicity of responses, avoidance of unnecessary specifications or details, pertinence to the situation of the respondent, clarity of purpose and questions, phrasing of items to facilitate summarization of responses, and possible precoding of the questionnaire in the interest of using tabulating machine cards for summarization. Questionnaires that go to local and state school systems, or to similar educational agencies, may well formulate questions in keeping with the items of official or regular reports.

As to form,[42] the structured questionnaire is definite, concrete, preordained in terms of items, with additional questions limited to those necessary to clarify inadequate answers or to elicit more detailed responses. The form of questions may be closed (categorical) or open-end (inviting free response). The check list (usually a closed form of questionnaire) is a set of categories for the respondent to check, as in listing

---

[41] Herbert H. Hyman, *op. cit.*, p. 151–72.
[42] Pauline V. Young, *op. cit.*, Chapters 8, 9.

frequency of performance of certain duties by school officers. The completeness of the original list is especially important, since the respondent is likely to consider it all-inclusive and may depend on the list so completely that he does not write in additional items. The check responses or similar answers in the closed form of questionnaire commonly provide categorized data that greatly facilitate tabulating and summarizing processes.

The open-end or free-response questionnaire frequently goes beyond statistical data or factual material into the area of hidden motivations that lie behind attitudes, interests, preferences, and decisions. Such questions are used extensively in depth and focused questionnaires and interviews, although the work of tabulating and summarizing is time-consuming and expensive.

The choice between open and closed questions in both questionnaire and interview surveys depends on the following criteria:[43] the objective or purpose, the respondent's level of information on the particular topic, the degree of structure that characterizes respondent opinions on the topic, ease with which the material can be communicated, and the investigator's knowledge and insight into the respondent's situation. The closed question is most appropriate when the investigator's objective is to classify the respondent, when there is little question as to the adequacy of respondent information, when the respondent's opinions on the specific topic are well structured, when there are no major barriers to communication, and when the investigator is well informed about the respondent. Conversely, when the opposite of the foregoing conditions prevails, the open question is preferable.

The nonstructured questionnaire commonly serves as an interview guide, especially for focused, depth, or nondirective interviews. It includes definite subject-matter areas, but the interviewer is largely free to arrange the form and timing of the questions.

A helpful summary of criteria for constructing questionnaires includes nine items:[44]

1. It must be short enough so as not to take too much time and so that the respondent will not reject it completely.

2. It must be of sufficient interest and have enough face appeal so that the respondent will be inclined to respond to it and to complete it.

[43] Robert L. Kahn and Charles F. Cannell, *op. cit.*, p. 164–65.
[44] Douglas E. Scates and Alice V. Yeomans, *The Effect of Questionnaire Form on Course Requests of Employed Adults*. Washington: American Council on Education, 1950. p. 2–4.

3. The questionnaire should obtain some depth to the response in order to avoid superficial replies.

4. The ideal questionnaire must not be too suggestive or too unstimulating, particularly with reference to choices.

5. The questionnaire should elicit responses that are definite but not mechanically forced.

6. Questions must be asked in such a way that the responses will not be embarrassing to the individual.

7. Questions must be asked in such a manner as to allay suspicion on the part of the respondent concerning hidden purposes in the questionnaire.

8. The questionnaire must not be too narrow, restrictive, or limited in its scope or philosophy.

9. The responses to the questionnaire must be valid, and the entire body of data taken as a whole must answer the basic question for which the questionnaire was designed.

Certain errors[45] in construction and pretesting of the questionnaire should be avoided, including questionnaires used for interview purposes.

1. Irrelevance of the research problem to respondents. If the study involves the social and psychological problems of aging, with emphasis on retirement from employment, the sample would include only respondents past sixty years of age.

2. Irrelevance or insufficiency of questionnaire items for the variable being investigated. In studying membership activity in a local union, the investigator cannot assume that what represents high activity to him will also represent high activity to his potential respondents; for example, regularity of attendance at union meetings might be an insufficient index of union activity for construction workers whose jobs frequently take them miles away from the town where the meetings are held.

3. Ambiguous or inappropriate item wording. Some people misunderstood the following question: "Which of the following groups do you think your family belongs in—upper class, middle class, working class, lower class?" Some people thought that the phrase "belongs in" meant "deserves to be in." The question was reworded to read, "If you were asked to put yourself (your family) in one of these groups—the upper class, middle class, working class, lower class—how would you answer?" Ambiguous questions result in equally confusing responses. A newspaper printed a questionnaire concerning the items read by its subscribers, without indicating for a family whether the checking should be done by one member, by the head of the family, or by each member of the family.

4. Inadequate categories for responses. Acceptable standard forms are: "Often—sometimes—hardly ever," "more—some—less," "very happy—fairly happy—not so happy." A dichotomous questionnaire on the administrative

[45] John T. Doby, Editor, *op. cit.*, p. 207-10.

policy of a college, with provision for answering "for" or "against," would not represent adequately the college faculty as respondents. A third alternative for each item, such as "no definite feeling or conviction," is needed, because it is as important to know that a faculty member is neutral toward a particular policy as to know that he has a strong conviction for or against the policy.

When a question involves a number of categories for checking (sometimes a dozen or more), they should be reasonably complete and detailed, and as a rule nonoverlapping and co-ordinate. The young investigator who studied teacher turnover in a county school system included in his questionnaire a classification of eight reasons for leaving a teaching position. In summarizing the results, he found that thirty-one additional reasons had been written in by the respondents. A tryout of the questionnaire would have revealed a more complete set of classes or categories.

5. Inappropriate item sequence; overlengthiness; insensitivity to the emotional impact on the respondent of an item or series of items. These sources of difficulty can be greatly minimized by careful pretesting.

In preparing directions for answering questions, there is the challenge of keeping between one extreme of completeness and detail that seems overwhelming to the respondent and the other extreme of incompleteness and vagueness that would brand the investigator as careless and superficial. Usually the investigator must work back and forth, shuttle-like, between the questions and directions, as he constructs a questionnaire satisfactory for his purpose, with necessary adjustments as work proceeds on all parts of the questionnaire pattern.

Some questions are for purposes other than obtaining information; for example, warming up or getting the respondent's mind on the subject or area, meeting the respondent's expectation that certain questions normally will be included, and catharsis or release of possible tensions.

There is a human tendency to answer "yes" when the respondent thinks that this is the expected answer. This tendency can be partially offset by inclusion of the opposite question, so as to have a number of such pairs of questions.

In many instances the questionnaire includes two or more questions, in order to make clear the answer to a single question; for example, "the number of college courses completed" would serve as a check on an item relating to "semester hours completed."

A device in questionnaire construction for placement of detailed lists of items or subjects is to print them at the end of the questionnaire, especially when such lists do not apply to every respondent. To cite an example, a questionnaire for the field of psychology, in the interest of gathering data for the National Register of Scientific and Technical

Personnel, covers two pages, with one question referring to a four-page list of specialties covering all the major fields of scholarship and research, with comprehensive coverage in the mathematical, physical and life sciences, and engineering, and less detailed coverage for social sciences and other professional areas. The item in the questionnaire proper that refers to the four-page specialties list reads as follows: "From the accompanying complete Specialties List, regardless of your current employment, please select and give below in order of decreasing competence up to six of these specialties in which you have had professional experience and/or training."

Tryout

Before the final form is prepared and distributed to the respondents, tryout or pretesting of the questionnaire is essential, for the purpose of validation in terms of practical use. This tryout probably will lead to revision of certain questions, deletion of useless questions, and addition of other items. Tabulation of the tryout responses in rough tables will indicate whether the answers can be tabulated satisfactorily and whether answers to the major questions are forthcoming. The manual of the United States Bureau of the Budget emphasizes that it is desirable to test the feasibility of the questionnaire survey in advance, with pretests designed and conducted to secure answers to such problems as the following:

Relative effectiveness and costs of alternative questionnaires, instructions, and operating procedures

Acceptability and intelligibility of the questions from the respondent's point of view

Possible misunderstandings of questions and procedure on the part of the interviewers

Clarity and applicability of definitions and classifications

Completeness of questions for correct coding and interpretation

Defects in the forms, maps, lists, instructions, etc.

Estimates of strata means and variances

Response rates.

Validity

The validity of a questionnaire and of its parts may be judged by the following types of evidence:[46]

[46] Douglas E. Scates and Alice V. Yeomans, *The Effect of Questionnaire Form on Course Requests of Employed Adults, op. cit.,* p. 4–7.

1. Is the question on the subject?

2. Is the question perfectly clear and unambiguous?

3. Does the question get at something stable, which is typical of the individual or of the situation?

4. Does the question pull or have extractive power? Will it be answered by a large enough proportion of respondents to have validity?

5. Do the responses show a reasonable range of variation?

6. Is the information consistent, in agreement with what is known, and in agreement with expectancy?

7. Is the item sufficiently inclusive?

8. Is there a possibility of obtaining an external criterion to evaluate the questionnaire?

Follow-up

Follow-up usually is necessary in reaching the goal of a high percentage of questionnaire returns (above 95 per cent). The following ingenious and persistent techniques of follow-up in a questionnaire analysis of a professional organization resulted in a return of 99 per cent from a membership list of 600:[47]

A card or letter calling attention to the questionnaire, one to two weeks after sending the blank.

Possibly a second reminder, probably only a post card.

Without waiting too long, a second mailing of the entire questionnaire, with a new cover page or accompanying letter; persons may have misplaced the first questionnaire, or it may have become buried on a desk.

Possibly a personal letter at this point, individually written and signed, as a special appeal for co-operation, with a return stamped envelope.

A short form of the questionnaire was mailed, asking for just a few questions or items of information (perhaps sent by airmail or special delivery), phrased so as to cover the items most essential to the study.

A second mailing of the short questionnaire was sent to a relatively small number by special delivery, with an encouraging personal letter. (It may be necessary to scratch off the list at intervals persons unduly irritated or those who have good reason for not responding; however, these names must be included in the count in calculating percentages.)

Supplementary material went to all those who had returned the abbreviated questionnaire, including a few more essential items of information, and informing them that this is the last round.

Other special means and techniques included mailing of a questionnaire

[47] Douglas E. Scates, "Analysis of a Professional Organization: The American Educational Research Association in 1948," *Growing Points in Educational Research.* 1949 Official Report of the A.E.R.A. Washington: The Association, 1949. p. 111–42.

to the member, partially filled out in advance with answers deemed likely for him, together with a personal letter, suggesting that the information would not be used without his approval and asking that he go the rest of the way to complete the questionnaire; forwarding of liberal postage, transportation, or communication expenses; long distance telephone; and telegraph.

Percentage of Returns

Although the goal of 90 to 100 per cent returns has not been achieved generally in questionnaire surveys, definite progress in this direction is being made through improved plans for sponsorship, formulation of questions, follow-up, checking results, and studying nonresponse. The mean percentages (rounded to the nearest whole number) of questionnaire returns from a large number of survey investigations[48] were as follows: 170 master's theses at Indiana State Teachers College, 72 per cent; 204 doctoral dissertations at Teachers College, Columbia University, 71 per cent; and 59 research studies reported in the *Journal of Educational Research*, 81 per cent.

As an example of bias or incompleteness of returns for mail questionnaires, during World War II a selected list of farmers was canvassed for the purpose of determining the need for farm laborers. Most of the large farm operators listed their shortages, but most of the small farmers were too busy doing their own work to take time to reply, with the result that a fantastic estimate of 3 or 4 laborers was indicated to meet the needs of the average farm.[49]

Editing, Tabulating, Summarizing

The investigator may need to check the returns to determine whether different parts of the questionnaire response are consistent, to correct plain errors, and to revise the summarizing categories as indicated by the responses. One respondent checked all possible answers, revealing later in an interview that a check mark was his way of showing that he had read or checked off every item in the questionnaire. Sometimes written notes on the margins must be read and interpreted, figures rearranged or moved to the correct column, or other details checked that go beyond mechanical and routine clerical operations. After tabulation of questionnaire returns, further re-examination of the data and editing of the returns may be necessary. In a job classification of the members of a research

[48] J. R. Shannon, "Percentages of Returns of Questionnaires in Reputable Educational Research." *Journal of Educational Research* 42: 138–41; October 1948.

[49] George W. Snedecor, "On the Design of Sampling Investigations." *American Statistician* 2: 6–9, 13; December 1948.

organization, when the 600 returns had been tabulated, two general categories were relatively high: "administrators not otherwise described," 26 cases; "none of the following descriptions fits me," 18 cases. The cards for these 44 cases were re-examined and, on the basis of position, title, and institution reported, most of the 44 were reclassified into more specific and meaningful categories of jobs. In the same questionnaire survey of membership, an editorial decision was made to the effect that persons who listed "Teachers College" and "Columbia University" as having granted their degrees were referring to the same institution (Teachers College of Columbia University), with the result that the two categories were combined (accompanied by an explanatory footnote).

In dealing with questionnaire returns for purposes of tabulation, there are three choices:

1. Sometimes the questionnaire can be used directly, without copying off the material before tabulation. This is likely to be true when the questionnaire is a single page, which permits the questionnaire to be handled much like a data card.

2. In an initial list table the responses for each questionnaire (or other case) may be put on a single line, which permits a preliminary overview of the results, by way of showing (perhaps better than data cards will) what the range is likely to be.

3. Data cards have their chief advantage for purposes of cross classification or tabulation, because they can be sorted once for a trait, and then sorted again on one or more secondary traits. Data cards also can be checked readily when tabulations are made. There is the physical advantage of allowing a sub-group of cards to be removed from the main pack for use at some other place.[50]

When tabulating machines are used to summarize questionnaire returns, the investigator probably will check back many times against original data, as in identifying the individuals at the extremes of a distribution, or listing by name in the report the individual cases at the extremes (or at the median) of a distribution.

We have already noted in this chapter the value of descriptive-survey studies in providing perspective concerning present status or current conditions, including novel or promising practices. In interpreting questionnaire results, perplexing questions concerning frequency of practice are present. Can cruciality or importance be inferred from frequency? Can the significance of an event or an activity for an individual be inferred from the frequency for the majority of the sample represented?

[50] Quoted from Carter V. Good and Douglas E. Scates, *op. cit.*, p. 630.

Literature on the Questionnaire

The procedures of the questionnaire survey, outlined only briefly in this section, are treated fully in the literature, including such details of technique as: classification and categories, enumeration, gathering data from documentary sources and records, analysis, coding, hand and machine tabulation, and evaluation and interpretation of data. Especially helpful are Payne's recommendations and examples with respect to major types of questions (free-answer, dichotomous, multiple-choice, and others), treatment of respondents, selection and use of appropriate words and language, and readability, as well as a summary list of 100 items at the end of the book;[51] and Parten's detailed treatment[52] of construction of schedules and questionnaires, procedures for the mail questionnaire, sources of bias, editing the schedule data, and coding and tabulating the data. Many additional references on the questionnaire are listed in the bibliographies at the beginning of this section and at the end of the chapter.

THE INTERVIEW[53]

In a treatment of interviewing, it is essential to consider the social and psychological meaning of the interview for the two parties involved, the cognitive and motivational processes affecting the behavior of the interviewer, the reactions of the respondent, and the relation of errors in

[51] Stanley L. Payne, *op. cit.*

[52] Mildred Parten, *op. cit.*, Chapters 6, 11–15.

[53] E. Anstey and E. O. Mercer, *Interviewing for the Selection of Staff*. London: George Allen and Unwin, for the Royal Institute of Public Administration, 1956. xiv+111 p.

W. V. Bingham and B. V. Moore, *How to Interview*. Third Revised Edition. New York: Harper & Brothers, 1941. 263 p.

Clifford E. Erickson, *The Counseling Interview*. New York: Prentice-Hall, 1950. 174 p.

R. A. Fear, *The Evaluation Interview*: Predicting Job Performance in Business and Industry. New York: McGraw-Hill Book Co., 1958. xii+288 p.

Anne F. Fenlason, *Essentials in Interviewing*: For the Interviewer Offering Professional Services. New York: Harper & Brothers, 1952. xi+352 p.

Leon Festinger and Daniel Katz, Editors, *op. cit.*, p. 327–80.

John F. Fraser, *A Handbook of Employment Interviewing*. Revised Edition. London: MacDonald and Evans, 1951. 214 p.

Merton Gill, Richard Newman, and Fredrick C. Redlich, *The Initial Interview in Psychiatric Practice*. New York: International Universities Press, 1954. 423 p.

Carter V. Good and Douglas E. Scates, *op. cit.*, p. 635–45.

William J. Goode and Paul K. Hatt, *op. cit.*, p. 184–208.

Herbert H. Hyman and Others, *Interviewing in Social Research*. Chicago: The University of Chicago Press, 1954. xvi+415 p.

the data to the behavior of the persons in interviewing situations of various types.[54]

Interviewing as Communication and Motivation[55]

The dynamics of interviewing begin with the concept that the interview is a process of communication or interaction. If the interviewer and the respondent share a common language and terminology that permit easy communication, there remains the challenge to the interviewer of motivating frank and complete answers from the respondent. The interviewer must be able to identify and, so far as possible, control the psychological forces present in the interview, which affect both the respondent and himself. The stimulus-response episodes of the interview involve the purposes, motives, attitudes, and beliefs of both the interviewer and the respondent. Of late, social scientists have gathered evidence concerning the process of communication between people and concerning sources of bias in the interview; social psychologists have observed how people communicate with each other in small groups; and clinical psychologists have studied the interaction between the therapist and the patient in the psychotherapeutic interview.

One major form of motivation for the respondent is the psychological

---

Marie Jahoda and Others, *op. cit.*, p. 151–208, 423–92.

Robert L. Kahn and Charles F. Cannell, *The Dynamics of Interviewing*: Theory, Technique, and Cases. New York: John Wiley & Sons, 1957. x+368 p.

Grace Langdon and Irving Stout, *Teacher-Parent Interviews*. New York: Prentice-Hall, 1954. 336 p.

Stanley G. Law, *Therapy Through Interview*. New York: McGraw-Hill Book Co., 1948. xiii+313 p.

John Madge, *op. cit.*, p. 144–253.

Thomas C. McCormick and Roy G. Francis, *Methods of Research in the Behavioral Sciences*. New York: Harper & Brothers, 1958. Chapter 6.

Robert K. Merton, Marjorie Fiske, and Patricia L. Kendall, *The Focused Interview*: A Manual of Problems and Procedures. Glencoe, Ill.: Free Press, 1956. 186 p.

C. A. Moser, *op. cit.*, Chapters 11, 13.

Mildred Parten, *op. cit.*, p. 331–82.

Stanley L. Payne, *op. cit.*

J. Francis Rummel, *op. cit.*, p. 75–86.

Harry S. Sullivan, *The Psychiatric Interview*. New York: W. W. Norton and Co., 1954. 246 p.

James D. Weinland and Margaret V. Gross, *Personnel Interviewing*. New York: Ronald Press, 1952. vii+416 p.

Helen L. Witmer, Editor, *Psychiatric Interviews with Children*. New York: Commonwealth Fund, 1946. viii+444 p.

Pauline V. Young, *Interviewing in Social Work*. New York: McGraw-Hill Book Co., 1935. 416 p.

Pauline V. Young, *Scientific Social Surveys and Research*, *op. cit.*, p. 205–28.

[54] Herbert H. Hyman and Others, *Interviewing in Social Research*, *op. cit.*, p. 3.

[55] Robert L. Kahn and Charles F. Cannell, *op. cit.*, p. 3–21, 65–91.

reward of talking to an understanding, permissive interviewer. A second type of motivation is that of accomplishing certain practical ends or purposes, as in giving information to the physician to improve one's health, to the personnel interviewer to secure a job, and to the social worker to secure advice or economic assistance. At the beginning of the interview the respondent may be motivated almost entirely by his own needs and purposes, but as the process of interaction progresses the respondent may find motivation in the psychological climate of the interview itself.

Values and Uses of the Interview[56]

Although the interview belongs to a class of methods that yield primarily subjective data, that is, direct descriptions of the world of experience, the interests of many social scientists call for such data, however crude the method of data-gathering may of necessity be. For example, the interview technique has certain advantages for collection of data relating to three of the most prominent emphases in social psychology, all implying subjective data: the emphasis on desires, goals, and values by students of personality; the current interest in social perception; and emphasis on the concept of attitude.

It is true that certain methods utilizing other personal documents (such as diaries, life histories, or letters) do yield an elaborate picture of the individual's world of desires and attitudes, but such techniques are relatively inflexible or inefficient for certain types of problems, in that they may not exist for the particular population of individuals to be studied, or these sources may be available only for some self-selected and possibly biased subsample of the particular population. Such life-history documents may not contain information relating to specific significant variables, since they are usually spontaneous in origin.

Many of the concepts and techniques of the questionnaire survey are useful in interviewing. The dynamics of interviewing, however, involve much more than an "oral questionnaire." Many types of information can be secured only through face-to-face contacts with people, especially data relating to personal history, family life, opinions, and attitudes. The interview has certain unique values, as compared with the questionnaire:

1. The interviewees may require the stimulus and confidential relationships of the interview in order to provide personal and confidential information which they would not ordinarily place on paper.

---

[56] Herbert H. Hyman and Others, *Interviewing in Social Research, op. cit.,* p. 15–19.

2. The interviewer may follow up leads and clues in a manner that is not possible by means of an instrument prepared in advance.

3. The interviewer may form some impression of the interviewee, in relation to the truth of the answers and the things that may have been left unsaid.

4. The interviewer may give information and develop attitudes on the part of the respondent, especially in a therapeutic relationship, sometimes encouraging exchange of ideas and information.

The self-administered questionnaire may provide subjective data from the respondent and has the advantages of cheapness because of the reduction of interviewer costs and the possibility of group administration, plus applicability on a systematic sampling basis, but has certain limitations not characteristic of the personal-interview technique:

1. The interview permits study of illiterates or near-illiterates for whom the written questionnaire is not applicable, which may be an important problem for investigations involving the national population, as in studies of recruits in the military forces with very limited education.

2. Since it is always possible for the respondent to read through the entire questionnaire first, or to edit earlier answers in the light of later questions, the advantages of saliency questions become dubious, and it is difficult to control the contextual effects of other questions upon a given answer. In the interview, later questions can be hidden from the knowledge of the respondent and, therefore, can have no effect on the results of an earlier question.

3. A resourceful interviewer with insight may produce certain favorable results not possible in the self-administering situation of the questionnaire, where the mistakes of the respondent have a quality of finality. For example, the interviewer may make ratings of given characteristics of the respondent, explain or amplify a given question, probe for clarification of an ambiguous answer or elaboration of a cryptic report, or even persuade the respondent to answer a question that he would otherwise skip.

Informal observation of behavior under natural conditions usually is not a flexible method, in that the environment may not provide any avenue for the expression of the behavior relevant to the particular problem. To discover a person's thoughts may require a question, as in the case of studies concerned with the past; for example, investigations of the reactions of certain populations to strategic bombing were not undertaken until after the end of hostilities, when the natural setting of the postwar world was not appropriate to observing the reaction to the bombing of three years earlier; hence it was necessary to reconstruct the past either through the memories of the respondent as reported in the course of interviewing or through historical records.

Sometimes an observational approach to attitudes is attempted by placing the subject in a specially contrived experimental or laboratory situation in which the behavior relevant to a given inference appears. However, the behavior exhibited in this laboratory situation is as much bound by the unstated conventions of the contrived situation, and by the explicit instructions characteristic of all experiments on humans, as is the verbal report restricted or limited by the nature of the formal interview. Observation under natural conditions or in real life deals with behavior conditioned by a host of unknown momentary factors operating in environment, just as the verbal report of an individual is bound or limited by the formal interview situation. One is always playing some role in relation to some situation—laboratory, everyday life, or the interview—and the real issue is the kind of situation in which the attitudinal findings are liberated, as well as the ability to relate the findings to the particular situation.

Many research problems merely require data that, by definition, are objective and consequently would not require interviewing. Even in many such instances, however, the interview technique has been applied extensively because of certain practical advantages; for example, the decennial census of the United States, governmental surveys of household possessions and the job record of the individual, insurance company surveys, and the political preference of the voter. The interview enables the investigator to relate the given datum to other characteristics of that same individual as measured simultaneously. For example, the records of an insurance company include a considerable amount of objective data on a health insurance policy covering a certain member of the population, but do not permit analysis of such coverage in relation to health needs and experiences, medical expenses, family income, and other significant variables. Voting records reveal the political behavior or preference of an individual, but do not indicate the social and psychological characteristics of the voter.

Often, the interview is used for practical purposes rather than to gather data for research. The following represent the variety of situations in which interviewing is appropriate, although in many instances it serves to accomplish the practical task at hand: student counseling, a variety of teacher and pupil-personnel contacts, occupational adjustment, applying for a position, employment offices, civil-service agencies, employer-employee relationships, public-opinion polls, radio and TV programs, commercial surveys and market studies, industrial surveys, advertising, censuses, social case work, psychiatric work, mental clinics, psychology, anthropology, sociology, journalism, and law. The interview is frequently employed in historical, experimental, and case-clinical studies.

Outline of Types of Interviews[57]

A working classification of interviews is as follows:

1. According to function (diagnostic, treatment, or research)
2. Number of persons participating (individual or group)
3. Length of contact (short or prolonged)
4. According to the roles assumed by the interviewer and interviewee, in relation to the sociopsychological process of interaction

    Nondirective (uncontrolled, unguided, or unstructured)

    Focused

    Depth

    Repeated, in order to trace change or development.

The Clinical Interview[58]

In clinical work some form of the interview or personal contact has been used in many kinds of situations to secure information about the client and to understand his problems. The two major purposes of the interview in clinical work are diagnosis and treatment. Social workers employ the interview to secure information about the client's problem, his past history, family relations, and job adjustment. Other persons than the client frequently are interviewed when the client is a child, a mental defective, or a psychotic, or when there are unusual discrepancies in the client's presentation of data about himself. The psychiatric examination and even the standardized individual psychological examination are interviewing procedures.

During the clinical interview, certain nonverbal behavior on the part of the patient has useful diagnostic value, including gait, expression, posture, rate of speech, topics avoided, digressions, and word choice. In addition to the general techniques that apply to any interview situation, special procedures may be needed to deal effectively with the problems that arise in the several types of clinical interviews: the intake or admission interview, concerned chiefly with the patient's complaints; the personal and social-history interview, to gather background data with a bearing on the complaints; the screening or diagnostic interview, to

---

[57] Pauline V. Young, *Scientific Social Surveys and Research, op. cit.,* p. 210–13.

[58] Sol L. Garfield, *op. cit.,* p. 192–94.

L. A. Pennington and Irwin A. Berg, Editors, *An Introduction to Clinical Psychology.* Second Edition. New York: Ronald Press, 1954. p. 125.

arrive at a judgment concerning the patient's condition; interviews before and after psychological test administration, and as a means of introducing the patient to therapy; the interview to assist friends and relatives in their dealings with the patient; and the exit or termination interview to facilitate the patient's discharge or transition from hospital to home.

Group and Individual Interviews[59]

Although there is little evidence concerning distinctive merits of group and individual interviews, certain relative advantages and disadvantages may be summarized briefly, with an introductory comment on the setting for the group interview. The size of the group should not be so large that it is unwieldy or inhibits participation by most members, and should not be so small that it lacks substantially greater coverage than in the individual interview. The optimum size is approximately 10 to 12 persons. Social, intellectual, and educational homogeneity are important for effective participation of all group members. A circular seating arrangement, with the interviewer as one of the group, is conducive to full and spontaneous reporting and participation.

The advantages of the group interview are as follows:

1. Release of inhibitions through personal comments and responses, with expressions of interest by the interviewer

2. A wider range of response as the result of a wider range of experience on the part of the group

3. Recall of forgotten details of experience through the process of group interaction.

Possible disadvantages of the group interview are as follows:

1. Group interaction may result in controversies or discussions unrelated to the stimulus situation or topic. The interviewer should redirect attention to the initial problem.

2. Articulate members may be accorded the status of "leader," with the result that others may look to the leader for guidance, or one or more leaders may monopolize the discussion.

3. Continuity of group discussion sometimes is interrupted by an informant or respondent, with the result that the topic is not explored in detail.

4. The group may have an inhibiting effect of two kinds, in that interviewees may hesitate to reveal certain attitudes or experiences in the quasi-public situation of the group interview, and articulate subjects may withhold significant responses on the assumption that others in the group want to express themselves.

[59] Robert K. Merton, Marjorie Fiske, and Patricia L. Kendall, *op. cit.*, p. 136–53.

Focused, Depth, and Nondirective Interviews

Nonstructured interviews and interview guides usually are labeled by the terminology "focused," "depth," "nondirective." Although definite subject-matter areas are involved, the interviewer is largely free to arrange the form and timing of the question. The focused interview concentrates attention on some particular event or experience rather than on general lines of inquiry about the event. The depth interview is intensive and searching, with emphasis on such psychological and social factors as attitudes, convictions, or emotions. The nondirective approach as an uncontrolled or unstructured technique permits much freedom on the part of the respondent to "talk about" the problems under study.[60]

The focused interview is a method for collection of data developed to determine the responses of individuals to specific communication situations such as a movie or a speech. The procedural and technical aspects of focused interviewing may well be considered in terms of its relationship to other methods for collection of data, namely, observational, interview and questionnaire, and projective methods. Although focused interviewing places primary emphasis on the subject's verbal report of his definition of a specific situation and response to it, the method also possesses certain characteristics resembling closely the techniques found in projective and observational studies. During the course of the interview, the interviewer may utilize certain projective techniques to evaluate and interpret discrepancies occurring between the investigator's appraisal and the subject's report of the stimulus situation. The interviewer's objective evaluation of the particular situation to which subjects are to be exposed resembles observational procedures, in that the investigator is enabled: (1) to develop an hypothesis regarding expected and appropriate subject responses, (2) to focus the interview upon the subject's definition of and his responses to a particular situation, and (3) to appraise and interpret discrepancies occurring between his objective definition and the subject's subjective definition of the situation. An inherent disadvantage of focused interviewing is its limitation to occasions or settings where the investigator is able to secure an objective measurement of the specific social situation to which all subjects will be exposed. This limitation is relatively serious in the social sciences where there has been only limited success in objectively defining any simple or complex social situation.

[60] Pauline V. Young, *Scientific Social Surveys and Research, op. cit.*, p. 205–28.

Focused interviewing involves an unstructured form, nondirective orientation, and artistic and empathic skills.[61]

In general the focused interview employs nondirective procedures
in encouraging the respondent to structure the stimulus situation by indicating aspects of the situation most significant and by progressively
exploring his responses. Nondirection in the focused interview means
reliance on unstructured questions, but varying degrees of structure may
be present:

1. *Unstructured question (stimulus and response-free)*

    For example, "What impressed you most in this film?" or "What
    stood out especially in this conference?"

2. *Semi-structured question*

    Type *A*: *Response-structured, stimulus-free*. For example, "What did
    you learn from this pamphlet that you hadn't known before?"
    Type *B*: *Stimulus-structured, response-free*. For example, "How did
    you feel about the episode of Joe's discharge from the army as a
    psychoneurotic?"

3. *Structured question (stimulus- and response-structured)*

    For example, "Judging from the film, do you think that the German
    fighting equipment was better, as good as, or poorer than the equip-
    ment used by Americans?" or "As you listened to Chamberlain's speech,
    did you feel it was propagandistic or informative?"

    Although especially useful in opening stages, relatively unstructured
    questions can be profitably used throughout the interview.[62]

Depth procedures in focused interviews enable the investigator
through depth responses to determine the respondent's degree of detach-
ment or personal involvement in the experience, and the peripheral or
salient character of the responses. The procedures of such depth interviewing are as follows:[63]

Flexibility of Interview Situation
Flexible interviews encourage orientation to stimulus situation, rather
than to interviewer, thus facilitating depth and curbing stereotyped reports.

Retrospective Focus
Focus on past experience, through reinstatement of stimulus situation,
promotes elaboration of reported responses.

[61] Robert K. Merton, Marjorie Fiske, and Patricia L. Kendall, *op. cit.*, xx+186 p.
Reviewed by Charles G. McClintock, *Contemporary Psychology* 2: 220–21; August
1957.
[62] Quoted from Robert K. Merton, Marjorie Fiske, and Patricia L. Kendall, *op.
cit.*, p. 12–17.
[63] Quoted from *ibid.*, p. 96–113.

Focus on Feelings

Questions explicitly referring to affective aspects (e.g., "How did you feel when. . . ?") encourage reports of depth responses.

Restatement of Implied or Expressed Feelings

Occasional restatements of implied or expressed feelings prove effective by (1) inviting progressive elaboration of response, and (2) establishing common ground for mutual understanding. When interviewee indicates that he is not yet ready to admit these feelings, restatements can be extensive (in group interview) or projective (in individual interview).

Comparative Situations

Suggested comparisons between stimulus situation and significant experiences that subjects are known or can be presumed to have had often aid verbalization of effect.

Guiding the Course of an Interview: Overview[64]

A check list of recommendations for conducting the interview is as follows:

1. An interviewer generally should open an interview by asking factual nonthreatening questions.
2. The interviewer should locate the major data by unstructured "lead" questions.
3. The interviewer should make use of occasional guide questions.
4. The interviewer should make an effort to pick up leads.
5. The interviewer should cut through generalities with well-formulated probes.
6. The interviewer should stick with the fruitful areas once they open up.
7. The interviewer should reflect on the meaning of emerging data and ask questions that clarify or amplify their meaning for the research problem.
8. The interviewer should be especially alert to follow up only areas where the respondent shows emotional involvement.
9. The interviewer should try to redirect the interview to more fruitful topics when useful data are not emerging.
10. The interviewer should be alert to "touchy" subject matters and not just blunder in.
11. The interviewer should try to turn back respondent's direct questions.
12. The interviewer should wind up the interview before the respondent becomes tired.
13. Whether an interviewer should take notes depends on the situation.

[64] John T. Doby, Editor, *op. cit.*, p. 240–48.

Ways of Opening the Interview

Methods of beginning the interview include the following procedures:

An indirect social approach, as when a teacher calls on the parents of one of her pupils

Spontaneous reaction to controlled stimuli, as in administering an intelligence test to a child who has not learned to read

Distribution of forms prior to the interview, especially for the purpose of collecting statistical data

A direct frank approach, usually employed for research interviews, especially when factual data are involved.

Questions and Responses

Interviewing is an art which requires appropriate training and guided experience as essential background. Careful preparation of questions for the interview is fully as important as has been emphasized in preparing the questionnaire. A well-conducted interview is not just a haphazard series of questions and answers or a pleasant conversation. The interviewer has a set of carefully prepared questions to serve as a thread of conversation, although he may vary the order of the questions to adapt to special circumstances. These characterizations apply especially to data-gathering studies; nondirective or client-centered counseling permits greater freedom by way of an unstructured interview.

Inadequate responses which call for probing or secondary questions may be partial response, nonresponse, irrelevant response, inaccurate response, or verbalized response. In addition to problems of motivation and conflict of motives, other causes of inadequate response[65] include the following:

1. The respondent may fail to understand the purpose of the question or the kind of answer needed.

2. The language or concepts may go beyond the respondent's comprehension.

3. The respondent may lack the information or background necessary to answer the question.

4. The respondent may not remember the information requested.

5. The respondent may not be able to verbalize his feelings, as in the case of intimate, "depth" questions or materials.

6. The respondent may feel that the question does not fit the purpose of the interview.

[65] Robert L. Kahn and Charles F. Cannell, *op. cit.*, p. 203–32.

7. The respondent may regard a question as going beyond the limits of what he is willing to confide in the interviewer.

8. The respondent may feel that the interviewer is unable to understand his true feelings.

Sources of Error and Bias

Factors conducive to successful interviews (neglect of which may lead to failure) include the following:

An adequate number and length of interviews

Rapport and sensitivity to the interviewee

A comfortable and relaxing physical setting

A favorable reputation on the part of the interviewer, in terms of integrity and knowledge of the subject under study.

The reliability of the information obtained through the interview is affected by such factors as the following:

The desire of many interviewees to make a good impression, particularly in answering questions relating to generally accepted standards of behavior

The reluctance of many subjects to reveal highly personal information that might appear damaging to the interviewee

An attitude of confidence in and respect for the interviewer, on the part of the interviewee.

In addition to basic psychological factors or processes (intellectual, perceptual, cognitive, or motivational) affecting the interviewer and the respondent's interaction within the context of social relations with the interviewer, there are other possible sources of error or bias:[66] content and form of questions, procedures established for the interview, physical setting, mode of recording, accidental distractions, and temporary state of the parties involved. Variation and bias are likely to result when interviewers have complete freedom to interview respondents of their choice, to ask any questions desired (in any form), to make comments as they choose, and to record answers as they prefer (particularly after the close of the interview). Standardized interview procedures, however, may at times break down under the pressure of a specific situation. The history of election-forecasting reveals that the successful forecasts of a dozen years did not preclude a failure in 1948.

Potential sources of error and bias in the interview include firmly fixed attitudes, personality characteristics, motives, and goals that fre-

[66] Herbert H. Hyman and Others, *Interviewing in Social Research, op. cit.*, p. 171–72, 275.

quently are related to group memberships and loyalties (age, sex, race, religion, income, and education). Although these psychological and social characteristics or factors are potentially biasing, it is only through behavior that bias can become operative. This behavior, on the part of the interviewer, includes asking questions, probing for additional information, recording responses, and motivating the respondent to communicate. Helpful investigations of these behavioral sources of error and bias have been made, especially in social psychology and sociology. To function effectively and without bias, the interviewer needs techniques for formulation of questions, for motivation of the respondent, and for focusing communication on the content objectives of the interview; he also needs a deep understanding of the dynamics of interaction and of the psychological forces that affect the processes of the interview.[67]

Rapport, Interpersonal Relations, and Subjectivity[68]

It is generally accepted that a friendly atmosphere of rapport and skillful probing for meaningful answers are essential to a good interview. We question the skill of an interviewer who obtains numerous "don't know" responses. In attempting to establish favorable rapport, however, the interviewer should not err in the direction of extreme chumminess with the respondent. In depth-probing to secure meaningful responses, the investigator should not pursue the question to the extreme of distorting the situation, since some people have no hidden depths and only superficial attitudes on certain issues. At such times, repeated probing may suggest inaccurate responses and may "salt the mine."

Both interviewer and respondent contribute to the effects of interpersonal relationships. While the interviewer enters the situation with certain attitudes and beliefs that operate to affect his perception of the respondent, his judgment of the response, and other relevant aspects of his behavior, the respondent also entertains beliefs and attitudes which influence the response he makes and are at least in part a product of the personal-interview procedure. Certain respondent reactions are independent of any act or conduct on the part of the individual interviewer, and are merely a function of the interpersonal nature of the interview situation. The involvement of any respondent in an interview situation includes two major components: "task involvement" (involvement with the questions and answers) and "social involvement" (involvement with

[67] Robert L. Kahn and Charles F. Cannell, *op. cit.*, p. 166–202.
[68] Herbert H. Hyman and Others, *Interviewing in Social Research*, *op. cit.*, p. 8, 12–14, 24, 83, 138–39.

the interviewer as a personality). Validity should increase in proportion to the extent of task involvement on the part of the respondent. So far as the respondent's reaction derives from social or interpersonal involvement, bias will result, since the response is primarily a function of the relation between the respondent and the interviewer rather than a response to the particular task (the questions and answers).

Removal of the interviewer from the physical environment, as in the case of self-administered questionnaires, is not a complete answer to the problem of interviewer effect. Subjects filling out questionnaires may take account of the prospective readers of their replies, and thus involve an "interviewer effect," even when no interviewer is present. It is true that the social component of involvement is increased as the interviewer looms larger in the psychological field of the respondent, which means that the respondent usually will be more sensitized to the "interviewer" when the latter is physically present.

Much of the criticism of the interview technique rests on the fact that the data are derived from interpersonal situations. We should remember, however, that even in experimentation with animals in physiology and psychology, certain "interpersonal" relationships or effects may be present, as illustrated by research on conditioning in animals, although criticism of such experiments is rarely in terms of peculiar interpersonal relations between animal subject and human experimenter.

Although interviewer effect is a difficult problem in the social sciences, there are parallel errors of observation and measurement or interpretation in other sciences; for example, observer differences in reading chest x-ray films, in interpreting the results of laboratory tests, in appraising the malnutrition of children from medical examinations, or in noting the transit of stars in a telescope. We may be willing to pay the price of some crudity in the interview technique to secure the gains of essential information.

Examples of subjective or qualitative effects in the interview are numerous in the fields of clinical psychology and counseling. Differences between psychiatrists in the subtle dynamics of their interviewing behavior, differences which are possibly relevant to the variations in results reported, have been demonstrated through the application of instruments previously developed to describe social interaction processes; for example, significant differences in the degree of "activity" (ratio of talk to silence) of two psychiatrists, and similar differences in two psychiatrists with respect to an index of "tempo," another formal dimension of verbal behavior. In clinical psychology and counseling there are similar problems.

In counseling, the great concern with the actual nature of the therapeutic procedure has led to a series of studies in which an accurate description of the entire content of the interview is available from electrical recordings. Comparison of the counselor's written report of interviews with an electrical transcription demonstrates that there are large and significant omissions of content in the written record, alterations in the time sequence of remarks, and lack of precision in the notes, leading to ambiguity. Presumptive evidence of differences in counseling behavior is available from studies of the attitudes of counselors toward given interviewing practices. Therefore, a basic issue is the magnitude of errors in the collection of data by interview, efficient ways of estimating the presence of such errors, and the safeguards or checks upon such errors.

Hyman found that skilled interviewers frequently have certain beliefs about their respondents and expectations as to answers, but that the existence of such role expectations, attitude-structure expectations, and probability expectations did not materially affect the behavior of interviewers so as to alter survey results. The skillful interviewer's expectations may have a foundation in truth and consequently may enhance validity.

Records and Recording

Clinical interview findings, together with other related material, usually are filed in a folder or case record, including four types of information: (1) historical or background data concerning the patient's past life; (2) quantitative, or test and measurement results; (3) impressionistic or nonverbal behavior, such as gestures and posture; and (4) the treatment record, or data on medical treatment and psychiatric interview notes.[69]

Helpful extracts from interviews and illustrative records of interviews are as follows:

Clinical interviews under such catchy topics as the envious man, beaten man, weak feet, bad conscience, struggle within, sacrifice, overburdened mouth, and color barrier[70]

The dynamics of interviewing, including the problems of cardiac symptoms and neurotic manifestations, experienced and inexperienced applicants for a clerical job, a production bottleneck and an office feud, and family and job adjustments of a discharged psychiatric patient[71]

[69] L. A. Pennington and Irwin A. Berg, Editors, *op. cit.*, p. 125.
[70] Felix Deutsch and William F. Murphy, *The Clinical Interview*, Vol. 2: Therapy. New York: International Universities Press, 1955. 335 p.
[71] Robert L. Kahn and Charles F. Cannell, *op. cit.*, p. 253–351.

Psychiatric interviews with children[72]
Therapy through interviews[73]
Interviews in the general area of professional services.[74]

Interviewers have made increasing use of instrumentation and forms of recording, including tape recording, the telephone,[75] radio, and television. Among the activities where tape recordings[76] may be used effectively are the following:

1. Exploratory interviewing, as when using an unstructured or nondirective technique

2. Pretest interviewing, permitting the interviewer to subject the record to objective and intensive analysis

3. Intensive unstructured or nondirective interviewing, freeing the investigator from the mechanics of note-taking and enabling him to devote full attention to meanings

4. Interdisciplinary research, permitting the representatives of each discipline to select the data most pertinent to their own problems and interests.

Some of the questions most frequently raised about the effect of tape recording on interview data are as follows:[77]

1. Will the use of tape recorders increase resistance to the interview and thereby raise the refusal rate? The answer to this question—based upon our own experience and that of other investigators—would appear to be a clear "no."

2. Will the presence of the tape recorder decrease or destroy interviewer-respondent rapport? Our experience also suggests a negative answer to this question.

3. Will the presence of the tape recorder alter the responses of the respondent? No unequivocal answer to this question can be given without further systematic research. However, our impression—based upon a general evaluation and the contrast of about 300 written interviews with the approximately 700 tape recorded interviews gathered in the course of our work—is that there is no noticeable or significant effect on interview data that can be attributed to the introduction of the tape recorder.

The basic advantages of tape recording over various forms of note-taking and memory reconstruction are as follows:[78]

[72] Helen L. Witmer, *op. cit.*
[73] Stanley G. Law, *op. cit.*
[74] Anne F. Fenlason, *op. cit.*
[75] Paul Widen, "The Telephone Intake Interview in a Child Guidance Clinic." *Social Casework* 38: 485–89; November 1957.
[76] Rue Bucher, Charles E. Fritz, and E. L. Quarantelli, "Tape Recorded Interviews in Social Research." *American Sociological Review* 21: 359–64; June 1956.
[77] Quoted from *ibid.*
[78] Quoted from *ibid.*

1. Apart from the operational problems of obtaining proper audibility and voice fidelity, no verbal productions are lost in a tape recorded interview.

2. The tape recorded interview eliminates a major source of interviewer bias—the conscious and unconscious selection on the part of the interviewer of the material to note down.

3. The tape recorded interview not only eliminates the omissions, distortions, elaborations, condensations, and other modifications of data usually found in written interviews, but it also provides an objective basis for evaluating the adequacy of the interview data in relation to the performance of the interviewer.

4. The tape recorded interview is a liberating influence on the interviewer, because it permits him to devote full attention to the respondent.

5. Other things being equal, the interviewer who uses a tape recorder is able to obtain more interviews during a given time period than an interviewer who takes notes or attempts to reconstruct the interview from memory after the interview has been completed.

Interview transcriptions and commentaries, and records of the practice interviews of trainees, are valuable devices for training the beginner. Other techniques for acquiring the essential skills of interviewing include role-playing, with the trainee acting in turn as interviewer, respondent, and observer. Rating scales also are used in helping the interviewer evaluate the effectiveness of his techniques of probing for information.

OBSERVATIONAL STUDIES[79]

Observation, as a general rule, is concerned neither with what a respondent places on paper nor with what he says in an interview, but deals with the overt behavior of persons in appropriate situations, sometimes under conditions of normal living and at other times with some special

[79] Russell L. Ackoff, *The Design of Social Research*. Chicago: The University of Chicago Press, 1953. Chapter 9.

Dorothy C. Adkins, "Principles Underlying Observational Techniques of Evaluation." *Educational and Psychological Measurement* 11: 29–51; Spring 1951.

Robert F. Bales, *Interaction Process Analysis*. Cambridge, Mass.: Addison-Wesley Publishing Co., 1950. 203 p.

Roger G. Barker and Herbert F. Wright, *Midwest and Its Children*: The Psychological Ecology of an American Town. Evanston, Ill.: Row, Peterson and Co., 1955. vii+532 p.

Roger G. Barker and Herbert F. Wright, *One Boy's Day*: A Specimen Record of Behavior. New York: Harper & Brothers, 1951. x+435 p.

Clarence W. Brown and Edwin E. Ghiselli, *Scientific Method in Psychology*. New York: McGraw-Hill Book Co., 1955. p. 193–202.

Leon Festinger and Daniel Katz, Editors, *op. cit.*, p. 243–99, 381–417.

Elizabeth Gellert, "Systematic Observation: A Method in Child Study." *Harvard Educational Review* 25: 179–95; Summer 1955.

Ruth Glassow and Others, "Photographical and Cinematographical Research Methods," *Research Methods Applied to Health, Physical Education, and Recreation.*

set of factors operating. In a questionnaire or interview, the respondent may tell what he thinks he does, but human beings are not generally accurate or reliable observers of themselves. Only direct observation of overt behavior can reveal what the subject actually does. It is sometimes desirable to observe the behavior of persons when completing a questionnaire, participating in an interview, or taking a standardized test, since significant aspects of behavior or personality may be revealed under such conditions.

Direct observation as a systematic research approach in the psychological and social areas has developed during the present century, with marked progress in educational studies during the second quarter of the century. Among the factors favorable to wider use of observation as an investigational procedure were the following: establishment of centers for research in child development; the demands of the newer or progressive education; a desire to probe aspects of behavior not accessible to the conventional paper-and-pencil test, interview, or laboratory technique; a wish to obviate certain of the judgmental errors likely to enter into the customary rating procedures; and emphasis on the need for studying children in natural or social situations, and for observing the functioning child (including his social and emotional behavior), rather than relying exclusively on cross-sectional measurements of mental and physical growth.[80]

Revised Edition. Washington: American Association for Health, Physical Education, and Recreation, 1952. p. 204–18.

Carter V. Good and Douglas E. Scates, *op. cit.*, p. 646–62.

William J. Goode and Paul K. Hatt, *op. cit.*, p. 119–31.

Marie Jahoda and Others, *op. cit.*, p. 129–50, 493–513.

Arthur T. Jersild and Margaret F. Meigs, "Direct Observation as a Research Method." *Review of Educational Research* 9: 472–82, 597–99; December 1939.

John Madge, *op. cit.*, p. 117–43.

C. A. Moser, *op. cit.*, Chapter 9.

J. Francis Rummel, *op. cit.*, p. 64–75.

Morris S. Schwartz and Charlotte G. Schwartz, "Problems in Participant Observation." *American Journal of Sociology* 60: 343–53; January 1955.

Saul B. Sells, "Observational Methods of Research." *Review of Educational Research* 18: 424–47; December 1948.

Saul B. Sells and Robert W. Ellis, "Observational Procedures Used in Research." *Review of Educational Research* 21: 432–49; December 1951.

R. M. W. Travers, *An Introduction to Educational Research*. New York: The Macmillan Co., 1958. Chapter 8.

Lovisa C. Wagoner and J. M. Castellanos, *Observation of Young Children*: Their Behavior and Their Teaching. Revised Edition. Oakland, Calif.: L. C. Wagoner, Mills College, 1951. xii+142 p.

Robert I. Watson, *The Clinical Method in Psychology*. New York: Harper & Brothers, 1951. p. 64–82.

Pauline V. Young, *Scientific Social Surveys and Research*, *op. cit.*, p. 154–75.

[80] Arthur T. Jersild and Margaret F. Meigs, *op. cit.*

Planning the Design of Observational Studies

The following list of factors that affect reliability of observation may serve as a check list or summary of problems in planning the design of observational investigations. Poor reliability may be a function of one or more of these factors:[81]

1. Inadequate sampling
2. Lack of precision in defining behavior
3. Complexity of method of recording
4. Rapid, complex interaction
5. Difference in perspective of observers
6. Individual differences in degree of decisiveness of activities of subjects observed
7. Constant errors due to observer bias (overweighting, timing, "halo" effects, etc.)
8. Requiring high-order inferences in classifying behavior
9. Demanding the simultaneous observation of too many variables
10. Excessively long periods of observation without interspersed rest periods
11. Inadequate training of observers
12. The effect of individual observers upon the behavior of the subjects
13. Degree of acquaintance with the subjects.

Another classification of factors important in planning and conducting observations was prepared originally for the field of psychology, but applies also to education and other social areas.[82]

1. Nature of the observing process
   a. Mechanisms involved in observing
   b. Active nature of observing
   c. "Mental sets" in observing
2. Scientist as observer
   a. Distinguishing facts and inference
   b. Safeguards in attitude
   c. Adequate training in observational techniques
   d. Mechanical supplements to observation
3. Temporal course of the observations
   a. Necessity for constant conditions of observation
   b. Temporal variations in subjects
   c. Temporal variations in apparatus

[81] Elizabeth Gellert, *op. cit.*
[82] Clarence W. Brown and Edwin E. Ghiselli, *op. cit.*

4. Number of observations
    a. Variability of behavior
    b. Replication of observations to achieve representativeness
    c. Statistical compared with practical significance
    d. Designing the study in order to increase the number of observations
5. Recording the observations
    a. Need for records
    b. Records to be comprehensive
    c. Accuracy of records varying with degree of conceptualization
    d. Limitations of apparatus recording
    e. Keeping a daily record.

To summarize briefly, the aspects of planning for observation include the following factors that affect the success of the investigation:[83]

An appropriate group of subjects to observe

Selection and arrangement of any special conditions for the group

Length of each observation period, interval between periods, and number of periods

Physical position of the observer and possible effect on the subject or subjects

Definition of specific activities or units of behavior to be observed

Entry of frequencies or tallies in the record, as a total for the entire observation period or by subdivisions of time within the observation period

Scope of observation, whether for an individual child or for a group

Form of recording, including consideration of mechanical techniques and such quantitative factors as number, time, distance, and spatial relationships

Training of the observer in terms of expertness

Interpretation of observations.

Participant Observation

Participant observation is a dynamic process of interaction, involving registering, interpreting, and recording.

The process and the kinds of data are influenced by continuing observed-observer transactions. The role of the observer may be passive or active. In either case affective involvement with the observed develops inevitably and may range from sympathetic identification to projective distortion. The form it takes is a function primarily of the observer's experience, awareness, and personality. Anxiety and bias are sources of distortion, and their adequate handling is a major problem in refining the human instrument for gathering data.[84]

[83] Carter V. Good and Douglas E. Scates, *op. cit.*
[84] Quoted from Morris S. Schwartz and Charlotte G. Schwartz, *op. cit.*

The investigator may play any one of several roles in observation of social situations, with varying degrees of participation,[85] as a visiting stranger, an attentive listener, an eager learner, or a more complete role as participant-observer. As indicated, participation or role-playing is not necessarily complete, since it is possible to take part in many of the activities of the group, as an accepted member, and at the same time act in the role of observer and interviewer. Quasi-participation is illustrated by a study of "corner boys" in an Italian slum.[86] The observer or investigator came in as the local historian under the auspices of a key member of a gang. In other words, the investigator may be disguised in such a manner as to be accepted as a member of the group, although he may not carry out exactly the same activities as the other members, in order to be accepted as a participant-observer. Obviously, if the group has accepted the observer as a participant, their behavior is least likely to be affected by the presence of the participant-observer.

The participant-observer commonly lives in the community or social setting under study, as he takes part in the activities and functions of the particular group or groups. In this way he gets the "feel" of what the various activities and processes mean to the regular participants. The participant-observer also plays a dual role, in that he must take an objective position after performing as a participant; otherwise his subjective reactions might distort his findings. Classic examples[87] are *Middletown* and *Middletown in Transition*.

Two interesting examples of participant observation represent a Negro subculture and a group which thought the world was coming to an end.

EXAMPLE: BLACKWAYS OF KENT[88]

In research method, the book shows a happy combination of anthropological field work technique and sociological participant-observational technique. Approaching the study of the Negro subculture in the manner of an anthropologist and sociologist, Hylan Lewis, in Part One, not only places

[85] Raymond L. Gold, "Roles in Sociological Field Observations." *Social Forces* 36: 217–23; March 1958.

William J. Goode and Paul K. Hatt, *op. cit.*, p. 120–24.

Marie Jahoda and Others, *op. cit.*, p. 134–48, 493–513.

Pauline V. Young, *Scientific Social Surveys and Research*, *op. cit.*, p. 157–64.

[86] William F. Whyte, *Street Corner Society*: The Social Structure of an Italian Slum. Enlarged Edition. Chicago: The University of Chicago Press, 1955. xxii+336 p.

[87] Robert S. Lynd and Helen M. Lynd, *Middletown*: A Study in Contemporary Culture. New York: Harcourt, Brace and Co., 1929. x+550 p.

Robert S. Lynd and Helen M. Lynd, *Middletown in Transition*: A Study in Cultural Conflicts. New York: Harcourt, Brace and Co., 1937. xviii+604 p.

[88] Quoted from review by Jitsuichi Masuoka, *American Sociological Review*

solidly the *Blackways of Kent* in their geographic, ecological, and demographic contexts but also in the broader cultural situation. In Part Two, he deals with contents of the subculture in terms of the institutions of courtship, marriage, and the family; the economics of Negro life; religion and salvation; teaching the children; government and social control; orientations and values; and social organization. He concludes the book by touching upon the consistency and coordination of ways of life, and briefly relates the Negro subculture to the dominant or "foreign" culture of Kent.

EXAMPLE: WHEN PROPHECY FAILS[89]

At the approach of midnight one December 20 not long ago, fifteen persons maintained anxious vigil in a "Lake City" living room. For all of them the occasion was momentous, but the reader of this remarkable book knows what a casual visitor to the gathering would not have guessed: for five members of the company the occasion had entirely different significance than for the other ten. Ostensibly, the entire group was awaiting spacemen who, at the appointed hour, were to rescue them in flying saucers from the worldwide cataclysm of earthquake and flood that they expected before dawn. In fact, five persons—a third of those present—were participant observers who had been following the band of believers for more than a month, awaiting opportunity to test some theoretically-based predictions about what happens in social movements "when prophecy fails." Fortunately for the reader, the prophecy did fail; less predictably, the prophecy was explicit and remained so to the crucial hour; the disconfirmation was unequivocal.

Clearly this is no routine research report. The book, an eminently readable one, represents a noteworthy venture in at least four respects, around which subsequent comments will be focused. First, it is an exemplary instance in which alert social psychologists with a theory to test were able to see the relevance of a passing event, and to respond to it in time and in sufficient force to capture the pertinent data. Incidental to testing their central hypothesis, secondly, the authors provide an inside account of a miniature apocalyptic movement, an account that is fascinating quite apart from its bearing on the authors' theory. Securing the necessary information from such a socially marginal group, in the third place, tested the resourcefulness of the observers. Their account of the unusual problems they encountered and how they attempted to solve them (given in a methodological appendix) will be of special interest to investigators not intimidated by the barrier between the laboratory and "real life." Finally, the authors' temerity and success in covertly penetrating others' privacy, essential as it was to the enterprise, raises some serious problems of research ethics, problems hardly encountered when psy-

---

21: 111–12; February 1956, of Hylan Lewis, *Blackways of Kent*. Chapel Hill: University of North Carolina Press, 1955. xxiv+337 p.

Also see John K. Morland, *Millways of Kent*. Third volume of "Field Studies in the Modern Culture of the South." Chapel Hill: University of North Carolina Press, 1958. xxii+291 p.

[89] Quoted from review by M. Brewster Smith, *Contemporary Psychology* 2: 89–92; April 1957, of Leon Festinger, Henry W. Riecken, and Stanley Schachter, *When Prophecy Fails*. Minneapolis: University of Minnesota Press, 1956. vii+256 p.

chologists confine themselves to the accustomed laboratory or clinic. The authors have elected to present their findings without discussing the ethical ambiguities that must have troubled them and their associates. The difficulties remain, however, and the rest of us would do well to face them more explicitly.

In summary, participant observation has certain advantages over such survey techniques as the questionnaire:[90]

1. The participant observer is not basically limited by prejudgment, but can reformulate the problem as he goes along.

2. Because of his closer contact with the field situation, he is better able to avoid misleading or meaningless questions.

3. The impressions of a participant field worker are often more reliable in classifying respondents than a rigid index based on one or two questions in a questionnaire.

4. The most expert and highest paid persons are in direct contact with the data in the field.

5. He can ease himself into the field situation at the appropriate pace and thus avoid rebuff by blundering into delicate situations or subject matter.

6. He can constantly remodify his categories to provide more meaningful analysis of problems under study.

7. He can generally impute motives more validly on the basis of the interlocking of aspersions and actual behavior, supplemented by occasional "feedback" reactions.

8. He can select later informants in such a way as to throw additional light on emerging hypotheses.

9. He can generally get at depth material more satisfactorily.

10. He may absorb considerable information which seems at the time irrelevant, but later proves valuable for perspective.

11. He can make use of selected informants' skills and insights by giving them free rein to report the problem situation as they see it.

12. He usually can move more easily back and forth between data-gathering in the field and desk analysis.

13. Through free data-gathering he probably distorts less the difficult-to-quantify situations or aspects of a problem.

14. While ostensibly just participating, he can do covert research in delicate areas.

15. Participant observation usually involves less expense.

Nonparticipant Observation

The nonparticipant observer takes a position where his presence is not disturbing to the group, such as a kindergarten or a nursery school.

[90] John T. Doby, Editor, *op. cit.*, p. 227-29.

He may follow in detail the behavior of only one child or may describe one or two behavior characteristics of a dozen or more children. This type of observation permits use of recording instruments and gathering of large quantities of data that may be treated statistically. Also observations of different investigators may be checked against each other in terms of relative accuracy. Variations in the observations of trained and reliable observers frequently are surprisingly large.[91] Nonparticipant observation is illustrated by observing and recording conditions in such settings as a nursery school, classroom, teachers' meeting, playground, home, Sunday school, summer camp, factories, retail stores, police station, or court.

Illustrative Observational Studies

Interest in the behavior of infants and young children stimulated development of the technique of direct observation, as did a desire for improved instructional and supervisory procedures. Many of the earlier observational investigations were "omnibus" reports of everything a child did or said over long periods of minute observation, but later observational studies have been concerned with more limited characteristics of behavior, sometimes measurements of one or two traits. The older omnibus or case-history types of data were not usually suitable for statistical treatment and often reflected the particular ability or attitude of the observer himself. The later studies of limited scope are more reliable, with less personal variation between observers, and compare favorably with the reliability of paper-and-pencil instruments. Examples of the more limited observational studies during recent years are as follows: interpersonal smiling responses in the preschool years over a two-year interval, including 150 recorded observations; the spontaneous remarks of 12 nursery-school children during a period of four weeks; the behavior and changes over a period of seven weeks induced in a seven-year-old girl who moved suddenly from a small city apartment to an elegant country estate; recorded speech sounds for "only" infants and for those with older siblings; and 1001 recorded remarks overheard in conversations among the population of Manhattan.[92]

To cite an example[93] of minute observation of behavior, a record of what a seven-year-old boy did in the situations confronting him in his home, school, and neighborhood from the time he awoke one morning until he went to sleep that night represents a minute-by-minute chron-

[91] Emory S. Bogardus, *The Development of Social Thought.* Third Edition. New York: Longmans, Green and Co., 1955. p. 628–29.
[92] Saul B. Sells and Robert W. Ellis, *op. cit.*
[93] Roger G. Barker and Herbert F. Wright, *One Boy's Day, op. cit.*

ology, showing him interacting with parents, teachers, adults, and other children. Eight trained observers took turns in gathering the data throughout the day. Each observational period was approximately 30 minutes in length, with brief notes made during the period and the observations dictated into a sound recorder immediately after the end of the period.

Barker and Wright have provided a sharp contrast to observation of one child's behavior in a description of 585 community settings and 10,406 episodes of child behavior. These 585 settings as a major source of data are described in 26 ways; for example, "occupancy" describes the total man-hours spent in each setting, while "penetration" indicates how important and central a person is in a setting (from leader down to spectator). If each participation in a setting in the role of a responsible functionary is taken as a performance, then the 721 midwest citizens accomplished a total of 5,659 performances, an average of about 7 performances per person per year. The second main source of data is 11 "specimen records," each describing one day's behavior of one child. Each of the 10,406 episodes in the eleven specimen records is described in terms of 29 variables, with the findings presented in the form of frequency distributions; for example, the action of midwest children toward other children shows the following characteristics in decreasing frequency: domination, appeal, resistance, nurturance, aggression, submission, compliance, and avoidance.[94]

Recording Techniques and Instruments

Methods and devices for recording observations include time-sampling procedures, shorthand records of conversations and of teacher and pupil participation in classroom lessons, still and motion-picture photography for infants and young children and in sports and physical activities,[95] a photographic dome with a one-way vision screen and tracks for movement of the camera, a clinical crib or isolation cabinet for infants, a one-way vision screen or mirror, sound-recording devices for studying language, an electric-eye ticker to count the number of autos or persons passing a given spot, a counting apparatus at the gate or door to keep a current record of attendance, an observer with a ticker device in his hand to count the number of persons passing a particular spot, mechanical recording devices attached to the radio or telephone, and an applause

[94] Roger G. Barker and Herbert F. Wright, *Midwest and Its Children, op. cit.* Reviewed by Alfred L. Baldwin, *Contemporary Psychology* 1: 149–50; May 1956.
[95] Ruth Glassow and Others, *op. cit.*, p. 204–18. Also see certain chapters on laboratory and experimental research, p. 182–203, 254–300.

meter. Recording of behavior has an element of objectivity, in that the observer may look at or hear the same record as often as desired, and comparisons may be made between the judgments of different persons who use the same record. Motion pictures have the advantage of presenting the action in slow motion. With mechanical methods of recording, it is important to include enough elements of behavior to represent typical social situations rather than to be limited to characteristics so narrow and simple that they are not significant in understanding behavior in actual social settings.

Special forms or types of observation are represented by the anecdotal technique and by procedures for study of small groups or group-behavior analysis. Anecdotal records are discussed in the chapter on case and clinical studies, and small-group studies are presented in the next section of the present chapter. In many of these investigations of small groups observation has provided all or part of the data.

Observation in Relation to Experimentation

The pressure of clinical problems during recent years has brought many psychologists to a realization that observation and description usually are necessary prior to experimentation. Psychology and biology are making mutual contributions to the technique of observation. Animal behaviorists with biological training have been doing the basic collecting of observational facts on animal species as a prerequisite to understanding details of behavior which can be subjected to experimentation. Intelligent planning of experiments on the effect of early experience requires a knowledge of normal behavioral events. The descriptive material throws new light on human development and suggests possibilities for research. Psychology has contributed to the technique of observation through use of duplicate observers, statistical techniques of reliability, studies of perception, and use of moving pictures in which behavioral situations may be exactly repeated and discrimination more easily taught than in most real-life situations. The training of psychology students may well include more emphasis on the technique of objective observation. Many of the important problems of human behavior lie in the area of social relationships and personality interaction where a paper-and-pencil test cannot duplicate real-life situations, which means that, as in clinical psychology, observation is the only satisfactory technique.[96]

Direct observation makes a contribution not usually present in con-

---

[96] J. P. Scott, "The Place of Observation in Biological and Psychological Science." *American Psychologist* 10: 61–64; February 1955.

trolled experimentation. Observational studies may deal with certain stimuli in a complex social setting to which the children react, with possible comparisons between different subjects. Such social settings are regarded as natural or normal, whereas many experimental situations and laboratory settings are considered artificial or unnatural in character. It is true that many of the conditions in carefully planned observational studies are similar to the requirements of controlled experimentation, with the exception of manipulating a variable factor, in that basic factors or conditions of observation are controlled by selection of the room, equipment, children, stimuli, and observers. Direct observation of learning in a regular classroom setting can provide us with running accounts of what happens from day to day in teaching a group of children some complex skill, generalization, or attitude, including errors and their origins, improvement and the causes, instructional difficulties and methods of correction, plateau periods in learning and remedial techniques, and levels of pupil progress from time to time or stage to stage.[97]

Objectivity and Preparation for Observation

Even the simplest observation in physics or in the more objective areas of psychology has in it the essence of a judgment or interpretation, and in the early days of psychology Helmholtz recognized that

the observation depends upon the past experience of the observer, his unconscious inferences and the resulting modification of the sensory core. . . . There is the influence of a "laboratory atmosphere" upon observational results, which means that investigators are likely to observe what they are trained to observe, and there is also the contrary fact that good observers have to be trained.[98]

The uncertainties and difficulties of correct observation are illustrated by the "flying saucers" of recent years, owing to indefinite concepts, exaggeration, error, imagination, and absence of essential facts.[99] Attempts at direct observation of earth satellites probably involve similar difficulties and uncertainties.

The problem of objectivity in observation has perplexed survey ex-

---

[97] William A. Brownell, "A Critique of Research on Learning and on Instruction in the School," *Graduate Study in Education.* Fiftieth Yearbook of the National Society for the Study of Education, Part 1. Chicago: The University of Chicago Press, 1951. p. 62–65.
[98] Quoted from Edwin G. Boring, *A History of Experimental Psychology.* Second Edition. New York: Appleton-Century-Crofts, 1950. p. 313.
[99] C. C. Wylie, "Those Flying Saucers." *Science* 118: 124–26; July 31, 1953.
Donald H. Menzel, *Flying Saucers.* Cambridge: Harvard University Press, 1953. 319 p.

perts and other students of administrative questions in higher education (and secondary schools as well). By the accrediting standards and procedures of some years ago, a too narrow conception of research and survey technique centered the attention of visiting committees on matters that could be enumerated or counted (students, courses, faculty members, books, average teaching loads, unit expenditures, laboratory and classroom space per student, and duties of administrative officers), to the partial neglect of careful observation and logical analysis by observers of insight. Many aspects of secondary schools and higher institutions, as appraised by accrediting teams of observers, are now reported at least in part in qualitative rather than statistical terms (including administrative organization, objectives, curriculum, instructional methods, evaluative techniques, personnel and guidance policies, and student-faculty morale).[100]

The investigator who plans to use direct observation of behavior as a research approach should realize that careful preparation and training are necessary. In the earlier days of the child-study movement the observational method was popular, partly because it was thought that no special preparation or apparatus was needed; one simply watched the child and reported what he saw. As an illustration of the thoroughness of training recommended for observations of the introspective type, "it is said that no observer who had performed less than 10,000 of the introspectively controlled reactions was suitable to provide data for published research from Wundt's laboratory. Some Americans, like Cattell, had the idea that the minds of untrained observers might also be of interest to psychology, and later a bitter little quarrel on this matter developed."[101]

SMALL-GROUP STUDY OR GROUP BEHAVIOR ANALYSIS[102]

In studying small groups or in group-behavior analysis, much of the discussion of the preceding section of this chapter is pertinent, including the topics of particular aspects of behavior observed and recorded, nonparticipant and participant observation, instruments for observation, forms of recording, categories or units of behavior, time units for tallying responses, length of the observation period, scope in relation to

[100] Norman Burns, "Higher Education." *Review of Educational Research* 22: 375–85; October 1952.

[101] Edwin G. Boring, "A History of Introspection." *Psychological Bulletin* 50: 169–89; May 1953.

[102] Michael Argyle, *The Scientific Study of Social Behavior*. New York: Philosophical Library, 1957. 239 p.

Robert F. Bales, *Interaction Process Analysis*. Cambridge, Mass.: Addison-Wesley Publishing Co., 1950. 203 p.

Leland P. Bradford and Jack R. Gibb, "Developments in Group Behavior in Adult Education." *Review of Educational Research* 23: 233–47; June 1953.

number of subjects, training and reliability of the observer, and interpretation of observational data.[103]

It is more time-consuming to study group-member interaction by direct observation of a group in some artificial or natural setting, as described in the preceding section. Large amounts of time are required to train judges or raters, who usually are more numerous than is true for sociometric or peer-group ratings. Direct observation is especially effective, however, in investigations that deal with such areas as communications and problem-solving. Many of the studies of group dynamics include some combination of observational and paper-and-pencil techniques.

Procedures and Instruments

During the second half of the 1950's, discussion and experimental activity concerned with group behavior continued at a vigorous rate, with further refinement of useful observational methods and increased knowledge of variables operating to bias and distort the observations

---

Dorwin Cartwright and Alvin Zander, *Group Dynamics*: Research and Theory. Evanston, Ill.: Row, Peterson and Co., 1953. 642 p.

Leon Festinger, Stanley Schachter, and Kurt Back, *Social Pressures in Informal Groups*. New York: Harper & Brothers, 1950. 240 p.

Eric F. Gardner and George G. Thompson, *Social Relations and Morale in Small Groups*. New York: Appleton-Century-Crofts, 1956. ix+312 p.

Harold Guetzkow, Editor, *Groups, Leadership, and Men*: Research in Human Relations. Pittsburgh: Carnegie Press, 1951. 293 p.

Paul Hare, Edgar F. Borgatta, and Robert F. Bales, *Small Groups*: Studies in Social Interaction. New York: Alfred A. Knopf, 1955. xv+666 p.

George C. Homans, *The Human Group*. New York: Harcourt, Brace and Co., 1950. 484 p.

Mary E. Roseborough, "Experimental Studies of Small Groups." *Psychological Bulletin* 50: 275–303; July 1953.

Muzafer Sherif and M. O. Wilson, *Group Relations at the Crossroads*. New York: Harper & Brothers, 1953. viii+379 p.

Eloise C. Snyder, "The Supreme Court As a Small Group." *Social Forces* 36: 232–38; March 1958.

F. L. Strodtbeck and A. P. Hare, "Bibliography of Small Group Research, from 1900 through 1953." *Sociometry* 17: 107–78; May 1954. Includes 1407 items.

F. L. Strodtbeck and Others, "Small Group Research." *American Sociological Review* 19: 651–781; December 1954.

Marvin Taylor and Harold E. Mitzel, "Research Tools: Observing and Recording Group Behavior," in "Methodology of Educational Research." *Review of Educational Research* 27: 476–86; December 1957.

Herbert A. Thelen, *Dynamics of Groups at Work*. Chicago: The University of Chicago Press, 1954. 379 p.

Herbert A. Thelen, "Educational Dynamics, Theory and Research." *Journal of Social Issues* 6: 1–96; 1950.

William A. Van Til and Others, "Research on Human Relations and Programs of Action." *Review of Educational Research* 23: 285–385; October 1953.

Alvin Zander, "Systematic Observation of Small Face-to-Face Groups," *Research Methods in Social Relations*. Edited by Marie Jahoda and Others. New York: Dryden Press, 1951. p. 515–38.

[103] Alvin Zander, *op. cit.*, p. 515–38.

themselves. A number of investigations have been concerned with locating and studying variables affecting group-member interaction; for example, a conceptual framework for observing both the social structure and the interaction within classroom groups (problem-solving, authority-leadership, power, friendship, personal prestige, sex, and privileges). Other studies have dealt with administrative and leadership relationships within an established, hierarchal organization, utilizing scales which produce sociometric data, and with peer- and self-ratings. These techniques are useful in obtaining intimate data about intragroup relations which are not easily accessible to the observer's eye or to other forms of paper-and-pencil tests.

The development and refinement of sociometric instruments are illustrated by a variety of studies: relationship between sociometric choices of preschool-age children and criteria of social behavior; a picture sociometric test for use with preschool-age children, utilizing large photographs of children in the same group and several oral sociometric-type questions; relationship between choices of friends and such variables (observed by a group of sophisticated judges in two-minute segments) as associative play, friendly approach, conversation, hostile interaction, attention, and no response; and development of social-relations instruments or scales which provide indexes of an individual's social-relations status in a group and indexes of social-group structure. Some of the activity in this area has been concerned with problems other than the development of new sociometric instruments: reliability and validity of the sociometric-type test in a variety of military, industrial, and educational settings; relations between sociometric choice and perceived similarity and dissimilarity; measures of prestige as revealed by a sociometric-type questionnaire and an anthropological field-worker's ratings; number of choices to be allotted the subject, in the construction of sociometric tests; ways of analyzing and charting or mapping the results of sociometric tests; and social growth of a group over a period of time, as revealed by test-retest sociometric data.[104]

Illustrative Studies and Problem Areas

Varied illustrations[105] of group-behavior studies may be listed in outline form, classified according to the problem area represented:

Communications: direction of remarks between members of the group in leaderless and in trainer-dominated sessions; relationship between the

[104] Marvin Taylor and Harold E. Mitzel, *op. cit.*
[105] *Ibid.*

type of participation in a small-group discussion and feelings of satisfaction; emotional responsiveness, as measured by a paper-and-pencil technique and by observation of the group

Group problem-solving: effectiveness of group versus individual problem-solving, development of criteria for measuring effectiveness, and the process of group problem-solving

Conformity behavior: amount of agreement between group participants in discussion, and effect of simulated group discussion or of a tape recording of a simulated group in producing conformity

Social-emotional climate: use of rating instruments and scales to assess the quality of social acceptance in a classroom, consistency of teacher behavior in the area of social-emotional climate, "esprit de corps" and "group effectiveness" components of morale, and group cohesiveness

Role behavior: structuring over a period of time of initially informal groups, role differentiation by the various members of a group, and relation between leadership, followership, and friendship in a group

Assessment and selection: use of group techniques in selection and training of candidates for critical jobs, primarily through development of situational tests that yield data relevant to prediction of individual performances on a job; a functional observation room for studying small groups, including comfort and space requirements, needs of research staff, visiting spectators, and the design of the experimental room; utility of leaderless-group discussions for evaluating leadership behavior; and factors affecting the validity of the judgment of assessors, pointing to a consensus of judges' ratings for valid results.

Bibliographical and Summarizing Reports

Helpful bibliographical and summarizing tools for the subject of group behavior are available:

A bibliography of small-group research for the period from 1900 through 1953, including 1,407 items[106]

A summary and interpretation of 169 experimental studies of small groups, covering the topics of contrasts and comparisons between the behavior of groups and individuals, manipulation of social-structure variables important to group functioning (authority relationships), effect of cultural variables (sharing of values and goals in a group), manipulation of situational conditions (such as group task, size of group, communication networks), and personality variables affecting group behavior[107]

A 94-item bibliography and summary of the research literature on group behavior for the period of the early 1950's, covering the topics of trends in small-group research, development in methodology, leader style and group atmosphere, communication in small groups, interpersonal perceptions, the

[106] F. L. Strodtbeck and A. P. Hare, *op. cit.*
[107] Mary E. Roseborough, *op. cit.*

decision-making process, emotional factors in group interaction, group size and the large meeting, and leadership and human-relations training[108]

A bibliography of 62 items and summary, dealing with the research tools for observing and recording group behavior, under the topics of measurement of group-membership interaction, sociometric instruments, direct observational techniques, communications, group problem-solving, conformity, social-emotional climate, role behavior, and assessment and selection.[109]

Next Steps

During the latter half of the 1950's, improvements and refinements in small-group study were marked by replication of earlier investigations, development of mathematical models, interdisciplinary research, and expenditure of large amounts of money for long-range studies in natural settings, as in the military services and in industry. Further progress in group theory and methodology will depend on continuous development of more rigorous techniques of locating and measuring variables connected with group characteristics and group structure, a closer relationship between theory and data-gathering, and greater uniformity in semantics or terminology.[110]

THE CRITICAL-INCIDENT TECHNIQUE[111]

The critical-incident technique is a set of procedures for collecting direct observations of human behavior in such a way as to facilitate their potential usefulness in solving practical problems and in developing broad psychological principles, with emphasis on observed incidents possessing special significance and meeting systematically defined criteria. An incident is any observable human activity sufficiently complete in itself to permit inferences and predictions about the person performing the act. To be considered critical, an incident must occur in a situation where the purpose or intent of the act seems fairly clear to the observer

---

[108] Leland P. Bradford and Jack R. Gibb, *op. cit.*

[109] Marvin Taylor and Harold E. Mitzel, *op. cit.*

[110] *Ibid.*

[111] John E. Corbally, Jr., "The Critical Incident Technique and Educational Research." *Educational Research Bulletin* 35: 57–62; March 14, 1956.

John C. Flanagan, "The Critical Incident Technique." *Psychological Bulletin* 51: 327–58; July 1954.

D. Wells Goodrich and Donald S. Boomer, "Some Concepts about Therapeutic Interventions with Hyperaggressive Children: Part 1." *Social Casework* 39: 207–13; April 1958. Critical-incident technique.

Lewis B. Mayhew, "The Critical Incident Technique in Educational Evaluation." *Journal of Educational Research* 49: 591–98; April 1956.

and where its consequences are sufficiently definite to leave little doubt concerning its effects.

Examples

The origin of the critical-incident technique may be found in time-sampling studies of recreational activities, controlled observation tests, and anecdotal records, although the method as such may be regarded as an outgrowth of studies in the Aviation Psychology Program of the United States Army Air Forces in World War II. Illustrations of these studies include an analysis of the specific reasons for failure in learning to fly, reasons for the failures of bombing missions, critical requirements of combat leadership, disorientation while flying, and factual incidents as a basis for research on the design of instruments and controls and the arrangement of these within the cockpit; other investigations have sought to determine critical requirements for the work of an officer in the United States Air Force, a commercial airline pilot, research personnel on a particular project, hourly wage employees in an industry, and for many other specific occupational groups or activities.

An example of the critical-incident technique is found in an analysis of approximately 2,000 responses revealing attitudes of students and adults in terms of excellent and poor citizenship, in that the study is a process of analyzing free responses to critical-incidents questions on citizenship, classified under 19 categories.[112]

Procedures and Applications

The five steps[113] in the critical-incident procedure are as follows:

1. Determination of the general aim of the activity, in the form of a brief statement from the authorities in the field that expresses in simple terms those objectives to which most people would agree

2. Development of plans and specifications for collecting factual incidents regarding the activity, with the instructions to the persons reporting their observations stated as specifically as possible with respect to the standards used in evaluating and classifying the observed behavior

3. Collection of data, with the incident reported in an interview or written up by the observer himself, so as to be objective and include all relevant details

---

[112] Citizenship Education Project, *Content Analysis Manual*: Classification System for Analysis of Responses to Four Questions on Citizenship. Publication No. 9. New York: Teachers College, Columbia University, 1950. 52 p.

Citizenship Education Project, *Building Better Programs in Citizenship*. New York: Teachers College, Columbia University, 1958. 320 p. Describes the nature of the project and the techniques for planning and promoting the program at the local school level.

[113] John C. Flanagan, *op. cit.*

4. Analysis of data, in the form of an effective summary and description which can be used for practical purposes

5. Interpretation and reporting of the statement of the requirements of the activity, indicating both limitations and values of the results.

The two basic principles of the critical-incident technique may be summarized concisely as follows:

1. Reporting of facts regarding behavior is preferable to the collection of interpretations, ratings, and opinions based on general impressions.
2. Reporting should be limited to those behaviors which, according to competent observers, make a significant contribution to the activity.

Applications of the critical-incident procedure have been made in the following areas:[114]

1. Measures of typical performance (criteria)
2. Measures of proficiency (standard samples)
3. Training
4. Selection and classification
5. Job design and purification
6. Operating procedures
7. Equipment design
8. Motivation and leadership (attitudes)
9. Counseling and psychotherapy.

Use in Education

In applying the critical-incident technique to education, it is essential to include the following aspects: observation of on-the-job behavior, evaluation of significant success or lack of success in meeting the aims of the job, reporting incidents which led to marked success or failure in meeting the aims of the job, and treatment of the data in such incidents so as to isolate and categorize the critical elements of the job. It should also be kept in mind that the technique was originally intended to study men at work on machines (including airplanes, scientific instruments, and assembly lines), whereas in the field of education men are studied as they work with men, involving human interaction and a number of variables. Therefore, certain cautions are significant:[115]

1. The use of the critical-incident technique in educational research should be restricted to studies of situations with limited complexity.

[114] *Ibid.*
[115] John E. Corbally, Jr., *op. cit.*

2. In designing a research project in which the critical-incident technique is to be applied, great care must be taken to insure that the problem is one in which aims and outcomes can be recognized by various competent observers with both validity and reliability.

3. Reports of critical-incident studies must stress that the technique is not designed to discriminate between several types of behavior with regard to their criticalness, except to indicate that some behaviors are critical and others are noncritical.

4. Efforts should be made to improve the method, but its use should not be discouraged because it seems to possess elements of subjectivity.

5. In reporting research using this method, great care must be taken to make clear the meaning of such terms as *critical element, critical incident,* or *noncritical elements.*

6. In view of the problems arising from the choice of observers and the interpretation of observers' reports, it is likely that the team approach can provide more fruitful results than can the individual approach.

In the area of educational evaluation, the critical-incident technique is thought to have certain values not obtainable by other techniques of measurement:[116]

1. Adequate collection of critical incidents places categories of human behavior on an empirical base, thus providing for greater validity for any subsequent measuring instrument.

2. Collections of critical incidents provide realistic bases for any of a variety of evaluation techniques, although the incidents do not of themselves comprise a measurement instrument.

3. The critical incidents themselves can frequently serve as a source for the raw material out of which evaluation items are constructed, since incidents expressed in the words of the students may overcome the tendency either to over- or under-shoot the level of the prospective examinees.

ACTION OR CO-OPERATIVE RESEARCH[117]

Action research (or co-operative research or co-operative-action research), as comparatively new terminology, has appeared in the literature primarily since the midpoint of the present century, although teachers have been urged for many years to be more consistent consumers of research and to conduct appropriate studies as a means of improving instruction. The term *operational research* sometimes has appeared as a synonym for action research. Such research in the schools

[116] Lewis B. Mayhew, *op. cit.*

[117] Association for Supervision and Curriculum Development, *Research for Curriculum Improvement.* 1957 Yearbook. Washington: The Association, 1957.

is an attempt to provide investigational procedures suitable for study and solution of school problems in relation to the total situation, and is a program to be conducted by teachers as part of their teaching activity, usually with the advice and co-operation of research specialists.

Characteristics and Procedures

The social psychology and group dynamics of action-research programs are based on the concept of bringing about desirable change step by step through group participation. In the early stage of a co-operative project, the role of participating observer separates study of the problem from possible fear of any change which might be required by the findings or recommendations. In later stages, participation as a member of the group identifies the individual with the project and develops attitudes favorable to support of the findings and recommendations.

Certain differences in emphasis have characterized basic or fundamental research (outlined below), as compared with action studies or programs:[118]

---

350 p. Especially Matthew B. Miles, "Human Relations in Cooperative Research," p. 187–226.

A Comprehensive Bibliography on Operations Research, through 1956 with Supplement for 1957. New York: John Wiley & Sons, 1958. 199 p.

Stephen M. Corey, *Action Research to Improve School Practices.* New York: Teachers College, Columbia University, 1953. xiii+161 p.

Stephen M. Corey, "Implications of Cooperative-Action Research for Teacher Education," *Eighth Yearbook of the American Association of Colleges for Teacher Education.* Oneonta, N. Y.: The Association, 1955. p. 164–72.

Bernard R. Corman, "Action Research: A Teaching or a Research Method?" in "Methodology of Educational Research." *Review of Educational Research* 27: 544–47; December 1957.

Arthur W. Foshay and Others, *Children's Social Values:* An Action Research Study. New York: Teachers College, Columbia University, 1954. 323 p.

Harold L. Hodgkinson, "Action Research—A Critique." *Journal of Educational Sociology* 31: 137–53; December 1957.

Ernest J. McCormick, *Human Engineering.* New York: McGraw-Hill Book Co., 1957. 467 p.

Aaron H. Passow and Others, *Training Curriculum Leaders for Cooperative Research.* New York: Teachers College, Columbia University, 1955. 158 p.

Abraham Shumsky, "Action Research and Modern Man." *Educational Theory* 8: 27–34; January 1958.

William A. Van Til and Others, "Research on Human Relations and Programs of Action." *Review of Educational Research* 23: 285–385; October 1953.

Kenneth D. Wann, "Action Research in Schools." *Review of Educational Research* 23: 337–45; October 1953.

[118] Carter V. Good and Douglas E. Scates, *op. cit.,* p. 883–84.

Stephen M. Corey, "Fundamental Research, Action Research and Educational Practices," *Growing Points in Educational Research.* Washington: American Educational Research Association, 1949. p. 261–65.

1. Formulation of new generalizations, explanatory principles, and scientific theories or laws that go beyond the populations and situations represented, with the expectation that some other person will bring about improvement in practice.

2. High value placed on sampling procedures as a basis for generalizations.

3. Careful planning in advance of the investigation and adherence to the design of the study throughout the project, with the reporting done in sufficient detail to permit repetition of the study.

4. Desirability of technical training or equipment which frequently involves statistical, sampling, testing, or experimental procedures.

5. Judgment of the quality of the investigation based on the possibility of generalizing the methods and findings beyond the sample and situation studied, thus adding to the body of knowledge in the particular field.

The contrasting major emphases in action research are as follows:

1. Usually stemming from an urgent practical or felt need, with a goal of application of results and improvement of practice in the particular setting where the group or investigator works, through processes of group planning, execution, and evaluation (by both research specialists and volunteer or lay participants).

2. Interest in the particular subjects investigated rather than in the total theoretical population represented by the sample under study.

3. A developmental design, with the hypothesis and method subject to modification during the course of the action program, and with due consideration of all interdependent groups concerned in any changes to be made.

4. Desirability of training in concepts of group dynamics as background for co-operative study of practical problems, with the guiding theory that of human interaction by which change is either facilitated or resisted, and with frequent difficulties of interaction with the particular community by way of choice of problem areas, specific formulation of the problem, selection of procedures, presentation of findings, and application to practices. The scientists or scholars in their role of democratic leaders stimulate and develop the talents of the group, and train and supervise the participants in the project.

5. Determination of the value of the action project in terms of the extent to which methods and findings make possible improvement in practice in a particular situation and realization of social and educational purposes.

A Teaching or a Research Method?[119]

Questions have been raised as to whether action research is a new investigational method or a form of in-service training for school workers. Some writers contrast co-operative or action research with so-called traditional or fundamental research, as outlined above, while other per-

[119] Bernard R. Corman, *op. cit.*

sons make a distinction on the basis of the kinds of problems investigated, adaptability of the findings to real situations, motivation of the workers, kinds of generalizations sought, intrinsic value of the investigation to the practitioner, and the individual who does the research (as summarized above in part). It is doubtful that any of these distinctions, even though significant, provides the foundations for new methodology in terms of a new way of organizing or analyzing phenomena, so as to lead to the development and testing of new hypotheses (or to improved methods of testing old hypotheses). In other words, the major contribution of action or co-operative research is to in-service training and stimulation of teachers rather than as a basic research methodology paralleling the historical, descriptive-survey, experimental, case-clinical, and developmental techniques. All of these fundamental methods of investigation are available for co-operative research on the part of field workers, with the assistance of research specialists. Probably the descriptive-survey approaches are more common in action programs; to cite a specific example in a social field:

> This is an account of an unusual social-action and sociological research project conducted in a community of 13,000 in the Piedmont region in Alabama, a project made possible by a grant to University of Alabama sociologists for the purposes of studying the processes of a community self-survey in health. The major part of the volume is devoted to description and explanation of the self-survey events, presented as an application of community status-structure analysis to a relatively specific action problem and as a demonstration of the advantages of studying social process through participation in action activities, specifically through participation in the community self-survey.[120]

Contributions and Next Steps

Many of the reports of action studies include statements to the effect that teachers have found cherished prejudices challenged, leadership developed, lines of communication made clearer, interest in research engendered, curriculum change facilitated, and success in incorporating the action approach both in the training of teachers and in the teaching of public-school classes. These statements suggest an emphasis on problem-solving in teacher education and in instruction as an important contribution for co-operative or action research to make. The action-research movement developed as a result of the partial failure of educa-

---

[120] Quoted from review by Warren A. Peterson, *American Journal of Sociology* 61: 393–94; January 1956, of Solon T. Kimball and Marion Pearsall, *The Talladega Story: A Study in Community Process.* University, Ala.: University of Alabama Press. 1954. xxxii+259 p.

tional research to play a significant role in changing practice and as a means of avoiding the separation of facts and values.

Certain problems or difficulties in conducting action or co-operative studies have included the reluctance of teachers to undertake research because of their concept of formal research, lack of time to conduct studies, difficulty of communication, and inadequate training for research activities. Suggestions for facilitating co-operative investigation have mentioned the need for a climate in the schools favorable to study and experimentation, ways to provide time for teachers to participate, and leadership and consultative help for the workers. In involving field workers more directly in programs of co-operative investigation, it will require time and effort to acquire the necessary tools and techniques of inquiry for sound research. The need for this training presents a real challenge to programs of teacher education. A second challenge relates to the amount and quality of co-operative research by teachers-college personnel themselves, which should be stimulated in several ways:[121]

1. To value and reward this type of study within the institution itself

2. To provide staff members with the research and professional literature, and with facilities for meeting together on their problems

3. To provide expert assistance in research methodology

4. To recruit staff members with an experimental attitude toward their work and a willingness to conduct research to improve it

5. To provide appropriate experience in doctoral programs in the procedures of co-operative-action research.

QUANTITATIVE OR CONTENT ANALYSIS OF DOCUMENTARY MATERIALS[122]

Like historical research, quantitative or content analysis of documentary materials uses as sources the collections of records already in existence. The survey type of documentary analysis expresses the results

[121] Stephen M. Corey, "Implications of Cooperative-Action Research for Teacher Education," *op. cit.*

[122] William M. Alexander and Others, "The Curriculum: Organization and Development." *Review of Educational Research* 24: 191–261; June 1954.

Frank Auld, Jr., and Edward J. Murray, "Content-Analysis Studies of Psychotherapy." *Psychological Bulletin* 52: 377–95; September 1955.

Milton L. Barron, "A Content Analysis of Intergroup Humor." *American Sociological Review* 15: 88–94; February 1953.

Bernard Berelson, *Content Analysis in Communication Research.* Glencoe, Ill.: Free Press, 1952. 220 p.

Bernard Berelson and M. Janowitz, *Reader in Public Opinion and Communication.* Glencoe, Ill.: Free Press, 1953. xi+611 p.

Citizenship Education Project, *Content Analysis Manual:* Classification System for

in quantitative terms, and in the studies of an earlier period was concerned with counting and frequencies rather than with the meaning or message within the documents analyzed. The investigator in this area must deal with problems of locating or bringing together an appropriate collection of documents, of determining what characteristics to count or measure, and of defining the aspects selected for study.

Earlier Studies

An earlier form of quantitative or content analysis used textbooks as sources, dealing with such frequencies or measures as: sentence length, word difficulty, pictures, tables, exercises for pupils, content topics and

Analysis of Responses to Four Questions on Citizenship. Publication No. 9. New York: Teachers College, Columbia University, 1950. 52 p.

Edgar Dale and Others, *Mass Media and Education*. Fifty-third Yearbook of the National Society for the Study of Education, Part 2. Chicago: The University of Chicago Press, 1954. x+290 p.

Leonard W. Doob, *Public Opinion and Propaganda*. New York: Henry Holt and Co., 1948. vii+600 p.

Leon Festinger and Daniel Katz, *op. cit.*, p. 419–70.

Carter V. Good and Douglas E. Scates, *op. cit.*, p. 665–77.

William J. Goode and Paul K. Hatt, *op. cit.*, p. 325–30.

Walter Hirsch, "The Image of the Scientist in Science Fiction: A Content Analysis." *American Journal of Sociology* 63: 506–12; March 1958.

Chester L. Hunt, "The Treatment of 'Race' in Beginning Sociology Textbooks." *Sociology and Social Research* 35: 277–84; March-April 1951.

Marie Jahoda and Others, *op. cit.*, p. 235–44, 539–60.

Solon T. Kimball and Marion Pearsall, "Event Analysis as an Approach to Community Study." *Social Forces* 34: 58–63; October 1955.

Harold D. Lasswell, Nathan Leites, and Others, *Language of Politics*. New York: Stewart Co., 1949. vii+398 p.

Donald V. McGranahan, "Content Analysis of the Mass Media of Communication," *Research Methods in Social Relations*. Edited by Marie Jahoda and Others. New York: Dryden Press, 1951. p. 539–60.

Nathaniel B. McMillian, *An Analysis of Regional Items in the Content of Southern State Education Association Journals*, 1935–49. Bulletin of the Bureau of School Service, Vol. 23, No. 4. Lexington: University of Kentucky, June 1951. 91 p.

Henry J. Otto and Donald McDonald, "Learning Materials." *Review of Educational Research* 21: 220–26; June 1951.

J. Galen Saylor and Others, "Curriculum Planning and Development." *Review of Educational Research* 27: 237–304; June 1957.

Robert C. Sorenson and Theodore C. Sorensen, "A Proposal for the Use of Content Analysis Evidence in Literary Infringement Cases." *Social Forces* 33: 262–67; March 1955.

Marvin Spiegelman, Carl Terwilliger, and Franklin Fearing, "The Reliability of Agreement in Content Analysis" and "The Content of Comics: Goals and Means to Goals of Comic Strip Characters." *Journal of Social Psychology* 37: 175–87, 189–203; May 1953.

T. D. Weldon, *The Vocabulary of Politics*. Baltimore: Penguin Books, 1953. 199 p.

Ralph K. White, *Value-Analysis:* The Nature and Use of the Method. New York: Society for the Psychological Study of Social Issues, Columbia University, 1951. 87 p.

space allotment, grade placement or difficulty of material, and vocabulary load. Although many of these earlier analyses of textbooks were regarded as mechanical, they proved valuable in textbook-writing and in instruction, as in using standard word lists to select the vocabulary appropriate for a certain age group or grade level.

Many of the earlier content analyses of documentary materials dealt with bodies of literature larger than a collection of a dozen or two textbooks. Such studies and textbook analyses were used extensively in curriculum development, based on the hypothesis that knowledge most frequently applied (or appearing in the literature) should be included in the instructional program. In the earlier analyses of relatively large bodies of literature, illustrative topics and sources are as follows: major fields of human concern, in terms of topics covered in periodical literature; column-inches of space devoted to topics in newspapers; distribution of space to topics in the volumes of a standard encyclopedia; topics covered in a weekly news magazine; duties and traits of a good citizen, as emphasized in newspaper editorials and magazine articles on citizenship; civic and social shortcomings identified in the editorials of newspapers and magazines; shortcomings in the written English of adults, as revealed in letters written for newspaper publication; and mathematics used in popular science, based on analysis of magazines and books.

Other earlier content analyses have been based upon specimens of child or adult usage or performance, including children's compositions and test papers, social letters, and other specimens of usage or performance. Vocabulary analysis has made possible basic word lists helpful in textbook-writing and in grade placement of curriculum materials. Error studies in such areas as reading, language usage, arithmetic, spelling, and writing have been useful in remedial and developmental aspects of instruction.

In interpreting frequency analyses of documentary materials, important questions of permanent values and social significance arise. Frequency of appearance of a topic or interest in the current literature may reflect only the passing fancy of the average reader rather than an appropriate goal or aim in improving interests and activities. In any given year the name of the leading batter in baseball or the most popular TV star probably will appear more frequently in the periodical literature than the names of George Washington or Thomas Jefferson. In interpreting error studies, as a basis for teaching the child, we need to know why he made certain mistakes and what objectives he should be able to attain, if we are to develop a sound psychology of learning. Studies of frequency of usage and errors may lead to overemphasis on very limited aspects of the child's activities and difficulties, and may fail to recognize even more important aspects of learning by way of purpose, interest, satisfaction, and emotional adjustment.

New Theory and Technique

The content analyses since approximately 1940 represent a more complex and subtle type of study, which should be differentiated from the rather mechanical and simple statistical studies of frequencies made during the 1920's and 1930's. As early as 1940, questions were being asked concerning a new type of content analysis; for example, analysis of propaganda in films, radio, and print in relation to responses elicited, and truth or falsity.

Especially since 1950, the complex content analyses have had little relation to the simple textbook analyses of the 1920's and 1930's, as illustrated by Berelson's survey of several hundred titles in the area of content analysis.[123] According to his findings, the content of communication includes that body of meanings through symbols (verbal, musical, pictorial, plastic, and gestural) which makes up the communication itself. Content analysis has been used to investigate such diverse topics as the following: the slogans of May Day propaganda in the U.S.S.R., dominant images in Shakespeare's plays, values in American plays as compared with German plays of the same period, treatment of minority ethnic groups in short stories published in popular magazines, comparison of newspapers and radio and their treatment of a sensational murder case, manner in which motion pictures reflect popular feelings and desires, similarities and differences in the political symbols that come to the attention of people in the major power states, and intelligence data secured from analysis of enemy propaganda.

A method for describing quantitatively and objectively any kind of verbal data (propaganda and public-opinion materials, autobiographies, clinical interviews, letters, conversational records, and other devices of personality study) includes appropriate consideration of emotional dynamics and certain psychological factors on which data can be obtained—hostility, self-approval, social perception (stereo-types), self-picture and ego-ideal, areas of frustration, and ability to take another's viewpoint.[124]

[123] Bernard Berelson, *Content Analysis in Communication Research, op. cit.*
[124] Ralph K. White, *op. cit.*

With the advent of sound recording of interviews, content-analysis studies of psychotherapy became quite common. These studies of psychotherapy may be divided into three general classes: methodological investigations, in which the aim was primarily to develop measures; descriptive studies of cases; and theoretically guided studies of therapy, that is, investigations of cause-and-effect relationships.[125]

Newspaper reading may be analyzed in terms of five types or classes of content: public affairs (delayed reward), human interest (immediate reward), comics, illustrations, and advertising. In relation to these five classes of content, *The Continuing Study of Newspaper Reading*, a series of leadership surveys made under the sponsorship of the Advertising Research Foundation, shows the following general patterns in newspaper reading:[126]

Comics, illustrations, and human interest are often read by more than half the readers.

Comics, illustrations, and human interest almost invariably have more readers for more items than public affairs or advertisements.

Most newspapers have fewer comics, illustrations, and human-interest items than public-affairs articles or advertisements. For example, many newspapers publish two to four times as many public-affairs articles as human-interest items.

Few public-affairs articles and few advertisements are read by more than half the readers. About 1 public-affairs article in 10 may be read by more than 50 per cent of a sample of readers.

Some newspapers are more successful than others in attracting readers to different classes of content. Family newspapers in small cities, for example, may have more readership of articles about local public affairs but less readership for comic strips than metropolitan dailies.

In analyzing the content of radio (and TV), common classifications[127] of programs are as follows:

Entertainment-type
    Music programs—popular and dance, semiclassical and classical, old familiar and western
    Drama programs—daytime serial or domestic, mystery, comedy
    Variety programs—quiz, sports, miscellaneous
Information-type
    News and commentators
    Farm
    Homemaking

[125] Frank Auld, Jr., and Edward J. Murray, *op. cit.*
[126] Edgar Dale and Others, *op. cit.*, p. 157–58.
[127] *Ibid.*, p. 195–204.

Orientation-type
Religious
Talks
Forums and panels.

Illustrative Studies

To begin with TV, an analysis of television programs is classified under seventeen headings: news, weather, public issues, public events, institutional, information, religion, drama, dance, music, fine arts, variety, personalities, quiz-stunts-contest, sports, homemaking, and children's programs.[128]

Other examples of content analysis since 1950 are as follows:

An analysis of journals published by state education associations, for the purpose of locating materials contributing to regional improvement, in terms of criteria relating to: a point of view of regionalism instead of traditional sectionalism; awareness of the South as a region; ample natural and human resources; deficiency of technological skill, capital wealth, and institutional services; waste of resources; a plan or program for alleviating a problem or relieving a deficiency; and progress in the direction of regional improvement.[129]

An analysis of the acts of the Indiana General Assembly relating to formal education, classified under the following subject headings: township schools, county seminaries, Indiana College (Indiana University), private educational institutions, school lands, school funds, school officials, fines and license fees, school taxes, education of special groups, and libraries.[130]

Textbook analyses in sociology: a content analysis of 12 widely used textbooks in beginning sociology, concerned with the treatment of race;[131] and a survey of 33 introductory texts in sociology, 28 social-problems texts, and 22 family texts published over the period 1926-45, in terms of treatment of personality, marriage and the family, social controls, social disorganization, and social change.[132]

---

[128] Dallas W. Smythe, "An Analysis of Television Programs." *Scientific American* 184: 15–17; June 1951.

[129] Nathaniel B. McMillian, *op. cit.*

[130] Velorus Martz and Stanley E. Ballinger, *A Guide to the Source Materials Relating to Education in the Laws of the State of Indiana, 1816–1851, Part I: 1816–1838.* Bulletin of the School of Education, Vol. 29, No. 4. Bloomington: Indiana University, July 1953. 96 p.

[131] Chester L. Hunt, *op. cit.*

[132] A. H. Hobbs, *The Claims of Sociology:* A Critique of Textbooks. Harrisburg, Penn.: The Stackpole Co., 1951. iv+185 p.

An analysis of 266 textbooks in the light of their handling of materials pertaining to intergroup relations.[133]

A content analysis of humor, based on three anthologies of jokes concerning three American ethnic groups; 300 Negro jokes, 160 Jewish, and 274 Irish, a total of 734 jokes; divided into six categories—dialect, theme, proper names, sex composition, occupations, and intergroup or intragroup composition.[134]

An analysis of approximately 2,000 responses revealing attitudes of students and adults in terms of excellent and poor citizenship; a process of analyzing free responses to critical-incidents questions on citizenship, classified under nineteen categories.[135]

A study of 5,188 terms, having 4,294 different bases or stems, necessary to understanding and interpreting the business and economic news available through the mass media.[136]

Summary of Uses of Content Analysis[137]

Seventeen types of uses (applications, functions) of content analysis have been identified.

CHARACTERISTICS OF CONTENT: SUBSTANCE

1. To describe trends in communication content
2. To trace the development of scholarship by way of interests and activities
3. To disclose international differences in communication content
4. To compare media or levels of communication
5. To audit communication content against objectives
6. To construct and apply communication standards
7. To aid in technical-research operations

[133] J. L. Hanley, *Intergroup Relations in Teaching Materials:* A Survey and Appraisal. Washington: American Council on Education, 1949. 231 p.
Maxwell S. Stewart, *Prejudice in Textbooks.* National Conference of Christians and Jews. Public Affairs Pamphlet No. 160. New York: Public Affairs Committee, 1950. 31 p.
[134] Milton L. Barron, "A Content Analysis of Intergroup Humor." *American Sociological Review* 15: 88–94; February 1953.
[135] Citizenship Education Project, *op. cit.*
Improving Citizenship Education: A Two-Year Progress Report of the Citizenship Education Project. Publication No. 29. New York: Teachers College, Columbia University, 1952. 44 p.
[136] Dean R. Malsbary, "A Study of the Terms That People Need to Understand in Order to Comprehend and Interpret the Business and Economic News Available Through the Mass Media." *Studies in Education,* 1952. Iowa City: State University of Iowa, January 1953. p. 199–204.
[137] Bernard Berelson, "Content Analysis," *Handbook of Social Psychology:* Theory and Method. Vol. 1. Edited by Gardner Lindzey. Cambridge, Mass.: Addison-Wesley Publishing Co., 1954. p. 488–522.

CHARACTERISTICS OF CONTENT: FORM

8. To expose propaganda techniques
9. To measure readability
10. To discover stylistic features

PRODUCERS OF CONTENT

11. To identify the intentions and other characteristics of the communicators
12. To determine the psychological state of persons and groups
13. To detect the existence of propaganda (primarily for legal purposes)
14. To secure political and military intelligence

AUDIENCE OF CONTENT

15. To reflect attitudes, interests, and values (cultural patterns) of population groups

EFFECTS OF CONTENT

16. To reveal the focus of attention
17. To describe attitudinal and behavioral responses to communications.

The units of content analysis have been the word, theme, character, item, and space-and-time measures.

The categories of content analysis have been as follows:

"What is said" categories—subject matter, direction, standard, values, traits, actor, authority, origin, target

"How it is said" categories—form or type of communication, form of statement, intensity, device.

SURVEY-APPRAISAL TECHNIQUES

The various survey-appraisal procedures, including index numbers, are beyond the scope and purpose of this book; they are treated extensively in the books on evaluation and measurement. In some of these techniques, direct judgment rather than some more objective form of evaluation is employed. The several types of direct judgment or rating are as follows:

Rating of specimens or items, as in pooling the judgments of a "jury" concerning the traits considered important for success as a teacher

Ranking of human beings, as in direct comparison of the pupils in a class with respect to some characteristic

Comparison with scaled specimens, as in a handwriting or composition scale

Check lists, with items to be marked "yes" or "no," "present" or "absent," as illustrated by check lists for school buildings, supervision of instruction, or characteristics of a successful teacher

Rating scales, with a scale of values for certain aspects or characteristics, as illustrated by a series of numbers, qualitative terms (excellent—strong—average—weak—poor), named attributes, verbal descriptions (applied to buildings, playgrounds, educational institutions, teachers, administrators, supervisors)

Score cards, usually somewhat more elaborate than rating scales, as illustrated by instruments for evaluating school plants and textbooks.

An index number is an average in the sense that it combines in one figure the average of a number of different factors or variable elements. This technique has been applied to certain phases of education and to many social and economic areas. The index numbers for the purpose of rating the state school systems usually have included such factors as: "per cent of school population attending school daily," "average number of days schools were kept open," "average expenditure per child in average attendance," "expenditure per teacher employed, for salaries," and so on. Other applications or forms of index numbers have included: changes in prices of commodities, cost of school supplies, interest rate for school bonds, cost of school buildings, cost of living (food, clothing, housing, fuel and light, house furnishings, and miscellaneous), wholesale prices, retail prices, increasing costs of education, and purchasing power of teachers' salaries.

For many educational, sociometric, and psychometric areas of appraisal, tests, rating scales, score cards, and check lists have been developed and used extensively, with applications to teachers, curriculum, home environment, social distance, socioeconomic status, attitudes, opinions, morale, social and personal behavior, personality and character, temperament, interests, and selection and evaluation of personnel. An extensive literature deals with the details of appraisal techniques.

CONCLUDING STATEMENT

The descriptive-survey investigations are too varied in type and technique to permit more than a summary of recent trends by way of challenging theoretical concepts, improved techniques, or standards of practice:

1. Support of foundation grants for status studies to determine the present position of education in our culture and thus provide a basis for comparison and future evaluation

2. Increased use of the processes of analysis and classification, especially in certain complex studies

3. Increased interest of social agencies and of the federal and state governments in social problems of local communities, as illustrated by social surveys

4. Studies of community schools to improve the school program and community

5. Trends in school surveys toward: the continuing survey (with a cooperative planning survey at appropriate intervals), recognition of the qualitative aspects of recommendations, and essential safeguards for consultants, school system, and survey agency

6. New standards, depths, and uses for the questionnaire

7. Recognition of the interview as a process of communication or interaction, and development of focused, depth, and nondirective interviewing

8. New skills and examples in both participant and nonparticipant observation

9. Further refinement of observational methods for studying group behavior and increased knowledge of variables that serve to bias and distort observations, with future progress dependent on development of more rigorous techniques of locating and measuring variables, closer relationship between theory and data-gathering, and greater uniformity of terminology

10. Invention of a critical-incident technique for collecting direct observations of human behavior, so as to facilitate their usefulness in solving practical problems and in developing broad psychological principles

11. Action or co-operative research, designed to involve field workers directly in programs of co-operative investigation, with future progress requiring time and effort on the part of teachers to acquire necessary tools and techniques of inquiry for sound research

12. New theory, technique, and use for content analysis of documentary materials

13. Development and application of a variety of educational, psychometric, and sociometric instruments of appraisal, including tests, scales, score cards, check lists, and indexes.

SELECTED REFERENCES

ABRAMS, Mark. *Social Surveys and Social Action*. London: William Heinemann, 1951. 153 p.

ACKOFF, Russell L. *The Design of Social Research*. Chicago: The University of Chicago Press, 1953. Chapter 9.

ADKINS, Dorothy C. "Principles Underlying Observational Techniques of Evaluation." *Educational and Psychological Measurement* 11: 29-51; Spring 1951.

ANASTASI, Anne. *Psychological Testing*. New York: The Macmillan Co., 1954. 682 p.

ANDERSON, Robert C. "The Guided Interview As An Evaluative Instrument." *Journal of Educational Research* 48: 203-9; November 1954.

ANGELL, Robert C., and FREEDMAN, Ronald. "Use of Documents, Records, Census Materials, and Indices." *Research Methods in the Behavioral Sciences*. Edited by Leon Festinger and Daniel Katz. New York: Dryden Press, 1953. Chapter 7.

ANSTEY, E., and MERCER, E. O. *Interviewing for the Selection of Staff*. London: George Allen and Unwin, for the Royal Institute of Public Administration, 1956. xiv+111 p.

ARENSBERG, Conrad M. "The Community-Study Method." *American Journal of Sociology* 60: 109-24; September 1954.

ARGYLE, Michael. *The Scientific Study of Social Behavior*. New York: Philosophical Library, 1957. 239 p.

ARNY, Clara Brown. *Evaluation in Home Economics*. New York: Appleton-Century-Crofts, 1953. xii+378 p.

AULD, Frank, Jr., and MURRAY, Edward J. "Content-Analysis Studies of Psychotherapy." *Psychological Bulletin* 52: 377-95; September 1955.

AULD, Frank, Jr., and WHITE, Alice M. "Rules for Dividing Interviews into Sentences." *Journal of Psychology* 42: 273-81; October 1956.

BACK, Kurt W., HILL, Reuben, and STYCOS, J. Mayone. "Interviewer Effect on Scale Reproducibility." *American Sociological Review* 20: 443-46; August 1955.

BALES, Robert F. *Interaction Process Analysis*. Cambridge, Mass.: Addison-Wesley Publishing Co., 1950. 203 p.

BARKER, Roger G., and WRIGHT, Herbert F. *Midwest and Its Children*: The Psychological Ecology of an American Town. Evanston, Ill.: Row, Peterson and Co., 1955. vii+532 p.

BARKER, Roger G., and WRIGHT, Herbert F. *One Boy's Day*: A Specimen Record of Behavior. New York: Harper & Brothers, 1951. x+435 p.

BARR, A. S., DAVIS, Robert A., and JOHNSON, Palmer O. *Educational Research and Appraisal*. Philadelphia: J. B. Lippincott Co., 1953. p. 51-62, 124-57.

BARRON, Milton L. "A Content Analysis of Intergroup Humor." *American Sociological Review* 15: 88-94; February 1953.

BEACH, Norton L. "Research Goes into Action." *Journal of Educational Research* 47: 351-58; January 1954.

BEALS, Ralph L. "The Village in an Industrial World." *Scientific Monthly* 77: 65-75; August 1953.

BECKMAN, Darold R. "Student Teachers Learn by Action Research." *Journal of Teacher Education* 8: 369-75; December 1957.

BENNEY, Mark, RIESMAN, David, and STAR, Shirley A. "Age and Sex in the Interview." *American Journal of Sociology* 62: 143-52; September 1956.

BERELSON, Bernard. "Content Analysis," *Handbook of Social Psychology*: Theory and Method. Vol. 1. Edited by Gardner Lindzey. Cambridge, Mass.: Addison-Wesley Publishing Co., 1954. p. 488-522.

BERELSON, Bernard. *Content Analysis in Communication Research.* Glencoe, Ill.: Free Press, 1952. 220 p.

BERELSON, Bernard, and JANOWITZ, M. *Reader in Public Opinion and Communication.* Glencoe, Ill.: Free Press, 1953. xi+611 p.

BINGHAM, W. V., and MOORE, B. V. *How to Interview.* Third Revised Edition. New York: Harper & Brothers, 1941. 263 p.

BLENKNER, Margaret. "Predictive Factors in the Initial Interview in Family Casework." *Social Service Review* 28: 65-73; March 1954.

BLENKNER, Margaret, and Others. "A Study of Interrelated Factors in the Initial Interview with New Clients." *Social Case Work* 32: 23-30; January 1951.

BORGATTA, Edgar F., and COTTRELL, Leonard S., Jr. "Directions for Research in Group Behavior." *American Journal of Sociology* 63: 42-48; July 1957.

BRADFIELD, James M., and MOREDOCK, H. S. *Measurement and Evaluation in Education.* New York: The Macmillan Co., 1957. 509 p.

BRADFORD, Leland P., CARTWRIGHT, Dorwin, and Others. "The Dynamics of Work Groups." *Adult Leadership* 2: 8-27; December 1953.

BRADFORD, Leland P., and GIBB, Jack R. "Developments in Group Behavior in Adult Education." *Review of Educational Research* 23: 233-47; June 1953.

BUCHER, Rue, FRITZ, Charles E., and QUARANTELLI, E. L. "Tape Recorded Interviews in Social Research." *American Sociological Review* 21: 359-64; June 1956.

BUGENTAL, J. F. T. "Explicit Analysis: A Design for the Study and Improvement of Psychological Interviewing." *Educational and Psychological Measurement* 14: 552-65; Autumn 1954.

BURCHARD, Waldo W. "A Study of Attitudes Toward the Use of Concealed Devices in Social Science Research." *Social Forces* 36: 111–16; December 1957.

BUROS, Oscar K., Editor. *The Fourth Mental Measurements Yearbook.* Highland Park, N. J.: Gryphon Press, 1953. 1189 p.

BURROUGHS, G. E. R. "A Study of the Interview in the Selection of Students for Teacher Training." *British Journal of Educational Psychology* 28: 37–46; February 1958.

CANNELL, Charles F., and AXELROD, Morris. "The Respondent Reports on the Interview." *American Journal of Sociology* 62: 177–81; September 1956.

CAPLOW, Theodore. "The Dynamics of Information Interviewing." *American Journal of Sociology* 62: 165–71; September 1956.

CARTWRIGHT, Dorwin, and ZANDER, Alvin. *Group Dynamics:* Research and Theory. Evanston, Ill.: Row, Peterson and Co., 1953. 642 p.

CHARTERS, W. W., Jr. "Beyond the Survey in School Board Research." *Educational Administration and Supervision* 41: 449–52; December 1955.

CHURCH, Harold H., and Others. *The Local School Facilities Survey.* Bulletin of the School of Education, Indiana University, Vol. 29, Nos. 1 and 2. Bloomington: Division of Research and Field Services, Indiana University, 1953. vii+96 p.

CHURCHMAN, C. W., ACKOFF, R. L., and ARNOFF, E. L. *Introduction to Operations Research.* New York: John Wiley & Sons, 1957. x+645 p.

Citizenship Education Project, *Content Analysis Manual:* Classification System for Analysis of Responses to Four Questions on Citizenship. Publication No. 9. New York: Teachers College, Columbia University, 1950. 52 p.

COCKING, Walter D. "The School Survey and Its Social Implications." *Educational Research Bulletin* 30: 169–78, 196; October 9, 1951.

CONGALTON, Athol A., Editor. *Hawera—A Social Survey:* A Report of a Community Venture. Hawera, New Zealand: Hawera and District Progressive Association and Hawera Star Publishing Co., 1954. xv+218 p.

CORBALLY, John E., Jr. "The Critical Incident Technique and Educational Research." *Educational Research Bulletin* 35: 57–62; March 14, 1956.

CORBALLY, John E., Jr. "A Second Look at the Critical Incident Technique." *Phi Delta Kappan* 38: 141–42; January 1957.

COREY, Stephen M. "Action Research in Education." *Journal of Educational Research* 47: 375–80; January 1954.

COREY, Stephen M. *Action Research to Improve School Practices.* New York: Bureau of Publications, Teachers College, Columbia University, 1953. xii+161 p.

CORNELL, Francis G. "Sample Surveys in Education," in "Statistical Methodology in Educational Research." *Review of Educational Research* 24: 359–74; December 1954.

CORNELL, Francis G., and Others. *The Index of Local Economic Ability in State School Finance Programs:* A Review of the Theory and Practice in the Use of Measures of Local Taxpaying Ability Based upon Economic Indexes. Washington: National Education Association, October 1953. 63 p.

COSTIN, Lela B. "The History-Giving Interview in Adoption Procedures." *Social Casework* 35: 393–400; November 1954.

DALE, Edgar, and Others. *Mass Media and Education.* Fifty-third Yearbook of the National Society for the Study of Education, Part 2. Chicago: The University of Chicago Press, 1954. x+290 p.

DEANE, Stephen R. "The Interview as a Tool of Adult Education Research." *Adult Education Bulletin* 14: 150–57; June 1950.

DEXTER, Lewis A. "Role Relationships and Conceptions of Neutrality in Interviewing." *American Journal of Sociology* 62: 153–57; September 1956.

DEYOUNG, John E. *Village Life in Modern Thailand.* Berkeley: University of California Press, 1955. xii+224 p.

DI VESTA, F. J. "Problems in the Use of Questionnaires for Studying the Effectiveness of Educational Programs." *Educational and Psychological Measurement* 14: 138–50; Spring 1954.

DOOB, Leonard W. *Public Opinion and Propaganda.* New York: Henry Holt and Co., 1948. vii+600 p.

DUBE, S. C. *Indian Village.* Ithaca, N. Y.: Cornell University Press, 1955. xiv+248 p.

DUNCAN, Marie C. "Recording Descriptive Data and Observer Reliability." *Pedagogical Seminary and Journal of Genetic Psychology* 78: 159–64; June 1951.

ERICKSON, Clifford E. *The Counseling Interview.* New York: Prentice-Hall, 1950. 174 p.

FENLASON, Anne. *Essentials in Interviewing:* For the Interviewer Offering Professional Services. New York: Harper & Brothers, 1952. xi+352 p.

FESTINGER, Leon, and KATZ, Daniel, Editors. *Research Methods in the Behavioral Sciences.* New York: Dryden Press, 1953. p. 15–97, 243–99, 327–535.

FESTINGER, Leon, SCHACHTER, Stanley, and BACK, Kurt. *Social Pressures in Informal Groups.* New York: Harper & Brothers, 1950. 240 p.

FLANAGAN, John C. "The Critical Incident Technique." *Psychological Bulletin* 51: 327–58; July 1954.

FOSHAY, Arthur W. "Action Research as Imaginative Hindsight." *Educational Research Bulletin* 34: 169–71; October 12, 1955.

FOSHAY, Arthur W. "Considerateness and Aggression: An Action Research Study." *Educational Research Bulletin* 32: 85–112; April 8, 1953.

FOSHAY, Arthur W., and GOODSON, M. R. "Some Reflections on Cooperative Action Research." *Educational Leadership* 10: 411–18; April 1953.

FRASER, John F. *A Handbook of Employment Interviewing.* Revised Edition. London: MacDonald and Evans, 1951. 214 p.

FRIED, Jacob. "Forty Years of Change in a Hawaiian Homestead Community: Anahole." *Rural Sociology* 20: 51–57; March 1955.

GADOUREK, I. *A Dutch Community:* Social and Cultural Structure and Process in a Bulb-Growing Region in The Netherlands. Publications of the Netherlands Institute of Preventive Medicine, XXX. Leiden: H. E. Stenfert Kroese N. V., 1956. xvi+555 p.

GAGE, N. L. "Explorations in the Understanding of Others." *Educational* and *Psychological Measurement* 13: 14–26; Spring 1953.

GAMBLE, Sidney D. *Ting Hsien:* A North China Rural Community. New York: International Secretariat, Institute of Pacific Relations, 1954. xxv+472 p.

GARDNER, Eric F., and THOMPSON, George G. *Social Relations and Morale in Small Groups.* New York: Appleton-Century-Crofts, 1956. ix+312 p.

GEDDES, Arthur. *The Isle of Lewis and Harris:* A Study in British Community. Edinburgh: Edinburgh University Press, 1955. xvi+340 p.

GEE, Wilson. *Social Science Research Methods.* New York: Appleton-Century-Crofts, 1950. p. 198–204, 300–329.

GELLERT, Elizabeth. "Systematic Observation: A Method in Child Study." *Harvard Educational Review* 25: 179–95; Summer 1955.

GERBERICH, J. Raymond. *Specimen Objective Test Items:* A Guide to Achievement Test Construction. New York: Longmans, Green and Co., 1956. ix+436 p.

GIEDT, F. Harold. "Comparison of Visual, Content, and Auditory Cues in Interviewing." *Journal of Consulting Psychology* 19: 407–16; December 1955.

GILL, Merton, NEWMAN, Richard, and REDLICH, Fredrick C. *The Initial Interview in Psychiatric Practice.* New York: International Universities Press, 1954. 423 p.

GILLIN, John, and Others. *For a Science of Social Man:* Convergences in

Anthropology, Sociology, and Psychology. New York: The Macmillan Co., 1954. 296 p.

GLACKEN, Clarence J. *The Great Loochoo:* A Study of Okinawan Village Life. Berkeley: University of California Press, 1955. xvi+324 p.

GLADWIN, Thomas, and SARASON, Seymour B. *Truk:* Man in Paradise. New York: Wenner-Gren Foundation for Anthropological Research, 1953. 651 p.

GLASSOW, Ruth, and Others. "Photographical and Cinematographical Research Methods," *Research Methods Applied to Health, Physical Education, and Recreation.* Revised Edition. Washington: American Association for Health, Physical Education, and Recreation, 1952. p. 204–18.

GOLDSMITH, Virginia. "Group Activities Used in Action Research in Education." *College of Education Record* 23: 20–23; January 1957.

GOOD, Carter V., and SCATES, Douglas E. *Methods of Research:* Educational, Psychological, Sociological. New York: Appleton-Century-Crofts, 1954. p. 255–688.

GOODE, William J., and HATT, Paul K. *Methods in Social Research.* New York: McGraw-Hill Book Co., 1952. p. 119–208, 232–95, 375–430.

GOODYKOONTZ, Bess. "Selected Studies Relating to Community Schools," *The Community School.* Edited by Nelson B. Henry. Fifty-second Yearbook of the National Society for the Study of Education, Part 2. Chicago: The University of Chicago Press, 1953. p. 64–82.

GORDEN, Raymond L. "Dimensions of the Depth Interview." *American Journal of Sociology* 62: 158–64; September 1956.

GREENE, Harry A., JORGENSEN, Albert N., and GERBERICH, J. Raymond. *Measurement and Evaluation in the Secondary School.* Second Edition. New York: Longmans, Green and Co., 1954. 690 p.

GRIEDER, Calvin. "School Surveys." *Review of Educational Research* 19: 322–33; October 1949.

GROSS, Neal, and MASON, Ward S. "Some Methodological Problems of Eight-Hour Interviews." *American Journal of Sociology* 59: 197–204; November 1953.

GUETZKOW, Harold, Editor. *Groups, Leadership, and Men:* Research in Human Relations. Pittsburgh: Carnegie Press, 1951. 293 p.

GULICK, John. *Social Structure and Culture Change in a Lebanese Village.* Viking Fund Publications in Anthropology, Number Twenty-One. New York: Wenner-Gren Foundation for Anthropological Research, 1955. 191 p.

HALLENBECK, Wilbur C. *American Urban Communities.* New York: Harper & Brothers, 1951. 617 p.

HALLENBECK, Wilbur C., Editor. *The Baumanville Community:* A Study of the First African Family Location in Durban. Durban: Institute for Social Research, University of Natal, 1955. vii+217 p.

HANLEY, J. L. *Intergroup Relations in Teaching Materials:* A Survey and Appraisal. Washington: American Council on Education, 1949. 231 p.

HARE, A. Paul, and DAVIE, James S. "The Group Interview: Its Use in a Study of Undergraduate Culture." *Sociology and Social Research* 39: 81–87; November-December 1954.

HARE, Paul, BORGATTA, Edgar F., and BALES, Robert F. *Small Groups:* Studies in Social Interaction. New York: Alfred A. Knopf, 1955. xv+666 p.

HEYNS, Roger W., and LIPPITT, Ronald. "Systematic Observational Techniques," *Handbook of Social Psychology:* Theory and Method. Vol. 1. Edited by Gardner Lindzey. Cambridge, Mass.: Addison-Wesley Publishing Co., 1954. p. 370–404.

HILDUM, Donald C., and BROWN, Roger W. "Verbal Reinforcement and Interviewer Bias." *Journal of Abnormal and Social Psychology* 53: 108–11; July 1956.

HOBBS, A. H. *The Claims of Sociology:* A Critique of Textbooks. Harrisburg, Penn.: The Stackpole Co., 1951. iv+185 p.

HODGKINSON, Harold L. "Action Research—A Critique." *Journal of Educational Sociology* 31: 137–53; December 1957.

HOIBERG, Otto G. *Exploring the Small Community.* Lincoln: University of Nebraska Press, 1955. xii+199 p.

HOLLINGSHEAD, August B. *Elmtown's Youth:* Impact of Social Classes on Adolescents. New York: John Wiley & Sons, 1949. xi+480 p.

HOLLINGSHEAD, August B., and REDLICH, FREDRICK C. *Social Class and Mental Illness*: A Community Study. New York: John Wiley & Sons, 1958. ix+442 p.

HOMANS, George C. *The Human Group.* New York: Harcourt, Brace and Co., 1950. 484 p.

HYMAN, Herbert H. *Survey Design and Analysis:* Principles, Cases and Procedures. Glencoe, Ill.: Free Press, 1955. xxviii+425 p.

HYMAN, Herbert H., and Others. *Interviewing in Social Research.* Chicago: The University of Chicago Press, 1954. xvi+415 p.

JAHODA, Marie, and Others. *Research Methods in Social Relations:* With Especial Reference to Prejudice. Part One: Basic Processes. New York: Dryden Press, 1951. p. 47–58, 91–208, 229–50, 423–513, 539–60, 569–75, 611–41, 681–711.

JONES, D. Caradog. *Social Surveys.* London: Hutchinson's University Library, 1949. 232 p.

JONES, Maxwell. *The Therapeutic Community.* New York: Basic Books, 1953. 727 p.

JORDAN, A. M. *Measurement in Education.* New York: McGraw-Hill Book Co., 1953. xi+533 p.

KADUSHIN, Alfred. "The Effect on the Client of Interview Observation at Intake." *Social Service Review* 31: 22–38; March 1957.

KADUSHIN, Alfred. "The Effects of Interview Observation on the Interviewer." *Journal of Counseling Psychology* 3: 130–35; Summer 1956.

KADUSHIN, Alfred. "Interview Observation as a Teaching Device." *Social Casework* 37: 334–41; July 1956.

KADUSHIN, Alfred. "Observing the Interview in Counselor Training and Supervision." *Personnel and Guidance Journal* 34: 405–8; March 1956.

KAHN, Robert L., and CANNELL, Charles F. *The Dynamics of Interviewing:*

Theory, Technique, and Cases. New York: John Wiley & Sons, 1957. x+368 p.

KAHN, Robert L., MARM, Floyd C., and SEASHORE, Stanley, Editors. "Human Relations Research in Large Organizations, II." *Journal of Social Issues* 12: 1–69; 1956.

KATONA, George. "The Function of Survey Research in Economics," in *Common Frontiers of the Social Sciences*. Edited by Mirra Komarovsky. Glencoe, Ill.: Free Press, 1957. p. 358–75.

KEATING, Elizabeth, and Others. "Validity of Work Histories Obtained by Interview." *Journal of Applied Psychology* 34: 6-11; February 1950.

KIMBALL, Solon T., and PEARSALL, Marion. "Event Analysis as an Approach to Community Study." *Social Forces* 34: 58-63; October 1955.

KIMBALL, Solon T., and PEARSALL, Marion. *The Talladega Story:* A Study in Community Process. University, Ala.: University of Alabama Press, 1954. xxxii+259 p.

KINCAID, Harry V., and BRIGHT, Margaret. "Interviewing the Business Elite." *American Journal of Sociology* 63: 304-11; November 1957.

KLEIN, Lawrence R., and Others. *Contributions of Survey Methods to Economics.* New York: Columbia University Press, 1954. viii+269 p.

KOGAN, Leonard S. "The Electrical Recording of Social Case Work Interviews." *Social Case Work* 31: 371-78; November 1950.

KOLAJA, Jiri. "A Contribution to the Theory of Participant Observation." *Social Forces* 35: 159-63; December 1956.

KUTNER, Bernard, and Others. *Five Hundred Over Sixty:* A Community Survey on Aging. New York: Russell Sage Foundation, 1956. 345 p.

KYTE, George C. "Survey and Analysis of Community Conditions," *The Principal at Work*. Revised Edition. Boston: Ginn and Co., 1952. p. 37-58.

LANGDON, Grace, and STOUT, Irving. *Teacher-Parent Interviews.* New York: Prentice-Hall, 1954. 336 p.

LASSWELL, Harold D., LEITES, Nathan, and Others. *Language of Politics.* New York: Stewart Co., 1949. vii+398 p.

LAW, Stanley G. *Therapy Through Interview.* New York: McGraw-Hill Book Co., 1948. viii+313 p.

LEVIN, Harry. "The Influence of Fullness of Interview on the Reliability, Discriminability, and Validity of Interview Judgments." *Journal of Consulting Psychology* 18: 303-6; August 1954.

LEWIS, Hylan. *Blackways of Kent.* Field Studies in the Modern Culture of the South. Vol. II. Chapel Hill: University of North Carolina Press, 1955. xxiv+337 p.

LINDQUIST, E. F., Editor. *Educational Measurement.* Washington: American Council on Education, 1951. 819 p.

LITWAK, Eugene. "A Classification of Biased Questions." *American Journal of Sociology* 62: 182-86; September 1956.

MACCOBY, Eleanor E., and MACCOBY, Nathan. "The Interview: A Tool of Social Science," *Handbook of Social Psychology:* Theory and Method. Vol. 1. Edited by Gardner Lindzey. Cambridge, Mass.: Addison-Wesley Publishing Co., 1954. p. 449-87.

MADGE, John. *The Tools of Social Science.* New York: Longmans, Green and Co., 1953. 332 p.

MAHL, G. F., and Others. "Facilities for the Sound Recording and Observation of Interviews." *Science* 120: 235-39; August 13, 1954.

MARRIOTT, McKim, Editor. *Village India:* Studies in the Little Community. Chicago: The University of Chicago Press, 1955. xix+269 p.

MATARAZZO, Joseph D., SASLOW, George, and GUZE, Samuel B. "Stability of Interaction Patterns During Interviews: A Replication." *Journal of Consulting Psychology* 20: 267-74; August 1956.

MAULDIN, W. P., and MARKS, E. S. "Problems of Response in Enumerative Surveys." *American Sociological Review* 15: 649-57; October 1950.

MAYHEW, Lewis B. "The Critical Incident Technique in Educational Evaluation." *Journal of Educational Research* 49: 591-98; April 1956.

McCLOSKEY, J. F., and COPPINGER, J. M., Editors. *Operations Research for Management.* Vol. II: Case Histories, Methods, Information Handling. Baltimore: Johns Hopkins Press, 1956. xxxvi+563 p.

McCORMICK, Thomas C., and FRANCIS, Roy G. *Methods of Research in the Behavioral Sciences.* New York: Harper & Brothers, 1958. ix+244 p.

McGRANAHAN, Donald V. "Content Analysis of the Mass Media of Communication," *Research Methods in Social Relations.* Edited by Marie Jahoda and Others. New York: Dryden Press, 1951. p. 539-60.

McMILLIAN, Nathaniel B. *An Analysis of Regional Items in the Content of Southern State Education Association Journals,* 1935-49. Bulletin of the Bureau of School Service, Vol. 23, No. 4. Lexington: University of Kentucky, June 1951. 91 p.

MEARES, Ainslie. *The Medical Interview:* A Study of Clinically Significant Interpersonal Reactions. Springfield, Ill.: Charles C Thomas, 1957. x+117 p.

MERTON, Robert K., FISKE, Marjorie, and KENDALL, Patricia L. *The Focused Interview:* A Manual of Problems and Procedures. Glencoe, Ill.: Free Press, 1956. 186 p.

MITCHELL, J. Clyde. *The Yao Village:* A Study in the Social Structure of a Nyasaland Tribe. Manchester, England: Manchester University Press, 1956. xviii+235 p.

MITCHELL, James V., Jr. "The Factor Analysis of a 'Guess-Who' Questionnaire Designed to Identify Significant Behavior Patterns in Children." *Journal of Personality* 24: 376-86; June 1956.

MOSER, C. A. *Survey Methods in Social Investigation.* New York: The Macmillan Co., 1958. xiii+352 p.

NIXON, John E. "The Mechanics of Questionnaire Construction." *Journal of Educational Research* 47: 481-87; March 1954.

NOLL, Victor H. *Introduction to Educational Measurement.* Boston: Houghton Mifflin Co., 1957. xx+437 p.

NORBECK, Edward. *Takashima:* A Japanese Fishing Community. Salt Lake City: University of Utah Press, 1954. xi+232 p.

OLIVER, Douglas L. *A Solomon Island Society:* Kinship and Leadership Among the Siuai of Bougainville. Cambridge: Harvard University Press, 1955. xxii+535 p.

PACE, C. R., and BROWNE, Arthur D. "Trend and Survey Studies." *Review of Educational Research* 21: 337–49; December 1951.

PARKER, Clyde A., WRIGHT, Wayne E., and CLARK, Selby G. "Questions Concerning the Interview as a Research Technique." *Journal of Educational Research* 51: 215-21; November 1957.

PARTEN, Mildred. *Surveys, Polls, and Samples:* Practical Procedures. New York: Harper & Brothers, 1950. p. 1–23, 82–85, 157–228, 331–484.

PAYNE, Stanley L. *The Art of Asking Questions.* Princeton: Princeton University Press, 1951. xiv+249 p.

PEIFFER, Herbert C., Jr., and WALKER, Donald E. "The Disciplinary Interview." *Personnel and Guidance Journal* 35: 347-50; February 1957.

PHILLIPS, William M., Jr. "Weaknesses of the Mail Questionnaire." *Sociology and Social Research* 35: 260-67; March-April 1951.

PIERCE, Truman M. *Controllable Community Characteristics Related to the Quality of Education.* Metropolitan School Study Council, Research Studies, No. 1. New York: Teachers College, Columbia University, 1947. 88 p.

PILTZ, Albert, and O'REGAN, William. "Non-Response and Non-Quantifiable Data in Sample Surveys." *Journal of Educational Research* 51: 143-47; October 1957.

PODELL, Lawrence. "An Interviewing Problem in Values Research." *Sociology and Social Research* 41: 121-26; November-December 1956.

PODELL, Lawrence. "The Structured Interview as a Social Relationship." *Social Forces* 34: 150-55; December 1955.

QUEEN, Stuart A., and CARPENTER, David B. *The American City.* New York: McGraw-Hill Book Co., 1953. 383 p.

QUINN, James A. "Concluding Comments, Symposium on Viewpoints, Problems, and Methods of Research in Urban Areas." *Scientific Monthly* 73: 37-50; July 1951.

REASON, Paul L., FOSTER, Emery M., and WILL, Robert F. *The Common Core of State Educational Information.* State Educational Records and Reports Series, Handbook 1. Washington: Government Printing Office, 1953. (The basic guide for state systems of educational records and reports and a major tool for comparability of educational information; contains the list of items of educational information, with their definitions, which each state department of education should have available, plus a glossary of terms.)

REDFIELD, Robert. *The Little Community:* Viewpoints for the Study of a Human Whole. Chicago: The University of Chicago Press, 1955. 182 p.

RIESMAN, David, and BENNEY, Mark, Editors. "The Interview in Social Research." *American Journal of Sociology* 62: 137-217; September 1956.

ROGERS, Virgil, and Others. *Gary, Indiana:* A Study of Some Aspects and Outcomes of a General School Survey. Washington: National Commission for the Defense of Democracy Through Education, N.E.A., June 1957. 40 p

Roseborough, Mary E. "Experimental Studies of Small Groups." *Psychological Bulletin* 50: 275-303; July 1953.

Rosen, Hjalmar, and Rosen, R. A. Hudson. "The Validity of 'Undecided' Answers in Questionnaire Responses." *Journal of Applied Psychology* 39: 178-81; June 1955.

Rummel, J. Francis. *An Introduction to Research Procedures in Education.* New York: Harper & Brothers, 1958. p. 57-148, 225-77.

Ryans, David G. "Are Educational Research Offices Conducting Research?" *Journal of Educational Research* 51: 173-83; November 1957.

Sachs, Benjamin M. "The Interview and the Curriculum." *Educational Administration and Supervision* 43: 369-82; October 1957.

Sanders, Irwin T. *Making Good Communities Better:* A Handbook for Civic-minded Men and Women. Lexington: University of Kentucky Press, 1950. 174 p.

Scates, Douglas E. "The Silent Side of Teaching: Key to Its Understanding." *Journal of Teacher Education* 4: 316-19; December 1953. (On depth studies.)

Scates, Douglas E., and Scates, Alice Yeomans. "Developing a Depth Questionnaire to Explore Motivation and Likelihood of Action." *Educational and Psychological Measurement* 12: 620-31; Winter 1952.

Scates, Douglas E., and Yeomans, Alice V. *Developing a Depth Essay Questionnaire to Assess the Market for Further Education Among Employed Scientists and Engineers.* Washington: American Council on Education, 1950. 128 p.

Scates, Douglas E., and Yeomans, Alice V. *Developing an Objective Item Questionnaire to Assess the Market for Further Education Among Employed Adults.* Washington: American Council on Education, 1950. 48 p.

Schwartz, Alfred, and Tiedeman, Stuart C. *Evaluating Student Progress in the Secondary School.* New York: Longmans, Green and Co., 1957. xi+ 434 p.

Schwartz, Morris S., and Schwartz, Charlotte G. "Problems in Participant Observation." *American Journal of Sociology* 60: 343-53; January 1955.

Scott, Frances Gillespie. "Mail Questionnaires Used in a Study of Older Women." *Sociology and Social Research* 41: 281-84; March-April 1957.

Scott, J. P. "The Place of Observation in Biological and Psychological Science." *American Psychologist* 10: 61-64; February 1955.

Sears, Jesse B. "School Surveys," *Encyclopedia of Educational Research.* Second Edition. Edited by Walter S. Monroe. New York: The Macmillan Co., 1950. p. 1126-33.

Seashore, Stanley E., and Likert, Rensis. "Action Research for Better Community Programs in International Affairs." *Adult Leadership* 2: 23-25; July-August 1953.

Seeley, John R., Sim, R. Alexander, and Loosley, Elizabeth W. *Crestwood Heights:* A Study of the Culture of Suburban Life. New York: Basic Books, 1956. xv+505 p.

Sells, Saul B., and Ellis, Robert W. "Observational Procedures Used in Research." *Review of Educational Research* 21: 432-49; December 1951.

SERVICE, Elman R., and SERVICE, Helen S. *Tobati:* Paraguayan Town. Chicago: The University of Chicago Press, 1954. xxix+337 p.

SHERIF, Muzafer. "Sociocultural Influences in Small Group Research." *Sociology and Social Research* 39: 1-10; September-October 1954.

SHERIF, Muzafer, and WILSON, M. O. *Group Relations at the Crossroads.* New York: Harper & Brothers, 1953. viii+379 p.

SHRYOCK, Henry S., Jr. "The Natural History of Standard Metropolitan Areas." *American Journal of Sociology* 63: 163-70; September 1957.

SHUMSKY, Abraham. "Teachers' Insecurity and Action Research." *Educational Research Bulletin* 35: 183-86; October 10, 1956.

SHYNE, Ann W. "Telephone Interviews in Casework." *Social Casework* 35: 342-47; October 1954.

SLOCUM, W. L., and Others. "Increasing Response to Questionnaires and Structured Interviews." *American Sociological Review* 21: 221-25; April 1956.

SMITH, Raymond T. *The Negro Family in British Guiana:* Family Structure and Social Status in the Villages. New York: Humanities Press, 1956. xvi +282 p.

SNEED, Ruth. *School Visits Home:* An Action Research Study of Home Visiting by Home Economics Teachers with Implications for the Total School Program. Bulletin of the Bureau of School Service, Vol. 30, No. 2. Lexington: University of Kentucky, December 1957. 63 p.

SORENSON, Robert C., and SORENSON, Theodore C. "A Proposal for the Use of Content Analysis Evidence in Literary Infringement Cases." *Social Forces* 33: 262-67; March 1955.

SPIEGELMAN, Marvin, TERWILLIGER, Carl, and FEARING, Franklin. "The Reliability of Agreement in Content Analysis" and "The Content of Comics: Goals and Means to Goals of Comic Strip Characters." *Journal of Social Psychology* 37: 175-87, 189-203; May 1953.

SPROTT, W. J. H. *Science and Social Action.* Glencoe, Ill.: Free Press, 1955. 164 p.

Standards for Statistical Surveys. Exhibit A, Circular No. A-46. Washington: Executive Office of the President, Bureau of the Budget, March 28, 1952. 10 p.

STANTON, Howard, BACK, Kurt W., and LITWAK, Eugene. "Role-Playing in Survey Research." *American Journal of Sociology* 62: 172-76; September 1956.

STEPHAN, F. F., and McCARTHY, P. J. *Sampling Opinions:* An Analysis of Survey Procedure. New York: John Wiley & Sons, 1958. 451 p.

STRAYER, George D., Jr. *Planning for School Surveys.* Bulletin of the School of Education, Indiana University, Vol. 24, No. 2. Bloomington: Division of Research and Field Services, Indiana University, 1948. 36 p.

STRODTBECK, F. L., and HARE, A. P. "Bibliography of Small Group Research, from 1900 through 1953." *Sociometry* 17: 107-78; May 1954. (Includes 1,407 items.)

STRODTBECK, F. L., and Others. "Small Group Research." *American Sociological Review* 19: 651-781; December 1954.

SULLIVAN, Harry S. *The Psychiatric Interview.* New York: W. W. Norton and Co., 1954. 246 p.

SUMPTION, M. R. "School and Community Relationships." *Review of Educational Research* 22: 317-28; October 1952.

A Survey of Surveys. Nashville, Tenn.: Division of Surveys and Field Services, George Peabody College for Teachers, 1952. 56 p.

TATE, H. Clay. *Building a Better Home Town:* A Program of Community Self-Analysis and Self-Help. New York: Harper & Brothers, 1954. xvi +236 p.

THELEN, Herbert A. *Dynamics of Groups at Work.* Chicago: The University of Chicago Press, 1954. 379 p.

THELEN, Herbert A. "Educational Dynamics, Theory and Research." *Journal of Social Issues* 6: 1-96; 1950.

THEODORSON, George A. "Elements in the Progressive Development of Small Groups." *Social Forces* 31: 311-20; May 1953.

THOMPSON, James D., and DEMERATH, N. J. "Some Experiences with the Group Interview." *Social Forces* 31: 148-54; December 1952.

THORNDIKE, Robert L., and HAGEN, Elizabeth. *Measurement and Evaluation in Psychology and Education.* New York: John Wiley & Sons, 1955. 550 p.

THORNE, Frederick C. *Principles of Psychological Examining.* Brandon, Vt.: Journal of Clinical Psychology, 1955. i+494 p.

TOOPS, Herbert A. "Questionnaires," *Encyclopedia of Educational Research.* Second Edition. Edited by Walter S. Monroe. New York: The Macmillan Co., 1950. p. 948-51.

TORGERSON, Theodore L., and ADAMS, Georgia S. *Measurement and Evaluation:* For the Elementary-School Teacher with Implications for Corrective Procedures. New York: Dryden Press, 1954. 489 p.

TRAVERS, R. M. W. *Educational Measurement.* New York: The Macmillan Co., 1955. 420 p.

TRAVERS, R. M. W. *An Introduction to Educational Research.* New York: The Macmillan Co., 1958. Chapters 5-11.

TYLER, Leona. "The Initial Interview." *Personnel and Guidance Journal* 34: 466-73; April 1956.

U. S. Bureau of the Budget, Office of Statistical Standards. *Statistical Services of the United States Government.* Revised Edition. Washington: The Bureau, 1952. 78 p.

VAN TIL, William A., and Others. "Research on Human Relations and Programs of Action." *Review of Educational Research* 23: 285-385; October 1953.

VIDICH, Arthur J. "Participant Observation and the Collection and Interpretation of Data." *American Journal of Sociology* 60: 354-60; January 1955.

VIDICH, Arthur J., and SHAPIRO, Gilbert. "A Comparison of Participant Observation and Survey Data." *American Sociological Review* 20: 28-33; February 1955.

VOGT, Evon Z. *Modern Homesteaders:* The Life of a Twentieth Century Frontier Community. Cambridge: Belknap Press of Harvard University Press, 1955. xi+232 p.

WAGLEY, Charles. *Amazon Town:* A Study of Man in the Tropics. New York: The Macmillan Co., 1953. xi+305 p.

WAGONER, Lovisa C., and CASTELLANOS, J. M. *Observation of Young Children: Their Behavior and Their Teaching.* Revised Edition. Oakland, Calif.: L. C. Wagoner, Mills College, 1951. xxi+142 p.

WANDT, Edwin, and OSTREICHER, Leonard M. *Variability in Observed Class-room Behaviors of Junior High School Teachers and Classes.* Publication 16. New York: College of the City of New York, June 1953. iv+31 p.

WARNER, William L., and Others. *Democracy in Jonesville.* New York: Harper & Brothers, 1949. xviii+313 p.

WARREN, Roland L. *Studying Your Community.* New York: Russell Sage Foundation, 1955. xii+385 p.

WARRINER, Charles K. "Leadership in the Small Group." *American Journal of Sociology* 60: 361-69; January 1955.

WAYLAND, S. R., and Others. *Aids to Community Analysis for the School Administrator.* New York: Teachers College, Columbia University, 1956. 51 p.

WEINLAND, James D., and GROSS, Margaret V. *Personnel Interviewing.* New York: Ronald Press, 1952. vii+416 p.

WELDON, T. D. *The Vocabulary of Politics.* Baltimore: Penguin Books, 1953. 199 p.

WHITE, Ralph K. *Value-Analysis:* The Nature and Use of the Method. New York: Society for the Psychological Study of Social Issues, Columbia University, 1951. 87 p.

WHYTE, William F. *Street Corner Society:* The Social Structure of an Italian Slum. Enlarged Edition. Chicago: The University of Chicago Press, 1955. xxii+366 p.

WIDEM, Paul. "The Telephone Intake Interview in a Child Guidance Clinic." *Social Casework* 38: 485-89; November 1957.

WILES, Kimball. "Can We Sharpen the Concept of Action Research?" *Educational Leadership* 10: 408-10; April 1953.

WILL, Robert F. *The State Department of Education Report.* Washington: Office of Education, 1953. vii+58 p.

WILLIAMS, W. M. *Gosforth:* The Sociology of an English Village. Glencoe, Ill.: Free Press, 1956. x+246 p.

WITMER, Helen L., Editor. *Psychiatric Interviews With Children.* New York: Commonwealth Fund, 1946. viii+444 p.

WOLFENSTEIN, Martha, and LEITES, Nathan. *Movies: A Psychological Study.* Glencoe, Ill.: Free Press, 1950. 316 p.

WOOD, Arthur E. *Hamtramck Then and Now:* A Sociological Study of a Polish-American Community. New York: Bookman Associates, 1955. 253 p.

WOODBURY, Coleman, Editor. *The Future of Cities and Urban Redevelopment.* Chicago: The University of Chicago Press, 1953. xix+764 p.

WOODBURY, Coleman, Editor. *Urban Redevelopment:* Problems and Practices. Chicago: The University of Chicago Press, 1953. xvi+525 p.

WRIGHTSTONE, J. Wayne, JUSTMAN, Joseph, and ROBBINS, Irving. *Evaluation in Modern Education.* New York: American Book Co., 1956. xi+481 p.

WRIGLEY, Charles. "Data Processing: Automation in Calculation," in "Methodology of Educational Research." *Review of Educational Research* 27: 528-43; December 1957.

WYLIE, Laurence. *Village in the Vaucluse.* Cambridge: Harvard University Press, 1957. 345 p.

YONGE, K. A. "The Value of the Interview: An Orientation and a Pilot Study." *Journal of Applied Psychology* 40: 25-31; February 1956.

YOUNG, Pauline V. *Interviewing in Social Work.* New York: McGraw-Hill Book Co., 1935. 416 p.

YOUNG, Pauline V. *Scientific Social Surveys and Research.* Third Edition. Englewood Cliffs, N.J.: Prentice-Hall, 1956. xx+540 p.

ZANDER, Alvin. "Systematic Observation of Small Face-to-Face Groups," *Research Methods in Social Relations.* Edited by Marie Jahoda and Others. New York: Dryden Press, 1951. p. 515-38.

ZEISEL, Hans. *Say It With Figures.* New York: Harper & Brothers, 1947. p. 4-65.

6

Developmental and Growth Studies

This chapter discusses developmental and growth studies in terms of purposes and uses, sources for genetic research, cross-section and longitudinal techniques of investigation, longitudinal study of cultural growth, the cross-cultural method, developmental techniques in relation to other methods, principles for analysis and interpretation of growth data, stages of maturity and developmental tasks, and illustrative studies and applications in major areas of development (physical, mental, social, personality, and learning).

PURPOSES AND USES

The increased interest of the twentieth century in genetic and developmental psychology is related to the rapid progress of biology, which explains in part the early emphasis of genetic research on physical and anatomical development. Other early influences contributing to the genetic approach in psychology and education include: recognition of the importance of the child as an individual, formulation and development of evolutionary theories, observational and questionnaire studies of the growth of infants and young children, certain psychological movements, and the invention and use of measuring and recording instruments (especially mental tests) in growth studies. Before World War I the topic of mental growth and its measurement received little attention in the psychological and educational literature.

As indicated in the preceding paragraph, the concept of development is fundamentally biological and has been most commonly associated with the organization of living structures and life processes, although a developmental concept sometimes is applied to physical systems, cultures, social institutions, or systems of ideas. This concept has been applied to educational, psychological, sociological, anthropological, historical, economic, political, artistic, and aesthetic phenomena.[1]

The purpose of genetic or developmental studies is to discover origin, direction, trend, rate, pattern, limit, and decline of growth, with a somewhat more recent interest in causes and interrelationships as factors affecting growth. For example, the relationships and pattern of development for mentality, emotional stability, and physical growth are more meaningful than separate analysis of each aspect of growth. Adequate interpretation of behavior includes consideration of direction of growth, rate, and optimal development. Direction indicates whether the child is moving forward, is stationary, or regressing. Rate indicates whether progress is slow or rapid. It is particularly important in the instruction of gifted children to know whether the level attained represents optimal development in relation to ability.

Investigations of developmental problems have been extended beyond the classroom, laboratory, nursery school, and child clinic to the church school, home, child-care agency, camp, playground, and discussion group, with interests going beyond the earlier physical and anatomical studies to phases of mental, social, and personality development. The genetic approach could be applied more readily in tracing the development of the insane, criminal, and maladjusted, if suitable methods were available for identifying the several types of abnormality or maladjustment at an early age, as has been done for the gifted, so as to permit a forward movement of observation through the several stages of growth or development (the longitudinal approach). In most studies of abnormality or maladjustment, it has been necessary to work backwards to origins or causes through case and clinical methods or the life history, since these cases usually have reached some critical stage before coming to the attention of persons equipped to make appropriate studies.

SOURCES OF GENETIC DATA

Among the sources[2] for study of child development are the following:

1. The present behavior of the child, including verbal output, as based

---

[1] Dale B. Harris, *The Concept of Development:* An Issue in the Study of Human Behavior. Minneapolis: University of Minnesota Press, 1957. x+287 p.

[2] John E. Anderson, "Methods of Child Psychology," *Manual of Child Psychology*. Second Edition. Edited by Leonard Carmichael. New York: John Wiley & Sons, 1954. p. 18–19.

on observations, measurements, and records in test or experimental situations, or on direct observation of behavior in play and social settings

2. Products of the child in the form of permanent records, including drawings, letters, and compositions

3. Records on file at home, school, and in a variety of agencies, covering school achievement, birth certificates, and health records

4. Introspections of the child

5. Memories of the child, or of the adult of his own earlier life, as based on the recording of conscious memories or of getting at more deeply buried memories by a free-association process or projective methods

6. Memories of the child's life as retained by those who have been associated with him

7. Measures of the parents, siblings, and other relatives of the child or of the environment, culture, or background in which he develops—a source that actually does not provide direct information concerning the child.

In describing the stages of maturity from 10 to 16, Gesell and associates have used the following sources of information:[3]

Developmental evaluation
> Developmental examination—naturalistic observations, organization and consistency of performance of simple tasks, standardized psychometric tests, projective techniques

> Visual examination—case history, visual analysis, visual skills

> Physical growth evaluation—observations of response to situation, standard physical-growth measures, standardized physique photographs

Subject interview
> Topics covering emotions, sense of self, interpersonal relationships, activities and interests, self-care and routines, action system, school, ethical sense, philosophical outlook

Teacher interview.

CROSS-SECTION AND LONGITUDINAL TECHNIQUES

The cross-section technique requires at least a single measurement for each individual within the particular groups represented, as when height is measured for each pupil in the first six grades of a public-school system. The central tendency for each of the six grades can be calculated, the result representing "norms" of growth in height or growth trends from grade to grade or year to year, although these central tendencies are not appropriate "norms" of growth in height for an

[3] Arnold Gesell, Frances L. Ilg, and Louise B. Ames, *Youth:* The Years from Ten to Sixteen. New York: Harper & Brothers, 1956. p. 506-7.

individual child. The cross-section technique has the advantage of gathering the data promptly, as in measuring at one time the height of children in the first six grades, rather than waiting for the pupils in the first grade to grow in height through a period of six years (a longitudinal technique), although cross-section studies present special problems in sampling and statistical procedure.[4]

In following growth in height of a particular group of children or of an individual through a period of months or years by the longitudinal method, the resulting series of measurements represents growth sequences for the same group or the same individual. The longitudinal approach is considered a sounder method than the cross-section technique, although the former involves an expenditure of time and resources in waiting a period of months or years for growth to take place. While problems of sampling and statistical procedure sometimes are perplexing in cross-section studies, there are other problems related to unpredictable and uncontrollable selective elimination in longitudinal investigations, because of the casualties of death, illness, moving of families, and changes in the co-operation of children and parents. The longitudinal technique provides a significant picture of growth not present in the successive cross sections of development for different groups, since the latter do not represent the developmental stages of an individual child. For example, the cross-section approach, on an age basis, groups together at the thirteen-year level girls who are well past puberty and other girls who are some months away from puberty. Therefore, it is incorrect to say that the average increment in height for this group of thirteen-year-old girls is typical, since a preadolescent girl at this age will have a much smaller gain in height than an adolescent girl who is passing through her stage of most rapid growth. Growth curves for adolescent groups tend to "smooth" this period and to conceal the usual spurt in height during adolescence, whereas individual curves at this period reveal a rapid increment in growth.

Although wider use of the longitudinal method has been recommended, adequate precautions are necessary in dealing with certain difficulties, some of which are common to cross-section studies:[5]

[4] Norman L. Munn, *The Evolution and Growth of Human Behavior.* Boston: Houghton Mifflin Co., 1955. p. 7–9.

[5] Florence L. Goodenough, "Some Special Problems of Nature-Nurture Research," *Intelligence:* Its Nature and Nurture. Thirty-ninth Yearbook of the National Society for the Study of Education, Part I. Bloomington, Ill.: Public School Publishing Co., 1940. p. 367–84.

W. F. Dearborn and J. W. M. Rothney, *Predicting the Child's Development.* Cambridge, Mass.: Sci-Art Publishers, 1941. p. 58–79.

1. Difficulties in population sampling, such as the selective elimination of many of the original subjects during the course of a long-term investigation

2. Maintenance of satisfactory working relationships among subjects, parents, schools, and investigators, particularly as personnel changes take place with the passing of time

3. Motivation of children to demonstrate full rather than perfunctory performance, a real challenge in the case of repeated testing over a period of months or years

4. Systematic errors of measurement in the administration or scoring of tests, mental or physical

5. Noncomparability or uncertain psychological equivalence of tests used at different age levels, especially when the time span is from early childhood to adolescence

6. Unequal experience of groups in terms of factors affecting the results of the measurement used, but not affecting the trait itself; for example, variation in previous experience with standardized tests

7. Recording and manipulation of data; for example, work of graduate students probably not as accurate and efficient as a highly trained permanent staff of skilled punch-card operators and statistical clerks

8. Mistakes of interpretation resulting from failure to take account of the principle of regression, particularly in its effects on measurements of gain or loss.

Bell, in partial solution of some of the difficulties of the longitudinal technique, suggested a method of combining the cross-section and longitudinal techniques in such a manner that long-range developmental changes may be estimated in a relatively short period of time.[6] He recommended that groups be selected so that final measurements on a younger group could be made at the same age as the initial measurements of the next-older group; for example, a longitudinal study that normally would take eight years might be accomplished over a two-year period if four slightly overlapping age groups were selected. Both absolute measurements and directions of development could be ascertained and used to help answer the question of whether age changes only were involved. Such a short-cut method would be especially helpful in studying transient populations or relatively unco-operative groups, and wherever extensive study leads to undesirable contamination of the population universe, as well as to point up special problems and to obtain initial results to further experimental design in longitudinal studies.

[6] Kai Jensen, "Physical Growth," in "Growth, Development, and Learning." *Review of Educational Research* 25: 369-414; December 1955.

LONGITUDINAL STUDY OF CULTURAL GROWTH

The "age-unit method," adopted and modified from the longitudinal study of human development, has been suggested for describing quantitatively the growth-maturity-senescence cycles of an economic, political, or entire cultural system and for analyzing the relationships among their component parts. Tentative examples[7] of factors that might enter into the determination of an economic age, a political age, and a cultural age are suggested below. Some of these ages, like height age in the study of human development, appear and are measurable from the time the organism (economy, political system, or cultural group) first exists as a separately definable entity. Others, like dental age in the child, represent late emerging characteristics and cannot be measured individually or averaged into an "organismic age" until they first appear.

Political age
    Behavior controls age
        Sacredness-secularness age
        Legal codification age
        Universality of legal applicability age
        Normative (moral) integration age
    Public works age
        Flood control age
        Road construction age
    Political unit age
    Taxation age
        Tax incidence age
        Tax utilization age
    Inclusiveness of "in-group" age (definition of "we the people")
    Defense-militarization age
    Governmental age
        Political participation age
        Functional division of governmental age
        Inclusiveness of governmental control age
        Determination of power incidence age

Economic age
    Specialization of labor age
    Producing unit age
    Tool (machine) production age
    Productivity per unit-of-work age
    Food source age
    Food processing age

[7] Thomas E. Parsons, "A Longitudinal Approach to the Study of Cultural Growth." *Social Forces* 34: 34–41; October 1955.

Product diversification age
Surplus goods age
Savings age
Investment age
Human conservation age
Wealth distribution age
Commercial exchange age
    Universality of exchange system age
    Credit extension age
    Banking age
Taxation age

Cultural age (Would include many of the component ages of Political age and Economic age plus others, some of which are suggested below. A list of universal culture traits might well provide both a systematic organization of subages and a theoretical framework within which to interpret or interrelate them.)
Sanitation age
Literary age
Graphic arts age
Architectural-structural age
Systematization of knowledge age
Population control age
Communication age
Transportation age.

This "age-unit method" consists essentially of:

(*a*) operationally defining the class of political, economic, social, or cultural divisions within which development is to be analyzed; (*b*) defining —again operationally, if possible—the cultural (etc.) subdivisions to be studied and the unitary structural or functional composition of these subdivisions for each developmental variable or growth factor under investigation; (*c*) determining (by direct measurement if possible) the units which comprise each growth factor within each cultural (etc.) subdivision; (*d*) repeating the latter operation at regular intervals through time; (*e*) computing age norms, or means of the obtained status values for each of the representative growth factors in the cultural (etc.) system at each chronological age (or point in time since the system's defined beginning) for which reliable data are available; (*f*) expressing the average measured status of each cultural (etc.) subdivision— and of each component growth factor within each subdivision—as the mean chronological age at which that status is attained within the culture (etc.) as a whole; and (*g*) plotting the obtained status values for all the growth factors and their means (within each subdivision being studied) as serial points on a grid which calibrates chronological time along the abscissa and equal time units of average growth (interpreted as units of time required to reach normal status in any growth factor) along the ordinate.[8]

[8] Quoted from *ibid*.

CROSS-CULTURAL METHOD[9]

The cross-cultural method has been in existence since approximately the 1880's, but not until recently has either its scope or its value been recognized, and there have been relatively few studies utilizing this method. Early examples of cross-cultural studies include: development of laws of marriage and descent, relationships between certain social institutions and stages of economic development, and constructs relating to kinship derived from evolutionary theory. In spite of the very limited amount of published research, however, the cross-cultural method has greatly influenced behavioral science and has proved a sensitive methodology for interdisciplinary research in the behavioral sciences. This approach employs statistical techniques to test theory and recently has had a major interest in matters of personality development in different cultures.

Since the late 1930's, interest has increased in an interdisciplinary approach to behavioral science, as indicated by attempts to pool the evidence and theory from the fields of anthropology, psychoanalysis, and experimental psychology. Examples of cross-cultural studies during the past few years include developmental investigations of: patterns of sexual behavior, relationship between the drinking of alcoholic beverages and anxiety, kinship terminology and its relation to certain phenomena (forms of marriage, descent, and social structure), relationship between sorcery and social control, relationship between the education of the child and art forms, relationship between the content of myths and education as these both relate to aggression, relationship between certain child-training variables and need achievement, and relationship between various techniques of education and the development of superego and other manifestations of personality.

One of the criticisms of cross-cultural studies relates to use of ethnographic sources written at different times by people with a variety of backgrounds and personal predilections. It is obvious that ethnographies already in existence cannot be completely rewritten, but such materials can be brought up to date in relation to a strict set of criteria.

[9] George W. Goethals and John W. M. Whiting, "Research Methods: The Cross-Cultural Method," in "Methodology of Educational Research." *Review of Educational Research* 27: 441–48; December 1957.

William Line and Margery R. King, "Cross-Cultural Research." *Journal of Educational Sociology* 29: 281–91; March 1956.

Carl Murchison, Editor, "Cross-Cultural Research and Methodology." *Journal of Social Psychology* 47: 157–405; May 1958.

Criticisms of this method have been met by anthropologists and behavioral scientists in general through provision of appropriate training, so that a group of anthropologists may collect field data in the same way, after having the benefit of methodological training (before going into the field).

In keeping with these new safeguards relating to existing data and to the collection of new information, recent cross-cultural studies with developmental implications have dealt with such problems as the following: techniques of education and the development of the superego from a sample of three cultures; relationship between pregnancy taboos, family structure, and dietary regulations; relationship of initiation ceremonies to child-training practices and to aspects of the kinship organization of various cultures; and relationship between kinship, education, and forms of marriage.

The implications of the cross-cultural method for educational research indicate that there is a broad range of methods or patterns[10] by which a child may be brought up, that we must be aware of both the virtues and the limitations of the untrained observer, and that there are ways of training persons to look at the phenomena of behavior with a strategy of reason, logic, and objectivity. The evidence from cross-cultural research is important in socializing the child as the school faces problems involving the emotions of both the individual child and of groups of children as they come together. This approach should help education correct the mistake of remaining "culture bound."

DEVELOPMENTAL TECHNIQUES IN RELATION TO OTHER METHODS

Certain types of genetic or developmental studies use methods similar to the techniques employed in other types of research. The cross-section approach, in terms of the data secured for each age group, is similar to a descriptive-survey investigation of status.[11] Genetic studies make extensive use of the data-gathering methods described in the chapter on descriptive-survey studies.

[10] Robert R. Sears, Eleanor E. Maccoby, and Harry Levin, *Patterns of Child Rearing.* Evanston, Ill.: Row, Peterson and Co., 1957. 549 p.

[11] Roger G. Barker and Herbert F. Wright, *Midwest and Its Children:* The Psychological Ecology of an American Town. Evanston, Ill.: Row, Peterson and Co., 1955. vii+532 p. Also see Herbert F. Wright, "Psychological Development in Midwest." *Child Development* 27: 265–86; July 1956.

Lewis M. Terman and Melita H. Oden, *The Gifted Child Grows Up:* Genetic Studies of Genius. Stanford, Calif.: Stanford University Press, 1947. xiv+450 p.

Both genetic and historical investigations are interested in the sequence or development of events, with genetic studies emphasizing growth sequences and a forward movement, while historical research involves the entire range of human events and a backward movement by means of documents and remains. The genetic and historical approaches most nearly meet in certain types of biography or autobiography with emphasis on the growth and development of the individual.[12]

Genetic investigations that use the co-twin control technique[13] in studying development are similar to experimentation. Some experimental factor affecting development is present for one twin, while his mate serves as the control. For example, one twin may be taught to climb the stairs, while the other proceeds to the activity of stair-climbing whenever he reaches his own stage of "readiness."

Genetic and case-clinical studies are similar in certain investigations of growth or development of an individual child, adolescent, or adult over a period of time.[14] Another example of a type of investigation where genetic and case studies meet is a series of cases concerned chiefly with diagnosis of defects and deviations of child development in such clinical areas as amentia, endocrine disorders, convulsive disorders, neurological behavior, cerebral injury, special sensory handicaps, prematurity, precocity, and environmental retardation.[15]

During the 1950's, studies of the intellectual growth of children increasingly applied projective methods, especially drawing and painting, as a means of exploring the more subtle changes in the child's inner world of thoughts and feelings; for example, doll play and spontaneous drawings and paintings in studying the emotional experiences and per-

---

[12] Harry L. Hollingworth, *Leta Stetter Hollingworth*. Lincoln: University of Nebraska Press, 1943. 204 p.

[13] Morton M. Hunt, "Doctor Kallmann's 7000 Twins." *Saturday Evening Post* 227: 20–21, 80–82; November 6, 1954. Co-twin control and genetics.

[14] Robert J. Havighurst, *Human Development and Education*. New York: Longmans, Green and Co., 1953. p. 177–253. Three cases.

Harold E. Jones, *Development in Adolescence*. New York: Appleton-Century-Crofts, 1943. 161 p. Development of one boy over a period of seven years.

For a highly detailed, contrasting study of behavior covering only one day, see Roger G. Barker and Herbert F. Wright, *One Boy's Day: A Specimen Record of Behavior*. New York: Harper & Brothers, 1951. x+435 p.

Lois B. Murphy and Others, *Personality in Young Children*. 2 vols. New York: Basic Books, 1956. Volume 2 is a detailed study of "Colin, A Normal Child," from his second through his fifth year.

Robert W. White, *Lives in Progress: A Study of the Natural Growth of Personality*. New York: Dryden Press, 1952. 376 p. Presents, interprets, and compares the lives (case studies) of three normal people.

[15] Arnold Gesell and Catherine S. Amatruda, *Developmental Diagnosis*. New York: Harper & Brothers, 1947. xvi+496 p.

sonality development of children. Other techniques for study of personality development include observation of behavior, interviews, questionnaires, personal documents, rating scales, certain psychometric and sociometric instruments, and the projective techniques of word association, story telling, play, psychodrama, and picture methods.[16]

The techniques of growth studies vary with the age of the subjects:[17] for infants—experiments, direct measurements, observations, one-way vision screen, the Gesell observation dome, and motion-picture recording; preschool children—direct observation and experiments; older children and adolescents—paper-and-pencil tests, indirect measurement techniques, one-way vision screen, recording of individual behavior in a social setting, and sociometric techniques in dramatic-play situations and in diagramming social relationships.

PRINCIPLES FOR ANALYSIS AND INTERPRETATION

Principles of Child Development

Certain principles of child development, which may be classified under the following abbreviated headings, are helpful as background for discussion of the several aspects of human growth and development:[18]

1. Developmental objectives
2. Levels of maturity
3. Differential rates of maturing
4. Variability in rate of maturing
5. Variability in differential rates of maturing
6. Differential developmental pre-eminence at various stages of growth
7. "Wholeheartedness and gradation" in emotional development
8. Indigenous motivation or spontaneous use, as a feature of growing ability
9. The principle of anticipation
10. "Laying by" or shedding as a feature of development

---

[16] Lawrence E. Abt and Leopold Bellak, Editors, *Projective Psychology:* Clinical Approaches to the Total Personality. New York: Alfred A. Knopf, 1950. xvii+485+xiv p.

Harold H. Anderson and Gladys L. Anderson, Editors, *An Introduction to Projective Techniques.* . . . New York: Prentice-Hall, 1951. xxiv+720 p.

Lydia Jackson and Kathleen M. Todd, *Child Treatment and the Therapy of Play.* Second Edition. New York: Ronald Press, 1950. xii+159 p.

[17] John E. Anderson, *op. cit.,* p. 32–33.

[18] Arthur T. Jersild and Charlotte Fehlman, "Child Development and the Curriculum: Some General Principles." *Journal of Experimental Education* 12: 130–42; December 1943.

11. Developmental revision of habits

12. Differentiation and integration

   a. Individuation

   b. Progression from generalized to more localized response

   c. Incorporation of separately practiced operations into larger activity systems

13. Priority of "large" over "small" muscular activities in certain sections of the body

14. Interaction between various aspects of growth

15. Vicarious extension of experience

16. Early establishment of some of the basic features of personality structure

17. The play of complementary and potentially conflicting forces

   a. Dependence—independence

   b. Self-centered and "outgoing" tendencies.

Initial Stage

In interpreting growth and development, certain stages and processes are significant.[19] The beginning or initial stage of development is important in genetic research. The initial stages of certain types of behavior in infancy are commonly as follows: in the first quarter of the first year he gains control of the muscles that move his eyes; second quarter, reaches out for things; third quarter, sits; fourth quarter, stands upright; second year, walks and runs, and articulates words and phrases; and in the third year, speaks in sentences, using words as tools of thought.[20]

Quantitative and Qualitative Changes

Growth or development is both quantitative and qualitative. Growth in vocabulary involves both the total number of words used (a quantitative change) and the effectiveness of usage in speaking or writing (a relatively qualitative phase of development). Qualitative changes in growth commonly are expressed in descriptive terms; for example, at different stages of development an infant commonly responds to the mirror situation as follows: at 40 weeks, smiles at his mirror image; at

---

[19] Nancy Bayley and Herbert S. Conrad, "Child Development—General Aspects," *Encyclopedia of Educational Research.* Second Edition. Edited by Walter S. Monroe. New York: The Macmillan Co., 1950. p. 139-42.

[20] Arnold Gesell and Others, *The First Five Years of Life.* New York: Harper & Brothers, 1940. p.13.

52 weeks, approaches his mirror image socially and even vocalizes; and at 56 weeks, brings his face close to his image, sometimes kissing it.[21]

Trends and Patterns

All growth probably is substantially gradual rather than irregular or in spurts, when due consideration is given to the relatively long period of preliminary preparation, as in walking without aid. The stages of behavior that ordinarily precede walking without aid include: at 32 weeks, in sitting the infant leans forward passively, although he sits erect for a brief period, and standing he supports his entire weight, although he leans forward with considerable hip flexion; at 40 weeks, when prone he pushes with his hands and regresses, and when standing supports himself by holding the crib side-rail; at 48 weeks, when prone he creeps, and unaided pulls himself to standing, cruises sidewise holding onto the crib rail, and may even walk forward if both hands are held; and at 56 weeks, he stands alone at least momentarily.[22] There are exceptions to the concept or principle of gradual development, such as the familiar growth spurt at adolescence, and even an occasional reversal, as illustrated by a decrease in the neck girth during the infant's first year.

Stages of Growth and Integration

Reasonable unity or integration in development prevails at a particular stage of growth, although there are many exceptions. The normal boy of 10 has reached similar stages of development intellectually, educationally, socially, and physically. On the other hand, an exceptional boy of 10 may be small in physical size but will answer questions on a quiz show at the college level in science and mathematics. Another exception to the concept of integrated growth at a particular stage is the adolescent boy who may be 6 feet in height but quite immature socially and emotionally. The vestibule of the ear is of adult size at birth, but the heart has not fully completed its growth at the age of 20. As a general rule, the several aspects of development tend to cluster around a "center of gravity of growth" for the individual.

Individuality of Growth

Although there are stages of maturation and behavior that reveal basic or common trends in development, not even identical twins grow

[21] Arnold Gesell and Helen Thompson, *The Psychology of Early Growth.* New York: The Macmillan Co., 1938. p. 158–63.
[22] *Ibid.,* p. 156–62.

up in exactly the same way. Individuality of behavior in motor activity relates to such items as output of energy, bodily activity and fatigability, and postural demeanor, with the latter noted to determine whether it is tense, relaxed, poised, steady, or variable. Adaptive behavior varies in terms of insight, inquisitiveness, originality, decisiveness, and initiative. Language is characterized by individual differences in articulation, flow of speech, inflections, inhibitions, conversational rapport, and expressiveness. Personal-social behavior reflects variations in emotional vitality; motivation; reaction to success, failure, and fatigue; reaction to novelty and surprise; and sense of humor.[23]

Limits of Growth and Old Age

The upper limits of physical growth or performance can be determined with considerable precision, as in height or speed of running, but little is known concerning maximum mental development or performance.[24] It may be that "quantitative" growth of intelligence continues until 18 or 19 years or even later, although qualitative and functional development of intelligence in terms of vocabulary, information, and insight or power in contrast to speed of reaction probably continues well beyond the age of 20. An attempt has been made to identify the most creative years of men of genius or the time during the life span when their "masterpieces" were produced. Many of these talented men produced their best works at a comparatively early age.[25]

In terms of physical and physiological development, adulthood is reached soon after the age of 20, followed by a few years at the peak of physical efficiency, and then some physical deterioration actually beginning as early as the late 20's, as is well known in the athletic sports. The peak of physical maturity and physiological equilibrium are lost in part only a few years after attainment. Fortunately, the relatively early deterioration of the anatomical and physiological functions may be offset by creative imagination, enriched experience, and good judgment, thus

---

[23] Arnold Gesell and Others, *The First Five Years of Life, op. cit.*, p. 296–308.

Arnold Gesell and Others, *Biographies of Child Development*. New York: Paul B. Hoeber, 1939. p. 13–309.

[24] L. G. Humphreys and P. L. Boynton, "Intelligence and Intelligence Tests," *Encyclopedia of Educational Research, op. cit.*, p. 600–610.

Irving Lorge and Floyd Ruch, "Adult Intelligence," *Encyclopedia of Educational Research, op. cit.*, p. 32–35.

[25] Harvey C. Lehman, *Age and Achievement*. Princeton: Princeton University Press, 1953. xiv+358 p.

Harvey C. Lehman, "The Chemist's Most Creative Years." *Science* 127: 1213–22; May 23, 1958. The 2500 ablest of the world's chemists attained their maximum production rate at ages 30 through 34.

permitting the intellect to operate in a socially effective manner. Changes in test performances of a quantitative sort during maturity and old age may be offset by qualitative aspects of intellectual performance. It is well known that senescence or disease may produce marked changes in behavior and even disintegration of personality.[26]

There is the remarkable story of a man who graduated from medical school at the age of 64, after earning seven other degrees: chiropody, bachelor of law, bachelor of science, two master's diplomas, doctor of philosophy, and doctor of judicial science. To cite another example of further growth and development at an advanced age, an eminent state commissioner of education after retiring went through law school and practiced law in his 70's. It would be interesting and profitable to follow the growth, development, and experience for a month or a year of a first-year teacher, a new supervisor, or a beginner in school administration.

During the 1950's there was increased study of the psychological adjustment of people as they grow older, but the concept of adjustment as applied to adults in a modern society is so complex that these studies have merely served to outline the problem and to suggest some useful approaches to it, leaving a thorough exploration to the future. An important characteristic of current research in gerontology is the amount of study being devoted to middle age rather than to old age. This signifies an interest in the process of aging and in knowledge which will provide a basis for a preventive mental hygiene that will help people make a better adjustment in their later years. The studies of aging and psychological adjustment during the 1950's may be classified under the following broad headings: meaning of psychological adjustment in the later years, measurement of psychological adjustment in later maturity, adjustment and social relations, living conditions and personal adjustment, retirement, public attitudes about aging, health and adjustment, and education for aging.

Scientists study psychological adjustment for two general purposes: the purely scientific purpose of getting an accurate description of the behavior of people, and to discover how to help people become happier,

[26] Jeanne G. Gilbert, *Understanding Old Age*. New York: Ronald Press, 1953. 442 p. Detailed treatment of gerontology; important physical aspects of the aging process and the intellectual, emotional, and psychosexual changes that take place in later years; normal and abnormal aging; 26 case histories based on the author's professional experience.

Robert J. Havighurst and Ruth Albrecht, *Older People*. New York: Longmans, Green and Co., 1953. xvi+415 p.

more successful in their pursuit of the goals of life, or better adjusted. Both purposes are illustrated in current research on adjustment in the later years.[27]

Pressey and Kuhlen's book emphasizes psychological development during the later years, with appropriate graphs and tables in a textual presentation which has been carefully organized.[28]

The warp of the fabric is the genetic or age order of development. Starting with infancy and following through age by age to senescence, growth is mapped in successive chapters on its physical side, then its intellectual, its educational, its emotional and motivational, its moral-religious, its interpersonal-social, its familial. The woof in the weave is the recognition of individual differences in most of the functions and at most of the stages, and their exploitation and interpretation against the background of individual history. . . .

The most nearly central theme of this book is a sort of longitudinal holism (as well as the currently well-accepted cross-sectional holism), a life-span, cradle-to-grave perspective. Even where the problems of old age are being canvassed, the reader is reminded that that period of life with its subculture and subsociety—the period which needs to be rescued from the "inane placidities of the Florida trailer camp or the narrow evangelism of certain religious groups"—must be seen in its continuity with childhood, youth, and maturity. . . .

Scattered through the chapters there are such queries as: Do the biological drives resume their earlier primary importance for motivation in the advanced years? Is the dichotomy of work versus play especially false in those years? What are the actual effects upon people—at all ages—of the ready-made fantasies stimulated by TV and other mass media? The age-trends toward conservatism: what are possible remedies? The age-changes in marital adjustment are highly multiple and complex: how may that relationship be kept optimal? And finally the all-pervading question: can one hope to approximate Browning's wishful insight?

> "Grow old along with me.
> The best is yet to be:
> The last of life for which the first
> was made."

---

[27] Robert J. Havighurst and Betty E. Orr, "Aging and Psychological Adjustment," in "Growth, Development, and Learning." *Review of Educational Research* 25: 477–86; December 1955.
James E. Birren, "Why Study Aging?" *American Psychologist* 13: 292–96; June 1958. The three major areas of problems for older persons are health, economics, and loneliness.
[28] Quoted from review by John F. Dashiell, *Contemporary Psychology* 2: 265–66; October 1957, of Sidney L. Pressey and Raymond G. Kuhlen, *Psychological Development Through the Life Span.* New York: Harper & Brothers, 1957. xxiii+654 p.

Diagnosis and Prognosis

Interest in developmental diagnosis and causation came later than the investigations limited to determination of growth norms or sequences. A common error in identifying causation is failure to recognize the combined effects of two or more causal factors that are interrelated functionally, as illustrated by the difficulty of separating the influence of nature from nurture on achievement. The causal factors that affect growth and development include: race; age; sex; familial heredity; prenatal conditions; birth trauma; birth order; maternal age at pregnancy; endocrine factors; nutritional factors; health factors; disease and infections; seasonal conditions; atmospheric conditions (temperature, humidity, and pressure); national-racial culture; socioeconomic status; educational agencies; social pressure; family and neighborhood; acquaintances and friends; intelligence; knowledge; experience, exercise, and training; interests and motivation; and emotional adjustments.[29]

Interest and progress in the area of developmental diagnosis are illustrated by a full-length treatise which presents in some detail a wide range of diagnostic problems: techniques for the developmental examination of behavior and norms of development; diagnosis of the defects and deviations of development (amentia, endocrine disorders, convulsive disorders, neurological diagnosis of infant behavior, cerebral injury, special sensory handicaps, prematurity, precocity, environmental retardation, and clinical aspects of child adoption); and protection of early child development, as related to diagnosis, guidance, and developmental supervision.[30]

The discussion in this chapter relating to causal factors affecting physical and mental growth suggests the difficulties of developmental prognosis and prediction.[31] Prediction in such areas as constancy of the I.Q., height, time of maturity, and age at which growth will cease is possible only to the extent that valid techniques or instruments of measurement are available, that early development provides a stable base from which subsequent growth proceeds, and that later development is affected by the same causal factors as operated in the earlier stages of growth. As indicated earlier in this chapter, it is much simpler to predict in the area of physical growth and performance than in the fields of mentality and personality development.

[29] Nancy Bayley and Herbert S. Conrad, *op. cit.*
[30] Arnold Gesell and Catherine S. Amatruda, *op. cit.*
[31] Leo F. Cain, John U. Michaelis, and Alvin C. Eurich, "Prognosis," *Encyclopedia of Educational Research, op. cit.,* p. 874–94.

DEVELOPMENTAL TASKS AND STAGES OF MATURITY

During the 1950's the developmental-task concept was applied to the field of education. This concept developed from the research on child and adolescent development during the 1930's and resulted in a science of human development cutting across disciplines in the biological and the social sciences. More recently this concept has been developed on the basis of psychological and sociological research on attitudes and social roles, and also has been applied to adulthood and old age.

A developmental task is one which "arises at or about a certain period in the life of the individual, successful achievement of which leads to his happiness and to success with later tasks, while failure leads to unhappiness in the individual, disapproval by society, and difficulty with later tasks."[32] Such tasks arise from three sources: physical maturation, cultural pressure (the expectations of society), and individual aspirations or values.

To cite an example, the central task of adolescence, "achieving identity," includes the following developmental tasks: learning a masculine or feminine social role, accepting one's body, achieving emotional independence of parents and other adults, selecting and preparing for an occupation, and achieving a scale of values and an ethical system to live by.

By way of illustration, the developmental tasks of middle childhood[33] include:

1. Learning physical skills necessary for ordinary games
2. Building wholesome attitudes toward oneself as a growing organism
3. Learning to get along with age-mates
4. Learning an appropriate masculine or feminine social role
5. Developing fundamental skills in reading, writing, and calculating
6. Developing concepts necessary for everyday living
7. Developing conscience, morality, and a scale of values
8. Achieving personal independence
9. Developing attitudes toward social groups and institutions.

Gesell and associates have outlined maturity traits and gradients of growth:[34]

[32] Robert J. Havighurst, "Research on the Developmental-Task Concept." *School Review* 64: 215–23; May 1956.

[33] Robert J. Havighurst, *Human Development and Education*, *op. cit.*, p. 25–41.

[34] Arnold Gesell, Frances L. Ilg, and Louise B. Ames, *Youth*: The Years from Ten to Sixteen, *op. cit.*, p. 35.

1. *Total action system:* physical growth, sex interest, health, tensional outlets, response to the examination and interview

2. *Self-care and routines:* eating, sleep, bath, clothes, care of room, money and work

3. *Emotions:* in general, anger, worries and fears, humor, affectivity, self-assertion, expressing feelings

4. *The growing self:* in general, self-evaluation, wishes and inclinations, the future

5. *Interpersonal relationships:* mother-child, father-child, siblings, family, same-sex friends, opposite-sex friends, crushes, parties

6. *Activities and interests:* outdoor activities, indoor activities, clubs and camps, reading, radio, television, phonograph, movies

7. *School life:* in general, school subjects and work, teacher-child relationship

8. *Ethical sense:* right and wrong, sense of fairness, response to reason, honesty, swearing, drinking, smoking

9. *Philosophical outlook:* time and space, death and deity.

As an illustration of stages of development,[35] the changes in "likes" from ten to sixteen are as follows:

Ten. "My mother and father, of course," is the outstanding answer to the question: "What do you like best in the world?" "Horses" comes next in frequency.

Eleven. As at ten years, "my mother and father" are mentioned most often as things liked best, and again "horses" is second in frequency. Few other likes are mentioned, except eating and travel.

Twelve. Mother and father still lead as best liked of anything, and animals of some kind—cats, dogs, horses—are next in frequency of mention. Sports have come in strongly, and eating, dancing, and reading are other favored activities. Nice clothes and "my home" are among the things most liked.

Thirteen. A real change appears at thirteen—great variety of likes occurs, and parents have dropped out in mention of best liked. Friends of the opposite sex are now most often mentioned, and are followed in frequency by eating, "my home," and automobiles. Items mentioned for the first time at thirteen include: a good time, the United States, peace and quiet, luxury, and popular music.

Fourteen. Fourteen's likes seem to be broad-ranging. Sports and friends of the opposite sex now lead in frequency, followed by travel and music. Likes first mentioned at fourteen include: knowledge, art and literature, just living, shelter.

Fifteen. Again, as at thirteen, great individual variation appears, with no two "best likes" alike. Among items mentioned are: reading, sailing, art, literature, just living. For the first time, security is named as a thing liked best.

[35] *Ibid.*, p. 372–75.

Sixteen. Great individual variety of likes, and many Sixteens find it difficult to indicate the thing they like best. Only one mentioned material objects ("car and radio"), while others have more general preferences, such as work, communication, "having other people like me."

An example of four stages of maturity in using measuring instruments, with specific applications to the school curriculum, is as follows:

Early Childhood: Becoming acquainted with common measuring instruments—Using ruler to measure paper, wood for construction; measuring curtains, wallpaper for playhouse; measuring paper for mural; helping fill aquarium; telling time; reading thermometer; finding dates on calendar; figuring how many more days before special holiday or excursion; keeping chart of weight or height; using such measures as cupful, spoonful, pint, quart, in following recipes; learning to tell time.

Later Childhood: Using common measuring instruments effectively—Using yardstick, ruler effectively; deciding whether ruler, tape measure, or yardstick is most suitable to measure given distances; finding how to use stop watch; investigating uses of compass in telling direction; finding how to use pints, quarts, other measuring instruments in the home; using scales to weigh self, other objects; reading speedometer; reading thermometer, barometer; making charts, maps, scale drawings; developing simple time chart in social studies.

Youth: Extending the range and variety of measuring instruments used —Using stop watch; using efficiently protractor or compass; using kitchen utensils to measure ingredients; laying out basketball court; using a T square for construction activities; using transit, angle mirror or other instruments for measuring heights or distances; using fine scales in experimental work; reading gasoline gauge, speedometer, and other indicators on car; reading directions from compass; using color charts; adjusting shutter and lens speed on camera; reading barometer; interpreting different types of thermometers, metric and other scales.

Adulthood: Using instruments of measurement appropriately in a variety of situations of adult life—Using precise instruments appropriate to one's vocation; recognizing when inaccurate instruments might throw measurements off, when more accurate instruments are needed; interpreting statements about industrial processes requiring precision measures; using surveying instruments; using scales in grocery store, scales to weigh self, children; reading utility meters; reading clinical thermometers; using barometer and thermometer to make weather predictions; using scale on light meter, other photographic equipment; reading automobile gauges.[36]

[36] Quoted from Florence B. Stratemeyer, Hamden L. Forkner, Margaret G. McKim, and A. Harry Passow, *Developing a Curriculum for Modern Living.* Second Edition. New York: Bureau of Publications, Teachers College, Columbia University, 1957. p. 208-9.

EXAMPLES AND APPLICATIONS

In a large measure, developmental and growth studies have been centralized and co-ordinated through such university centers as California at Berkeley, Columbia, Chicago, Harvard, Iowa, Michigan, Minnesota, Stanford, and Yale,[37] as illustrated in the footnotes and bibliography of this chapter. Another example of a center is found in the work of the Fels Research Institute for the Study of Human Development at Antioch College, which was founded to study human growth and development from the prenatal period through maturity by the longitudinal method of research, by means of repeated measurements and observations of the same children over long periods of time. More than 300 children from Yellow Springs and neighboring communities have participated in the program of investigation, with staff members in the fields of biochemistry, physical growth, psychophysiology, and psychology engaged in experimental and cross-section research, as well as longitudinal investigation. One of these longitudinal problems is a study of individual differences in mental-growth rate or individual patterns of change in the measured intelligence of children, including an investigation of the relationship between I.Q. change and the personality structure of the child.[38]

Physical Growth

Physical growth is a biological process that involves rates, directions, and patterns of change and development affected by a variety of diverse and complex external and internal factors and causes. It encompasses a diversity of detectable and measurable changes in size, shape, or function occurring in living organisms with the passage of time. Many scientific disciplines study physical growth from a variety of angles at different levels with increasingly refined and ingenious methods and techniques. Challenging and rewarding fields for study have included: genetic origins and backgrounds; reproduction; cell multiplication; protein synthesis; the role of chemical excitors and inhibitors; cell migration; prenatal development; birth phenomena; developmental history of special

[37] Lois M. Stolz, "Youth: The Gesell Institute and Its Latest Study." *Contemporary Psychology* 3: 10–15; January 1958. Reviews the projects in child development completed at Yale University.

[38] Lester W. Sontag, Charles T. Baker, and Virginia L. Nelson, *Mental Growth and Personality Development:* A Longitudinal Study. Monographs of the Society for Research in Child Development, Vol. 23, Serial No. 68, No. 2, 1958. Lafayette, Ind.: Child Development Publications, Purdue University, 1958. 143 p.

tissues, organs, and intact organisms; increases in body measurements and changes in shape; comparative growth of groups, interindividual and intraindividual growth; and environmental conditioners and impacts.[39]

Mental Development

Before the middle of the present century, investigations of mental development dealt primarily with the period of childhood and adolescence. Longitudinal studies now have begun to provide information on age changes later in the life span of individuals first tested in childhood or adolescence. During the 1950's, research workers showed an active interest in the consistency of test performance at different ages and in factors related to change in test performance; effect of environmental variables on mental development; role of emotional and motivational factors; extent to which I.Q. changes represent true changes in relative standing or are attributable instead to test construction, test standardization, or other psychometric factors; group and individual differences; test performance of institutional and defective children; studies of various socioeconomic and ethnic groups; differential responses of groups with different physical and mental disorders; and mental development of the infant in relation to predictive value of tests given in infancy.[40] The specific topics under which the studies of mental development during the 1950's were reviewed include the following: abilities at different developmental levels, adult mental abilities, constancy of the I.Q., intelligence and achievement, sex differences in intelligence, intelligence and socioeconomic status, differences among ethnic groups, bilingualism, genetic influences on intelligence, institutionalized and defective children, mental abilities in psychiatric groups, intelligence and personal and social adjustment, and mental, physical, and physiological relationships.

Learning

The development of a universally accepted definition of learning is greatly needed and would not necessarily limit either the number or variety of studies or the differences in perceptual or theoretical framework of the investigators. An acceptance of such a definition, however, not only would provide a more effective opportunity to synthesize for the use of research but would also enable the investigator to make contributions more in harmony with the total field than at present. Although

---

[39] Kai Jensen, *op. cit.*

[40] Samuel R. Pinneau and Harold E. Jones, "Mental Development in Infancy and Childhood and Mental Abilities in Adult Life," in "Growth, Development, and Learning." *Review of Educational Research* 25: 415–37; December 1955.

the name used to identify a particular phenomenon is not of significance in itself, the assumptions upon which experimentation is based are highly significant. It is often easier to make an assumption from the name given than from the reality itself.

A number of trends in the literature on learning indicate that a new frame of reference is being accepted: a change from concern for facts to a concern for generalizations and laws; a change of focus from the experimenter to the learner, from emphasis on outcomes to emphasis on process, from judgment based on magnitude to that based on rate, from the cross-section to the longitudinal basis, from specifics to patterns or configurations, and from independent findings to findings related to each other.[41]

Personality and Social Development

Modern personality theories assign a leading role in personality formation to the events of the preschool years. Although the need for knowledge and understanding of the important early processes has long been acutely experienced, the relative dearth of sound studies of early personality development indicates a hiatus between theory and observation. The scarcity of relevant studies probably is the result of several factors: a lack of technical devices for assessment of the behavior of young children comparable to the procedures currently utilized in studies of adults, and the cultural lag that permits less recognition of efforts in this area than of work in the more adequately financed and currently fashionable fields.[42] The use of conventional psychometric devices has not proved adequate, with interest focused on projective and play techniques. The Rorschach Test has been a common projective device selected for young children, with recent studies concentrated on the normative aspects of performance. The studies of personality development in infancy and the preschool years during the 1950's may be classified under the headings of child-rearing practices (demographic differences and relation to development), family relationships and attitudes (mother-child relationships, early separation, father-child relationships, and sibling relationships), frustration and aggression, adjustment, behavior disorders, prematurity, hospitalization, measuring instruments, and play therapy.

[41] Arthur R. Delong, "Learning," in "Growth, Development, and Learning." *Review of Educational Research* 25: 438–52; December 1955.
[42] Harold H. Anderson, Charles Hanley, and John R. Hurley, "Personality Development in Infancy and the Preschool Years," in "Growth, Development, and Learning." *Review of Educational Research* 25: 453–68; December 1955.

Personality and social development during the 1950's received considerable attention from psychologists, psychiatrists, sociologists, and anthropologists, which suggests an interdisciplinary approach. The individual is being viewed increasingly as a unique, unified, and whole personality with the ability to act according to his own self-determination and not just in response to present and past occurrences, which places major emphasis on striving and goal-directed behavior. The investigations of the 1950's dealing with personality and social development during childhood and adolescence may be classified under the large headings of adolescence, juvenile delinquency, sociometric investigations, relationship to academic success, and techniques for evaluation.[43]

CONCLUDING STATEMENT

Approximately 5,000 references are listed in the nine issues of the *Review of Educational Research* devoted to growth and development, with much of this research sponsored in child-study divisions of higher institutions and with helpful support from the foundations. These resources, however, are not adequate for the expensive and time-consuming longitudinal investigations, which suggests the need for public interest and support, including the co-operation of teachers, administrators, parents, and children. The concepts, procedures, and applications of developmental or growth investigations may be summarized briefly as follows:

1. An interest in origin, direction, trend, rate, pattern, limit, and decline of growth

2. Encouragement of carefully planned longitudinal investigations, and improved sampling procedures in cross-section studies

3. Application of the longitudinal approach to study of the growth-maturity-senescence cycles of an economic, political, or entire cultural system

4. Use of the cross-cultural method in the behavioral sciences, with statistical techniques employed to test theory, and recently with a major interest in matters of personality development in different cultures

5. Formulation of basic principles for analysis and interpretation of genetic data

6. Further progress in identification of maturity traits and gradients of growth, stages of development or maturity, and developmental tasks

[43] Cameron W. Meredith, "Personality and Social Development During Childhood and Adolescence," in "Growth, Development, and Learning." *Review of Educational Research* 25: 469–76; December 1955.

7. Increased interest and recently devised procedures in certain major areas of development (physical, mental, social, personality, learning, and old age).

SELECTED REFERENCES

ALMY, Millie. *Child Development.* New York: Henry Holt and Co., 1955. xvii+490 p. (Chapters 3 and 4 deal with procedures and problems in studying child development.)

ANDERSON, Harold H., and Others. "Growth, Development, and Learning." *Review of Educational Research* 25: 365-540; December 1955.

ANDERSON, John E. *The Psychology of Development and Personal Adjustment.* New York: Henry Holt and Co., 1949. xvi+720 p.

AUSUBEL, David P. *Theory and Problems of Adolescent Development.* New York: Grune and Stratton, 1954. 600 p.

AUSUBEL, David P. *Theory and Problems of Child Development.* New York: Grune and Stratton, 1958. xiv+650 p.

BALDWIN, Alfred L. *Behavior and Development in Childhood.* New York: Dryden Press, 1955. xviii+620 p.

BARKER, Roger G., and WRIGHT, Herbert F. *Midwest and Its Children:* The Psychological Ecology of an American Town. Evanston, Ill.: Row, Peterson and Co., 1955. vii+532 p.

BARKER, Roger G., and WRIGHT, Herbert F. *One Boy's Day:* A Specimen Record of Behavior. New York: Harper & Brothers, 1951. x+435 p.

BARNES, Melvin W. "The Nature and Nurture of Early Adolescents." *Teachers College Record* 57: 513-21; May 1956.

BAYLEY, Nancy. "Individual Patterns of Development." *Child Development* 27: 45-74; March 1956.

BAYLEY, Nancy. "On the Growth of Intelligence." *American Psychologist* 10: 805-18; December 1955.

BAYLEY, Nancy, and FREEMAN, Frank N. "Child Development," *Encyclopedia of Educational Research.* Second Edition. Edited by Walter S. Monroe. New York: The Macmillan Co., 1950. p. 137-39.

BAYLEY, Nancy, and Others. "Growth and Development." *Review of Educational Research* 17: 301-403; December 1947.

BERNARD, Harold W. *Adolescent Development in American Culture.* Yonkers-on-Hudson: World Book Co., 1957. xii+644 p.

BLAIR, Arthur W., and BURTON, William H. *Growth and Development of the Preadolescent.* New York: Appleton-Century-Crofts, 1951. viii+221 p.

BOSSARD, James H. S. *The Sociology of Child Development.* Revised Edition. New York: Harper & Brothers, 1953. 788 p.

BOUSFIELD, W. A., and Others. "A Study of Developmental Changes in Conceptual and Perceptual Associative Clustering." *Journal of Genetic Psychology* 92: 95-102; March 1958.

BREEN, Leonard Z. "Some Problems of Research in the Field of Aging." *Sociology and Social Research* 41: 412-16; July-August 1957.

BURLINGHAM, Dorothy. *Twins:* A Study of Three Pairs of Identical Twins.

New York: International Universities Press, 1953. x+92 p. + 30 developmental charts.

CARMICHAEL, Leonard, Editor. *Manual of Child Psychology*. Second Edition. New York: John Wiley & Sons, 1954. ix+1295 p.

COLE, Luella. *Psychology of Adolescence*. Fourth Edition. New York: Rinehart, 1954. xvi+712 p.

CORNELL, Ethel L., and ARMSTRONG, Charles M. "Forms of Mental Growth Patterns Revealed by Reanalysis of the Harvard Growth Data." *Child Development* 26: 169-204; September 1955.

CROW, L. D., and CROW, Alice. *Adolescent Development and Adjustment*. New York: McGraw-Hill Book Co., 1956. xiv+555 p.

CRUZE, Wendell W. *Adolescent Psychology and Development*. New York: Ronald Press, 1953. 584 p.

DAVITZ, Joel R. "Contributions of Research with Children to a Theory of Maladjustment." *Child Development* 29: 3-7; March 1958.

DENNIS, Wayne. "The Age Decrement in Outstanding Scientific Contributions: Fact or Artifact?" *American Psychologist* 13: 457-60; August 1958.

DEWEY, Richard, and HUMBER, W. J. *The Development of Human Behavior*. New York: The Macmillan Co., 1951. 832 p.

DONAHUE, Wilma T., Editor. *Education for Later Maturity:* A Handbook. New York: Whiteside, and William Morrow, 1955. xiii+338 p.

DUNN, L. C., Editor. *Genetics in the 20th Century*. New York: The Macmillan Co., 1951. xi+634 p.

DUVALL, Evelyn M. *Family Development*. Philadelphia: J. B. Lippincott Co., 1957. vii+533 p.

EMERSON, Alfred E. "Dynamic Homeostasis: A Unifying Principle in Organic, Social, and Ethical Evolution." *Scientific Monthly* 78: 67-85; February 1954.

ESSERT, Paul L., LORGE, Irving, and TUCKMAN, Jacob. "Preparation for a Constructive Approach to Later Maturity." *Teachers College Record* 53: 70-76; November 1951.

ESSERT, Paul L., and Others. "Adult Education." *Review of Educational Research* 23: 191-283; June 1953.

FOREST, Ilse. *Child Development*. New York: McGraw-Hill Book Co., 1954. 286 p.

FREEMAN, Frank S., and MILES, Catharine C. "Sex Differences," *Encyclopedia of Educational Research*. Second Edition. Edited by Walter S. Monroe. New York: The Macmillan Co., 1950. p. 1201-8.

FROEHLICH, Gustav J., and Others. "Growth and Development." *Review of Educational Research* 20: 341-440; December 1950.

GARRISON, Karl C. *Growth and Development*. New York: Longmans, Green and Co., 1952. xii+559 p.

GARRISON, Karl C. *Psychology of Adolescence*. Fourth Edition. New York: Prentice-Hall, 1951. 510 p.

GESELL, Arnold. *Infant Development:* The Embryology of Early Human Behavior. New York: Harper & Brothers, 1952. 108 p.

GESELL, Arnold. *Studies in Child Development*. New York: Harper & Brothers, 1948. x+224 p.

GESELL, Arnold, and AMATRUDA, Catherine S. *Developmental Diagnosis: Normal and Abnormal Child Development, Clinical Methods and Practical Applications.* Revised Edition. New York: Harper & Brothers, 1947. xvi+496 p.

GESELL, Arnold, and ILG, Frances L. *Child Development.* New York: Harper & Brothers, 1949. xii+403, xxxii+475 p. 2 vols. in one.

GESELL, Arnold, ILG, Frances L., AMES, Louise B., and BULLIS, Glenna E. *The Child From Five to Ten.* New York: Harper & Brothers, 1946. 475 p.

GESELL, Arnold, ILG, Frances L., and AMES, Louise B. *Youth:* The Years from Ten to Sixteen. New York: Harper & Brothers, 1956. xv+542 p.

GILBERT, Jeanne G. *Understanding Old Age.* New York: Ronald Press, 1953. 442 p.

GOOD, Carter V., and SCATES, Douglas E. *Methods of Research:* Educational, Psychological, Sociological. New York: Appleton-Century-Crofts, 1954. p. 800-831.

HARRIS, D. B., Editor. *The Concept of Development:* An Issue in the Study of Human Behavior. Minneapolis: University of Minnesota Press, 1957. x+287 p.

HAVIGHURST, Robert J. *Human Development and Education.* New York: Longmans, Green and Co., 1953. ix+338 p.

HAVIGHURST, Robert J. "Research on the Developmental-Task Concept." *School Review* 64: 215-23; May 1956.

HAVIGHURST, Robert J., and ALBRECHT, Ruth. *Older People.* New York: Longmans, Green and Co., 1953. xvi+415 p.

HORROCKS, John E. *The Psychology of Adolescence:* Behavior and Development. Boston: Houghton Mifflin Co., 1951. 614 p.

HUNT, Morton M. "Doctor Kallmann's 7000 Twins." *Saturday Evening Post* 227: 20-21, 80-82; November 6, 1954. (Co-twin control and genetics.)

HURLOCK, Elizabeth B. *Adolescent Development.* Second Edition. New York: McGraw-Hill Book Co., 1955. 590 p.

HURLOCK, Elizabeth B. *Child Development.* Second Edition. New York: McGraw-Hill Book Co., 1950. xvi+669 p.

HURLOCK, Elizabeth B. *Developmental Psychology.* New York: McGraw-Hill Book Co., 1953. 556 p.

HUXLEY, Julian. *Evolution in Action.* New York: Harper & Brothers, 1953. 182 p.

ILG, Frances L., and AMES, Louise B. *Child Behavior.* New York: Harper & Brothers, 1955. xi+364 p.

JERSILD, Arthur T. *Child Psychology.* Fourth Edition. New York: Prentice-Hall, 1954. v+676 p.

JERSILD, Arthur T. *The Psychology of Adolescence.* New York: The Macmillan Co., 1957. xii+438 p.

JERSILD, Arthur T. "Self-Understanding in Childhood and Adolescence." *American Psychologist* 6: 122-26; April 1951.

KINSEY, A. C., and Others. *Sexual Behavior in the Human Male.* Philadelphia: W. B. Saunders Co., 1948. xvi+804 p.

KINSEY, A. C., and Others. *Sexual Behavior in the Human Female.* Philadelphia: W. B. Saunders Co., 1953. xxx+842 p.

KOCH, Helen L. "Methods of Studying the Behavior and Development of Young Children," *Methods of Psychology.* Edited by T. G. Andrews. New York: John Wiley & Sons, 1948. Chapter 21, p. 624-63.

KUHLEN, Raymond G. *The Psychology of Adolescent Development.* New York: Harper & Brothers, 1952. xvii+675 p.

KUHLEN, Raymond G., and THOMPSON, George G. *Psychological Studies of Human Development.* New York: Appleton-Century-Crofts, 1952. 533 p.

LANDIS, Paul H. *Adolescence and Youth:* The Process of Maturing. Second Edition. New York: McGraw-Hill Book Co., 1952. xii+461 p.

LANDRETH, Catherine. *The Psychology of Early Childhood.* New York: Alfred A. Knopf, 1958. xviii+412+xiii p.

LEHMAN, Harvey C. *Age and Achievement.* Princeton: Princeton University Press, 1953. xi+358 p.

LINE, William, and KING, Margery R. "Cross-Cultural Research." *Journal of Educational Sociology* 29: 281-91; March 1956.

MALM, Marguerite, and JAMISON, Olis G. *Adolescence.* New York: McGraw-Hill Book Co., 1953. 512 p.

MARTIN, William E., and STENDLER, Celia B. *Child Development:* The Process of Growing Up in Society. New York: Harcourt, Brace and Co., 1953. xxii+519 p.

MARTIN, William E., and STENDLER, Celia B. *Readings in Child Development.* New York: Harcourt, Brace and Co., 1954. 513 p.

MERRY, Frieda K., and MERRY, Ralph V. *The First Two Decades of Life.* Second Edition. New York: Harper & Brothers, 1958. 626 p.

MILLARD, Cecil V. *Case Inventory for the Study of Child Development.* Minneapolis: Burgess Publishing Co., 1950. 29 p.

MILLARD, Cecil V. *Child Growth and Development in the Elementary School Years.* Boston: D. C. Heath and Co., 1951. xiv+511 p.

MILLARD, Cecil V. *School and Child:* A Case History. East Lansing: Michigan State College Press, 1954. xv+210 p.

MILLARD, Cecil V., and ROTHNEY, John W. M. *The Elementary School Child:* A Book of Cases. New York: Dryden Press, 1957. xii+660 p. (Case histories of development, including a developmental curve, achievement record, elementary-school marks, mental characteristics, mental-test results, observation notes, and teachers' summaries.)

MOHR, G. J., and DESPRES, Marian A. *The Stormy Decade:* Adolescence. New York: Random House, 1958. 272 p.

MONTAGUE, M. F. Ashley. *The Direction of Human Development:* Biological and Social Bases. New York: Harper & Brothers, 1955. 404 p.

MULLER, H. J. "Genetic Principles in Human Populations." *Scientific Monthly* 83: 277-86; December 1956.

MUNN, Norman L. *The Evolution and Growth of Human Behavior.* Boston: Houghton Mifflin Co., 1955. xi+525 p.

MUNN, Norman L. *Psychological Development:* An Introduction to Genetic Psychology. Boston: Houghton Mifflin Co., 1938. xxv+582 p.

MURPHY, Lois B., and Others. *Personality in Young Children.* 2 vols. New York: Basic Books, 1956. (Volume 2 is a detailed study of "Colin, A Normal Child," from his second through his fifth year.)

Mussen, Paul H., and Conger, John J. *Child Development and Personality.* New York: Harper & Brothers, 1956. xii+569 p.

Northway, Mary L. "A Plan for Sociometric Studies in a Longitudinal Programme of Research in Child Development." *Sociometry* 17: 272-81; August 1954.

Olson, Willard C. *Child Development.* Boston: D. C. Heath and Co., 1949. xiii+417 p.

Parsons, Thomas S. "A Longitudinal Approach to the Study of Cultural Growth." *Social Forces* 34: 34-41; October 1955.

Pressey, S. L., and Kuhlen, R. G. *Psychological Development Through the Life Span.* New York: Harper & Brothers, 1957. xxiii+654 p.

Shock, N. W. *Trends in Gerontology.* Second Edition. Stanford, Calif.: Stanford University Press, 1957. viii+214 p.

Shock, N. W., and Others. "The Age Problem in Research Workers." *Scientific Monthly* 72: 353-67; June 1951.

Sigel, Irving E. "The Need for Conceptualization in Research on Child Development." *Child Development* 27: 241-52; June 1956.

Soddy, Kenneth, Editor. *Mental Health and Infant Development.* Vol. I: Papers and Discussions. Vol. II: Case Histories. Proceedings of the International Seminar held by the World Federation for Mental Health, Chichester, England, 19 July–10 August 1952. New York: Basic Books, 1956. xix+308 p., v+289 p.

Sontag, Lester W., Baker, Charles T., and Nelson, Virginia L. *Mental Growth and Personality Development:* A Longitudinal Study. Monographs of the Society for Research in Child Development, Vol. 23, Serial No. 68, No. 2, 1958. Lafayette, Ind.: Child Development Publications, Purdue University, 1958. 143 p.

Stephens, J. M. *Educational Psychology:* The Study of Educational Growth. New York: Henry Holt and Co., 1951. xxiii+692 p.

Stevens, S. S., Editor. "Growth and Development," *Handbook of Experimental Psychology.* New York: John Wiley & Sons, 1951. p. 236-386.

Stoke, Stuart M., and Others. "Growth, Development, and Learning." *Review of Educational Research* 22: 387-525; December 1952.

Stone, L. J., and Church, Joseph. *Childhood and Adolescence:* A Psychology of the Growing Person. New York: Random House, 1957. xvii+456 p.

Stott, L. H. *The Longitudinal Study of Individual Development.* Detroit: Merrill-Palmer School, 1955. x+115 p.

Strang, Ruth. *The Adolescent Views Himself:* A Psychology of Adolescence. New York: McGraw-Hill Book Co., 1957. xiv+581 p.

Strang, Ruth. *Introduction to Child Study.* Third Edition. New York: The Macmillan Co., 1951. xi+705 p.

Terman, Lewis M., and Oden, Melita H. *The Gifted Child Grows Up:* Genetic Studies of Genius. Stanford, Calif.: Stanford University Press, 1947. xiv+450 p.

Terrell, Glenn. "The Need for Simplicity in Research in Child Psychology." *Child Development* 29: 303-10; June 1958.

Thompson, George. *Child Psychology.* Boston: Houghton Mifflin Co., 1952. xxxiii+667 p.

THORPE, Louis P. *Child Psychology and Development*. Second Edition. New York: Ronald Press, 1955. 700 p.

THORPE, Louis P., and CRUZE, Wendell W. *Developmental Psychology*. New York: Ronald Press, 1956. v+670 p.

TIBBITTS, Clark, and DONAHUE, Wilma. "Developments in Education for Later Maturity." *Review of Educational Research* 23: 202-17; June 1953.

TRAVERS, R. M. W. *An Introduction to Educational Research*. New York: The Macmillan Co., 1958. Chapter 12.

WAGONER, Lovisa C., and CASTELLANOS, J. M. *Observation of Young Children, Their Behavior, Their Teaching*. Revised Edition. Oakland, Calif.: L. C. Wagoner, Mills College, 1951. 142 p.

WATSON, ERNEST H., and LOWERY, George H. *Growth and Development of Children*. Chicago: Year Book Publications, 1951. 260 p.

WATTENBERG, W. W. *The Adolescent Years*. New York: Harcourt, Brace and Co., 1955. 510 p.

WHITE, Robert W. *Lives in Progress:* A Study of the Natural Growth of Personality. New York: Dryden Press, 1952. (Presents, interprets, and compares the lives or case studies of three normal people.) 376 p.

WHITING, John W. M. "The Cross-Cultural Method," *Handbook of Social Psychology:* Theory and Method. Vol. 1. Edited by Gardner Lindzey. Cambridge, Mass.: Addison-Wesley Publishing Co., 1954. p. 523-31.

WIENER, Norbert. *Ex-Prodigy:* My Childhood and Youth. New York: Simon and Schuster, 1953. xii+309 p.

WILES, Kimball, and Others. "The Educational Program: Adolescence." *Review of Educational Research* 24: 1-104; February 1954. (Chapter 11 lists needed research.)

WRIGHT, Herbert F. "Psychological Development in Midwest." *Child Development* 27: 265-86; July 1956.

ZUBEK, John P., and SOLBERG, Patricia A. *Human Development*. New York: McGraw-Hill Book Co., 1954. 478 p.

7

Clinical and Case Studies

This chapter presents the several types of case study, applications and uses of clinical and case techniques, sequence or stages in case study and case work (symptoms, examination and history, diagnosis, therapy, and follow-up), clinical and case records, ethical standards, relationship between case-clinical and statistical methods, and illustrative case histories.

TYPES OF CASE STUDY

The basic approach of the case study is to deal with all pertinent aspects of one thing or situation, with the unit for study an individual, a social institution or agency such as a family or a hospital, or a community or cultural group such as a rural village, a steel town, or a trailer camp, as illustrated by numerous titles in the chapter bibliography. The case is some phase of the life history of the unit of attention, or it may represent the entire life process.

Case studies of individuals may be an autobiography of a mental patient or of a criminal, a personal account of a psychoanalysis, a biography of child development, an autobiography of an evolving philosophy and psychology of teaching, or the childhood and youth of a prodigy.

Case studies have been made of such social institutions or agencies as the family, marriage, a higher institution of learning, a hospital clinic, and a movie.

Case studies of communities or cultural groups have included such units as a rural village, an industrial community, a war-boom community, a factory setting, a ghetto, and a trailer camp. Many community studies mentioned in the chapter on descriptive-survey research may also serve as examples of the case approach.

A distinction sometimes is made between case study, case work, and case method. From the point of view of research, case study means intensive investigation of the case unit, especially with respect to initial status or symptoms, collection of explanatory data, and diagnosis or identification of causal factors, looking toward remedial or developmental treatment. Case work frequently is interpreted as the process of therapy and follow-up in relation to developmental, adjustment, or remedial procedures. Although case study and case work frequently are done by different persons or agencies, they are complementary. The case method of instruction is a plan of organizing and presenting materials in such fields as law, medicine, social work, psychology, and education, based on case materials produced through case-study investigation.

APPLICATIONS AND USES

Case-study procedures have been extensively followed in such fields as law and juvenile delinquency, medicine, psychiatry, psychology, education, counseling and guidance, anthropology, sociology, social work, economics, business administration, political science, and journalism. Although case study was once limited primarily to problems of maladjustment, such as truancy or failure in school, a broken or poverty-stricken home, or an underprivileged or malfunctioning community, this approach more recently has been extended to investigation of normal or bright children, successful institutions and agencies, and well-organized communities or effectively functioning cultural groups. Case study has been helpful in providing classifications or categories of individuals referred to such agencies as a bureau of juvenile research or a juvenile court; information on social and institutional group patterns in families, schools, and communities; case materials for teaching purposes; supplementary interpretations and illustrations for statistical findings; and generalizations through the accumulation of careful case reports, especially in the field of medicine.

The usefulness of the clinical and case approach may be illustrated by the field of clinical psychology in general, and more specifically by personality study and counseling psychology. Clinical psychologists perform a variety of services in many settings, dealing with a wide range of human problems. However, within this apparent diversity of clinical psychology there is considerable unity. Psychologists first try to achieve an understanding, based on the hypotheses and techniques of their professional field of knowledge. Then they apply their understanding, so as to help the people help themselves, with such activities frequently labeled "diagnosis" and "therapy." Clinical psychology has grown not so much by the invention of new basic functions as by the extension and development of fundamental procedures; for example, in the diagnostic area, methods for assessing and describing broader aspects of personality are supplementing the older techniques for testing intelligence and school achievement.[1]

Clinical psychology has been of service in a variety of centers and settings, including especially long-standing service in the psychological clinic at the University of Pennsylvania, the Institute for Juvenile Research for the State of Illinois, the Training School at Vineland in New Jersey, Worcester State Hospital, the Menninger Foundation, and the Wichita Guidance Center. Government agencies with large-scale programs of clinical psychology include the Veterans Administration, United States Army, United States Navy, United States Air Force, and the Public Health Service. Clinical centers concerned primarily with mental-health problems include the medical school psychiatric clinic, the psychological-service center, private clinical practice, the old-age counseling center, the clinic for alcoholics, the student-counseling bureau, and industrial-employee counseling. Clinical centers dealing primarily with antisocial behavior include the municipal court, the juvenile court and youth authority program, the training school for delinquents, and prison. Clinical centers concerned primarily with educative, remedial, and rehabilitative problems include the rehabilitation center, school system, reading clinic, hearing clinic, and speech clinic.

Factors that have played a compelling part in promoting clinical and case studies of personality are as follows:

(1) a national situation (press) consisting of an increased awareness of an increasing incidence of mental illness; (2) in response to this invasion of the field of mental illness by humanitarians (need to relieve suffering), by social reformers (need to correct societal defects), and by scientists (need for knowledge and understanding), and as a result of these forces, the construction of new and enlarged hospitals and clinics with facilities for research under the direction of psychiatrists; (3) technical developments within the field of psychology—the perfection of intelligence tests, word-association tests, projective tests, etc., also the accomplishments of applied psychologists in World Wars I and II; (4) in recognition of their technical abilities, the creation of jobs in hospitals and clinics affording livelihood to

[1] Eli A. Rubinstein and Maurice Lorr, Editors, *Survey of Clinical Practice in Psychology.* New York: International Universities Press, 1954. xvii+363 p.

clinical psychologists; (5) the acquisition by psychologists of certain medical principles and practices, especially the case method.[2]

Counseling psychology is a specialty within the area broadly designated as applied psychology, and utilizes concepts, tools, and techniques also used by several other specialty groups, notably social, personnel, and clinical psychology. Historically, counseling psychology has drawn upon three distinct movements: vocational guidance, psychological measurement, and personality development.

Currently, the specialty of counseling psychology is approaching a balance among emphases upon contributions to (*a*) the development of an individual's inner life, (*b*) the individual's achievement of harmony with his environment, and (*c*) the influencing of society to recognize individual differences and to encourage the fullest development of all persons within it. Although counseling psychology leaves to other psychologists the major responsibility for treating psychological disasters, the counseling psychologist may be found working in the full range of social settings. He has unique resources, e.g., tests and other methods of psychological evaluation, for helping individuals to achieve harmonious relationships with their environments. He is willing to work directly with other persons and groups with whom his clients must deal outside of the counseling office. His goal is to further the fullest possible self-realization of those who live in a particular social setting.[3]

In many instances case study is supplementary to or related to other investigational procedures. The life history of an individual, of an institution, or of a community resembles historical research in sources and techniques. Case investigation uses many of the data-gathering instruments described in the chapter on descriptive-survey studies. Case and genetic investigations of an individual have common interests in growth and development, although ordinarily the direction of movement in case study is backward, whereas in genetic research the movement is forward as growth takes place.

SEQUENCE OR STAGES IN CASE STUDY AND CASE WORK

The characteristics and skills[4] of case study and case work include the following items:

[2] Quoted from Arthur Burton and Robert E. Harris, Editors, *Clinical Studies of Personality*. Vol. 2 of Case Histories in Clinical and Abnormal Psychology. New York: Harper & Brothers, 1955. p. 12–13.

[3] Quoted from Harold B. Pepinsky and Others, "Counseling Psychology as a Specialty." *American Psychologist* 11: 282–85; June 1956.

[4] Gordon Hamilton, *Theory and Practice of Social Case Work*. Second Edition. New York: Columbia University Press, 1951. vii+328 p.

1. Continuity of data and procedure. Although continuity in gathering evidence, diagnosis, and therapy is a logical sequence, in a concrete life situation the movement may be shuttle-like. While interviewing an individual to gather information, certain treatment may take place, or during adjustment or therapeutic procedures, additional evidence may be secured.

2. Completeness and validity of data, including symptoms relating to initial status, examination results (psychophysical, health, educational, and mental), and health, school, family, and social history.

3. Synthesis in the form of an adequate diagnosis which identifies causal factors, with a prognosis that points toward therapy in the form of corrective treatment or developmental procedures. The social skills of case work or of adjustment procedures include social insight, empathy, and a positive social behavior; ability to communicate by transmitting an experience or sharing a common experience; co-operation and participation in working with others; and effective counseling and guidance. It is recognized that the concepts of nondirective or client-centered therapy tend to minimize the process of diagnosis as a basis for therapy.[5]

4. Confidential recording and relationships, as exemplified in the field of medicine.

Expressed in one way, the standards of case study and case work are similar to the major requirements of clinical psychology: high levels of academic and professional qualifications for the worker, a practitioner who is familiar with the trends of recent research even though not actually engaged in investigation, and sound ethics emphasizing long-term aims by way of service to society.[6]

The cycle of complementary steps[7] in case study and case work is as follows:

1. Recognition and determination of the status of the phenomenon to be investigated; for example, reading disability.

2. Collection of data relating to the factors or circumstances associated with the given phenomenon; factors associated with learning difficulty or reading disability may be physical, intellectual, pedagogical, emotional, social, or environmental.

3. Diagnosis or identification of causal factors as a basis for remedial or developmental treatment; defective vision may be the cause of difficulty in reading.

4. Application of remedial or adjustment measures; correctly fitted glasses may remove the cause of the poor performance in reading.

[5] Carl R. Rogers, *Client-Centered Therapy:* Its Current Practice, Implications, and Theory. Boston: Houghton Mifflin Co., 1951. xii+560 p.
[6] L. A. Pennington and Irwin A. Berg, Editors, *An Introduction to Clinical Psychology.* Second Edition. New York: Ronald Press, 1954. p. 22.
[7] Carter V. Good and Douglas E. Scates, *Methods of Research:* Educational, Psychological, Sociological. New York: Appleton-Century-Crofts, 1954. p. 732-33.

5. Subsequent follow-up to determine the effectiveness of the corrective or developmental measures applied.

INITIAL STATUS OR SYMPTOMS OF THE CASE

The first step in case study is to identify the unit for investigation in the form of some aspect of behavior, or phase of the life process, or need-situation, as in truancy, delinquency, exceptional talent, or a broken home. Whereas the case has commonly centered on the need-situation as the unit of attention, client-centered or nondirective therapy has focused attention on the individual or subject. With increased knowledge and improved techniques, cases in new areas have been identified for corrective or developmental treatment; for example, in the field of special education recognizing in turn the need for therapy of the physically handicapped, then cases of low mentality, special talents, and deficiencies in the school subjects, and later the various types of social maladjustment involving personality difficulties and behavior disorders. With increased knowledge, cases of child delinquency have become subdivided to represent such problems as parental rejection, parental overprotection, poverty and low social status, emotional immaturity, and rebellion against authority. It is not possible even to count the several types of cases for remedial or developmental attention until the scope of the various categories is defined as a basis for labeling a child as exceptional: the extent of deficiency necessary in vision or hearing to be labeled subnormal, the level of general intelligence or of special talent to be considered superior, and the line between normality and social, emotional, personality, or behavior disorders. Many of the data-gathering instruments and procedures discussed in the chapter on descriptive-survey research are available for the first step of case study and also for later steps, especially in collection of data through the examination and case history.

EXAMINATION AND HISTORY AS SOURCES OF DATA

Determination or identification of the status of the situation or unit of attention leads into the collection of data through the examination and life history, which suggests that the first and second steps of case study are supplementary. The emphasis in the second stage, however, is on evidence that may serve as a basis for diagnosis through identification of the explanatory or causal factors. This step in case study has available for use the several descriptive-survey instruments and procedures, as well as the life history, biography, autobiography, letters, and diaries. The case study usually includes an examination[8] of psychophysical, health, educational, and mentality factors, as well as a health, school, family, and social history. Certain of the common testing instruments may be characterized briefly.

Testing Instruments

Intelligence-testing in modern clinical psychology is far more than the automatic administration of routine test procedures. It involves a judicious choice of instruments, precise knowledge of the characteristics of intelligence scales, skill in interpreting test results, ability to evaluate the results of highly controversial research, and formulation of insightful hypotheses to account for a patient's behavior. In short, the clinician is both a proficient laboratory experimenter and an impartial, understanding observer of human behavior.[9]

From personality, interest, and achievement tests the clinician secures information which often can be gathered from no other source. Scores from these inventories may suggest hypotheses to the clinical psychologist, who must then verify them and integrate his data into an adequate descriptive picture of his patient for the purposes of diagnostic, prognostic, and treatment problems.

Projective methods utilize ambiguous stimuli to which subjects are encouraged to respond freely in their own way, as illustrated by ink blots, pictures, art and drama media, and paper-and-pencil techniques. It is assumed that attention is selective and that perception is motivated by the wishes and attitudes of the responding person, with the result that the content perceived and the manner of organizing the material reveal significant dynamic aspects of personality (useful for diagnosis, prognosis, and research).[10]

Life History

As sources of data for case study, from an analytical rather than a historical approach, more frequent and better use may well be made of such personal documents as the life history, biography, autobiography, diaries and journals, letters, records of dreams, and expressive interviews. Such personal materials include retrospective autobiographies, contem-

[8] Cecil V. Millard, *Case Inventory for the Study of Child Development.* Minneapolis: Burgess Publishing Co., 1950. 29 p.
[9] L. A. Pennington and Irwin A. Berg, Editors, *op. cit.*, p. 154–55, 181.
[10] *Ibid.*, p. 215.

poraneous life histories, and episodic and topical documents. Data obtained from personal documents may make a contribution by way of supplementing ecological and statistical information, so as to provide a more inclusive interpretation of the problem, and may serve as a basis for prediction of human behavior.

As a longitudinal observation of culture, the life history emphasizes the natural history of the individual, his reactions to early social stimuli which have led to development of attitudes and values, evolution of a philosophy of life, personal experiences, anecdotes, mental and social conflicts, crises, adjustments, accommodations, and release of tensions. As an intimate personal document or confession which records through introspection inward stresses and attitudes rather than external events, the life history differs from the usual autobiography secured from famous persons (with one eye on publication). The life history, dealing with individuals who have encountered mental and social crises or conflict situations, does not stress judgments of merit. The subject may tell his own story or an interviewer may record the life history, as "a deliberate attempt to define the growth of a person in a cultural milieu and to make theoretical sense of it." Basic criteria for evaluating the life-history approach[11] are as follows:

1. The subject must be viewed as a specimen in a cultural series.

2. The organic motors of action ascribed must be socially relevant.

3. The peculiar role of the family group in transmitting the culture must be recognized.

4. The specific method of elaboration of organic materials into social behavior must be shown.

5. The continuous related character of experience from childhood through adulthood must be stressed.

6. The social situation must be carefully and continuously specified as a factor.

7. The life-history material itself must be organized and conceptualized.

The purposes and procedures of a particular life history or autobiography[12] may be generally helpful as background for understanding this approach:

[11] John Dollard, *Criteria for the Life History*. New Haven: Yale University Press, 1935. p. 3. Reprinted in 1949 by Peter Smith.
Pauline V. Young, *Scientific Social Surveys and Research*. Third Edition. Englewood Cliffs, N. J.: Prentice-Hall, 1956. p. 230-39.
[12] Leo W. Simmons, Editor, *Sun Chief: The Autobiography of a Hopi Indian*. New Haven: Yale University Press, for the Institute of Human Relations, 1942. xii+460 p.

1. To prepare a relatively full and reliable account of an individual's experience and development from birth on, or a comprehensive life history emphasizing personality problems

2. To accumulate and arrange in natural order a socially and culturally oriented record of an individual in a "primitive society" for the purpose of developing and checking certain hypotheses in the field of culture

3. To attempt at least a partial interpretation of the individual's development and behavior

4. To utilize the investigation for the formulation of generalizations and the testing of theories in the field of individual behavior with respect to society and culture (reserved for further study).

Autobiography, Biography, and Diaries

Autobiography, biography, and diaries have been resorted to frequently as sources in historical studies. Autobiography as historical narration and the diaries of distinguished persons who have anticipated publication usually have been relatively formal documents. The movement in autobiography and biography is backward (written in retrospect), whereas the movement in a diary is forward, with entries recorded as events take place. Autobiography contributes to case study through providing the life history of an individual, a tribe, race, or community; is helpful in studying reticent or resistant persons; is economical for use in groups; and may serve therapeutic purposes for the subject by release of tensions and insight into his own life. Diaries kept without undue concern for publication may reveal interests, desires, tensions, and conflicts not apparent in the more formal autobiography (usually written for publication), although the persons who keep diaries and permit their use are a rather select group of individuals. The general principles of historical research apply in dealing with personal documents.

To cite as an example the autobiography of an educator, Spaulding has written in two volumes what is substantially his life history to the end of his administrative work in the public schools. The first volume[13] carries the story to the completion of his graduate study in Europe and at Clark University, including early life on a farm in New Hampshire, schooling in the district and college-preparatory schools in New England, four years at Amherst College, a doctoral program at the University of Leipzig, and postdoctoral year at Clark University. The second volume[14]

[13] Frank E. Spaulding, *One School Administrator's Philosophy:* Its Development. New York: Exposition Press, 1952. 352 p.
[14] Frank E. Spaulding, *School Superintendent in Action in Five Cities*. Rindge, N. H.: Richard R. Smith, 1955. xx+699 p.

is substantially an anecdotal history or case study of the development of the city superintendency during the first quarter of the twentieth century. It is the story of the evolution and application of a philosophy of education to the organization and administration of the public schools. The individual probably is not fully aware of the pattern and sources of his own philosophy until he attempts what Spaulding has done in his autobiography or life history.

Another autobiography[15] is the story of an 81-year-old man who began to teach at the age of seventeen in a one-teacher school in Pennsylvania in 1891. His long years of service were as teacher, principal, superintendent, and teacher or executive in 17 American colleges in 10 states, as author, organizer of professional groups, editor, and lecturer before many thousands of educational and professional groups. The autobiography is to a considerable extent an anecdotal history of education and of the education of teachers, covering almost the entire modern period of educational history and teacher education during the twentieth century. Here are the beginnings of teaching as a profession, the development of small local school systems, the struggles of boards of education on professional problems, the efforts of school administrators to professionalize their staffs in larger cities, and the organization of a program to prepare the professors who staff the teachers colleges.

An especially interesting group of personal documents is an approach to the history of psychology through the autobiographies of a number of eminent psychologists.[16]

Yet another example is the autobiography of a schizophrenic, although this description may be inaccurate, since the author set out to prove that he was never "insane" and perhaps not even mentally ill; yet he does demonstrate that mental illness is misunderstood and badly mistreated even in some of our better hospitals.

As a case history the book does not arouse the same clinical interest and speculative excitement that come with a reading of Schreber's *Memoirs*, or the autobiography written by Sechehaye's patient, or comparable documents by Beers, Custance, and others; but as a very human and moving statement of a young man's struggle to maintain personal integrity and dignity in the face of a practical, well-meaning, but uncomprehending world, [it] will touch deeply every reader. It is difficult to say whether the author succeeds better in demonstrating that the ideas and beliefs of non-inmates of mental institutions

[15] Ambrose L. Suhrie, *Teacher of Teachers*. Rindge, N. H.: Richard R. Smith, 1955. 418 p.
[16] Herbert S. Langfeld and Others, Editors, *A History of Psychology in Autobiography*, Vol. 4. Worcester, Mass.: Clark University Press, 1952. xii+356 p.

are just as irrational as his own, or that he is entitled to maintain his own irrational beliefs without undue interference by authority, however well intentioned. Certainly he presents a dramatic and often frightening picture of what it means to someone who has lost his way in the world to be suddenly confronted by the loving therapeutic zeal involved in hospitalization, electric shock, insulin convulsions, and medical logic. The reader, whether professional or otherwise, is bound to experience that compassion and uneasiness which come with sharing intimately in the life-and-death struggle which is psychosis.[17]

A book of nine word portraits[18] or type-persons or case histories may offer suggestions for similar studies of the teacher, supervisor, administrator, or professor. Bauer and his colleague have created type-persons as they live, think, and act in the Soviet milieu. The data are true, based on interviews with escaped refugees from the Soviet Union, who have reported their own experiences and have revealed their knowledge of conditions within their motherland. The portraits are fiction, composites of the data collected, with the smallest amount of fabrication necessary to make them into stories. The nine synthesized types of persons are: the student (three of them), the woman collective farmer, the woman doctor, the Party secretary, the housewife, the writer, the factory director, the tractor driver, and the secret police agent. These portraits are not actual case histories, nor are they even exactly fiction, since the characteristics of the people and the events of their stories are always subordinated to the facts of the records; the persons themselves are synthesized types.

An application of psychoanalytic psychology to the biographical data of famous creative individuals has the two purposes of comprehending the subject of the biography in terms of the dynamic forces of his developmental experience, and of understanding the nature of the creative man and the creative process. For these purposes, the main value of psychoanalytic psychology lies in its ability to analyze and to structure meaningfully highly complex and diverse biographical information, by way of establishing cause-and-effect relationships between the data of infancy, childhood, and adult life.[19]

[17] Quoted from the review by Milton Wexler, *Contemporary Psychology* 1: 306; October 1956, of William L. Moore, *The Mind in Chains:* The Autobiography of a Schizophrenic. New York: Exposition Press, 1955. 315 p.
[18] Raymond A. Bauer and Edward Wasiolek, *Nine Soviet Portraits*. New York: John Wiley & Sons, 1955. ix+190 p. Reviewed by Edwin G. Boring, *Contemporary Psychology* 1: 149; May 1956.
[19] Edward Hitschmann, *Great Men:* Psychoanalytic Studies. New York: International Universities Press, 1956. xiii+278 p.

CAUSATION AND DIAGNOSIS

Diagnosis[20] seeks to formulate a theory or hypothesis of causation, pointed toward the adjustment or development of the individual, institution, or community. Diagnosis and treatment may at times be parallel or even move shuttle-like. Diagnosis is prognostic in recommending therapy, and when adjustment procedures fail, further search for causal factors and a second diagnosis may be necessary. If adjustment proves only temporary, as revealed in the last step of follow-up, further diagnosis and therapy are indicated. For evidence, diagnosis depends on the data gathered in the earlier phases of case study. It has already been indicated in this chapter that nondirective or client-centered therapy minimizes the diagnostic process in advance of psychotherapy, although recognizing the basic necessity for physical diagnosis in dealing with organic disease.[21]

Adequate diagnosis[22] of difficulties must meet certain basic requirements relating to significant objectives, valid evidence of strengths and weaknesses, objectivity, reliability, specificity, comparable and exact data, practicability, and expertness. Most of the data-gathering instruments and procedures described in the chapter on descriptive-survey research can be adapted to provide evidence on which successful diagnosis rests. Diagnosis as an aspect of case study, like other research approaches, finds the problem of causation complex and perplexing. To cite examples, factors that may be associated with learning difficulty are physical, intellectual, pedagogical, emotional, social, and environmental. Causes of poor performance in reading may be perceptual (visual and auditory), motor, intellectual, linguistic, emotional, and methodological. Factors affecting the behavior of the problem child may be hereditary, physical, mental, familial, economic, cultural, social, and educational. Defects and deviations of development may be in the form of amentia, endocrine disorders, convulsive disorders, neurological defects, cerebral injury,

---

[20] Ralph F. Berdie and John G. Darley, "Student Personnel Work: Diagnostic Techniques," *Encyclopedia of Educational Research*. Second Edition. Edited by Walter S. Monroe. New York: The Macmillan Co., 1950. p. 1305-10.
   Cora Kasius, Editor, *A Comparison of Diagnostic and Functional Casework Concepts*. New York: Family Service Association of New York, 1950. 169 p.
   Robert I. Watson, *The Clinical Method in Psychology*. New York: Harper & Brothers, 1951, p. 21-153, 527-761.
[21] Carl R. Rogers, *op. cit.*, p. 219-28.
[22] Leo J. Brueckner, "Diagnosis in Teaching," *Encyclopedia of Educational Research, op. cit.*, p. 314-21.
   Robert I. Watson, Editor, "Diagnostic Methods," *Readings in the Clinical Method in Psychology*. New York: Harper & Brothers, 1949. p. 183-443.
   Gordon Hamilton, *op. cit.*, p. 213-36.

special sensory handicaps, prematurity, precocity, and environmental retardation.[23] It usually is necessary to look beneath the surface to find the basic or primary cause of maladjustment; on the surface we may see only a secondary, tertiary, or contributory cause or condition. For example, difficulty in reading as a primary cause of maladjustment may lead to failure in the school subjects, truancy, and misbehavior (probably only secondary or tertiary factors in this instance).

To cite an example in the area of counseling, school psychologists, guidance specialists, and school social workers need a common knowledge of psychological principles and of educational aims and practices. It is highly desirable that school psychologists be equipped, like competent high-school counselors, to do diagnostic and counseling work. It is equally desirable that counselors, deans, and visiting teachers be better trained in the psychological principles and techniques that are appropriate. The school psychologist may well be an educationally oriented clinical psychologist, in contrast to the medically oriented clinical psychologist, who serves as a diagnostician, therapist, and consultant in the preventive and alleviative work of adjustment.[24]

THERAPY AND DEVELOPMENTAL ADJUSTMENT

Purposes

The purpose of diagnosis is realized in some form of effective therapy or developmental adjustment. Therapy and follow-up sometimes are labeled as case work, as distinguished from case study or case investigation, and in many instances these later steps are the work of other specialists (as in medicine). It has been indicated earlier that there is no sharp division between the earlier steps of case investigation and diagnosis, and the later phases of therapy and follow-up. In gathering information through the examination and case history, certain treatment or therapy may be possible, and in the stage of treatment additional evidence may appear. The supplementary and co-operative relationships of the specialists engaged in the several steps of case study and case work may be illustrated by the type of conference frequently arranged for planning

[23] Arnold Gesell and Catherine S. Amatruda, *Developmental Diagnosis:* Normal and Abnormal Child Development, Clinical Methods and Practical Applications. Revised Edition. New York: Harper & Brothers, 1947. xvi+496 p.
[24] Stanley S. Marzolf, *Psychological Diagnosis and Counseling in the Schools*. New York: Henry Holt and Co., 1956. xiv+401 p. Reviewed by Donald E. Super, *Contemporary Psychology* 2: 35–37; February 1957.

the therapy of the problem child, with participation by such workers and agencies as the clinic staff, school, visiting teacher, court, probation officer, child-placing agency, family agency, and children's institution.

Frequently, complex or multiple causation of maladjustment may lead to a diagnosis and to therapy requiring the co-operation of a number of specialists. Child-guidance clinics and mental-hygiene programs, working with problem and delinquent children, have combined the resources of psychiatrists, physicians, psychologists, social workers, sociologists, and sometimes teachers and specialists in the field of education. Adequate treatment in child guidance requires the co-operation of clinic, community, home, school, case-working organization, recreational program, and child-placement agency.

The primary purpose of therapy is development of the potentialities of the individual for growth and improvement. In a learning situation this means focusing of attention on the pupil in relation to a specific difficulty or opportunity for growth rather than on the formal organization of a subject of instruction as such. To cite another illustration, the purposes of social treatment or therapy are concerned with preventing social breakdown, conserving strength, restoring social function, making life more comfortable or compensating, creating opportunities for growth and development, and increasing the capacity for self-direction and social contribution.[25] More specific examples of assistance given to a client by a case worker would include financial aid, help in seeking employment, facilitating health plans, entrance into an appropriate group activity, and modifying the attitudes of associates.

Preventive Measures and Self-Help

Adjustment procedures are outlined in this chapter with recognition of the desirability of preventive measures,[26] as illustrated by current emphases in medicine, dentistry, and the field of health in general. Regular physical and health examinations, including the testing of sight and hearing, may indicate corrective measures which will prevent later maladjustments. Effective programs of education, work, recreation, and guidance in school, home, community, church, and other social institutions and agencies will do much to prevent the maladjustment known as the "youth problem," including juvenile delinquency.

[25] Gordon Hamilton, *op. cit.*, p. 237-70.
[26] Sheldon Glueck and Eleanor Glueck, *Delinquents in the Making:* Paths to Prevention. New York: Harper & Brothers, 1952. viii+214 p.
Pauline V. Young, *Social Treatment in Probation and Delinquency:* Treatise and Casebook for Court Workers, Probation Officers, and Other Child Welfare Workers. Revised Edition. New York: McGraw-Hill Book Co., 1952. xxvi+536 p.

In all forms of therapy, the importance of self-help is recognized, as illustrated by the patient's will or desire to recover from an illness. This basic principle of therapy or treatment is recognized in such concepts as encouraging the subject in his own efforts, thinking things through together, and increasing the capacity for self-understanding and self-direction.

Favorable mental attitudes on the part of specialists, parents, and child contribute materially to the process of therapy. Effective remedial or developmental treatment is based on genuine concern for the well-being of the child or client, cordial relationships of mutual confidence, and understanding and control of prejudices and emotional reactions. Favorable initial attitudes are especially significant in short contacts, as in large school systems and social transient work, where critical decisions may be made in one or two brief interviews; for example, employment of a teacher or arrangements to return a young traveler to her distant home.

The principle of self-help in the process of therapy is illustrated by nondirective or client-centered procedures,[27] which have revealed certain improvements in the subject:

1. Change or movement in therapy, as revealed in the type of verbal comment presented by the client; for example, from talk about his problems and symptoms, to insightful statements showing some self-understanding of relationship between his past and current behavior, to discussion of new actions in accord with his new understanding of the situation.

2. Change in the client's perception of and attitude toward self: (*a*) sees himself as a more adequate person, with increased worth and greater possibility of meeting life; (*b*) draws on more experiential data, thus achieving a more realistic appraisal of himself, his relationships, and environment; (*c*) tends to place the basis of standards or values within himself rather than in the experience or perceptual object.[28]

Treatment of Learning Difficulties

Basic principles underlying therapy or treatment of learning difficulties[29] are as follows:

1. Treatment must be based on a diagnosis.
   a. Locate weaknesses that require correction.
   b. Establish the type of treatment needed.
   c. Clearly formulate the remedial program.

[27] Carl R. Rogers, *op. cit.*, p. 131–96.
[28] Robert I. Watson, *The Clinical Method in Psychology, op. cit.*, p. 21–153, 527–761.
[29] Leo J. Brueckner and Guy L. Bond, *The Diagnosis and Treatment of Learning Difficulties.* New York: Appleton-Century-Crofts, 1955. p. 77–100.

  d. Modify the program as may be advisable.

  e. Use a variety of remedial techniques.

  f. The child should help formulate the program of treatment.

2. The child's personal worth must be considered.

  a. Avoid stigmatizing pupils in classification and grouping.

  b. Consider the child's emotional state.

  c. Correct faulty attitudes.

  d. Recognize the importance of group as well as individual work.

3. Corrective treatment must be individualized.

  a. Outcomes and methods should be commensurate with the child's ability.

  b. Treatment should be specific and not general.

  c. Fatigue should be noted and practice spaced.

4. The program must be well motivated and encouraging to the child.

  a. The teacher must be optimistic.

  b. Success of the student must be emphasized.

  c. Errors should be pointed out in a positive way.

  d. Growth should be made apparent to the child.

  e. Treatment should not conflict with other enjoyable activities.

  f. Purpose should always be established.

  g. The results of the learning experience should be utilized and evaluated.

5. Materials and exercises must be carefully selected.

  a. Materials must be suitable in level of difficulty and type.

  b. Materials must be suitable in interest and format.

  c. Materials must be abundant and not artificial.

6. The entire environment of the child must be considered.

  a. Adjustments must be made in the child's school program.

  b. The home environment must be favorable.

7. Continuous evaluations must be made.

  a. A cumulative record must be kept.

  b. A follow-up is necessary.

8. Sound teaching procedures must be utilized in the treatment of learning difficulties.

Principles and Techniques of Psychotherapy

Psychotherapy is limited or handicapped by the tendency of some clinicians, teachers, and students to overemphasize certain approaches at the expense of others, thus failing to recognize at least three major sources of error in therapy.[30]

  1. No single approach to psychotherapy has been found that can explain the behavior of all individuals or is pertinent to all persons.

  2. An individual with a specific problem may fail to respond to a single

[30] James L. McCary and Daniel E. Sheer, Editors, *Six Approaches to Psychotherapy*. New York: Dryden Press, 1955. p. 4-5.

type of therapy; as the individual's needs change the therapeutic techniques must be changed, if the patient is to derive maximum benefit.

3. Since therapists differ in personality structure, need systems, and value systems, the therapeutic technique must be suited to the needs of the therapist.

Psychological research has identified the wide range of individual differences in physical, intellectual, pedagogical, emotional, social, and environmental factors that must be considered in diagnosis and therapy. To illustrate by a specific example, variations in the treatment of children with individual problems of adjustment include: (1) change of environment through the foster home or institutional placement; (2) modification of environment through adjustments in the parents' attitudes, family relationships, school and instructional program, clubs, groups, and camps; and (3) treatment of the individual through a variety of therapeutic approaches, including psychoanalysis, nondirective interviewing and therapy, group psychotherapy, projective techniques, play therapy, physical treatment, occupational therapy, psychodrama, sociodrama, and hypnodrama.

The variety and complexity of the problems of clinical and case study may be illustrated in further detail from the field of psychotherapy. The varieties of psychotherapy include supportive therapy, insight therapy with re-educative goals, and insight therapy with reconstructive goals.[31]

Among the techniques and procedures utilized in supportive therapy are guidance, environmental manipulation, externalization of interests, reassurance, prestige suggestion, pressure and coercion, persuasion, emotional catharsis and desensitization, muscular relaxation, hydrotherapy, drug therapy, shock and convulsive therapy, and inspirational group therapy.

Insight therapy with re-educative therapeutic approaches includes "relationship therapy," "attitude therapy," distributive analysis and synthesis, interview psychotherapy, therapeutic counseling, therapeutic casework, reconditioning, re-educative group therapy, semantic therapy, and bibliotherapy.

Insight therapy with reconstructive goals includes the three main "types": "Freudian psychoanalysis," "non-Freudian psychoanalysis," and "psychoanalytically oriented psychotherapy."

[31] Lewis R. Wolberg, *The Technique of Psychotherapy*. New York: Grune and Stratton, 1954. xiv+869 p.

Supportive, re-educative, and reconstructive therapies have certain similarities and differences with respect to the duration of therapy, frequency of visits, taking of detailed histories, routine psychologic examinations, kinds of communications obtained from the patient, general activity of the therapist, frequency of advice-giving to the patient, handling of transference, general relationship of the patient to the therapist, physical position of the patient during therapy, handling of dream material, and adjuncts utilized during treatment.

The beginning phase of treatment in psychotherapy includes a number of problems relating to the initial interview: the first contact with the patient, collating essential data, making a diagnosis, formulating the tentative dynamics, estimating the prognosis, estimating the patient's general condition, making practical arrangements for psychotherapy, securing essential consultations, and dealing with inadequate motivation.

The principal techniques by which the therapist helps the patient in the acquisition of insight include interview procedures, free association, dream analysis, and the examination of attitudes toward the therapist (including transference).

In the terminal phase of psychotherapy, success is judged from the standpoint of the patient, of society, and of the therapist, and in terms of the "ideal" objectives of mental health.

Adjunctive aids in psychotherapy include group therapy, hypnotherapy, narcotherapy, and bibliotherapy.

Among the emergencies that sometimes develop during psychotherapy which require prompt and cautious handling are: suicidal attempts; psychotic attacks; excitement, overactivity, and antisocial behavior; panic states; acute alcoholic intoxication; acute barbiturate poisoning; severe psychosomatic symptoms; and intercurrent incurable somatic illness.

Certain kinds of conditions make extensive therapeutic objectives difficult to achieve, and require specific techniques or combinations of methods, especially in dealing with problems often encountered in the treatment of the different neurotic, psychophysiologic, personality, and psychotic disorders.

The variety of techniques in psychotherapy is illustrated in convenient form by the following list of "supportive" methods.[32] An equally long list of "reconstructive" methods has been compiled by the same authors.

[32] James L. McCary and Daniel E. Sheer, *op. cit.*, p. 3.

1. Bibliotherapy
2. Color therapy
3. Conditioned-reflex therapy
4. Correction of physical defects
5. Dance therapy
6. Desensitization
7. Environmental manipulation
8. Hypnotherapy
9. Inspirational group therapy
10. Motivational procedures (such as rewards and punishments)
11. Music therapy
12. Narcotherapy
13. Negative practice
14. Occupational therapy
15. Persuasion and reasoning
16. Physiotherapy
17. Placebos
18. Pressure and coercion
19. Progressive relaxation
20. Reassurance
21. Recreation
22. Re-education
23. Religious approaches
24. Rest
25. Suggestion and advice
26. Selected types of group therapy
27. Verbal catharsis and abreaction.

Group psychotherapy has been used to good effect with patients suffering from a variety of psychosomatic disorders and with addicts, alcoholics, stutterers, unmarried mothers, mothers of emotionally disturbed children, delinquents, and the aged. It has been of value in mental hospitals, child guidance, family service, marital counseling agencies, community mental-health programs, and industry. As a rule, group psychotherapists have been more willing than individual therapists to record their sessions by mechanical and observational methods, which augurs well for improvement of the therapeutic process and for future development of group psychotherapy.[33]

The literature of the 1950's includes dozens of full-length treatments of therapy, as listed in the chapter bibliography.

FOLLOW-UP

The final stage in case and clinical work is follow-up to determine whether the treatment is successful, as illustrated by the physician's attention to the patient during the stage of convalescence. Failure to make satisfactory progress following treatment may require a new diagnosis and another form of therapy. It is common to utilize the techniques of experimentation in evaluating the success of treatment, especially in the field of medicine. By way of example of follow-up, case study has been used as one approach in following a group of bright children over a period of years through school into maturity.[34] The school, home, and

[33] S. R. Slavson, Editor, *The Fields of Group Psychotherapy.* New York: International Universities Press, 1956. xiii+338 p. Reviewed by Norman A. Polansky, *Social Service Review* 30: 372–73; September 1956.

[34] Lewis M. Terman and Melita H. Oden, *The Gifted Child Grows Up:* Genetic Studies of Genius. Stanford, Calif.: Stanford University Press, 1947. xiv+450 p.

other environmental conditions may be thought of as the therapy or treatment for the bright children, with a follow-up to determine the adjustment of the subjects after reaching maturity.

CLINICAL AND CASE RECORDS[35]

Desirable Characteristics

Adequate case records serve useful purposes in treatment, especially when the regular worker or client moves to another locality, or when a case is reopened; as a medium for study of social problems; and for instructional materials in training students. Adequate records possess the attributes of accuracy and objectivity, conciseness and clarity, ease of reference and visibility, and uniformity and "up-to-dateness," with suitable provision for cumulative recording of interviews, the narrative, letters, anecdotal information, summaries, and interpretation and treatment.

Accuracy goes beyond the recording of information as received to insure the correctness of the data in relation to the truth, as discussed in the chapter on the historical method (with respect to the reliability of witnesses and the criticism of documents).

Effective recording in case study, like adequate reporting in any area of investigation, must be an active process of attention and discriminating selection from a considerable mass of materials, with a balance to strike somewhere between the completeness necessary for objectivity and the brevity essential for clarity. Many of the comments of the chapter on technical reporting and of the section on note-taking in the chapter on historical research are appropriate and suggestive in case-recording and in the preparation of case reports. Uniformity of records within the agency, institution, or school system, and between similar social or educational services in different territories, facilitates research, interchange of information, and ready use.

With respect to the recording of interviews in case study, the discussions of interviewing and of mechanical techniques of observation and recording in the descriptive-survey chapter are pertinent. In social case-recording, the narrative usually begins with the first interview. When conditions are favorable, the first interview should be reasonably complete. It is relatively simple to record information concerning identity, address, legal residence, financial status, and units of food, shelter, or education,

[35] Gordon Hamilton, *Principles of Social Case Recording.* New York: Columbia University Press, 1946. vii+142 p.
        Kenneth R. Hammond and Jeremiah M. Allen, *Writing Clinical Reports.* New York: Prentice-Hall, 1953. p. 169–231.

but both interviewing and recording become more complex in dealing with human relationships and with the related process and movement within the interview.

The narrative or running record in case study may be entered either chronologically or topically, or by some appropriate combination, as discussed in the chapter on historical writing. In chronological recording, the contacts and interviews are entered in diary fashion as they occur, although some marginal headings may give a superficial appearance of topical organization. The chronological narrative may have large sub-divisions corresponding approximately with the case-study stages of initial status, examination, diagnosis, therapy, and follow-up. These large headings also are suitable for topical or thematic organization of materials. Topical recording combines and condenses information from a number of contacts or interviews under such large themes as family and home setting, neighborhood and group life, cultural background, education, recreational activities and interests, health, mental attitude, occupation, and income and resources. Topical recording presents original data or subject matter, whereas the several types of "summaries" condense and point up material which has previously appeared in the record.

Since letters and written reports frequently serve as substitutes for direct contacts in the form of personal visits and interviews, they are an important part of case records, especially as a medium of communication between social-work, medical, clinical, legal, and educational agencies. Letters and reports today stress the immediate situation and the therapy or adjustment rather than present a complete summary of the case. Certain forms or blanks have been developed for routine types of communication between agencies, especially between the public schools and other social agencies.

Cumulative and Anecdotal Records[36]

Clinical work and case study, as well as counseling in the schools,

[36] Wendell C. Allen, *Cumulative Pupil Records:* A Plan for Staff Study and Improvement of Cumulative Pupil Records in Secondary Schools. New York: Teachers College, Columbia University, 1943. 69 p.
A. E. Hamalainen, *An Appraisal of Anecdotal Records.* Contributions to Education, No. 891. New York: Teachers College, Columbia University, 1943. 88 p.
Gordon Hamilton, *Principles of Social Case Recording, op. cit.*
Gordon Hamilton, *Theory and Practice of Social Case Work, op. cit.,* p. 133-41.
Kenneth R. Hammond and Jeremiah M. Allen, *op. cit.*
Judith I. Krugman and J. Wayne Wrightstone, *A Guide to the Use of Anecdotal Records.* Educational Research Bulletin of the Bureau of Reference, Research and Statistics, No. 11. New York: Board of Education, May 1949. 33 p.
A. E. Traxler, *The Nature and Use of Anecdotal Records.* Revised Edition. Educational Records Supplementary Bulletin *D.* New York: Educational Record Bureau, 1949. p. 4-8.

depend to a large extent on the data in cumulative records, including anecdotal records. The cumulative record is maintained for a client or pupil over a considerable period of time, usually a number of years, with additions to the record at relatively frequent intervals; for example, marks in the school subjects, educational and aptitude test scores, social and character ratings, school attendance, health, home conditions and family history, participation in the activities program, interests, and attitudes. Cumulative records are useful in meeting instructional needs, for discovery of causes of behavior difficulties and failures, identification of talents and special abilities, placement, and counseling on a variety of problems.

In filing all pertinent information concerning the individual in one place as a unit, a folder is essential for samples of school work, test forms, behavior deviations, and adjustment or treatment procedures. Childguidance clinics, for example, have sought especially to integrate into a unit record the medical, psychological, psychiatric, social, and also the school evidence.

Anecdotal materials have come to be a significant part of the cumulative record. A type of cumulative individual record which emphasizes episodes of behavior important in the development of character or personality is known as the anecdotal-behavior journal. These anecdotes include not only maladjustment, but also positive and constructive episodes, the admirable behavior of well-adjusted pupils, and the outstanding accomplishments of the superior or talented. The anecdote as a revealing episode of conduct is in the form of a word picture or verbal snapshot. To be most helpful, anecdotes should possess the characteristics of objectivity, factual emphasis, clarity, and subjectivity (in the sense that an artistically composed photograph is subjective, with a center of attention and with subordination of inconsequential details). Anecdotal records serve useful purposes by way of mutual understanding between faculty and pupils, counseling relationships, curriculum development, appraisal of outcomes, and case instruction in professional programs for preparation of teachers and others.

Although highly standardized or formalized procedures are incompatible with the nature of anecdotal recording, certain steps or sequential stages are desirable in introducing the plan into a school:[37]

1. Enlisting the co-operation of the faculty, including counselors, and development of an understanding and acceptance of the ideal of individualized education.

[37] Judith I. Krugman and J. Wayne Wrightstone, *op. cit.*, p. 8–14, 23–24. Arthur E. Traxler, *op. cit.*, p. 9–22.

2. Deciding how much should be expected of observers who write anecdotes, possibly a reasonable minimum number per week.

3. Preparing forms, which are usually very simple, as illustrated by forms in current use; an outline adapted to most situations provides blank spaces for identifying the pupil, class, and observer, with separate columns for date, incident, and comment.

4. Obtaining the original records, including a plan for jotting down the name of the pupil and an appropriate catch word at the time of the incident, with a period set aside toward the end of the day for recording the anecdotes concerning significant behavior episodes observed during the day; a reasonable, although not equal, distribution of anecdotes among the pupils is desirable.

5. Central filing, as emphasized in the earlier discussions of cumulative records, in order that incidents described by different observers over a period of time may be assembled and compared to note trends.

6. Periodic summarizing, preferably under topical headings, as recommended earlier in the discussion of case-recording.

Certain precautions and procedures are essential in dealing with problems which frequently arise in the preparation of anecdotes:[38]

1. Accuracy and objectivity in observation and in recording are imperative, as emphasized in the discussion of case-recording; statements of opinion must be separated from the report of the incident itself.

2. Anecdotal records should not be used as a defense mechanism by the teacher to justify some action on his part, such as loss of temper or harsh discipline.

3. In many instances, a brief description of the background against which a behavior incident occurred is necessary, since there is a grave danger of misinterpretation in isolating an episode from its social setting.

4. In summarizing and interpreting anecdotal records, one must be on guard against acceptance of a relatively small number of anecdotes as a valid picture of the total behavior pattern of the pupil; an understandable picture is based on some degree of repetition of similar behavior reported from a number of situations in different areas of conduct.

5. As in case study in general, anecdotal records must have professional and confidential treatment, in order that unfortunate behavior incidents may not prejudice the future adjustment and success of the pupils represented.

6. A workable plan for handling the load of clerical work and for summarizing anecdotes is necessary before a school commits itself to the writing of anecdotes.

7. Urgent needs for adjustment, as revealed through anecdotes, should not encourage hasty generalizations and should not be used as excuses for short cuts in personality adaptation, which is usually a long-term process.

8. Observers should strive to record evidence of growth and favorable adjustment even more diligently than examples of undesirable behavior.

[38] Judith I. Krugman and J. Wayne Wrightstone, *op. cit.*, p. 3–5, 15–20. Arthur E. Traxler, *op. cit.*, p. 22–26.

9. Teachers must be on guard against overemphasizing inconsistencies in behavior or incidents that are not at all typical of the behavior of the particular pupil; sometimes behavior at the beginning of the school year is atypical, although anecdotes recorded during the first few weeks may possess some significance as single incidents for understanding the pupil; however, without repetition episodes give little insight for determining developmental patterns of behavior, and deviations cannot be recognized until the usual patterns have been established through a repetition of incidents in different situations.

ETHICAL STANDARDS[39]

Since the primary function of records is to render treatment of the case more effective in terms of adjustment of the client, and to serve community interests in dealing with social problems, the ethical implications of case-recording are important. It may be wise to omit personal or nonessential information of a confidential nature that throws little light on diagnosis and therapy, although other possibilities or alternatives are to inform the client in advance of the nature and use of case records, to label such personal material "confidential," or to assume that all case records are confidential and will be so treated. Problems arise in deciding what use to make of evidence concerning the efficiency of staff members, the mistakes of fellow workers, and the policies of the agency or institution. Accuracy and objectivity require that the facts be entered in the record, where they usually speak for themselves, and may prove useful in improvement of both staff and program. Workers must keep within their own bounds of training and experience in making diagnoses and interpretations; for example, a teacher may communicate certain objective facts concerning a pupil's health or mental level, but diagnosis and treatment usually must be left to the physician or psychologist. Safeguarding of confidential records is a heavy responsibility, and ordinarily professional workers will not risk using case records outside the office where they are filed.

A summary of ethical principles formulated for psychology is generally applicable to other clinical fields, especially in the diagnosis and treatment relationships with the client.[40]

[39] Nicholas Hobbs and Others, *Ethical Standards of Psychologists.* Washington: American Psychological Association, 1953. xv+171 p.
Wayne H. Holtzman and Others, "Standards of Ethical Behavior for Psychologists." *American Psychologist* 13: 266–71; June 1958.
A. M. Lee, "Responsibilities in Sociological Research." *Sociology and Social Research* 37: 367–74; July-August 1953. Ethics of sociology.
[40] *Ethical Standards of Psychologists:* A Summary of Ethical Principles. Washington: American Psychological Association, 1953. 19 p.

1. The worth of a profession is measured by its contribution to the welfare of man.

2. The psychologist has ethical obligations as a scientist, teacher, practitioner, and citizen.

3. The psychologist's ultimate allegiance is to society, and his professional behavior should demonstrate an awareness of his social responsibilities.

4. The psychologist in practice, mindful of the significance of his work in the lives of others, must strive at all times to maintain highest standards of excellence.

5. A cardinal obligation of the psychologist is to respect the integrity and protect the welfare of the client with whom he is working.

6. The psychologist should guard professional confidences as a trust.

7. The psychologist is obligated to inform his client of all aspects of the clinical relationship, including the handling of materials derived therefrom, that might reasonably be considered important factors in the client's decision to enter the relationship.

8. The psychologist should present his clinical findings in a manner most likely to serve the best interests of his client.

9. Fees charged by an individual or agency in the practice of clinical psychology should be established with careful regard for the welfare of all concerned, to insure that the client is not unduly burdened by the cost of psychological assistance, that the psychologist or the agency involved is assured of adequate recompense, and that the profession is recognized as fair in financial matters and worthy of public support and confidence.

10. In clinical or consulting practice, the psychologist must refer his client to an appropriate specialist when there is evidence of a difficulty with which the psychologist is not competent to deal.

11. The psychologist who engages in psychotherapy is obligated to make adequate provision for the diagnosis and treatment of medical problems arising in his work.

12. If he advertises or makes public announcements of his services, the psychologist is obligated to describe his services with accuracy and dignity, adhering to professional rather than to commercial standards.

13. The psychologist should encourage students in their quest for knowledge, giving them every assistance in the free exploration of ideas.

14. A teacher of psychology should respect the student's right to privacy and not require him to give information which he may wish to withhold; neither should the teacher reveal information which a student has given with the reasonable assumption that it will be held in confidence.

15. Psychologists giving instruction in the use of clinical techniques should insist that their students adhere to all applicable principles governing the practice of clinical psychology.

16. Psychologists advising students electing psychology as a major field of study with the intent of entering the profession should be sure that students understand opportunities and requirements in the field, e.g., that few positions as psychologists are open to those with only a bachelor's degree, that there is considerable screening of candidates at the graduate level, and that the .

doctorate is required for many positions. Students with personality problems so severe that they are unlikely to be effective in graduate study or in later professional work should be discouraged from entering areas of psychology in which effective interpersonal relationships are crucial.

17. In the conduct of research the psychologist should adhere to the highest standards, following procedures judged by him to be appropriate to the problem on which he is working.

18. The psychologist, like other scientists, should protect the welfare of his research subjects, both animal and human.

19. As a scientist the psychologist is expected wherever possible to communicate the results of his research to other investigators, provided that he judges the results to be of value for the development of psychology as a science or for the welfare of the general public.

20. The public requires dependable sources of psychological information, and it is in the interest of the profession that the public be well supplied.

21. In the publication of books, theoretical articles, or the results of research, the psychologist should fairly apportion credit for the work accomplished.

22. A psychologist writing on scientific and professional subjects should, in the interest of the advancement and dissemination of knowledge, be thoroughly familiar with previous work of others on his subject and should deal objectively and frankly with controversial issues, even when his interpretations of data lead him to take an unpopular position.

23. Tests and diagnostic aids should be released only to persons who can demonstrate that they have the knowledge and skill necessary for their effective use and interpretation.

24. Psychologists assuming responsibility for testing programs or activities (including testing, supervising or sponsoring testing, and teaching courses in testing) obligate themselves to participate actively in the programs, either by actually carrying out the work or by planning, supervising, and checking it.

25. Representatives of publishers of psychological tests who are not themselves highly trained in psychological or educational measurement should serve only as distributors of materials and takers of orders, not as consultants on testing problems.

26. Psychologists should offer tests for publication only to publishers who are familiar with testing procedures and problems, who represent and present their tests in a professional way, and who limit the sale of tests to qualified users, or to publishers who are willing to set up adequate standards and secure professional help in venturing into test publication.

27. Publishers should make tests available to practitioners for routine use only when adequate reliability and validity data are available and can be published in detailed form.

28. The publication of actual tests or parts of tests in popular magazines and books, whether for self-evaluation or for illustrative purposes, is an abuse of professional materials and may be detrimental to public interest and to private welfare.

29. Instructors should manage the administration of psychological tests and other devices, use of which might be spoiled if the general public becomes familiar with their specific contents or underlying principles, in such a way as to limit access to them to persons who have a professional interest and will exercise safeguards against abuse of them.

30. High standards of conduct in professional relationships are as essential as professional competence if psychology is to retain the confidence of related professions and of the public.

31. There are a number of courtesies which professional workers owe to each other in the interest of harmony and efficient work. Thus, a psychologist who plans to initiate professional activity likely to encroach upon a recognized field of work of a colleague is expected, as a matter of professional courtesy, to consult with him before proceeding.

32. The welfare of society, the profession, and the individual concerned should be the primary consideration in recommending candidates for psychological degrees, positions, advancement, or membership in associations.

33. Ethical problems of concern to psychologists may arise in the seeking of positions and in the relationships between employer and employee.

34. When psychologists or persons identifying themselves as psychologists violate ethical standards or offer inferior professional service, it is the obligation of psychologists who know firsthand of their activity to attempt to rectify the situation.

RELATION BETWEEN CASE-CLINICAL AND STATISTICAL METHODS

A major problem of methodology in clinical psychology is to determine the relation between the clinical and the statistical or actuarial methods of prediction. In the actuarial or statistical type of prediction, we may classify the subject on the basis of objective facts from his life history, his scores on psychometric tests, behavior ratings or check lists, or possibly subjective judgments secured from interviews. We check this classification against a statistical or actuarial table which gives the statistical frequencies of behavior of various sorts for persons belonging to the particular class.

In the clinical or case-study method of prediction, we may arrive at some psychological hypothesis regarding the structure and dynamics of a particular individual, on the basis of interview impressions, other data from the life history, and possibly certain psychometric information, as in a psychiatric staff conference.

Various terms are applied to the method or approach preferred; for example, those who favor the statistical method have referred to it as "operational, communicable, verifiable, public, objective, reliable, behavioral, testable, rigorous, scientific, precise, careful, trustworthy, experimental, quantitative, down-to-earth, hardheaded, empirical, mathematical, and sound." Those who dislike the statistical method have labeled it as "mechanical, atomistic, additive, cut-and-dried, artificial, unreal, arbitrary, incomplete, dead, pedantic, fractionated, trivial, forced, static, superficial, rigid, sterile, academic, oversimplified, pseudoscientific, and blind."

The clinical method, on the other hand, is labeled by its proponents as "dynamic, global, meaningful, holistic, subtle, sympathetic, configural, patterned, organized, rich, deep, genuine, sensitive, sophisticated, real, living, concrete, natural, true to life, and understanding." The critics of the clinical method are likely to view it as "mystical, transcendent, metaphysical, supermundane, vague, hazy, subjective, unscientific, unreliable, crude, private, unverifiable, qualitative, primitive, prescientific, sloppy, uncontrolled, careless, verbalistic, intuitive, and muddleheaded."[41]

It is a common error to group together the terms *quantitative, statistical*, and *experimental*, setting them in opposition to *qualitative, clinical*, and *nonexperimental*. Some phenomena of behavior cannot be studied satisfactorily in the laboratory, and some quantification of clinical evidence is desirable. What we need is a balanced approach in selecting techniques appropriate for the problem at hand.[42]

ILLUSTRATIONS OF CASE HISTORIES

Students of psychology have not been fully trained to construct adequate case histories, to gather the relevant information, and to organize and interpret the findings. Other factors have interfered with the development of a library of case histories (normal and abnormal), including the conditions that make it difficult to obtain the data necessary for an understanding of any personality:[43]

1. Every life is long and complicated to the psychologist, and many hours are required for the exploration of even a few segments of it.

2. Man's power to recall his past is limited.

[41] Paul E. Meehl, *Clinical Versus Statistical Prediction:* A Theoretical Analysis and a Review of the Evidence. Minneapolis: University of Minnesota Press, 1954. p. 3–9, 136–38.
[42] Emory S. Bogardus, "Sociology and Social Philosophy." *Sociology and Social Research* 37: 260–64; March-April 1953.
Carlton W. Berenda, "Is Clinical Psychology a Science?" *American Psychologist* 12: 725–29; December 1957.
Starke R. Hathaway, "A Study of Human Behavior: The Clinical Psychologist." *American Psychologist* 13: 257–65; June 1958.
Pauline V. Young, *Scientific Social Surveys and Research, op. cit.*, p. 239–45.
[43] Arthur Burton and Robert E. Harris, *op. cit.*, p. 15–16.

3. Man tends to guard his reputation when scientific scrutiny seeks to look at some crucial area of his secret life.

4. The psychologist's conscience, acknowledging that every man is entitled to his privacy, forbids unscrupulous intrusions.

Additional factors which have interfered with building a body of case histories are the difficulties in making dependable observations under clinical or experimental conditions, in formulating correct interpretations, in publication of a revealing, recognizable portrait of a still living person, and in finding a publisher and an audience.

In spite of the difficulties in producing adequate case histories, the dozens of book-length treatments in the chapter bibliography contain hundreds of illustrative case and clinical studies in such fields as education, psychology, psychiatry, mental hygiene, guidance and counseling, therapy, behavior problems and delinquency, child development, social work, and sociology. Selected examples follow.

EXAMPLE: CHILDHOOD EMOTIONAL DISABILITIES[44]

The cases presented in this volume include a wide range of disorders, although they are not necessarily a representative sample of the range of child disabilities that one commonly encounters in a child-guidance clinic. Each case opens with a developmental history and a brief description of the emotional interrelationships within the family, which is followed by a detailed account of the collaborative treatment that includes the child and the simultaneous treatment of one or both parents. Considerable case material, interspersed with interpretive comment, is presented to illustrate therapeutic methods and patterns of family dynamics. Although little direct verbatim material is included, the abstracts of the therapeutic sessions seem to convey adequately the flavor of the therapeutic interaction. Reading through these cases one is impressed with the therapists' sensitivity to the patients' needs and the considerable flexibility in treatment. At a time when therapeutic rituals and rule-of-thumb methods are prevalent, these papers make for refreshing and instructive reading. Unfortunately, apart from the therapists' general impressions, little attempt is made to evaluate the procedures and outcomes through the use of data external to the therapeutic process.

Most of our clinical methods and classification systems have been designed primarily for the purpose of individual diagnosis and few adequate procedures have been developed for yielding a family diagnosis. The articles in this volume demonstrate how the case method can be used successfully to give a comprehensive picture of the constellation of intrafamily relationships and the changes in the family pattern during treatment. The limitations of the case

[44] Quoted from review by Albert Bandura, *Contemporary Psychology* 2: 14–15; January 1957, of George E. Gardner, Editor, *Case Studies in Childhood Emotional Disabilities*. Vol. 2. New York: American Orthopsychiatric Association, 1956. vii+368 p.

method, nevertheless, tend to make these papers better as a source of hypotheses for more definitive studies than as a source of systematic knowledge about family disturbances.

The types of disorders and problems represented in these cases are as follows:

Collaborative treatment of mother and boy with fecal retention, soiling, and a school phobia

The planned return of a placed child to own family

The defense mechanisms of a six-year-old

The use of a therapeutic nursery school in co-operation with clinical treatment of an acute separation problem

Pupils psychologically absent from school

The dynamics of encopresis

On the significance of the anal phase in pediatrics and child psychiatry

Brother identification in an adolescent girl

The dynamic significance of the mother-child relationship in the case of a young delinquent with psychotic mechanisms

Ego treatment causing structural change in personality

Is trying enough? A report of treatment during the latency period of a girl with atypical development

The psychological problems of the congenitally blind child

Two phases in the treatment of a hyperactive, destructive boy

Treatment of the adolescent delinquent

A technical problem in the beginning phase of psychotherapy with a borderline psychotic child.

EXAMPLE: DISTURBED CHILDREN[45]

This book, which is a companion piece to the author's *Love Is Not Enough*, presents the detailed case studies of four children and their rehabilitation at the Orthogenic School. These are children who had suffered such injury in human contact and such impoverishment in the human ties offered them that ego development was arrested or crippled in its early stages. They had been so severely damaged that psychotherapy could not be employed while they remained in their own homes or foster homes. They required a special environment, now provided by a few institutions throughout the country, in which every aspect of the program is designed to meet the extraordinary requirements of such disturbed children, and in which the daily care and education are provided by psychiatrically trained personnel.

[45] Quoted from review by Selma Fraiberg, *Social Casework* 37: 242–43; May 1956, of Bruno Bettelheim, *Truants From Life*. Glencoe, Ill.: Free Press, 1955. 511 p.

EXAMPLE: THREE PATIENTS IN ONE[46]

A bewildered young woman sought treatment for severe headaches. She turned out to be three patients in one. Her two psychiatrists studied their patient with the best traditional care together with special checks and modern methods. Evidently these authors, like a number of their predecessors in the field, were completely surprised to find that their patient was a multiple personality. They tested every possibility of play-acting, escape, fraud, and fun. They avoided reading accounts of other cases while working with this one. They scrutinized their own interests and asked themselves, after Bernheim, "Who is hypnotizing whom?" They checked the patient's statements with statements from the same personality, other personalities, relatives, friends, other observers, and records. They observed naive persons' reactions to the several personalities; they exhibited the several personalities to professional colleagues for interpretation; and, from experts who knew as little as possible about the patient, for each personality they obtained interpretations of the handwriting, the results of intelligence tests, projective tests, and Osgood and Luria's semantic differential test. They obtained electroencephalograms, sound recordings and sound films.

The recordings and sound films the authors used as part of the therapy. The case, like a number of the earlier ones in the literature, was worked through to an excellent synthesis; one which, though the authors say they cannot be sure about this, seems durable.

The entire study supports the observations of prior authors about multiple personality: the build-up of meanings that can make for stress; conflicts in childhood and maturity; lapses; relevant sleepwalking; neurotic symptoms; hallucinations engendered by a co-conscious personality; transitional syncopes; various amnesias; the several personalities' differences in facial expression, manner, voice, speech, handwriting, interests, thought, character, and maturity; between personalities, barriers neither perfect nor wholly unchanging; one-way amnesia between certain personalities, and mutual amnesia, for a time, between others; each personality's striving to function as fully as possible; use of hypnosis to recover dreams, other memories, and larger organizations; light on psychotherapy; the changing, growing self; the integrative role of an inclusive interest; and the throes of coalescence or synthesis.

The findings are thought new, to the effect that one of the personalities, Eve Black, could not be hypnotized; one, Jane, emerged with mature powers, general orientation, and language, but with no specific memories; each of the most disparate personalities, Eve White and Eve Black, was sad at having to "die," and the most inclusive of the three personalities, Jane, was sad to "lose" her erstwhile "sisters." New too, and significant, are the special methods of study as applied to multiple personality, and the whole picture of a contem-

[46] Quoted from review by William S. Taylor, *Contemporary Psychology* 2: 289–90; November 1957, of Corbett H. Thigpen and Hervey M. Cleckley, *The Three Faces of Eve*. New York: McGraw-Hill Book Co., 1957. ix+308 p.
Evelyn Lancaster with James Poling, *The Final Face of Eve*. New York: McGraw-Hill Book Co., 1958. x+290 p.

porary young woman, with her playfulness, selfishness, affection, humanity, idealism, and practical judgment most revealingly tried, segregated, and finally synthesized in a normal urge to live as a mature person.

EXAMPLE: RECORDED THERAPY SESSIONS[47]

Alice, a 32-year-old married woman, with a life-long history of severe eczema, was treated psychotherapeutically by Dr. Abramson. More than 300 of Alice's therapy sessions were electrically recorded, and the volume consists primarily of verbatim transcriptions of segments selected from the interviews.

With the major exception of Rogers and his colleagues, psychotherapists have not made available for public scrutiny substantial samples of their therapeutic work. Most of the publications dealing with the theory and technique of psychotherapy present only brief, illustrative examples of patient or therapist behavior. The aspiring psychotherapist in a prepracticum graduate seminar is, perforce, asked to deal with a complex phenomenon which he looks at through a conceptual reducing screen.

EXAMPLE: HUMAN RELATIONS[48]

The major part (160 pages) of *School Problems in Human Relations* consists of selections from over 5500 cases dealing with school and community problems in human relations. The authors had accumulated these materials over a ten-year period of teaching and research. Each of the nine chapters in Part 2 includes several cases related to some central problem. Chapter 4, for example, includes seven that have most pertinence to the beginning teacher. The cases, generally, are short, running from a dozen lines to a maximum of two or three pages. They are "disguised" and are presented for analysis and discussion as a kind of training in human relations. The authors include a brief note on "case teaching" in which they stress variation in the use of such materials.

EXAMPLE: CASE STUDY OF A Y.M.C.A.[49]

Institutions find it relatively easy to experiment with phases of their life and to make improvements in segments of their work. The distinctive quality of the San Francisco Y.M.C.A. project is its comprehensiveness. Many different things are described as having been done as parts of a common design and with resolute effort to deal with the institution as a totality. Depending on tested and known processes, it would have been possible to improve membership enlistment, equipment, group procedures, instruction materials, super-

[47] Quoted from review by Zanwil Sperber, *Contemporary Psychology* 2: 232; September 1957, of Harold A. Abramson, *The Patient Speaks*. New York: Vantage Press, 1957. xxi+239 p.

[48] Quoted from review by Stephen M. Corey, *Contemporary Psychology* 2: 242–43; September 1957, of Lloyd Cook and Elaine Cook, *School Problems in Human Relations*. New York: McGraw-Hill Book Co., 1957. xi+292 p.

[49] Roy Sorenson and Hedley S. Dimock, *A Case Study in Institutional Change*. New York: Association Press, 1955. p. vii–viii.

vision, parent participation, appraisal of results, public relations, administration, or other aspects of the life and work of this Y.M.C.A. Any such single venture would have been commendable. We know, however, that the *total life* of an institution—a school, a house, a church, a community, or a Christian Association—is a major determiner of the nature of its influence. Various aspects or segments of institutional life are each intrinsically important, but all are interrelated in a manner that determines the real significance of each and of the organization as a whole. Here is described an earnest attempt to change an Association as a whole—its goals, its methods, its administration—and that comprehensive factor, its *total climate*. All who compose the institution—members, leaders, supervisors, administrators, officers, related families, and community supporters—will, it is hoped and planned, come to hold those common expectations composing the climate which is the effective determiner of quality.

Each aspect of the San Francisco Y.M.C.A. takes on new dimensions when seen in the context of the whole. Each development is made in the light of a new perspective on the Association as a totality, and that outlook makes distinctive demands on every phase of the project.

The threefold character of this project is revealing of the manner in which dependable change comes in an institution. Concepts have been re-thought and have taken on a living reality for all involved. Steps in transition —how to get from where we are to new positions—have been carefully taken with the best of procedures for re-education. Records have been kept all along the way. These steps are interrelated—they do not come in an orderly sequence but each is seen and described clearly. Each makes its vital contribution to the adventure as a whole.

EXAMPLE: THE FIELD OF SOCIAL WORK[50]

This book covers the specialized social services found in specific settings —social services in a family agency and in a local welfare department, welfare services for children, psychiatric social work, medical social work, the correctional services, school social work, social services for the aged, social group work, and community organization. . . . A well-chosen case illustration follows each chapter, showing the purposes and goals of the agency, the specific problems encountered in the particular family or individual situation, and some of the methods employed by the social worker to help the family or individual in trouble. The progress achieved is explained and evaluated.

EXAMPLE: A SELLING GROUP[51]

This study describes the behavior patterns emerging from the interpersonal relations of the members of a small group of 20 salesgirls. It describes

[50] Quoted from review by Mary S. Branch Scoville, *Social Service Review* 29: 436–37; December 1955, of Arthur E. Fink, Everett E. Wilson, and Merrill B. Conover, *The Field of Social Work*. Third Edition. New York: Henry Holt and Co., 1955. ix+630 p.

[51] George F. F. Lombard, *Behavior in a Selling Group:* A Case Study of Interpersonal Relations in a Department Store. Boston: Harvard University Graduate School of Business Administration, 1955. p. v–vi.

the relation of these emergent behavior patterns to the need satisfaction of the particular members of the group and to the achievement of the group's purposes. The emergent behavior patterns satisfied the personal need of each girl to maintain her beliefs about herself and also secured organized purposes in ways considered unusually successful by both the salesgirls and the executives concerned. Nevertheless, the group processes through which these results were obtained made difficult changes of behavior that would have resulted in more satisfaction to either customers or salesgirls. Indeed, the girls' beliefs brought it about that in most instances when one of them changed her behavior in these ways, she would be punished for the change.

The study regards the assumptions about behavior underlying the executives' evaluations of service as the single most important influence restricting the development of new behavior patterns in the department as a whole. The executives' need to maintain their beliefs about themselves by behaving in conformity to the existing logics of management made it difficult for them to examine and change these assumptions.

The conclusions of the study point to a need for the re-education of executives in sensitivity to group behavior patterns and in awareness of the effects of their own behavior on others.

EXAMPLE: PERSONNEL SECURITY[52]

The 50 cases presented here have been collected in the course of a study of several hundred cases arising under the various Federal personnel security programs. These histories are collected, with the consent of the employees involved, from the files of the lawyers who advised or represented them. The reports are of necessity incomplete, because the Government file, which was not released to the employee, was also not available to our interviewers. While we realize that the usefulness of a study of this kind is circumscribed by the limitations on the available material, we feel that it will provide useful and indeed essential material for an understanding of how the security programs operate from day to day. We have tried to eliminate possible bias, by employing carefully selected lawyer-interviewers; by relying in the main on documentary materials, such as the written charges, the employee's written response, and the transcript of the hearing; and by identifying information based on statements by the employee or his counsel.

The 50 cases in this collection are taken from a current total of 230 cases from 12 cities. In each instance, the employee is asked, through his lawyer, whether he would be willing to release the report of his case for general distribution, and the cases appearing here are among those in which such a release has been obtained.

[52] Adam Yarmolinsky, Compiler, *Case Studies in Personnel Security*. Washington: Bureau of National Affairs, 1955. p. iii. The cases include government civilian employees, industrial employees, military personnel, port security, and international organization employees.

EXAMPLE: PERSONNEL AND INDUSTRIAL RELATIONS[53]

Two different types of materials have been included in the book. Forty-four cases, each written around a situation which actually occurred in a business concern, provide facts and information which give the student practice in developing his ability to think through a problem. There is no single solution to any of these problems. It should be emphasized that the most important benefits gained by the student will not come from whatever solution is decided upon, but rather from the opportunity to discuss and analyze problem situations.

The second part of the book consists of seven summary case problems in which the student evolves a complete personnel program from the individual cases he has been studying. Thus the student learns to look at a situation objectively, to plan logically sound solutions, and to use intelligent initiative, ingenuity, and imagination. The cases and problems deal with personnel programming, personnel research and standards, employment, training and development, health and medical care, safety, employee services, and employee relations.

EXAMPLE: CASE STUDY OF A FACTORY GROUP[54]

This report is a study of behavior in an industrial work group. The group, consisting of fourteen workers and their foreman, formed one department of a small instrument manufacturing company. It was referred to as "the machine shop." The purpose is to demonstrate through description and diagnosis how social organization in a group develops from the web of work and nonwork behavior. We want to demonstrate why this social organization is so important to the men involved and to the enterprise for which they work. We also want to show, however, that social organization can become "frozen" unless leadership is exercised to challenge the adaptive capacities of individuals and their group.

The plan for our field work was simple in design, but difficult in execution. The data we wanted to get consisted of actual behavior in the group and how the men perceived this behavior. The major method for research was observation, informal interviewing, and examination of records where appropriate. The methodology was similar to that followed by the social anthropologist in field work. Over a period of almost six months we spent part of each workday in the shop and part in recording data and in discussion with colleagues. The data were present in the group itself and available to all members, with the possible exception of the information in the personnel records. But, to lift up these data, to fit them into a consistent pattern of behavior and to see their significance required some understanding

[53] Edgar G. Williams and John F. Mee, *Cases and Problems in Personnel and Industrial Relations.* New York: Ronald Press, 1955. p. iii.

[54] Abraham Zaleznik, *Worker Satisfaction and Development:* A Case Study of Work and Social Behavior in a Factory Group. Boston: Harvard University Graduate School of Business Administration, 1956. p. 1, 2, 5, 9–10.

of theoretical material on small group behavior as well as skill in observation and diagnosis.

From this analysis, we attempt to restate the central problem for the administration of work groups. This problem is two-fold: First, how can work groups be helped to develop an effective social organization? Second, how can the ingredients for growth and creativity be introduced to prevent the social organization from becoming static?

EXAMPLE: CASE HISTORIES IN OPERATIONS RESEARCH[55]

Operations Analysis in the United States Air Force

Traffic Delays at Toll Booths

The Influence of Vehicular Speed and Spacing on Tunnel Capacity

Road Safety and Traffic Research in Great Britain

Revising New York's Subway Fare Structure

Ore-Handling at British Ports

Analysis of a Railroad Classification Yard

Queing Theory and Cost Concepts Applied to a Problem in Inventory Control

Strip Mining Phosphate Rock with Large Walking Draglines

Operational Research in the British Coal Industry

Operational Research in Underground Mining

Utilization of Training Aircraft

A Study of Combat Stress in Korea: Bio-Social Research in Operations Research.

CONCLUDING STATEMENT

Significant trends and emphases in clinical and case study may be summarized briefly as follows:

1. Extension of the case approach to include study of social institutions or agencies and communities or cultural groups

2. Application and use in a number of professional fields and to a wide range of human problems

3. Recognition of the complementary functions of the several stages in case study and case work

4. Fuller and better use of such personal documents as the life history, autobiography, biography, diaries and journals, letters, records of dreams, and expressive interviews

5. Recognition of the significance of multiple causation in diagnosis and of the corresponding need for a variety of therapeutic techniques

[55] Joseph F. McCloskey and John M. Coppinger, Editors, *Operations Research for Management:* Case Histories, Methods, Information Handling. Vol. 2. Baltimore: Johns Hopkins Press, 1956. xxxvi+563 p.

6. A concept of therapy as development of the potentialities of the individual for growth and improvement, including adjustment procedures in the form of preventive measures, self-help, and client-centered techniques

7. Development and application of a variety of methods of psychotherapy, including group therapy

8. Further improvement in case records, as well as wider use of cumulative and anecdotal records

9. Formulation of ethical principles or standards, particularly in the field of psychology, but with applications to other clinical and case areas (especially in diagnosis and treatment)

10. Recognition of the supplementary functions of case-clinical and statistical methods

11. Appearance of a considerable body of case-history material, in spite of certain difficulties in producing and publishing adequate case histories.

SELECTED REFERENCES

ABRAHAMSON, Arthur C., Editor. *Social Work Practice in Canada:* Case Records and Examples for Study and Teaching. Vancouver: School of Social Work, University of British Columbia, 1955. 252 p.

ABT, Lawrence E., and BELLAK, Leopold, Editors. *Projective Psychology:* Clinical Approaches to the Total Personality. New York: Alfred A. Knopf, 1950. xvii+485+xiv p.

ADAMS, Leonard P., and ARONSON, Robert L. *Workers and Industrial Change:* A Case Study of Labor Mobility. Ithaca, N. Y.: New York State School of Industrial and Labor Relations, Cornell University, 1957. xi+209 p.

ADAMSON, LeMay, and DUNHAM, H. Warren. "Clinical Treatment of Male Delinquents: A Case Study in Effort and Result." *American Sociological Review* 21: 312-20; June 1956.

ALEXANDER, V. K. "A Case Study of a Multiple Personality." *Journal of Abnormal and Social Psychology* 52: 272-76; March 1956.

ALEXANDER, William M. "Cooperation in In-Service Education: A Case Study." *Educational Leadership* 15: 279-85; February 1958.

ALLBAUGH, Leland G. *Crete:* A Case Study of an Underdeveloped Area. Princeton: Princeton University Press, 1953. 592 p.

ALLEN, R. M. *Personality Assessment Procedures:* Psychometric, Projective, and Other Approaches. New York: Harper & Brothers, 1958. xi+541 p.

American Psychological Association Education and Training Board. "Criteria for Evaluating Training Programs in Clinical or in Counseling Psychology." *American Psychologist* 13: 59-60; February 1958.

ANDERSON, Harold H., and ANDERSON, Gladys L., Editors. *An Introduction to Projective Techniques.* . . . New York: Prentice-Hall, 1951. xxiv+720 p.

ANDERSON, Robert P. "Physiological and Verbal Behavior During Client-Centered Counseling." *Journal of Counseling Psychology* 3: 174-84; Fall 1956.

ANDREW, Gwen. "An Investigation of Methods for Follow-Up of Child-Guidance Clinic Cases." *Social Service Review* 31: 74-80; March 1957.

ANDREWS, Kenneth R., Editor. *Human Relations and Administration; The*

Case Method of Teaching: An Interim Statement. Cambridge: Harvard University Press, 1953. xvi+271 p.

ANTHONY, Joseph. *The Invisible Curtain:* Psychoanalytic Cases of Louis Montgomery. New York: Rinehart & Co., 1957. 250 p.

APTEKAR, Herbert H. *The Dynamics of Casework and Counseling.* Boston: Houghton Mifflin Co., 1955. 262 p.

APTEKAR, Herbert H. "Evolving Concepts in Casework and Counseling." *Social Service Review* 28: 74-82; March 1954.

ARGYRIS, Chris. *Diagnosing Human Relations in Organization:* A Case Study of a Hospital. New Haven: Labor and Management Center, Yale University, 1956. vii+120 p.

BACH, George R. *Intensive Group Psychotherapy.* New York: Ronald Press, 1954. xi+446 p.

BAKAN, David. "Clinical Psychology and Logic." *American Psychologist* 11: 655-62; December 1956.

BAKWIN, Harry, and BAKWIN, Ruth M. *Clinical Treatment of Behavior Disorders in Children.* Philadelphia: W. B. Saunders Co., 1953. xi+495 p.

BALSER, Benjamin H., Editor. *Psychotherapy of the Adolescent.* New York: International Universities Press, 1957. 270 p.

BARRON, Frank, and LEARY, Timothy F. "Changes in Psychoneurotic Patients with and without Psychotherapy." *Journal of Consulting Psychology* 19: 239-45; August 1955.

BARRY, Ruth, and Others. *Case Studies in College Student-Staff Relationships.* New York: Bureau of Publications, Teachers College, Columbia University, 1956. ix+117 p.

BAUER, Raymond A., and WASIOLEK, Edward. *Nine Soviet Portraits.* New York: John Wiley & Sons, 1955. ix+190 p.

BAUER, Ronald C. *Cases in College Administration.* New York: Columbia University Press, 1955. 213 p.

BAXTER, John C. "Multiple Management Matures: A Case History." *Personnel Journal* 35: 254-57; December 1956.

BEALS, Ralph L. "The Village in an Industrial World." *Scientific Monthly* 77: 65-75; August 1953.

BEATMAN, Frances L. "Family Interaction: Its Significance for Diagnosis and Treatment." *Social Casework* 38: 111-18; March 1957.

BECK, Dorothy F. "The Dynamics of Group Psychotherapy as Seen by a Sociologist: Part I, The Basic Process." *Sociometry* 21: 98-128; June 1958.

BECK, Dorothy F. "The Dynamics of Group Psychotherapy as Seen by a Sociologist: Part II, Some Puzzling Questions on Leadership, Contextual Relations, and Outcomes." *Sociometry* 21: 180-97; September 1958.

BEIER, E. G. "Client-Centered Therapy and the Involuntary Client." *Journal of Consulting Psychology* 16: 332-37; October 1952.

BELLOWS, Roger M. *Case Problems in Personnel Management.* Dubuque, Ia.: William C. Brown and Co., 1955. 148 p.

BENDIG, A. W. "The Personality of Judges and Their Agreement with Experts in Judging Clinical Case Histories." *Journal of Consulting Psychology* 20: 422; December 1956.

BENDIG, A. W. "Ranking Methodology: The Development of a Judgmental Criterion with Clinical Case Histories." *Journal of Consulting Psychology* 20: 75-78; February 1956.

BENDIG, A. W. "The Reliability of Adjustment Ratings and the Length of Case Histories." *Journal of Consulting Psychology* 19: 463-67; December 1955.

BENDIG, A. W. "Reliability of Case History Ratings and Intellectual Ability of Graduate Raters." *Journal of Consulting Psychology* 20: 142-44; April 1956.

BENNETT, John W., and ISHINO, Iwao. "Futomi: A Case Study of the Socio-Economic Adjustments of a Marginal Community in Japan." *Rural Sociology* 20: 41-50; March 1955.

BENNEY, Celia. "The Role of the Caseworker in Rehabilitation." *Social Casework* 36: 118-23; March 1955.

BERENDA, Carlton W. "Is Clinical Psychology a Science?" *American Psychologist* 12: 725-29; December 1957.

BERG, I. A. "Measures before and after Therapy." *Journal of Clinical Psychology* 8: 46-50; January 1952.

BERG, I. A. "The Use of Human Subjects in Psychological Research." *American Psychologist* 9: 108-11; March 1954.

BERKMAN, Herman G. *The Delineation and Structure of Rental Housing Areas: A Milwaukee Case Study.* Wisconsin Commerce Reports, Vol. 4, No. 5. Madison: University of Wisconsin School of Commerce and Bureau of Business Research and Service, 1956. 144 p.

BERKOWITZ, Sidney. "Some Specific Techniques of Psychosocial Diagnosis and Treatment in Family Casework." *Social Casework* 36: 399-406; November 1955.

BERNSTEIN, Arnold. *On the Nature of Psychotherapy.* Garden City, N. Y.: Doubleday & Co., 1954. ix+36 p.

BERRIEN, F. K., and BASH, Wendell H. *Human Relations:* Comments and Cases. Second Edition. New York: Harper & Brothers, 1957. xii+564 p.

BETTELHEIM, Bruno. *Truants From Life.* Glencoe, Ill.: Free Press, 1955. 511 p.

BIESTEK, Felix P. *The Casework Relationship.* Chicago: Loyola University Press, 1957. 149 p.

BIESTEK, Felix P. "The Principle of Client Self-Determination." *Social Casework* 32: 369-75; November 1951.

BLAIR, G. M. *Diagnostic and Remedial Teaching.* New York: The Macmillan Co., 1956. xvi+409 p.

BLENKNER, Margaret. "Obstacles to Evaluative Research in Casework." *Social Casework* 31: 54-60, 97-105; February, March 1950.

BLENKNER, Margaret, and Others. "A Study of Interrelated Factors in the Initial Interview with New Clients." *Social Casework* 32: 23-30; January 1951.

BLOCH, Helen I. "Casework Services in a Geriatric Clinic." *Social Casework* 39: 228-35; April 1958.

BLOCH, Herbert A., and FLYNN, Frank T. *Delinquency:* The Juvenile Offender in America Today. New York: Random House, 1956. xii+612 p. (Two cases are reported at some length.)

BOEHM, Werner W. "The Terminology of Social Casework: An Attempt at Theoretical Clarification." *Social Service Review* 28: 381-91; December 1954.

BONE, Harry, Editor. *Case Reports in Clinical Psychology.* Vol. 3, Nos. 3 and 4. Brooklyn: Department of Psychology, Kings County Hospital, 1956. p. 111-79. (An issue devoted to psychotherapy.)

BOYD, Gertrude, and SCHWIERING, O. C. "Remedial Instruction and Case Records: A Survey of Reading Clinical Practices." *Journal of Educational Research* 44: 443-55; February 1951.

BRITTON, Clare. "Casework Techniques in Child Care Services." *Social Casework* 36: 3-13; January 1955.

BROWER, Daniel, and ABT, Lawrence E., Editors. *Progress in Clinical Psychology.* Vol. 2. New York: Grune and Stratton, 1956. viii+364 p.

BROWN, C. A. P. "Social Status As It Affects Psychotherapy." *Journal of Educational Sociology* 25: 164-68; November 1951.

BÜHLER, Charlotte B. "Techniques for Studying Individual Children." *California Journal of Elementary Education* 21: 58-63; February 1953.

BURCH, Thomas K. "Postwar Japan: A Case Study in Population Policy and Social Disorganization." *American Catholic Sociological Review* 19: 45-53; March 1958.

BURTON, Arthur, and HARRIS, R. E., Editors. *Clinical Studies of Personality.* Vol. 2. Case Histories in Clinical and Abnormal Psychology. New York: Harper & Brothers, 1955. xiii+836 p.

BYCHOWSKI, Gustav, and DESPERT, J. Louise, Editors. *Specialized Techniques in Psychotherapy.* New York: Basic Books, 1958. xii+371 p.

CAIN, Leo F., MICHAELIS, John U., and EURICH, Alvin C. "Prognosis," *Encyclopedia of Educational Research.* Second Edition. Edited by Walter S. Monroe. New York: The Macmillan Co., 1950. p. 874-94.

CALLIS, Robert, and Others. *A Casebook of Counseling.* New York: Appleton-Century-Crofts, 1955. ix+352 p.

CARR, Lowell J., and STERMER, James E. *Willow Run:* A Study of Industrialization and Cultural Inadequacy. New York: Harper & Brothers, 1952. xxii+406 p.

CARTER, Genevieve W. "Theory Development in Social Work Research." *Social Service Review* 29: 34-42; March 1955.

"Case Report: An Autobiography of a Schizophrenic Experience." *Journal of Abnormal and Social Psychology* 51: 677-89; November 1955.

Casework Papers, 1955. From the National Conference of Social Work. New York: Family Service Association of America, 1955. 154 p.

CASTORE, George F. "Attitudes of Students Toward the Case Method of Instruction in a Human Relations Course." *Journal of Educational Research* 45: 201-13; November 1951.

CAUDILL, William. *The Psychiatric Hospital as a Small Society.* Cambridge, Mass.: Harvard University Press, for the Commonwealth Fund, 1958. xxii+406 p.

CLARK, Burton R. "Organizational Adaptation and Precarious Values: A Case Study." *American Sociological Review* 21: 327-36; June 1956.

COFFEY, Hubert, and Others. "A Technique of Group Psychotherapy." *Journal of Social Issues* 6: 25-36; 1950.

COLBY, Kenneth. *A Primer for Psychotherapists.* New York: Ronald Press, 1951. viii+167 p.

COLLIER, Rex M. "A Basis for Integration Rather Than Fragmentation in Psychotherapy." *Journal of Consulting Psychology* 14: 199-205; June 1950.

CONGALTON, Athol A., Editor. *Hawera—A Social Survey:* A Report of a Community Venture. Hawera, New Zealand: Hawera and District Progressive Association and Hawera Star Publishing Co., 1954. xv+218 p.

CONNERY, Maurice F. "The Measure of Effective Recording." *Social Casework* 35: 445-48; December 1954.

CONRAD, Dorothy C. "An Empirical Study of the Concept of Psychotherapeutic Success." *Journal of Consulting Psychology* 16: 92-97; April 1952.

CORSINI, Raymond J. *Methods of Group Psychotherapy.* New York: McGraw-Hill Book Co., 1957. xi+251 p.

CORSINI, Raymond J., and ROSENBERG, Bina. "Mechanisms of Group Psychotherapy: Processes and Dynamics." *Journal of Abnormal and Social Psychology* 51: 406-11; November 1955.

CREGAN, Robert F. "Case Methods 'Unlimited'?" *School and Society* 74: 214-16; October 6, 1951.

CRONON, Edmund D. *Black Moses:* The Story of Marcus Garvey and the Universal Negro Improvement Association. Madison: University of Wisconsin Press, 1955. 278 p.

CULBERTSON, Jack. "The Case for Cases in the Study of Administration." *Educational Administration and Supervision* 42: 420-27; November 1956.

CUSTANCE, John. *Wisdom, Madness and Folly:* The Philosophy of a Lunatic. New York: Pellegrini and Cudahy, 1951. 254 p. (Mostly written in a mental hospital by a manic-depressive patient.)

DAVID, Henry P., and SPRINGFIELD, Franklyn B. "Phones, Phonies, and Psychologists: II, Four Years Later." *American Psychologist* 13: 61-64; February 1958.

DE GRAZIA, Sebastian. *Errors of Psychotherapy.* Garden City, N. Y.: Doubleday & Co., 1952. 288 p.

DEJOGHN, Jan F. "A European Experiment in Casework Teaching." *Social Casework* 34: 9-17; January 1953.

DEUTSCH, Felix, and MURPHY, William F. *The Clinical Interview.* Vol. 1, *Diagnosis.* New York: International Universities Press, 1954. 613 p.

DEUTSCH, Felix, and MURPHY, William F. *The Clinical Interview.* Vol. 2, *Therapy.* New York: International Universities Press, 1955. 335 p.

DEUTSCHER, Verda, and DEUTSCHER, Irwin. "Cohesion in a Small Group: A Case Study." *Social Forces* 33: 336-41; May 1955.

DEVEREUX, George. *Therapeutic Education:* Its Theoretical Bases and Practice. New York: Harper & Brothers, 1956. xxviii+435 p. (Includes 77 brief cases.)

DeYoung, John E. *Village Life in Modern Thailand.* Berkeley: University of California Press, 1955. xii+224 p.

Dittmann, Allen T. "The Interpersonal Process in Psychotherapy: Development of a Research Method." *Journal of Abnormal and Social Psychology* 47: 236-44; April 1952.

Dollard, John. *Caste and Class in a Southern Town.* Second Edition. New York: Harper & Brothers, 1949. xvi+502 p.

Dollard, John. *Criteria for the Life History.* New Haven: Yale University Press, 1935. vi+288 p. Reprinted in 1949 by Peter Smith.

Dollard, John, Auld, Frank, and White, Alice. *Steps in Psychotherapy.* New York: The Macmillan Co., 1953. 222 p.

Dollard, John, and Miller, Neal E. *Personality and Psychotherapy:* An Analysis in Terms of Learning, Thinking, and Culture. New York: McGraw-Hill Book Co., 1950. xiii+488 p.

Dube, S. C. *Indian Village.* Ithaca, N. Y.: Cornell University Press, 1955. xiv+248 p.

duMas, Frank M. "Clinical Statements as Scientific Propositions and Social Decisions." *Journal of Consulting Psychology* 19: 255-58; August 1955.

Edwards, A. L., and Cronbach, Lee J. "Experimental Design for Research in Psychotherapy." *Journal of Clinical Psychology* 8: 51-59; January 1952.

Elson, Miriam. "Does Present Casework Practice Foster Integration of the Adopted Child within Himself, His Family, His Community?" *Social Service Review* 29: 137-47; June 1955.

Embree, R. B. "Developments in Counseling Bureaus and Clinics." *Educational and Psychological Measurement* 10: 465-75; Autumn 1950.

Erickson, Clifford E. *Counseling Interview.* New York: Prentice-Hall, 1950. 174 p.

Ethical Standards of Psychologists: A Summary of Ethical Principles. Washington: American Psychological Association, 1953. 19 p.

Evans, Jean. "Case Reports: Miller." *Journal of Abnormal and Social Psychology* 45: 359-79; April 1950.

Evans, Jean. *Three Men:* An Experiment in the Biography of Emotion. New York: Alfred A. Knopf, 1954. xviii+298 p. (Case reports.)

Ewalt, J. R., Strecker, E. A., and Ebaugh, F. G. *Practical Clinical Psychology.* Eighth Edition. New York: McGraw-Hill Book Co., 1957. xiv+457 p.

Eysenck, H. J. "The Effects of Psychotherapy: An Evaluation." *Journal of Consulting Psychology* 16: 319-24; October 1952.

Faatz, Anita J. *The Nature of Choice in Casework Process.* Chapel Hill: University of North Carolina Press, 1953. vii+141 p.

Fensterheim, Herbert, and Birch, Herbert G. "A Case Study of Group Ideology and Individual Adjustment." *Journal of Abnormal and Social Psychology* 45: 710-20; October 1950.

Fenton, Norman, and Louttit, C. M. "Child-Guidance Clinics," *Encyclopedia of Educational Research.* Second Edition. Edited by Walter S. Monroe. New York: The Macmillan Co., 1950. p. 197-99.

Fenton, Norman, and Louttit, C. M. "Problem Children and Delinquents,"

Encyclopedia of Educational Research. Second Edition. Edited by Walter S. Monroe. New York: The Macmillan Co., 1950. p. 868-74.

FIEDLER, Fred E. "The Concept of an Ideal Therapeutic Relationship." *Journal of Consulting Psychology* 14: 239-45; August 1950.

FINESTONE, Samuel. "The Scientific Component in the Casework Field Curriculum." *Social Casework* 36: 195-202; May 1955.

FINK, Arthur E., WILSON, Everett E., and CONOVER, Merrill B. *The Field of Social Work.* Third Edition. New York: Henry Holt and Co., 1955. ix+630 p.

FISHER, V. E. *The Meaning and Practice of Psychotherapy.* New York: The Macmillan Co., 1950. xv+411 p.

FOOTE, Estelle. *Six Children.* Springfield, Ill.: Charles C Thomas, 1956. ix+317 p. (Psychiatric case studies.)

FOULKES, S. H., and ANTHONY, E. J. *Group Psychotherapy:* The Psycho-Analytic Approach. Baltimore: Penguin Books, 1957. 263 p.

FRAIBERG, Selma. "Some Aspects of Casework with Children: Part I, Understanding the Child Client." *Social Casework* 33: 374-81; November 1952.

FRAIBERG, Selma. "Some Aspects of Casework with Children: Part II, Helping with Critical Situations." *Social Casework* 33: 429-35; December 1952.

FRAIBERG, Selma. "Some Aspects of Residential Casework with Children." *Social Casework* 37: 159-67; April 1956.

FRANCIS, Roy G., and STONE, Robert C. *Service and Procedure in Bureaucracy: A Case Study.* Minneapolis: University of Minnesota Press, 1956. vi+201 p. (Empirical study of a public employment agency.)

FREEMAN, Lucy. *Fight Against Fears.* New York: Crown Publishers, 1951. 332 p. (A personal account of a woman's psychoanalysis.)

FRENCH, David G. *An Approach to Measuring Results in Social Work.* New York: Columbia University Press, 1952. xiv+178 p.

FRIEDLANDER, Walter A., Editor. *Concepts and Methods of Social Work.* Englewood Cliffs, N. J.: Prentice-Hall, 1958. ix+308 p.

FRINGS, John. "Experimental Systems of Recording." *Social Casework* 38: 55-63; February 1957.

FRINGS, John. "What About Brief Services?—A Report of a Study of Short-Term Cases." *Social Casework* 32: 236-41; June 1951.

FROMM-REICHMANN, Frieda. *Principles of Intensive Psychotherapy.* Chicago: The University of Chicago Press, 1950. xv+246 p.

FROMM-REICHMANN, Frieda, and MORENO, J. L., Editors. *Progress in Psychotherapy.* New York: Grune and Stratton, 1956. xii+352 p.

GAMBLE, Sidney D. *Ting Hsien:* A North China Rural Community. New York: International Secretariat, Institute of Pacific Relations, 1954. xxv+472 p.

GARDNER, George E., Editor. *Case Studies in Childhood Emotional Disabilities.* Vol. 2. New York: American Orthopsychiatric Association, 1956. vii+368 p.

GARFIELD, Sol L. *Introductory Clinical Psychology:* An Overview of the Functions, Methods, and Problems of Contemporary Clinical Psychology. New York: The Macmillan Co., 1957. xiii+469 p.

GARFIELD, Sol L., HEINE, Ralph W., and LEVENTHAL, Morton. "An Evaluation of Psychological Reports in a Clinical Setting." *Journal of Consulting Psychology* 18: 281-86; August 1954.

GEDDES, Arthur. *The Isle of Lewis and Harris:* A Study in British Community. Edinburgh: Edinburgh University Press, 1955. xvi+340 p.

GEE, Wilson. *Social Science Research Methods.* New York: Appleton-Century-Crofts, 1950. p. 230-51.

GERBER, Israel. *Man On a Pendulum:* A Case History of an Invert Presented by a Religious Counselor. New York: American Press, 1956. 320 p.

GESELL, Arnold, and AMATRUDA, Catherine S. *Developmental Diagnosis:* Normal and Abnormal Child Development, Clinical Methods and Practical Applications. Revised Edition. New York: Harper & Brothers, 1947. xvi+496 p.

GILBERT, Jeanne G. *Understanding Old Age.* New York: Ronald Press, 1953. 442 p. (Twenty-six case histories based on the author's professional experience.)

GINZBERG, Eli, and BRAY, Douglas W. *The Uneducated.* New York: Columbia University Press, 1953. xxv+246 p. (Case histories from civilian and military life.)

GIOSEFFI, William. "The Relationship of Culture to the Principles of Casework." *Social Casework* 32: 190-96; May 1951.

GLACKEN, Clarence J. *The Great Loochoo:* A Study of Okinawan Village Life. Berkeley: University of California Press, 1955. xvi+324 p.

GLADFELTER, Millard E. "Community College Case History." *School and Society* 71: 353-56; June 10, 1950.

GLADWIN, Thomas, and SARASON, Seymour B. *Truk:* Man in Paradise. New York: Wenner-Gren Foundation for Anthropological Research, 1953. 651 p.

GLICKMAN, Esther. *Child Placement through Clinically Oriented Casework.* New York: Columbia University Press, 1957. xii+448 p.

GLUECK, Sheldon, and GLUECK, Eleanor. *Delinquents in the Making:* Paths to Prevention. New York: Harper & Brothers, 1952. viii+214 p.

GLUECK, Sheldon, and GLUECK, Eleanor. *Unraveling Juvenile Delinquency.* New York: Commonwealth Fund, 1950. xv+399 p.

GONDOR, Emery I. *Art and Play Therapy.* Garden City, N. Y.: Doubleday & Co., 1954. x+61 p.

GOOD, Carter V., and SCATES, Douglas E. *Methods of Research:* Educational, Psychological, Sociological. New York: Appleton-Century-Crofts, 1954. p. 726-99.

GOODE, William J., and HATT, Paul K. *Methods in Social Research.* New York: McGraw-Hill Book Co., 1952. p. 330-40.

GORDON, Henrietta L. *Casework Services for Children:* Principles and Practices. Boston: Houghton Mifflin Co., 1956. xii+493 p.

GORLOW, L., HOCH, E. L., and TELSCHOW, E. *The Nature of Nondirective Group Psychotherapy.* New York: Bureau of Publications, Teachers College, Columbia University, 1952. viii+143 p.

GREEN, Harold R., HANSON, John J., and SEEMAN, Julius. "A Stereophonic Sound System for Play Therapy Observation." *Journal of Consulting Psychology* 21: 499-500; December 1957.

GREEN, Sidney L. "Psychoanalytic Contributions to Casework Treatment of Marital Problems." *Social Casework* 35: 419-23; December 1954.

GREENACRE, Phyllis. *Swift and Carroll:* A Psychoanalytic Study of Two Lives. New York: International Universities Press, 1955. 306 p.

GREENWOOD, Ernest. "Social Science and Social Work: A Theory of Their Relationship." *Social Service Review* 29: 20-33; March 1955.

GREENWOOD, Ernest. "Social Work Research: A Decade of Reappraisal." *Social Service Review* 31: 311-20; September 1957.

GREENWOOD, Ernest, and MASSARIK, Fred. "Some Methodological Problems in Social Work Research." *American Sociological Review* 15: 546-50; August 1950.

GREGORY, Jean L. "The Generic and Specific Aspects of a Family Casework Program." *Social Casework* 31: 284-91; July 1950.

GRIFFITHS, Daniel E., and HOBDAY, Arthur F. "A New Kind of Case Study." *Educational Research Bulletin* 31: 19-21, 28; January 16, 1952.

GROSS, Neal, MASON, Ward S., and MCEACHERN, Alexander W. *Explorations in Role Analysis:* Studies of the School Superintendency Role. New York: John Wiley & Sons, 1958. 379 p.

GULICK, John. *Social Structure and Culture Change in a Lebanese Village.* Viking Fund Publications in Anthropology, Number Twenty-One. New York: Wenner-Gren Foundation for Anthropological Research, 1955. 191 p.

GUNTRIP, Henry. *Psychotherapy and Religion.* New York: Harper & Brothers, 1957. 206 p.

GUTHEIL, Emil A., Editor. *The Autobiography of Wilhelm Stekel:* The Life Story of a Pioneer Psychoanalyst. New York: Liveright, 1950. ix+293 p.

HADLEY, J. M. *Clinical and Counseling Psychology.* New York: Alfred A. Knopf, 1958. xv+682+xix p.

HAHN, Milton E., and MACLEAN, Malcolm S. *General Clinical Counseling in Educational Institutions.* New York: McGraw-Hill Book Co., 1950. xi+375 p.

HAIGH, Gerard, and KELL, Bill L. "Multiple Therapy as a Method for Training and Research in Psychotherapy." *Journal of Abnormal and Social Psychology* 45: 659-66; October 1950.

HALPERN, Joel M. *A Serbian Village.* New York: Columbia University Press, 1958. xxii+325 p.

HAMILTON, Gordon. *Principles of Social Case Recording.* New York: Columbia University Press, 1946. vii+142 p.

HAMILTON, Gordon. *Psychotherapy in Child Guidance.* New York: Columbia University Press, 1947. 340 p.

HAMILTON, Gordon. "The Role of Social Casework in Social Policy." *Social Casework* 33: 315-24; October 1952.

HAMILTON, Gordon. *Theory and Practice of Social Case Work.* Revised Edition. New York: Columbia University Press, 1951. vii+328 p.

HAMLIN, R. M., and Others. "The Clinician as Judge." *Journal of Consulting Psychology* 18: 233-50; August 1954.

HAMMER, E. F., Editor. *The Clinical Application of Projective Drawings.* Springfield, Ill.: Charles C Thomas, 1958. xxii+663 p.

HAMMOND, Kenneth R., and ALLEN, Jeremiah M. *Writing Clinical Reports.* New York: Prentice-Hall, 1953. 288 p.

HARRIS, Joseph P. "The Senatorial Rejection of Leland Olds: A Case Study." *American Political Science Review* 45: 674-92; September 1951.

HARRIS, Marvin. *Town and Country in Brazil.* New York: Columbia University Press, 1956. xx+302. (Anthropological study of Minas Velhas and its environs.)

HASSLER, Alfred. *Diary of a Self-Made Convict.* Chicago: Henry Regnery Co., 1954. 182 p.

HATHAWAY, Starke R. "Clinical Intuition and Inferential Accuracy." *Journal of Personality* 24: 223-50; March 1956.

HAVIGHURST, Robert J. *Human Development and Education.* New York: Longmans, Green and Co., 1953. p. 177-253.

HAVIGHURST, Robert J., and MORGAN, H. Gerthon. *The Social History of a War-Boom Community.* New York: Longmans, Green and Co., 1951. xix+356 p.

HECK, Arch O., and Others. "Pupil Personnel Work," *Encyclopedia of Educational Research.* Second Edition. Edited by Walter S. Monroe. New York: The Macmillan Co., 1950. p. 909-48.

HERZOG, Elizabeth G. "One Research Project—A Case History." *Social Casework* 34: 191-98; May 1953.

HERZOG, Elizabeth G. "What Social Casework Wants of Social Science Research." *American Sociological Review* 16: 68-73; February 1951.

HINCKLEY, Robert G., and HERMANN, Lydia. *Group Treatment in Psychotherapy.* Minneapolis: University of Minnesota Press, 1951. 136 p.

HITSCHMANN, Edward. *Great Men:* Psychoanalytic Studies. New York: International Universities Press, 1956. xiii+278 p.

HOBBS, Nicholas, and Others. *Ethical Standards of Psychologists.* Washington: American Psychological Association, 1953. xv+171 p.

HOCHWALD, Hilde L. "The Use of Case Records in Research." *Social Casework* 33: 71-76; February 1952.

HOEY, Jane M. "Social Work: Its Base, Skills, and Relation to Other Fields." *Social Casework* 31: 399-410; December 1950.

HOLLINGSHEAD, August B. *Elmtown's Youth:* The Impact of Social Classes on Adolescents. New York: John Wiley & Sons, 1949. xi+480 p.

HOLLIS, Ernest V., and TAYLOR, Alice L. *Social Work Education in the United States:* Report of a Study Made for the National Council on Social Work Education. New York: Columbia University Press, 1951. xviii+422 p.

HOLLIS, Florence. "The Generic and Specific in Social Casework Reexamined." *Social Casework* 37: 211-19; May 1956.

HOLLIS, Florence. "The Relationship between Psychosocial Diagnosis and Treatment." *Social Casework* 32: 67-74; February 1951.

HOLT, Robert R. "Some Statistical Problems in Clinical Research." *Educational and Psychological Measurement* 10: 609-27; Winter 1950.

HUNT, J. McV. "Toward an Integrated Program of Research on Psychotherapy." *Journal of Consulting Psychology* 16: 237-46; August 1952.

HUNT, J. McV., BLENKNER, Margaret, and KOGAN, L. S. *Testing Results in*

Social Casework. New York: Family Service Association of America, 1950. 64 p.

HUNT, J. McV., and KOGAN, L. S. *Measuring Results in Social Casework.* New York: Family Service Association of America, 1950. 79 p.

HUNT, Rockwell D. *"Mr. California":* Autobiography of Rockwell D. Hunt. San Francisco: Fearon Publishers, 1956. 380 p.

HUNT, William A. *The Clinical Psychologist.* Springfield, Ill.: Charles C Thomas, 1956. xi+206 p.

HUNT, William A. "Clinical Psychology—Science or Superstition." *American Psychologist* 6: 683-87; December 1951.

HUSTON, P. E. "Some Observations on the Orientation of Clinical Psychology." *American Psychologist* 8: 191-96; May 1953.

INGHAM, Harrington V., and LOVE, Leonore R. *The Process of Psychotherapy.* New York: McGraw-Hill Book Co., 1954. ix+270 p.

IRVINE, May. "Communication and Relationship in Social Casework." *Social Casework* 36: 13-21; January 1955.

IVES, Kenneth. "The Preparation of Case Balance Sheets." *Journal of Psychology* 35: 45-58; January 1953.

JACKSON, Lydia, and TODD, Kathleen M. *Child Treatment and the Therapy of Play.* Second Edition. New York: Ronald Press, 1950. xii+159 p.

JACOBSON, Eugene, and SCHLACHTER, Stanley, Editors. "Cross-National Research: A Case Study." *Journal of Social Issues* 10: 2-68; 1954.

JACQUES, Elliott. *The Changing Culture of a Factory.* New York: Dryden Press, 1952. xxi+341 p. (Three-year case study of the psychological and social forces affecting the group life, morale, and productivity of a London industrial community; includes description, diagnosis, and treatment.)

JAHODA, Marie, and HAVEL, Joan. "Psychological Problems of Women in Different Social Roles: A Case History of Problem Formulation in Research." *Educational Record* 36: 325-35; October 1955.

JARRARD, Leonard E. "Empathy: The Concept and Industrial Applications." *Personnel Psychology* 9: 157-67; Summer 1956.

JENKINS, Gladys G., SHACTER, Helen, and BAUER, William W. *These Are Your Children.* Expanded Edition. Chicago: Scott, Foresman and Co., 1953. 320 p. (Numerous case studies.)

JENKINS, Richard L. "Understanding Psychiatrists." *American Psychologist* 9: 617-20; October 1954.

JESSOR, Richard. "Social Values and Psychotherapy." *Journal of Consulting Psychology* 20: 264-66; August 1956.

JOEL, Walther, and SHAPIRO, David. "Some Principles and Procedures for Group Psychotherapy." *Journal of Psychology* 29: 77-88; January 1950.

JOHNSON, Marjorie S. "A Study of Diagnostic and Remedial Procedures in a Reading Clinic Laboratory School." *Journal of Educational Research* 48: 565-78; April 1955.

JONES, Maxwell. *The Therapeutic Community.* New York: Basic Books, 1953. 727 p.

JOURARD, Sidney M. *Personal Adjustment:* An Approach through the Study of Healthy Personality. New York: The Macmillan Co., 1958. 462 p.

KARDINER, Abram, and OVESEY, Lionel. *The Mark of Oppression:* A Psychosocial Study of the American Negro. New York: W. W. Norton and Co., 1951. xvii+396 p. (Case histories of 25 American Negroes.)

KARSH, Bernard, and Others. "The Union Organizer and His Tactics: A Case Study." *American Journal of Sociology* 59: 113-22; September 1953.

KASIUS, Cora. "Casework Developments in Europe." *Social Casework* 32: 281-88; July 1951.

KASIUS, Cora, Editor. *A Comparison of Diagnostic and Functional Casework Concepts.* New York: Family Service Association of New York, 1950. 169 p.

KASIUS, Cora, and Others. "Family Casework in the Interest of Children." *Social Casework* 39: 61-182; February-March 1958.

KATZENELBOGEN, Solomon. *Analyzing Psychotherapy.* New York: Philosophical Library, 1958. 126 p.

KEITH, Arthur. *An Autobiography.* New York: Philosophical Library, 1950. vi+721 p. (An eminent pioneer among anthropologists tells of his life and work.)

KENT, Grace H. *Mental Tests in Clinics for Children.* New York: D. Van Nostrand, 1950. xii+180 p.

KERKHOFF, Jack. *How Thin the Veil:* A Newspaperman's Story of His Own Mental Crack-up and Recovery. New York: Greenberg, 1952. 311 p.

KIMBALL, Solon T., and PEARSALL, Marion. *The Talladega Story:* A Study in Community Process. University, Ala.: University of Alabama Press, 1954. xxxii+259 p.

KINSEY, A. C., and Others. *Sexual Behavior in the Human Female.* Philadelphia: W. B. Saunders Co., 1953. xxx+842 p.

KINSEY, A. C., and Others. *Sexual Behavior in the Human Male.* Philadelphia: W. B. Saunders Co., 1948. xvi+804 p.

KIRKPATRICK, Clifford. *The Family:* As Process and Institution. New York: Ronald Press, 1955. viii+651 p.

KOESTER, George A. "A Study of the Diagnostic Process." *Educational and Psychological Measurement* 14: 473-86; Autumn 1954.

KOGAN, Leonard S. "The Electrical Recording of Social Casework Interviews." *Social Casework* 31: 371-78; November 1950.

KOGAN, Leonard S., and BROWN, B. H. "A Two-Year Study of Case Record Uses." *Social Casework* 35: 252-57; June 1954.

KOGAN, Leonard S., and Others. "Validation of Caseworker Impressions by Verbatim Interview Recording." *Social Casework* 32: 376-81; November 1951.

KOMAROVSKY, Mirra. "Continuities in Family Research: A Case Study." *American Journal of Sociology* 62: 42-47; July 1956.

KORNBERG, Leonard. *A Class for Disturbed Children:* A Case Study and Its Meaning for Education. New York: Teachers College, Columbia University, 1955. viii+157 p.

KORNER, Anneliese F. "Theoretical Considerations Concerning the Scope and Limitations of Projective Techniques." *Journal of Abnormal and Social Psychology* 45: 619-27; October 1950.

KOSTLAN, Albert. "A Method for the Empirical Study of Psychodiagnosis." *Journal of Consulting Pyschology* 18: 83-88; April 1954.

KRAMER, Edith. *Art Therapy in a Children's Community.* Springfield, Ill.: Charles C Thomas, 1958. xvii+238 p.

KRAMISH, A. A. "Problems in the Non-Directive Therapist's Reflection of Feeling." *Journal of Social Psychology* 39: 201-9; May 1954.

KRUG, Othilda. "The Dynamic Use of the Ego Functions in Casework Practice." *Social Casework* 36: 443-50; December 1955.

KUBIE, Lawrence S. "Research in Psychiatry Is Starving to Death." *Science* 116: 239-43; September 5, 1952.

KVARACEUS, William C. "What the Elmtowners Think of the Elmtown Study." *School Review* 60: 352-57; September 1952.

LANGFELD, Herbert S., and Others, Editors. *A History of Psychology in Autobiography.* Vol. 4. Worcester, Mass.: Clark University Press, 1952. xii+356 p.

LANTZ, Herman R. *People of Coal Town.* New York: Columbia University Press, 1958. 310 p.

LEARY, Timothy. *Interpersonal Diagnosis of Personality.* New York: Ronald Press, 1957. xix+518 p.

LEBO, Dell. "Age and Suitability for Nondirective Play Therapy." *Journal of Genetic Psychology* 89: 231-38; December 1956.

LEBO, Dell. "A Formula for Selecting Toys for Non-Directive Play Therapy." *Journal of Genetic Psychology* 92: 23-34; March 1958.

LEBO, Dell. "The Present Status of Research on Nondirective Play Therapy." *Journal of Consulting Psychology* 17: 177-83; June 1953.

LEE, A. M. "The Clinical Study of Society." *American Sociological Review* 20: 648-53; December 1955.

LEE, A. M. "Responsibilities in Sociological Research." *Sociology and Social Research* 37: 367-74; July-August 1953. (Ethics of sociology.)

LEFEVER, D. Welty, and Others. "Guidance and Counseling." *Review of Educational Research* 21: 71-167; April 1951.

LEMERT, Edwin M. "Is There a Natural History of Social Problems?" *American Sociological Review* 16: 217-23; April 1951.

LEWIS, Hylan. *Blackways of Kent.* Field Studies in the Modern Culture of the South. Vol. 2. Chapel Hill: University of North Carolina Press, 1955. xxiv+337 p.

LEWIS, Oscar. *Life in a Mexican Village:* Tepoztlan Restudied. Urbana: University of Illinois Press, 1951. xxvii+512 p.

LEWIS, Oscar. "Urbanization without Breakdown: A Case Study." *Scientific Monthly* 75: 31-41; July 1952.

LIPPMAN, Hyman S. *Treatment of the Child in Emotional Conflict.* New York: McGraw-Hill Book Co., 1956. x+298 p.

LLOYD, A. Katharine. "Helping a Child Adapt to Stress: The Use of Ego Psychology in Casework." *Social Service Review* 31: 11-21; March 1957.

LOKSHIN, Helen. "Casework Counseling with the Older Client." *Social Casework* 36: 257-63; June 1955.

LOMBARD, George F. F. *Behavior in a Selling Group:* A Case Study of Interpersonal Relations in a Department Store. Boston: Harvard University, 1955. xx+259 p.

LORAND, Sandor. *Clinical Studies in Psychoanalysis.* New York: International Universities Press, 1951. 272 p.

LOUTTIT, C. M., and Others. *Clinical Psychology of Exceptional Children.* Third Edition. New York: Harper & Brothers, 1957. xii+573 p.

LUCHINS, Abraham S. "A Functional Approach to Clinical Psychology." *Journal of Genetic Psychology* 89: 153-63; December 1956.

LUCHINS, Abraham S. "Patients View the Therapist: A Training and Research Device." *Journal of Consulting Psychology* 15: 24-31; February 1951.

LUCHINS, Abraham S. "A Variational Approach to Empathy." *Journal of Social Psychology* 45: 11-18; February 1957.

MAHER, Brendan A. "Clinical Psychology in Britain: A Laboratory for the American Psychologist." *American Psychologist* 12: 147-50; March 1957.

MALMO, Robert B., and Others. "Motor Manifestation of Conflict in Interview: A Case Study." *Journal of Abnormal and Social Psychology* 52: 268-71; March 1956.

MANNELLO, George, Jr. "Student Strike at an Asian University: A Case History." *American Association of University Professors Bulletin* 43: 249-62; June 1957.

MARCUS, Grace F. "The Advance of Social Casework in Its Distinctive Social Usefulness." *Social Casework* 36: 391-98; November 1955.

MARMOR, Judd. "Indications for Psychiatric Therapy or Social Casework." *Social Casework* 36: 60-63; February 1955.

MARRIOTT, McKim, Editor. *Village India:* Studies in the Little Community. Chicago: The University of Chicago Press, 1955. xix+269 p.

MARTIN, John B., Reporter. *My Life in Crime:* The Autobiography of a Professional Criminal. New York: Harper & Brothers, 1952. 279 p.

MARZOLF, S. S. *Psychological Diagnosis and Counseling in the Schools.* New York: Henry Holt and Co., 1956. xiv+401 p.

MASSERMAN, Jules H. "Evolution vs. 'Revolution' in Psychotherapy: A Biodynamic Integration." *Behavioral Science* 2: 89-100; April 1957.

MASSERMAN, Jules H. *Science and Psychoanalysis:* Integrative Studies. Vol. 1. New York: Grune and Stratton, 1958. vi+201 p.

MASSERMAN, Jules H., and MORENO, J. L., Editors. *Progress in Psychotherapy:* Anxiety and Therapy. Vol. 2. New York: Grune and Stratton, 1957. viii+264 p.

McCARY, James L., Editor. *Six Approaches to Psychotherapy.* New York: Dryden Press, 1955. vii+402 p.

McCORD, Joan, and McCORD, William. *Psychotherapy and Delinquency.* New York: Grune and Stratton, 1956. x+230 p. (Evaluation of therapy with seriously disturbed delinquents.)

McCORMICK, Mary J. *Diagnostic Casework in the Thomistic Pattern.* New York: Columbia University Press, 1954. xiv+239 p.

McCORMICK, Mary J. "The Old and the New in Casework." *Social Casework* 35: 432-38; December 1954.

MEEHL, Paul E. *Clinical Versus Statistical Prediction:* A Theoretical Analysis and a Review of the Evidence. Minneapolis: University of Minnesota Press, 1954. x+149 p.

MEEHL, Paul E., and Others. "Symposium on Clinical and Statistical Prediction." *Journal of Counseling Psychology* 3: 163-73; Fall 1956.

MEIER, Elizabeth G. "Interrelationship of Social Causes and Casework in Child Welfare." *Social Casework* 31: 105-12; March 1950.

MENNINGER, William C. "The Relationship of Clinical Psychology and Psychiatry." *American Psychologist* 5: 3-15; January 1950.

MENSH, Ivan U. "Statistical Techniques in Present-Day Psychodiagnostics." *Psychological Bulletin* 47: 475-92; November 1950.

MESSINGER, Sheldon L. "Organizational Transformation: A Case Study of a Declining Social Movement." *American Sociological Review* 20: 3-10; February 1955.

MIDELFORT, C. F. *The Family in Psychotherapy.* New York: McGraw-Hill Book Co., 1957. 203 p.

MILES, Arthur P. *American Social Work Theory:* A Critique and a Proposal. New York: Harper & Brothers, 1954. 246 p.

MILLARD, Cecil V. *Case Inventory for the Study of Child Development.* Minneapolis: Burgess Publishing Co., 1950. 29 p.

MILLARD, Cecil V. *School and Child:* A Case History. East Lansing: Michigan State College Press, 1954. xvi+221 p.

MILLARD, Cecil V., and ROTHNEY, J. W. M. *The Elementary School Child:* A Book of Cases. New York: Dryden Press, 1957. xii+660 p.

MILLER, Lebern N. "Using Law Case Materials to Teach Ethical Behavior." *Journal of Educational Research* 51: 349-54; January 1958.

MINTON, Eunice. "The Effect of the Setting on Casework Practice in Public Assistance." *Social Casework* 37: 61-68; February 1956.

MITCHELL, Lucy S. *Two Lives:* The Story of Wesley Clair Mitchell and Myself. New York: Simon and Schuster, 1953. 575 p. (A personal and professional autobiography.)

MOORE, W. L. *The Mind in Chains:* The Autobiography of a Schizophrenic. New York: Exposition Press, 1955. 315 p.

MORENO, J. L., and ENNEIS, J. M. *Hypnodrama and Psychodrama.* New York: Beacon House, 1950. 56 p.

MORRIS, Cherry, Editor. *Social Case-work in Great Britain.* London: Faber and Faber, 1950. 223 p.

MOSHER, Arthur T. *Case Study of the Agricultural Program of Acar in Brazil.* Washington: National Planning Association (Technical Cooperation in Latin America), 1955. xiv+63 p.

MOUSTAKAS, Clark E. *Children in Play Therapy:* A Key to Understanding Normal and Disturbed Emotions. New York: McGraw-Hill Book Co., 1953. ix+218 p.

MOWRER, O. H., and Others. *Psychotherapy:* Theory and Research. New York: Ronald Press, 1953. xviii+700 p.

MUDD, Emily H., and Others, Editors. *Marriage Counseling:* A Casebook. New York: Association Press, 1958. 488 p.

MURPHY, Lois B., and Others. *Personality in Young Children.* 2 vols. New

York: Basic Books, 1956. (Volume 2 is a detailed study of "Colin, A Normal Child," from his second through his fifth year.)

NATENBERG, Maurice. *The Case History of Sigmund Freud:* A Psychobiography. Chicago: Regent House, 1955. 245 p.

NORBECK, Edward. *Takashima:* A Japanese Fishing Community. Salt Lake City: University of Utah Press, 1954. xi+232 p.

NUNNALLY, Jum C. "A Systematic Approach to the Construction of Hypotheses About the Process of Psychotherapy." *Journal of Consulting Psychology* 19: 17-20; February 1955.

ORMSBY, Ralph. "Group Psychiatric Consultation in a Family Casework Agency." *Social Casework* 31: 361-65; November 1950.

PARKER, Clyde A. "Empathy." *Personnel and Guidance Journal* 34: 89-93; October 1955.

PARLOFF, Morris B. "Some Factors Affecting the Quality of Therapeutic Relationships." *Journal of Abnormal and Social Psychology* 52: 5-10; January 1956.

PASCAL, G. R., and ZAX, Melvin. "Psychotherapeutics: Success or Failure." *Journal of Consulting Psychology* 20: 325-31; October 1956.

PASCAL, G. R., and Others. "Prognostic Criteria in the Case Histories of Hospitalized Mental Patients." *Journal of Consulting Psychology* 17: 163-71; June 1953.

PAUL, Benjamin D., Editor, and MILLER, Walter B. *Health, Culture, and Community:* Case Studies of Public Reactions to Health Programs. New York: Russell Sage Foundation, 1955. viii+493 p.

PECK, Harris B., and BELLSMITH, Virginia. *Treatment of the Delinquent Adolescent:* Group and Individual Therapy with Parent and Child. New York: Family Service Association of America, 1954. 147 p.

PENNINGTON, L. A., and BERG, Irwin A. *An Introduction to Clinical Psychology.* Second Edition. New York: Ronald Press, 1954. viii+709 p.

PEPINSKY, Harold B., and PEPINSKY, Pauline N. *Counseling Theory and Practice.* New York: Ronald Press, 1954. viii+307 p.

PERLMAN, Helen H. "The Basic Structure of the Case-Work Process." *Social Service Review* 27: 308-15; September 1953.

PERLMAN, Helen H. "The Caseworker's Use of Collateral Information." *Social Casework* 32: 325-33; October 1951.

PERLMAN, Helen H. "The Lecture as a Method in Teaching Case Work." *Social Service Review* 25: 19-32; March 1951.

PERLMAN, Helen H. *Social Casework:* A Problem-solving Process. Chicago: The University of Chicago Press, 1957. xv+268 p.

PERLMAN, Helen H. "Teaching Case Work by the Discussion Method." *Social Service Review* 24: 334-46; September 1950.

PERRY, Stewart E. "Observations on Social Processes in Psychiatric Research." *Behavioral Science* 1: 290-302; October 1956.

PHILLIPS, Ewing L. *Psychotherapy:* A Modern Theory and Practice. Englewood Cliffs, N. J.: Prentice-Hall, 1956. xviii+334 p.

PHILLIPS, Helen U. *Essentials of Social Group Work Skill.* New York: Association Press, 1957. x+180 p.

PIERSON, Donald. *Cruz das Almas:* A Brazilian Village. Washington: Government Printing Office, 1951. viii+226 p.

POLLAK, Otto. "Cultural Dynamics in Casework." *Social Casework* 34: 279-84; July 1953.

POLLAK, Otto. "Relationships Between Social Science and Child Guidance Practice." *American Sociological Review* 16: 61-67; February 1951.

POLLAK, Otto, and Others. *Social Science and Psychotherapy for Children.* New York: Russell Sage Foundation, 1952. 242 p.

PORTER, E. H., Jr. *An Introduction to Therapeutic Counseling.* Boston: Houghton Mifflin Co., 1950. xi+223 p. (Extracts from cases serve as a test for counselors.)

PORTER, E. H., Jr. "On the Nature of Psychotherapeutic Interpretation." *Journal of Consulting Psychology* 16: 343-46; October 1952.

POTTER, Muriel. "The Use of Limits in Reading Therapy." *Journal of Consulting Psychology* 14: 250-55; August 1950.

POWDERMAKER, Florence B., and FRANK, Jerome D. *Group Psychotherapy:* Studies in Methodology of Research and Therapy. Cambridge: Harvard University Press, 1953. xv+615 p. (Report of a group psychotherapy research project of the U. S. Veterans Administration.)

PRESTON, Malcolm G., and Others. "An Experimental Study of a Method for Abstracting the Content of Social Case Records." *Journal of Abnormal and Social Psychology* 45: 628-46; October 1950.

PRESTON, Malcolm G., MUDD, Emily H., and FROSCHER, Hazel B. "Factors Affecting Movement in Casework." *Social Casework* 34: 103-11; March 1953.

QUEEN, Stuart A., and ADAMS, John B. *The Family in Various Cultures:* A Survey of Eleven Family Systems in Eleven Cultural and Historical Settings throughout the World. Philadelphia: J. B. Lippincott Co., 1952. vii+280 p.

RAIMY, Victor C., Editor. *Training in Clinical Psychology.* New York: Prentice-Hall, 1950. xix+253 p.

RALL, Mary E. "The Casework Process in Work with the Child and the Family in the Child's Own Home." *Social Service Review* 28: 270-78; September 1954.

RALL, Mary E. "The Effective Use of Case-Work Principles in the Family Agency." *Social Service Review* 24: 327-33; September 1950.

RASEY, Marie I. *It Takes Time:* An Autobiography of the Teaching Profession. New York: Harper & Brothers, 1953. x+204 p. (Case history of an evolving philosophy and psychology of teaching.)

RECKLESS, Walter C. "Juvenile Delinquency," *Encyclopedia of Educational Research.* Second Edition. Edited by Walter S. Monroe. New York: The Macmillan Co., 1950. p. 643-47.

Red Dust: Autobiographies of Chinese Communists. As Told to Nym Wales. Stanford, Calif.: Stanford University Press, 1952. 238 p.

REDFIELD, Robert. "The Natural History of the Folk Society." *Social Forces* 31: 224-28; March 1953.

REDFIELD, Robert. *A Village That Chose Progress:* Chan Kom Revisited. Chicago: The University of Chicago Press, 1950. xiv+187 p.

REGENSBURG, Jeanette. "Application of Psychoanalytic Concepts to Casework Treatment of Marital Problems." *Social Casework* 35: 424-32; December 1954.

REIZEN, Paul. "Family Casework with Boys under Court Jurisdiction." *Social Casework* 36: 208-14; May 1955.

"Research Design in Clinical Psychology; Symposium." *Journal of Clinical Psychology* 8: 3-98; January 1952.

REVIE, Virgil A. "The Effect of Psychological Case Work on the Teacher's Concept of the Pupil." *Journal of Counseling Psychology* 3: 125-29; Summer 1956.

RIPPLE, Lilian. "Motivation, Capacity, and Opportunity as Related to the Use of Casework Service: Theoretical Base and Plan of Study." *Social Service Review* 29: 172-93; June 1955.

ROE, Anne. *A Psychological Study of Eminent Biologists.* Washington: American Psychological Association, 1951. iii+68 p. (Reports data from the life histories and from three psychological tests of twenty eminent research biologists.)

ROGERS, Carl R. *Client-Centered Therapy.* Boston: Houghton Mifflin Co., 1951. xii+560 p.

ROGERS, Carl R. "The Interest in the Practice of Psychotherapy." *American Psychologist* 8: 48-50; January 1953.

ROGERS, Carl R. "The Necessary and Sufficient Conditions of Therapeutic Personality Change." *Journal of Consulting Psychology* 21: 95-103; April 1957.

ROGERS, Carl R., and DYMOND, Rosalind F., Editors. *Psychotherapy and Personality Change.* Co-ordinated Research Studies in the Client-Centered Approach. Chicago: The University of Chicago Press, 1954. x+446 p.

RONKEN, Harriet O., and LAWRENCE, Paul R. *Administering Changes:* A Case Study of Human Relations in a Factory. Boston: Harvard University, 1952. xvii+324 p.

ROSEN, Elizabeth. *Dance in Psychotherapy.* New York: Bureau of Publications, Teachers College, Columbia University, 1957. xx+178 p.

ROSENTHAL, Leslie. "Group Psychotherapy in a Child Guidance Clinic." *Social Casework* 32: 337-42; October 1951.

ROSS, M. G. *Case Histories in Community Organization.* New York: Harper & Brothers, 1958. ix+259 p.

RUBENSTEIN, Eli A., and LORR, Maurice, Editors. *Survey of Clinical Practice in Psychology.* New York: International Universities Press, 1954. xvii+363 p.

SARASON, Seymour B. *The Clinical Interaction.* New York: Harper & Brothers, 1954. x+425 p.

SARGANT, William. *Battle for the Mind:* How Evangelists, Psychiatrists, Politicians and Medicine Men Can Change Your Beliefs and Behavior. Garden City, N. Y.: Doubleday & Co., 1957. 263 p.

SARGENT, Cyril G., and BELISLE, Eugene L. *Educational Administration:* Cases and Concepts. Boston: Houghton Mifflin Co., 1955. xiii+474 p.

SCHARY, Dore. *Case History of a Movie.* New York: Random House, 1950. xix+242 p.

SCHRAGER, Jules. "Child Care Staff Recording in a Treatment Institution." *Social Casework* 36: 74-81; February 1955.

SEELEY, John R., SIM, R. Alexander, and LOOSLEY, Elizabeth W. *Crestwood Heights:* A Study of the Culture of Suburban Life. New York: Basic Books, 1956. xv+505 p.

SEELEY, John R., and Others. *Community Chest:* A Case Study in Philanthropy. Toronto: University of Toronto Press, 1957. 593 p.

SELBY, Lola G. "Supportive Treatment: The Development of a Concept and a Helping Method." *Social Service Review* 30: 400-14; December 1956.

SERVICE, Elman R., and SERVICE, Helen S. *Tobati:* Paraguayan Town. Chicago: The University of Chicago Press, 1954. xxix+337 p.

SEWARD, Georgene. *Psychotherapy and Culture Conflict.* With Case Studies by Judd Marmor. New York: Ronald Press, 1956. ix+299 p.

SEWARD, Georgene, Editor. *Clinical Studies in Culture Conflict.* New York: Ronald Press, 1958. 587 p.

SHAFFER, G. Wilson, and LAZARUS, Richard S. *Fundamental Concepts in Clinical Psychology.* New York: McGraw-Hill Book Co., 1952. 540 p.

SHAFFER, L. F., and SHOBEN, E. J., Jr. *The Psychology of Adjustment.* Second Edition. Boston: Houghton Mifflin Co., 1956. xxi+672 p.

SHERMAN, Murray H. "Psychotherapy with Adolescent Girls in a Court Clinic." *Journal of Genetic Psychology* 92: 3-9; March 1958.

SHOBEN, E. J. "The College, Psychological Clinics, and Psychological Knowledge." *Journal of Counseling Psychology* 3: 200-5; Fall 1956.

SHOBEN, E. J., and Others. "Behavior Theories and a Counseling Case: A Symposium." *Journal of Counseling Psychology* 3: 107-24; Summer 1956.

SHRYOCK, Henry S., Jr. "The Natural History of Standard Metropolitan Areas." *American Journal of Sociology* 63: 163-70; September 1957.

SHYNE, Ann W. "Telephone Interviews in Casework." *Social Casework* 35: 342-47; October 1954.

SHYNE, Ann W. "What Research Tells Us About Short-Term Cases in Family Agencies." *Social Casework* 38: 223-31; May 1957.

SILLS, David L. *The Volunteers—Means and Ends in a National Organization.* Glencoe, Ill.: Free Press, 1958. xx+320 p. (A case study.)

SIPORIN, Max. "Family-Centered Casework in a Psychiatric Setting." *Social Casework* 37: 167-74; April 1956.

SKINNER, B. F. "A Case History in Scientific Method." *American Psychologist* 11: 221-33; May 1956.

SLAVSON, S. R. *Analytic Group Psychotherapy with Children, Adolescents, and Adults.* New York: Columbia University Press, 1950. ix+275 p.

SLAVSON, S. R. *Child Psychotherapy.* New York: Columbia University Press, 1952. 332 p.

SLAVSON, S. R. *An Introduction to Group Therapy.* New York: International Universities Press, 1953. xvi+352 p.

SLAVSON, S. R., Editor. *The Fields of Group Psychotherapy.* New York: International Universities Press, 1956. xiii+338 p.

SLOTKIN, J. S. *The Peyote Religion:* A Study in Indian-White Relations. Glencoe, Ill.: Free Press, 1956. vii+195 p. (Ethnohistorical case study using sociological approach.)

SMITH, Harvey L. "Psychiatry: A Social Institution in Process." *Social Forces* 33: 310-16; May 1955.

SMITH, John C. "Casework on the Campus." *Social Casework* 33: 423-29; December 1952.

SMITH, Raymond T. *The Negro Family in British Guiana:* Family Structure and Social Status in the Villages. New York: Humanities Press, 1956. xvi+282 p.

SONNE, Thomas R., and GOLDMAN, Leo. "Preferences of Authoritarian and Equalitarian Personalities for Client-Centered and Eclectic Counseling." *Journal of Counseling Psychology* 4: 129-35; Summer 1957.

SORENSON, Roy, and DIMOCK, Hedley S. *Designing Education in Values:* A Case Study in Institutional Change. New York: Association Press, 1955. xiv+365 p. (Change in San Francisco Y.M.C.A.)

SPAULDING, Frank E. *One School Administrator's Philosophy:* Its Development. New York: Exposition Press, 1952. 352 p.

SPICER, Edward H., Editor. *Human Problems in Technological Change:* A Casebook. New York: Russell Sage Foundation, 1952. 301 p.

STACY, Chalmers L., and DeMARTINO, Manfred F., Editors. *Counseling and Psychotherapy with the Mentally Retarded:* A Book of Readings. Glencoe, Ill.: Free Press, 1957. 478 p.

STANDAL, Stanley W., and VAN DER VEEN, Ferdinand. "Length of Therapy in Relation to Counselor Estimates of Personal Integration and Other Case Variables." *Journal of Consulting Psychology* 21: 1-9; February 1957.

STEIN, Harold. "Preparation of Case Studies: The Problem of Abundance." *American Political Science Review* 45: 479-87; June 1951.

STEIN, Harold, Editor. *Public Administration and Policy Development:* A Case Book. New York: Harcourt, Brace and Co., 1952. 860 p. (Applied to the area of public administration, including the executive branches of the federal, state, and local governments; for example, a case study of the Office of Education Library.)

STEWART, David A. *Preface to Empathy.* New York: Philosophical Library, 1956. 157 p.

STONE, G. Raymond. "Prediction in Clinical Psychology and Behavior Theory." *Psychological Review* 59: 95-97; March 1952.

STRANG, RUTH. *Group Work in Education.* New York: Harper & Brothers, 1958. x+322 p.

STRUPP, Hans H. "An Objective Comparison of Rogerian and Psychoanalytic Techniques." *Journal of Consulting Psychology* 19: 1-7; February 1955.

STRUPP, Hans H. "Psychotherapeutic Technique, Professional Affiliation, and Experience Level." *Journal of Consulting Psychology* 19: 97-102; April 1955.

STRUPP, Hans H. "The Psychotherapist's Contribution to the Treatment Process." *Behavioral Science* 3: 34-67; January 1958.

STUBBINS, Joseph, and NAPOLI, Peter J. "Counseling with the Neuropsychiatric

Patient: A Case Study." *Journal of Counseling Psychology* 3: 185-92; Fall 1956.

SULLIVAN, Harry S. *Clinical Studies in Psychiatry*. Edited by Helen S. Perry, Mary L. Gawel, and Martha Gibbon. New York: W. W. Norton and Co., 1956. 386 p.

SULLIVAN, Harry S. *The Psychiatric Interview*. New York: W. W. Norton and Co., 1954. 246 p.

SYMONDS, P. M. *Dynamics of Psychotherapy:* Principles. Vol. I. New York: Grune and Stratton, 1956. 224 p.

SYMONDS, P. M. *Dynamics of Psychotherapy:* The Psychology of Personality Change. Vol. II: Process. New York: Grune and Stratton, 1957. xlv+175-398 p.

SYMONDS, P. M. *Dynamics of Psychotherapy:* The Psychology of Personality Change. Vol. III: Procedures. New York: Grune and Stratton, 1958. xxxv+399-607 (209) p.

SYMONDS, P. M., and HESSEL, Martha G. "Development and Educational Significance of Projective Technics in Personality Measurement." *Review of Educational Research* 20: 51-62; February 1950.

TABA, Hilda, BRADY, Elizabeth H., and ROBINSON, John T. *Elementary Curriculum in Intergroup Relations:* Case Studies in Instruction. Washington: American Council on Education, 1950. xiii+248 p.

TAFT, Jessie. "A Conception of the Growth Process Underlying Social Casework Practice." *Social Casework* 31: 311-18; October 1950.

TALBERT, Robert H. *Cowtown—Metropolis:* Case Study of a City's Growth and Structure. Fort Worth: Texas Christian University, 1956. xvii+274 p.

TATE, H. Clay. *Building a Better Home Town:* A Program of Community Self-Analysis and Self-Help. New York: Harper & Brothers, 1954. xvi+236 p.

TAYLOR, Alice L. "Case Recording: An Administrative Responsibility." *Social Casework* 34: 240-46; June 1953.

TAYLOR, James W. "Relationship of Success and Length in Psychotherapy." *Journal of Consulting Psychology* 20: 332; October 1956.

TAYLOR, Robert K. "The Social Control Function in Casework." *Social Casework* 39: 17-21; January 1958.

"Technical Recommendations for Psychological Tests and Diagnostic Techniques." Supplement to the *Psychological Bulletin* 51: 1-38; March 1954.

THOMAS, Dorothy V. "The Relationship between Diagnostic Service and Short-Contact Cases." *Social Casework* 32: 74-81; February 1951.

THOMPSON, Albert S., SUPER, Donald E., and NAPOLI, Peter J. "Developing a VA Counseling Psychology Training Program: A Case History of University-Hospital Cooperation." *American Psychologist* 10: 283-88; July 1955.

THOMPSON, Clare W., and BRADWAY, K. J. "Teaching of Psychotherapy through Content-Free Interviews." *Journal of Consulting Psychology* 14: 321-23; August 1950.

THOMPSON, Laura. *Culture in Crisis:* A Study of the Hopi Indians. New York: Harper & Brothers, 1950. xxiv+221 p.

THORNE, F. C. "An Evaluation of Eclectically Oriented Psychotherapy." *Journal of Consulting Psychology* 21: 459-64; December 1957.

THORNE, F. C. "Rules of Evidence in the Evaluation of the Effects of Psychotherapy." *Journal of Clinical Psychology* 8: 38-41; January 1952.

TOWLE, Charlotte. "Client-Centered Case Work." *Social Service Review* 24: 451-58; December 1950.

TOWLE, Charlotte. "The Contribution of Education for Social Casework to Practice." *Social Casework* 31: 318-26; October 1950.

TOWLE, Charlotte. "Selection and Arrangement of Case Material for Orderly Progression in Learning." *Social Service Review* 27: 27-54; March 1953.

TOWNSEND, Gladys E. "Short-Term Casework with Clients Under Stress." *Social Casework* 34: 392-98; November 1953.

TUMIN, Melvin M. *Caste in a Peasant Society:* A Case Study in the Dynamics of Caste. Princeton: Princeton University Press, 1952. 300 p.

VAN PRAAG, Philip H. "Basic Concepts of Social Work." *Social Service Review* 31: 183-91; June 1957.

VIRTUE, Maxine B. *Family Cases in Court:* A Group of Four Court Studies Dealing with Judicial Administration. Durham, N. C.: Duke University Press, 1956. xxxvii+291 p.

VOGT, Evon Z. *Modern Homesteaders:* The Life of a Twentieth Century Frontier Community. Cambridge: Harvard University Press, 1955. xi+232 p.

WAGLEY, Charles. *Amazon Town:* A Study of Man in the Tropics. New York: The Macmillan Co., 1953. xi+305 p.

WALKER, Charles R. *Steeltown:* An Industrial Case History of the Conflict between Progress and Security. New York: Harper & Brothers, 1950. xv+284 p. (Case study of an industrial town, with relation to a decision of the steel company to abandon the town and the plant; one of a series of studies on decision-making.)

WALKER, Charles R. *Toward the Automatic Factory:* A Case Study of Men and Machines. New Haven: Yale University Press, 1957. xxii+232 p.

WALLEN, Richard W. *Clinical Psychology:* The Study of Persons. New York: McGraw-Hill Book Co., 1956. 400 p.

WARREN, James V. *Methods in Medical Research.* Volume 7. Chicago: Educational Year Book, 1958. 250 p.

WARTERS, Jane. *Techniques of Counseling.* New York: McGraw-Hill Book Co., 1954. viii+384 p. (A number of chapters on observational, descriptive-survey, and case techniques.)

WATSON, Robert I. "A Brief History of Clinical Psychology." *Psychological Bulletin* 50: 321-46; September 1953.

WATSON, Robert I. *The Clinical Method in Psychology.* New York: Harper & Brothers, 1951. xii+779 p.

WATSON, Robert I. "Research Design and Methodology in Evaluating the Results of Psychotherapy." *Journal of Clinical Psychology* 8: 29-33; January 1952.

WATSON, Robert I., and MENSH, Ivan N. "The Evaluation of the Effects of Psychotherapy: I, Sources of Material." *Journal of Psychology* 32: 259-73; October 1951.

WATSON, Robert I., and MENSH, Ivan N. "The Evaluation of the Effects of Psychotherapy: II, A Case Study." *Journal of Psychology* 32: 275-91; October 1951.

WATSON, Robert I., MENSH, Ivan N., and GILDEA, Edwin F. "The Evaluation of the Effects of Psychotherapy: III, Research Design." *Journal of Psychology* 32: 293-308; October 1951.

WATTENBERG, William W., and REDL, Fritz. "Mental Hygiene," *Encyclopedia of Educational Research.* Second Edition. Edited by Walter S. Monroe. New York: The Macmillan Co., 1950. p. 733-45.

WEINBERG, Henry, and HIRE, A. W. *Casebook in Abnormal Psychology.* New York: Alfred A. Knopf, 1956. 320 p.

WERTHEIMER, Rita, and McKINNEY, Fred. "A Case History Blank as a Projective Technique." *Journal of Consulting Psychology* 16: 49-60; February 1952.

WHITAKER, Carl A., and MALONE, Thomas P. *The Roots of Psychotherapy.* Philadelphia: Blakiston Co., 1953. (Available at McGraw-Hill Book Co.) xvii+236 p.

WHITE, Robert W. *The Abnormal Personality.* Second Edition. New York: Ronald Press, 1956. 644 p. (Illustrated by case histories.)

WHITE, Robert W. *Lives in Progress:* A Study of the Natural Growth of Personality. New York: Dryden Press, 1952. 376 p. (Presents, interprets, and compares the lives, case studies, of three normal people.)

WIENER, Norbert. *Ex-Prodigy:* My Childhood and Youth. New York: Simon and Schuster, 1953. xii+309 p.

WILLIAMS, Edgar G., and MEE, John G. *Cases and Problems in Personnel and Industrial Relations.* New York: Ronald Press, 1955. 204 p.

WILLIAMS, W. M. *Gosforth:* The Sociology of an English Village. Glencoe, Ill.: Free Press, 1956. x+246 p.

WILLIAMSON, E. G., SARBIN, Theodore R., and Others. "Student Personnel Work," *Encyclopedia of Educational Research.* Second Edition. Edited by Walter S. Monroe. New York: The Macmillan Co., 1950. p. 1290-1362.

WILTSE, Kermit T. "Social Casework and Public Assistance." *Social Service Review* 32: 41-50; March 1958.

WINDLE, Charles. "Psychological Tests in Psycho-Pathological Prognosis." *Psychological Bulletin* 49: 451-82; September 1952.

WOLBERG, L. R. *Technique of Psychotherapy.* New York: Grune and Stratton, 1954. xiv+869 p.

WOLFF, Werner, Editor. *Projective and Expressive Methods of Personality Investigation.* New York: Grune and Stratton, 1950. 76 p.

WOLFF, Werner. *Success in Psychotherapy.* New York: Grune and Stratton, 1952. 196 p.

Woman at Work: The Autobiography of Mary Anderson as Told to Mary N. Winslow. Minneapolis: University of Minnesota Press, 1951. 266 p.

WOOD, Arthur E. *Hamtramck Then and Now:* A Sociological Study of a Polish-American Community. New York: Bookman Associates, 1955. 253 p.

WOOD, Austin B. "Transference in Client Centered Therapy and in Psychoanalysis." *Journal of Consulting Psychology* 15: 72-75; February 1951.

WOODWARD, C. Vann. *The Strange Career of Jim Crow.* New York: Oxford University Press, 1955. xi+155 p.

WOOLF, Maurice D., and WOOLF, Jeanne A. *Remedial Reading:* Teaching and Treatment. New York: McGraw-Hill Book Co., 1957. viii+424 p. (Includes case reports.)

WYLIE, Laurence. *Village in the Vaucluse.* Cambridge: Harvard University Press, 1957. 345 p.

YARMOLINSKY, Adam, Compiler. *Case Studies in Personnel Security.* Washington: Bureau of National Affairs, 1955. ix+310 p.

YOUNG, Kimball. "Social Psychology and Social Casework." *American Sociological Review* 16: 54-61; February 1951.

YOUNG, Leontine. "Diagnosis as a Creative Process." *Social Casework* 37: 275-80; June 1956.

YOUNG, Pauline V. *Scientific Social Surveys and Research.* Third Edition. Englewood Cliffs, N. J.: Prentice-Hall, 1956. Chapters 10, 15-18.

YOUNG, Pauline V. *Social Treatment in Probation and Delinquency:* Treatise and Casebook for Court Workers, Probation Officers, and Other Child Welfare Workers. Second Edition. New York: McGraw-Hill Book Co., 1952. xxvi+536 p.

ZALEZNIK, Abraham. *Worker Satisfaction and Development:* A Case Study of Work and Social Behavior in a Factory Group. Boston: Harvard University Graduate School of Business Administration, 1956. xv+148 p.

8

Experimental Designs

This chapter on controlled experimentation includes the topics of independent and dependent variables, control of variables, pre-experimental designs, true experimental designs, other special classifications of experimental designs, inference and generalization, training for experimentation, appropriate problems for experimental investigation, role of the teacher in classroom experimentation, relations of experimentation to other research techniques, and instrumentation.

Since the typical reader of this book is a graduate student in his first year or two of study following the bachelor's degree, with only limited training in statistics, measurement, and quantitative methods, this chapter is a descriptive account of controlled experimentation. The statistical and mathematical details of experimental design are treated fully in the references listed in the chapter bibliography. Such concepts are commonly presented in a second-level statistics course. In presenting the several types of experimental design, the limitations of older methods of experimentation (one group, parallel group, and rotation group) and of exhaustive person-for-person matching or pairing have been recognized, these techniques having given way to the newer methods of statistics and experimental design.

CHARACTERISTICS OF CONTROLLED EXPERIMENTATION

Independent and Dependent Variables

Experimentation differs from descriptive-survey methods and from other techniques of investigation, in that the experimenter has some degree of control over the variables involved and the conditions under which the variables are observed. The relationship between socioeconomic status and opinion on some issue can be determined by a survey investigation through appropriate observation (questionnaire, interview, or some other appropriate data-gathering instrument). In this instance the two variables, socioeconomic status and opinion, are fixed, and the investigator has no control over the variables; he does not manipulate or change either socioeconomic status or opinion.[1]

In experimentation the investigator controls (manipulates or changes) certain independent variables and observes the changes that take place in the form of dependent variables. The investigator may wish to note the effect of a film strip or a lecture (an independent variable) on the performance of the subjects, as measured by an appropriate test (a dependent variable). To cite other examples of the simplest form of experimentation, involving an independent variable and at least one dependent variable, a blow (independent or experimental variable) delivered to the patellar tendon of the bended knee causes the leg to straighten (dependent variable or result). An independent or experimental variable (a loud noise producing the condition of being startled) may result in an increase in arterial pulse rate, perspiration, and an increased diameter of the pupils of the subject's eyes (dependent variables or results).[2]

In a well-known experiment,[3] Dr. Jonas Salk tested polio vaccine in 1954, first on animals and then on human beings. It was a large-scale experiment, including children from every part of the United States, especially from areas where there was a high incidence of polio. Three injections of vaccine were given to 440,000 school children, placebo or "dummy" shots were given to 210,000 youngsters as a control group, and no injections at all to approximately 1,180,000 children as a second control group. To achieve maximum similarity of conditions for the experimental and control groups, each bottle of injection material was made to appear exactly alike, with identification by a code number which was known only to the scientists who planned the experiment but not to the doctors who injected the vaccine. Many experts in statistics and experimental design aided in planning the experiment and analyzing the results, including information on age, sex, the area in which the child lived, the kind of health and educational facilities available, and other related data.

[1] Allen L. Edwards, "Experiments: Their Planning and Execution," *Handbook of Social Psychology:* Theory and Method. Vol. 1. Edited by Gardner Lindzey. Cambridge, Mass.: Addison-Wesley Publishing Co., 1954. p. 260–61.

[2] John C. Townsend, *Introduction to Experimental Method:* For Psychology and the Social Sciences. New York: McGraw-Hill Book Co., 1953. p. 52–57.

[3] Philip Goldstein, *How to Do an Experiment.* New York: Harcourt, Brace and Co., 1957. p. 44–46.

Many hundreds and even thousands of other examples of experiments may be found in the references of the chapter bibliography, the *Encyclopedia of Educational Research*, *Review of Educational Research*, *Psychological Abstracts*, and *Annual Review of Psychology*.

Control of Variables

In experimentation the investigator seeks to control variables for three purposes: to isolate the determiners of activity or behavior individually and in combinations; to vary them as magnitudes either singly or in combinations; and to describe quantitatively the extent of their expression and their interacting effects, again, either as single determiners or as combinations of determiners.[4]

The simple and narrow concept of the "rule of the single variable" was formulated at a time in the earlier period of experimentation when it was believed that all variables (independent) must be held constant except one, with a "one-to-one" correspondence between a particular cause and a specific effect, as when one end of a lever is pushed down, the other end goes up (a predictable amount). Today many specialists in statistics and experimental design regard such a theory of causation as narrow and mechanical, and as characteristic of past investigations in physical science, since the efficient statistical methods and experimental designs now available make it possible to handle several independent variables in the same design and to have as many dependent variables as may seem necessary.

. . . The seventeenth, eighteenth, and nineteenth centuries formed the period in which physical science learned how to analyze two-variable problems. Thus during that three hundred years, science developed the experimental and analytical techniques for handling problems in which one quantity —say, a gas pressure—depends primarily upon a second quantity—say, the volume of the gas. . . . These two-variable problems are essentially simple in structure, and precisely for the reason that the theories or the experiments related to them need deal with only two quantities, changes in one of which cause changes in the other.[5]

While this simple type of experimental design contributed to progress in the earlier stages of physical science, scientists more recently have gone beyond the simple two-variable problems to attack problems involving a large number of factors, resulting in statements of probability. Certain complex problems of the human and behavioral sciences do not lend

[4] Clarence W. Brown and Edwin E. Ghiselli, *Scientific Method in Psychology*. New York: McGraw-Hill Book Co., 1955. p. 76.
[5] Quoted from Warren Weaver, Editor, *The Scientists Speak*. New York: Boni and Gaer, 1947. p. 1, 2.

themselves to either the ordinary experiment or the probability approach, and await solution through some appropriate combination of statistical and experimental methods.

Factors Requiring Control

Among the factors, variables, or determiners of behavior requiring control[6] in psychological and educational investigations are the following:

Schooling: academic incentives, level of success in different areas of subjects, amount of training in different areas, curriculum likes and dislikes, speed and accuracy of work in different fields or subjects

Skills: sports, hobbies, musical instruments, mechanical; physical handicaps

Maturity: chronological, physiological, psychological, developmental experience in special areas

Culture: foreign language and ideologies, American, regional

Social activities and experiences: likes and dislikes, participation in activities (social, sports, hobbies)

Physiological factors: physiological development, emotional development, general physical well-being, specific physical impairments, susceptibility to particular diseases, level of energy output.

Control Through Physical Manipulation

In certain types of experimentation, particularly in psychology, control of variables may be effected through some form of physical manipulation:[7]

Mechanical means: insulating material for sound-proofing a room, a light-proof room, or a tachistoscope for exposing perceptual stimuli

Electrical means: generation of sounds for experiments in hearing, screening out a distracting noise, or use of telechron and other constant speed motors for driving apparatus, controlling relays, and measuring time intervals

Surgical means: surgical removal of glands, such as the thyroid or the adrenals

Pharmacological means: drugs, change of diet, or feeding of gland extracts, as illustrated by use of dilantin in the treatment of epilepsy.

Control Through Selection

Control of variables through selection[8] enables the experimenter to achieve results not possible through the method of physical manipulation of the determining variables.

---

[6] Clarence W. Brown and Edwin E. Ghiselli, *op. cit.*, p. 80–82.
[7] *Ibid.*, p. 82–83.
John C. Townsend, *op. cit.*, p. 64–67.
[8] Clarence W. Brown and Edwin E. Ghiselli, *op cit.*, p. 84–85.

Selection of materials: for example, in studying the relation between the amount of material to be learned and the time required for learning, to provide (select) a sufficiently large number of units of material which are comparable in terms of the ease of learning. Any difference in the difficulty of the material would introduce a spurious factor which might affect the speed of learning.

Selection of subjects: to consider such factors as experience, age, ability, interest, attitude.

Selection of data: as illustrated by such primary sources as the records of public institutions, collections of vital statistics, government census reports, and certain types of records for institutions where the behavior of the subjects could not be subjected to experimental control (as in a reform school or a state prison).

Control over Intraprocedural Factors

In psychological and educational experimentation, determinant variable factors (intraprocedural factors) sometimes are present within the experimental procedures themselves. Certain techniques of control over potentially disturbing intraprocedural factors,[9] with examples of physical-response factors, are as follows:

1. Equal exposure of the subject to the experimental conditions: equal time to work; or time required to complete the task and the nature and number of errors committed

2. Minimizing the contribution of the spatial arrangement of procedural factors: spatial relation of the apparatus to the subject, or the direction of the adjustive movement (right-left or left-right)

3. Minimizing the contribution of temporal factors within an experimental sitting: time intervals between trials in most conditioning experiments of a few seconds, and time intervals of a number of hours in some maze experiments

4. Minimizing the contribution of factors arising from the order of the experimental conditions: counterbalancing of the temporal order of conditions in experiments in memory and in work involving carrying forward practice or fatigue effects from one gradation or condition to another

5. Counterbalancing of the order of experimental conditions through their random assignment to subjects: similar to counterbalancing experimental conditions in time.

The importance of randomization may be illustrated simply. If the problem is to divide 30 pupils in a class into a control group of 15 and an experimental group of the same size, with 5 seats to a row, the experimenter might consider taking all pupils in the first three rows for one

[9] *Ibid.*, p. 280–86.

group and all pupils in the last three rows for the other group. However, if girls commonly sit near the front of the room and boys near the rear, possible sex interests and achievements in arithmetic might bias the experiment from the beginning.

Another procedure would be to place the 30 names in a hat or bowl, each on a separate slip, shuffle them thoroughly, and then draw out 15 names. Another less desirable plan is to alphabetize the 30 names, and place the odd-numbered pupils in one group and the even-numbered persons in the other group. The best method is to number the pupils from 1 through 30 (or from 0 through 29) and draw 15 numbers within this range from a table of random numbers.[10]

Development of Experimental Designs

Helen Walker summarizes concisely the development of the literature of experimental design during a third of a century:[11]

From Thorndike on, many individual research workers were vividly aware of the danger of bias and took great precautions to keep extraneous factors from influencing the outcome of their work, but many others were not so careful. McCall's *How to Experiment in Education*, published in 1923, was probably the first book dealing explicitly with this important matter and apparently had a tonic effect upon educational research. Before the first issue of the *Review* at least 15 books on research methods in education appeared, most of them showing McCall's influence.[12]

Fisher's *Design of Experiments*, 1935, introduced novel ideas and patterns which made use of the technic of analysis of variance.[13] To the statistician, design means primarily the decision as to what subjects shall be employed, how many, and how distributed over the categories with which a study is concerned. Fisher showed how the design must control the analysis, and startled his readers by the statement, now generally accepted, that an "unfortunate consequence only ensues when a method of diminishing the real errors is adopted, unaccompanied by their elimination in the statistical analysis." This was a blow to research workers who had spent long hours in matching subjects but had not taken account of that matching in their statistical treatment of the data.

The first paper on research designs in the *Review*, by C. C. Peters,[14]

[10] Julian C. Stanley, "Controlled Experimentation in the Classroom." *Journal of Experimental Education* 25: 195–201; March 1957.

[11] Quoted from Helen M. Walker, "Methods of Research," in "Twenty-five Years of Educational Research." *Review of Educational Research* 26: 323–43; June 1956.

[12] W. A. McCall, *How to Experiment in Education*. New York: The Macmillan Co., 1923. 282 p.

[13] R. A. Fisher, *The Design of Experiments*. Sixth Edition. New York: Hafner Publishing Corp., 1951. xv + 244 p.

[14] C. C. Peters and Others, "Research Methods and Designs." *Review of Educational Research* 15: 377–93; December 1945.

appeared in December 1945. A very considerable development took place in the next three years, so that in the 1948 issue Lev was able to discuss randomized blocks, Latin squares, factorial designs, and split-plot designs and to quote 51 studies applying such designs to educational research.[15] In December 1951, a chapter of 15 pages by Norton and Lindquist had as its chief purpose "to draw attention to some of the more serious or more frequently recurring errors that are currently being made in experimental design and analysis in educational research," and commented that "on the whole, the authors have been none too favorably impressed with the general quality of contemporary educational research so far as experimental design and analysis are concerned."[16] In December 1954, there was a separate chapter by Kogan on applications of variance-covariance designs.[17]

The era of exhaustive person-for-person matching appears now to be over. The newer statistical methods at the same time facilitate more efficient use of data, make possible greater economy in design, and require that the statistician shall have a part in the initial planning of a study before the data are gathered.

Stanley's concise summary of the literature on experimental design, appearing during the middle 1950's, supplements Walker's review, indicates the complexity of the concepts, and emphasizes the extensive training needed to understand the rudiments of experimental design.

Many of the contributions to experimental design during the past three years should be incorporated rapidly into statistics textbooks designed for students in education and psychology. Authors of such books need the ability and willingness to translate into simpler but still accurate form relevant material published by mathematical statisticians. Then by studying for at least a year, and preferably longer, under a well-qualified instructor, graduate students may come to understand the rudiments of experimental design. To do less than this and still hope for properly designed experiments is asking for a miracle.[18]

PRE-EXPERIMENTAL DESIGNS[19]

Much research in social science has relied upon the *"one-shot"* case *study*, in which a single individual or group is studied in detail only once,

[15] Joseph Lev, "Research Methods and Designs." *Review of Educational Research* 18: 410–23; December 1948.

[16] Dee W. Norton and Everet F. Lindquist, "Applications of Experimental Design and Analysis." *Review of Educational Research* 21: 350–67; December 1951.

[17] Leonard S. Kogan, "Applications of Variance-Covariance Designs in Educational Research," in "Statistical Methodology in Educational Research." *Review of Educational Research* 24: 439–47; December 1954.

[18] Quoted from Julian C. Stanley, "Research Methods: Experimental Design," in "Methodology of Educational Research." *Review of Educational Research* 27: 449–59; December 1957.

[19] Donald T. Campbell, "Factors Relevant to the Validity of Experiments in Social Settings." *Psychological Bulletin* 54: 297–312; July 1957. This helpful analysis is the basis for the review of pre-experimental and true experimental designs on succeeding pages of this book.

and in which the observations are attributed to exposure to some prior situation. This design does not merit the title of an experiment, since the minimum of useful scientific information involves at least one formal comparison and therefore at least two careful observations.

The *one-group pretest-posttest design* provides for one formal comparison of two observations and is still widely used. In this design, however, four or five categories of extraneous variables may be left uncontrolled and thus become rival explanations of any difference between the two observations or measurements, confounded with the possible effect of the experimental variable or event.

History: During the time span between the two observations or measurements, many events have occurred in addition to the experimental variable or event. Although experimental isolation, through the employment of experimental settings in which all extraneous stimuli are eliminated, may be approximated in physical and biological research, such control is difficult or even impossible in social psychology and in other social sciences.

Maturation: Certain effects are systematic with the passage of time and not, like history, a function of the specific events involved. Between the two observations the subjects may have grown older, hungrier, or tireder, and these conditions may have produced the difference between the two observations or measurements, independently of the experimental variable. While maturation is unlikely to be a source of change in the typical brief experiment in the psychology laboratory, it has been a real problem in research in child development, social psychology, and education.

Testing: The effect of testing itself may explain the difference between the two observations, apart from the effect of the experimental variable. In many instances persons taking a test for the second time make scores systematically different from individuals taking a test for the first time; for example, a second mean for intelligence tests may run as much as 5 I.Q. points higher than the first one. In general, any measurement procedure which makes the subject self-conscious or aware of the fact of the experiment may introduce an effect other than the experimental variable or event; for example, measurement of weight, introduced into an experimental design involving adult American women, probably would stimulate weight reduction (through the mere process of noting weight) apart from any experimental variable involving food or nutrition.

Instrument decay: This variable may be illustrated by the fatiguing of a spring scales. In educational and social psychology, education, and other social fields, fatiguing is an especially acute problem when human beings are part of the measuring apparatus or procedure, as in the case of judges, observers, raters, or coders. The two observations may differ because the raters have become more experienced, more fatigued, better adapted, or informed about the purpose of the experiment. Conditions are especially crude when observers or interviewers or coders are different for the two observations.

Statistical regression: Shifts toward the mean may occur owing to random imperfections of the measuring instrument or random instability within the population, as reflected in the test-retest reliability. In general, regression operates like maturation, in that the effects increase systematically with the time interval between the two observations or measurements. Failure to control this factor results in especially serious mistakes of interpretation in remedial research.

Another pre-experimental design is the *static group comparison*, in which there is a comparison of a group which has experienced the experimental variable with a group which has not, for the purpose of establishing the effect of the variable or event. In this design, there is no means of certifying that the groups were equivalent at some prior time. The prevalence of this design in the social sciences and its weaknesses have been recognized. Any difference between the two observations might have come about through biased selection or recruitment of the persons making up the groups, or they might have differed without the effect of the experimental variable. Exposure to the experimental variable may have been voluntary, and therefore the two groups have an inevitable systematic difference on the factors determining the choice involved, a difference which no amount of matching can remove.

Experimental *mortality* may be confounded with the effect of the experimental variable. Even though the groups may have been equivalent at some prior time, differences between the two observations may result because individuals have dropped out, as illustrated in studies seeking to compare the attitudes of college freshmen and college seniors.

TRUE EXPERIMENTAL DESIGNS[20]

The difficulties of confounded extraneous variables in the pre-experimental designs led psychologists during the first quarter of the twentieth century to search for true experimental designs. The *pretest-*

[20] *Ibid.*

posttest control group design was formed by adding a control group to the one-group pretest-posttest design. This experimental design seeks to control the main effects of history, maturation, testing, instrument decay, regression, selection, and mortality. If the differences between the two observations for the experimental group are due to intervening historical events, then they should also show up in the results for the control group, although there may be certain complications in achieving control. If the respondents operate as groups, with only one experimental session and one control session, then there is no control over the unique internal histories of the groups, possibly involving a chance distracting factor appearing in one or the other group. If only one experimenter is involved, he ordinarily cannot make a simultaneous initial observation or measurement for the two groups and likewise cannot make a second or end measurement of the two groups at the same time. If two experimenters are available, one working with the experimental respondents, and the other with the control subjects, differences between the two experimenters probably introduce extraneous variable factors. Therefore, for a true experiment, the experimental and control groups should be tested and exposed individually or in small subgroups, with sessions of both types temporally and spatially intermixed.

If maturation or testing contributes to a difference between the two observations, this should appear also in the results of the control group. To make sure the design controls for instrument decay, it is necessary to use the same experimenter or a small-session approximation to the simultaneity needed for controlling historical events. Therefore the running of the experimental group and the control group at different times is ruled out; otherwise the observers may have become more experienced, more hurried, more careless, or the equipment or apparatus changed in some respect. When more than one experimenter or observer is used, counterbalancing the experimenter, time, and group is desirable, with the balanced Latin square frequently serving a useful purpose.

Although regression is controlled in the design as a whole, secondary analyses of effects may be made for extreme pretest scores in both experimental and control groups.

Selection is handled by the sampling equivalence insured through the randomization employed in assigning persons to groups, supplemented by matching procedures, with the initial observations of the experimental and control groups serving as a check on possible sampling differences.

With respect to experimental mortality, if the experimental and control groups do not differ in the number of lost cases or in their pretest scores, the experiment can be judged internally valid on this point. However, mortality reduces generalization of effects, as applied to the original population from which the groups were selected.

Although the pretest-posttest control group design was highly regarded in the social sciences for some thirty years, by 1940 serious criticism was voiced, in the form of an interaction effect of testing. The effects of history, maturation, and testing, in the language of analysis of variance, are main effects, manifesting themselves in mean differences independently of the presence of other variables, and capable of adding on to other effects, including the effect of the experimental variable. In contrast, interaction effects (a joint effect) may occur even when no main effects are present; for example, applied to the testing variable, the interaction effect might involve not a shift due solely or directly to the measurement process, but rather a sensitization of subjects to the experimental variable.

As a concrete example of interaction it is pertinent to cite the NORC study of a United Nations information campaign in Cincinnati,[21] in which two equivalent samples of a thousand each were drawn from the city's population. After one of these samples was interviewed, Cincinnati was subjected to an intensive publicity campaign using the various mass media of communication, including special features in the newspapers and on the radio, bus cards, and public lectures. At the end of two months the second sample of 1,000 persons was interviewed and the results compared with the first 1,000. There were no differences between the two groups except that the second group was somewhat more pessimistic about the likelihood of Russia's co-operation for world peace, which could be attributed to history rather than to the publicity campaign in Cincinnati. As a result of the publicity campaign of two months, the second sample was no better informed than the first about the United Nations, nor had it been sensitive to the publicity campaign itself. The initial sample was reinterviewed at the same time that the second sample was interviewed (after the publicity campaign), with the first group showing significant attitude changes, a high degree of awareness of the campaign, and important increases in information. The interaction effect was in the form of sensitizing the initial group (through the initial interview) to the topic of the United Nations, so as to make the subsequent publicity campaign effective for them.

[21] Shirley A. Star and Helen M. Hughes, "Report on an Educational Campaign: The Cincinnati Plan for the United Nations." *American Journal of Sociology* 55: 389–400; January 1950.

A *four-group design* has been suggested by Solomon to control the problem of interaction effects.[22] This design involves adding to the traditional two-group experiment two groups that are not pretested. The design enables the experimenter to control and measure both the main and interaction effects of testing, and the main effects of a composite of maturation and history. These possibilities recommend the design highly to social scientists.

The *posttest-only control group design* is illustrated by Fisher's typical agricultural experiment,[23] which involves no pretest; equivalent plots of ground receive different experimental treatments, and the subsequent yields are measured. To cite an illustration in a social area, by way of testing the influence of a motion picture upon attitudes, two randomly assigned audiences would be selected, one exposed to the movie, and the attitudes of each audience measured subsequently for the first time. This design has been criticized as vulnerable to selection bias, especially where random assignment is not possible. Where naturally aggregated units such as classes are employed intact, these should be used in large numbers and assigned at random to the experimental and control conditions. If but one or two intact classrooms are available for each experimental treatment, the pretest-posttest control group design is preferable. Other advantages of the pretest-posttest control group design over the posttest-only control group design are in terms of greater precision, dealing with experimental mortality (through comparing pretest scores of lost cases in both experimental and control groups), and studying the relationship of pretest attitudes to kind and amount of change. For the posttest-only control group design, there are certain social settings in which it is feasible; for example, whenever the social contact represented by the experimental variable is made to single individuals or to small groups, and where the response to that stimulus can be identified in terms of individuals or type of exposure to the experimental variable (as illustrated by direct mail and door-to-door contacts).

It is traditional in discussions of experimental design in psychology, education, and such social fields as sociology to think of exposure to the experimental variable as opposed to absence of the experimental variable. While this condition may be possible in the stimulus-isolated laboratory in the physical sciences, it is difficult to think of a setting in the social sciences as empty of potentially change-inducing stimuli. The experience

[22] Richard L. Solomon, "An Extension of Control Group Design." *Psychological Bulletin* 46: 137–50; March 1949.
[23] R. A. Fisher, *op. cit.*

of the control group, in social experimentation, may be described as another type of exposure to the experimental variable (a control experience) rather than complete absence of an experimental variable. Frequently, in the social areas, we are not so much interested in the qualitative fact of effect or no-effect as in the degree of effect for varying degrees of the experimental variable, which leads to designs in which multiple groups are used, each with a different degree of the experimental variable. When different degrees of the experimental variable are given to the same group, with different groups receiving the variable in different orders, the technique of counterbalancing is essential.

It is necessary to test for effects extended in time, since the longer-range effects of persuasive experimental variables may be qualitatively as well as quantitatively different from immediate effects. Experiments may be designed to measure the effect of the experimental variable at extended periods of time by adding two separate groups for each post-test period (including the additional control group). The additional control group is necessary; otherwise the effects of intervening history, maturation, instrument decay, regression, and mortality are confounded with the delayed effects of the experimental variable.

OTHER CLASSIFICATIONS OF EXPERIMENTAL DESIGNS

The techniques of the recent statistical approaches and forms of experimental design are beyond the scope of an introductory, descriptive account of research methodology, but these methods may be illustrated further by a list of the significant chapter headings[24] of a comprehensive book in this field. Study of such concepts usually is preceded by an introductory course in statistical method.

Completely Randomized, Randomized Block, and Latin Square Designs
Factorial Experiments
Confounding
Factorial Experiments in Fractional Replication

[24] William G. Cochran and Gertrude M. Cox, *Experimental Designs*. Second Edition. New York: John Wiley & Sons, 1957. xiv+611 p. Also see:

Walter T. Federer, *Experimental Design*: Theory and Application. New York: The Macmillan Co., 1955. xix+544+47.

Oscar Kempthorne, *The Design and Analysis of Experiments*. New York: John Wiley & Sons, 1952. xix+631 p.

E. F. Lindquist, *Design and Analysis of Experiments in Psychology and Education*. Boston: Houghton Mifflin Co., 1953. xix+393 p.

Benton J. Underwood, "Research Design," *Psychological Research*. New York: Appleton-Century-Crofts, 1957. p. 85-173.

Factorial Experiments with Main Effects Confounded: Split-Plot Designs
Factorial Experiments Confounded in Quasi-Latin Squares
Methods for Study of Response Surfaces
Balanced and Partially Balanced Incomplete Block Designs
Lattice Designs
Incomplete Block Designs
Lattice Squares
Incomplete Latin Squares.

To cite another approach, by way of classification of 1,000 experiments in education, dating from 1909 to 1952, Shannon has identified seventeen headings or types.[25]

Groups of subjects
   In single formation
      1. Treated once, not in series (or in series with the same act repeated and no changing factor involved), and perhaps with comparison with earlier practice or with the mode of practice
      2. Treated in series with a changing factor and with comparison from stage to stage
   In parallel formation
      3. Equivalent, with a single variable
      4. Not known to be equivalent, with a single variable
      5. Known not to be equivalent, usually with no variable factor, to determine the degree of nonequivalence in performance
   In reversed formation
      6. Equivalent, with a single variable
      7. Not known to be equivalent, with a single variable
      8. Known not to be equivalent
Single subjects
   In single formation
      9. Treated once, not in series (or in series with the same act repeated and no changing factor involved), and perhaps with comparison with earlier practice or with the mode of practice
      10. Treated in series with a changing factor and with comparison from stage to stage
   In parallel formation
      11. Equivalent, with a single variable
      12. Not known to be equivalent, with a single variable
      13. Known not to be equivalent, usually with no variable factor, to determine the degree of nonequivalence in performance
   In reversed formation
      14. Equivalent, with a single variable

[25] J. R. Shannon, "Experiments in Education: A New Pattern and Frequency of Types." *Journal of Educational Research* 48: 81–93; October 1954.

15. Not known to be equivalent
16. Known not to be equivalent

Materials and instruments

17. Materials, material facilities, or instruments relating to schools or to formal instruction (inanimate objects or procedures rather than live subjects either as individuals or in groups).

Shannon found that the majority of the experiments in education have been in the area of teaching methods. The prevailing types of experimental procedure or technique have been parallel groups, with the groups not known to be equivalent (but apparently presumed to be approximately so) or with the experimental factors so well controlled, according to Shannon, that the groups were known to be equivalent in the significant characteristics involved. The single-group type has been second in frequency of use in educational experimentation.

To summarize the essential characteristics of a good experimental design:[26]

1. It will insure that the observed treatment effects are unbiased estimates of the true effects. (The term *treatment* refers to any induced or selected variation in the experimental procedures or conditions whose effect is to be observed and evaluated.)

2. It will permit a quantitative description of the precision of the observed treatment effects regarded as estimates of the "true" effects.

3. It will insure that the observed treatment effects will have whatever degree of precision is required by the broader purposes of the experiment.

4. It will make possible an objective test of a specific hypothesis concerning the true effects.

5. It will be efficient.

INFERENCE AND GENERALIZATION

Statisticians and experts in experimental design[27] frequently are asked for advice about making inferences from the results of experiments, sometimes after the investigation has been completed. Since the making of sound inferences depends on the way in which the experiment was carried out, the time to think about statistical inference and to seek advice is when the experiment is being planned. The statistician or expert in experimental design can make a valuable contribution beyond advice on some technical matter of statistical theory by getting the investigator to explain clearly why he is doing the experiment, to justify the experi-

[26] E. F. Lindquist, *op. cit.*, p. 1, 6–7.
[27] William G. Cochran and Gertrude M. Cox, *op. cit.*, p. 9–11.

mental treatments whose effects he proposes to compare, and to defend his claim that the completed treatment will enable its objectives to be realized. The statement of objectives may assume the form of the questions to be answered, the hypotheses to be tested, or the effects to be estimated. (A general treatment of the formulation and testing of hypotheses has been presented in the chapter on the development of the problem.)

In experimentation, generalization beyond the specific group studied can be made only to other comparable groups;[28] for example, if certain results are found when male college students are subjects, to what extent would this result hold true for female subjects, for high-school subjects, or for older subjects? If a specified amount of fertilizer applied to units of land in a section of Iowa results in greater production of corn than any other specified amount of fertilizer tested, to what extent could a generalization be made for land units in a different part of Iowa or in Nebraska? In this instance the varying amounts of fertilizer represent an independent variable, and the yield of corn a dependent variable. Soil differences may represent important independent variables in the sense that they are related to the results obtained from the applications of the different amounts of fertilizer; a particular amount of fertilizer may work well with certain kinds of land and have little or no effect when applied to other kinds.

EVALUATION OF EDUCATIONAL EXPERIMENTATION

Obstacles to controlled experimentation in the field of education and in the classroom include three factors: the very limited training for experimentation offered in the field of education, as compared with prolonged exposure of doctoral candidates in psychology to experimental psychology, statistics, and measurement; the relatively small amount of experimentation done by professors of education; and the neutral or even negative attitude toward experimentation on the part of school administrators and parents.

Training for Experimentation

It is essential for the graduate student or investigator interested in controlled experimentation to have the necessary training in statistics (especially the analysis of variance) and research methods before attempting to design an experiment, and to work closely from the beginning with

[28] Allen L. Edwards, *op. cit.*, p. 265.

a competent specialist. One answer is to take courses in statistics and experimental design usually offered in the psychology departments of major universities and relatively less frequently in graduate departments of education. It is common for experts in experimental design in education and psychology to consult each other and the mathematical statisticians. Although the specialist in experimental design may not know the investigator's subject-matter field thoroughly, he can point out logical flaws and methodological imperfections that might nullify otherwise commendable efforts. A number of the book-length treatises in the chapter bibliography are used as texts in experimental-design courses in psychology and education.

A critical comment on controlled experimentation in the classroom points out that we have neglected this technique to our great detriment:

> Most decisions about methods have been based upon colloquial, anecdotal, or administrative considerations rather than experimentation. Seldom are adequate control groups incorporated into classroom experiments. The necessity for long-range experimental design is not usually appreciated by teachers and administrators. The principle of randomness is often misunderstood or ignored in favor of elaborate matching, which has several disadvantages. Worst of all, few teachers, including those with doctoral degrees, get even minimal training for modern experimentation. Our professional literature is virtually devoid of well controlled experimental studies in the classroom. We continue to pool ignorance via conferences, questionnaires, rating scales, opinionnaires, and ineffective correlational studies, all of which are valuable for certain purposes but not sufficient in themselves.[29]

Appropriate Problems for Experimental Study

A critical comment on the educational research of the second quarter of the present century, including experimentation, indicates the need for adequate standards of investigation and the overemphasis on purely local, trivial, or temporary problems. The suggestion is made that members of such groups as the American Educational Research Association can do much as individuals and as members of the organization to improve the quality and influence of educational research.

The fetish of empiricism leads to elaborate and expensive attempts to demonstrate experimentally, at rather modest levels of confidence, hypotheses whose truth could be defended on rational grounds with much greater degrees of certainty. Is it necessary, for example, to demonstrate experimentally that a teacher who gives some time to individual instruction in a large class has more time available for individual instruction per pupil if the class becomes smaller?

---

[29] Quoted from Julian C. Stanley, "Controlled Experimentation in the Classroom." *Journal of Experimental Education* 25: 195–201; March 1957.

Is it even necessary to show experimentally that a teacher, unused to spending much time in individual instruction because of the pressure of large classes, will not automatically begin to do more individual instruction when the size of her class is reduced? The techniques used in educational research studies are frequently inadequate. Specific testable hypotheses are not identified before the experiment begins. There is too much tendency to seek global answers to complex questions such as, "Is teaching by television effective?" There is too easy yielding in the face of difficulties of adequate experimental control— too many woefully inadequate studies whose only defense is that this was the best that could be done under the circumstances. Because of the nature of the problems studied, and the techniques employed, the findings of many educational research studies are of temporary local value only, or contradictory and inconclusive.[30]

As indicated above, at times zeal for experimentation may become a fetish. There is a place for the exercise of good judgment in attempting to bring about social and educational improvements, without seeking an answer through controlled experimentation, as illustrated by Andrew Carnegie's establishment of libraries and Abraham Flexner's reform of medical education. To provide teachers with a better knowledge of their subject matter is a worthwhile activity, but to secure and analyze such evaluative data as can be gathered may prove more costly than the results justify. A pertinent example of a project that does not lend itself to experimental evaluation is the program of the American Association for the Advancement of Science and the National Science Foundation, which involves sending sets of books about science and scientists to more than 100 high schools, mainly to schools with meager library facilities of their own.

We can get records of how many times each book was withdrawn. We can get the judgments of teachers about the usefulness of the program. But the real purpose of the traveling libraries is to supplement the library and teaching resources of the schools and, we hope, to stimulate a few bright students and help them to decide whether or not they want to become scientists. Because we do not know any feasible method of finding out how successfully we accomplish this real purpose, we are not planning to make elaborate evaluative studies. The project seems well worth doing, but we shall have to rely on unverified judgments in deciding whether or not it is worth continuing.[31]

[30] Quoted from Robert L. Ebel, "The Role of Educational Research." *AERA Newsletter* 9: 1–2; January 1958.
  Also see J. G. Taylor, "Experimental Design: A Cloak for Intellectual Sterility." *British Journal of Psychology* 49: 106–16; May 1958. Maintains that there is a dearth of serious theorizing and an excess of trivial experimentation.
  [31] Quoted from Dael Wolfle, "The Fetish of Experiment." *Science* 125: 177; February 1, 1957.

The characteristics of the social object and the social context of the experimenter are sufficiently different from experimentation in the physical sciences to warrant special consideration. There are differences between physical data and social data which must be considered before the experimental method is carried over bodily from physical science to social science. The social scientist encounters difficulties in holding extraneous influences constant, and is seldom in a position to remove these influences physically, although society sometimes creates situations in which such extraneous influences are physically held constant. In taking over the experimental method from the older sciences, the social scientist is compelled to examine it in terms of problems and assumptions in relation to the specific social problem for investigation.[32]

Classroom Experimentation and the Teacher

As a setting for experimentation the classroom is a complex human situation. The pupils in a classroom act not only as individuals, but together react as a social system. The school is a part of the political subdivision and of a community of educational institutions. The school itself is a system, of which the classroom is a part. Within the classroom many sources (sometimes unseen) are at work—a reference group to which each individual feels himself accountable, a pedagogical tradition that dictates subject matter and method, and a culture (societal needs, the peer culture, and the professional culture represented by the school and the teacher).[33]

Since experimentation is the most difficult and technically exacting research method for studying human and behavioral problems, if teachers do not understand the scientific spirit of inquiry and the requirements of controlled experimentation, they may make departures from the rules and design prescribed for the experiment. The teacher's values, attitudes, interests, motives, and sentiments may affect the procedure and results, since the natural inclination of the teacher is to try to "help" the pupils, the experiment, and investigator appear in the best possible light. Certainly it seems desirable for the classroom teacher to have a knowledge of the fundamentals of experimental methods and of illustrative investigations, but not to attempt formal experimental studies without the counsel of an

[32] Arnold M. Rose, "Conditions of the Social Science Experiment," *Theory and Method in the Social Sciences.* Minneapolis: University of Minnesota Press, 1954. p. 273–81.

[33] Arthur W. Foshay and James A. Hall, *Research for Curriculum Improvement.* 1957 Yearbook. Washington: Association for Supervision and Curriculum Development, National Education Association, 1957. p. 8–11.

appropriate expert in statistics and experimental design. Objective, impartial participation by teachers in appropriate experimentation should have a stimulating effect on both teachers and pupils and cultivate a spirit of exploration in the adventure of teaching (a personal value or by-product of the experiment).

Ethics

In the behavioral sciences many of the techniques for manipulation of variables involve deception, prevarication, and misdirection of the subject. In working with human subjects the experimenter is obligated to keep in mind his responsibilities to the subject and the ethics of experimentation. One of the difficulties in classroom experimentation is that the subjects are children, who for ethical reasons must not be subjected to conditions that may harm them. The investigator may be handicapped by the popular attitude of "no experimenting with children." The experimenter should perform some service for the subjects in exchange for their help; for example, to give the subjects (if mature enough to comprehend) a full explanation at the conclusion of the experiment, even though it may require more time for explanation and discussion than it took to do the experiment. If this explanation is well done, the subjects will feel that they have learned something and have not wasted their time.[34]

EXPERIMENTATION IN RELATION TO OTHER TECHNIQUES

Psychometric and Statistical Research

Some investigators differentiate between experimental research and psychometric research (studies in which psychometric techniques are used to investigate relations between variables, but excluding such procedures in assessing individuals for clinical or other applied psychological work). Since experimental and psychometric techniques are basically similar in purpose, they can be combined in areas traditionally restricted to one or the other.

In an investigation of the relation between, let us say, reaction time and alcoholic content of blood, variations in alcoholic content of blood are likely to be produced experimentally by feeding comparable groups of subjects different amounts of alcohol. The groups are treated in different ways, subjected to different conditions. On the other hand, in studying the relation

[34] Leon Festinger and Daniel Katz, *Research Methods in the Behavioral Sciences.* New York: Dryden Press, 1953. p. 170.

between memory and intelligence, for example, variations in intelligence are obtained psychometrically by selecting individuals who vary with respect to scores on an intelligence test. In both cases we vary each of at least two variables in order to determine the relation between them, but the method of producing variation is different. In experimental investigations the investigator produces variation by changing the external environment, or internal state, or both, of his subjects. In psychometric research no attempt is made to produce any change in the individual subject. Rather, the subject is assumed to stay put with respect to the property (e.g., intelligence) in which the investigator is interested, and variation in that property is obtained by selecting individuals who differ with respect to it. The experimentalist obtains variation by subjecting a given group of subjects to different experimental conditions, the psychometric researcher achieves it by moving from individual to individual.[35]

We are reminded that statistical and experimental methods represent one approach to problems but not the only scientific method, although the prestige of statistics and experimentation is great, in part deriving from the high repute of mathematics and logic. Strong professional societies are devoted to the advancement of mathematics and statistics, and hundreds of technical books and journals in the fields of statistics and experimentation are published annually. We must keep in mind, however, that important parts of the scientific process do not now lend themselves to mathematical, logical, or any other formal treatment, as illustrated particularly by certain of the studies cited in the chapter on case and clinical techniques.

Statistical techniques serve a useful function, but they have acquired a purely honorific status which may be troublesome. Their presence or absence has become a shibboleth to be used in distinguishing between good and bad work. Because measures of behavior have been highly variable, we have come to trust only results obtained from large numbers of subjects. Because some workers have intentionally or unconsciously reported only selected favorable instances, we have come to put a high value on research which is planned in advance and reported in its entirety. Because measures have behaved capriciously, we have come to value skillful deductive theories which restore order. But although large groups, planned experiments, and valid theorizing are associated with significant scientific results, it does not follow that nothing can be achieved in their absence.[36]

[35] Quoted from Dalbir Bindra and Ivan H. Scheier, "The Relation Between Psychometric and Experimental Research in Psychology." *American Psychologist* 9: 69–71; February 1954.
Lee J. Cronbach, "The Two Disciplines of Scientific Psychology." *American Psychologist* 12: 671–84; November 1957. Experimental and correlational psychology.
[36] Quoted from B. J. Skinner, "A Case History in Scientific Method." *American Psychologist* 11: 221–33; May 1956.

The Experimental Clinician

Many graduate students in psychology (and some in education) have experienced frustration in attempting to mold themselves in the image of the "experimental clinician." The graduate student seeks to find some appropriate middle ground in his training and profession between the goal of research as the pursuit of understanding and the ideal of service as the welfare of the client. (The relationship of the clinical and statistical approaches to problem-solving has been discussed in the chapter on clinical and case studies.)

To many, there appears to be an irreconcilable schism between the rather rigid, controlled methodology of the experimentalist, on the one hand, and the flexible, eclectic approach extolled as the clinician's *modus operandi*, on the other. And many feel that this schism will never be reached. It appears to be the logical dividing line between two mental attitudes which, although possibly lying on a continuum, form the polar aspects of this continuum with no present-day intermediate steps. It is the difference between a data-centered and a client-centered approach, between a research-centered and a service-centered attitude which makes the difference here. . . .

When an experimental psychologist sets about experimenting, he is quite careful to control rigidly his variables, to manipulate precisely his parameters, and to adhere religiously to an explicit procedure. Emulating the mother science, he strives to approach the situation of quantitatively plotting the concomitant changes in a dependent variable against the measured changes in an independent variable. Adherence to stated rules, quantification, and explicit control are the hallmarks of the experimental psychologist's procedure, and this is as it should be. Summarily stated, then, this is the experimental methodology as taught in our universities. When results are presented, they are presented, with confidence, as a function of the stated conditions, i.e., the manipulated variables.

But the other half of our "experimental clinician" faces problems of its own. In a client-centered, service-oriented profession the clinician is opportuned to follow the lead of his patient, to be flexible, and to consider the patient first and society second. Multidimensional manipulation of variable complexes, clinical intuition, and qualitative insights are the hallmarks of clinical psychology. This is the psychotherapeutic methodology as taught in our universities today.[37]

The student's predicament is shared by the profession of psychology as a whole. Psychologists have yet to learn how to test in the laboratory the induced hypotheses of the therapy room and to develop a theoretical framework which will deductively support both clinical insight and experimental inquiry.[38]

[37] Quoted from Lawrence N. Solomon, "The Paradox of the Experimental Clinician." *American Psychologist* 10: 170–71; April 1955.

[38] George A. Kelly, "I Itch Too." *American Psychologist* 10: 172–73; April 1955.

Observational or Descriptive-Survey Studies

For certain purposes direct observation of a descriptive-survey type may prove more rewarding than controlled experimentation, as in noting the particular stimuli in a complex social setting to which the individual child reacts, consistency of reaction for an individual, and variability in response between the different members of the group. From this point of view, controlled experiments in laboratories and in many classrooms are regarded as artificial or unnatural. Some observational studies may even satisfy the requirements of controlled observation, in that certain controls are used in selecting the room, equipment, children, stimuli, and observers. The simpler technique of observation of behavior, as compared with controlled experimentation, is useful in securing accurate running accounts of what happens from day to day in teaching a group of children some complex skill, generalization, or attitude.

On the other hand, if the experimenter succeeds in controlling the conditions under which an event occurs, he has certain advantages over an observer who simply watches the course of events without exercising any control: the experimenter can make the event occur when he wishes; he can repeat his observation under the same conditions for verification; and he can vary the conditions systematically and note the variation in results.

Psychologists sometimes have used the term *qualitative* in contrast to *quantitative* in discussing experimentation. Woodworth points out that important variables are qualitative rather than quantitative: the role of the different senses in revealing the environment as an important psychological problem; training with "understanding" differs from routine drill; an animal will approach one object and avoid another; and a human subject likes one odor and dislikes another. "How could chemistry ever have become quantitative without first being interested in the various kinds of elements and compounds? A qualitative survey is often necessary to show up the important problems and suggest hypotheses for more exact testing."[39]

Examples may be cited of investigational techniques used in conjunction with experimentation, actually as part of the experimental design. Use of eye-movement photography, for the purpose of establishing central tendencies, is descriptive-survey in character, but may become a first step in experimentation when reading content is varied (from prose to poetry to written problems in arithmetic). As a co-twin control tech-

[39] Robert S. Woodworth and Harold Schlosberg, *Experimental Psychology*. Revised Edition. New York: Henry Holt and Co., 1954. p. 6–7.

nique, using identical twins, one infant may be taught to climb the stairs, while the other waits until he has reached a stage of stair-climbing "readiness." This study may be so analyzed and reported as to possess the characteristics of case-study and genetic procedures, as well as experimentation.

INSTRUMENTATION

Instruments play an important part in modern science, technology, and business organization, and also in the design of controlled experimentation (with relatively greater use in psychological research than in educational experiments). Achievements made possible by modern instruments include the development of sensing devices capable of operating under extreme conditions and sensitive to physical changes far beyond the range of human sense organs, computing machines of extreme rapidity, and devices for automatic control of machining and assembling operations. Many current discoveries would have been impossible without the aid of the specially designed instruments made possible by modern technology. Improved instruments are essential for research progress in the future. Scientists can expect and even demand more assistance from machines in handling scientific data, including the processes or techniques of integrated and electronic data-processing.[40] The numerous instruments for mechanical recording and for data-gathering, as described in the chapter on descriptive-survey studies, are available for use in controlled experimentation.

It was early recognized by some psychologists, including Helmholtz, that elaborate instrumentation was not so important as the human mind and the insight of the teacher or investigator.

As a teacher, he [Helmholtz] seems to have rather disdained the current trend toward spectacular methods in the teaching of science. According to contemporary writers, the custom of the time was for each scientist to try to outdo all other scientists in this respect: they used huge charts that could be raised and lowered mechanically, a darkened auditorium for showing slides, large models of the eye and the ear, and "hundreds of animals, large and small . . . sacrificed, and in one case even a horse . . . introduced to show heart action." Textbooks were "almost useless . . . except for review"; the trend was all toward demonstration, and several assistants were kept continually occupied by each lecturer in preparing for the next day's lecture.

---

[40] Graham DuShane, "Instruments and Man." *Science* 124: 771; October 26, 1956.
Karl F. Heumann, "Data Processing for Scientists." *Science* 124: 773–77; October 26, 1956.

One chemistry laboratory—that of Kolbe—was decorated with the motto: "God made the world according to number, weight, and measure."

Helmholtz apparently left these elaborate demonstrations to his assistants and taught a small group of advanced students with no other aid than a blackboard. On this he would work out complicated equations, sometimes finding errors in his calculations, and always preferring to work out problems as he went along rather than to prepare every lecture beforehand. According to Hall, he had a habit of thinking out loud in lecture room and laboratory, and he used to spend some hours each day discussing experiments with his student assistants. But all these attributes, which might seem progressive today, apparently could not eradicate the impression—at least as far as Hall was concerned—that Helmholtz was a man "far more gifted in discovery than in teaching."[41]

CONCLUDING STATEMENT

In experimentation the investigator controls (manipulates or changes) certain independent variables and observes the changes that take place in the form of dependent variables. The "rule of the single variable" is now considered a narrow and mechanical theory of causation. The efficient statistical methods and experimental designs of today make it possible to handle several independent variables in the same design and to have as many dependent variables as may seem necessary. These true experimental designs have been developed by psychologists who sought to overcome the difficulties of confounded extraneous variables in the pre-experimental designs widely used during the first quarter of the twentieth century and even later.

Obstacles to controlled experimentation in the field of education and in the classroom involve three factors: limited graduate training for experimentation in the field of education, relatively little experimentation by professors of education, and a neutral or even negative attitude toward experimentation on the part of school administrators and parents. It is essential that the graduate student or investigator interested in controlled experimentation have the necessary training in statistics (especially the analysis of variance) and in research methods before attempting to design an experiment, and that he work closely from the beginning with a competent specialist.

At times, zeal for experimentation has become a fetish. There is a place for the exercise of good judgment and logic in attempting to bring

[41] Quoted from Howard Gruber and Valmai Gruber, "Hermann von Helmholtz: Nineteenth-Century Polymorph." *Scientific Monthly* 83: 92–99; August 1956.
   G. S. Hall, *Founders of Modern Psychology*. New York: Appleton-Century-Crofts, 1924. vii+470 p.

about social and educational improvements, without insisting on an answer through controlled experimentation.

If teachers do not understand the scientific spirit of inquiry and the requirements of controlled experimentation, they may invalidate an investigation as the result of departures from the rules and design prescribed for the experiment. Objective, impartial participation by teachers in appropriate experimentation should have a stimulating effect on both teachers and pupils as a personal value or byproduct of the experiment.

SELECTED REFERENCES

ACKOFF, Russell L. *The Design of Social Research*. Chicago: The University of Chicago Press, 1953. xi+420 p.

American Association for Health, Physical Education, and Recreation. *Research Methods Applied to Health, Physical Education, and Recreation*. Revised Edition. Washington: The Association, National Education Association, 1952. p. 182-203, 254-314.

ANDERSON, John E. "Methods of Child Psychology," *Manual of Child Psychology*. Second Edition. Edited by Leonard Carmichael. New York: John Wiley & Sons, 1954. p. 44-52.

ANDREWS, T. C., Editor. *Methods of Psychology*. New York: John Wiley & Sons, 1948. xiv+716 p.

BARTLEY, S. Howard. *Beginning Experimental Psychology*. New York: McGraw-Hill Book Co., 1950. viii+483 p.

BERG, Irwin A. "The Use of Human Subjects in Psychological Research." *American Psychologist* 9: 108-11; March 1954.

BEVERIDGE, William I. B. *The Art of Scientific Investigation*. New York: W. W. Norton and Co., 1950. 171 p.

BIJOU, Sidney W. "A Systematic Approach to an Experimental Analysis of Young Children." *Child Development* 26: 161-68; September 1955.

BINDRA, Dalbir, and SCHEIER, Ivan H. "The Relation between Psychometric and Experimental Research in Psychology." *American Psychologist* 9: 69-71; February 1954.

BINGHAM, Walter V. "Psychology as a Science, as a Technology and as a Profession." *American Psychologist* 8: 115-18; March 1953.

BLACKWELDER, R. E., and HOYME, L. E. "Statistics, Experiment, and the Future of Biology." *Scientific Monthly* 80: 225-29; April 1955.

BLOMMERS, Paul, and LINDQUIST, E. F. "Experimental and Statistical Studies: Applications of Newer Statistical Techniques." *Review of Educational Research* 12: 501-20; December 1942.

BLUMER, Herbert. "Sociological Analysis and the 'Variable.'" *American Sociological Review* 21: 683-90; December 1956.

BOGARDUS, Emory S. "Experimental Research in Sociology." *Sociology and Social Research* 33: 33-40; September-October 1948.

BORING, Edwin G. *A History of Experimental Psychology*. Second Edition. New York: Appleton-Century-Crofts, 1950. xxi+777 p.

BRENNAN, R. E. *History of Psychology*. New York: The Macmillan Co., 1945. 277 p.

BROWN, Clarence W., and GHISELLI, Edwin E. *Scientific Method in Psychology*. New York: McGraw-Hill Book Co., 1955. xii+368 p.

BROWN, Clinton C., and SAUCER, Rayford T. *Electronic Instrumentation for the Behavioral Sciences*. Springfield, Ill.: Charles C Thomas, 1958. 176 p.

BROWNELL, W. A. "Critique of Research on Learning and on Instruction in the School," *Graduate Study in Education*, p. 52-66. Fiftieth Yearbook, National Society for the Study of Education, Part 1. Chicago: The University of Chicago Press, 1951. 369 p.

BRUNSWIK, Egon. *Perception and the Representative Design of Psychological Experiments*. Berkeley: University of California Press, 1956. xii+154 p.

BRUNSWIK, Egon. *Systematic and Representative Design of Psychological Experiments*. Berkeley: University of California Press, 1947. 60 p.

BUGELSKI, B. R. *A First Course in Experimental Psychology*. New York: Henry Holt and Co., 1951. xxiii+421 p.

BUROS, Oscar K., Editor. *The Fourth Mental Measurements Yearbook*. Highland Park, N. J.: Gryphon Press, 1953. 1,189 p.

CAMPBELL, Donald T. "Factors Relevant to the Validity of Experiments in Social Settings." *Psychological Bulletin* 54: 297-312; July 1957.

CHAPIN, F. Stuart. *Experimental Designs in Sociological Research*. Revised Edition. New York: Harper & Brothers, 1955. xxii+295 p.

CHAPIN, F. Stuart. "Experimental Design in Sociology: Limitations and Abuses." With rejoinders by J. E. Hulett, Jr., and Stuart A. Queen, *Social Forces* 29: 25-32; October 1950.

COCHRAN, William G., and Cox, Gertrude M. *Experimental Designs*. Second Edition. New York: John Wiley & Sons, 1957. xiv+611 p.

CORNELL, Francis G., and MONROE, Walter S. "Experiment," *Encyclopedia of Educational Research*. Second Edition. Edited by Walter S. Monroe. New York: The Macmillan Co., 1950. p. 414-16.

CRAFTS, L. W., and Others. *Recent Experiments in Psychology*. Second Edition. New York: McGraw-Hill Book Co., 1950. xvii+503 p.

DENNIS, Wayne, Editor. *Readings in Child Psychology*. New York: Prentice-Hall, 1951. xi+624 p.

DENNIS, Wayne, Editor. *Readings in the History of Psychology*. New York: Appleton-Century-Crofts, 1948. 598 p.

DOBY, John T., Editor. "Principles of Experimentation," *An Introduction to Social Research*. Harrisburg, Penn.: The Stackpole Co., 1954. p. 101-22.

EDWARDS, Allen L. *Experimental Design in Psychological Research*. New York: Rinehart & Co., 1950. xiv+445 p.

EDWARDS, Allen L. "Experiments: Their Planning and Execution," *Handbook of Social Psychology:* Theory and Method. Vol. 1. Edited by Gardner Lindzey. Cambridge, Mass.: Addison-Wesley Publishing Co., 1954. p. 259-88.

EDWARDS, Allen L., and CRONBACH, Lee J. "Experimental Design for Research in Psychotherapy." *Journal of Clinical Psychology* 8: 51-56; January 1952.

FARNSWORTH, P. R., and McNEMAR, Quinn, Editors. *Annual Review of Psychology*. Vol. 8. Stanford, Calif.: Annual Reviews, 1957. ix+502 p.

FARRELL, B. A. "On the Limits of Experimental Psychology." *British Journal of Psychology* 46: 165-77; August 1955.

FEDERER, Walter T. *Experimental Design:* Theory and Application. New York: The Macmillan Co., 1955. xix+544+47 p.

FESTINGER, Leon, and KATZ, Daniel, Editors. *Research Methods in the Behavioral Sciences.* New York: Dryden Press, 1953. p. 98-172.

FINNEY, D. J. *Experimental Design and Its Statistical Basis.* Chicago: The University of Chicago Press, 1955. 169 p.

FISHER, R. A. *The Design of Experiments.* Sixth Edition. New York: Hafner Publishing Corp., 1951. xv+244 p.

FISHER, Seymour, and FISHER, Rhoda. "Relationship Between Personal Insecurity and Attitude Toward Psychological Methodology." *American Psychologist* 10: 538-40; September 1955.

FLUGEL, J. C. *A Hundred Years of Psychology.* Second Edition. New York: The Macmillan Co., 1951. 424 p.

GARRETT, Henry E. *Great Experiments in Psychology.* Third Edition. New York: Appleton-Century-Crofts, 1951. 400 p.

GEE, Wilson. *Social Science Research Methods.* New York: Appleton-Century-Crofts, 1950. p. 330-60.

GLUECK, Sheldon, and GLUECK, Eleanor. *Delinquents in the Making:* Paths to Prevention. New York: Harper & Brothers, 1952. viii+214 p. (A briefer, less technical version of *Unraveling Juvenile Delinquency.*)

GOLDSTEIN, Philip. *How to Do an Experiment.* New York: Harcourt, Brace and Co., 1957. 192 p.

GOOD, Carter V., and SCATES, Douglas E. *Methods of Research:* Educational, Psychological, Sociological. New York: Appleton-Century-Crofts, 1954. p. 689-725.

GOODE, William J., and HATT, Paul K. *Methods in Social Research.* New York: McGraw-Hill Book Co., 1952. p. 74-102.

GREENWOOD, Ernest. *Experimental Sociology:* A Study in Method. New York: King's Crown Press, 1945. xiii+163 p.

GRINGS, William W. *Laboratory Instrumentation in Psychology.* Palo Alto, Calif.: National Press, 1954. vi+282 p.

HARLOW, Harry F. "Experimental Analysis of Behavior." *American Psychologist* 12: 485-90; August 1957.

HERRICK, Virgil E., and HARRIS, Chester W. "Handling Data," *Research for Curriculum Improvement.* 1957 Yearbook. Washington: Association for Supervision and Curriculum Development, National Education Association, 1957. p. 83-118.

HILLWAY, Tyrus. *Introduction to Research.* Boston: Houghton Mifflin Co., 1956. p. 153-74.

HOTELLING, Harold. "The Impact of R. A. Fisher on Statistics." *Journal of the American Statistical Association* 46: 35-46; March 1951.

HUMPHREY, George. *Thinking:* An Introduction to Its Experimental Psychology. New York: John Wiley & Sons, 1951. xi+331 p.

JAHODA, Marie, and Others. *Research Methods in the Study of Social Rela-*

tions: With Especial Emphasis on Prejudice. Vol. 1. New York: Dryden Press, 1951. p. 58-85.

KEMPTHORNE, Oscar. *The Design and Analysis of Experiments.* New York: John Wiley & Sons, 1952. xix+631 p.

KOGAN, Leonard S. "Applications of Variance-Covariance Designs in Educational Research," in "Statistical Methodology in Educational Research." *Review of Educational Research* 24: 439-47; December 1954.

LACEY, Oliver L. *Statistical Methods in Experimentation:* An Introduction. New York: The Macmillan Co., 1953. xi+249 p.

LANGFELD, Herbert S., and Others, Editors. *A History of Psychology in Autobiography.* Vol. 4. Worcester, Mass.: Clark University Press, 1952. xii+356 p.

LEV, Joseph. "Research Methods and Designs." *Review of Educational Research* 18: 410-23; December 1948.

LINDQUIST, E. F. *Design and Analysis of Experiments in Psychology and Education.* Boston: Houghton Mifflin Co., 1953. xix+393 p.

LUCHINS, Abraham S. "Towards an Experimental Clinical Psychology." *Journal of Personality* 20: 440-56; June 1952.

LUNDBERG, George A. "Alleged Obstacles to Social Science." *Scientific Monthly* 70: 299-305; May 1950.

MADGE, John. *The Tools of Social Science.* New York: Longmans, Green and Co., 1953. p. 254-89.

MANN, H. B. *Analysis and Design of Experiments.* New York: Dover Publications, 1949. x+198 p.

MAXWELL, A. E. *Experimental Design in Psychology and the Medical Sciences.* New York: John Wiley & Sons, 1958. 144 p.

McCANDLESS, Boyd R., and ROSENBLUM, Sidney. "Psychological Theory as a Determiner of Experimental Pattern in Child Study." *Review of Educational Research* 22: 496-525; December 1952.

McCANDLESS, Boyd R., and SPIKER, Charles C. "Experimental Research in Child Psychology." *Child Development* 27: 75-80; March 1956.

MILLER, Delbert C. "The Shaping of Research Design in Large-Scale Group Research." *Social Forces* 33: 383-90; May 1955.

MORENO, J. L. *Sociometry, Experimental Method and the Science of Society.* New York: Beacon House, 1951. xiv+220 p.

MOWRER, O. H. "Learning Theory." *Review of Educational Research* 22: 475-95; December 1952.

MURPHY, Gardner. *Historical Introduction to Modern Psychology.* Revised Edition. New York: Harcourt, Brace and Co., 1949. xiv+466 p.

NORTON, Dee W., and LINDQUIST, Everet F. "Applications of Experimental Design and Analysis." *Review of Educational Research* 21: 350-67; December 1951.

O'NEIL, W. M. *An Introduction to Method in Psychology.* Melbourne, Australia: Melbourne University Press, 1957. ix+155 p.

OSGOOD, Charles E. *Method and Theory in Experimental Psychology.* New York: Oxford University Press, 1953. vi+800 p.

PETERS, Charles C., TOWNSEND, Agatha, and TRAXLER, Arthur E. "Research

Methods and Designs." *Review of Educational Research* 15: 377-93; December 1945.

QUENOUILLE, M. H. *The Design and Analysis of Experiment.* New York: Hafner Publishing Corp., 1953. xiii+356 p.

REISS, Albert J., Jr. "Unraveling Juvenile Delinquency: II, An Appraisal of the Research Methods." *American Journal of Sociology* 57: 115-20; September 1951.

"Research Design in Clinical Psychology: Symposium." *Journal of Clinical Psychology* 8: 3-98; January 1952.

ROBACK, A. A. *History of American Psychology.* New York: Library Publishers, 1952. xiv+426 p.

ROSE, Arnold M. "Conditions of the Social Science Experiment," *Theory and Method in the Social Sciences.* Minneapolis: University of Minnesota Press, 1954. p. 273-81.

ROSE, Edward, and FELTON, William. "Experimental Histories of Culture." *American Sociological Review* 20: 383-92; August 1955.

ROSEBOROUGH, Mary E. "Experimental Studies of Small Groups." *Psychological Bulletin* 50: 275-303; July 1953.

RUBIN, Sol. "Unraveling Juvenile Delinquency: I, Illusions in a Research Project Using Matched Pairs." *American Journal of Sociology* 57: 107-14; September 1951.

RUMMEL, J. Francis. *An Introduction to Research Procedures in Education.* New York: Harper & Brothers, 1958. p. 203-24.

RUSSELL, Wallace A. "An Experimental Psychology of Development: Pipe Dream or Possibility?" *The Concept of Development.* Edited by Dale B. Harris. Minneapolis: University of Minnesota Press, 1957. p. 162-74.

RYANS, David G. "Research Designs for the Empirical Validation of Tests and Inventories." *Educational and Psychological Measurement* 17: 175-84; Summer 1957.

SHANNON, J. R. "Experiments in Education: A New Pattern and Frequency of Types." *Journal of Educational Research* 48: 81-93; October 1954.

SHERIF, Muzafer, WHITE, B. Jack, and HARVEY, O. J. "Status in Experimentally Produced Groups." *American Journal of Sociology* 60: 370-79; January 1955.

SOLOMON, Lawrence N. "The Paradox of the Experimental Clinician." *American Psychologist* 10: 170-71; April 1955.

SPEARMAN, C. E. *Psychology Down the Ages.* Vols. 1, 2. London: Macmillan and Co., 1937. xii+454, viii+355 p.

STANLEY, Julian C. "Research Methods: Experimental Design," in "Methodology of Educational Research." *Review of Educational Research* 27: 449-59; December 1957.

STEVENS, S. S. "Problems and Methods of Psychophysics." *Psychological Bulletin* 55: 177-96; July 1958.

STEVENS, S. S., Editor. *Handbook of Experimental Psychology.* New York: John Wiley & Sons, 1951. xi+1436 p.

TINKER, Miles A., and RUSSELL, Wallace A. *Introduction to Methods in Ex-*

perimental *Psychology.* Third Edition. New York: Appleton-Century-Crofts, 1958. x+282 p.

TOWNSEND, John C. *Introduction to Experimental Method:* For Psychology and the Social Sciences. New York: McGraw-Hill Book Co., 1953. ix+ 220 p.

TRAVERS, R. M. W. *An Introduction to Educational Research.* New York: The Macmillan Co., 1958. Chapters 13, 14.

UNDERWOOD, Benton J. *Experimental Psychology:* An Introduction. New York: Appleton-Century-Crofts, 1949. vii+638 p.

UNDERWOOD, Benton J. "Research Design," *Psychological Research.* New York: Appleton-Century-Crofts, 1957. p. 85-173.

VALENTINE, Willard L., and WICKENS, Delos D. *Experimental Foundations of General Psychology.* Third Edition. New York: Rinehart & Co., 1949. xxi+472 p.

WALKER, Helen M. *Statistical Inference.* New York: Henry Holt and Co., 1953. xi+510 p.

WEAVER, Warren, Editor. *The Scientists Speak.* New York: Boni and Gaer, 1947. 369 p.

WILSON, E. Bright. *Introduction to Scientific Research.* New York: McGraw-Hill Book Co., 1952. 375 p.

WOLFLE, Dael. "The Fetish of Experiment." *Science* 125: 177; February 1, 1957.

WOLFLE, Dael, and Others. "Standards for Appraising Psychological Research." *American Psychologist* 4: 320-28; August 1949.

WOODWORTH, Robert S., and SCHLOSBERG, Harold. *Experimental Psychology.* Revised Edition. New York: Henry Holt and Co., 1954. xi+948 p.

YOUDEN, W. J. "The Fisherian Revolution in Methods of Experimentation." *Journal of the American Statistical Association* 46: 47-50; March 1951.

9

The Technical Report and Communication

This chapter discusses the technical or research report in relation to communication and implementation of findings, major parts of the report, development of the problem, presentation of evidence, summary and conclusions, bibliographical technique, documentation, style, and readability.

COMMUNICATION AND IMPLEMENTATION

The technical or research report is an exposition type of composition, with emphasis on communication of ideas and evidence in such form as to be readily understood by the reader. In the technical report the soundness of the data and insight in interpretation are the important considerations rather than form and style as such, although commonly there is a relationship between careful organization of materials, sound interpretation of data, and effective style. To make it possible for the reader to give undivided attention to content and interpretation, it is essential to meet standards of usage with respect to certain details of form, style, and readability. Many examples of the time requirements and other essential conditions for effective research and technical reporting are included in the chapters on formulation of the problem and on historical writing.

Scientists are cautioned against attempting, in a "popular" description of their efforts, the same precision and detail as would be appropriate in communicating with colleagues. "Communicative accuracy," or the effective accuracy of a written statement, depends primarily upon the reader's interpretation.

The events of the past few months have emphasized something we have known all along—that it is important for scientists to describe their activities to the public in such a way that they will be generally understandable and properly informative. This runs into the practical difficulty that some scientists, when they attempt a "popular" description of their labors and of their ideas, insist on achieving almost the same precision and completeness of statement which they would, quite properly, use in talking to their scientific colleagues. "You must not expect me to say that genes are distributed along a chromosome like different sizes and colors of beads along a string, for I have no satisfactory evidence that genes are as discrete as separate beads, and also I don't know about their sizes and shapes." Such scientists feel the urge to attach to each general statement of a popular exposition all the cautionary qualifications, all the modifying details, and all the scholarly footnotes that they would use in a technical report.

It may be helpful to suggest to such scientists that they consider the concept of "communicative accuracy." This concept rests upon the fact, not always recognized, that the effective accuracy of a written statement depends primarily upon the interpretation given to it by the reader. A statement may be said to have communicative accuracy, relative to a given audience of readers or hearers, if it fulfills two conditions. First, taking into account what the audience does and does not already know, it must take the audience closer to a correct understanding. The better an example of communicative accuracy it is, the more gain in understanding it will achieve—but the basic point is simply that it must gain ground in the right direction. Second, its inaccuracies (as judged at a more sophisticated level) must not mislead, must not be of a sort which will block subsequent and further progress toward the truth. Both of these criteria, moreover, are to be applied from the point of view of the audience, not from the more informed and properly more critical point of view of an expert.

Communicative accuracy is important to all of us all of the time. Consider the illuminating example, recently offered by a newspaper reporter, of the two men coming home from work and greeting their wives. One says, "My dear, when I look into your face, time stands still." The other remarks, "My dear, your face would stop a clock."[1]

In discussing reporting as a process of communication, it is pertinent to note Whitehead's answer when he was asked whether facts or ideas are more important; he replied: "Ideas *about* facts." In illustrating the difficulty of communication in words, Whitehead pointed out that something could be said about one's personality, but much would remain that could not be put into words. He believed that a marked limitation of philosophy is the supposition that language is an exact medium and that a verbalized philosophical idea is stated for all time; to overcome this difficulty, when ordinary verbal methods failed Plato, he came nearer to

[1] Quoted from Warren Weaver, "Communicative Accuracy." *Science* 127: 499; March 7, 1958.

the truth by giving us a myth. When Whitehead was collaborating on a book with Bertrand Russell, the latter satisfied his craving for expression by composing directly in words and thus satisfying his ideas of things, whereas Whitehead composed in concepts and then tried to find words into which the concepts could be translated.[2]

The importance of communication in the field of educational research was stressed in the First International Conference on Educational Research, sponsored by the American Educational Research Association in co-operation with UNESCO. Adequate communication will contribute to the development of research and to applications of its findings in improvement of education at the personal, community, national, and international levels. Many of the sources of information and media of communication are listed in the chapter on library guides and techniques. Procedures for extending and improving communication,[3] especially at the national and international levels, are as follows:

1. Compilation and publication of a list of primary sources of information about educational research.

2. Preparation and publication of abstracts of the more important studies in certain fields of research selected because they are considered to be of international concern.

3. Compilation and publication of sources of information about research methods.

4. Clarification of technical terminology.

5. Compilation and publication of a list for all countries of sources of information about agencies of educational research, especially those which produce or publish the various types of instruments required for evaluation and measurement.

6. Greater international utilization of existing national periodicals carrying reports of research.

7. Development, where they do not already exist, of national centers for the collection, dissemination, and co-ordination of information about educational research and, in those national centers which already exist, a re-examination of their functions and responsibilities with respect to communication.

8. Expansion of the personal mailing list of individual research workers.

9. Widening the coverage of related studies that are reviewed before a piece of contemplated research is undertaken.

[2] *Dialogues of Alfred North Whitehead.* As Recorded by Lucien Price. New York: New American Library of World Literature, 1954. p. 149–50, 271–72, 295–96.
[3] Ben S. Morris and Others, "Communication in the Field of Educational Research," *Report of the First International Conference on Educational Research.* Educational Studies and Documents, No. 20. Paris: UNESCO, 1956. p. 10–15.

10. Use of ephemeral publications to reduce the time lag in communication.

11. More frequent movement of research workers from one country to another.

12. Greater recognition by research workers of their professional responsibility for improving the utilization of the results of research.

The foregoing procedures for extending and improving communication cover most of the techniques sometimes discussed under the topic of implementation of the results of research. The opening chapter presents a related discussion of the social responsibility of the scholar and scientist in making certain that the discoveries of research are used for the benefit of society. Scientific communication and improved relations between science and society will be advanced greatly if every practicing scientist assists in representing to the public the way in which science advances, the need for tests of the validity of conclusions, the logical processes of science, the demands for objectivity, the need for adequate and valid data, and the difference between claims and proved results (with his own research reports so written as to be models of objectivity and clarity).[4]

STRUCTURE OF THE REPORT

Standards of technical reporting and publication have taken form in a series of parts or sections that should be generally observed. These items of mechanical make-up are known as *format*. While the manuals and handbooks in the chapter bibliography are generally helpful, many publishing houses, editors of journals, and graduate schools or departments have their own sample pages, style sheets, or outlines for preparation of the book, thesis, or technical report.

Relatively short reports of less than forty or fifty pages usually do not lend themselves to a chapter form of organization, but can be divided into sections, with appropriate headings and subheadings. The parts[5] of the longer technical report or thesis and the usual sequence are commonly as listed below. The several sections or subdivisions of this book may serve as examples of the different parts of the research report.

Title Page

Acknowledgment (if any)
(The terms *Preface* or *Foreword* ordinarily are used in printed books, and sometimes an *Editor's Introduction* is included.)

[4] Fred W. Decker, "Scientific Communications Should Be Improved." *Science* 125: 101–5; January 18, 1957.
[5] Carter V. Good and Douglas E. Scates, *Methods of Research*: Educational, Psychological, Sociological. New York: Appleton-Century-Crofts, 1954. p. 842.

Table of Contents

List of Tables (if any)

List of Figures (if any)

Formulation and Definition of the Problem
(One or more chapters dealing with such items as the problem, sources, procedure, and related literature)

Presentation and Interpretation of Data
(Commonly divided into several chapters)

Summary and Conclusions
(Restatement of problem, sources, and procedure; conclusions and their limitations; application and recommendations; needed research)

Bibliography

Appendix (if any)

Index (if any)
(Customary only in printed volumes)

Preparation of the research or technical report is an aspect of the investigation that may move shuttle-like in relation to the various stages of formulation of the problem, development of the data-gathering procedure, gathering of evidence, and analysis and interpretation of data. In preference to waiting until the end of the investigation before preparing the report, first drafts of sections relating to formulation of the problem and the related literature may be prepared early in the project, and helpful notes at different stages of the study will simplify greatly preparation of the complete report.

Certain skills of outlining, briefing, and note-taking are basic to preparation of an adequate report. While the outline should be prepared before the report is written, in order to serve as a framework of organization, revision of the outline takes place as the study progresses and even as the report is being written. The brief, a more advanced stage than outlining, expresses concisely the principal statements under each topic. From the outline and brief may be phrased the appropriate headings and subheadings for the report. It is helpful to place the headings and subheadings of the outline and the different statements of the brief on separate slips of paper, in the interest of revision or rearrangement of the outline and brief. The chapters of this book may serve as illustrations of outlining and of headings. Note-taking has been discussed in some detail in the chapter on the related literature.

The pages of this chapter in particular and of this book as a whole include many illustrations of form with respect to formulation of the problem, presentation of evidence, summarizing, conclusions, headings, footnotes, bibliographies, quotations, and other matters of format. The graduate student and others may turn to the numerous manuals and handbooks listed in the chapter bibliography for many details of form and usage which cannot be presented within the limited scope and space of the present chapter. Skill in proofreading of manuscripts and printer's proof is an important asset, as appropriately expressed in the following anonymous verses, probably written by some harried proofreader:

> The typographical error is a slippery thing and sly,
> You can hunt till you are dizzy, but it somehow
> will get by;
> Till the forms are off the presses it is strange how
> still it keeps;
> It shrinks down in a corner, and it never stirs or
> peeps.
> That typographical error, too small for human
> eyes,
> Till the ink is on the paper, when it grows to
> mountain size.
>
> The boss he stares with horror, then he grabs his
> hair and moans,
> The copyreader drops his head upon his hands
> and groans,
> The remainder of the issues may be clean as clean
> can be,
> But that typographical error is the only thing you
> see.

TITLE OF THE REPORT

The title of an investigation should be concise and as adequately descriptive as preferably two lines of space will permit. Certain forms of expression and phrasing are either redundant or superfluous; for example, aspects of, comments on, study of, investigation of, inquiry into, analysis of. Exceptions to this statement are helpful attempts to indicate the research procedure involved; for example, experimental investigation of, developmental study of, case study of. Many of the titles in the references of this book, in the *Review of Educational Research*, and in the *Encyclopedia of Educational Research* are suggestive. The particular graduate school or department usually has its own style sheet for the title page of the thesis or dissertation.

ACKNOWLEDGMENT

The terms *acknowledgment, preface,* and *foreword* are commonly used as synonyms in the preparation of graduate studies and similar typed reports, although the printed book frequently makes distinctions between these expressions. The usual designation for this preliminary part of the thesis or dissertation is acknowledgment. It is appropriate to recognize substantial assistance and co-operation in concise and temperate language, although tributes to the graduate advisory committee, librarians, typists, and clerks seem out of order.

TABLE OF CONTENTS

If the working outline and brief are logical and well organized, the design or structural pattern of the report should be clearly apparent, with the table of contents serving as a synopsis or headline display. Since the typed report or thesis usually has no index, a reasonably complete table of contents is essential for the guidance of the reader. It is advantageous for a heading in the body of the report and in the table of contents to keep within one line of space. The table of contents and the index of this book may serve illustrative purposes.

TABLES AND FIGURES

Titles of tables and figures should be listed accurately on separate pages in the front matter or section of the report, numbered consecutively in one list for tables and in another list for figures. Figures may include all types of graphic representation or illustrations, whether called graphs, charts, diagrams, maps, or photographs. Titles of tables and figures should include information concerning who, what, when, where, and how many. It is advantageous to phrase the titles concisely within two lines, avoiding such wording as "showing," "table showing," or "graph showing." Titles or legends are placed above tables and below figures.

A table is appropriate for any series of items that involve frequencies. For purposes of interpretation, it is well to confine each table to a single page, sometimes breaking up unwieldy tables into smaller tables, and placing each table in the manuscript as near the point of first reference as possible. Sometimes an especially lengthy or complex table of several or more pages can be placed to advantage in the appendix, with a shorter summary table in the body of the thesis for purposes of discussion and interpretation. A practical test of the effectiveness of a table or figure is whether it is understandable apart from the text or discussion of the technical report.

Figures should be used only when they make a real contribution to interpretation of the data or tables, never to impress the reader. The general arrangement of a figure is from left to right, and the lettering is placed so as to be easily read from the base as the bottom or sometimes from the right-hand edge of the figure as the bottom. The horizontal scale for curves usually reads from left to right, and the vertical scale from bottom to top.

The details of tabular and graphic representation are such that an adequate treatment is not possible within the limits of this chapter. Therefore, the writer of a technical report that includes tables or figures is referred to the available handbooks or manuals.[6]

FORMULATION OF THE PROBLEM

The formulation and development of the problem may require one or more chapters to present an analysis of the problem into its constituent elements, limits or scope of the study, related literature, sources of data, method or technique, technical terminology, initial assumptions, and hypotheses. Since these details have been presented at some length in the chapter on the development of the problem, only brief comment will be made at this time. If the sequence in a well-organized report is to tell the reader where he is going, take him there, and then tell him where he

[6] Herbert Arkin and Raymond R. Colton, *Graphs*: How to Make and Use Them. New York: Harper & Brothers, 1940. xviii+236 p.

Darrell Huff, *How to Lie with Statistics*. New York: W. W. Norton and Co., 1954. 142 p.

R. R. Lutz, *Graphic Presentation Simplified*. New York: Funk and Wagnalls, 1949. xx+202 p.

Rudolf Modley, *How to Use Pictorial Statistics*. New York: Harper & Brothers, 1937. xviii+170 p.

Rudolf Modley and Others, *Pictographs and Graphs*: How to Make and Use Them. New York: Harper & Brothers, 1952. 186 p.

Publication Manual of the American Psychological Association. 1957 Revision. Washington: The Association, 1957. 70 p.

John L. Ridgway, *Scientific Illustration*. Stanford, Calif.: Stanford University Press, 1938. xiv+173 p.

Calvin F. Schmid, *Handbook of Graphic Representation*. New York: Ronald Press, 1954. vii+316 p.

Helen M. Walker and Walter N. Durost, *Statistical Tables:* Their Structure and Use. New York: Bureau of Publications, Teachers College, Columbia University, 1936. v+76 p.

Hans Zeisel, *Say It with Figures*: How to Make Figures Make Sense—a Guide for Those Who Use and Read Statistics. Fourth Revised Edition. New York: Harper & Brothers, 1957. xviii+257 p.

has been, the first purpose should be accomplished in the section devoted to formulation and development of the problem. In this sense, the introductory chapter looks forward, and also looks backward through the medium of the related literature and historical background. The opening chapter may well begin with a direct statement of the purpose of the study. This overview section of the research report may be prepared to advantage early in the investigation, with necessary revisions as the study progresses. A functional test of the effectiveness of the introductory chapter is to ask whether one who has never heard of the investigation could secure, through the statement of the problem, a satisfactory understanding of the purpose, sources of data, and technique.

BODY OF THE REPORT

The body of the research report presents the evidence. The inexperienced writer frequently leaves gaps in his report, partly because he is so familiar with the investigation that he overlooks the importance of certain details and of a unified organization for the reader. A careful outline, meaningful headings, and a brief of key statements will aid materially in developing a unified report. The body of the report varies in keeping with the content and research method represented. The historical narrative usually is presented in a series of chronological or topical chapters. The case-clinical report may have a series of chapters dealing with the different types of cases, or a number of sections on the several steps in case study and case work, or some combination of these two forms of organization of content. Unity can be promoted within a chapter and within the report as a whole through introductory, transitional, and summary statements; appropriate cross references; placement of lengthy tables, questionnaires, tests, and other exhibits in the appendix; skill in handling quotations; and avoidance of overloading of the text with statistical details.

SUMMARY AND CONCLUSIONS

The chapter of summarization and conclusions looks backward, and also forward through consideration of applications, recommendations, and needed research. The final chapter should be an illustration of the adage that the whole is greater than the sum of the parts. Although chapter summaries are helpful in preparing the closing chapter, the mere process of adding these details together falls short of the synthesis or integration expected at the end of the report. The summarizing chapter is especially valuable to many readers, particularly in business and industry, who may not go outside the closing chapter (sometimes the summary is the opening section in business reports) for information concerning problem, sources of evidence, method or technique, conclusions and their limitations, applications and implementation, recommendations, and needed research. The final chapter should recapitulate the answer to the opening question or hypothesis of the study. The investigator should plainly label all instances where he has depended on his own judgment rather than directly on the data in presenting limitations, applications, recommendations, and problems for future research.

BIBLIOGRAPHY AND DOCUMENTATION

Adequate bibliographical and summarizing work as a phase of the investigation has been characterized as the "pilot" of research. This view has been emphasized in the chapters on formulation of the problem and on the library guides. The rules of professional ethics require adequate documentation of ideas and quotations from other sources. Appropriation of ideas from another author, without proper recognition, is a type of intellectual dishonesty known as plagiarism. The ethical standards of psychologists, as summarized in the chapter on case-clinical studies, present statements relating to professional relationships, research, writing, and publishing. Specific examples of plagiarism or literary piracy include theft of ideas without documentation, use of figures or drawings without credit lines, direct or indirect quotations without proper documentation, and sometimes reproduction for class use of large portions of copyrighted works without permission from the publisher or author. As a general rule, permission to quote is not necessary in an unpublished thesis or typewritten report. In writing for publication, however, when quoting more than a few lines from a published source it is wise to secure permission from the copyright holder. Extremes of documentation are to be avoided; there is a common body of knowledge in each field which belongs to the discipline itself rather than to an individual author. A major purpose of direct quotations is to portray accurately the language and thought of the particular author. This book includes numerous illustrations of direct and indirect quotations and documentation (in footnotes):

> Direct quotations of more than a few lines in smaller type (single space in a typed manuscript)

Shorter direct quotations within double quotation marks as part of the
paragraph of discussion

Indirect quotations (paraphrasing or borrowing of ideas) without quotation marks but with appropriate documentation in footnotes.

In technical or research reports, it is common practice to place a
complete bibliography of all pertinent references immediately after the
summary chapter, arranged alphabetically by authors, although chapter
bibliographies sometimes are listed, as illustrated in the *Review of Educational Research*. The references in the bibliography must be numbered
consecutively, if a cross-reference system of citation from the body of
the report to the bibliography is preferred to footnotes. In the interest
of uniformity and completeness of information, it is necessary to translate references of different styles from a variety of sources into the form
adopted by the particular graduate school or publisher. In this chapter
and book are hundreds of illustrations of bibliographical form for the
several types of references: books not identified with a series, publications (monographs, yearbooks, and certain books) identified with a series,
journals or periodicals, and unpublished studies (including theses and
dissertations).

In this book the reader will find hundreds of illustrations of footnote
usage, relating to such items as: consecutive numbering throughout each
chapter or section of the report, listing of the author's name in normal
order (rather than surname first), use of *ibid.* and *op. cit.*, and the system
of cross reference to a consecutively numbered chapter bibliography.
Ibid. is an abbrevation of *ibidem*, meaning "in the same place"; it is used
when succeeding uninterrupted citations of a work occur on the same
page or within a space of a few pages. *Op. cit.* is the abbreviation of
opere citato, meaning "in the work cited"; it is used (following the
author's name) when other references intervene between different citations of a particular work or when a number of pages have intervened
since the work was cited in full. Some writers prefer a system of cross
reference to a consecutively numbered bibliography, rather than numerous footnotes, as illustrated in the *Review of Educational Research* and
Encyclopedia of Educational Research. John Brown's report (12: 80–90)
would mean that pages 80–90 of item 12 in the bibliography contain the
quotation or material cited.

APPENDIX

The appendix serves a useful purpose in providing a place for cum-
bersome or voluminous materials which tend to break the continuity of

discussion and interpretation for the reader (in the body of the report). However, the appendix should not be made a convenient dumping ground for irrelevant materials, sometimes placed there in an attempt to impress the reader or to swell the volume of the report. The pertinent materials assigned to the appendix should be grouped in homogeneous parts, provided with appropriate numbers and headings, and listed in the table of contents. Cross references in the body of the report may be made to the appendix in connection with such materials as lengthy tables, raw data, questionnaires, schedules, interview forms, standard tests, form letters, formulas, and lengthy quotations from documents (for example, constitutions, laws, and court decisions).

STYLE AND READABILITY

The details of style, usage, and readability cannot be discussed within the scope of this chapter and must be left to the manuals, handbooks, and dictionaries listed in the chapter bibliography. The dictionaries of education, psychology, and sociology are also listed in the chapter dealing with the related literature and library guides. A number of illustrations of style are presented in the chapter on historical writing.

The manuals may be consulted for assistance in diction (the choice and use of words), phraseology (the arrangement of words in groups), and style, which is concerned with certain more general characteristics of writing, especially individuality of expression. Scientists and research workers at times are accused of being inarticulate and at other times are charged with writing in a language that few persons can understand. A technical or research report may well use a style that is simple, direct, and effective, without ornateness or literary embellishments, but with whatever skill in language the reporter possesses. Formality in reporting should not be permitted to stifle an effective individual style of writing, although there is something about technical or research reporting which sometimes freezes the pen of an author. As illustrated in the chapter on historical writing, able scholars have varied greatly in style. Ebbinghaus and William James wrote with sufficient scientific rigor, yet in a lucid and interesting manner, with glimpses of the author as a human personality, whereas Wundt almost overwhelmed the reader with a mass of facts, arguments, and dicta. Gibbon experimented extensively before he could find a middle ground between a dull chronicle and a rhetorical declamation.

An apparently anonymous report of a conversation between a

graduate student and his professorial adviser includes humorous illustrations of the simple language in the student's draft of his manuscript and the ornate language supposedly suggested by the professor:

Student: "It will be hard to provide enough schools for the children entering in 1960."

Professor: "The phenomenon of fecundity has confronted American education with a challenge of Herculean proportions. An evaluation of the implication to the tax structure of state governments in providing adequate educational facilities is a difficult and complex task."

Student: "Professor Blank's scheme of teaching reading was tried, but it did not work."

Professor: "The writer does not choose to disparage the efficacy of Professor Blank's method of teaching reading. It is not inappropriate, however, to point out that careful scrutiny of the method shows it to be what might be called ineffective."

Student: "The federal government has no control over local schools."

Professor: "The federal government has no plenary jurisdiction over local school matters. Moreover, since government in the United States is administered at federal, state, and local levels, the implications to government are several, rather than single, and affect each of these three levels of government in separate and differing fashion."

Student: " 'Early to bed and early to rise, makes a man healthy, wealthy, and wise,' strikes me as an effective form of expression."

Professor: "It is better to say: 'Early retirement is a significant factor in one's physical development, pecuniary success, and intellectual stature.' "

Certain principles of readability[7] in reporting research may be summarized as follows:

1. Appeal and interest increase readability.

2. Personalization means putting human interest into the report: through a review of previous investigations as a story of other persons' successes and failures, an account of how the author collected and treated the data, illustrative cases, and deviations from central tendencies.

3. Pattern or design should be made plain to the reader.

4. Through appropriate emphasis the reader should get the important points.

5. Too great density or concentration of ideas may make reading difficult, requiring some expansion or dilution.

6. Plain words are important in making a report readable.

[7] Ruth Strang, "Principles of Readability Applied to Reporting Research," *Improving Educational Research.* Washington: American Educational Research Association, 1948. p. 41-43.

CONCLUDING STATEMENT

As an exposition type of composition, the major purpose of the technical report is communication of ideas and evidence, with the emphasis of the interpretation on ideas *about* facts. Effective communication will contribute to the development of educational investigation and to the application of research findings to improvement of education at personal, community, national, and international levels. Preparation of the report is an integral part of the total research project which may move shuttle-like in relation to the several stages of development of the problem, gathering evidence, and analysis and interpretation of data rather than waiting until the end of the investigation before starting the writing of the report. In the interest of readability and communication, the technical report should have a style that is simple and direct, without rhetorical flourishes, but with every bit of language skill the reporter possesses.

SELECTED REFERENCES

ALEXANDER, Carter, and BURKE, Arvid J. *How to Locate Educational Information and Data.* Third Edition. New York: Bureau of Publications, Teachers College, Columbia University, 1950. xix+441 p.

American Association for Health, Physical Education, and Recreation. *Research Methods Applied to Health, Physical Education, and Recreation.* Revised Edition. Washington: The Association, National Education Association, 1952. p. 478-517.

ANDERSON, Wayne. "Readability of Readers." *American Psychologist* 11: 147-48; March 1956.

ARKIN, Herbert, and COLTON, Raymond R. *Graphs:* How to Make and Use Them. New York: Harper & Brothers, 1940. xviii+236 p.

ASHMEAD, John. "Publish or Perish—Socrates!" *American Association of University Professors Bulletin* 41: 716-20; Winter 1955.

BAKER, John R. "English Style in Scientific Papers." *Science* 123: 713-14; April 27, 1956.

BALL, John, and WILLIAMS, Cecil B. *Report Writing.* New York: Ronald Press, 1955. 407 p.

BARZUN, Jacques, and GRAFF, Henry F. *The Modern Researcher.* New York: Harcourt, Brace and Co., 1957. p. 229-354.

BEBELL, Clifford S. "Getting Meaning from Research," *Research for Curriculum Improvement.* 1957 Yearbook. Washington: Association for Supervision and Curriculum Development, National Education Association, 1957. p. 119-51.

BINGHAM, Walter V. "How to Make a Useful Index." *American Psychologist* 6: 31-34; January 1951.

Borg, Walter R. "Teachers as Intelligent Consumers of Research." *School and Society* 73: 357-59; June 9, 1951.

Brieland, Donald M. "The Psychologist as Speaker." *American Psychologist* 5: 409-11; August 1950.

Campbell, W. G. *Form and Style in Thesis Writing*. Boston: Houghton Mifflin Co., 1954. vi+114 p.

Colton, F. Barrows. "Some of My Best Friends Are Scientists." *Scientific Monthly* 69: 156-60; September 1949.

David, Henry P. "Book Reviewing and Language Barriers." *Contemporary Psychology* 1: 131-33; May 1956.

Davidson, Henry A. *Guide to Medical Writing: A Practical Manual for Physicians, Dentists, Nurses, Pharmacists*. New York: Ronald Press, 1957. vii+338 p.

Davis, R. A. "Writing a Thesis in Education." *Peabody Journal of Education* 27: 285-95; March 1950.

Decker, Fred W. "Scientific Communications Should Be Improved." *Science* 125: 101-5; January 18, 1957.

Dugdale, Kathleen. *A Manual of Form for Theses and Term Reports*. Bloomington: Indiana University, 1950. vi+58 p.

DuShane, Graham. "Pitfalls of Prepublication." *Science* 127: 623; March 21, 1958.

Dvorak, Earl A. "General Guide to a Study of Research Reports." *Peabody Journal of Education* 34: 141-44; November 1956.

Eells, Walter C. "Journals Publishing Articles on College Teachers and College Teaching." *American Association of University Professors Bulletin* 43: 458-60; September 1957.

Emberger, Meta R., and Hall, Marian R. *Scientific Writing*. W. Earl Britton, Editor. New York: Harcourt, Brace and Co., 1955. 468 p.

English, Horace B. "The -iles That Plague Elementary Statistics." *Psychological Bulletin* 54: 421-22; September 1957.

English, Horace B., and English, Ava C. *Comprehensive Dictionary of Psychological and Psychoanalytical Terms*. New York: Longmans, Green and Co., 1958. xiv+594 p.

Faculty of Teachers College, University of Cincinnati. *A Guide for the Preparation of Dissertations, Theses, and Field Reports*. Cincinnati: University of Cincinnati, 1952. iii+55 p.

Fairchild, H. P., Editor. *Dictionary of Sociology*. New York: Philosophical Library, 1944. viii+342 p.

Festinger, Leon, and Katz, Daniel, Editors. *Research Methods in the Behavioral Sciences*. New York: Dryden Press, 1953. p. 579-646.

Fishbein, Morris. *Medical Writing: The Technic and the Art*. Third Edition. New York: McGraw-Hill Book Co., 1957. 272 p.

Flesch, Rudolph. *The Art of Plain Talk*. New York: Harper & Brothers, 1946. xiii+210 p.

Flesch, Rudolf. *The Art of Readable Writing*. New York: Harper & Brothers, 1949. xvi+237 p.

FLESCH, Rudolf, and LASS, A. H. *The Way to Write*. Revised Edition. New York: Harper & Brothers, 1949. x+342 p.

FROMAN, Lewis A. " 'Communication Skills' of College Faculties." *Educational Record* 35: 257-60; October 1954. (Terminology.)

GIRDEN, Edward, and DENNIS, Wayne. "Book Reviewing in American Psychological Journals." *American Psychologist* 9: 251-53; June 1954.

GIRDEN, Edward, and DENNIS, Wayne. "Publication Trends in American Psychology—A Five-Year Extrapolation." *American Psychologist* 9: 632-35; October 1954.

GOOD, Carter V., Editor. *Dictionary of Education*. Second Edition. New York: McGraw-Hill Book Co., 1959. xxx+676 p.

GOOD, Carter V., and SCATES, Douglas E. *Methods of Research:* Educational, Psychological, Sociological. New York: Appleton-Century-Crofts, 1954. p. 832-96.

GOOD, Ruth. "Medical Writing: Notes on Grammar and Diction." *University of Michigan Medical Bulletin* 20: 245-52; September 1954.

GOODE, William J., and HATT, Paul K. *Methods in Social Research*. New York: McGraw-Hill Book Co., 1952. Chapters 3, 4, 21.

GORDON, Robert. "A Question of Style." *American Association of University Professors Bulletin* 43: 23-32; Spring 1957.

GREEVER, Garland, JONES, E. S., and JONES, Agnes L. *The Century Collegiate Handbook*. Third Edition. New York: Appleton-Century-Crofts, 1950. xv+460 p.

HAMMOND, Kenneth R., and ALLEN, Jeremiah M. *Writing Clinical Reports*. New York: Prentice-Hall, 1953. xii+235 p.

HARRIMAN, Philip L. *New Dictionary of Psychology*. New York: Philosophical Library, 1947. 364 p.

HEBB, D. O., and BINDRA, Dalbir. "Scientific Writing and the General Problem of Communication." *American Psychologist* 7: 569-73; October 1952.

HILBISH, Florence M. A. *The Research Paper*. New York: Bookman Associates, 1952. 292 p.

HILL, John W., and PAYNE, James E. "Scientists Can Talk to the Layman." *Science* 117: 403-5; April 17, 1953.

HILLWAY, Tyrus. *Introduction to Research*. Boston: Houghton Mifflin Co., 1956. p. 231-62.

HODGSON, James G. "Bibliographical Citations for Modern Scholars." *School and Society* 73: 289-91; May 12, 1951.

HOLT, Robert R., and Others. "Publication Problems in Psychology." *American Psychologist* 8: 235-42; June 1953.

HUFF, Darrell. *How to Lie with Statistics*. New York: W. W. Norton and Co., 1954. 142 p.

IVEY, John E., Jr. "A University Experiments in Research Translation." *Educational Record* 31: 383-404; October 1950.

JOHNSON, Granville B., Jr. "A Method for Evaluating Research Articles in Education." *Journal of Educational Research* 51: 149-51; October 1957.

JOHNSON, Loaz W. "Educational Research and Its Dissemination." *Educational Leadership* 10: 423-27; April 1953.

JURGENS, Marion A. "Research Publication: A Federal Responsibility?" *Science* 110: 209-12; August 26, 1949.

KAESS, W. A., and BOUSFIELD, W. A. "The Use of Citations of Authorities in Textbooks of Introductory Psychology." *American Psychologist* 9: 144-48; April 1954.

KAPLAN, Bert. "Dissemination of Primary Research Data in Psychology." *American Psychologist* 13: 53-55; February 1958. (Techniques of microcopy.)

KIERZEK, John M. *The Macmillan Handbook of English*. Third Edition. New York: The Macmillan Co., 1954. 579 p.

LEGGETT, Glenn, MEAD, C. David, and CHARVAT, William. *Prentice-Hall Handbook for Writers*. Second Edition. Englewood Cliffs, N. J.: Prentice-Hall, 1954. 544 p.

LEGGETT, Glenn, and YAGGY, Elinor. *Writing a Paper:* From Idea to Finished Copy. New York: Ronald Press, 1955. 192 p.

LUTZ, R. R. *Graphic Presentation Simplified*. New York: Funk and Wagnalls, 1949. xx+202 p.

A Manual of Style. Revised and Enlarged. Chicago: The University of Chicago Press, 1949. x+498 p.

McCANN, Lloyd E. "Presenting That Idea in the Professional Journal." *Phi Delta Kappan* 39: 173-76; January 1958.

McCORMICK, Thomas C., and FRANCIS, Roy G. *Methods of Research in the Behavioral Sciences*. New York: Harper & Brothers, 1958. Chapters 8, 10.

MODLEY, Rudolf. *How to Use Pictorial Statistics*. New York: Harper & Brothers, 1937. xviii+170 p.

MODLEY, Rudolf, and Others. *Pictographs and Graphs:* How to Make and Use Them. New York: Harper & Brothers, 1952. 186 p.

MOSER, C. A. *Survey Methods in Social Investigation*. New York: The Macmillan Co., 1958. Chapter 15.

MURRAY, Robert K. "The 'Technical' Art of Manuscript Reporting." *American Association of University Professors Bulletin* 40: 631-37; Winter 1954-55.

NELSON, J. R. *Writing the Technical Report*. Second Edition. New York: McGraw-Hill Book Co., 1947. xiv+388 p.

NEWMAN, Edwin B. "Public Relations—For What?" *American Psychologist* 12: 509-14; August 1957.

OWEN, John E. "This Pressure to Publish." *American Association of University Professors Bulletin* 40: 638-42; Winter 1954-55.

PARTEN, Mildred. *Surveys, Polls, and Samples:* Practical Procedures. New York: Harper & Brothers, 1950. Chapter 17.

PFEIFFER, John. "Making Popular Science More Popular." *Science* 127: 955-57; April 25, 1958.

Publication Manual of the American Psychological Association. 1957 Revision. Washington: The Association, 1957. 70 p.

PURPUS, E. R. "Scientific and Technical Literacy." *Journal of Higher Education* 25: 475-78; December 1954.

REDFORD, Grant H. "Publish or Else." *American Association of University Professors Bulletin* 38: 608-18; Winter 1952-53.

RIDGWAY, John L. *Scientific Illustration.* Stanford, Calif.: Stanford University Press, 1938. xiv+173 p.

RUJA, Harry, and JOHNSON, Sam. "Citing References Accurately." *American Psychologist* 10: 306-7; July 1955.

RUMMEL, J. Francis. *An Introduction to Research Procedures in Education.* New York: Harper & Brothers, 1958. p. 278-345.

SANDERS, Chauncey. *An Introduction to Research in English Literary History.* New York: The Macmillan Co., 1952. p. 277-315.

SCHMID, Calvin F. *Handbook of Graphic Representation.* New York: Ronald Press, 1954. vii+316 p.

"On Scientific Editorial Problems." *Science* 121: 526-40; April 15, 1955.

SHANNON, J. R. "Art in Writing for Educational Periodicals: The Ending." *Journal of Educational Research* 46: 333-45; January 1953.

SHANNON, J. R. "Art in Writing for Educational Periodicals: The Introduction." *Journal of Educational Research* 44: 599-610; April 1951.

SHANNON, J. R. "Art in Writing for Educational Periodicals: The Main Body." *Journal of Educational Research* 47: 489-504; March 1954.

SHANNON, J. R. "Tips to Writers from Seventy-Five Editors of Educational Periodicals." *Journal of Educational Research* 44: 241-68; December 1950.

SHAW, Ralph R. "Copyright and the Right to Credit." *Science* 113: 571-73; May 18, 1951.

SHEFFIELD, Edward F. "That Thesis Outline." *Educational Forum* 17: 355-64; March 1953.

SKILLIN, Marjorie E., GAY, Robert M., and Others. *Words into Type:* A Guide in the Preparation of Manuscripts; for Writers, Editors, Proofreaders and Printers. New York: Appleton-Century-Crofts, 1948. xx+585 p.

SOUTHER, J. W. *Technical Report Writing.* New York: John Wiley & Sons, 1957. xi+70 p.

STEVENS, Neil E. "The Moral Obligation to Be Intelligible." *Scientific Monthly* 70: 111-15; February 1950.

SYMONDS, Percival M. "A Research Checklist in Educational Psychology." *Journal of Educational Psychology* 47: 100-9; February 1956.

THISTLE, M. W. "Popularizing Science." *Science* 127: 951-55; April 25, 1958.

THOMA, Henry F. "Good Morning, Professor, Want to Write a Textbook?" *College English* 19: 45-50; November 1957.

THURBER, James. "The Psychosemanticist Will See You Now, Mr. Thurber." *Science* 123: 705-7; April 27, 1956.

TRAVERS, R. M. W. *An Introduction to Educational Research.* New York: The Macmillan Co., 1958. Chapter 15.

TRELEASE, Sam F. *The Scientific Paper, How to Prepare It, How to Write It:* A Handbook for Students and Research Workers in All Branches of Science. Second Edition. Baltimore: Williams & Wilkins Co., 1951. 163 p.

TUTTLE, Robert E., and BROWN, C. A. *Writing Useful Reports:* Principles and Applications. New York: Appleton-Century-Crofts, 1956. xiv+635 p.

ULMAN, Joseph N., Jr. *Technical Reporting.* New York: Henry Holt and Co., 1952. xiv+289 p.

VERPLANCK, William S. *A Glossary of Some Terms Used in the Objective Science of Behavior.* Supplement to the *Psychological Review,* Vol. 64, No. 6, Part 2. Washington: American Psychological Association, November 1957. viii+42 p.

WALDO, Willis H. *Better Report Writing.* New York: Reinhold Publishing Corp., 1957. 238 p.

WALKER, Helen M., and DUROST, W. N. *Statistical Tables:* Their Structure and Use. New York: Teachers College, Columbia University, 1936. viii+76 p.

WALKER, Helen M. "Statistics, Sense and Nonsense." *Teachers College Record* 56: 68-73; November 1954.

WARREN, H. C. *A Dictionary of Psychology.* Boston: Houghton Mifflin Co., 1934. x+372 p.

WELD, Walter E. *How to Chart:* Facts from Figures with Graphs. Norwood, Mass.: Codex Book Co., 1947. xiv+218 p.

WHITMORE, Charles E. "The Language of Science." *Scientific Monthly* 80: 185-91; March 1955.

WHITNEY, F. L. *The Elements of Research.* Third Edition. New York: Prentice-Hall, 1950. p. 404-35, 485-519.

WILLIAMS, C. B., and STEVENSON, A. H. *A Research Manual for College Studies and Papers.* Revised Edition. New York: Harper & Brothers, 1951. 194 p.

WOOLLEY, Edwin C., SCOTT, Franklin W., and BRACHER, Frederick. *College Handbook of Composition.* Fifth Edition. Boston: D. C. Heath and Co., 1951. x+344 p.

ZEISEL, Hans. *Say It with Figures:* How to Make Figures Make Sense—a Guide for Those Who Use and Read Statistics. Fourth Revised Edition. New York: Harper & Brothers, 1957. xviii+257 p.

Index